A

Gravity's

Rainbow

Companion

A *Gravity's Rainbow* Companion

Sources and Contexts for Pynchon's Novel

Second Edition, Revised and Expanded

by Steven C. Weisenburger

The University of Georgia Press

Athens and London

Set in Trump Medieval by The Composing Room
of Michigan, Inc.

Printed digitally in the United States of America

Library of Congress Cataloging-in-Publication Data
Weisenburger, Steven.
A Gravity's rainbow companion : sources and
contexts for Pynchon's novel / by Steven C.
Weisenburger.—2nd ed., rev. and expanded.
xii, 412 p., [8] p. of plates : ill., maps ; 23 cm.
Includes bibliographical references (p. [385]–395) and index.
ISBN-13: 978-0-8203-2811-9 (alk. paper)
ISBN-10: 0-8203-2811-1 (alk. paper)
ISBN-13: 978-0-8203-2807-2 (pbk. : alk. paper)
ISBN-10: 0-8203-2807-3 (pbk. : alk. paper)
1. Pynchon, Thomas. Gravity's rainbow.
I. Title.
PS3566.Y55 G7395 2006
813'.54—dc22   2006011956

British Library Cataloging-in-Publication Data available

Contents

Acknowledgments (1988) / vii

And More Acknowledgments
(2006) / ix

Introduction / 1

Part 1
Beyond the Zero / 13

Part 2
*Un Perm' au Casino Hermann
Goering* / 121

Part 3
In the Zone / 175

Part 4
The Counterforce / 319

Bibliography / 385

Index / 397

Acknowledgments (1988)

I N many ways doing this book was fun. It meant readings in American pop and material culture, the occult, varieties of pseudoscience, real science, vernacular geography, and forty-year-old news periodicals—to mention just a few fields I wandered into. A new discovery each week, at the peak of my research, sometimes tedious but always-enjoyable work because of friends and colleagues who took an interest. I am grateful to all who helped it along. Roger Sale, for two reasons: for showing that one could enjoy these serendipitous paths of scholarship and for sharing his reading of *Gravity's Rainbow* when the novel was first published. Malcolm Griffith, for suggesting (in 1978) that I should write this book. I put the idea aside for four years, but once the project was under way it was helped by a number of friends and colleagues. Staff members at the M. I. King Library at the University of Kentucky provided invaluable assistance, and I especially want to thank Roxanna Jones and Barbara Wight of interlibrary loan, as well as Rob Aken, Dan Barkley, Brad Grissom, and Laura Rein of King Library's reference department. Steven Moore, fresh from a similar project on Gaddis's *The Recognitions*, made wise suggestions as I prepared the first draft. Molly Hite gave suggestions and encouragement. To all of Pynchon's scholarly readers, acknowledged in the notes and listed in the bibliography, I owe innumerable debts. Colleagues at the University of Kentucky answered what must have seemed the oddest possible salmagundi of queries and requests. For their help and encouragement I am especially grateful to Tom Adler, Gerald Alvey, Roger Anderson, Tom Blues, Joe Bryant, John Cawelti, Guy Davenport, Joe Gardner, and John Shawcross. Thanks to Bob Hemenway for supporting the work while he was chairman and, in particular, for helping me find funds and time off from my departmental responsibilities at a crucial time. The research and preparation of the book were assisted by grants from the University of Kentucky Research Foundation. To complete the final draft, I also managed to steal time from another project that was being assisted by a grant from the National Endowment for the Humanities. Janis Bolster did an epic job of copyediting, down to the last line-number reference. And at the University of Georgia Press, Debra Winter has guided this project with care for all the details that matter. Again, thanks to all.

Finally, to Susan, still my best friend, who knows this project as an oral history: this book's for you.

Lexington, Kentucky

And More
Acknowledgments (2006)

S INCE this book first appeared Pynchon has published two novels, *Vineland* (1990) and the long-awaited *Mason & Dixon* (1997). He's less the invisible writer. He wrote (for example) the liner notes for a disk of Spike Jones classics (*Spiked!*, 1994), contributed a *New York Times* essay on sloth to a quirky series on the seven deadly sins and a fine introduction to the Centennial Edition of George Orwell's *1984* (2003). He was written up on (but said nothing publicly about) winning a 1988 McArthur "Genius Award." We heard that he married, became a father. One day while walking with his son Jackson he was photographed publicly for the first time in decades. In 2003 he made a television voice-over appearance on an episode of *The Simpsons*—a cool move, given his satires of The Tube in *The Crying of Lot 49* and *Vineland*. *Gravity's Rainbow* itself had a cameo on "The John Laroquette Show" in 1993. More significantly, Penguin published a special paperback edition of *Gravity's Rainbow* honoring it—in company with novels like *Heart of Darkness*, *Swann's Way*, *The Age of Innocence*, *The Grapes of Wrath*, *On the Road*, and *Beloved*—as one of twenty "Great Books of the Twentieth Century." Thirty years after its release his novel stands as a classic.

New readers keep coming to the book, old ones keep turning back to it, and occasionally I hear from one such person. Weeks after this *Companion* was published in 1988 I began receiving and have periodically found in my campus mailbox various cards, e-mails, letters, even packages from readers wishing to correct and/or add to these annotations. Gracious, kind, and uniquely cultured, every one of these good people has contributed to this revised second edition. I thank each and all for their earnest care over detail and meanings. In many instances these correspondents were providing information others had previously submitted (my errors were that apparent). In some instances, they supplied—at last!—long sought answers to enigmatic references in *Gravity's Rainbow*. A number glossed quite technical matters in electronics or mathematics, others heard Pynchon riffing on song lyrics or movie dialogue that I—child of the next generation after Pynchon—wouldn't have caught. Receiving these submissions over the past eighteen years has been a delight.

Here I get the space to name these correspondents along with others who variously contributed to this book. So at last I send my gratitude and blessings to Professor C. Greg Anderson, formerly of the University of California, Berkeley, for advice on mathematics and especially on Roger Mexico's Whittaker and Watson math textbook, and to Mr. Robert C. Anderson of Salt Lake City, Utah, for detail on things like Frick & Frack. Mr. William E. Bailey provided some useful comments on statistics; Mr. David Blumberg, formerly of the University of California, Berkeley, German Department, helped with Pynchon's German; Mr. Robert G. Bramscher, of Kenosha, Wisconsin, offered a handful of good tips; Dr. William Bradford Jr. sent tidbits on Harvard University and Cambridge, Massachusetts; and Mr. Alan Bryden of Chesapeake, Virginia, wrote with information about the physics of heat transfer. I thank Mr. David Carr of Sheffield, England, for Marx Brothers film references; Professor Michael Crumb of New Mexico for sending his studies of Pynchon's Uruboros images; and Ms. Sydney Darby, my research assistant in 1995, for tirelessly and meticulously photocopying and scanning the 1988 *Companion* and then correcting those scans, thus providing a freshly digitized manuscript that would enable me (eventually) to input the revisions for this edition (*gracias*, Syd, wherever you are!). Mr. Paul di Filippo posted information on Pynchon-L (a Pynchon electronic mailing list) that solved the mystery of the "Kenosha Kid"; Professor Andrew Dinn of Heriot-Watt University, Edinburgh, Scotland, sent several helpful e-mails and posted a number of helpful messages; Professor Bernard "Duffy" Duyfhuizen, of the University of Wisconsin, Eau Claire, a gracious and careful scholar and friend and coeditor of *Pynchon Notes,* has over the years provided incisive remarks regarding my work on the chronology of *Gravity's Rainbow* (partly by annotating my annotations) while also uncovering in his own critical work valuable new sources for Pynchon's historical references to the Nazi military-industrial complex. Mr. Hartwin Gebhardt gave advice on German spellings and usage; Professor John (Jody) Keith Gilbert, of Simon Fraser University, posted a number of helpful messages on the list; Mr. John Hellegers sent me, along with his *Companion* containing his own marginal notes, materials on Pynchon's references to Pavlov and abreaction and other matters; Professor Luc Herman of the Universitaire Instelling Antwerpen, another friend (thanks to *Gravity's Rainbow*), helped with Pynchon's Dutch, Low-Country geography and history, and references to Antwerp among other things; and Professor Molly Hite of Cornell University sent along several items. Mr. Mark Irwin, formerly of the University of Virginia, clarified some musical allusions; Professor Theodore Kharpertian of the Hudson County Community College offered a canny suggestion on a Pynchon pun; Professor John Krafft, of Miami University, Ohio, coeditor of *Pynchon Notes* and a friend whom I first met at a Modern Language Association Pynchon session in 1977, has over the years sent a continuous stream of items culled from Pynchon criticism and oddments from the Web; Mr. Glenn Laing, of St. Joseph, Missouri, forwarded a wonderfully detailed sheaf of notes on my notes; Dr. Paul Lantos of the University of Connecticut School of Medicine helped with matters biochemical and medical; and then there is Professor Don Larsson, of Mankato State University, who maintains a uniquely valuable Web site, "A *Companion*'s Companion" (all readers will appreciate Larsson's work on Pynchon's pop culture references and his fine set of linked illustrations), that has been a great help. Mr. Juan Cires Martinez advised on Pynchon's Spanish; Professor William McCarron of East Texas State University has over the years sent items, including offprints of published notes and articles; Mr. Harry L. McDonald of Edwardsville, Illinois, wrote me about various technical and engineering matters; Professor Oisín McGuinness of Fordham University is another who tutored my math illiteracy; Mr. Doug Millison passed along several excellent finds; and Professor Stephen Moore caught an array of notable allusions I had missed. Mr. Bob Orlowsky supplied a bunch of useful postings to the list; Mr. Conrad Planas of Davie, Florida, sent eight densely scripted pages of corrections and annotations; Mr. Austin Pratt of Seattle corrected my glosses on naval nomenclature and service slang; Mr. Chris Pyle, formerly of the University of Kentucky, helped enormously with Pynchon's comic book references; and my lifelong friend Mr. Fredric Rosenberg of Palmdale, California, advised on sixties-era drug subculture references and practices, and Los Angeles geography. Ms. Martha Salyers of Asheville, North Carolina, sent seven pages of annotations; Professor Georg Schmundt-Thomas, formerly of the Northwestern University English Department, provided authoritative advice on Pynchon's German usage and cultural references; Professor Andreas Selmeci helped me to obtain a copy of his remarkable 1995 book (coauthored with Dag Henrichsen), *Das Schwarzkommando*; Mr. Harrison Sherwood of Takoma Park, Maryland, patiently explained Pynchon's Argentine Spanish; and Mr. James E. Shirk of Tampa, Florida, clarified various engineering references. Southern Methodist University, my new academic home, has provided the congenial surroundings and fresh resources—especially the precious resource of the time—needed to complete these revisions; Mr. Jay Stevens of Ft. Mitchell, Kentucky, offered several juicy tidbits; the late Professor Brian Stonehill (*requiescat in pace*), of the Pomona College English Department, forwarded several excellent catches, and we all thank him for networking the Pynchon community in April 1995 when he launched the Pynchon list. Professor Joe Tabbi, of the University of Illinois, among other things solved the problem of Pynchon's source for the Wernher von Braun quote used as an epigraph to the novel; Mr. Ben Teague, a scientific and technical translator as well as a meticulous and generous scholar from Athens, Georgia, provided a detailed set of corrections to and additional annotations for the first edition, which notes are now available online (see the bibliography to this edition). The University of Kentucky Graduate School funded a research assistantship crucial to the early stages of my revising work; Prof.-Dr. Dirk Vanderbeke, in English and American Studies at Ernst Moritz Arndt Universität, Greifswald, Germany, gave permission to use his excellent map of Tyrone

Slothrop's European Progress; my brother Gary Weisenburger, wooden boat-builder extraordinaire, clarified details about historic sailing craft and sailing terminology; Mr. D. S. Wentz II, of Hampton, Virginia, sent information on precision gauges and devices; Mr. Alan Westrope posted a number of excellent finds on the Pynchon list; Mr. Skip Wolfe solved one of Pynchon's punning riddles; and Mr. Steven Woods of Seattle, Washington, sent me a number of helpful new notes and revisions.

Some years ago I heard from Professor Brett Scott Rogers of the University of Missouri History Department about a find he made. While working through an archive at the Western Historical Manuscript Collection, the Peter C. Tamony papers, he came across a February 4, 1966, letter from Pynchon to Tamony inquiring whether there was any better dictionary of American slang for the period 1876–1888 than the Harold Wentworth and Stuart Berg Flexner *Dictionary of American Slang*, a standard reference. He'd found that it didn't "give a clear notion of who used what words under what circumstances." Pynchon understood very well how context matters greatly. Did he, Tamony, know of a better resource? Then Pynchon puzzled out loud:

> I ask myself, who gives a shit anyway? What's the point of being histori-cally accurate, nobody's going to notice one way or another. A sticky question, one I've puzzled for a long time, how much you have a right to make up out of your own head.

My experience: *they notice, man! They really do notice!* Readers of *Gravity's Rainbow* and of my *Companion* have demanded that one be "histori-cally accurate" even in treating the most minor details, such as the precise spelling of idiomatic foreign expressions. With great good humor they have trounced my work for its errors and needled Pynchon's (many fewer) errors too, despite all that he clearly did to get things right in *Gravity's Rainbow*—even down to his characters' Argentine Spanish slang. I trust that this revised second edition of the *Companion* better lives up to that shared faith and joy in fact and fiction.

Dallas, Texas

Introduction

THE first draft of *Gravity's Rainbow* was written out in neat, tiny script on engineers' quadrille paper. The idea had grown, parts of it during a stint in Mexico, from *V.*, Pynchon's first novel. It had been put aside for a second book, *The Crying of Lot 49* ("in which I seem to have forgotten most of what I thought I'd learned up till then," Pynchon would later lament, too harsh a critic of his own work [*Slow Learner* 22]). It was completed in southern California and New York. Visitors to his cave-like rooms perched two blocks up from the Pacific in Manhattan Beach, a Los Angeles suburb, recall only a cot, desk, and some bookshelves. One ruling mood of the place was a monkish impermanence; another, his warm, nonchalant eccentricity. Arranged on the shelves were an assortment of piggy banks and several books about swine. He delighted in a friend's wife who could parody Shirley Temple singing "On the Good Ship Lollipop." On his desk were deposited, in strata, various letters, miscellanea, and those quadrille sheets. Atop them stood a rocket constructed much like one of Picasso's found objects: it was made out of a pencil-type eraser (the kind from which you peel off the corkscrew wrapper) in which a needle had been inserted to form a nose and to which a bent paper clip had been attached to serve as a launching pad.

Gravity's Rainbow was released on February 28, 1973, under the astrological sign of Pisces, the watery house of dreams and dissolution. "Madness spews forth in torrents, Pandora's evils incarnate!" wrote *Publishers Weekly*. Richard M. Nixon, satirized in the novel's final pages as Richard M. Zhlubb, was referring to "the Watergate mess" as an obsessive fabrication of newswriters, and much of the nation still believed him.

Thomas Pynchon's big book quickly confirmed him as one of the few novelists of unprecedented genius to emerge in the postwar era. Here was the Great American Novel at last. The reviewers' favorite comparisons were to *Moby Dick* and *Ulysses*. There was a remarkable flap over the Pulitzer awards, with judges so sharply divided against trustees over the book that no award in fiction was given—the only year that's ever happened. The novel won a National Book Award (shared it, with Isaac Bashevis Singer, for *A Crown of Feathers*), and it was awarded a Howells Medal in 1975 (though, speaking on Pynchon's behalf, stand-up comic Irwin Corey made light of the honor). That early hoopla has long since yielded to more sober assessments of Pynchon's achievement, but scholarly critics have also tended toward superlatives. Tony Tanner (*Thomas Pynchon* 75), for instance, hails the book as "both one of the great historical novels of our time and arguably the most important literary text since *Ulysses*." Translations of the novel attest to its international importance. *Gravity's Rainbow* has been published in French (as *Rainbow*, 1975), German (as *Die Enden der Parabel*, 1981), and Spanish (as *El arco iris de la gravedad*, 1978). Episodes of the book have been translated into Japanese. Through all of this, Pynchon has militantly guarded his privacy. His public appearances are, at best, like skyrockets: brief, brilliant, unexpected, consisting in a few jacket blurbs, letters, introductions to his own and others' work, and a (short and very crotchety) cover essay for the *New York Times Book Review*. There are persistent rumors of forthcoming work. Still, we know little at all about the author himself; in an age when all manner of novelists are routinely interviewed about their work and composing processes, Pynchon is mum. With *Gravity's Rainbow*, to alter a sentence Pynchon once got from Wittgenstein, "the text" is all that is the case.

ABOUT THIS BOOK

I began this study because a set of basic textual and critical questions needed answers. At a minimum, these questions included: What is the structure of *Gravity's Rainbow*? What are its most persistent and significant stylistic features? What focuses its satires and parodies? What are the source texts Pynchon transformed into fiction? The points of connection between (on the one hand) procedures of science and technology and (on the other) the rituals of religion and occultism? Perhaps most basic of all, I wanted to gain a more coherent, readerly understanding of the simple when and where of story events. The obvious strategy was to begin annotating the text.

A *"Gravity's Rainbow" Companion* is intended to serve as a sourcebook on Pynchon's novel, as comprehensive as one might make it. The following notes were written to ease the demands of the novel's multilanguaged style, its obscure and brilliantly pointed references. They are meant to document sources and to spin readers outward from the text itself, into contexts that open the reading in new and unsuspected ways. The *Companion* was conceived as a line-by-line guidebook; indeed, as eight resources in one: a source study, encyclopedia, handbook, motif index, dictionary, explicator, gazetteer, and list of textual errors (nearly twenty-five in the Bantam edition).

On the whole, this commentary is as attentive as I can presently make it, though some items have doubtless escaped notice. For example, Pynchon has a remarkable ear for popular song lyrics—from thirties jazz tunes to sixties rock 'n' roll. He riffs on the rhythms of dialogue in Plasticman comics and snippets of speech from the film *Casablanca*—and other ears will surely recognize echoes I have missed. My aim was not completion, a desire *Gravity's Rainbow* laughs away by reference to Murphy's Law, but comprehension, a sense of the field. The commentary also had to walk a thin line between supplying information and offering interpretation. I found, for example, that a rare coincidence of the occidental calendar occurred in 1945: Easter Sunday fell on April Fool's Day. Further, the Feast of the Transfiguration fell on Sunday, August 6, when the first atomic bomb was released to the pull of gravity over Hiroshima. For Pynchon, fictions followed from these facts, and they all participate in the stunningly ambiguous cyclical structure of the novel. What Pynchon's critics eventually make of that pattern remains to be seen. For now, however, it would be folly to ignore its interpretive potential.

A brief analogy: readers familiar with Gifford and Seidman's annotations for *Ulysses*, their *Notes for Joyce* (1974), will remark that I have copied the format and so could have as easily followed their model with respect to content as well by providing factual, interpretively neutral annotations. But Gifford and Seidman, like their readers, already had access to extensive descriptions of the structure and style of *Ulysses*. Their notes laid a wealth of filigree on an existing model.

I wish this had been the need when I began annotating *Gravity's Rainbow*, but it was not. Indeed, the prevailing impression was that Pynchon's book stood on the landscape like a formless monster with little, if any, organizing skeleton. This impression is still quite pronounced among many of Pynchon's poststructuralist, deconstructionist readers. They wish to make strong claims for his contemporaneity, and therefore they tend to come out swinging against virtually any hint that a particular signifier might totalize one's reading of the novel. Given this reception of the book, these notes have had to sketch in broad strokes patterns of narrative order at the same time that they have had to acknowledge the theoretical assumptions involved in doing so. Throughout, I have been guided by the unwritten axiom that textual sources and facts suggest interpretations, and I have welcomed that interplay.

In my view, the most significant revelation of the annotations is that *Gravity's Rainbow* unfolds according to a circular design. Across the novel's four parts, historical events intersect the Christian liturgical calendar, suggesting possibilities for return and renewal, but possibilities that Pynchon's satire hopelessly equivocates on. This means that readers might have a novel as elegantly modeled as Joyce's *Ulysses* and have their deconstructionism too. Indeed, one might well read *Gravity's Rainbow* as a satire on the very desire for grand plots or metanarratives, a desire the narrative unmasks as the terrible dynamic of a culture huddling on the brink of nuclear winter. I take up these interpretive problems again, briefly, at the end of this introduction.

HOW TO USE THIS BOOK

These notes refer to the principal American editions of *Gravity's Rainbow*: the Viking (1973), which appeared in both hardcover and as a Penguin trade paperback; the Bantam (1974), with its smaller and lengthier format; and the most recently released, repaginated Penguin (2000). Items from the narrative are listed, in boldface, by page and line numbers for editions— "V" for the Viking/Penguin (1973), "B" for the Bantam (1974), and "P" for the Penguin Great Books of the Twentieth Century (2000).

Sources and contextual references are from items generally listed in the bibliography, and many annotations are cross-referenced using the 1973 Viking/Penguin numbers (all that's needed to move around in the *Companion*) and the abbreviation "n." To locate references on their pages of *Gravity's Rainbow* more quickly, it helps to know that uninterrupted pages in the Viking/Penguin editions generally have forty-one lines of text and the Bantam forty-two. In these notes, line numbers refer only to actual lines of text; blank lines don't count.

Ideally, one would prefer to have an annotated edition of the novel. One might then "look down at the bottom of the text of the day, where footnotes will explain all," as the narrator remarks (V204.26–27). One solution is simply to put the *Companion* under or alongside the novel and follow an interrupted reading with a more fluent, second turn. Another solution is to read an episode and then the annotations—the best way, in my view, as it more closely approximates the inferential processes of reading. Indeed, the reader soon begins tracking back and forth in the narrative, an activity encouraged by both the cross-referencing and the index. For simplicity, these employ Viking/Penguin numbers only. But this poses no problem for Bantam readers since all entries include the corresponding Bantam and 2000 Penguin page- and line-number references.

One of my ideas in undertaking these notes is that scholarly studies can be user-friendly. If *Gravity's Rainbow* sets in motion "the Night's Mad Carnival" (V133.38) of intertextual entertainments, then these annotations succeed if they get more readers aboard more of the rides.

FOR FURTHER STUDY

To open *Gravity's Rainbow* is to step into a shifting field of languages, each with its own spatiotemporal uniqueness. Part 3 represents this field as a horizontal "Zone," an uncertain, skeptical, often violent ground where an old hierarchy of values has been leveled. Everywhere in the novel, words are caught up in the cataclysmic change they describe. Yet the reading must begin with them, and the complexity of that task is apparent from a listing of only those formal discourses we encounter, including

—Hebrew (imaged through Kabbalistic writings)
—German (through the narrator's references to technical sources on
    rocketry, the poetry of Rainer Maria Rilke, and Teutonic mythology)
—Kazakh (prior to and during its clash with Soviet bureaucracy)
—Russian (through a score of bureaucratic designations)

—Spanish (via Argentine literary icons: Hernández, Lugones, and Borges)

—French (a source of some conversational puns)

—Japanese (in references to the kamikaze squadrons and haiku)

—Herero (as preserved first by nineteenth-century German philology and then in the Herero people's fateful clash with German colonialism)

To date, the critical commentary on *Gravity's Rainbow* has mostly side-stepped the implications of this great, encyclopedic heteroglossia, though it is full of possibilities. One line of questions should certainly take up the ways a whole language is represented, or refracted, through a specialized jargon or argot: Hebrew, for instance, by way of Kabbalistic mysticism; or Russian, by way of bureaucratic acronyms and the like. Another line of inquiry ought to take up the ways one language is refracted through, or even demolished by, another: Kazakh, for example, as it collides with the bureaucratizing needs of Soviet overlords during the twenties; or Herero, under the boot of General von Trotha's colonialist *Venichtungsbefehl* (extermination order) in 1904. Then there is the larger question of how the novel's "foreign" discourses nuance meanings within its English-language narration. A fine example occurs in episode 4 of part 2, unforgettable (the Pulitzer trustees evidently raged against it) for its depiction of Katje Borgesius as a sable-draped "Domina Nocturna," engaging Brigadier General Pudding in a gut-wrenching act of urolagnia and coprophagia. As the annotations show, Pynchon has brought together two mythologies (the Teutonic and the Kabbalistic) in this episode to produce a satiric inversion of the Kabbalistic ascent to the Merkabah, or divine throne, a narrative technique that is in fact characteristic of many other moments in the book and whose success hinges here as elsewhere on the means by which a person's profoundest nightmares are colonized and used for purposes of control.

Turning next to the variety of *informal* discourses in the narration, one faces a still more uncertain flux. From the word-hoard of English Pynchon has grabbed varieties of pop cultural and subcultural discourses that include, at a minimum,

—popular slang (picked up from jokes, street ditties, song lyrics, comic books, street speech, and popular cinema)

—ethnic usage (black English, the Hispanic slang of *pachuco* zoot-suiters, others)

—underworld cant (especially as it pertains to black marketeering in drugs and contraband)

—regional dialects (from the American Southwest, Boston, and Britain)

—service slang (from both the American and the British military services, probably gleaned from *Partridge's Dictionary of Forces' Slang*)

—esoteric cant (by way of astrology, black magic, freemasonry, Rosicrucianism, and the like)

—folk usage (as found in children's lore and games, folktales, material culture, and so on)

—professional jargon (cinematography, ballistics, statistics, chemistry, behavioral and Pavlovian psychology, and many more)

It would be hard to overestimate the importance of these extraliterary languages in *Gravity's Rainbow*. The book's foremost source of surprise, incongruity, bathos, and recognition—in short, of satiric laughter—this heteroglossia nuances every narrative turn. This unofficial side of modern discourse provides a rich store of curses and words related to excretory and sexual indecencies and fantasies, as well as terms connected with compulsions toward states of inebriation and anesthesia. Such "unauthorized" languages are common to preterite souls everywhere, and in them the narration discovers specific points of view on the world, unsuspected orderings of things and values. Sometimes such views stand in sharp opposition to the official side; they often serve up ready-made parodies of it. So these languages may reveal a delightful absence of repression and sublimation, a bluntness that even verges on political aggression, as, for example, in the hard-won sexual intimacy of Roger Mexico and Jessica Swanlake or when Roger and "Pig" Bodine break up the "Krupp wingding" (V711.17) of part 4 with strings of obscene, alliterative epithets. Yet kinds of unofficial discourse may just as often be routinized, subordinated, and dominated by other languages as, for instance, in the case of Brigadier Pudding's humiliating coprophagia or the satirical fantasy of the "Toilet-ship" in part 3.

This unofficial side of ordinary language also supplies the novel with a welter of ready-made folkloric genres: puns, rhyming speech, jokes and ditties, popular lyrics, children's games, and pantomimes. All are integrated into the novel's satirical project. Consider, for example, the closing episode of part 1, in which Roger Mexico spends Boxing Day at a pantomime of Hansel and Gretel, that Pynchon doubtless selected for its harsh judgments against parents, symbolized in the witch whose *Kinderofen* has its analogue in the V-2 rocket used to sacrifice a young boy, Gottfried, in the novel's climactic scene. Or the reference in episode 28 of part 4 to the street game popular among children in Berlin, *Himmel und Hölle* (Heaven and Hell), a form of hopscotch involving ten steps, beginning from a zero space called *Erde* (Earth), leading through *Hölle*, and ending in *Himmel* (see V567.24–25n). The game corresponds to a great variety of homewarding, ten-stage motifs in *Gravity's Rainbow*, most notably the countdown preceding a rocket launch.

Whatever their source, these folkloric genres are all redirected by the radical undertaking of Pynchon's novel. Traditionally vital to the acculturation of both children and adults, in *Gravity's Rainbow* they contribute to a vastly articulated defamiliarization of history and culture. This is even the case with the novel's simplest structuring device, its division into four parts, which satirizes a traditional schema from hagiographic and heroic narratives: (1) the disclosure of the hero's miraculous gifts, (2) his education, (3) his testing during a course of travels, and (4) the confirmation of his powers, a revelation. This plot is projected onto a lower plane; the narration pulls it down, not only by inversion but also by means of everyday lore and lingo, those unofficial languages outlined above.

Reading that plot, it quickly becomes apparent that building up networks of detail is one key aspect of Thomas Pynchon's style, his creative technique. For example, in Marion Cooper's 1933 film *King Kong*, the "giant scapeape" (V275.34) originates from a South Seas place called Skull Island. The V-2 rocket originated from Peenemünde, an island off the Usedom coast of northern Germany, long a pleasant resort on the Baltic Sea yet glimpsed from above (on maps from Pynchon's sources) as a skull—or so the narrator remarks. On the fictional page this detail momentarily links both monstrosities, ape and rocket, in a web of narrative inferences. Pynchon is drawn to these possibilities for fictional transformation. The moments that speak most resonantly for him are those when lowly, seemingly preterite stuff is raised up, when its hidden signs and broader humanness stand redeemed. The black and evil-smelling coal tars of nineteenth-century organic chemistry are recalled for yielding up a rainbow of colorful dyestuffs. "'All the shit is transmuted to gold,'" as one of his stoned characters puts it (V440.23). The novel's epigraph from Nazi (and later, U.S.) rocket man Wernher von Braun puts it another way: "Nature does not know extinction; all it knows is transformation."

In the minutest of the myriad details of its composition, *Gravity's Rainbow* reveals this idea at work. Images on film are transmuted into facts; folk sayings suddenly inspire acts. Characters become the forces signaled from deep in the provenance of their names. And everywhere in the book footnotes (subtexts) are raised from the bottoms of the pages in Pynchon's sources and integrated into fictional text. Horsley Gantt, Pavlov's translator, footnotes *gorodki*, a favorite game of Russian peasants; in playing, they lay waste to wood-block "cities" by heaving rough-hewn bats (*gorodki* sticks) over considerable distances. Considering how V-2 rockets were fired on London, Pavlov's "old *gorodki* stick" therefore cuts a significant figure in a poem (done after the manner of T. S. Eliot) by the fictional Pavlovian, Pointsman, as rockets fall about him (V226.33n). It's but one of many instances where marginal, footnoted material is transmuted into fictional reference and event.

There are several patterns in Pynchon's borrowings that are worth further attention. The first is that many of the novel's episodes draw their backgrounds, references, and even details of plotting from a central source text: the two volumes of Pavlov's *Lectures* in several episodes of part 1; a technical handbook on rocketry by Dutch scientists Kooy and Uytenbogaart in episodes of parts 1 and 2; Richard Sasuly's *IG Farben* on German manufacturing cartels and the dyestuff/chemical industry in parts 2 and 3; an anthropological dissertation on the Herero for episodes treating South-West Africa; Thomas Winner on the Kazakhs; General Walter Dornberger on day-to-day activities and conditions at Peenemünde. A second pattern is that, in working with such texts, Pynchon's eye seems preternaturally alert to moments of personal testimony, comments often buried in footnotes or beneath heaps of technical data and objective detail. Pavlov's *gorodki* stick; his use of himself as subject of study; Dornberger's recollections of local-color detail; the memories of travelers, anthropologists, wives of rocket engineers, Japanese kamikaze pilots—these and many more are woven into *Gravity's Rainbow*.

I hope these annotations will help to rebut those impatient Pecksniffs (the Pulitzer trustees, John Gardner in *On Moral Fiction*, and Gore Vidal, to name just a few) who have condemned *Gravity's Rainbow* as a careless, amoral, and malignant book. Pynchon's better readers, too taken by matters technical and theoretical, have mostly written around the fringes of this issue. But Pynchon's is no limp, value-free historicism. Everywhere in *Gravity's Rainbow* the testimony of his witnesses stands in relation to a moral vision. For example, in their voluminous recollections ex-Nazis like Walter Dornberger and Wernher von Braun wave aside the issue of slave labor at Peenemünde with euphemisms like "foreign construction workers" and neither of them ever treats the use of death-camp labor at the final assembly plant at Nordhausen. In one of the really chilling ironies of it all, virtually the only Nazi associated with the rocket program to remember those death-camp inmates was Albert Speer, sentenced to life imprisonment in Spandau Prison while both Dornberger and von Braun went on to the United States, Dornberger ending up sitting on the board at Bell Helicopter and von Braun heading up NASA during the Apollo moon launches. This is the context one is asked to bear in mind when the narrative suggests that Blicero, an embodiment of everything truly evil and deadly in the German romance of rocketry, has gone on to the United States, remarking that to find him readers should "look among the successful academics, the presidential advisers, the token intellectuals who sit on boards of directors. He is almost surely there. Look high, not low" (V749.10–12). At the novel's actual (if not virtual) center, the story of Franz Pökler (episode 11 of part 3) stands against that collective loss of memory. Pökler's struggle with these moral cruxes, including finally his simple act of empathy at the Nordhausen concentration camp, does establish a normative base for Pynchon's satirical aggressions even though the account of this struggle is composed mainly from Dornberger's testimony. In their composition, other episodes also contribute to such a reading. Against the novel's critics, there is thus a great deal more to be said about the politics and morality of its fiction making.

Careful attention to *Gravity's Rainbow* also discloses patterns of structure. Especially in part 1, a number of episodes trace a complex, circular motion. Episode 9, for example, begins with Jessica Swanlake standing at a window and then moves through a sequence of analepses (or flashbacks), cuts that also involve shifts in focalization, all without any of the spatiotemporal markers that conventionally signal shifts to readers, until it finally concludes with Jessica standing, once more, at the window. Again in part 1, episode 14 is a much more complex variant on this cyclical pattern. It opens at Pirate Prentice's London maisonette with Katje Borgesius standing before the lens of Osbie Feel's movie camera; the first analepsis, focalized through Katje, discloses Blicero, Gottfried, and Katje at the rocket battery in Holland; the second, focalized now through Blicero, takes us to South-West Africa during the Herero insurrection of 1922. Then we return momentarily to the second-order time (at the Holland rocket battery) in order to begin a third analepsis, this time focalized through one of Katje's seventeenth-century ancestors, Frans van der Groov, on the island of Mauritius; the narration ends by cycling readers back to the place where we began but a little while later, with Katje still standing before the camera eye, the film of her having been completed. Other episodes and bits of episodes (the "Tamara/Italo drill" [V261.39–40] of episode 6 in part 2, the circular group grope of episode 14 in part 3) are similarly shaped. To adopt a term from the narrator's own discussions of organic chemistry, this episodic structuring of *Gravity's Rainbow* is "heterocyclic" (V249.26): rings are looped together in still larger polymerized rings that are looped together in the still larger cycling of its four parts.

Indeed, when annotating *Gravity's Rainbow*, one of my greatest surprises came with the discovery that details of story reveal a narrative chronometrics that can be concisely plotted. I mean detail of the most unobtrusive sort: images of the moon, remarks about weather, movies playing at London theaters, a song playing over the radio, references to BBC programs and newspaper headlines and saints' days. Many of these were available to Pynchon through one of his main sources, the *Times* of London. Collectively, they enable one to pinpoint the story time of many episodes, sometimes to within an hour.

This chronology unfolds according to a carefully drawn circular design. *Gravity's Rainbow* is not arch-shaped, as is commonly supposed. It is plotted like a mandala, its quadrants carefully marked by Christian feast days that happened to coincide, in 1944–45, with key historical dates and ancient pagan festivals. The implications of this design are several—and wonderfully complex.

Part 1 begins on December 18, 1944, in the Advent season, and it ends nine days later on Boxing Day, December 26, when Christmas comes to the British servant classes. A saturnalian office party in episode 20 invokes the pagan counterpart to the Judeo-Christian feasts of Hanukkah (celebrated on the 25th of Kislev) and Christmas. Part 2 commences around Christmas, with Slothrop newly arrived at Monaco, and it concludes on May 20, 1945—Whitsunday, or Pentecost, when Christians celebrate the descent of the Holy

Ghost to the disciples, seven weeks after Easter. On that "White Sunday" in the novel, Pointsman is visited by auditory hallucinations while vacationing at Dover's white cliffs. Part 3 opens with an obscure reference to four saints' days in mid-May and ends on the Feast of the Transfiguration, celebrated on August 6 in the Roman Catholic church to mark Christ's final earthly revelation of his divinity—a blaze of illumination followed by a white cloud—witnessed by Peter, James, and John as they stood atop a mountain. But August 6, 1945, was also the day Hiroshima was bombed. Part 4 begins with an analepsis to that day, with Tyrone Slothrop on a mountaintop in central Germany, where he "becomes a cross himself, a crossroads" (V625.3–4), and thereupon begins to disappear from the novel. Transfiguration: Hiroshima. After scattered references to the A-bomb, and narrative insinuations that bomb and rocket are technologies soon to be joined, part 4 ends, nominally, around September 14, 1945, on the Feast of the Exaltation (or "Raising") of the Holy Cross, whose fictional counterpart is the "rocket raising" of V-2 number 00001 by Enzian and his Herero comrades. Figurally, part 4 ends with an almost simultaneous prolepsis and analepsis. The proleptic jump forward in time takes us to Los Angeles and the Orpheus Theater, circa 1970. The analeptic jump cut reveals the firing of Rocket 00000, with its sacrifice of Gottfried (God's peace), which finally occurs after much anticipation from the Lüneburg Heath, at noon, during Easter of 1945. But in 1945 the Easter holy day fell on April Fool's. Easter: April Fool's. That coincidence had occurred only forty-three times since A.D. 500; it occurred again in 1956 but would not happen again during the twentieth century.

This is the shape of *Gravity's Rainbow*: a mandala, its four quadrants marked by crucial dates on the Christian liturgical calendar, that traces a motion in which the circle of redemptive death, or foolishness (read it however you will) is nearly closed. It reveals a design formed as much by traditional, orderly patterning as by contemporary, purely coincidental events. The liturgical structure seems to focus the novel around a theme of salvation, a redeeming earthly savior. Equally as well, the pagan coincidences suggest that the whole enterprise is a *poisson d'avril*, a red herring, a fool's quest. And one can find nothing in the novel to resolve this antinomy. Everywhere in *Gravity's Rainbow* the parabolic arch symbolizes disease, dementia, and destruction. Its counterpart is the circular mandala, a symbol of opposites held in delicate equipoise. In the novel drinking games and dances move in circles; the Herero villages used to be arranged mandala-like; and in every episode there are windmills, buttons, windows, eyes, Ferris wheels, roulette wheels, rocket insignia, and other cast-down indexes of the novel's grand cycling. Pynchon's lowly, preterite souls come together around such symbols. Indeed, this circular structure is introduced to readers in the opening episode, when Pirate Prentice watches the sunrise blaze through the contrail of a newly launched V-2 and imagines its parabolic trajectory transformed into a rainbow that can only be a perfect circle high over the North Sea (see V6.33–35n). And the narrator reminds us of this event near the close, commenting that the rainbow is "not, as we might imagine, bounded below by the line of the Earth it 'rises from' and the Earth it 'strikes' No But Then You Never Really Thought It Was Did You Of Course It Begins Infinitely Below The Earth And Goes On Infinitely Back Into The Earth it's only the peak that we are allowed to see" (V726.17–21). Put another way, only gravity's rainbow is arch-shaped; the shape of *Gravity's Rainbow* is circular.

The literary precursors of this design, at least those that come most directly to mind, are Joyce's *Ulysses* and Melville's great satire, *The Confidence-Man*. Both involve cyclical plots unfolding over exactly three-fourths of a solar day. *Gravity's Rainbow* unfolds over nine months, three-fourths of a solar year. And like Melville, Pynchon sets the decisive action of his book, the firing of Rocket 00000, on Easter/April Fool's. As in *The Confidence-Man*, this one detail renders hopelessly equivocal any theme of salvation.

Thomas Pynchon ends his great satire on that wholly ambiguous crux. The ninth month of his narrative draws to a close with swarms of characters chasing various red herrings and arriving "too late" at the Holy Center (V752.12). Like the "Holy-Center-Approaching" (V508.35) he satirizes, Pynchon's novel ends on the threshold of a tenth month; the rocket crew runs through its ten-stage countdown; surely, then, some revelation is at hand. Yet the book refuses to dish up that summarizing symbol. The narrative approaches, but avoids, closure. It combines the elegance of a preordained structure and the unintelligibility of pure coincidence. Does it see history as plotted or accidental? Is the rocket descending on the last page a symbol of divinely prefigured salvation or the triumph of an absolute violence? *Gravity's Rainbow* will not say, and neither can the notes in this book. They are offered to fuel that process of transformation that is reading.

POSTSCRIPT (2006)

Reading and rereading *Gravity's Rainbow* for this revised edition, while also working into the book new information other readers have sent and that I discovered over the years, has brought me here—I think—to a much more complete *Companion*. The text itself grew by a quarter of its 1988 size. All of the significant "unknowns" have been identified—most notably, for example, the source of Pynchon's epigraph from Wernher von Braun, and his enigmatic "Kenosha Kid" references. Pynchon's allusions to and quotations from pop and material culture items—movies and songs and comics, as well as brand names and place names and strange foods and arcane objects—are much more fully and accurately annotated in this edition. The ears and eyes of other readers have been vital in that work; equally and unexpectedly crucial to the revisions has been the awesome power of search engines roving through digitized databases. Doing this research without something like Google seems impossible, now.

Rereading with a critical eye the 1988 *Companion*, I found that its claims about Pynchon's circular design for *Gravity's Rainbow* have held up well. I therefore decided to leave claims related to that design untouched; indeed in a few places they've been sharpened. At the same time, I found it necessary to back away somewhat from some claims I made about the dates and times of episodes. At key moments in the novel Pynchon can be very concise—for example, in pegging events at the close of part 3 and the beginning of part 4 pretty nearly to the fateful moment when U.S. Army Air Corps Colonel Paul Tibbetts opened the bomb-bay doors of his B-29, the *Enola Gay*, and dropped the first atomic bomb, over Hiroshima. Yet Pynchon's chronology is at times also, as Bernard Duyfhuizen has shown, loose and much more impressionistic than one might expect from the narrative's concision elsewhere. I amended these pages to reflect that wiser sense of what happens in the novel's story world, attempting to avoid overnaturalizing a fiction that so accents fantasy and dreamscapes, as well as historical events shrouded and nimbused by uncertainty, haunted by ghosts.

Part 1 *Beyond the Zero*

P ART 1 of *Gravity's Rainbow* (herein abbreviated *GR*), entitled "Beyond the Zero," spans nine days of the Advent and Christmas season, from December 18 through December 26, 1944. There are also a number of carefully orchestrated analepses: to the day several months earlier when the first V-2 rocket fell on England; to an Easter 1942 air raid by Allied bombers on the German city of Lübeck, which first prompted Hitler to warn of the coming *Vergeltungswaffe,* or "revenge weapons"; to prewar Britain; to the seventeenth-century Dutch colony of Mauritius; and to Puritan America, with all its millennial hopes. Braiding these separate strands of narrative together is a strong theme of anticipated redemption. Characters feel as though they stand poised at the edge of some sought-after revelation from "beyond the zero" of empirical knowledge. The Advent season suggests one form that revelation might assume—the Nativity story. Yet Pynchon's depictions of technological, psychological, and paranormal research all demonstrate how modern culture secularizes that redemptive hope.

Indeed, Pynchon's satire quickly erases the boundary between sacred and secular, and this erasure is signaled vividly in his epigraph to part 1. Long unknown but now identified thanks to Joseph Tabbi's excellent sleuthing (see his *Postmodern Sublime* 5–6), the source was a little homily by Werner von Braun, the Nazi and then NASA "Inventor & Space Expert" (which is how the author is identified at the beginning of the piece), that raises questions about scientific responsibility and about that responsibility in relation to a human afterlife, two major themes in *GR*. Pynchon's source was William Nichols's *Third Book of Words to Live By* (1962), which reads as follows:

Why I Believe in Immortality

I believe . . . that the soul of Man is immortal and will be treated
with justice in another life respecting its conduct in this.
　　—Benjamin Franklin

Today, more than ever before, our survival—yours and mine and our children's—depends on our adherence to ethical principles. Ethics alone will decide whether atomic energy will be an earthly blessing or the source of mankind's utter destruction.

Where does the desire for ethical action come from? What makes us want to be ethical? I believe there are two forces which move us. One is belief in a Last Judgment, when every one of us has to account for what we did with God's great gift of life on the earth. The other is belief in an immortal soul, a soul which will cherish the reward or suffer the penalty decreed in a final Judgment.

Belief in God and in immortality thus give us the moral strength and the ethical guidance we need for virtually every action in our daily lives.

In our modern world many people seem to feel that science has somehow made such "religious ideas" untimely or old-fashioned.

But I think science has a real surprise for skeptics. Science, for instance, tells us that nothing in nature, not even the tiniest particle, can disappear without a trace.

Think about that for a moment. Once you do, your thoughts about life will never be the same.

Science has found that nothing can disappear without a trace. Nature does not know extinction. All it knows is transformation!

Now, if God applies this fundamental principle to the most minute and insignificant parts of His universe, doesn't it make sense to assume that He applies it also to the masterpiece of His creation—the human soul? I think it does. And everything that science has taught me—and continues to teach me—strengthens my belief in the continuity of our spiritual existence after death. Nothing disappears without a trace.

Pynchon's epigraph radically trims the German rocket man's implicit claims that modern science will validate transcendentalist beliefs in an afterlife. Still more significantly, Pynchon excises von Braun's claims that a belief in immortality creates a human desire for ethical action or "transformation," in particular a need to prevent nuclear holocaust that is itself a possible consequence of the brainchildren of applied scientists like Von Braun. The irony of von Braun's concern is one that a few perceptive critics—like Joel Dana Black (23–24)—have understood even without having the source text. Indeed, with respect to such ironies note that Pynchon further excises the text's own epigraph from Ben Franklin (an earlier, kite-in-the-sky space expert) and its thoughts about divine justice, a deletion that *GR* might be said to massively backfill by figuring von Braun's V-2 rocket as epitome of modern war machinery and terror. In any case, von Braun's text corresponds thematically with Pynchon's concern throughout part 1 of *GR* with "the other side," with paranormal and metaphysical being.

Numerological correspondences also shape part 1. Discounting analepses, the narration is carefully plotted through nine winter days; in turn, the novel spans nine months, from mid-December to mid-September of 1945. There are twenty-one episodes in part 1; the tarot deck has twenty-one numbered cards, if one omits the Fool, which is a zero or null card with no assigned place in the tarot sequence. And this part begins a sequence of astrological correspondences. Events in these episodes unfold under the sign of Pisces. Sagittarius, the ninth house in the astrological calendar, would be the *actual* sign; but symbolically, *virtually*, the action everywhere takes place on a Piscean aspect because this house, the twelfth, stands for death and dissolution, for contact with the supernatural, as well as for warfare and strife. In part 2 Aries will emerge as a sign of renewals and departures.

EPISODE I

The novel opens around dawn in the London cottage of Pirate Prentice. Episodes 1 through 5 all occur on the same day, which subsequent allusions pinpoint as Monday, December 18, 1944. This episode begins with Pirate dreaming about the evacuation from London of its preterite souls who pass under "the final arch," symbol of "a judgment from which there is no appeal" (V4.2–4). With the end-times motif thus established in a nightmare vision, Pirate awakens to the fall of a comrade, whom he manages to save, and to the impending fall of a V-2 rocket, just launched from Holland, against which he and the Allied forces are powerless to save anyone. Watching the morning sun illuminate its vapor trail over the North Sea, Pirate imagines the light refracting into a rainbow that could only be not a parabola, but a perfect circle.

V3.3, B3.3–4, P3.3   The Evacuation still proceeds, but it's all theatre.
Historically, this is a fair analogy. When Germany began its V-1 or buzz bomb offensive in June 1944, one and a half million civilians were evacuated from London. Minister of Home Security Herbert Morrison was also prepared to order an almost total evacuation if the expected barrage of rockets proved as devastating as he feared. British intelligence experts had predicted that the rocket would carry a warhead of seven tons, and Hitler was boasting that Nazi rockets would deliver five hundred tons of explosives each hour. However, when the first V-2 dropped on Chiswick in September, British intelligence quickly realized that the weapon would be much weaker (it carried not seven tons of amatol explosive but one) and nowhere near as prolific (1517 hit London during the entire seven months of V-2 assault). Still, the V-2's proved an effective weapon of terror, and to calm citizens the British Home Security office proceeded with some of its evacuation plans. Irving (*Mare's Nest* 80, 280–81, 287–88) sees the evacuations as good public relations with Londoners needing assurances.

V3.7, B3.8–9, P3.7–8   the fall of a crystal palace   A reference to the glass-and-iron display hall designed by Sir Joseph Paxton for the Great Exhibition of 1851. From 1854 (when it was put back up after having been dismantled in 1851) until 1936, when it was razed by fire, the structure stood—a symbol of Victorian progress—in London's Hyde Park. Two of its towers survived the fire but were dismantled in 1940 to prevent German bomber crews from using them as landmarks.

V3.14, B3.16, P3.14   second sheep   In the terms of Calvinist theology, second sheep are *preterite,* those predestined for abandonment at the moment of Christ's apocalyptic return, in contrast to the *elect* who are predestined for redemption. Here Pynchon commences a string of theological references to the doctrine of preterition, which his distant ancestor William Pynchon—like an ancestor of the novel's protagonist Tyrone Slothrop—undermined in his theological writings (see especially V555.29–31).

V3.29, B3.35, P4.5   naphtha winters   Naphtha is the flammable liquid obtained from the distillation of coal and used to fire gaslights and heaters. The first of many coal derivatives mentioned in the narrative.

V3.34, B4.3, P4.10   Absolute Zero   The centigrade temperature of minus 273.15 degrees, at which matter possesses the least energy; thus a *physically* inert condition. In Pavlov's neuropsychiatric writings, however, the term assumes a parallel meaning Pynchon will soon reference: "An unreinforced conditioned reflex without any repetitions . . . ends in every case in extinction, [returns] to an absolute zero" (*Lectures* 2:121). Here, it signifies total nonresponsiveness to external stimuli, thus a *psychologically* inert condition, the imagined death in Pirate's dream.

V4.36, B5.7–8, P5.9   un-Hoovered rugs   That is, unvacuumed, after the popular brand of vacuum cleaner manufactured in Ohio. For as ads in the *Times* of London used to claim, "Post-war as Pre-war for Your Ideal Home, Be It Castle or Cottage, the World's Best Cleaner Is THE HOOVER."

V5.3, B5.17, P5.17   His name is Capt. Geoffrey ("Pirate") Prentice   Whose nickname refers us to the 1879 Gilbert and Sullivan opera *The Pirates of Penzance; or, The Slave of Duty*. In its opening act we learn how the hero, Frederic, was bound over as an indentured servant to a quite unsuccessful (because too merciful) pirate band: his nursemaid, Ruth, had misheard the instructions of Frederic's father, who envisioned his boy as apprentice—or, 'prentice—to a ship's *pilot*. In her first song from act 1, Ruth explains her error to Frederic's master, the Pirate King:

> I was a stupid nurserymaid,
> On breakers always steering
> And I did not catch the word aright,
> Through being hard of hearing;
> Mistaking my instructions,
> Which within my brain did gyrate,
> I took and bound this promising boy
> Apprentice to a *pirate*.
>
> A Sad mistake it was to make
> And doom him to a vile lot.
> I bound him to a pirate—you—
> Instead of to a pilot.

V5.15, B5.30–31, P5.29   The Special Operations Executive   Pirate's employer, the British equivalent of the U.S. Office of Strategic Services (OSS), was charged with gathering strategic and technical intelligence. Irving (*Mare's Nest* 209) discloses that during March of 1944 eleven SOE commandos were, like Pirate, parachuted into France and Holland to glean anything they could about the new German V-weapons.

V5.21–22, B5.37–38, P5.35–36   a maisonette . . . the Chelsea Embankment   Baedeker's *London* (158–59) describes the Embankment as "a fine boulevard constructed in 1871–74," extending along the north bank of the Thames "from Chelsea Bridge to Battersea Bridge, a distance of over a mile." Corydon Throsp is fictional; his first name, deriving from the character in Greek poet Theocritus's pastoral works, means "ready for war" but also invokes André Gide's 1924 *Corydon*, a defense of homosexuality as both socially and naturally a sign of advanced civilization. Throsp appears to be Pynchon's creation, while his "maisonette" (cottage) is characteristic of the area. Moreover, Pirate's bohemianism extends a tradition: Oscar Wilde lived at No. 16 Chelsea Embankment from 1884 until his trial in 1895 and the boulevard also skirts Cheyne Walk, once the home of Dante Gabriel Rossetti and Algernon Charles Swinburne, whose drunken carryings-on became legendary stuff.

V5.35–36, B6.12, P6.9 flew the Rio–to–Ascension–to–Fort-Lamy run Thus explaining how bananas would come to London during wartime: from Rio de Janeiro in Brazil, to the British mid-Atlantic naval station on Ascension Island, then to Fort-Lamy (now N'Djamena), the capital city of Chad (the French colony in equatorial Africa), then to England.

V6.9, B6.29, P6.23 climbs a spiral ladder ringing to the roof garden An allusion perhaps to the opening of *Ulysses*. James Joyce's novel opens with "stately plump Buck Mulligan" rising a "winding stairs" in his "dressinggown," while Pirate Prentice in his "wool robe" has climbed this "spiral ladder" to overlook a landscape and ready himself for breakfast, much as Mulligan does. For more, see McCarron ("Openings").

V6.21, B7.1, P6.35 A new star Here, the burst of illumination from a launched rocket. Soon, though, references to various other kinds of stars will emerge in *GR*: for example, the stars children put on their calendars during the Advent season; the star over Bethlehem; patterns of the zodiac; and the (apparently) fateful stars on Tyrone Slothrop's map of his sexual conquests throughout London.

V6.26–27, B7.8, P6.40–41 it's a vapor trail Pynchon's source for this detail is the *Times* of London. V-2 rockets were launched on London from The Hague, 195 miles distant. Nevertheless, from their rooftops and upper windows Londoners might have observed the white starburst of a launch and the vapor trail of a rocket climbing over the North Sea. Many of the missiles were launched at dawn, when the low winter sun would brilliantly illuminate their exhaust. For example, a letter in the *Times* of December 12, 1944 (5, col. 7) describes just such a "bright trace" and subsequent days' editions printed several letters from others who described what Prentice sees on this day.

V6.30, B7.12, P7.3 "Incoming mail" Infantryman's slang for hostile, arriving ordnance; but see V11.10–11n for an occasion when the metaphor is literally fulfilled and Pirate receives word of a communiqué sent to him by V-2 express.

V6.33–35, B7.17–19, P7.7–9 the sun . . . striking the rocket's exhaust . . . making them blaze clear across the sea A fascinating image: the missile's vapor trail would bend the rays of sunlight into a rainbow, not arch-shaped, as one initially suspects, but perfectly circular. Here is why. Later in part 1 (V100.36), Pynchon notes that the rockets were launched from The Hague on London at a compass bearing of 260 degrees WSW, a detail he found in Kooy and Uytenbogaart (*Ballistics of the Future* 285). In mid-December, when Pirate observes this dawn firing, the sun would be nearing its lowest southern latitudes, approximately over South-West Africa (now Namibia), the topos for many of Pynchon's Herero references. The sun would be ascending at a bearing of about 170 degrees ESE, or perpendicular to the rocket's line of trajectory and forming, incidentally, a cross in the sky. Now since a rainbow of illuminated light moves in a direction opposite to that of its source—that is, since the rainbow falls as the sun rises—then this imagined rainbow would be high overhead relative to any observer who might be standing one-half to one mile east-southeast of the rocket's airborne vapor trail. Such an imaginary observer would see a circular rainbow and not the arch we normally witness, one-half of which plunges into the earth. Pynchon reminds us of this fact as *GR* draws to a close: "Of Course It Begins Infinitely Below The Earth and Goes On Infinitely Back Into the Earth" (V726.19–20). Note that Pirate's rainbow is *imagined*: to observe it under these circumstances one would have to be perched high over the North Sea.

V6.37, B7.22, P7.11 Brennschluss Available to Pynchon from a variety of his technical sourcebooks, but most notably Dornberger (9n), who explains: "*Brennschluss*, the 'end of burning'; the German word is preferred to the form 'all-burnt,' which is used in England, because at Brennschluss considerable quantities of fuel may still be left in the tanks." In the V-2 this stage occurred at an altitude of 112.3 miles.

V6.39, B7.24, P7.13–14 But the rocket will be here In the Bantam, "rocket" here is misprinted as "racket." This is the first of many typographical errors in the Bantam edition.

V7.3–4, B7.29–30, P7.18–19 the operations room at Stanmore Thirteen miles northwest of London; home of the Special Operations Executive.

V7.5, B7.31–32, P7.21 Less than five minutes Hague to here Dornberger (*V-2* 14) gives the flight time as "two-ninety-six seconds."

EPISODE 2

The time is later the same morning; the scene, still Pirate's maisonette, then greater London. Pirate prepares a lavish "Banana Breakfast" (V8.28–29) before superiors call him away to retrieve a message come down by rocket. His departure for Greenwich triggers a lengthy analepsis concerned with the "Eastern Question" of 1914. This spins into one of the novel's more eccentric nightmares about a monstrous Adenoid poised to swallow the city of London. Pirate's duty as "fantasist-surrogate" (V12.38–39) is to hold these strands together.

V7.36, B8.25, P8.10   table stakes, B.O.Q.   In poker-playing jargon, "table stakes" is a variable wagering limit fixed by the amount of money on the table at the time of any one bet. "B.O.Q.": a military abbreviation for a Bachelor Officers' Quarters.

V8.11, B9.2, P8.22   "A4, yes"   Pirate uses the German name for the V-2 rocket in its operational configuration (or *Aggregat*) after three earlier versions (so *Aggregat-4*).

V9.3, B9.38, P9.17   Miss Grable   With her virtuoso display of legs in a series of 1943 publicity photos and then in the 1944 film *Pin-up Girl*, American actress Betty Grable (1916–73) became the serviceman's heartthrob of World War II, though all knew she was married to singer and bandleader Harry James (V685.39n).

V9.4, B9.39, P9.18   V-E Day   Allied abbreviation for "Victory in Europe," officially declared on May 8, 1945: Pynchon's eighth birthday, President Harry Truman's sixty-first, and a day of increasing significance as *GR* continues (see V269.32n and V628.4n). The Allies began using the term in August 1944.

V9.5, B9.40, P9.19   grand in Civvie Street   In other words, during peacetime, when soldiers resumed wearing their civilian clothes, or "civvies." Larsson also points out that American actor (and Slothrop look-alike, see V18.25n) George Formby starred in a 1946 film, *George in Civvy Street*.

V9.14, B6–7, P9.28   Bartley Gobbitch, DeCoverly Pox   Bartley's surname would seem to stem from the Middle English "*gobbet*" or "*gobbit*," the noun (according to the *OED*) for a part or piece or lump of something, usually a mass of flesh (but also even a passage) from a body (or text), while Mr. Pox's first name recalls a Middle English variant (again, see the *OED*) for things done secretly or "covertly"—although in Addison and Steele's *Spectator* essays Roger DeCoverly appeared frequently as epitome of the genteel country squire, and Roger DeCoverly (whelped in 1904) was the patriarch of a now legendary line of English setters, the ideal gentleman's shooting dog from breeder George Ryman.

V9.26, B10.22, P9.41   Vat 69   As *Times* of London advertisements used to note, "A Luxury Blend Scotch Whiskey, 25/9 per Bottle."

V9.29, B10.24–25, P10.3   the Jungfrau   German (literally) for "young lady" but generalized in common usage to signify a virgin; also a mountain located in the Interlaken region of Switzerland, outside Zurich, with an elevation of 4,158 meters (13,514 feet).

V9.40, B10.39, P10.15   struggle into Sam Brownes   A type of belt, with a diagonal shoulder strap and often a sidearm holster, designed by one-armed British general Sir Samuel Browne (d. 1901).

V10.9, B11.10–11, P10.25   musaceous odor of Breakfast   The odor from a species of *Musacae*, the banana family of plants.

V10.28, B11.33, P11.3   *C'est magnifique, mais ce n'est pas la guerre*   An exclamation ("It's magnificent, but it's not war!") widely attributed to French general Pierre Bosquet as he observed the Battle of Balaclava, October 25, 1854. The occasion was the brief but bloody Charge of the Light Brigade under Lord Cardigan, whose light-horse company charged across the valley at Balaclava, outside Sevastopol (then under siege by English, French, and Turkish troops), against greatly superior Russian troops. General Bosquet observed the charge from a hillside, on the left flank. Tennyson's well-known ballad (see V270.14–15n) expresses the popular sense of it as a moral victory in the face of certain defeat.

V11.10–11, B12.18, P11.25–26   waiting at Greenwich   The mail-carrying rocket has impacted near the Royal Observatory in Greenwich, the point defined as having a zero degree of longitude.

V11.24–25, B12.34–35, P11.40   east over Vauxhall Bridge . . . green Lagonda . . . his batman   Pirate's route, from the Chelsea Embankment to Greenwich, takes him eastward over the Thames River via the Vauxhall Bridge. The Lagonda was a luxury sedan with separate driver's compartment; its color, green, will be Pirate's once again in part 4. A batman is the traditional soldier-aide assigned to a British officer but it also recalls legendary comic-book hero Bruce Wayne (the creation of DC Comics' artist/writer Bob Kane), who made his Batman debut in May 1939 in that month's *Detective Comics* issue (no. 27).

V11.27, B12.38, P12.2   crew of American sappers   Military engineers, those who dig (or "sap") fortifications.

V11.34, B13.4, P12.9   narodnik   Soules ("What to Think about *Gravity's Rainbow*" 104) points out that the term derives from "the Russian *narod*, 'people.' Intellectual trying to metamorphose peasants into revolutionaries. The *narodniki* flourished in the late 1860s. In the late 1960s, Student Nonviolent Coordinating Committee activists were referred to as *narodniks*. By show-offs."

V11.35, B13.5, P12.10   Iasi . . . men of the League   During the 1930s Romania found itself caught between Germany and Russia, with their crumbling Nazi-Soviet Pact. Corneliu Codreanu organized his League of the Archangel Michael and its military wing, the Iron Guard, a Fascist brotherhood based in the city of Iasi. Iron Guardsmen wore green shirts and carried little bags of Romanian soil—symbolizing their love of the fatherland—tied to thongs around their necks. Under Codreanu, Romania maintained an alliance with Hitler through August 1944, when Britain and France assisted the deposed young king, Michael, in a successful coup. Still, the political situation remained unstable and was a frequent topic of discussion in the *Times* of London throughout the fall and winter of 1944–45. The Russians had been fomenting an underground struggle, and in March 1945 a Communist faction directed by the Russian commissar Andrei Vyshinski seized control. Here, the significant points are that in 1936 Pirate was having, or "managing" (V12.3), the fantasies of a fictional Romanian anti-Fascist and royalist and that it all satirizes those in the British Foreign Office who, as Hitler's power grew, kept applying scenarios from the previous war.

V12.7, B13.18, P12.21 cup and bleed The archaic medical practice of "drawing blood by scarifying the skin and applying a 'cup' or cupping-glass, the air in which is rarefied by heat or otherwise" (*OED*).

V12.14–15, B13.28, P12.28–29 the words of P. M. S. Blackett Can be traced, Javaid Qazi ("Source Materials for Thomas Pynchon's Fiction" 9) finds, to a book by the 1948 physics Nobel laureate (for developing the cloud chamber) Patrick M. S. Blackett (1897–1974) entitled *Fear, War and the Bomb* (New York, 1948).

V12.22, B13.36, P12.36 I don't even get to ask for whom the bell's Recalls Ernest Hemingway's best-selling novel of the Spanish civil war, *For Whom the Bell Tolls* (1940), the title of which references John Donne's "Meditation XVII" from the *Devotions on Divergent Occasions* (1623): "Any man's death diminishes me because I am involved in mankind, and therefore never send to know for whom the bell tolls; it tolls for thee."

V12.30, B14.5, P13.5 a walking stick with W. C. Fields's head Note the pun with "Joaquin Stick" (V9.28) (pronounced hwa-kēn). Fields (1880–1946) was the irascible, bibulous, strawberry-nosed dandy of American comic cinema.

V13.1, B14.17–18, P13.15 the mark of Youthful Folly This is Meng, fourth hexagram of *The I Ching; or, Book of Changes*. The upper trigram of this figure depicts a mountain, the lower one a pool of water. Here is Richard Wilhelm's interpretation (20): "Keeping still is the attribute of the upper trigram; that of the lower is the abyss. Stopping in perplexity at the brink of a dangerous abyss is a symbol of the folly of youth. However, the two trigrams can also show a way of overcoming the follies of youth. Water is something that of necessity flows on. When the spring gushes forth, it does not know at first where it will go. But its steady flow fills up the deep place blocking its progress, and success is attained." The figure of this hexagram and its symbolism will later apply to Tyrone Slothrop (V378.12n).

V13.11, B14.30, P13.25 two Girl Guides British version of the Girl Scouts, founded in 1910 by Robert Baden-Powell and his sister Agnes.

V13.14, B14.34, P13.29 pixilated Slang for "inebriated," as if led by pixies.

V13.26–27, B15.8–9, P14.2 rather a Eugène Sue melodrama Perhaps one of his novels about pirate exploits, such as *Plik et plok* or *La salamandre*, which led critics to call Sue (1804–57) the French James Fenimore Cooper.

V13.28, BlS.10, P14.3 dacoits Members of a nineteenth-century Burmese robber band. In the twelve Fu-Manchu novels by Sax Rohmer (Arthur Sarsfield Ward), *dacoits* serve as bodyguards and assassins for the megalomaniacal oriental genius, Dr. Fu-Manchu.

V13.30–31, B15.13–14, P14.6–7 during his Kipling Period, beastly Fuzzy-Wuzzies . . . Oriental sore The term "Fuzzy Wuzzy" was British military slang for the Sudanese insurgents who became infamous during campaigns of the 1880–90s for their ferocity in battle, their expert use of both American-made Remington rifles and native-made spears, and their strategy of poisoning water wells before British troops arrived. In "Fuzzy Wuzzy," one of his *Barrack-Room Ballads* (1892), poet Rudyard Kipling refers to British troopers' begrudging respect for them:

> So 'ere's *to* you, Fuzzy-Wuzzy, at your 'ome in the Soudan;
> You're a pore benighted 'eathen but a first-class fightin' man;
> We gives you your certificate, an' if you want it signed
> We'll come an' 'ave a romp with you whenever you're inclined.

Dracunculiasis is a swelling caused by an infestation of Dracunculus worms in the leg and arm muscles of those living in tropical environments, like the Indies. Oriental sore: a skin ulcer occurring in the Indies, also known as the Aleppo boil. In 1935, the time of these oriental fantasies of Pirate's "Kipling Period," the famous poet (b. 1865) was a year away from his death.

V13.34–35, B15.18–19, P14.10–11 no Cary Grant larking in . . . medicine in the punchbowls In the 1952 Ben Hecht and Howard Hawks comedy *Monkey Business*, Cary Grant, as chemist Barnaby Fulton, develops a marvelous elixir, a kind of psychedelic. When they accidentally ingest it, Barnaby and his coworkers regress to a zany, playful childhood, which finds them hanging from chandeliers and such. Given the Kipling context, however, the exact reference, as Loranger ("'His Kipling Period'") first pointed out (see also Larsson, "A *Companion*'s Companion"), is to Cary Grant's "larking" about India (and spiking the regimental punchbowl with "elephant medicine") in George Stevens's 1939 *Gunga Din*, a film adaptation of the writer's famous poem.

V13.39–40, B15.25, P14.16 Sandy MacPherson playing The source for this snippet of local texture is the BBC broadcasting schedules listed in the *Times* of London. MacPherson, "on his organ," was occasionally featured in the evenings.

V14.4, B15.31–32, P14.21 his John the Baptist, his Nathan of Gaza Respectively, the prophet and precursor of Jesus (see Matt. 3:1–16) and the prophet to David (see 2 Sam. 12:1–15). Nathan of Gaza was also the name adopted by the seventeenth-century Jewish mystic and Kabbalist, a forerunner to the famed mystic Sabbatai Zvi (see V639.18–19n).

V14.7, B.35, P14.24 no one's fantasy but H. A. Loaf With the idea that, as Larsson points out, half a loaf is, as they say, better than none (or no fantasy) at all.

V14.12, B15.42, P14.30   the red-cap section   British military police were identified by a red band around their cap, hence in service slang, "red-caps" (see also V607.18n).

V14.22–23, B16.13, P14.40–41   one proper Sherlock Holmes London evening   Fog and preternatural quiet are the usual conditions in Conan Doyle's detective novels.

V14.30–31, B16.23, P15.8   It was a giant Adenoid   The fantastic creature disappears from *GR* after this analeptic appearance, but a thinly disguised Richard M. Nixon, as "adenoidal" theater manager Richard M. Zhlubb, will reappear in the final, proleptic moments of the narrative (see V754.34). In typical monster-movie fashion, this creature is "as big as St. Paul's, " the London cathedral atop Ludgate Hill measuring 250 by 515 feet. Lodged in the pharynx of Lord Blatherard Osmo, this roving Adenoid satirizes the nasal characteristics of upper-crust British speech; at least, it satirizes how that speech sounds to preterite ears. Since medical references to "adenoids" nearly always use the plural, Pynchon probably refers here to Charlie Chaplin's role as the Jewish barber and then dictator of Tomania, "Adenoid Hynkel," a thinly veiled Adolph Hitler in *The Great Dictator* (1940). Indeed the film's closing speech, in which Chaplin drops the Hitler-mask and appeals directly to viewers, rather deftly capsulizes *GR*'s core themes:

> The misery that is now upon us is but the passing of greed, the bitterness of men who fear the way of human progress: the hate of men will pass and dictators [will] die and the power they took from the people will return to the people and so long as men die, liberty will never perish.
>
> Soldiers—don't give yourselves to brutes, men who despise you and enslave you—who regiment your lives, tell you what to do, what to think and what to feel, who drill you, diet you, treat you as cattle, as cannon fodder.
>
> Don't give yourselves to these unnatural men, machine men, with machine minds and machine hearts. You are not machines. You are not cattle. You are men. You have the love of humanity in your hearts. You don't hate—only the unloved hate. Only the unloved and the unnatural. Soldiers—don't fight for slavery, fight for liberty.

V14.34–36, B16.28–30, P15.12–14   Novi Pazar . . . this obscure sanjak   Before World War I, Novi Pazar existed as a small *sanjak* or principality sandwiched between Serbia and Montenegro in a mountainous region with few passes. The 1878 Treaty of Berlin empowered Austria-Hungary to garrison the area, while specifying that civil administration was to remain in Turkish hands. In 1908 Austria-Hungary announced plans to run a rail line through the pass at Novi Pazar. It would have been commercially insignificant but militarily critical in providing a crucial land bridge to Macedonia and Bulgaria, thereby completing the encirclement of Serbia. These strategic problems were central to the "Eastern Question," occupying the major European powers from 1908 until the outbreak of war in August 1914. Then plans for the railway were shelved, so Pirate's image of getting to the *sanjak* via the legendary Orient Express is romantic fancy.

V15.2, B16.36, P15.19 Pack up my Glad-stone A light luggage piece, usually of leather, with a rigid frame that opens into two compartments; named for William Ewart Gladstone, British prime minister repeatedly from 1868 to 1894.

V15.7, B16.42, P15.24–25 naughtily attired in Busbies Tall fur caps with a bag-like crown hanging down their right-hand sides; part of the ceremonial dress for artillerymen, hussars, and engineers of the British army.

V15.12–13, B17.5–6, P15.29–30 Mayfair . . . East End First the Adenoid moves due east, with no regard for the social status of the neighborhoods he destroys. Mayfair, once the most fashionable residential quarter of London, by 1944 was mostly home to retail businesses, especially the city's better clothiers (hence the "tophats" strewn about the Adenoid's path). The East End includes not only London's "Bloody Tower" and the docks but also the densely populated boroughs of Shoreditch, Whitechapel, and Stepney. East End is London's haven for the preterite: diaspora Jews moved in during the late nineteenth century, and the Salvation Army was instituted there in 1865. In Rohmer's Fu-Manchu novels, it is a warren of opium dens and "the Yellow Peril"—a criminal underground of inscrutable Asians.

V15.20–21, B17.16, P15.37 in Hampstead Heath The Adenoid has circled counterclockwise, moving north and west into this upper-class borough.

V15.26, B17.22, P16.3 the Cavendish Laboratory The scientific institute at Cambridge University named for classical physicist Henry Cavendish (1731–1810). Before World War II it was home to nuclear physicists Rutherford and Bohr, who first proposed the planetary model of the atom and later made the discoveries that enabled researchers to split atoms of uranium.

V15.38, B17.36–37, P16.15 occupies all of St. James's The Adenoid has closed the circle. St. James Park borders on Whitehall, home of the British War Office, the Admiralty, the Treasury, and Scotland Yard.

V16.5, B18.2, P16.22 daily *démarche* A daily strategic update or diplomatic plan of action.

V16.15–16, B18.14–15, P16.32 a *croix mystique* on the palm of Europe In palmistry, two lines that intersect, cross-like, on the Lunar Mound; symbolic of great clairvoyant power, of contact with the Other Side and therefore perhaps of death.

EPISODE 3

The time is noon of the same "dripping winter" day (V17.9); the scene, headquarters of ACHTUNG, just off Grosvenor Square. Teddy Bloat, spared a broken neck by Pirate's quick reflexes in episode 1, photographs the cubicle of his American coworker, Lt. Tyrone Slothrop. Thus, before meeting the character himself in episode 4, we are first introduced to Slothrop's possessions. To Bloat, the main item of interest is the map, speckled rainbow-like with colored stars, each signifying the site of one of Slothrop's London sexual conquests.

V17.5, B19.5–6, P17.20 capsicum Meloids for a Mellow Voice Capsicum is a (hot) derivative of the tropical pepper plants. Meloids is the trademark of a British throat "pastille" made and marketed by the Boots Group PLC, Nottingham, England. Meloids were small squares like Sen Sen, and ads for them in the *Times* of London used to tout their uses ("For a Mellow Voice"). The Meloids ad printed the ingredients: licorice, menthol, and capsicum.

V17.7, B19.8–9, P17.22–23 flaming SHAEF sword, which Mother had Garrard's make up All servicemen connected with SHAEF, the Supreme Headquarters, Allied Expeditionary Force, wore a shoulder patch depicting a flaming sword with a rainbow arching over it. Garrard and Company Ltd. are the Crown Jewelers located on Regent Street and would be *the* place to have one's "twin silver hairbrushes" engraved with such an insignia.

V17.9, B19.11, P17.24 this dripping winter noon From the eleventh until the eighteenth of December 1944, London was held in the grip of a cold fog that blew in from the south. Temperatures held in the upper thirties. "Bleak in the Streets" is how the Times described it on December 15. The afternoon of December 18, the fog broke and a cold drizzle began falling (see also V20.1–3n).

V17.11, B19.13–14, P17.26 Grosvenor Square Located in the Mayfair district, the square is the London home of the American Embassy and Consulate General and thus the residence and workplace of numerous Americans connected with the diplomatic corps. Oxford Street (V17.14–15) is the major thoroughfare two blocks north of the square.

V17.26, B19.31, P18.5 ATS Acronym for the Auxiliary Territorial Services, one of many British wartime support groups, such as the WRENS (Women's Royal Naval Service), WAAFS (Women's Auxiliary Air Force), WRACS (Women's Royal Air Corps), and NAAFI (Navy, Army, Air Forces Institutes). The ATS was an "Official Canteen Organization for His Majesty's Forces" that served around the world, thus comparable to the American USO clubs.

V17.34, B20.3, P18.14 lino British slang for "linoleum."

V17.36, B20.5, P18.16　his Jesus College friend　Of Oxford University, that is.

V17.36–37, B20.6, P18.17　Lt. Oliver ("Tantivy") Mucker-Maffick　Terrill Shepard Soules ("What To Think about *Gravity's Rainbow*") has pinned down two sources for this moniker: the noun "tantivy" meaning "a galloping gait" and the verb "maffick," coined to describe the jubilant celebrating after British troops successfully defended Mafeking, during the Boer War. A "mucker" is British slang for one who engages in low pursuits (from the noun "muck," meaning "waste" or "excrement").

V18.3, B20.10, P1.19　the ETO　European Theatre of Operations.

V18.8–38, B20.17–21.11, P18.25–19.13　Things have fallen roughly into layers . . . a News of the World　Among this list of objects on Slothrop's desk are items, allusions, and brand names associated with him throughout the novel. He began "chain-smoking," we are told, with the first rocket strikes (V21.22), so the flints for his Zippo brand lighter are a must. Mother Nalline would have had to mail him Thayer's slippery elm throat lozenges because the Henry Thayer Company (formerly of Cambridge, now of Concord, Massachusetts) marketed the product only in New England. The box still stresses how a lozenge "eases smoker's throat." Incidentally, "Nalline" is itself the proprietary name of a pharmaceutical product, Nalorphine, once widely employed by police to test for the presence of opiates, especially heroin, in a suspect's blood. "Johnny Doughboy Found a Rose in Ireland" (lyrics by Kay Twomey, music by Allan Roberts) was introduced in the 1942 John Auer film, *Johnny Doughboy* (Republic Pictures), starring Henry Wilcoxon (see also V559.11–14), and later that year the piece was a hit song for bandleader James King Kern "Kay" Kyser (1906–85). Slothrop will eventually give up ukulele for harmonica, but Tantivy's comparing him to George Formby (1904–61), the ukulele-strumming British screen comic of the forties, may tell us something about Slothrop's singing voice: Formby's was a high screech. Kreml hair tonic is a bygone product, but the countless advertisements for it in American magazines from the period (see *Time* or *Life*) all stress the Lothario factor: a Kreml man was a "love-pirate," as one ad put it, because "he always steals away the loveliest looking girls." Some of these objects exercise a proleptic force. Among the "lost pieces to different jigsaw puzzles," the eye of the "Weimaraner" will reappear in Ned Pointsman's dream about a 1941 champion Weimaraner named Reichssieger von Thanatz Alpdrucken (V142.32) and then again in *Alpdrücken*, a film by the character Gerhardt von Göll (V395.6). Similarly, the "orange nimbus of an explosion" anticipates the news photo Slothrop finds in part 4 of the atomic bomb exploding over Hiroshima after being dropped from a B-29 (rather than a B-17) Flying Fortress referred to in this passage. The can of Nugget shoe polish anticipates the analepsis to rag-popping shoeshine boy Malcolm X, working the Rose-

land Ballroom lavatory in 1939 (see V63.3n), which by circuitous routes
will lead to the semantic meditation on "Shit 'n' Shinola" (V687.5). At
the end of this catalog we also glimpse Slothrop's reading materials:
pamphlets and guidebooks distributed to foreign servicemen by the
British "F.O.," or Foreign Office. Finally note that Slothrop reads the
gossipy and sensationalistic London daily paper *News of the World*
along with reports from "G-2," or U.S. Army intelligence.

V19.5, B21.21, P19.22   G-loads   Engineers' abbreviation for the gravitational "load," or stress, on an object due to acceleration or deceleration.

**V19.12–14, B21.29–32, P19.29–31   near Tower Hill . . . up to Hampstead
Heath**   The mapping of Slothrop's sexual delights and V-2 rocket strikes
shows a pattern flowing westward. The idea for this map probably came
from Irving. One map in *The Mare's Nest* (228) shows the "number of
flying bombs per square kilometer"; another (262), the distribution of
rocket strikes around the city, with the strongest concentrations in the
east and a thinning pattern as the flow works west.

V19.30, B22.9, P20.6–7   the pantechnicon   In British usage, from circa
1830, the name of a bazaar on Motcomb Street in London's Belgravia
section; from the 1890s on, it signified the type of large-furniture moving van that took wares to and from that market—the reference here.

**V19.31–32, B22.11, P20.8   quid wager on the Blackpool-Preston North
End game**   A "quid" is British slang for the monetary denomination of
one pound sterling; the game is British football (American soccer), results of which were posted in each Monday's *Times* of London, after Saturday's matchups. Blackpool and Preston North End competed in the
North League of London's Football Association. As was customary, the
two teams played each other twice, on successive weekends: on October
7, 1944, the match produced a 1–1 tie, in a game broadcast over the BBC
General Forces Programme at 4:15 P.M.; the next Saturday, the four-
teenth, Preston North End narrowly beat Blackpool, 1–0. The dates
establish the time of Bloat's analeptic memories in this passage.

**V19.37, B22.16–17, P20.14–15   He moves back down the beaverboard
maze**   Beaverboard, formerly a trademark, is that form of building material made from compressed wood chips and commonly used to divide
office space into cubicles (see V538.14).

EPISODE 4

The time: afternoon of the "dripping winter" day of the prior episodes.
Events unfold on the road back from Greenwich, where Pirate's "incoming mail" arrived. Slothrop has also visited the bombsite, and we finally
meet him. Most of the narrative consists of analepses to incidents of
Slothrop's girl-chasing about London, his childhood in western Massachu-

setts, his nine generations of Puritan ancestors and their slowly wasted fortunes as the New World grew older.

V20.1–3, B22.22–24, P20.18–20   Wind has shifted . . . rain-clouds   Consistent with the *Times* weather information for December 18.

V20.4, B22.26, P20.21   out to zero longitude   Again, the Royal Observatory.

V20.10, B22.33, P20.27   Mark III Stens set on automatic   The Mark III was a silenced version of the British Sten machine gun, a weapon designed especially for commandos: it was lightweight, mechanically simple, very deadly.

V20.15, B22.38, P20.32   from T.I.   Pirate's counterpart is from the British Army's "Technical Intelligence" wing.

V20.16, B23.2, P20.33   a '37 Wolseley Wasp   Inexpensive two-door sedan, first produced by the Wolseley Automobile Company in 1935.

V20.18–19, B23.5, P20.36   distributing Lucky Strikes   A popular cigarette brand since 1871, when the R. A. Patterson Company introduced it as the U.S.'s first manufactured cigarette. In late 1944 the American Tobacco Company (having acquired the brand in 1905) launched an extensive advertising campaign: white packs replaced the long-familiar green, and the packaging featured a new acronym—"L.S.M.F.T." (for "Lucky Strike Means Fine Tobacco"). But Slothrop would be unlikely to have "the last Lucky Strike in all Switzerland"; ads for three years had proclaimed, "Lucky Strike Green Has Gone to War," and as the second best-selling brand *worldwide* in the 1940s, they'd have been plentiful in occupied Europe.

V20.21, B23.3, P21.1   a graphite cylinder   Graphite is a highly heat-resistant material, which is why the V-2 rocket steering vanes were made of it, and why this cylinder has "survived" (with message intact) at this blast site.

V20.36–37, B23.26–27, P21.17   sending him TDY some hospital   That is, sending him on a tour of "temporary duty" to the (fictional) St. Veronica's Hospital for Respiratory and Colonic Diseases, locus of episode 10.

V21.3–4, B23.31–32, P21.21–22   Some more of that Minnesota Multiphasic shit   On the Minnesota Multiphasic Personality Inventory and Slothrop's character as measured by such tests, see V81.22n, V81.23–24n, V90.8n.

V21.9–10, B23.40, P21.28   with those buzzbombs   The V-1, also known in Allied circles as the "doodlebug," was a pilotless aircraft propelled by a pulse-jet engine (hence the "farting sound" Slothrop hears) and fitted with a one-ton amatol warhead. Irving (*Mare's Nest* 123–25), Pynchon's likely source, explains that V-1s were either launched from a ramp or dropped from a bomber. In flight, they reached subsonic velocities of around 470 mph over a maximum range of 160 miles. Ten seconds after a preset engine cutoff, the V-1 dove toward earth, as described here. The initial attack of V-1 bombs on London commenced just before midnight on June 15, 1944, and by 5 A.M. the following day 244 had been launched, 73 falling directly on London.

V21.19, B24.9, P21.37   then last September the rockets came   Specifically, at 6:43 P.M. on September 8, 1944, at Chiswick, killing three people and seriously injuring seventeen more (see V26.23n).

V21.36, B24.29, P22.13   got them both 86'd   The origins of the phrase "eighty-sixed" are controversial but one explanation is that it came into existence as a rhyming synonym for the slang verb "nix," meaning "to deny" or "to reject," which appears to be the sense of the term here— that Slothrop and Mr. Pox were tossed out of the Junior Atheneum.

V22.2, B24.39, P22.21–22   subdeb legs   The legs of a "subdebutante," designating girls generally less than sixteen years old (here, from Cedar Rapids, Iowa).

V22.3, B24.40, P22.22–23   a build out of the chorus line at the Windmill   Marjorie, the second of Slothrop's girls, could work (thinks Tantivy, assigned to bird-dog all of Slothrop's amorous conquests for clues to his magical penis) at one of the "Non-Stop Revues" listed daily on the *Times* of London entertainments page. The Windmill Theatre was located on Great Windmill Street, just off Piccadilly Circle. The Windmill opened in 1931 as a venue for stage drama but poor receipts forced a turn to variety theater. "Revudeville," begun in 1932 and evidently the first of its kind in London, spotlighted low comedy and chorus lines of Parisian-style nearly nude dancing girls, "cont. dly. 12:15–9:30," according to the *Times*. Through the Blitz, the Windmill was the one theater that never closed, its performers often sleeping overnight during the worst bomber, V-1, and V-2 attacks.

V22.4, B24.41, P22.23–24   the Frick Frack Club in Soho   London's Soho district, now known as the hub of London filmmaking, once was home to clubs of low repute and numerous secondhand shops; the Frick Frack Club is unknown, but the phrase "frick and frack" was war-era slang for any two persons or objects related or nearly identical to each other. The phrase itself derived from a Swiss ice-skating duo known for their comical routines; they appear in the 1944 film *Lady, Let's Dance* (Monogram Pictures), in which war refugee Belita (an actual dancer, as herself) plays a waitress picked by a producer (James Ellison) to be a lead dancer when his show's prima donna walks off. Belita performs all manner of dances—ballroom, ballet, and even ice dancing—accompanied by the comical Frick & Frack.

V22.12, B25.8–9, P22.31–32   a lindy-hopping girl   The lindy hop, named for aviator Charles Lindbergh, was a popular dance of the thirties. Malcolm X describes the wild abandon (the windmilling arms and hopping step) of it in the "Homeboy" chapter of his *Autobiography*, a principal source for episode 10.

V22.24–27, B25.23–26, P23.3–6 "I know there is wilde love . . . of God's owne planting" David Seed has identified this obscure passage from Thomas Hooker as deriving from a 1637 sequence of sermons, *The Soules Implantation into the Natural Olive*. The general context is Christian redemptive hope, in which "Adam was the old and wild Olive, Christ the true Vine, and the new Olive" (180). Fallen man must therefore be severed from his unregenerate root and grafted onto, "implanted in," Christ; the last sermon, "Spirituall Love and Joy," sets worldly love against the fulfillment that stems from this humbling, enlightening influence of the Divinity. Hooker (180) acknowledges mundane passion in the passage Pynchon quotes: "I know there is wilde love and joy enough in the world, as there is wilde Thyme and other herbes, but wee would have garden-love and garden-joy, of Gods own planting, for such hypocriticall love and joy we will not meddle her." Seed's commentary ("Thomas Hooker") is useful: "Pynchon cuts out the dismissive comment at the end of the passage and renders Hooker's whole distinction ironic by quoting it within such a profane context. Indeed Tyrone Slothrop, the novel's closest candidate for protagonist, embodies two of the sins that Hooker rails against—drunkenness and adultery."

V22.27–29, B25.27–29, P23.68 Teems with virgin's-bower . . . love-in-idleness Slothrop's mapped garden of earthly delights further ironizes Hooker's image of the divine garden. The virgin's bower (genus *Clematis*) is an American plant with white flowers; the forget-me-not (*Myosotis*), a European plant with clusters of small blue or purple flowers; and rue (*Ruta*), also known as "herb of grace," a Eurasian plant with red flowers. Note the eastwarding progress of these three, for in a sense it summarizes "Slothrop's [eastward] Progress" (V25.6) from the United States back to the longitudes his forefathers left behind. As for the fourth herb, love-in-idleness (*Viola*), Pynchon correctly identifies this common pansy, which comes in all colors, as growing "all over the place."

V23.10, B26.14, P23.31 cup of Bovril Brand of English beef tea (broth).

V23.19, B26.27, P23.41 "Your two Wrens . . ." See V17.26n.

V24.13–14, B27.24, P24.36 the same aging Humber According to Georgano (*Complete Encyclopedia of Motor Cars*), "the company's staple products were upper-middle-class family sedans." Humbers served the Allied forces with distinction in World War II as "the standard of [the] British motor pool."

V24.14–15, B27.25–26, P24.37 a Saint George after the fact St. George is the patron saint and romance hero of Britain. Slothrop's dragon is the rocket, "the Beast" whose "droppings," or exploded parts, lie scattered over the blast site; a further point is that Slothrop, no hero, arrives too late to battle it.

V24.19, B27.31, P24.41 RAF dogs Royal Air Force, used to hunt for survivors and corpses.

V24.30, B28.1–2, P25.12 under a Morrison shelter Named for Minister of Home Security Herbert Morrison, these "crushproof steel tables" were designed to double as bomb shelters (Irving, *Mare's Nest* 80) but proved useless against V-2s.

V24.34, B28.6–7, P24.16 a Thayer's Slippery Elm See V18.8–38n.

V24.39, B28.13, P24.21 a Shirley Temple smile After the cute, innocent child star of American pre–World War II cinema (see also V466.4n).

V25.6–7, B28.21, P25.28–29 Slothrop's Progress, London the secular city instructs him Figures Tyrone as profane pilgrim, perhaps a secular version of John Bunyan's hero in the Puritan classic of 1678, *The Pilgrim's Progress, from this World to that which is to Come (Delivered under the Similitude of a Dream)*. Or, more interestingly, an expansive version of William Hogarth's series of eight paintings (later lithographed), "The Rake's Progress" (1733–34). As McCarron ("Pynchon and Hogarth") first pointed out, in Hogarth's narrative sequence his antihero Tom Rakewell, having inherited his miserly father's slowly accumulated fortune, is seen descending from the company of gentlemen and artists, to drinking excessively among bawdy women, gambling, getting arrested for debts, marrying for money, then landing in debtor's prison and, finally, the Bedlam madhouse. The eight guises of Tom Rakewell's progress through secular London correspond, loosely, to Slothrop's eight identities as he moves through London and Europe.

V25.28, B29.7, P26.9 the Bond Street Underground station Getting off work, Slothrop would walk from his Grosvenor Square office to the intersection of Oxford and Bond streets and then into the underground station of London's Central Line. Chiswick, where the first V-2 falls, is just over two miles away.

V25.31–32, B29.12, P26.13 *memento-mori* A "remembrance of death"; a death's-head or skull (unhyphenated in the Penguin edition).

V25.32–37, B29.12–18, P26.13–14 a sharp crack. . . . "Some bloody gas main" The source for these impressions of the first V-2 (the "crack," the double "thunder," the possibility of it being a buzz bomb or an exploded "gas main") is Irving (*Mare's Nest* 285–86).

V26.23, B30.8, P27.3 The Moment was 6:43:16 British Double Summer Time Again, the source is Irving (286). To conserve energy resources, Britain moved the clocks an hour ahead in winter and two hours in summer, hence the phrase "double summer time."

V26.30–31, B30.17–18, P27.10 back home in Mingeborough . . . hand of God emerges from a cloud A fictional Massachusetts locale (though Pynchon will soon [V28.21–39] situate it in the Berkshire Mountains, near the actual towns of Stockbridge, Pittsfield, and Lenox) first introduced in his 1964 short story "The Secret Integration" (published originally in *The Saturday Evening Post* and reprinted in *Slow Learner*). The place-name may hide a bit of English obscenity (the noun "minge" is slang for a vagina or "quim," and as an verb "to ming" means "to smell foul"), or it may (also) refer to the kind of small, biting fly or midge (genus *Unoxiphus*) common to forestlands throughout North America. The hand on Constant's headstone, if it is a right hand emerging from the cloud palm up, would recall the image that Waite uses for the Ace of Pentacles in drawings for the tarot deck. Its meaning: fruitfulness, productivity in one's enterprises and ventures.

V26.37–38, B30.25–26, P27.18–19   Death is a debt to nature due . . . so must you   To Puritan ears there is heresy in Constant Slothrop's epitaph. The debt, as Hooker and other Puritan divines would insist, is due not to nature but to God—a crucial difference.

V27.4–6, B30.31–33, P27.23   his son Variable Slothrop . . . the nine or ten generations tumbling back   Note the play of opposites, constant and variable. This is also the first of many instances of hysteron proteron: a trope of backward motion, regression, and reversals of cause and effect. Also, in a similar way Thomas Ruggles Pynchon Jr. is "nine or ten generations" removed from his ancestors, John Pynchon (1626–1702) of Springfield, Massachusetts, and William Pynchon (1590–1662), founder of Springfield and Roxbury. William was a patentee and treasurer of the Massachusetts Bay Company and author of theological treatises ruled heretical by Puritan divines.

V27.11, B30.39, P27.30   Masonic emblems   Perhaps the square, Masonic symbol of this earth, or the compass, symbol of the heavens; also likely are a gavel, a sign of force, and a twelve-inch ruler, sign of reason.

V27.13, B31.1–2, P27.32   eyes peeking Kilroy-style   A reference to the popular servicemen's logo of the war years. A quality control checker at the Fore River shipyard near Quincy, Massachusetts, James Kilroy (the story goes) used to chalk the phrase "Kilroy was Here" on riveted sections he had checked. Kilroy's ships traveled and so did the phrase; soon a logo was added (the top of a man's head peaking over a fence, eye-high, with his nose hanging over, its origin unknown), an image U.S. that servicemen begin leaving on surfaces wherever they went.

V27.26, B31.15–16, P28.6   bagged his epitaph from Emily Dickinson   Frederick Slothrop's epitaph is lifted from poem 712 in the Dickinson canon, lines written in 1863 and originally published (in 1890) as "The Chariot."

V27.31–34, B31.20–23, P28.11–12   They began as fur traders, cordwainers . . . gone to necropolis   Larsson ("From the Berkshires to the Brocken") identifies the source of these details about early western Massachusetts occupations, including the quarrying of marble (for headstones, among other things), as a guide entitled *The Berkshire Hills* that was produced under the (U.S.) Depression-era Federal Writers Project.

V28.2, B31.30–31, P28.19   converted acres at a clip into paper   Again see Larsson ("From the Berkshires to the Brocken"), who finds that *The Berkshire Hills* discusses Berkshire paper firms that devastated the forests after one of them pioneered the making of paper from wood pulp instead of rags. Another, Crane and Company, specialized in bonded papers, including (from 1879 on) that used in printing United States currency.

V28.4–5, B31.38, P28.22   No Slothrop ever made it into the Social Register or the Somerset Club   In print since 1887, the *Social Register* (now published by Forbes Media) bills itself as "the definitive listing of America's most prominent families, serving as an exclusive and trusted medium for learning about and communicating with their peers. It includes names, addresses, club memberships, college affiliations and other pertinent information." The *Register*'s information on "club memberships" might include many a listed family's affiliation with the exclusive Somerset Club, established in 1872 at 42 Beacon Street, Boston, a Greek Revival mansion overlooking Boston Common that has served as the inner sanctum for generations of Cabots, Lodges, Lowells, and their fellows. Exactly why, in Edith Wharton's *The Age of Innocence*, Newland Archer dines there while visiting Boston.

V28.12–13, B32.2–3, P28.29–30   around the time Emily Dickinson . . . was writing   This next poem is 997 in the Dickinson canon, written during 1865 as the Civil War was winding down but not published until 1945 in *Bolts of Melody*. Pynchon quotes the final stanza.

V28.26, B32.18, P29.5–6   in long rallentando   The musical term signifies a gradual slowdown of tempo. In this context, another instance of hysteron proteron.

V28.33–34, B32.26–27, P29.12–13   Harrimans and Whitneys gone   The Aspinwall Hotel fire (see below) destroyed the last great summer watering place in the Berkshires. Before that, as Larsson ("From the Berkshires to the Brocken") found in *The Berkshire Hills*, President Grover Cleveland's Secretary of the Navy William C. Whitney had in 1886 founded a vacation colony in Lenox, and the Harriman family was also prominent in the area. By the early twentieth century these Elect had transformed Saratoga, sixty miles northwest in New York, into their summer hideout.

V28.38, B32.32–33, P29.17   In 1931 . . . year of the Great Aspinwall Hotel Fire   Located outside Lenox, the Aspinwall was a four-story wooden structure of four hundred rooms. Reporting the spectacular blaze in its late edition of April 25, 1931, the *New York Times* described the building (in a front-page story) as "one of the most fashionable hostelries in the Berkshires and a social center for summer activities." John D. Rockefeller and Chauncey Depew were once regular guests; other wealthy financiers and robber barons had drifted through. The fire began at

1:00 A.M. on the morning of the twenty-fifth and was thought to have started when several drunken youths left behind a lighted cigarette. Here is the *Times*: "The blaze spread to the woodland and did widespread damage before [it was] finally gotten under control. The burning hotel made a spectacular blaze, the flames rising high and being visible over the mountains for many miles around. Hundreds of residents left their beds and drove to the scene. . . . By 3 o'clock the hotel was reduced to a heap of smoldering ruins."

EPISODE 5

Still December 18, but evening now; the location, someplace vaguely identified as "Snoxall's" (V32.29), where Roger Mexico and Jessica Swanlake attend a séance. These moments of occult contact with the Other Side introduce us to Blicero, the Teutonic deity of death soon to be revealed in an actual character. This episode begins with an account of a séance in which we are introduced to Roger and Jessica, and (like many episodes) it is related by what seems to be a traditional omniscient third-person narrator. But then the séance starts to be focalized *through* Pirate Prentice, whose memories take us back to his tour of duty in the Persian Gulf in the thirties, and to a woman he loved and lost. Pirate senses a similar loss approaching in Roger's life; whereupon the episode concludes with glimpses of a snuggling Roger and Jessica that bring us back full circle in both point of view and time.

V29.31, B33.29–30, P30.8　a "sensitive flame"　So called because such a flame appears to serve as a check against hoaxes (the idea being that the flame would detect actual—as opposed to spiritual—motion in the room). In his 1972 study of Victorian spiritualism Ronald Pearsall (42–43) summarizes the "rules" for a séance: "The people who composed the circles should be of opposite temperaments, 'as positive and negative,' not marked by any repulsive disease, not obviously struggling under mental handicap. The number of persons should not be less than three, nor more than twelve, eight being the ideal number. No person of strong magnetic temperament should be present, as he or she would quash the power of the spirits. The room should not be overheated, and should be well ventilated; bright light was anathema to successful dealings with spirits." Pearsall also describes some of the hoaxes characteristic of the period: gloves sprayed with phosphorescent powder, to give the appearance of a materialized hand, and musical instruments that leapt into action as spirits "played" them. But Snoxall's runs a respectable séance: "None of your white hands or luminous trumpets here" (V29.36–37), as Pynchon notes, and thus no leaps of the "sensitive flame" revealing other shenanigans. The "spirit" speaking on the following pages is

Roland Feldspath (Old German for "feldspar," the word for a crystalline mineral that forms in rock), whose "medium" is Carroll Eventyr (from the Danish "*eventyr*," "adventure"). Selena (whose name alludes to the ancient moon goddess) is the surviving wife of Feldspath, and she would be seated opposite Eventyr. The "control" in a séance is another name for the spirit of a deceased who speaks for, or about, the spirit in question; here it is Peter Sachsa, a German Communist and lover of Leni Pökler; we subsequently learn that he was killed during a Berlin street demonstration in 1930 (on the etymology of his name, see V218.10n). These constitute the "basic, four-way entente" (V31.27) of the evening's encounter with the Other Side.

V30.1, B33.38, P30.15   Camerons officers   Also known as the Scottish Rifles, a British army regiment; the "trews" are their tartan trousers.

V30.12, B34.13, P30.26   "into the realm of Dominus Blicero"   In short: into Death's domain. Pynchon's source is Grimm's *Teutonic Mythology* (849–50). "*Blicero*" is one of the many Germanic nicknames for death. Grimm traces the etymology from "*bleich*" (pale) and "*blechend*" (grinning), and from these he derives other nicknames, such as "*Der Blecker*" (The Grinning Death) and "*Der Bleicher*" ("The Bleacher," for what death does to bones). "*Dominus*" (Lord), from the Latin, recalls the appellation accorded both to Roman emperors by their underlings and to Christ in Latin translations of the Gospels.

V30.30, B34.34–35, P31.7   "A market needed no longer . . . the Invisible Hand"   The allusion is to Adam Smith's famous metaphor in *The Wealth of Nations* (1776). Arguing for the beneficial prospects of a true laissez-faire economy, Smith reasons that anyone seeking his own benefit will also be guided, as though by an unseen force, to benefit his society. Such a person, he claims, "neither intends to promote the public interest, nor knows how much he is promoting it. By preferring the support of domestick to that of foreign industry, he intends only his own security and by directing that industry in such a manner as its product may be of the greatest value, he intends only his own gain, and he is in this, as in many other cases, *led by an invisible hand* to promote an end which was no part of his intention" (456; my emphasis). A large vein of Protestant belief in Providence and election feeds Smith's metaphor, and Pynchon has already mined it with the image of the "hand of God" (V26.30) emerging from a cloud on Constant Slothrop's headstone. But the war economy has "dispensed with God" (V30.33), as Roland Feldspath claims. As the narrative will frequently suggest, the new industrial cartels erased any distinction between Smith's "foreign" and "domestic" manufacturers.

V30.37, B35.1, P31.14   "More Ouspenskian nonsense"   That is, ideas from a follower of Petr Demianovich Ouspensky (1878–1947), the Russian esoteric and occult philosopher who was a student of the Armenian-born mystic George Ivanovich Gurdjieff (1872–1949) for nine years before a disagreement caused them to split up and brought Ouspensky to London, where he lectured until war broke out in 1939. His philosophical writings sought to synthesize everything from Nietzsche's Superman to the tarot, yoga, astrology, the Kabbalah, Jungian dream analysis, and Christian iconography. *Tertium Organum: The Third Canon of Thought, a Key to the Enigmas of the World* (1920) is his best-known version of these attempts.

V30.39–40, B35.3–4, P31.15–16   Sous le Vent . . . Jessica Swanlake, a rosy young girl   The odor (other than the diesel fuel) is from the French perfume Sous le Vent (translation: "Under the Wind") released in 1933 by Guerlain. It is significant considering the "secular . . . personal wind" (V30.20) blowing through this séance. Jessica's surname certainly recalls Peter Tchaikovsky's 1877 grand ballet, *Swan Lake*, in which the heroine Odette is transformed by the wicked sorcerer Rothbart into a swan, then saved by the hero Siegfried, who fell in love with the girl during the few daily hours in which she was restored to human form. The ballet, however, concludes two different ways: one in which Odette and Siegfried tragically drown, and another in which they live happily ever. The allusion thus begs several questions: for this Swan Lake–style girl, who is her "Rothbart"? Is it Pointsman or Mexico? Or, if Roger Mexico is her "Siegfried," loving her as he does during the midnight hours, then is it their fate either to live happily together or (somehow) to drown?

V31.2, B35.7, P31.19   probably from Harrods   As *Times* of London ads used to boast, a department store with "the finest selection of quality goods in the world."

V31.17, B35.26–27, P31.34   achieved perfect tripos   At Cambridge University the tripos are any of the examinations for a baccalaureate degree; a perfect score constitutes the highest academic achievement.

V31.41, B36.13, P32.18   "Automatic texts"   That is, produced by "automatic writing"; unpremeditated, free-association composition produced with the least, or the least conscious, effort (see below), perhaps deriving from the writer's "unconscious" mind and therefore, perhaps, linked to spiritual domains and beings. A practice of the modernist poet William Butler Yeats, of surrealist writers like André Breton, and of European spiritualists from the late nineteenth century forward.

V32.5–11, B36.18–26, P31.23–30   "Well. Recall Zipf's Principle of Least Effort . . . a sort of bow shape"   The reference is not to George Kingsley Zipf's 1949 book, *Human Behavior and the Principle of Least Effort*. Instead, the text for this complex, arresting reference is his 1935 study, *The Psycho-Biology of Language*. Zipf was a professor of philology and linguistics at Harvard during the time of Slothrop's fictional attendance there. In the 1935 book he approached language as "a natural psychological and biological phenomenon to be investigated in the spirit of the exact sciences" (v). Examining everyday speech, he found patterns of abbreviation—the linguistic trace of his "Principle of Least Effort"—to be important in unlocking the dynamics of language. Much of his work relies on various statistical and probabilistic tests applied to recorded samples of ordinary discourse, and the text is chock-full of "word-frequency graphs" plotting on double-logarithmic charts the frequency of occurrence of a word, with abscissas indicating the number of words in the sample and ordinates the number of occurrences of the word. These are the "axes" Milton Gloaming describes to a perplexed Jessica Swanlake. The arresting thing, however, is that Zipf (*Psycho-Biology* 224) found natural speech always yielding a straight line in the graphs, a line that could be described by a simple mathematical formula concisely homologous to that "for gravity." However, in pathological and artistic usage, Zipf found that this law no longer applies. As Gloaming explains to Jessica, the graphs of schizophrenic speech yield, instead of a straight line, "a sort of bow shape." This appropriation of Zipf's data thus tallies with numerous other images in *GR*, where the arch, the parabola, and the bow loom as signs of disturbance and pathology. For useful background on Gloaming's comments see Zipf on "Pathological Language" (*Psycho-Biology* 216–18).

V32.26, B37.2, P33.5 Falkman and His Apache Band Another band name lifted from the *Times* of London BBC broadcasting schedules. Only once in December was Falkman the featured, live act (at 7:30 P.M. on December 26), but his recordings might have appeared on the "Top Ten" or "Forces Favorites" shows that aired every evening, ten to midnight.

V32.29, B37.6, P33.8–9 at here at Snoxall's A misprint in the Viking edition, corrected in the Bantam to read "as here at Snoxall's."

V32.36, B37.13–14, P33.15 your Dennis Morgan chap One of Warner Brothers' highest-paid stars of the forties, Dennis Morgan (1910–94) was noted for his wise-guy grin. During the war, Morgan played a pilot in four different films; here the reference is to his role as pilot (a daring ace with the Flying Tigers of the Far East) and narrator Bob Scott in *God Is My Co-Pilot* (1944)—hence the image of Bob's grinning at "every little bucktooth yellow rat he shoots down."

V33.17, B37.38, P33.37 sitreps Military jargon for "situation reports."

V33.26, B38.7–8, P34.5 the Witchcraft Act's more than 200 years old That is, the 1735 act of Parliament that repealed statutes against witchcraft in England and Scotland, the last witchcraft trial having occurred in 1712. Larsson, however, mentions the historical context pertinent to this episode ("A *Companion*'s Companion"). During the war a Scottish housewife and spiritualist named Helen Duncan (1897–1956) was tried, convicted and imprisoned for witchcraft (despite the repeal of the act two hundred years earlier). Her trial included testimony about a 1942 séance during which Duncan invoked the spirit of a dead sailor whose cap bore the name of a ship, the HMS Barham, the sinking of which the Royal Navy was keeping secret. That séance was one of many that brought Duncan fame for "materializing" in the presence of grieving family members the specters of dead servicemen, but the 1942 event had caught the attention of military security experts who feared, at the time of her January 1944 arrest, that she might disclose other state secrets such as the D-Day invasion date. Appeals of her conviction began immediately, turned on the question of whether mediums are witches, transformed her into a cause célèbre, and took years.

V33.31–32, B38.14, P34.11   "away to the Scrubs"   London's Wormwood Scrubs prison, completed in 1890 and home to some fifteen hundred felons.

V34.6, B38.31, P34.25   "on his EEG"   Electroencephalogram, the graphic representation of a patient's brain-wave activity, developed in 1929 by German neurophysiologist Hans Berger.

V34.21–22, B39.8, P34.41–35.1   agency known as PISCES   A fictional acronym. The twelfth house on the astrological calendar (February 19–March 20) and a water sign (the Fishes), symbolizing confinement, life reined in by institutions, social responsibilities, and death. Under its influence one also expects contact with unknown forces in the universe. It is the ruler of narrative action in part 1.

V34.28–30, B39.16–18, P35.7–9   Free French plotting . . . ELAS Greeks stalking royalists   A brief catalog of some principal struggles and realignments of European power occurring at this time. By December of 1944 the Free French under Charles de Gaulle were not only "plotting" revenge but trying those who collaborated with the Nazis. During late 1944 and into 1945 the Polish Committee of National Liberation based at Lublin carried out the overthrow of a "Varsovian" (that is, Warsaw-based) puppet government. These developments all received daily treatment in the *Times* of London, Pynchon's main source. But throughout December only the German counterattack in Holland got more newsprint than the struggles in Greece. The ELAS Greeks were a Communist-led faction who took to their side various captured Nazis and, mounting a mid-December attack against Athens, attempted to remove Allied forces led by the British general Roland Scobie, who was under the strictest orders to keep the Greek royalist faction in power.

V35.3, B39.35–36, P35.24   a Behaviorist here, a Pavlovian there   The Pavlovian is Dr. E. W. A. Pointsman, who, with the full baggage of his theories, will be introduced to us in coming episodes. Behaviorist psychology dates from the work of John and Rosalie Watson in the twenties; a reference to their work will soon occur in the general context of Tyrone Slothrop's conditioning, in 1920, when he was an infant or toddler (see V84.39–85.3n).

V35.21, B40.16, P36.2   a mixed AA battery   Once again Pynchon's source was the *Times* of London, here the issue of December 21 and its story entitled "Improper Conduct in Mixed Battery." The "mixed" antiaircraft batteries were necessary because of manpower shortages, and fraternization between the men and women during long winter nights had evidently become a concern. On the NAAFI see V17.26n.

V35.26, B40.22, P36.7   "a T. S. Eliot April"   Because "April is the cruelest month," according to the opening lines of Eliot's poem *The Waste Land*.

V35.32–34, B40.30–31, P36.13–15   Bahrein . . . Muharraq   Cities on the Persian Gulf, where Pirate was stationed during the early years of oil exploration/extraction there.

V36.11–12, B41.12–13, P36.35   what the lyrics to "Dancing in the Dark" are *really* about   About desperate love? Last days? Death? Composed by Howard Deitz and Arthur Schwartz in 1931, ten years later the song became a million seller for Artie Shaw and the Gramercy Five. Here are the lyrics:

> Dancing in the dark,
> Till the tune ends,
> We're dancing in the dark,
> And it soon ends—
>
> We're waltzing in the wonder of why we're here—
> Time hurries by,
> We're here and gone,
> Looking for the light
> Of a new love, to brighten up the night—
> I have you, love,
> And we can face the music together . . .
> Dancing in the dark.
>
> What though love is old?
> What though song is old?
> Through them we can be young—
> Hear this heart of mine,
> Make yours part of mine—
> Dear one, tell me that we're one,
> Dancing in the dark!

V37.5, B42.11, P37.29–30   the cutters and the sleek hermaphrodites   Here, ships, projected onto that "sky-sea behind." A cutter is a single-masted fore-and-aft rigged sailer with a running bowsprit and two or more headsails; a hermaphrodite is a boat with a square-rigged foremast and a fore-and-aft rigged mainmast.

V37.10–11, B42.19, P37.36   Fred Roper's Company of Wonder Midgets

Fred Roper and His Wonderful Midgets, apparently twenty or so in number, used to tour acts like their "Toy Soldier Parade" during the thirties, featuring Roper in his busby cap and military greatcoat (see Larsson, "A *Companion*'s Companion").

EPISODE 6

The time is midnight and early morning of the nineteenth as Roger Mexico and Jessica Swanlake drive southeast out of London, through a light rain, for a rendezvous with Dr. Pointsman. A short episode, analeptically revealing Roger and Jessica's "'cute meet'" (V38.36) and their wordless retreats to an empty house in one of London's evacuated zones, it foreshadows romantic complications: Jessica is attached to a battery mate named Jeremy, Roger to his "mother" (V39.15), the war.

V37.19–20, B42.30, P38.3–4   hunched Dracula-style inside his Burberry The Burberry is the British (luxury) brand of woolen overcoat, here in black with its wide lapels turned up, in the style of Bela Lugosi acting the lead in director Tod Browning's 1931 film version of Bram Stoker's *Dracula*.

V37.24, B42.36, P38.8   before the clock of St. Felix chimes one. And when the mice run down   St. Felix was the bishop of East Anglia during the seventh century, whom residents of Suffolk commemorate with St. Felix Church, at Felixstowe. However, that is ninety miles east-northeast of London, whereas Roger and Jessica are headed "south of the Thames," probably into Kent. A scan of Baedeker's *England* for *any* St. Felix church, hospital, school, or other institution (preferably with clock) in Kent and East Sussex turned up nothing. Its imaginary mice, in any case, clearly riff on the traditional nursery rhyme: "Hickory, dickory, dock, / The mouse ran up the clock. / The clock struck one, / The mouse ran down! / Hickory, dickory, dock."

V37.32, B43.5–6, P38.17–18   "he's a Pavlovian . . . a Royal Fellow"   On Pointsman's institutional connections see V47.3n and V42.15n, respectively.

V38.6, B43.18, P38.28   "the boy friend dear old Nutria"   Roger mocks Jessica's nickname for Jeremy. Instead of "Beaver" he uses the noun for a cheap, ersatz beaver pelt that is derived from a South American rodent, the *coypu*, which the British call "nutria."

V38.19, B43.33, P39.4   that awful *Going My Way*   Awful because of its sentimental depiction of Father Chuck O'Malley (played by Bing Crosby), a witty, optimistic, young Catholic priest matched against the cynical, opinionated old pastor of a poor, inner-city parish. Crosby won an Oscar for this 1944 role.

V38.37, B44.12, P39.23   heart of downtown Tunbridge Wells   Town located twenty-seven miles south of London.

V38.38, B44.13, P39.24   the vintage Jaguar   Vintage indeed. From 1936
until 1945, the Jaguar was one of nine *models* produced at the S. S. Cars
factory of Coventry. Few were made, but they won a small following because of their speed and handling at fairly affordable prices. After V-E
Day, Jaguar became the *make* name of a new motorcar line.

V39.1–2, B44.18–19, P39.28–29   "backstage at the old Windmill"   See
V22.3n.

V39.7, B44.25, P39.34   "called up the Girl Guides yet"   See V13.11n.

V39.11, B44.30, P39.38   "Nearly to Battle"   A town located twenty miles
south of Tunbridge, on the trunk road from London to Hastings.

V40.9, B45.35, P40.37   Roger's only a statistician   The Bantam
misprints this as "satistician."

V40.13–14, B45.41, P41.1   all the definitely 3-sigma lot   In statistics,
sigma is the designation for a standard deviation. When the frequencies
of an event are plotted against an attribute of it they will yield the classic bell curve. And, provided the distribution is normal or "Gaussian,"
the range from 1 standard deviation (s.d.) above normal to 1 s.d. below
normal will contain approximately one-half of all cases; the range between 2 s.d above/below, about three-fourths of all cases; and the range
between 3 s.d. above/below will contain (on either side of the bell curve,
under its far left and right edges) over 98 percent of all cases. Three-
sigma therefore designates an event (or person) that is quite beyond the
ordinary. See later references at V523.39 and V635.35.

**V40.18, B46.3–4, P41.6   outside the chi-square calculations . . . the Zener
cards**   A Zener deck contains twenty-five cards, with five symbols
(cross, wave, rectangle, circle, and star) depicted on them. They are commonly used while testing subjects for extrasensory abilities. Afterward,
the data might be subjected to a chi-square test to determine if the statistically expected frequencies of successful guessing matched the observed frequencies. But under the rocket barrage ("outside the chi-square
calculations") and with the subject's "mortality always goading," how
then to trust the results?

V40.36, B46.26, P41.24   a coal-black Packard   In the United States, a
moderately priced sedan but exported to England as a luxury-grade sedan
for American military brass and the diplomatic corps.

EPISODE 7

Another short episode, placed somewhere to the southeast of London,
around 1:00 A.M. on December 19. Roger and Jessica have found Dr.
Pointsman at the site of a house smashed earlier that day in a rocket blast.

Roger assists him in a slapstick chase after a shell-shocked dog prowling the ruins; during it Pointsman gets his foot stuck in a toilet bowl.

V42.15, B48.17, P43.10   F.R.C.S.   Dr. Pointsman is a Fellow of the Royal College of Surgeons, the official educational and professional standards organization for surgeons in England and Wales ever since King Henry VIII chartered it in 1450 (as the Company of Barber-Surgeons).

V42.24, B48.29, P43.19–20   fumed-oak   Oak wood that has been artificially aged by having been cured in an atmosphere of ammonia.

V42.36, B49.4–5, P43.31–32   the electric lantern   British nomenclature for a flashlight, also known in Britain as a torch.

V43.12–13, B49.21–22, P44.5–6   some woman's long-gathered nest, taken back to separate straws   Another instance of hysteron proteron.

V43.18–19, B49.29, P44.11   the boot of the car   British nomenclature for the trunk.

V43.28, B49.41, P44.20   "this *gillie* or something"   In Scotland, the attendant who caters to wealthy hunters and fishermen; he portages and maintains the equipment.

V44.4, B50.20, P44.37   fumbling a flashlight   After such care for proper British nomenclature above, Pynchon slips back into his American idiom.

V44.17–18, B50.36–37, P45.9–10   "Why it's Mrs. Nussbaum!"   That is, Mrs. Pansy Nussbaum (pronounced "Noose-bomb") of *Allen's Alley*, the American radio program that played over the CBS network beginning in 1943. The format centered on Fred Allen, who used to walk down his back alley, pausing to knock on the neighbors' doors. The comedy stemmed from the resulting exchanges—for example, with Mrs. Nussbaum, played by Minerva Pious, remembered for her Jewish accent and her phonetic errors and grammatical inversions. Harmon records a typical exchange (*Great Radio Comedians* 169–70): "Why it's Mrs. Nussbaum!" Allen exclaims, and she replies: "You were expecting maybe the Fink Spots?" Despite Pynchon's claim, "Allen's Alley" did not appear over BBC channels on Wednesday nights or on any other night. *Some* Wednesday evenings brought "The Bob Hope Show" or "The Jimmy Durante Show," but BBC programmers evidently followed no set schedule.

V44.20, B50.39, P45.12   "ekshpecting maybe Lessie?"   That is, Lassie, the Academy Award–winning dog that made its screen debut in *Lassie Come Home* (1943), with Roddy MacDowell and Elsa Lanchester in the supporting roles.

V46.40–41, B53.33–34, P47.33   Hospital of St. Veronica of the True Image   St. Veronica met Jesus on the road to Calvary, lent him a handkerchief, and found afterward that it bore an image of his face. There was no such London hospital, in any event.

V47.3, B53.37, P47.36   The Book   Here and throughout *GR*, "The Book" refers to volume 2 of the *Lectures on Conditioned Reflexes* by Russian physiologist Ivan Petrovich Pavlov (1849–1936), which was published four years after Pavlov's death and that represented his effort to branch out of physiological studies and into psychology. One of Pavlov's American collaborators, Dr. Horsley Gantt, did the English translation (1941). As for the secrecy of Pointsman, Spectro, and other devotees, who "rotate" their lone copy, we soon learn the reason for the book's preciousness to them (see V87.38–39n).

EPISODE 8

Yet another short episode. After 2:00 A.M., at the "Abreaction Ward" of St. Veronica's Hospital, Drs. Kevin Spectro and Edward Pointsman talk shop (Pavlovian psychology) and in particular about the puzzling case of Tyrone Slothrop. Their dialogue turns on problems of causality: first because Slothrop experiences sexual excitation at the sites of *future* rocket strikes; moreover (and this was widely reported at the time), when V-2 impacted, observers first saw the blast then heard the sound of the missile coming in. The symmetry of these reversals (further instances of hysteron proteron) gets Pointsman going, and other narrative threads introduced in his meditations will prove significant: these are Slothrop's link to a Dr. Jamf and Pointsman's conditioning of an octopus named Grigori.

V48.14, B55.16, P49.7 Abreactions C. G. Jung's essay "The Therapeutic Value of Abreaction" (*Collected Works* 16:129–38) supplies a gloss. In 1928 Jung's concern was "the neuroses resulting from the Great War, with their essentially traumatic etiology" in otherwise healthy patients. Abreaction is a form of therapy for such traumas, hinging on the "dramatic reversal of the traumatic moment, its emotional recapitulation" in the presence of a therapist. The therapist's role is to guide the patient through a representation of the injury and to stand as a point of transference for the patient's neurosis. Jung writes that the transference is crucial and often takes much time: "It is imperative that the doctor should get into the closest possible touch with the patient's line of psychological development. One could say that as the doctor assimilates the intimate psychic contents of the patient into himself, he is in turn assimilated as a figure into the patient's psyche." But there is the hitch. That transference must be "freely negotiated," not a "slavish and humanly degrading bondage." In comparison, *GR* teems with instances of "slavish" abreaction. Pointsman, for example, puts his commanding officer, Brigadier General Pudding, through a nightmarish rehearsal of his Great War traumas (in episode 4 of part 2). Slothrop's forced replay of his own neuroses during the sodium amytal session of the next episode is yet an-

other example of Pointsman's manipulative "therapy." This is why
Kevin Spectro doubts the ethic of his technique: "'I don't like it, Pointsman'" (V48.16). The issue here and elsewhere in the novel is control.

**V48.25, B55.28–29, P49.18–19   "If he hadn't been one of Laszlo Jamf's
subjects"**   Slothrop, that is. The name "Jamf," the subject of Slothrop's
meditations later in the novel (see V161.34–35n), apparently derives
from an acronym popularized by jazz artist Charlie Parker, to designate a
"jive-ass-motherfucker" (see Gold, *Jazz Talk* 148).

**V48.29–31, B55.34–35, P49.22–23   The reversal. . . . a few feet of film run
backwards**   Focalized through Pointsman, this trope for the apparent reversal of cause and effect in the rocket's blast is another instance of hysteron proteron.

V48.34, B55.39, P49.27   "ideas of the opposite"   See V49.1–2n.

**V48.38–39, B56.2–4, P49.31–32   into one of the transmarginal phases . . .
past "equivalent" and "paradoxical" phases**   Sends us into "The Book."
According to Pavlov, the intensity of a conditioned reflex depends obviously on the intensity of the stimulus used in its conditioning, be it
from a bell, a metronome, or any sensory apparatus. Yet the intensity depends just as importantly, though less obviously, on the magnitude of
such unconditioned factors as the subject's motivation or emotional
state. Let Pavlov's translator, Horsley Gantt, take it from there (*Lectures*
2:13–14): "Beyond a certain maximal intensity, variations may lead to
certain phases—the equivalent (in which strong and weak stimuli produce the same effect), the paradoxical (in which the weak stimuli give a
greater response than the strong), the ultraparadoxical (in which the excitatory conditioned stimuli become inhibitory, and vice-versa). Such
. . . stimuli, too strong to give the maximal conditioned reflex, Pavlov
terms *transmarginal*."

V49.1–2, B56.7–8, P49.36   Pavlov writing to Janet   Sends readers once
more to "The Book," specifically to chapter 54, "Les Sentiments D'Emprise and the Ultraparadoxical Phase." Originally the passage quoted
here was published in a French scholarly journal as an open letter from
Pavlov to Pierre Janet, the great French psychologist. Janet had recently
published a paper on feelings of persecution and paranoia in his patients
(the *sentiments d'emprise*). He explained their feelings as stemming
from the patients' weakened states (brought on by depression, disease,
trauma, or terror), during which they are confused by "ideas of the opposite." Categories such as mine/theirs, giving/receiving, or master/slave
become blurred. Soon, Janet theorized, the patient projects the pain of
this conflict outside, objectifying the conflict by personifying it in others. In short, the patient becomes paranoid, feels persecuted. Janet called
for a psychoanalytic therapy, but Pavlov, ever the physiologist, argued
for chemical cures. Pavlov surmised that the "ideas of the opposite,"
which seemed irrefutably tied to the switch-like, on/off functions of cor-

tical cells, would become confused in an addled, stressed, or terrified cortex. It therefore seemed a simple matter of the patient's having gone transmarginal, as defined above. Thus Pavlov (*Lectures* 2:148; the italics in *GR* are Pynchon's): "It is precisely the ultraparadoxical phase which is the base of the weakening of the idea of the opposite of [not Pynchon's "in"] our patients." Pavlov's remedy? He wrote (149): "In their turn, chemistry first, and then physics will be nearest these phenomena and their mechanism, approaching a final solution."

V49.13–14, B56.23–24, P50.8–9   "M. K. Petrova was first to observe it" Petrova was a research associate at Pavlov's laboratory in the Russian village of Koltushy. Her experiments with the hypnosis of dogs, one result of which Pynchon summarizes here, are described in volume 2 of the *Lectures*, chapter 47 ("Contributions to the Physiology of the Hypnotic State of the Dog"), especially pp. 75–77.

V49.31–50.1, B56.43–57.14, P50.26–38   as once again the floor. . . . two o'clock dawn The abreaction of a St. Veronica's patient, who relives the V-2 striking a cinema in which he was seated, anticipating the novel's closing moments.

V50.22, B57.38–39, P51.17   Realpolitik dreams Originally formulated in Ludwig von Rochau's *Grundsätze der Realpolitik* (1853), realpolitik had its greatest proponent in German chancellor Otto von Bismarck. Realpolitik elevates the strategic interests of the state—its relative security—over liberal domestic reform. Or, as Bismark once put it: "The great questions of our day cannot be solved by speeches and majority votes . . . but by blood and iron" (*ODQ*).

V50.25, B57.43, P51.21   St. Veronica's Downtown Bus Station Fictional.

V51.6, B58.27, P52.2   AWOL bags A small overnight bag, usually of canvas, so called because a serviceman might take it with him when "absent without leave."

V51.30, B59.15, P52.27   a gigantic, horror-movie devilfish The Bantam misprints this as "develfish."

V51.31–32, B59.17, P52.29   the Ick Regis jetty Unknown, if not fictional, though it seems to play on the southern seacoast town of Lyme Regis, or Ickford (Buckinghamshire) and Ickleton (Cambridgeshire), and perhaps to play still further with place-names, in a pun: the "Egregious jetty."

V52.23–24, B60.16–17, P53.22–23   "the damned Rundstedt offensive . . . P.W.E. won't fund anything" Pointsman frets over the constraints of foreign policy on funding. General Karl Gerd von Rundstedt, whose stature in the German high command was second only to that of Hitler's long-time associate and SS head Heinrich Himmler, directed the German counteroffensive in Holland, widely known as the Battle of the Bulge. It began on Sunday, December 16, 1944. The PWE was the Political Warfare Executive, an intelligence gathering and propaganda wing of SHAEF.

V52.39, B60.35, P53.41   "over Deptford"   London parish located four miles southeast of London Bridge, on the south bank of the Thames.

EPISODE 9

Early in the morning of December 20, Roger and Jessica lie sleeping in the abandoned house we learned of in episode 6. Like many of the episodes in *GR* this one has a circular movement. A rocket blast awakens Jessica, who leaves the bed to stand at a frosted window. Focalized through her, the narrative segues analeptically into Roger explaining statistical principles to Jessica, then into an omniscient analepsis in which Roger and Pointsman debate the efficacy of statistical versus deterministic views of the correspondence between rocket strikes and Slothrop's erections. The episode ends by returning us to Jessica at her frosted window and a discussion she and Roger once had about prewar England.

V53.6, B61.3, P54.8   their dollful and piteous cries   Perhaps a misprint. "Doleful" fits the context, but so too would "doll-like," the grammatically correct form in context with the previous line: "smooth as dolls." Is "dollful" one of Pynchon's portmanteau words?

V53.25–26, B61.27–28, P54.29   frost gathering on the panes . . . out into the snow   The night of December 19–20 was, according to the *Times*, a cold one. Temperatures in London ranged down to 32–35 degrees Fahrenheit, and there was a "persistent fog" that turned to light snow in some areas. For a remarkably similar image that frames episode 14, with Katje Borgesius watching "the long rain in silicon and freezing descent" upon her windows, see V93.34–35n.

V53.33, B61.37, P54.37   AR-E forms   Probably, Air Raid Evacuation forms, Home Security's attempt to keep track of the one and a half million people evacuated from London during the German V-bomb blitz.

V54.25, B62.36, P55.29   his Poisson equation   Named for the French mathematician Siméon Denis Poisson (1781–1840), the formula is useful in calculating the probability of exceedingly rare but possible events occurring. For example, the Poisson equation is commonly used in calculating the probability of radioactive emissions or in figuring, for actuarial purposes, the chances of one's dying, for example, in a bridge collapse. As Roger says, one can "look it up" (V54.40) in any handbook of mathematics; a working out of the formula appears at V140.6–10.

V55.11–12, B63.26–27, P56.17–18   Roger's old Whittaker and Watson   That is, his university math textbook, *Modern Analysis* by E. T. Whittaker and G. N. Watson, published by Cambridge University Press and in print continuously since 1902 with Whittaker as sole author in the first edition, but with Whittaker and Watson as coauthors in subsequent editions of 1915, 1920, and 1927 (the fourth edition, still reprinted); their names are now commonly attached to many of the formulae analyzed within it. Roger's training, for example in statistical uses of the Poisson distribution, would have come from his poring over pages of this text.

V55.22, B63.40, P56.29   table-rapping   A derogatory term for séances (V29.31n).

V55.29–30, B64.5–7, P56.37–38   "Summation," "transition," . . . "reciprocal induction"   A short catalog of Pavlovian "laws," most likely drawn from chapter 43 of volume 2 of the *Lectures*, "A Brief Outline of the Higher Nervous System" (esp. 48–50). According to Pavlov's "law of summation," the combination of "a number of weak conditioned stimuli" will result in "their exact mathematical sum" (48). The "law of transition" holds that if a conditioned positive stimulus continues unabated, it eventually "passes into a state of inhibition," a process Pavlov called "transition" (48). According to the "law of irradiation and concentration," the "processes of excitation and inhibition, originated at definite points of the cortex under the influence of corresponding stimuli, necessarily irradiate over a larger . . . area of the cortex, and then again concentrate in a limited space" (49). Finally, along with these processes a "reciprocal induction" may occur, that is, "intensification of one process by another taking place either in succession at the same point or simultaneously at two neighboring points" (50).

V55.36–37, B64.15, P57.3–4   his Kyprinos Orients   Advertised in tiny, front-page notices in the *Times* of London as "a Delightful, Fragrant Cigarette with a Rich, Satisfying Flavour." Generally the British prefer cigarettes made from Virginia tobaccos, but like Ian Fleming's character James Bond, Pointsman prefers a Near Eastern blend, here from the island of Cyprus. There is more. "Kyprinos" derives from the Greek "*kypris*," recalling Cyprian Aphrodite, or Venus. According to Graves (*White Goddess* 140): "The cypress was sacred to Hercules . . . and the word cypress is derived from Cyprus, which was called after Cyprian Aphrodite, his mother." So it is appropriate that Pointsman smokes this brand because, as we soon see, it was the "submontane Venus" (V88.10) of Pavlovian research that called him, as though he were Tannhäuser, out of traditional medicine and into the labyrinth of neurophysiology. Similarly, it is the same White Goddess of love-in-death that calls to the zany kamikaze pilots Tachezi and Ichizo when they gather luminescent white cypridinae from the Pacific surf (see V690.40n).

V56.8, B64.28, P57.15   "That's the Monte Carlo Fallacy"   So called because, on a roulette wheel (for example), the fact that one number comes up does not mean that its chances of coming up again are lessened. According to an axiom of statistics, with every new spin of the wheel the number has an equal chance against all others. With rockets, this means (as Roger says), "Everyone's equal. Same chances of getting hit. Equal in the eyes of the rocket" (V57.6–7).

V56.14, B64.35–36, P57.21   no reflex arc, no Law of Negative Induction Returns readers once more to Pavlov's *Lectures*. The concept of a reflex arc is a cornerstone in Pavlov's mechanistic theory. He represents the "arc" as a virtual "path" of cerebral causes and effects, from the time sensation is received until the body reacts to it. In volume 1 (117) he writes: "I represent the nervous path of the . . . reflex arc as a chain of three links—the *analyzer, the connection* or lock, and the *effector* or working part of the apparatus." The "law of negative induction" appears later in Pavlovian theory, essentially as a version of the "ultraparadoxical" phenomenon (see V48.38–39n). According to this law, a positive stimulus will, under certain conditions of trauma and stress, induce a negative response (*Lectures* 2:176).

V56.24, B65.5–6, P57.31   Reverend Dr. Paul de la Nuit Literally translated it is Paul "of the Night," but note as well the double pun: pall *de l'ennui* (pall of boredom).

V57.8, B65.34, P58.16   her Fay Wray look In *King Kong* (1933), actress Fay Wray's "look"—wide eyes, tense neck muscles, lips puckered on the verge of a scream—is something she first practices for director Carl Denham aboard ship, in a highly erotic scene, then puts to unfeigned use on Skull Island, when she first sees Kong.

V57.31, B66.19–20, P59.2   "another kind of Beveridge Proposal" The 1944 report "Social Insurgence and Allied Services," by Lord William H. Beveridge (1876–1963), became a foundation piece in English policy regarding the displaced persons of war-torn Europe. Beveridge argued that the last should be first, that those who suffered most should stand first in line for Allied aid. The "Bitterness Quotient" and "Evaluation Board" are Roger's exaggerations.

V58.38, B67.36–37, P60.10   bleached by the Star's awful radiance A Christmas tableau, with the Christ child in his manger, but "bleached" again calls up the image of Blicero (V30.12n).

V59.1–2, B67.42–68.1, P60.14–15   staticky Frank Bridge Variations . . . over the BBC Home Service Throughout the war two BBC "programmes" were broadcast on two different radio frequencies on the dial: one for the Home Service, another for the General Forces. The "Frank Bridge Variations" refers to British composer Benjamin Britten's homage to one of his teachers, "Variations on a Theme by Frank Bridge," op. 10 (1937).

V59.3, B68.1–2, P60.16   bottle of Montrachet From the tiny, exclusive vineyard of Montrachet, in the Côte de Beaune district of France. A very expensive bottle of wine.

V59.16, B68.19–20, P60.32–33   "Oh, Edward VIII abdicated. He fell in love with—" With Mrs. Wallis Warfield Simpson, the American divorcée whom the king married in 1937, after abdicating the throne in 1936 amid a storm of protest (see also V177.28–29n).

V59.30, B68.36, P61.6 **"And one cried wee, wee, wee, all the way"** Jessica quotes the old Mother Goose rhyme: "This little piggy went to market / This little piggy stayed home / This little piggy had roast beef / This little piggy had none / And this little piggy cried 'wee, wee, wee' all the way home." The pig/home motif will recur (see for example V114.12–13n).

EPISODE 10

The setting for this grotesquely surreal episode is St. Veronica's, the fictional hospital in London's East End where Tyrone Slothrop reports for his temporary duty as a testing subject. The date is unspecified, but it's probably December 18–20. Injected with sodium amytal, he lapses into an induced hypnotic vision, segments of which comprise the stream-of-consciousness "action" of this episode. In search of a fallen, lost harmonica, Slothrop journeys down a toilet in Boston's Roseland Ballroom, circa 1939. Then, in a western setting, a cowboy named Crutchfield the Westwardman prepares for a showdown with a bad figure named Toro Rojo. These visions introduce some of the most significant semantic contraries of *GR*: white/black, north/south, the word/shit. The prevalence of the color red is also noteworthy, and several motifs—the underground journey, westwarding progress, the lawless frontier—will reappear in the novel. In addition, like episodes 5 and 9 before it, this one seems to come full circle: it begins and ends with semantic play on an enigmatic phrase, "You never did the Kenosha Kid."

V60.5, B69.15, P61.23 **Bonechapel Gate, E1** A fictional London postal address, although the E1 designation would put this hospital around Whitechapel Road in the city's East End.

V60.8, B69.18, P61.26 **The Kenosha Kid** For decades, one of the outstanding enigmas in *GR*. Speculation has been that this Kid might be Slothrop himself, who will recall sitting in a "white tile greasy-spoon" Kenosha restaurant (V696.10–11); or that he might be the colonel "from Kenosha," whose apparently fatal haircut is played out to Slothrop's unwitting accompaniment on the recovered harmonica (see V643.11); or the "loony" Japanese radarman named Old Kenosho (V691.11), or even actor Don Ameche (see V381.6n). Readers (Poirier, "Rocket Power" 169; Crumb, "Uroboric Imagery" 76) have also made much of the fact that Kenosha, Wisconsin, is the birthplace of Orson Welles (on May 6, 1915). It turns out, however, that the Kenosha Kid was the creation of pulp writer Forbes Parkhill. From the 1920s through the 1940s, Parkhill published sixty-plus western stories in pulp magazines like *Popular Western* and *Ace-High Magazine,* and several more in the *Saturday Evening Post;* he also wrote screenplays, such as the 1935 Bob Steele western, *Alias John Law.* Parkhill's novelette, "The Kenosha Kid," appeared in the August 1931 issue of *Western Rangers* (published by Popular Publications). This story's hero makes his living playing poker, so effectively interpreting the "tells" of his opponents that he virtually controls action at the table. A kind of Robin Hood, he uses his seemingly uncanny powers to bring evil con men and crooks to financial ruin and stacks of dollars to the downtrodden. The Kenosha Kid enters the story riding a sorrel pony—perhaps an inspiration for the horse named "Snake," ridden by Crutchfield the Westwardman in Slothrop's sodium amytal fantasy (below).

V60.26–30, B70.2–7, P62.12–15   the "Charleston" . . . all them dances, I did the "Castle walk," and . . . the "Lindy," too!   The Charleston was a swing dance of the twenties and thirties, known for its "no-contact" positioning of the partners; the Big Apple was another swing dance, of the thirties, done to a fast six-beat count; the Castle Walk was named for Vernon and Irene Castle, the dynamic duo of pre–Great War ballroom dance (he died during the war); and the Lindy or Lindy Hop was a novelty dance, with exaggerated jumping and feet pendulously swinging, named for Charles Lindbergh's 1927 transatlantic flight.

V61.17, B70.26–27, P62.35   10% Sodium Amytal   An intermediate-strength barbiturate, sodium amytal is the popular "truth serum" of countless Hollywood movies. Therapeutically, it can be used to induce a trancelike state. The drug comes in three dosage forms: intravenous (IV), intramuscular (IM), and blue capsules for oral induction. Its psychological effects range from profound states of hypnotic trance to mild sedation. Slothrop receives a strong intravenous jolt. Later he will recognize the drug's effects in another character (see V512.1). One other thing: note the pun, amytal/amatol (the V-2 rocket's explosive, see V312.21n).

V61.24–62.2, B70.36–71.12, P63.7–19   Snap to, Slothrop . . . Slothrop, snap to!   Sung to the tune of "Bye, Bye Blackbird," a song Eddie Cantor popularized in the late twenties. Compare the actual lyric (written by Mort Dixon):

> Pack up all my cares and woe,
> Here I go, singin' low,
> Bye-bye, blackbird.
>
> Where somebody waits for me,
> Sugar's sweet, and so is she,
> Bye-bye, blackbird.

No one seems to care, or understand me,
Oh what hard luck stories they all hand me.
Make my bed, and light the light;
I'll be home, late tonight,
Blackbird, bye-bye.

V61.30, B71.6, P63.13   Just give me my "ruptured duck"   When they
were honorably discharged from the U.S. Army, soldiers were given a
brass lapel button with a "screaming eagle" embossed on it. In popular
slang these buttons were known as "ruptured ducks" (A. Marjorie Taylor, *The Language of World War II* 172).

V61.34, B71.10, P63.17   mike my brain   Measure it with a micrometer.

V62.4, B71.15, P63.21–22   the Negroes, in Roxbury   A suburb of Boston
and a black ghetto since the twenties, Roxbury was founded in 1630 by
William Pynchon (McIntyre, *William Pynchon* 9)

V62.20, B71.31–32, P64.2   "gage" smoke   In African American slang
from the thirties and forties, marijuana.

V62.22, B71.34, P64.4   my brain a process!   In African American slang,
"a process" refers to a tortuous method of straightening hair by applying
a pomade (called "congolene") that contains lye (see V67.31n). Also
known as "a conk." Malcolm X describes the terrors of his first one in
The Autobiography (51–55). Here, a conk for the brain.

V63.3, B72.18, P64.23   men's room at the Roseland Ballroom   The Roseland State Ballroom, on Massachusetts Avenue in Roxbury. During the
summer of 1940, Malcolm X worked as a shoeshine boy in the Roseland
men's room and saw the young Harvard men with their girls from Rad-
cliffe College. Pynchon has derived details about the Roseland from
chapters 3 ("Homeboy") and 4 ("Laura") of *The Autobiography*.

V63.5, B72.21, P64.25   bottle of Moxie   Trade name of an American soft
drink now marketed by the Monarch-Nugrape Company. Originally created in 1876 by Massachusetts physician Augustin Thompson and marketed as "Moxie Nerve Food," it was a bitter syrup derived from sugar
cane, gentian root, and various herbal extracts concocted to treat (in the
doctor's words) "recovered paralysis, softening of the brain, locomotor
ataxia and insanity when caused by nervous exhaustion." These medicinal promises faded but the brand name held, and two years before Coca-
Cola made its debut in 1884 Thompson was marketing Moxie, a syrupy
beverage thinned with carbonated water, as a soft drink. Its heyday came
in the twenties, when advertisements billed Moxie as "The Drink for
Those Who Are at All Particular" and featured celebrity endorsements.

V63.6, B72.21, P64.26   a Clark bar   Brand name of an American candy
bar (a chocolate coating around a brittle center) created by Irish immigrant D. L. Clark several years after he founded the Clark Company in

1886, in Alleghany, Pennsylvania. Clark began packaging individual bars for shipment to U.S. servicemen during World War I, afterward selling them for a nickel each.

V63.14, B72.31, P64.34   in his snow-white Arrow   Since the 1851 founding in Troy, New York, of collar, cuff, and shirt makers Cluett, Peabody and Company, a popular American brand of men's shirts.

V63.22, B72.41, P65.1   Red, the Negro shoeshine boy   This is Malcolm X, whose nicknames included "Red" (because of his hair) and "Homeboy" (because he'd come to Boston from the midwestern town of Lansing). See chapter 3 of *The Autobiography*.

V63.23–25, B73.1–3, P65.2–3   "Cherokee" comes wailing up . . . moving rose lights   The recollection derives from Malcolm X (47), who describes hearing the gaiety from above, in the lavatory: "From down below, the sound of the music had begun floating up . . . a few couples already dancing under the rose-colored lights." Two pages further on he recalls "Charlie Barnett's 'Cherokee,'" a song written by Ray Noble and a late-thirties hit for several jazz bands. Pynchon refers to the lyric as "one more lie about white crimes" (V63.27). Here are the words:

> Sweet Indian maiden,
> Since I first met you,
> I can't forget you—
> Cherokee sweetheart.
>
> Child of the Prairie,
> Your love keeps calling,
> My heart enthralling—
> Cherokee.
>
> Dreams of summertime,
> Of lover-time gone by,
> Throng my memory—
>
> So tenderly, I sigh!
>
> My sweet Indian maiden,
> One day I'll hold you,
> In my arms fold you—
> Cherokee! Cherokee!

V63.32–37, B73.12–18, P65.11–16   "Yardbird" Parker is finding out . . . Dan Wall's Chili House   The details probably derive from Max Harrison's book about saxophonist Charles ("Yardbird") Parker, who was nineteen when he played at Dan Wall's Chili House in Harlem. Parker began at that time to experiment with his playing, and he recalled the importance of those New York gigs in an interview Harrison quotes (8–9): "I remember one night I was jamming in a chili house on Seventh Avenue between 139th and 140th. It was December 1939. Now I'd been getting bored with the stereotyped changes that were being used all the time and I kept thinking there's bound to be something else. I could hear it sometimes but I couldn't play it. Well, that night I found that by using the higher intervals of a chord as a melody line and backing them with appropriately related changes I could play the thing I'd been hearing." Harrison explains how these "changes" or chord progressions involved thirty-second notes, or demisemiquavers (which word Pynchon wants us to say in a midget "Munchkin voice," as if we were in *The Wizard of Oz*). Charlie Parker died on March 12, 1955, in the New York apartment of Baroness Konigswater-Rothschild, of acute stomach ulcers and severe liver cirrhosis—both the result of his addictions to alcohol and heroin. It is the "dum-de-dumming" (V63.39) of his wasteful death that Pynchon wants us to hear as accompaniment to this historical digression. Note, however, that he has fudged the chronology: Slothrop's scene at the Roseland, like Charlie Parker's chili-house gig, occurred in December 1939; but Malcolm X did not begin shining shoes at the Roseland until June of 1940.

V64.13, B73.36, P65.32   the cold Lysol air   After the Lysol brand of disinfectant cleanser.

V64.24, B74.8, P66.2   "any of those Sheiks in the drawer?"   American brand of condom. Malcolm X (48) tells of dispensing prophylactics to wealthy white boys—he would buy condoms at the drugstore for a quarter and deal them in the men's room for a dollar.

V64.28–29, B74.13–14, P66.7   like topo lines up a river valley   That is, lines on a topographical map; anticipates the song (at V68.12–16).

V65.9, B74.40, P66.29   Burma Shave signs   In 1926, to advertise its brand of shaving cream, the Burma Shave Company launched an ingenious and highly successful campaign involving roadside jingles, one line per sign, as in "Don't take / That curve / At 60 per / We hate to lose / A customer."

V65.16, B75.7, P66.37   Fu's Folly in Cambridge   Perhaps fictional (like Sidney's Great Yellow Grille, at V65.27), this Harvard-area restaurant was named after Rohmer's Fu-Manchu tales (see V277.34–38n). In chapter 2 of Pynchon's *V.*, a character named Fu runs with the Whole Sick Crew and evidently overhears a whispered compliment about (fictional) sax player McClintic Sphere, who "plays all the notes Bird [Charlie Parker] missed" (60).

V65.20, B75.11, P66.40   here's Dumpster Villard   An apparent suicide (because he cannot master the differential equations of calculus?) who will reappear in another of Slothrop's dreams (V255.20).

V65.27, B75.20, P67.6   Sidney's Great Yellow Grille   Unknown if not fictional eatery.

V65.33, B75.28, P67.12   Jack Kennedy, the ambassador's son   Reappears in "Mom Slothrop's Letter to Ambassador Kennedy" (V682–83). Joseph Kennedy Sr. (1888–1969) was ambassador to England from 1937 until November 1940, when he stepped down to "keep America out of war"

(Wheeler, *Founding Father* 293). John F. Kennedy had returned from England to Harvard University in 1939 to finish his senior thesis on prewar English diplomacy, a study that later became his first book, *Why England Slept* (New York, 1940).

V66.12, B76.9, P67.34   Slothrop like an MTA subway train   As in Boston's Metropolitan Transit Authority.

V66.39, B77.1, P68.21   dust under the Capehart   American brand of radio receiver ("Your Private Window on the World," as the advertisements used to claim).

V67.8–9, B77.12, P68.30   Decline and fall works silently   Echoing the title of Edward Gibbon's monumental history, *The Decline and Fall of the Roman Empire* (1788).

V67.31, B77.38, P69.11   kid with the Red Devil lye in his hair   Here is the recipe for congolene according to Malcolm X (53): "can of Red Devil lye, two eggs, and two medium-sized potatoes."

V68.1, B77.8–9, P69.20   Half an Ark's better than none   As in, "half a loaf"? In any case the logic's clear: Noah's ark gave sanctuary to all the animals, two-by-two, but with Crutchfield *"the only,"* there is always "only one" of everything. So: half an ark.

V68.12, B78.21, P69.31   RED RIVER VALLEY   Pynchon parodies the traditional lyric of western cowboys:

> From this valley they say you are going,
> We will miss your bright eyes and sweet smile;
> For they say you are taking the sunshine,
> That has brightened our pathways awhile.
>
> Come and sit by my side if you love me,
> Do not hasten to bid me adieu;
> Just remember the Red River Valley,
> And the cowboy who loved you so true.

V68.23, B78.33, P70.5   His little pard   The term "baffles" Fowler, but it's a common, friendly shortening of the western slang term "pardner"; it appears throughout Mark Twain's *Roughing It* (1872), for example. Moreover, in the "Red Ryder" comic strips (beginning in 1938), as in the Dell comic book (beginning in 1940), and in the initial film *Adventures of Red Ryder* (Republic, 1940) as well as the twenty-three B-western *Red Ryder* movies released from 1944 to 1947, our hero (named for his red hair) sometimes refers to "Little Beaver," the Navajo Indian boy who is his sidekick, as "little pard."

V68.27, B78.38, P70.8   San Berdoo   Slang for the town of San Bernardino, in the California desert east of Los Angeles.

V69.12, B79.23–24, P70.30   in Eagle Pass from a faro dealer   Eagle Pass is a border town on the Rio Grande, about eighty miles upriver from Laredo, Texas. Faro is a card game that was well known throughout nineteenth-century western towns. In Wichita faro, the dealer lays out a "soda" card that counts for nothing and then, moving through the deck two at a time, turns both a "losing" and a "winning" card over and over. Before each turn players might wager on numbers, from ace through king, and lose or win depending on whether the number on which they'd put their chip or "marker" turned up in the "losing" or "winning" hole (that is, less than or greater than what the dealer turns). They might further let those bets "ride" as their chips increased or disappeared. A few other kinds of bets follow from this basic pattern.

V69.16, B79.28, P70.34   back home at "Rancho Peligroso"   This "Perilous Ranch" evokes the castle or seige perilous of Arthurian legend (see V321.6–7). Larsson ("A *Companion*'s Companion") also hears an allusion to director Fritz Lang's 1952 western film starring Marlene Dietrich, *Rancho Notorious*.

V69.32, B80.7, P71.10   "Toro Rojo"   "Red Bull."

V69.39, B80.16, P71.17   Los Madres   "The Mothers," the Sierra Madres range of northern Mexico. But the article should be feminine—"Las."

V70.4, B80.24, P71.24   platanos   Banana-like plantains, though in Spanish it should be accented: *plátanos*.

V70.29–30, B81.9–10, P72.8–9   ten thousand stiffs humped under the snow in the Ardennes   Soldiers fallen in the Battle of the Bulge (V52.23–24n), in the next line imagined as taking on the "sunny Disnified look of numbered babies under white wool blankets"—as if arrayed for viewing at the hospital, in a Walt Disney cartoon.

V70.32, B81.12–13, P70.11   Newton Upper Falls   A Middlesex County suburb, about eight miles west-southwest of downtown Boston, Massachusetts.

V70.36, B81.18, P70.16   segway   That is, "segue," radio announcers' musical terminology for a transition, a bridge between songs, an advertisement and a song, or parts of a musical composition; here given a phonetic spelling.

V71.2, B81.27, P72.23   Beacon Street   Runs through Boston westward to Brookline and Newton.

EPISODE 11

The time and setting of this episode are the same as for episode 9. By a bizarre method, Pirate decodes the message he received from that V-2 rocket of December 18. Later we learn that the note conveyed information about plucking Katje Borgesius out of Holland.

V71.11, B81.39, P72.32   "Kryptosam"   A (fictional) compound whose name Pynchon derives from the Greek *"kryptos"* (hidden) and the German *"samen"* (semen). Here it is a form of "tyrosine," an (actual) aromatic homocyclic amino acid (one of twenty-seven that form proteins in sets of two or more amino acids); tyrosine is convertible in skin cells to melanin, which controls skin pigmentation, light-to-dark. The invisible message in this scene is made visible—darkened or "developed" for decryption—by the application of (in this instance, Pirate's) seminal fluids.

V71.12, B81.40, P72.33   IG Farben . . . research contract with OKW   The Interessengemeinschaft Farbenindustrie Aktiengesellschaft, or Dye Industry Community of Interests Incorporated (IG Farben, for short), was Germany's largest industrial cartel during the thirties and, with the Krupp firm, a kingpin of the German rearmament program. Beginning in the nineteenth century as a patentee of the new coal-tar dyes, IG Farben metastasized into a multinational cartel concerned with drugs, synthetic fibers and rubber, films and dyes, and a variety of industrial chemicals. The firm plays a key role in *GR* from this moment on, and Pynchon's primary sources for details about it were Hermann Levy's *Industrial Germany* (1935) and Richard Sasuly's *IG Farben* (1947); another minor source, as Hite (*Ideas of Order* 165, n8) and Moore (*The Style of Connectedness* 145) both point out, was Josiah Dubois's book *Generals in Grey Suits* (1953). OKW was an acronym for the German Oberkommando der Wehrmacht, or Armed Forces High Command, with whom IG Farben maintained extensive research contracts.

The core issue in the late-nineteenth- and early-twentieth-century cartelization of modern industry was, as Levy succinctly put it, the problem of how "to reconcile the new monopolist movement" with long-standing ideals on the side of "a system of individualism and free competition" (11). Indeed, Pynchon's core concern is with the status of the individual in a system of increasingly state-integrated, rationalized, and internationalized capitalism. For Levy in 1935 the cartel was quite simply the leading edge of a "quite new order of public life" entailing not simply, or even crudely, strategems for price-fixing (which did occur) but for fully rationalized industrial complexes and workers' housing tied to state-organized infrastructures—especially, regulated public transportation and power. Levy is very clear about how German economic theorists imagined cartelization redressing potentially anarchic free markets in unregulated modern capitalism and even envisioned cartelization's *cultural* potentials for recapturing an idealized "medieval" condition of top-down communal integrity and stability (11–12). Levy leaves things at that, but in retrospect these cultural ideals were deeply consistent with an emerging Nazi ideology stressing nostalgia for premodern *Volkisch* community. He does however recognize the key paradox: that support for cartelization arose among "the ranks of the very hottest opponents of the capitalist system," even as "private industrial monopolies" had become "the most powerful exponents of the capitalist order" (12). They had moreover become, he realized, despite or even because of national support and regulation, increasingly transnational organizations, precursors in sum of the global capitalism that emerged during the post–World War II period. Levy thus provides the theoretical context and Sasuly the practical accounting for how cartelization reaches this climactic stage when it integrates with the war-making machineries, collectivities and powers of the modern state. In sum: Pynchon's thematic concerns throughout *GR*.

V71.24, B82.12, P73.7 Agfa, Berlin Here is Dr. Laszlo Jamf's employer, circa 1934: Agfa (or Aktiengesellschaft für Anilinenfabrikation) was a subsidiary of IG Farben specializing in the manufacture of dyes, photographic films, and reagents (Levy, *Industrial Germany* 72). Its American cousin, Agfa-Ansco, became the American IG Company in 1929, changing its name in 1939 to General Aniline and Film, or GAF. Levy sees that move as representing a classic example of the potential for globalization in the cartel movement (86–88). During the war, GAF property and cash was ordered seized by a U.S. District Court acting on authority of the Trading with the Enemy Act. After the war, Interhandel, the Swiss holding company also known as IG Chemie, sued the U.S. Attorney General for return of 93% of GAF property and cash, arguing that GAF had cut all ties with IG Farben in the 1920s. Attorneys for the U.S. countered that Interhandel had been part of a conspiracy to cloak ownership and control of GAF on behalf of IG Farben. The case dragged on for fifteen years; finally, on March 4, 1963, Attorney General Robert Kennedy announced that his brother President John Kennedy had authorized settlement of the Interhandel suit, a settlement that entailed the sale of GAF interests to U.S. buyers who would be able to continue to use the GAF trademark (on these post-war seizures and cases, see Sasuly, *IG Farben* 27, 34, 182; Dubois, *Generals in Grey Suits* 4, 24; and Borkin, *Crime and Punishment of I.G. Farben* passim).

V71.26, B82.14, P73.9 GEHEIME KOMMANDOSACHE Or "Top Secret Document" stamped on the page (see the photostat of such a document in Irving, *Mare's Nest* 298).

V71.27, B82.15–16, P73.10 after the style of von Bayros or Beardsley Aubrey Beardsley (1872–98) was a British graphic artist who had only begun to attract widespread attention when he died at age twenty-six. His grotesques, perhaps his drawings of Venus for an illustrated version of Richard Wagner's *Tannhäuser,* are the background here. Like Beardsley, the Marquis Franz von Bayros (1866–1924) was known principally as a graphic artist and an illustrator. His black-and-white drawings for turn-of-the-century German erotica by Hans Butsch and Max Somneraus won him a coterie following; his best-known work was a series of drawings for an edition of Dante's *Divine Comedy*.

V71.30, B82.20, P73.13–14 a De Mille set The reference is to film director Cecil B. DeMille's *Cleopatra* (1934), with its immense sets and arrangements of diaphanous silk scrims behind which brown-skinned girls fan the empress (played by Claudette Colbert) in her milk bath. See also V559.16–17n.

V72.27–28, B83.18, P74.6–7 like Wuotan and his mad army In Teutonic mythology Wuotan is "above all the arranger of wars and battles," and those who fall in battle will return to him. Ranging across the sky, Wuotan is accompanied by his "furious host," the *Wütende Heer*, or "Mad Army," of northern European legend (Grimm 132–35).

V72.29, B83.19, P74.8 Pirate's own robot hands begin to search The Bantam misprints this as "hands being to search."

EPISODE 12

S taff members at "The White Visitation" discuss their plans for Tyrone Slothrop. These include a "projective test" (with an octopus) that will lead off part 2. (In brief, a psychological projective test is designed to use a subject's responses to unstructured stimuli as measures of personality.) We also learn a good deal about the jealousies of and internecine fights between these scientists and pseudoscientists. Internal references put the date as December 21, the onset of winter.

V72.32–34, B83.24–27, P74.11–13 WAS TUST DU FÜR DIE FRONT . . . FÜR DEUTSCHLAND GETAN? A Nazi poster exhortation: "What are you doing for the front? For victory? What have you done for Germany today?"

V72.34, B83.26, P74.13 the walls read ice This roughly coincides with the *Times* of London weather report for December 21.

V73.5, B83.35–36, P74.21 taken at the manic whim of Henry VIII King Henry VIII plundered the Catholic monasteries after his 1536 break with Rome.

V73.23–27, B84.21–27, P75.3–7 "I can hear the Lord of the Sea. . . . Bert" The source of Reg Le Froyd's exclamations is Grimm's etymological somersaults in *Teutonic Mythology* (272–82). The goddess Bertha appears in the myths (as does the masculine god Berchtold, or Bert) as (1) "the promoter of navigation among men" and thus a "Lord of the Sea"; (2) a white figure, for Grimm explains that "*behrt* or *brecht* signifies bright, light, white"; (3) a being whose host includes the souls of children (comparable to Pynchon's man-child in this narrative digression); and (4) a figure whose festival occurs on the winter solstice (December 21). The suicide leap of Reg Le Froyd ("Reginald the Cold") corresponds with later references to the Gadarene swine and the rush of lemmings into the sea (V555.24–28n).

V73.32, B84.33, P75.12 Ick Regis See V51.31–32n.

V73.34, B84.35, P75.14 overflow from Brighton England's most popular seaside resort town, located fifty-three miles south of London on the English Channel in East Sussex.

V73.34, B84.36, P75.14 Flotsam and Jetsam A comedy show on the BBC Home Service Programme; according to the *Times* of London schedules it was featured on Wednesday evenings, usually at 9:30.

V74.13–14, B85.18, P75.34–35 the BBC's eloquent Myron Grunton Evidently fictional. The broadcaster's name derives from *"grunten,"* Middle English for marine fishes of the genus *Haemulon* that produce grunting sounds, and the Greek *"muron,"* meaning "sweet" or "delightful." Thus a "Myron Grunton" is a "sweet grunter."

V74.19, B85.25, P75.40 P/W interrogations Like POW, an abbreviation for prisoner of war.

V74.20, B85.26, P75.41 the brothers Grimm That is, Wilhelm (1786–1859) and Jacob (1785–1863) Grimm, the famous German philologists and folklorists, authors of the world-famous collection of fairy tales. Jacob's magisterial study, *Teutonic Mythology*, is one of Pynchon's principal sources.

V74.21, B85.27, P76.1 Dawes era flashes In 1924, former Brigadier General Charles Gates Dawes (1865–1951), then serving as director of the U.S. Bureau of the Budget, put forward a plan according to which Germany would begin making reparations payments to Allied governments involved in World War I. Through the mediation of British prime minister Ramsey MacDonald, the Dawes Plan was accepted and the payments continued for eight years, until Hitler's rise to power (A. J. P. Taylor, *English History* 215–16). Dawes went on to become vice president under Coolidge (1925–29) and then moved into banking.

V75.12, B86.26, P76.34 the name "Schwarzkommando" Translated, the "Black Command," a (mostly) fictional detachment of troops originally from, or descended from immigrants out of, the former German colony in South-West Africa. In *GR*, a (fictional) remnant of the Herero people who (in historical fact) were nearly annihilated in 1904 in accordance with the extermination order issued by German general Lothar von Trotha; they serve in *GR* as a special force of the SS assigned to the A4 rocket forces. Beneath that fiction there are, as Selmeci and Henrichsen have shown, nuggets of historical detail: chiefly, archival information and photographs revealing Herero tribesmen employed *prior to* the 1904 genocide in the service of German military units throughout South-West Africa. These *Offiziersburschen und Polizeidiener* (Officers' Boys and Police Footmen) rode and drilled with *Schutztruppe* (Rifle Troops) as servants and wore their masters' Prussian style uniform, including the "wideawake hat" and other regalia (see V361.7–13n). Before the 1904 uprising, these black troopers' varied work as translators and cultural go-betweens proved crucial to German efforts to regulate the colony. Afterward, German troops defined the 650 or so Herero who still had "regular jobs with the armed forces" in much more servile terms, but it is notable that they still wore the hats, uniforms, and regalia of the occupiers who had carried out von Trotha's extermination order against their own people.

V75.30–31, B87.5–6, P77.11–12   Dr. Porkyevitch, who worked with Pavlov himself at the Koltushy institute   Porkyevitch is fictional and part of the webwork of pig references in *GR* (e.g., Porky Pig, see V545. 4–5). Otherwise the source for details in this passage is Horsley Gantt's Introduction to volume 2 of Pavlov's *Lectures* (31–32). Koltushy was the village located outside Leningrad where Pavlov established an experimental lab, the Institute of Experimental Medicine. In 1929 the village was renamed Pavlovo in his honor.

V76.2–6, 87.22–26, P77.25–28   drops of saliva . . . castration   A catalog of Pavlovian experimental and surgical techniques for working with dogs: measuring their saliva flow as a sign of the strength of any conditioned response; conditioning their reflexes by using a metronome as a sound stimulus; using bromides to give the dogs a calmer disposition; cutting afferent nerves that send impulses from extremities to the spinal cord and thus the brain; and surgically castrating them when bromides failed (see, for example, Pavlov's discussion in chapter 2 of *Conditioned Reflexes*).

V76.6, B87.26–27, P77.29   a colony *dégagé*   French for a "free colony," one that is relaxed and unrestricted.

V76.12, B87.33–34, P77.34–35   M.O. in Thunder Prodd's regiment   An M.O. is a medical officer. The name of this fictional Great War commander contains a pun: Thunar (also known as Donar) was the Teutonic god of storm and rain, a son of Wuotan; Thunar's bolts of lightning were like "prods."

V76.29–33, B88.12–16, P78.10–14   colonies of that Mother City . . . the F.O. Political Intelligence Department at Fitzmaurice House   A brief catalogue of British agencies that fight wars using more virtual than actual violence: the Political Warfare Executive, the (state-sponsored) British Broadcasting Company's European programming division, the Foreign Office in St. James Park, and somewhat opposite it Fitzmaurice House, on Berkeley Square, where the Foreign Office's Political Intelligence wing operated during the war. The point, here, is that these entities are spawned "colonies of that Mother City" which is War's program of "systematic death." And complicating things still further, they all have to interface with their U.S. counterparts (below).

V76.34, B88.17–18, P78.15   their OSS, OWI   Respectively, the U.S. Office of Special Services (forerunner of the Central Intelligence Agency) and the Office of War Information. A few lines further on, Pynchon also mentions their political affiliations. The OSS was begun in June 1942 under the leadership of William J. ("Wild Bill") Donovan, who recruited the likes of Allen Dulles and William H. Jackson, lawyers and (in Jackson's case) venture capitalists whom the narrator (focalizing through Pudding) rather accurately refers to as "eastern and moneyed Republicans" (V77.3–4). After V-E Day Dulles and Jackson both returned to the agency, renamed the CIA, and steered it into the cold war. Whereas the OSS carried out overt operations, the OWI handled overt activities associated with the media. Under Robert Sherwood, an old New Dealer by 1942, there gathered a group of fairly liberal newspapermen like Richard Hollander (of the *Washington Daily News*) and Robert Bishop (of the *Chicago Sun-Times*).

V77.10–11, B88.38–39, P78.32–33 filth of the Ypres salient A key World War I battle zone of the western front, the low country outside the Belgian town of Ypres was the site of three massive battles. In the first, from October 14 to 27, 1914, Allied forces halted the Germans' northward advance after they had taken Antwerp; this battle was marked by the desperate move of Belgian King Albert, who ordered the sluices opened to flood the lowlands and thwart the German advance, an act that allowed Allied forces to advance but that terribly mired the battle. Allied and German forces later having dug in, the second battle occurred from April 24 to May 24, 1915, and became infamous for the Germans' use of chlorine gas. The third Ypres battle, commonly known for the fiercely contested valley and ridgeline of Passchendaele, lasted from July 18 to November 6, 1917. The Ypres salient's abominably muddy conditions come up again at V79.36–41.

V77.22–23, B89.11–12, P79.3 "Bereshith, as it were" *"Bereshith"*—"In the beginning"—is the first Hebrew word in the Book of Genesis, and in the Gospel of John.

V77.23, B89.12, P79.4 "Ramsey MacDonald can die" And so the former British prime minister did, in 1937. He had been the prime minister for two terms, 1929–31 and 1931–35, and until the abdication of King Edward VIII in early 1937 he kept his post as Lord President of the Privy Council. When Edward stepped down MacDonald lost his power; he died several months later.

V77.35–36, B89.27–28, P79.16–17 Couéists . . . Dale Carnegie zealots This is a short catalog of some pop psychology movements of the twenties and thirties. Emile Coué (1857–1926), a self-proclaimed psychotherapist from France, was best known for his proverbial formula "Every day in every way I am getting better and better." His patients were counseled to repeat it, mantra-like, sotto voce. Couéism centered on this type of autosuggestion as a means of subduing the will and thereby "healing" mental and physical ailments. After the publication of his book, *My Method* (1923), Coué attracted large audiences on a lecture tour through England and the United States. On Ouspenskian beliefs, see V30.37n. Pynchon's mention of the Skinnerites is an interesting one, but not because it is (as Fowler claims) anachronistic. B. F. Skinner's first book, *The Behavior of Organisms*, was published in 1938 as an expanded version of his Harvard dissertation, developing on his theory of "operant conditioning" that became widely known by 1940. Still more interesting, during the war Skinner directed a University of Minnesota project (under the acronym ORCON, for "Organic Control") that involved animals (pigeons) as a possible "guidance system" for rockets. The birds were shown film of a target and conditioned to guide the missile toward it by pecking at a control panel. Skinner tells the story of this secret research in "Pigeon in a Pelican," an essay included in *Cumulative Record: A Selection of Papers* (1972). There are striking resemblances to the method he details there and the operant conditioning of Octopus Grigori in *GR*. Finally, then, there is Dale Carnegie, best known for his 1937 book, *How to Win Friends and Influence People*, with its Couéist enthusiasm for "positive thinking" as a cure-all.

V78.6, B89.40–41, P79.27   blindfolded subjects call Zener-deck guesses That is, in a test for extrasensory perception (see V40.18n).

V78.12–13, B90.6–7, P79.33–34   like Cecil Beaton's photograph of Margot Asquith Beaton was one of *Vogue* magazine's most famous photographers of the twenties and thirties; Margot Asquith was the wife of British prime minister Sir Herbert Asquith (1852–1928). Originally published in *Vogue*, the photo shows Mrs. Asquith from behind, hair elegantly styled atop her head, hooped earrings, shoulders bared above a striped gown of some sheer fabric that is gathered at the derriere in a kind of fan; her left hand is poised at the arm of a chair, her right hand on her hip. A copy of the picture, dated 1931 and signed by Beaton, appears as the frontispiece to Margot Asquith's autobiography, *More or Less about Myself* (1934).

V78.20, B90.16, P79.41   The metronome at 80 per second Probably a misprint or error. At eighty per second a metronome would sound like a low-pitched buzz; eighty per *minute* would make more sense for this device that is "sovereign here in the lab."

V78.32–33, B90.30–31, P80.12–13   the traditional orange Pavlovian Cement of rosin, iron oxide, and beeswax The source is a footnote in *Conditioned Reflexes* (18), though Pavlov describes it there as "Mendeleef's Cement," after his chemistry professor at the University of St. Petersburg. The mixture was used to attach glass tubes to the surgically rerouted salivary ducts of dogs, tubes designed to drain (for measuring) through the cheek. The recipe: "Colophonium [resin], 50 grammes; ferric oxide, 40 grammes; yellow beeswax, 25 grammes."

V78.39, B90.39, P80.21 he has moved into "equivalent" phase See
V48.38–39n. Pynchon's fictional example of equivalence is textbook
perfect.

V79.13, B91.15, P80.35 Webley Silvernail Since 1887 the English firm
Webley and Sons has manufactured .455 caliber service revolvers; these
weapons were widely used by British officers in World War II. Larsson
("A *Companion*'s Companion") also reports that Pynchon's source on
western Massachusetts, *The Berkshire Hills*, mentions a "Silvernail
House" as one of the oldest houses in West Stockbridge.

V79.18, B91.21, P80.40 Géza Rózsavölgyi In Hungarian his family
name means "evil valley." Larsson ("A *Companion*'s Companion")
notes that it is also the name of a Budapest music store famous for publishing works by Franz Liszt, Béla Bártok, and others.

**V79.31–32, B91.37–39, P81.12–14 what Haig . . . once said at mess about
Lieutenant Sassoon's refusal to fight** Sir Douglas Haig was field marshal of the British Expeditionary Force in the Great War. His secretary
was Sir Philip Sassoon, cousin of Lt. Siegfried Sassoon, the poet, a soldier
with the Royal Welsh Fusiliers. Siegfried's battalion-mates called him
"Mad Jack" because of his reckless courage (he once attacked a trench
full of Germans with only hand grenades and after routing them sat
down among the dead to read a book of poems). When wounded in the
neck he used his recuperation in England to compose a series of bleak
and bloody poems about the war whose argument was that the struggle
had been transformed from one of national defense and liberation to one
of aggression and conquest. He claimed that the War Department was
misrepresenting its aims to the British, and thereafter he was derogato-
rily labeled a pacifist. Presumably this would be the context of Haig's unknown (perhaps apocryphal) remark, as the fictional Pudding relates it.

V79.38, B92.3–4, P81.19 duckboarded Soules ("What To Think about
Gravity's Rainbow" 105) explains that "duckboards are what, in order
not to walk in it, you lay across mud."

V79.41, B92.8, P81.22–23 the whole Passchendaele horror Lloyd
George, the British prime minister, called it "the battle of the mud"
(A. J. P. Taylor, *English History* 86). On July 31, 1917, Field Marshal Haig
launched a third—and, it was hoped, decisive—attack near Ypres, in
Flanders. It was called Passchendaele (literally, "Valley of the Passion")
after the bloodiest of its wooded battle zones. The British historian
A. J. P. Taylor (87) sums it up:

> Everything went wrong. The drainage system of Flanders broke down,
> as had been foretold. To make matters worse, it was the rainiest Au-
> gust for many years. Men struggled forward up to their waists in mud.
> The guns sank in the mud. The tanks could not be used. Haig had de-
> clared his intention to stop the offensive if the first attack failed. He
> did not do so. The futile struggle went on for three months. The

British advanced, in all, four miles. This made their salient more precarious than before, and they evacuated without fighting when the Germans took the offensive in March 1918. Three British soldiers were killed for every two German. The British lost a third of a million men to casualties at Passchendaele.

V80.2–3, B92.10–11, P81.25   cucurbitaceous improbabilities   That is, using the pulp of one of the *Cucurbitaceae* family—including pumpkins, squashes, and cucumbers—for General Pudding's "Gourd Surprise."

V80.12, B92.23, P81.35   a beet *rissolé*   This would be a triangular pastry canapé that has been deep-fried to cook the "beet-mash" within.

V80.13, B92.24, P81.36   some lovely pureed samphire   Somewhat like the iceplant that grows along the Pacific shores of the United States, samphire has thick fleshy leaves and white flowers; it appears in great profusion along the coasts of Flanders and Dover.

V80.16, B92.28, P81.39   none resemble . . . any ordinary "Toad"   The reference is to Pudding's surprise "Toad-in-the-Hole" recipe, but see the electrified Eisenkröte, or Toad-in-the-Urinal, the "ultimate test of manhood" (at V603.40–41).

V80.17–18, B92.29, P81.40   Young Chaps from Kings Road   The main thoroughfare of Chelsea, home of Pirate Prentice, Osbie Feel, and the crew we met in episodes 1 and following.

V80.20–22, B92.33–34, P82.3–4   eight bars, from "Would You Rather Be a Colonel with an Eagle on Your Shoulder, or a Private with a Chicken on Your Knee?"   In U.S. Army slang, a "bird" or "chicken" colonel is a full colonel. A. Marjorie Taylor supplies a helpful gloss (*Language of World War II*): "A Colonel's eagles [his insignia] were called 'chickens' in World War I, as noted in this popular song of 1918 by Sidney Mitchell and Archie Gottlieb, popular again during World War Two."

V80.24, B92.37–38, P82.6   the Electra House group   Near Waterloo Bridge, Electra House is the London headquarters of British Cable and Wireless Ltd.; during the war it housed the British broadcasting and radio propaganda offices.

V81.2, B93.18–19, P82.26   Maybe because this is 1945   Maybe someone fell asleep, for in the narrative chronology "this is" December of 1944.

V81.4, B93.20–21, P82.28   the Führer-principle   Literally the "leader-principle" but more specifically the concept of charismatic leadership (see below).

V81.8–9, B93.25–26, P82.32–33   charisma . . . its rationalization should proceed   In *The Theory of Social and Economic Organization*, German sociologist Max Weber analyzes three types of authority in society: the traditional or dynastic form in which power is handed along by right of birth; the rational or bureaucratic, with its abstract currencies and impersonal organization; and the charismatic, which is spontaneous and unstable and allied with ideals of love and brotherhood. Charismatic orders are in Weber's view (364) fleeting: "In its pure form charismatic authority may be said to exist only in the process of originating. It cannot remain stable, but becomes either traditionalized or rationalized, or a combination of both." Translations of Weber variously call this process of stabilizing the dynamic power of charisma its "routinization" or "rationalization," and Pynchon will use both terms interchangeably throughout *GR*.

V81.22, B93.43, P83.5   the MMPI was developed about 1943   Actually, the Minnesota Multiphasic Personality Inventory was developed in 1940 and made available to the military, which contracted for it, in 1943. See V90.8n for more detailed discussion.

V81.23–24, B94.1–3, P83.6–7   Allport and Vernon's Study of Values, the Bernreuter Inventory as revised by Flanagan in '35   The Allport and Vernon Study was prepared by psychologists G. W. Allport, P. E. Vernon, and G. Lindzey in the early thirties. According to Anne Anastazi (*Psychological Testing* 487–90), whose undergraduate textbook was probably a main source for much of this detail, "this inventory was designed to measure the relative strengths of six basic interests, motives or evaluative attitudes": theoretical, economic, aesthetic, social, political, and religious. Professor R. G. Bernreuter developed the Bernreuter Inventory for the Stanford University Press in 1931. His test measures self-sufficiency, introversion-extroversion, dominance-submission, and neurotic tendencies; it was especially targeted for young-adult populations and was designed to be answered with simple "yes-no-don't know" responses. J. C. Flanagan, who later became a major figure in psychological testing, noticed that the four Bernreuter categories of neurosis, introversion, submission, and low self-sufficiency were all statistically correlated, and to a very high degree of predictability. These discoveries led to a further refinement of the Bernreuter test, accurately pinpointed in *GR* as occurring in 1935.

V81.34–35, B94.13–15, P83.17–18   "a *so-called*, 'projec-tive' test . . . the Rohrschach *ink*-blot"   Making allowances for Géza Rószavölgyi's Hungarianized English speech rhythm, this summary of projective tests is substantially the same as that in Anastazi (*Psychological Testing* 493–94). The Rorschach test was first described in 1921 and more formally developed by Swiss psychoanalyst Hermann Rorschach in 1942. It consists of ten cards, each printed with a bilaterally symmetrical inkblot, which the subject is asked to interpret by telling what he or she "sees" in it. Implicit in the whole procedure, as Anastazi (495–99) points out, are the assumptions that test responses are typical of how a subject always perceives and that personality traits influence perception.

V81.41–82.1, B94.22–23, P83.24–25   resembling . . . his most famous compatriot   Hungarian-born compatriot Bela Lugosi (1882–1956), famous for his title role in director Tod Browning's *Dracula* (Universal, 1931).

V82.3, B94.26, P83.27   crawling headfirst down the north façade   That is, with supernatural powers like those of Dracula in Bram Stoker's novel.

V82.31, B95.17–18, P84.15   giant Gloucestershire Old Spots   In his biographical essay for *Playboy*, Jules Siegal recalls a late-sixties visit to Pynchon's apartment in Manhattan Beach, a Los Angeles suburb. His bookcase, Siegal (170) recalls, "had rows of piggy banks on each shelf and there was a collection of books and magazines about pigs." Reading these books, perhaps a book like Sillar's *The Symbolic Pig* (5), Pynchon may well have come across a description of Britain's native pig breeds: "Wessex Saddlebacks" (see also V5.27), "Large Black (and Little Black) Berkshires," "Dorset Gold Tips," and "Gloucester Old Spots."

V82.36–37, B95.24–25, P84.20–21   The W.C.s contain frescoes of Clive and his elephants stomping the French at Plassy   Fancy, patriotic toilet facilities (water closets). "Plassey," as most sources spell it, is a Bengal village on the river Bhagirathi, outside Calcutta. Not long after British colonial occupants of that city were massacred in the Black Hole atrocity, the British East India Company empowered Baron Clive (1725–74) to retake the city. He faced a native army of vastly superior numbers, and its nabob had also enlisted the help of French artillery troops. On June 23, 1757, Clive led his forces (assisted by elephant packtrains) against the French artillery, routing it in what proved the decisive battle of Clive's campaign. The victory was famous for solidifying the East India Company's hold over the region.

V82.37–38, B95.26, P84.22   Salome with the head of John   For the story of how young Salome danced for King Herod and won John the Baptist's head on a tray, see Matt. 14:1–12.

V83.9–10, B95.41–42, P84.34–35   no two observers, no matter how close they stand, see quite the same building   A visual example of indeterminacy resulting from parallax views. Also, another Bantam error: "not matter how."

EPISODE 13

Internal evidence shows that this episode occurs on December 22, on the Dover coast. The subject of the characters' discussion is once again Slothrop's enigmatic sexual member and what should be done to crack its "code." Interestingly, Brigadier General Pudding is the only one to raise the issue of Slothrop's welfare. Shaping the narration is a philosophical debate pitting the determinist view of Ned Pointsman against the statistical approach of Roger Mexico.

V83.25, B96.18, P85.9   The Nayland Smith Press   Named for Sir Dennis Nayland Smith of Scotland Yard, intrepid fictional hero of Sax Rohmer's Fu-Manchu books. Note the date on this fictional catalog of insults: in 1933 Slothrop was fifteen years old, about thirteen years beyond the time of his "conditioning" at the hands of Dr. Laszlo Jamf.

V84.3–4, B96.33–35, P85.23–24   if Watson and Rayner could successfully condition their "Infant Albert"   John B. Watson and his wife Rosalie Ravner Watson were the parents of behavioral psychology. Their 1918 conditioning of eleven-month-old "Infant Albert" is summarized in *The Psychological Care of Infant and Child* (1928). They first put into Albert's playpen a variety of furry animals and toys, which he displayed no natural predisposition to fear. Then an assistant began clanging "a carpenter's hammer" on a steel bar held just behind Albert's head. They repeated this procedure each time one of the animals was introduced and Albert reached for it. Terrified by the unseen noise, Albert quickly associated it with the animals and began registering his terror each time one was brought near him. His terror soon included *all* "furry objects," including his mother's feather boa, an item he'd previously associated with Mother's loving care. "You may think that such experiments are cruel," conceded Watson and Rayner (54), "but they are not cruel if they help us to understand the fear life of millions of people around us and give us practical help in bringing up our children."

V84.9–10, B97.5, P85.29–30   Kekulé's own famous switch into chemistry from architecture   Friedrich August Kekulé von Stradonitz (1829–96) was the German chemist who laid the groundwork for the theory of structure in organic chemistry, beginning with his discovery of the cyclical, or "ring," structure of the benzene molecule. At the University of Giessen he was initially enrolled as an architect but switched to chemistry at the urging of his teacher, Justus von Liebig. On Kekulé's famous dream that anticipated the discovery of the benzene ring, see V410.34n.

V84.21, B97.19–20, P86.7   the Larson-Keeler three-variable "lie detector"   John A. Larson was the author of *Lying and Its Detection* (1932), the first thorough analysis of lie-detection methods and machinery. His own device utilized a correlation of blood pressure and respiration data, improving on the simple blood pressure machine devised by William A. Marston in 1915 and already a part of American criminological folklore by the thirties. Leonarde Keeler was an associate of Larson's in the Berkeley, California, Police Department, but by the thirties he had moved on to Northwestern University and its newly founded Crime

Detection Laboratory. There he devised a third variable, a card test designed to enhance a subject's faith in the machinery and to locate the so-called peak-tension moments when the subject was most likely to be concealing some guilty knowledge. In the film *Northside 777* it is Keeler himself who administers the lie-detector test to Richard Conte in his Joliet Prison cell, confirming what Jimmy Stewart has thought all along: that he is not guilty of the crime for which he's been sentenced.

V84.39–85.3, B97.41–98.5, P86.25–30   as Ivan Petrovich himself said, "Not only must we speak of partial or of complete extinction . . . beyond the zero"   The quotation derives, verbatim, from chapter 4 ("Extinction") of Pavlov's *Conditioned Reflexes* (57; the emphasis is Pynchon's— or Pointsman's). In Pavlov's theory, the question of conditioned reflexes existing "beyond the zero" involves the way some will "spontaneously recover their full strength" after a long time-lapse. Occasionally, as in Slothrop's case, the recovery of that extinguished reflex may be "paradoxical" (see V48.38–39n).

V85.12–13, B98.16, P86.39–40   Infant Tyrone   Or "IT," in this elaborate game of tag?

V85.37, B99.2–3, P87.23   The stars fall in a Poisson distribution   Poisson's equation (see V54.25n) describes the probabilistic distribution of rockets over London. The precise correlation of Slothrop's "stars" with rocket strikes would be a coincidence of extremely low probability, but it would not be impossible.

V86.11, B99.20, P87.38–39   That points to the V-1   The Bantam edition misprints this as "The points to the V-1."

V85.15, B99.22, P88.1–2   Slothrop instead only gets erections when this sequence happens in reverse   Note the hysteron proteron again.

V86.32–33, B100.5, P88.19–20   Pointsman in Glastonburys . . . British warm   Against the cold, Pointsman wears sheepskin gloves made in Glastonbury, England (famous for its glovemakers from the early nineteenth century onward) and a scarf.

V86.39, B100.12–13, P88.26   The very bottom of the year   That is, the winter solstice, on December 21–22. In 1944 it occurred on Friday, December 22. Next day the *Times* of London reported that the twenty-second had been "one of the coldest days" thus far; temperatures ranged in the low thirties, with heavy frosts, just as Pynchon describes it here.

V87.17, B100.34, P89.4   a flight of B-17s   The Flying Fortress, built by the Boeing Company of America from 1934 until 1943. One writer (Angellucci 136) calls it "the most celebrated strategic aircraft of the war." Crewed by ten airmen, it was widely used in Allied bombing raids over Europe after 1942.

V87.22–23, B100.41, P89.9–10   curves of fuselage or nacelle   Specifically, here, the metal cowling or fairing around an airplane engine. More generally and in earlier usage the nacelle was the streamlined fuselage of an airplane, though Pynchon's phrasing indicated he intends the specific meaning here.

V87.32–34, B101.10–13, P89.20–22   Pavlov's open letter to Janet . . . and of Chapter LV, "An Attempt at a Physiological Interpretation of Obsessions and of Paranoia"   Pavlov's "open letter" is chapter 54, *"Les Sentiments D'Emprise* and the Ultraparadoxical Phase," in volume 1 of the *Lectures* (see V49.1–2n), which is followed by the chapter Pynchon mentions here.

V87.38–39, B101.18–19, P89.26–27   (most existing copies had been destroyed in their warehouse early in the Battle of Britain)   Indeed, according to William Sargent (*Battle for the Mind* 3), most copies of the *Lectures* had been destroyed during the German air bombardments known as the Battle of Britain, so that copies of Gantt's translations (see below) were very scarce. This explains the intense secrecy of Pointsman, Spectro, and their colleagues over their copy (see V47.3n).

V88.3, B101.25–26, P89.32–33   Dr. Horsley Gantt's odd translation   Of Pavlov's *Lectures*, volumes 1 and 2.

V88.9–10, B101.32–33, P89.38–39   the first Forty-One Lectures . . . at age 28   Volume 1 of the *Lectures* was published in English translation in 1928, when Edward Pointsman was "age 28," and the calling came to him as if from a "submontane Venus," which is to say, as if from the goddess of Tannhäuser legend (see V727.6–10).

V88.11, B101.34–35, P89.40   to abandon Harley Street   Around the corner from the Royal Society of Medicine, on London's Harley Street, "the leading medical practitioners have their consulting rooms" (Baedeker's *London* 165).

V88.12–17, B101.36–102.1, P90.1–6   thirteen years along the clew . . . Venus and Ariadne!   The Greek mythical hero Theseus sails to Crete intending to stand in for the seven young men and seven young women that King Minos demanded as an annual tribute from the Athenians. The fourteen were offered as sacrificial victims to the Minotaur, and Minos's bargain is that if Theseus slays the monster then his fellow citizens go free. Minos's daughter, Ariadne, falls in love with Theseus and seeks aid from Daedalus, who designed the Cretan labyrinth. Daedalus suggests that Theseus should carry with him a skein of thread (or "clew," see V457.2n) to unroll and mark his pathway out. After killing the Minotaur, Theseus takes Ariadne with him but abandons her (some versions say) on Cyprus. The Cypriot cult of Venus, goddess of love, used to regard Venus and Ariadne as the same goddess.

V88.29–31, B102.15–18, P90.18–21   "Pierre Janet. . . . 'The act of injuring and the act . . . joined in the . . . whole injury.'"   Pointsman is quoting from volume 2 of Pavlov's *Lectures* (147). Pavlov, in turn, was quoting from Janet's 1932 essay "Feelings in the Delusions of Persecution" for the *Journal de psychologie*.

V88.34, B102.21, P90.24 yang-yin rubbish In the dualistic philosophy of Chinese Buddhism, yang is the active, masculine principle of being, which always exists complementarily with the passive, feminine principle known as yin. Yang is the sun and enlightened consciousness; yin is the moon, and shadowed unconsciousnessness. Together they form a circular whole, a mandala. See also V.278.16n.

V89.36, B103.35–36, P91.28 "your P.R.S. categories" Pointsman means to say "S.P.R.," acronym for the London-based Society for Psychical Research (see also V153.11).

V90.8, B104.9, P91.41 "You've seen his MMPI. His F Scale?" The Minnesota Multiphasic Personality Inventory (see also V81.22n) includes four validity scales to help evaluate test results. The F Scale serves to indicate "undesirable behavior" during the test, for example, "deliberate malingering" or "gross eccentricity" or even "simple carelessness." The F Scale also tends to correlate with other indications of psychosis that may crop up in the main body of the test. Or it may indicate that the subject was trying to outwit the test, perhaps because he or she suffers from paranoid psychosis (Anastazi, *Psychological Testing* 498–505).

V91.37–38, B106.12–13, P93.30–31 cylindrical blocks to cripple the silent King Tigers The Königstiger or King Tiger was Germany's largest operational battle tank, an awesome weapon built from components manufactured in Krupp and Porsche factories during the war's closing period, from 1944 to 1945. Fitted with nearly impenetrable armor and 88-millimeter cannon capable of destroying Allied tanks at a range of two miles, the German King Tiger—nearly five hundred of which were produced by war's end—dominated battlefields on the eastern and western fronts. In preparation for a Nazi landing that Hitler never ordered, Britain's south coasts were thronged with such things as barbed wire, bunkers, and (as an antitank obstacle) the cylindrical blocks described here.

V91.41, B106.17, P93.34 improbable as a Zouave In the nineteenth century, Zouave tribesmen were recruited into the French army out of Algeria, given colorful uniforms, and sent back to fight the enemies of colonialism. The dignified black skater here has just been used in the film produced as propaganda by Operation Black Wing. By V112.29 he is on his way back to his regiment in North Africa (see also V442.36n).

EPISODE 14

Like episodes 5, 9, and 10 before it, this one also takes a circular form. It begins on December 22 in the London maisonette belonging to Pirate Prentice. Katje Borgesius (her name seemingly an homage to Argentine poet and short story writer Jorge Luis Borges) has just been snatched out of Holland and stands before a camera that is filming the visual material to be used in the operant conditioning of Octopus Grigori. Then begins a narrative analepsis treating Katje, Blicero, and Gottfried with the V-2 battery in Holland. The narrative circles still farther inward and back in time as we get glimpses—focalized through Blicero—of South-West Africa from his tour of duty there during the twenties. The narrative returns momentarily to the second-order time (at the V-2 battery) in order to begin one more analepsis, this time focalized through one of Katje's seventeenth-century ancestors, Frans van der Groov ("Frank the Groove"). His enthusiasm for the annihilation of the dodo (*Didus ineptus*) on the island of Mauritius extends the theme of colonization across nonhuman fields. The episode ends by cycling us back to the spot where we began, Katje still before the camera, but just a while later and her filming now completed. The German folktale of Hansel and Gretel and the theme of colonial domination provide continuity over these narrative shifts.

V92.29, B107.11, P94.22–23   this rainiest day in recent memory   And so the *Times* of London reported on December 23, about the previous day's weather: rain, at times turning to freezing rain, as temperatures held in the low- to mid-thirties (see also V93.34n below).

V93.2–3, B107.23–24, P94.32   *Amanita muscaria* . . . relative of the poisonous Destroying Angel   *Amanita verna* is the poisonous mushroom popularly known as the Destroying Angel. *Amanita muscaria*, its cousin, is as Robert Graves (*The White Goddess* 45) notes, "a spotted toadstool called 'flycap,'" which "Dionysius's centaurs, satyrs and maenads, it seems, actually ate," giving "them enormous muscular strength, erotic power, delirious visions, and the gift of prophecy."

V93.25, B108.13–14, P95.18   Huntley & Palmers biscuit tin   These biscuits were a top-quality product, with His Majesty King George IV pictured on the tin lid, and they were frequently advertised in the *Times* of London. In Joseph Conrad's *Heart of Darkness* (1899), Charlie Marlow says of the "tin-pot steamboat" he is to pilot upriver that it "rang . . . like an empty Huntley & Palmer bisquit-tin kicked along a gutter" (175).

V93.26, B108.15, P95.19   Rizla liquorice cigarette paper   Like Slothrop's mouth harp (V63.1), another "jive accessory." Originally trademarked in 1881 by Lacroix Fils (in France) but produced for generations at the Imperial Tobacco factory in Pontypridd, Wales, red and blue packages of Rizla rice papers with their cross logo have long been part of marijuana-smokers' underworld. The name derives from *"riz"* (French for "rice") and *La* (for Lacroix).

V93.34–35, B108.25–26, P95.28   the long rain in silicon and freezing descent   The phrase concisely anticipates the details of a moment twenty pages later, when "invisible tattooing needles" of ice strike "the nerveless window glass" while Octopus Grigori watches the film of Katje

(V113.30–33). See also V53.25–26n for discussion of a similar image framing the ninth episode.

V94.3–5, B108.37–40, P95.37–40   the frock . . . from Harvey Nicholls, a sheer crepe . . . a rich cocoa shade   Pynchon gives close attention to Katje's dresses throughout *GR*, and usually for a reason: here, because this frock will be the one she wears when Slothrop "saves" her from the octopus in part 2 (V186.3). Harvey Nicholls was a fashionable clothier located near Harrods, in Knightsbridge, and a frequent advertiser in the *Times*.

V94.17–18, B109.13, P96.12   the *soignée* surface   In this context, a polished one.

V94.20, B109.15–16, P96.14   to *Der Kinderofen*   A reference to the German folktale "Hansel and Gretel," number seventy-two in *Grimm's Fairy Tales*. The term, however, does not appear in Grimm, where *der Backofen* (literally, an "oven" as distinct from a furnace [*Brennofen*]) is used throughout. Pynchon's compound noun aptly conveys the cannibalistic idea of the story about an old crone who pushes children into her oven to bake them into breadstuffs.

V94.21–22, B109.18, P96.15–16   the yellow teeth of Captain Blicero   See V30.12n for the etymology. "Blicero" is Captain Weissmann's adopted code name while stationed with the German rocket battery in Holland (see also V152.21).

V94.26, B109.23, P96.20   Gottfried   At this point it will help to consider the origins of his name. It means "God's peace" (as Pynchon notes at V465.11), from the German "*Gottes*" and "*Frieden*." Yet these etymological strands weave a still finer, broader net in *GR*. "*Frieden*" is related specifically to the ancient Teutonic god Frey, also known as Freyr and Frigg. Like his sister, Freya, he was a fertility god, a brother to the Greek god Priapus, deriving from the Indo-European root "*prij*" (love). Frey was at the same time a god of peace and sexual love, and our slangy sexual terms "fuck" and "prick" stem from these roots. Branston (*Gods of the North* 134) reports that Frey's worship was celebrated with orgies. The god's disappearance underground is also related to the myths of Tammuz, Adonis, and Orpheus. Grimm (*Teutonic Mythology* 212–14) has also shown that the worship of Frey involved the sacrifice of pigs—a point that attests to the Tammuz/Adonis links—and that northern Europeans sacrificed a Yuletide boar in honor of Frey. This is striking because, as Branston comments, the word "*Frey*" often appears as a title of Christ: for example, in the Old English *Dream of the Rood*. Priapus, Orpheus, Adonis, Christ, Frey, peace, love, prick—the name Gottfried enmeshes all of these. Did Pynchon know sources like Branston and Grimm? Beyond a doubt: later in this episode he will quote a verse of Middle Dutch poetry from the very pages in Grimm's *Teutonic Mythology* where the origins of Frey/Freyr are set forward.

V94.35–37, B109.35–37, P96.30   a mathematical function that will expand . . . a power series with *no general term*   A power series is the sum of successively higher integral powers of a variable or sum of variables, each of which is multiplied by a "general term" or constant coefficient, perhaps out to infinity. The Poisson equation contains a power series. A power series "with no general term" would not yield a computation for the series' numerical value. In the instance here, possible referents of Blicero's cryptic phrases expand like a power series; yet with no common coefficient, these referents might be unrelated or at least involve wild leaps, as below.

V94.38, B109.38–39, P96.32   his phrase *Padre Ignacio* unfolding into Spanish inquisitor   *Padre Ignacio: or, A Song of Temptation* (1900) is a novella by Owen Wister. For kindly, wise Padre Ignacio of Wister's gold-rush California to "unfold" or regress to the punishing figure of a sixteenth-century Spanish Inquisitor is some leap backward—quite an instance of hysteron proteron—but that is just the idea. Wister's padre, incidentally, is "tempted" mainly by such worldly pleasures as opera, the works of Rossini in particular. In the end he decides to stay with his Pacific Indians on the California shore. Meanwhile he receives word that the opera-loving "young scapegrace" who visited, and embodied his temptation, has died.

V94.41, B109.42, P96.35–36   children out of old Märchen   That is, out of old fairy tales.

V95.3, B110.3, P96.38   her NSB credentials   That is, as a member of the Dutch Nationaal-Socialistische Beweging, or National Socialist Movement (see V97.9–10n).

V95.6, B110.8, P97.1   merkin of sable   The *Random House Dictionary* partially identifies a merkin as "false hair for the female pudenda." But from its description here it is most certainly a transsexual aid, known in underworld argot as a "cheater."

V95.17, B110.21, P97.11   expanses of polder, toward Wassenaar   Polder, drained land protected from the sea by dikes, is common in the Low Countries. Wassenaar is a district at the north end of The Hague. Pynchon's source on Holland as a V-2 launching site is Kooy and Uytenbogaart (*Ballistics of the Future* 283–84), who write about a "Sonderkommando (Special Commando)" of rocket troops arriving in Wassenaar on September 7, 1944, and remaining until late March of 1945.

V95.33, B110.40, P97.27   near Schußstelle 3   From Kooy and Uytenbogaart (284): "The Germans had marked all cars, apparatures and suchlike 'Schuszstelle 1' and 'Schuszstelle 2' (sites 1 and 2)." They also report that "firing site 3" was located at "de Beukenhorst," near the Duindigt race course. Pynchon uses the proper German spelling.

V95.36–37, B111.3, P97.31–32   the Captain's own "Hexeszüchtigung"   In German a *Hexe* is a witch; here, the reference is to a punishment meted out to suspected witches; literally, a "witch's whipping" or "chastisement."

V96.18–22, B111.29–34, P98.12–16 Late in October, not far from this estate, one fell back . . . killing 12 of the ground crew . . . fuel and oxidizer had gone off Again the source is Kooy and Uytenbogaart (284–85). Compare the closeness of the narrative in GR to theirs in *Ballistics of the Future*:

> On Friday the 27th of October at 2 P.M. the first great failure took place. A rocket launched from site no. 3 rose to a height of about 300 feet and then fellback [sic] on the site, which was destroyed. Twelve of the crew were killed.
>
> After this the site was abandoned and the launching was interrupted for about a week. The damage done to buildings in the neighborhood was limited to roofs and windowpanes. The latter were even broken a distance of about 700 meters from the centre of the explosion. Immediately after the failure the Germans spread the rumour that the charge of this rocket had not exploded, but that the oxygen and ethyl alcohol alone had caused the damage. This was not true; the charge had also exploded.

V96.31–32, B112.3–4, P98.25–26 Spitfires come roaring in low Duyfhuizen reports ("A Long View of V-2" 17) on "numerous" references in the fall 1944 *Times* of London to British Spitfire airplanes attacking German rocket sites. A tactical fighter aircraft, the Spitfire was produced continuously from 1937 to 1945 in forty different models; over twenty thousand planes were built in all.

V97.9–10, B112.27, P99.4 her record with Mussert's people Anton Adriaan Mussert headed up the Dutch Nazi Party, or NSB (V95.3n), and collaborated without reservation in all operations the Nazis carried out in Holland, including the deportation of Jews to concentration camps and the deployment of V-weapons used against England. He was quickly tried and hanged after the Allies liberated Holland in 1945.

V97.11–12, B112.29–30, P99.6 a Luftwaffe resort near Scheveningen To the immediate west of The Hague lies the coastal resort of Scheveningen, a town the German air force (the Luftwaffe) used for recreating and resting crews. It is also the site where Pirate Prentice picks up Katje for her trip to England.

V97.17–18, B112.36–37, P99.11–12 "Want the Change," Rilke said, "O be inspired by the Flame!" The quote is from sonnet 12 in part 2 of Rainer Maria Rilke's *Sonnets to Orpheus* (1922). In the German this sonnet begins with the exhortation "Wolle die Wandlung. O sei für die Flamme begeistert." Pynchon uses the Leishman translation of 1957. The context of Blicero's thoughts just following this quotation makes it clear that he regards love from the standpoint of a decadent and very *literary* romanticism: "To laurel, to nightingale, to wind . . . ," he thinks, recalling subjects of the great romantic odes—Shelley's "Ode to the West Wind" and Keats's "Ode to a Nightingale," for instance.

V97.27, B113.7–8, P99.22–23 her questing shoulders like wings On first glance the simile would seem to make of Katje a type of angel. Later, one will look back with the knowledge that Leni Pökler has similarly wing-like shoulders (see V162.37 and V218.31), and that one of Vaslav Tchitcherine's lovers, Luba, is similarly endowed (see V339.35n). There is in sum a striking homology among the various women, something deepened by subsequent images of the Angel of Death that "swooped in" on Walter Rathenau (V164.37) or of Rilke's "Tenth-Elegy angel coming, wingbeats already at the edges of waking" (V341.37–38). This angel appears to presage a transition to the Other Side, to Death's other kingdom.

V97.34–35, B113.16, P99.31 all Märchen und Sagen Respectively, the Germanic fairy tales and myths.

V98.1–2, B113.25–26, P99.37–38 *Und nicht einmal . . . this Tenth Elegy* Pynchon cribs his translation from Leishman and Spender's edition; see V98.7–8 for his rendering of the German. The reference throughout this paragraph is to the tenth of Rilke's *Duino Elegies*, especially lines 104–5:

> Einsam steigt er dahin, in die Berge des Urleids,
> Und nicht einmal sein Schritt klingt aus dem tonlosen Los.

Leishman and Spender translate them as follows:

> Alone he climbs to the mountains of Primal Pain,
> And never once does his step resound from the soundless Fate.

Note how Pynchon diverges from this: he has "ring" instead of "resound," "not" for "never," and "Destiny" instead of "Fate."

V98.7, B113.32–33, P100.2–3 wildly alien constellations overhead Because Weissmann has journeyed to the southern hemisphere and doesn't know the constellations there. In Rilke's "Pain Land," the Angel teaches the traveler names for these "new" stars "up in the southern sky" ("Elegy 10," 88–95). See also V99.35.

V98.16, B114.1, P100.11 Young Rauhandel His name means "rough trade," slang for prostitution, especially homosexual rough sex (e.g., sadomasochism).

V98.24, B114.11–12, P100.19–20 the Ufa-theatre on the Friedrichstrasse See Kracauer's description (*From Caligari to Hitler* 48) of the "Ufa-Palast am Zoo," Berlin's "largest movie theatre" located on the Friedrichstrasse. "Ufa" stands for Universum Film A.G. During the Great War it was Germany's premier film studio, mainly because of backing from a War Department that wanted films made on nationalistic themes. Kracauer (36) describes how "the official mission of Ufa was to advertise Germany according to government directives. These asked not only for direct screen propaganda, but also for films characteristic of German culture and films serving the purpose of national education." After the war these controls were removed and Ufa became home to Germany's best-known, most creative directors, including Fritz Lang (1890–1976), Ernst Lubitsch (1892–1947), and Georg Wilhelm Pabst (1885–1967) (see V112.33n).

V98.39, B114.30, P100.35   royal moths the Flame has inspired   That "Flame" is once more the fire of transformation in Rilke's sonnet 12 (see V97.17–18n). The royal moth is the *Saturnia pavonia* of Europe and Asia Minor, noted for its high-flying abilities when the moon is full.

V99.2, B114.35, P100.39   a Wandervogel   The term is best defined in a generic sense, as it applies to the remarkable proliferation of youth movements in Germany from 1900 to 1930. Ideologically varied, all the *Wandervogel* (wayward-bird) groups put the highest premium on organic wholeness, usually expressed as a pantheistic love of nature with an emphasis on the formation of mystical bonds to the fatherland. They romanticized medieval Germany as a refuge from petty commercialism and fragmented knowledge. Strong Oedipal forces were also behind the movement: its first "historian," Hans Bluhler, explicitly claimed in 1913: "The period that produced the *Wandervogel* . . . [was] characterized by a struggle of youth against age," in which Germany's alienated youth sought to form "a great confederation of friendship" (quoted in Bullock, *Hitler* 38). In practice, this meant that a powerful air of homoeroticism was soon noticeable in many of the groups. The *Wandervogeln* often planned visits to venerable ruins, where they celebrated with plenty of folksinging around campfires, and during the twenties one group of *Wandervogel* songs were best sellers in Germany for ten years. In literature, the groups preferred Stefan George and Rilke; in daily life, they were fastidious about their diet and health, usually forbidding the use of alcohol and tobacco and often also meat. This, then, was the generation of Germans who marched enthusiastically toward the battlefields of World War I and who, after the bitter truce, were ready to follow Adolf Hitler.

V99.4–5, B114.38, P101.1   nicht wahr?   "Is it not?"

V99.24–25, B115.19–21, P101.20–21   to Südwest . . . the Kalahari   Another reference to South-West Africa and its dominant geographical feature, the Kalahari Desert.

V99.34–35, B115.33, P101.31   new stars of Pain-Land   The reference is to lines 88–90 of Rilke's tenth elegy:

And higher, the stars. New ones. Stars of the Land of Pain.
Slowly she [the Angel] names them.

V99.38, B115.37, P101.34   to crush the great Herero Rising   South-West Africa became a German territory in 1884, under Chancellor Bismarck. Charitably described, the colonial plan amounted to little more than a protection scam. The Hereros, who had often been at war with neighboring tribes of Hottentots and Bondels, were offered "protection" in exchange for mineral rights to the precious diamond fields. The Herero chieftains soon saw through all this, however, and they rose up in rebellion against the German overlords in 1904. In August of that year the rebels were dealt a crushing defeat and the surviving Hereros fled across the scorching Kalahari; those who made the trek had little more than their lives. What followed, for the Germans, was a mopping-up operation conducted for almost two years in a brutal, genocidal manner. Under the *Vernichtungsbefehl* (extermination order) posted by General Lothar von Trotha, any Hereros refusing to submit voluntarily to life in the relocation camps could be summarily executed. By 1906 over two-thirds of the Herero population had perished. The "rising" Pynchon refers to occurred later, in 1922, when the remaining Hereros banded together with their old enemies, the Bondels and Hottentots, to rise up against the white landowners. Pynchon has written a fictional account of those events in chapter 9 of *V.* German cavalry units, supported by light artillery, put down the insurrection in two months.

V100.2–3, B116.2–3, P101.40–41   *We make Ndjambi Karunga now, omuhona* Luttig, Pynchon's principal source on the Herero, devotes the first chapter of his dissertation to Ndjambi Karunga, the divine creator of all Herero people, according to their myths. What is more interesting in this context of homosexual love is that the god is also bisexual. Ndjambi Karunga appears in Herero creation tales as the father of all being and generally a benevolent deity. But while he is thus "the god of life," he is also "the master of death" (Luttig 8); and in that aspect he is, in sum, the Herero version of Lord Death, Blicero. The god's bisexuality is signified, Luttig explains (9), in the name itself: "Ndjambi reveals more the characteristics of a [masculine] heavenly god and Karunga those of a [feminine] god of the earth." He passes on these dual traits— lord of the "other world" of the dead, as well as lord of *this* world— to Mukuru, the mythical first man. And in his turn the *omuhona*, Mukuru's embodiment in Herero society, also serves a dual role according to Luttig: he's not only a "chief" but a "living Mukuru" and thus a lineal descendent of the mythical creation tree, the *omumborumbanga* (see V321.40–322.1n). As "one who has been proven" to be the inheritor of these traits, the *omuhona* also embodies the bisexual principle of his origin (Luttig 33–34). As one aspect of his lineal descent from Ndjambi Karunga, the *omuhona* maintains a leather thong tied in knots signifying each member of the tribe.

V100.7–8, B116.8, P102.4–5   like the Rhenish Missionary Society who corrupted this boy In 1799, members of Reformed and Lutheran churches in Wuppertal, Germany, formed a *Missions Gesellschaft* (mission society). By 1828, they had expanded and renamed it the Rhenish Missionary Society, with the stated purpose of sending representatives to Africa and winning converts to Christianity. Their first missionaries to South-West Africa arrived at the settlement of Windhoek during Christmas of 1842. As Drechsler has shown (*"Let Us Die Fighting"* 18–24), the missionaries were, however, implicated practically from the beginning in colonial politics. Their settlements flew the Prussian flag, they assisted in the importation of weapons and ammunition, they served essentially as secret agents gathering intelligence from rival tribal chiefs for colonial administrators to use, and indeed they "corrupted" the Herero with bribes of tobacco and liquor (Drechsler 48).

V100.25, B116.31, P102.22   deep in the Harz   The Harz Mountains of central Germany, site of the Nordhausen underground rocket works.

V100.27, B116.32–33, P102.24   said auf Wiedersehen   "Good-bye."

V100.34–38, B116.42–117.4, P102.31–35   The Bodenplatte . . . red circle with a thick black cross inside   Once more the source is Kooy and Uytenbogaart: for the compass bearing of 260 degrees (285) and, a few pages further (287), for the detail about how trees were used in "determining the direction of London with respect to the launching site. The trees were always provided with marks for that purpose. The launching table (that is, the Bodenplatte) was then placed in the triangle bounded by those trees." The "red circle with a thick black cross" inside is from the same text (467); comparing it to "a rude mandala" or a "swastika" is Pynchon's touch.

V101.1–2, B117.9–10, P102.40   scratched in the bark . . . the words IN HOC SIGNO VINCES   A wonderful allusion. The Latin proclaims: "In this sign you shall conquer." According to Edward Gibbon (ch. 20), whose source was the Roman historian Eusebius, the emperor Constantine was converted to Christianity when "the miraculous sign [of the cross] was displayed in the heavens whilst he meditated for the Italian expedition." The phrase was inscribed horizontally on that airborne crucifix, and its truth was affirmed when Constantine's troops were victorious. Like his predecessor, Diocletian, Constantine was also called *"Dominus."* Also, since this is a novel that takes care over cigarette and cigarette paper brands, readers might want to examine the insignia on a package of Pall Mall cigarettes, with its two lions rampant in the heraldic design and the same phrase inscribed below them. Still, the sure source of this detail is Kooy and Uytenbogaart (467) again; they tell of "a German who wrote in Duindigt Park at Wassenaar, under one of the familiar red circles with the black cross with two nails in the middle[,] . . . *In hoc signo vinces.* He did not live to see his prophecy fulfilled."

V101.7–9, B117.17–19, P103.5   black India-rubber cables . . . the Dutch grid's 380 volts   From Kooy and Uytenbogaart (284): "Some india-rubber cables were laid from the Rijksstraatweg via the Rus en Vrengdlan, which established connection with the normal electrical network (voltage 380 volts/50 cycles)."

V101.9, B117.19, P103.6 *Erwartung* German for a sense of anticipation, foreboding. *Erwartung* is also the title of a 1922 monodrama by composer Arnold Schönberg. His libretto presents a woman looking for her lover in the middle of a pitch-black forest. The woman's estrangement, coupled with the imagined horrors of the dark, soon overwhelms her with feelings of *Erwartung* regarding the man's fate. When she finds him dead she lapses into insanity. Theodor Adorno (*Philosophy of Modern Music* 42–43) wrote of the opera's musical score that it "is polarized according to extremes: towards gestures of shock resembling bodily convulsions on the one hand, and on the other towards a crystalline standstill of a human being whom anxiety causes to freeze in her tracks." *Erwartung*, he continues, can be interpreted as the analytic case study, in music and verse, of "fashionable alienation," even the enjoyment of psychic pain. Like Rilke's depiction of "Pain Land" in the *Duino Elegies* (1922, the year *Erwartung* was composed and the year Weissmann goes to South-West Africa), Schönberg's opera is yet another reference point for the state of Captain Weissmann's psyche, as shaped by German expressionism.

V101.19–20, B117.33, P103.16–17 **a color-negative, yellow and blue** The most useful discussion of color symbolism in *GR* appears in Hayles and Eiser, who identify white, red, and black as "the basic triad"; within it, red consistently symbolizes a burst of passion deflecting characters from the routinized, mechanically achromatic opposition, white/black. Yellow and blue are complements: yellow appears yellow because it absorbs light in the blue range; the opposite holds for blue. Combining blue and yellow wavelengths yields white; shining blue light on a yellow background makes it appear black. As Hayles and Eiser (11) explain, this "complementarity is the physical basis for the code connecting Gottfried and Enzian, and explains how they can literally be each other's shadow-images." Still more interesting, Gottfried and Enzian will both be launched aloft in V-2 rockets: the white, Gottfried, in the 00000 while clad in the black Imipolex shroud (see Greta Erdmann's recollection, at V488.2); the black, Enzian, in the 00001, while trying not only to repeat Gottfried's firing but also to counterbalance his whiteness and thus to "recreate the coming together of opposites that marked the center of the Herero village" (Hayles and Eiser 12; but see also V321. 3–4n). This always-insufficient approach to the "Holy Center" is, as Hite argues ("'Holy Center-Approaching'"), one of Pynchon's organizing metaphors for *GR*. Note, for example, that its accomplishment could only exist outside the novel, after the V-2 falls in the last episode of *GR*. Another instance of incompletion.

V101.23–26, B117.38–41, P103.21–24 **Bringt doch der Wanderer . . . gelben und blaun Enzian** These yellows and blues are from Rilke's ninth elegy, lines 29–31. Leishman and Spender translate them:

For the wanderer doesn't bring from the mountain slope
A handful of earth to the valley, untellable earth, but only
Some word he has won, a pure word, of yellow and blue gentian.
Hence the character's name—Enzian/gentian—with the implied color
opposition.

**V102.14–15, B118.34–35, P104.13 the archer and his son, and the shoot-
ing of the apple** A reference to the story of Wilhelm Tell—for example,
in the Rossini opera.

V102.29, B119.9, P104.27 a Stuka pilot The German-produced Junkers
87, or "Stuka," a two-man dive-bomber used throughout the war.

V103.5, B119.30, P105.4 Mutti German: mother.

**V103.10–11, B119.37–38, P105.9–10 *If you cannot sing Siegfried at
least you can carry a spear*** In actor's idiom, a spear-carrier is an extra.

**V103.25–26, B120.14–15, P105.25–26 the word *bitch* . . . will give him
an erection** This turns into a bit of vital information—it's what will
become the cue in Gottfried's Pavlovian conditioning. Not only does
it remind one of Slothrop's seeming erection reflex; in part 3 we also
discover that "the word bitch" works the same magic on Franz Pökler
(V429.21–22n). So the reference links all three characters, as if in a
rocket clan.

V104.18, B121.12–13, P106.19 a precious TerBorch Gerard Terborch
(1617–81), a Dutch artist known for his portraits of commoners and depictions of everyday scenes.

**V104.19, B121.13, P106.20 Bombs fall to the west in the Haagsche
Bosch.** According to Kooy and Uytenbogaart (286–87), "Schuszstelle
16" (their transliteration of the German Schußstelle) was located in this
Bosch, or wood, but only "three or four" rockets were launched from
there.

V104.25, B121.21, P106.27 oude genever Dutch: an "old" or aged gin.

**V104.30–31, B121.27–28, P106.32–33 where the great airborne adven-
ture lies bogged for the winter** Troops from Britain's First Airborne division under the command of Field Marshal Montgomery were parachuted along the Lower Rhine river at Arnhem on September 17, 1944,
as American Eighty-second Airborne troops were dropped well to the
north, behind German lines. This plan, dubbed Operation Market Garden, was designed to pinch German occupiers at Arnhem and bring a
swift end to the European war. It failed. German troops held, and around
three-fourths Montgomery's First Airborne troops were killed or captured before the remnant safely retreated to the south and rejoined Allied comrades. So by December the Allied forces were still stretched
along the Rhine, but they were holding. During the interim Allied forces
had also bogged down in the effort to clear from the lowlands around the
captured port of Antwerp other resisting German forces, and the first
troop ship wasn't able to offload in that city until December 11, 1944.

Five days later German troops broke through Allied lines and drove toward Antwerp, opening the Battle of the Bulge.

V105.20, B122.21, P107.21   flimsies   British secretarial slang for thin sheets of paper used to make carbon copies of documents.

V106.6, B123.13, P108.7–8   a bulky, ancient Schwarzlose   An 11-millimeter, oil-cooled machine gun manufactured in Austria and used principally during the Great War.

V106.12, B123.20–21, P108.13–14   the windmill known as "The Angel"   The Dutch often name their windmills. "The Angel," Katje's rendezvous point with Pirate, will be described in greater detail at V535.36–536.2. Then its wheel blossoms into a mandala-like image that *seems* to be reflected in Blicero's eyes on the day when Rocket 00000 is fired (V670.15–16n). Prior to this we have also noted London's Windmill Theatre in Piccadilly (V39.1–2n).

V106.33–37, B124.4–9, P108.35–39   Bela Lugosi . . . perhaps *Dumbo*   Osbie Feel's "All-Time List" of his favorite films takes no special order. *White Zombie* (1932) stars Bela Lugosi and Madge Bellamy in the story of an island sugar mill operated by zombies under the control of a megalomaniac (Lugosi). *Son of Frankenstein* (1939) stars Lugosi, Basil Rathbone, and Boris Karloff; in this chapter of the saga the famous doctor's son meets his father's monster. In concentrating on modalities of life-after-death (zombies) and mechanically induced life (Frankenstein's "monster") these films correspond with *GR*'s core themes. *Flying Down to Rio* (1933) stars Dolores del Rio and Gene Raymond, with appearances by Fred Astaire and Ginger Rogers; the plot is light comedy, with Raymond torn between flying airplanes and playing piano. *Freaks* (1932) will appear several more times in *GR*. Since its release, the film has slowly won recognition as a classic of horror. It initially brought storms of protest because of the midgets, Siamese twins, and other "freaks of nature" cast by director Tod Browning. At first it was banned in most European countries, England included; but underground showings were common enough so that, as Sadoul (*Dictionary of Films*) notes, it was acclaimed at Cannes in 1962. *Dumbo* (1941) is the Walt Disney animated film that almost disappeared, for a time, because of its racist depiction of the character Jim ("Hush Mah Beak") Crow. Here, Osbie hallucinates the face of Labor Minister Ernest Bevin in place of young Dumbo the elephant, who thinks a white feather gives him powers of flight. Larsson ("A *Companion*'s Companion") also reports that American servicemen serving in the Pacific theater dubbed the B-17 bomber "Dumbo."

V107.23, B124.40, P109.24   "the bloody Mendoza"   A lightweight machine gun developed in 1934 by Rafael Mendoza, for the Mexican army. The gun weighed 11 kilograms, over three times the 3.5 kilograms of the British Sten gun (V20.10n). Most of the Mendoza's features were traditional; the unique thing about it was the double-ended firing pin. In case of a broken pin—a common fault in light-action machine guns—one could quickly remove the firing bolt and reverse the pin; no need to rummage through one's kit bag for a replacement while an enemy advanced. This is the basis for Pirate's trade-off. The Mendoza was much heavier and used an odd-sized shell, but it was safer.

V107.26, B125.1, P109.27 Portobello Road A narrow winding street in London's North Kensington district, with shops and covered markets on one side and covered stalls on the other. Until 1948 it was home to the Caledonian Market, nicknamed "The Stones" because that is what its impoverished tradesmen slept on. Portobello has lost its rough edges and its preterite, but Pynchon knows it through books—Baedeker's, no doubt—where its reputation as a mean street would make it a likely place to find a scarce size of ammunition ("7 mm Mexican Mauser") for Pirate's Mendoza.

V107.34–35, B125.12, P109.35 *façonné* velvet Katje wears a stiff, formal gown of red molded velvet (and so looks like a "statue").

V108.12–13, B125.32–33, P110.12–13 ic heb u liever . . . goude ghewracht The source of this Middle Dutch lyric is Grimm (*Teutonic Mythology* 213), whose translator (Stallybrass) renders the lines like this:
I hold you dearer than a boar-swine
All were it of fine gold y-wrought.
Grimm notes that the lines derive from a Middle Dutch romance, *Lantslot ende Sandrin*, verse 374, wherein the gentle knight makes this tender declaration of love to his lady. As Grimm explains, the Norse god Freyr (also Frey), a god of peace and love, often appeared with a boar in attendance (see V94.26n). At Yuletide, "atonement boars" were offered up to the god in anticipation of a year's peace and fruitfulness. Other "golden boars" in Norse and Teutonic myth attest to Freyr's popularity, for the god embodied a wholly creative, generative principle. He may even have been as powerful a god, in primitive Teutonic culture, as Wuotan or Thunar.

V108.17–18, B125.40–41, P110.17–18 off to Mauritius . . . toting his haakbus The Dutch twice tried to colonize the island of Mauritius, off the coast of East Africa. In 1638 they tried to garrison a port where trading ships could reprovision, but they abandoned the effort in 1658. Six years later the Dutch East India Company, with whom Frans van der Groov is associated, came to the island in force, attempting agricultural development and the construction of permanent buildings. The company pulled out in 1700, leaving behind over a hundred black slaves. The agricultural development had failed because of inclement weather, rats, and shortages of manpower and tools. During this second attempt the dodo bird (*Didus ineptus*) was brought to extinction, partly because the Dutch hunted the clumsy creatures, but mostly because they brought in foraging pigs that ate the dodoes' eggs, which lay unprotected in clumps of grass. Like Pirate Prentice, Frans also prefers to carry an outmoded firearm. The *haakbus*, or in German *hak-büchse* (or "arquebus"), was a "hook gun." Curved jaws held a piece of serpentine that was threaded into the gun's touchhole, where (when lit) it ignited the powder charge. The design was in wide use throughout Europe in the fifteenth century, but by the late sixteenth most soldiers preferred the *snaphaan*, a flint-lock weapon. Its serrated metal wheel scraped against a flint, sparking the powder charge. This was more expensive, more delicate, and more prone to malfunction than the *haakbus*.

V109.30, B127.19, P111.30 motionless as any Vermeer The Dutch painter Jan van der Meer, or Vermeer for short (1632–75), whose depictions of everyday scenes often seemed to freeze motion in a kind of photographic stasis.

V110.6, B127.40, P112.6 This furious host were losers Frans's Dutch cohorts as a parody, or preterite version, of the *Wütende Heer*, or "Mad Army" of Wuotan (V72.27–28n).

V110.22–23, B128.19, P112.23–24 the island of Reunion A former French colony, 110 miles southwest of Mauritius.

V111.7–9, B129.8–11, P113.9–11 *For as much as they are the creatures of God . . . eternal life to be found* The source of this, perhaps a prayer for new colonial subjects, is unknown. In any case the application of it to the doomed Dodoes, here, is significant in light of the heresy detailed later (see V555.29–31). Slothrop's Puritan ancestor William's treatise, *On Preterition*, is described as having extended eternal salvation to all—including the preterite. Why not to colonized animals, as well? Even to the least of them? Even to dodoes.

V112.22, B130.37, P114.26 Charing Cross station Near Whitehall and Trafalgar Square, where Katje departs for the vicinity of Dover and "The White Visitation."

V112.29, B131.4–5, P114.34–35 The Zouave has gone back to his unit The Algerian tribesman (see V91.41n) has returned to fight for France ("the Cross of Lorraine").

V112.33, B131.9, P114.38 Lang, Pabst, Lubitsch The Ufa directors, master craftsmen of German expressionist cinema (see V98.24n).

V112.39, B131.17, P115.4 Flit A U.S. brand of over-the-counter pesticide, still marketed by the Exxon Corporation.

V113.1, B131.21, P115.7 Meillerwagen A mobile trailer used to transport V-2 rockets to their launching sites; described and pictured in Kooy and Uytenbogaart (*Ballistics of the Future* 364–67).

V113.11, B131.33, P115.17 rocket-firing site in the Rijkswijksche Bosch Wooded site of "Schuszstelle 19," according to Kooy and Uytenbogaart (287).

V113.36–37, B132.22–23, P116.3–4 old, tarnished silver crown Brings readers back full circle to Katje's octopus-conditioning outfit, from the opening of this episode. In part 2 she appears in the same dress, with the same silver crown (see V186.3ff).

EPISODE 15

Internal references establish the date as on or around December 23, 1944. Slothrop, released after "these recent days" (V114.10) of confinement in St. Veronica's, had returned to his cubicle off Grosvenor Square, met one of his previous girls, and wound up with her in the East End flat of a Mrs. Quoad (Latin for "as much as"). Next, a "hopeless holocaust" (V118.12) in Slothrop's mouth when they gorge themselves on peppered British wine jellies, the prelude to vigorous intercourse.

V114.5, B132.29, P116.9   a Section 8   A discharge for U.S. servicemen deemed unfit for further duty because they were "unable to adapt" to military life (A. Marjorie Taylor, *Language of World War II*). Usually a Section Eight was given for reasons of mental instability, the sense at V182.9–10 when Slothrop uses the term in the context of a reference to "raving maniacs." David Mesher ("Corrigenda" 14) remarks on a seeming anachronism, in that "Slothrop's allusion is to a remote but real hope of being disqualified from further military service under Section Eight, Army Regulation 615-360. That regulation was in force only until July, 1944." The term nonetheless remained part of service slang for years after the regulation was revised.

V114.12–13, B132.37–133.1, P116.16–17   on the order of the old woman's arrangement for getting her pig home over the stile   A reference to an old folktale. The best version can be found in *Clouston's Popular Tales and Fictions* (1:295–96). Stith Thompson's *Motif-Index* (5:546) also lists a number of variants, scattered worldwide. Clouston calls it the story of "The Old Woman and the Crooked Sixpence" and catalogues it with cumulative stories, such as "The House That Jack Built." Here, the old woman of the tale finds a crooked coin and buys a pig with it, but the pig balks at her stile. She asks a dog to bite the pig, but the dog refuses; so she asks a stick to hit the dog, and it refuses; whereupon she turns to fire (to burn the stick), water (to douse the fire), an ox (to lap up the water), a butcher (to slaughter the ox), a rope (to hang the butcher), a rat (to gnaw the rope), and a cat (to eat the rat). They all decline in their turn. Yet when the cat asks for a bowl of milk from a nearby cow, and the cow gives milk after being given hay, the old woman has milk for the cat, which eats the rat, which chews the rope, and so on, until the dog bites the pig, which jumps over the stile.

Clouston traces the tale to a sacred hymn in the Hebrew Talmud; it has ten intermediary steps, just as there are ten intermediaries standing between the straw for the cow (a gift, eaten) and the pig leaping over the stile (a command, obeyed). Note also that the motif of ten, along with the hysteron proteron trope, recurs in the launch countdown. And Pynchon will later also link the motif to the ten-stage order of the Kabbalah. Incidentally, there are also ten sounding holes on Slothrop's Hohner harmonica, and there are ten generations of Slothrops (and Pynchons). There are further references to Rilke's tenth elegy (98.1–2), to an "aethereal Xth Programme" over the BBC (V147.7), a ten-step children's game called *Himmel und Hölle* (V567.25), Slothrop's ten thousand days of life (V624.18), and the ten-card spread in the Celtic method of tarot divination (V738.7), among many others. However, the main point in this context is Slothrop's desire to return home and his being lost in a search for the key to some recursive formula, or the catalyst of a chain reaction, that will bring him back.

V114.19, B133.8, P116.23   Woolworth's   In 1879 Frank Woolworth opened his first department store in Utica, New York, and then grew the company into a nationwide chain. He took it to England in 1909, from whence F. W. Woolworth's has spread throughout the British Commonwealth. Here, probably the store located in London's Marylebone district.

V114.20, B133.10, P116.24–25   little-kid-size Enfields   The British Arsenal is located at Enfield Lock, the place-name that has been used for decades as if it were the brand name for the various service rifles manufactured there.

V114.21–22, B133.11, P116.26   his Humber   See V24.13–14n.

V114.37–38, B133.30–31, P117.6–7   hair flying in telltales, white wedgies clattering . . . an adorable tomato   Of these slang terms, Partridge (in *Forces' Slang*) tells us that "wedgies" are any women's "wedge-heeled shoes," and he dates the term from "circa 1945." A "tomato" was originally Australian service slang for "an attractive girl," but U.S. servicemen adopted it "circa 1943." "Telltales" are apparently undocumented by students of slang, but a friend explains that they are a way of dressing the hair in pigtails so that they dangle over the ears. Larsson ("A *Companion*'s Companion") also reports that they are "short pieces of yarn, ribbon, thread, or tape attached to the sail [of a boat] which are used to show the air flow over the sail; or when attached to the shroud indicate apparent wind direction."

V115.3–4, B133.36–38, P117.10–11   greensickness . . . a touch of scurvy   These "antiquated diseases" will have turned Mrs. Quoad into nothing less than a rainbow-colored, toad-skinned old hag. Greensickness is an iron-deficiency anemia that turns the skin green. Tetter is an umbrella term for a variety of skin diseases—such as worms, herpes, eczema, pimples, pustules, blisters, and milk-blotches. The third, kibes, is a reddish inflammation or chilblain of the feet. Purples are livid blotches, spots, or pustules; the term also sometimes refers to the bubo of the plague. Mrs. Quoad's fifth ailment, imposthumes, appears as open abscesses of the skin, and the next, almonds in the ears, describes the condition of swollen lymph glands. Seventh and last, scurvy is the subcutaneous bleeding, especially at the lips, resulting from a vitamin C deficiency.

V115.16–17, B134.9–10, P117.22–23   the dome of faraway St. Paul's Though several miles away, the dome of St. Paul's Cathedral, atop Ludgate Hill, would be visible from this East End room.

V115.19, B134.13, P117.25   Primo Scala's Accordion Band Played over the BBC's General Forces Programme on Saturday, December 23, at 10:30 P.M., and at no other time during the month.

V115.32–33, B134.28–29, P117.39–40   all the Compton Mackenzie novels on the shelf If we exclude the sixty or so nonfictional books he published during his long lifetime (1883–1972), even then Mrs. Quoad has a hefty shelf of books. Sir Anthony Edward Montagu Compton Mackenzie published as many novels as there are letters in his name: thirty-six in all. And they are long novels, written as if the aim was to crowd every page with detail.

V115.33, B134.29–30, P117.33   glassy ambrotypes The phrase is somewhat redundant, the "glassy" being implicit in the word "ambrotype" itself. In this nineteenth-century photographic process, the light tones are produced on glass by plating it with silver, while the darks are made with black paper backing.

V115.35, B134.31–32, P118.1   Michaelmas daisies They bloom for the Feast of St. Michael on September 29.

V115.36–37, B134.33–34, P118.2–3   a Wardour Street shop Located in London's Soho district, which once, as Baedeker (*London* 153) explains, was "synonymous with imitation-antique furniture"; now it is the center of London's film industry.

V116.21, B135.21, P118.29   says Lafitte Rothschild The two *t*'s in "Lafitte" are notable, for as Alexis Lichine comments (Fifield, ed., *Alexis Lichine's Encyclopedia of Wines and Spirits*), only the very earliest nineteenth-century labels of Chateau Lafite Rothschild used that spelling. The wine is one of France's best, a rich and expensive red bordeaux.

V116.23, B135.24–25, P118.31   "the Bernkastler Doktor" Lichine (133) refers to it as "the most famous great Moselle wine," a white German vintage.

V116.24–25, B135.26, P118.32–33   "slimy elm things, maple-tasting with a touch of sassafras" Mrs. Quoad means Slothrop's throat aids, Thayer's slippery elm throat lozenges (V18.8–38n). Billed as "Nature's Gentle Demulcent," since 1847 Thayer's has contained dextrose, elm bark, and vegetable stearate.

V116.35, B135.39, P119.2–3   Gilbert & Sullivan   During their twenty-three-year collaboration, British dramatist William S. Gilbert (1836–1911) wrote the librettos, and composer Arthur Sullivan (1842–1900) the scores, for such light operas as *The Pirates of Penzance* and *The Mikado*, operas in which Darlene here could be playing the "ingenue" role.

V117.8, B136.11, P119.15   pure Nightingale compassion   After Florence Nightingale (1820–1910), pioneer of nursing and a founder of the Red Cross.

V117.15–16, B136.20–21, P119.22–23   Hop Harrigan ... Tank Tinker ... playing his ocarina   Short-lived as a syndicated comic strip in 1941, *Hop Harrigan* did very well as an American radio serial. From 1942 until 1950, Hop ("America's Ace of the Airwaves") used to appear over ABC stations during the early evening hours. He was the pilot and Tank Tinker his ocarina-playing mechanic of "Aircraft CX-4," which flew them through innumerable melodramatic adventures that by 1945 made this duo "the best known juvenile heroes of the war" (Dunning, *Tune in on Yesterday* 287). Why the ocarina? Because the U.S. Army issued these little yam-shaped instruments to servicemen headed overseas. Eastman Plastics manufactured ocarinas out of a revolutionary material, tennite, also used in airplanes. And as a 1944 Eastman ad in *Time* explains: "Ocarinas made of Tennite have furnished the jive for many a jam-session held in fox-holes, in canteens behind the lines, and on troop convoys." The army even issued "monthly hit kits," music sheets for popular songs.

V117.38–39, B137.7, P120.6   a Mills-type hand grenade   The pin-and-lever, pineapple-shaped grenade developed for British troops in the Great War.

V118.1, B137.10, P120.9   a .455 Webley cartridge   For decades after its introduction in 1868, the Webley was a standard "constabulary" re-volver, especially popular in the colonies. Closely resembling the American Colt, it came in calibers of .445, .45, and .455.

V118.2, B137.11, P120.10   a six-ton earthquake bomb   A twelve-thousand-pound bomb (the second-largest nonnuclear device dropped during the war), carried aloft in British Lancaster bombers on night raids. Some were used in the August 17, 1943, raid against Peenemünde (Irving, *Mare's Nest* 114–21). For more on that raid see V423.56n.

V118.3, B137.12, P120.11   a licorice bazooka   This is technically out of place in Mrs. Quoad's arsenal of "prewar" (V116.6) candies, because this antitank weapon was manufactured and named during the war. The name itself stems from American comedian Bob Burns (1896–1956), who played a crude wind instrument—somewhat resembling the weapon—he dubbed the "bazooka."

V118.31, B138.7, P120.40   the Meggezone   British tradename for a throat lozenge or pastille whose active ingredient is Eucalyptus-derived menthol, still registered for U.S. import.

V119.11, B138.30, P121.20   Bond Street or waste Belgravia   Bond Street
is located just two blocks from Slothrop's ACHTUNG "cubicle" (V18.3)
off Grosvenor Square. Baedeker (*London* 96) calls Bond Street "the most
fashionable shopping district in London for over a century." Similarly,
Belgravia is "the most fashionable residential quarter of London" (ibid.
84), located just west of Buckingham Palace. The adjective "waste" escapes me.

V119.15, B138.35, P121.24   tourmalines in German gold   Tourmaline
names any of several precious gems, columnar silicoborate crystals of
various color that have a vitreous luster; typically, they come from Cey-
lon and are generally set in gold.

V119.16, B138.36, P121.25   ebony finger-stalls   These provide protection
for the digits during procedures "in some handicrafts, in dissection, or
when the finger is diseased" (*OED*).

**V119.30–31, B139.12–13, P121.40–41   usurped the throne in 1878 during
the intrigues over Bessarabia**   During the summer of 1878 Europe's
great diplomats—chief among them Bismarck of Germany and Beacons-
field of England—met in Berlin to settle the "Eastern Question." Russia's defeat of Turkey in the 1876 war, insurrections in several Balkan
states (Serbia, Bosnia, Montenegro, Herzegovina), as well as the compet-
ing interests of Austria, Germany, and Russia—all these factors necessi-
tated a "summit" conference. Each nation wanted a piece of the strategic action around the Dardanelles. Britain, for example, wanted to rein
in the Russians and needed both access to and stability in the Dardanelles for the benefit of its Middle Eastern and African colonies. It was
at the 1878 Berlin conference that Austria was allowed to garrison the
sanjak of Novi Pazar (V14.34–36n); the nation-state of Bulgaria was created; Greece obtained Crete, Thessaly, and a portion of Macedonia; and
Russia was given a strip of Bessarabia, while Romania lost a portion of
it. Pynchon aptly calls the conference a business of "intrigues." The
Balkan states and Bessarabia had glimpsed a promise of independence
when Russia defeated their Turkish overlords. England and Germany,
however, maneuvered to install new overlords (the Austro-Hungarian
Empire) in an effort to buttress the region against Russian expansion.
England thus helped put into motion the sequence of events that led up
to the Great War and, by extension, World War II. King Yrjö is wholly
fictional, a carryover from Pynchon's 1964 short story, "The Secret Integration." In this scene he is remembered touching Mrs. Quoad's throat,
to cure her scrofula by the "miracle touch" associated with kings (see
Vl19.33n, Vl19.37n).

V119.32, B139.14, P122.1   golden galloons   From the French noun "*ga-
lon,*" a gold or silver braid or lace.

V119.33, B139.16, P122.2   King's Evil   Scrofula, a condition affecting the
tissues of young victims (like Mrs. Quoad, whose reminiscence harks

back more than sixty years before 1944). Usually the affliction takes the form of lymphatic swelling, jaundice, respiratory infection, or tuberculosis. Those tracing the manifold references to pigs in *GR* will note that "*scrofa*" is the Latin for "sow" and that scrofula got its name from the swelling in the "small sows" or lymphatic glands, which is why Mrs. Quoad must be touched in "the hollow of [her] throat" (V119.36–37). Scrofula was once known as "the King's Evil" in France and England, but the practice of royal cures was eradicated with the death of Queen Anne in 1714; five years later the office for this ceremony was removed from *The Book of Common Prayer*.

V119.37, B139.20, P122.6   the miracle touch   Here, the cure for King's Evil. Yet the phrase also functions as a bridge into episode 16, which opens with the analeptic recall of "the very first touch" (which proved rather a miracle) of Roger and Jessica. The idea of touching also forms an invitation at novel's end: "There is time, if you need the comfort, to touch the person next to you."

EPISODE 16

A chapter of chronologically unstructured analepses focalized through Roger and Jessica that concludes by returning readers to the night of December 23. This date is established through several references to Christmas caroling, references taken from that day's *Times* of London stories. The Advent season and the carols establish a theme of anticipated redemption.

V120.29–30, B140.20–21, P123.3–4   She came twice . . . important to both of them   Note that the reversal of cause and effect, of intercourse and orgasm or stimulus and response, is another instance of hysteron proteron. And the homology of these events with V-2 rocket strikes and other "transmarginal" phenomena in *GR* might explain why this is "important to both of them." Their romance coincides, chronologically and virtually, with the rocket blitz.

V121.13–14, B141.8–9, P123.25–26   at the Tivoli watching Maria Montez and Jon Hall   The Tivoli Theatre is located on the Strand in central London. A *Times* of London "Picture Theatres" guide reveals that from November 20 until December 10 the film *Gypsy Wildcat* starring Montez and Hall was featured at the Tivoli.

V121.14–15, B141.9–10, P123.26–27   peccaries in Regents Park Zoo   By 1940 the Zoological Gardens in Regents Park (in north-central London) housed the largest known collection of captive animals, nearly seven thousand species. Of them the peccary, common throughout the Americas, would interest Pynchon because it's a small pig-like animal, the *Tayassu tacaju*.

V121.23, B141.21, P123.35   the Bofors   A Swedish-made antiaircraft cannon.

V121.25, B141.23, P123.37   The Mayfair Hotel   Should be "May Fair," the hotel located on Berkeley Street in London's Mayfair district.

V121.29, B141.28, P123.41   "Time enough for several assignations"   Roger riffs on T. S. Eliot's 1917 poem, "The Love Song of J. Alfred Prufrock":

> And time yet for a hundred indecisions,
> And for a hundred visions and revisions
> Before the taking of a toast and tea. (11.32–34)

V121.35–36, B141.35–36, P125.5–6   Roland Peachey and his Orchestra playing "There, I Said It Again"   The band is another (like Falkman and his Apache Band) that Pynchon found in the *Times* of London BBC broadcasting schedules. The timing of this analepsis is indeterminate, as is the date of Peachey's performance. The song title is in error; it should be "There! I've Said It Again." The lyric, written in 1941 by Redd Evans and Dave Mann, was a million-seller for Boston bandleader Vaughn Monroe in 1944 (and twenty years later a number one hit again, for Bobby Vinton):

> I love you, there's nothing to hide,
> It's better than burning inside;
> I love you, no use to pretend,
> There! I've said it again.

And so on, in the same vein.

V122.24–25, B142.31–32, P124.38   blue-petaled pergolas   In ornate, high-ceilinged houses, a trelliswork pergola will have vines and flowering plants trained over it. It thus images another parabolic archway for us.

V122.28–29, B142.37–38, P125.2   motoring up . . . near Lower Beeding   On the trunk road from "The White Visitation" (near Brighton) to London, Roger and Jessica would pass through the village of Lower Beeding, a few miles north of Tunbridge Wells.

V123.18, B143.29, P125.30   ctenophile   Pynchon's portmanteau word, from the Greek *"kten-"* (comb) and *"-philos"* (loving); thus a "comb lover."

V124.12, B144.30, P126.24   bit of the je ne sais quoi de sinistre   Bit of the "sinister something-or-other."

V124.24–25, B145.5–6, P126.39   Turn off that faucet, Dorset   In the same spirit as "Girl in distress, Jess?" (V127.15) or "Got a fag, Mag?" (V127.18). A. Marjorie Taylor (*Language of World War II*) compiled a list of rhymes like these, many of which became popular wartime songs, such as "A Fellow on a Furlough," and "Good Bye, Mama, I'm Off to Yokohama."

V125.19, B146.5, P127.31   a Merseyside Labour branch   A British Labour

Party branch operating out of the industrial city of Liverpool, on the river Mersey.

V125.21, B146.7, P127.33   on demob   In British wartime slang, "on demobilization," that is, released from military service.

V125.22, B146.8, P127.34   the G-5-to-be   A. Marjorie Taylor (*Language of World War II* 88) explains that G-5 was designated as that "section of the Army set up to take over local government in lands occupied by invasion forces. Other sections are G-1 personnel, G-2 Intelligence, G-3 Training and Plans, G-4 Supply and Evacuation."

V125.25, B146.12–13, P127.37   were-elves   Unknown in the annals of folklore.

V126.19, B147.12–13, P128.32   this seventh Christmas of the War   A miscount: from the German invasion of Poland in September 1939 until V-J day in August 1945, this war encompassed six Christmas days. On the next page Pynchon gets it right: "six years of slander, ambition and hysteria" (V127.12–13).

V126.22, B147.16, P128.35   stale Woodbines   A medium-priced brand of British cigarette, frequently advertised in the *Times* of London.

V127.10, B148.8–9, P129.22   Grafty Green, Kent   A village situated in the heart of Kent, in southeast England, several miles from the village of Headcorn and Leeds Castle; it is still a popular holiday roost.

V127.16, B148.16, P129.28   On the Tannoy   Registered trademark for a British radio (or, loudspeaker), comparable to the American Capehart (V66.39n).

V127.19–20, B148.20–21, P129.31–32   like a bloody Garbo film . . . nicotine starvation   In films like *Grand Hotel* and *Mata Hari*, actress Greta Garbo characteristically appears with a cigarette in hand.

V128.2–3, B149.6, P130.13–14   the Star ready to be pasted up   The reference is to the traditional Advent calendar, marking off the days to Christmas.

V128.8, B149.12, P130.19   but def   Slang abbreviation for "but definitely" and an instance, also, of Zipf's "Principle of Least Effort."

V128.35, B150.3, P131.6   High Holborn Street   Jamaicans took, from London, the name for this downtown Kingston street.

V129.6–7, B150.18, P131.19   a compline service   Held during the last of the seven canonical hours just before retiring, usually at 8 P.M.

V129.8–16, B150.20–29, P131.21–29   Thomas Tallis, Henry Purcell, even a German macronic . . . attributed to Heinrich Suso . . . Alpha *es et O*   The word "macronic" (in the Viking; it is corrected in the Bantam) is a misprint; it should be "macaronic," a lyric composed in several different languages. The details for this interlude of caroling derive directly and indirectly from a story entitled "Macaronic Carols" in the *Times* of London (December 22, 1944, 6). The writer takes Suso's carol, "In dulci jubilo," as an example, commenting:

No simpler or more persuasive demonstration of the unity of Christendom (even at the very time of the Reformation) and the universality
of Latin could well be found than this example of macaronic verse, in
which the vernacular and Latin are arranged so closely as to preserve
the syntax of both tongues. There is argument over whether carols
have a popular or clerical origin. The conclusion of the argument, according to Richard Leighton Greene in *The Early English Carols*, is
that while the carol is not pure folk song, i.e. a product of communal
growth and oral transmission, it is popular in its use of familiar phrases,
and the Latin tags do not take it beyond the reach of the illiterate man
who heard them constantly in church.

Suso was a German composer of the late fifteenth and early sixteenth
centuries. The subject of this carol is Christ's Nativity; the *Times* gives
the following translatation:

In sweet jubilation
Let us our homage sing
Our hearts' joy
Reclines in the manger
And shines like the sun
In his mother's lap
Alpha he is, and Omega.

The *Times* article does not mention the other two composers, but
Greene's Early English Carols, to which Pynchon evidently turned next,
gives the background. Thomas Tallis (1505–85) was organist at the
Chapel Royal under Henry VIII and Queen Mary. Henry Purcell (1659–
95) was also employed, like Tallis, at the Chapel Royal. He was a composer of devotional songs and, before his early death, wrote a number of
songs for the Restoration stage. The *Times* also gives notice of caroling
scheduled for the London area on Saturday, December 23, the time of
Roger and Jessica's stop at this church.

V130.6, B151.27, P132.18   the Wrens work late   See V17.26n.

V130.15, B151.35, P132.28   from Harrow to Gravesend   Harrow, twelve
miles northwest of central London, is home to Harrow School. There,
future Byrons and Churchills (two of its illustrious graduates) might be
brushing their teeth before "quicksilver mirrors." Gravesend, twenty-
four miles east of London on the mouth of the Thames, once was a popular resort. The two towns are also the rough boundaries within which
the V-2 rockets fell, according to Irving's map (*Mare's Nest* 262).

V130.24, B152.4, P132.37   Household Milk   A packaged, price-controlled,
dehydrated milk product sold to the British throughout the war under
the auspices of the Ministry of Foods. Like the dried eggs at V252.16–17,
it was frequently advertised in the *Times* with recipes.

V131.1, B152.26, P133.14   ein Volk ein Führer   Nazi propaganda slogan
that translates as "One people, one Leader!" Recall Crutchfield the
Westwardman's "only one" of everything (see V68.1n).

V131.11, B152.38–39, P133.23–24   the Rundstedt offensive   See V52.23–24n.

V131.22–24, B153.10–13, P133.34   Will he show up under the Star . . . Bring to the serai gifts of tungsten, cordite, high-octane?   A serai is the palace of an eastern sultan (*OED*), here imagined in a scene inverting Christ's Nativity: these "Magi" bring gifts to the sultan's palace, not to the Savior's preterite birth site in a stable. And—instead of gold, frankincense, and myrrh—bring modern war materials: here motor fuel, explosives, and tungsten for light bulb filaments (compare Matt 2:10–11).

V132.3–4, B153.38–39, P134.16   the prisoners are back from Indo-China   The source was a *Times* of London story entitled "Ordeal of War Prisoners" (December 20, 1944, 2). In September 1944 some twenty thousand British prisoners of war were rescued from labor camps in Siam (now Thailand). The Japanese had used sixty thousand prisoners of varying nationalities to build roads through the jungles. Of these, some twenty thousand died of malnutrition, disease, and brutal beatings. The *Times* story concerns the difficulty of their return to British society. Most had psychological problems, as signified by their "eyes from Burma, from Tonkin" (V132.14).

V132.11, B154.5–6, P134.23   Mr. Morrison   Herbert Stanley, Baron Morrison (1888–1964), England's wartime minister of Home Security (see also V24.3n).

V132.16, B154.11–12, P134.28   headaches no Alasils can cure   An American brand of aspirin pain-relieving tablets.

V132.20–21, B154.16–18, P134.32–33   If these Eyeties sing . . . bet it's not "Giovinezza" but . . . *Rigoletto* or *La Bohème*   What the "Horst Wessel Lied" was to German Nazis, "Giovinezza" (Youth) was to the Italian Fascists under Benito Mussolini. After the Italian surrender, they would be careful to sing, instead, bits from comic operas by (respectively) Verdi and Puccini.

V132.26, B154.24, P134.39   Boxing Day   December 26, when the British give gifts, especially to servants and workers.

V132.31–32, B154.31–32, P135.4–5   *no mano morto* for the Englishmen back from CBI   The former prisoners recently returned from the China-Burma-India theater of war are given no magical remedy. Folk superstition holds that a dead hand (the *mano morto*) has various powers as charm and miracle cure (see S. Thompson, 6:859–60). For an illicit, black magic use of such a hand see V750.33n.

V132.37, B154.38, P135.9–10   If the brave new world should also come about   Recalling Aldous Huxley's vision of a completely routinized society in his novel *Brave New World* (1932), the title of which was bagged from Shakespeare's *Tempest* (5.1.183): "O brave new world, / That has such people in it!"

V133.3–4, B155.5–6, P135.17–18   children have unfolded last year's toys and found reincarnated Spam tins   Spam is the brand of canned meat product, and the source for this otherwise curious detail is a *Times* of London story entitled "Toys from Spam Tins" (December 9, 1944, 2): "Months of painstaking, spare-time effort by men and women in barrage units and anti-aircraft batteries in Greater London have been largely responsible for the production of over 6,000 toys for Abbey District Entertainments, which intends to distribute the toys at children's parties and among hospitals, clinics, and day care nurseries in eight London boroughs at Christmas." The toy "railway engines, lorries, tanks, dolls, and animals, which are both attractive and durable," were made from the tins of Spam and canned fish by folks like Jessica and Jeremy, in their A-A batteries.

V133.14–15, B155.19, P135.29   the Radio Doctor asking, What Are Piles? The *Radio Doctor* was a regular, weekly, five-minute program of the BBC Home Service Programme. At 6:25 P.M. on December 14, for example, he answered the question "What Are Boils?" Larsson ("A *Companion*'s Companion") reports that he was former British government minister Charles Hill (1904–89).

V133.29–30, B155.37, P136.3   even Big Ben will be fast now The (accelerated) bell that sounds the hours at Westminster, in London.

V134.24–25, B156.39–40, P136.40–41   strange thousand-year *sigh—eia*, wärn wir da! Another line from Suso's "In dulci jubilo," the translation of which (were we but there) Pynchon derives from the *Times* story (V129.8–16n).

V134.32–33, B157.11, P137.8   just left behind with your heart, at the Stage Door Canteen On March 2, 1942, the American Theater Wing opened the Stage Door Canteen in New York City's 44th Street Theater Building, serving free sandwiches, coffee, and doughnuts to all servicemen and -women, officers and enlisted men, white and black, but the Canteen's feature attraction was the table service and entertainment by a host of the city's finest performers from the stage and cinema. In 1943, Irving Berlin's hit musical *This Is the Army* featured his song "I Left My Heart at the Stage Door Canteen," the lyric of which Pynchon here riffs on:

> Old Mister Absent-Minded, that's me
> Just as forgetful as I can be
> I've got the strangest sort of a mind
> I'm always leaving something behind.

> I left my heart at the Stage Door Canteen,
> I left it there, with a girl named Eileen.

> I kept her serving doughnuts,
> Till all she had were gone
> I sat there dunking doughnuts
> Till she caught on.

I must go back, to the Army routine,
And every doughboy knows what that will mean
A soldier boy without a heart
Has two strikes on him, from the start;
My heart's at the Stage Door Canteen.

The Canteen's success also inspired a star-studded 1943 film, *Stage Door Canteen* (United Artists).

V134.38, B157.16, P137.14–15 your mother hoping to hang that Gold Star Since 1928 the Gold Star Mothers Incorporated have been a federally chartered U.S. organization for mothers of sons killed in military service. It grew from a World War I practice inspired by President Wilson, who encouraged mothers of sons killed in combat to honor them by wearing a black armband with a gold star. During World War II, the Gold Star Mothers established the practice of representing with blue stars on a banner each living son serving in the military. If one died, the mother would place a gold star over the blue one.

V134.40–135.1, B157.18–19, P137.16–17 Mr. Noel Coward . . . packing them into the Duchess for the fourth year The play was Coward's *Blithe Spirit*, and the edition of the *Times* of London that discussed the macaronic carols also proclaimed the "Fourth Year" for the play at the city's Duchess Theatre, on Catharine Street. The action centers on a writer, Charles Condamine, who holds a séance; havoc breaks loose when his late wife materializes. Pynchon's dislike of Coward's genteel comedies dates to his early story, "Lowlands."

V135.2–3, B157.21–22, P137.19–20 Walt Disney causing Dumbo the elephant to clutch to that feather See V106.33–37n.

V135.7, B157.27, P137.24 the 88 fell A German 88-millimeter cannon shell.

V135.33, B158.18, P138.10–11 SPQR Record-keeping The acronym stands for *Senatus Populusque Romanus* (The Senate and People of Rome), an official inscription on governmental documents of the Roman Empire. In financial circles, it also means "small profits and quick returns."

V135.38, B158.23–24, P138.15 "Wendell Willkie . . . Churchill? . . . 'Arry Pollitt!" Respectively they are Wendell Willkie (1892–1944), the surprise American presidential candidate of the 1940 election, whose book *One World* was a best seller and whose death in October 1944 might mean that a chaplain's prayers would be for a safe passage heavenward; Winston Churchill (1874–65), Britain's prime minister from 1940 to 1945; and Harry Pollitt (1890–1960), leader of the British Communist Party during the thirties, and again after 1941.

V135.39, B158.25, P138.16 tippin' those Toledos That is, being weighed on a scale produced by the Toledo Scale Corporation, founded in 1901 by Henry Theobald and based in Columbus, Ohio.

V136.6–7, B158.35–36, P138.25–26 *O Jesu parvule,* / Nach dir ist mir so

weh   Two more lines from Suso's carol, "In dulci jubilo." The *Times* translation gives: "O little Jesus, / I am so sad for you " Sad? Exactly: for he is born in such humble (seemingly preterite) surroundings and is fated to die on the Cross.

EPISODE 17

The time of this episode is indistinct, though from its placement it would seem to occur on Sunday, December 24, 1944. By the time of "this late English winter" day Slothrop, having evidently been whisked away, already "ought to be on the Riviera" (V143.24), the general location for part 2 of *GR*. The timing here is noteworthy: within a day of his release from St. Veronica's, Slothrop has been sent to the south of France; moreover, we learn in this episode that a V-2 has struck the ward in which Slothrop had his chemically induced excremental fantasies and his rocket-dowsing penis's erections. Pointsman sees this coincidence as confirming the determinist interpretation of Slothrop's enigmatic sex organ, and he imagines himself winning the Nobel Prize for finding the pathway through this mazy mystery. In fact, the story of Theseus's triumph over the Minotaur and the Cretan labyrinth emerges in this episode as the mythic counterpart to Pointsman's Pavlovian science of the brain.

V136.25, B159.18, P139.4   Paradoxical phase   Pointsman here diagnoses the effects of his own exhaustion, much as (according to Horsley Gantt) Pavlov used to diagnose the progressive effects of his own senility. On the paradoxical phase see V48.38–39n.

V136.27, B159.20, P139.6   Mosquitoes and Lancasters   The Mosquito was the war's first radar-equipped night fighter, a light, fast, dual-engine British airplane in service from 1942 on. The Lancaster was a four-engine bomber plane in use from 1940 on.

V137.20, B160.16–17, P139.34   You set out to the left   As Borges notes in his story "The Garden of Forking Paths" (*Ficciones* 93), in negotiating a labyrinth one turns to the left because "such was the common formula for finding the central courtyard." The left is also the "sinister" side (see V138.3) and that of the unconscious mind. Discussing mandala symbolism, Jung (*Collected Works* 12:127) explains how "a leftward movement is equivalent to movement in the direction of the unconscious, whereas a movement to the right is 'correct' and aims at consciousness." Elsewhere in his writings Jung connects rightward and leftward movement to, respectively, clockwise and counterclockwise cycles. These motifs correspond with examples of mandalas that have labyrinthine patterns, where a leftward, counterclockwise pathway leads to the center (see fig. 4 in vol. 9 of *Collected Works*). By thus turning leftward, counterclockwise, and into the unconscious, Pointsman in his dream becomes one of many characters in *GR* (like Slothrop and Enzian) who approach a "Holy Center" but never reach it. For an excellent discussion of this trope, see Hite (*Ideas of Order* 21–32).

V138.22, B161.27, P140.40   Spectro$_E$ Subscript-E because the late Kevin Spectro calls the word "Foxes" to Pointsman through Carroll Eventyr, whom we recall as the medium at the séance of episode 5.

V138.30, B161.38, P141.8   the old Ick Regis Abbey   Now this "eggregious" locale even has an abbey (see V51.31–32n).

V138.35–36, B162.2–3, P141.14   helping fill out the threes prediction   The Poisson equation can yield a prediction for the possibility of *three* rocket strikes per square of mapped territory. It is *very* low.

V139.14, B162.16, P141.33   The mummy's curse, you idiot   In another one of those events from 1922 (annus mirabilis in *GR*), the tomb of King Tutankhamun (more popularly known as King Tut) was discovered in Egypt by British archaeologist Howard Carter. Six weeks later, Lord Carnavon, who funded Carter's expedition, died after entering the tomb, sparking the legend that the pharaohs and their gods laid a curse on any who disturbed their tombs.

V139.36, B163.8–9, P142.14   back to pigs   Pigs are blocks of crude, impure cast iron. Notice also the hysteron proteron trope in this "Abreaction" (V139.34) from "faired" metal back to sheet metal back to "pigs" and then to "ore" and "Earth."

V140.5–10, B163.21–26, P142.24   this power series . . . number of wars per year   The mathematical formula here is a working out of Poisson's equation. The variable terms—2!, 3!, and so on—correspond to the possibility of events that are extremely unlikely to occur but that nonetheless can since there are many opportunities. In "Fishy Poisson," Khachig Tölölyan has shown that Pynchon's likeliest source was George U. Yule and M. G. Kendall's *Introduction to the Theory of Statistics*, a standard textbook in use for decades. In addition to deriving the formula (190), they also mention (193–94) exactly the examples Pynchon uses here and discuss a 1948 study of flying-bomb (V-1) strikes over greater London. Statistician R. D. Clarke had divided the city into a grid of 144 squares and found that the 576 V-1s were distributed very much as Poisson's equation predicts. He concluded: "There appears no evidence that the bombs 'clustered' otherwise than by chance."

V141.2, B164.23, P143.20   stayed in Harley Street   See V88.11n.

V141.18, B164.42, P143.36   sails and churchtops of Stockholm   Pointsman dreams of traveling to Stockholm, Sweden, to receive his Nobel Prize, the "yellow telegram" of his fantasy bringing the news. Pavlov was a 1904 Nobel recipient for his work on the digestive system.

V141.21, B165.4, P143.40   the Grand Hotel   Travel handbooks list this castlelike hotel, with its 105 elegant rooms, as the finest in Sweden. It is located twenty minutes outside of Stockholm, in the seaside area of Saltsjobaden.

V141.32–33, B165.16–17, P144.9–10   Norrmalm . . . Old City   Residential areas and districts of Stockholm.

V142.14, B166.1–2, P144.32–33   a Minotaur waiting for him   Like Theseus encountering the Minotaur of Greek myth (see V88.12–17n).

V142.32–33, B166.23–25, P145.9–10   Reichssieger von Thanatz Alpdrucken . . . champion Weimaraner for 1941   The dog's name will fragment, its parts metamorphosing into *Alpdrücken* (but note that Pynchon doesn't use the umlauted "u" in the dog's name), a (fictional) film by Gerhardt von Göll (the title of which means "nightmare") that links together many of the novel's characters (see V387.36n), and also into the character Miklos Thanatz (from the Greek "*thanatos*," "death"), who first appears in the narrative at V461.29. A *Reichssieger* is a "national champion."

V143.12, B167.8, P145.31   the icy noctiluca   A noctiluca is a "nightlight" or atmospheric glow; thermite is the name of an incendiary explosive made from powdered aluminum and iron oxide that burns intensely at ignition.

V143.16, B167.13, P145.35   Ariadne   Theseus's lover (see above).

V143.24, B167.23, P146.3   Slothrop ought to be on the Riviera by now   The first mention of Slothrop's hasty transfer to the south of France, which transfer anticipates the setting of part 2. By V168.10, Pointsman is getting "news from the Riviera."

V144.1–2, B168.3–4, P146.21–22   *sentiments d'emprise*, old man   This is Pointsman, warning himself against paranoia, Pierre Janet's "feelings of persecution" (V49.1–2n), because Slothrop, now on the French Riviera, was just two days earlier with "his Darlene" near St. Veronica's.

V144.13–14, B168.17–18, P146.33–34   "irradiation," for example, and "reciprocal induction"   Pavlovian terminology. Irradiation is the spreading of connections among cortical cells, so that a specific reflex begins to generalize and to shape others in the organism (*Lectures* 2:49). Reciprocal induction is the process by which an excitatory stimulus creates an inhibitory pattern of response; it is thus inversely symmetrical with the normal process of conditioning (ibid. 1:347).

V144.26, B168.34, P147.6   in Whitehall   In this main district of central London are located all the key government offices: for example, the War Office, the Admiralty, the Treasury, and the prime minister's residence.

EPISODE 18

Once again the time of this episode is indistinct. It consists of analepses to Berlin, circa 1930, and to Palm Sunday, in 1942, when a group of British airmen experience a vision over the city of Lübeck. It is through these historical moments that the medium, Carroll Eventyr, first gains access to the Other Side in episode 5, in particular to Peter Sachsa, the "control" Eventyr uses in his séances. Sachsa was killed during a Berlin street riot in 1930.

V145.4, B169.11, P147.22   the Embankment   North bank of the river Thames in central London, from Charing Cross Bridge to Blackfriars Station.

V145.15–16, B169.25, P147.34   the screever's wood box   A screever is an artist who draws on sidewalks with colored chalks. Bert (Dick Van Dyke) in Disney's 1964 film *Mary Poppins* is a screever; he draws such marvelous pictures that children are able to walk into their imaginary space.

V145.20, B169.31, P148.1–2   to stand inside the central pentagon   Waite, in *The Book of Black Magic and of Pacts* (191–93), discusses the function of this symbol. The pentagon itself appears in the center of a pentacle, and in the process of occult divination they are often drawn with "the blood of a black cock that has never engendered." In addition, the figures are inscribed on "virgin parchment" and in accord with a number of astrological and ritual prescriptions. To stand inside them is thought to guarantee safety from whatever demonic spirits one may intentionally or accidentally summon up.

V145.25–26, B169.37, P148.6–7   called up the control   During a séance the "control" is that deceased person who speaks through the medium; in episode 5, it was Peter Sachsa.

V145.36–37, B170.12–13, P148.18   under Rollo Groast's EEG   Groast as in "grossed"? The EEG is an electroencephalogram (see below).

V146.1–7, B170.15–21, P148.20–25   a stray 50-millivolt spike . . . slow delta-wave shapes . . . "subdued petit-mal spike-and-wave alteration"   This encephalographic record shows oscillating brainwaves, represented in millivolts, from different areas of the cortex. A "spike" is a sporadic, sharply peaked wave that may indicate a brain lesion of some kind, perhaps one that will cause a seizure. The "50-millivolt spike" would be strong enough to suggest as much. Unlike the alpha waves of a resting brain (oscillating at 8–12 cycles per second) or the beta waves of an active brain (18–25 cps), the so-called delta waves (1–3 cps) arise from an area of localized brain damage. This would be consistent with the spike. However, delta waves are normal in infants and children, so this one might indicate a deeply psychotic reversion to childhood states of consciousness, a possibility consistent with the "petit-mal" indications. Complexes of spike-and-wave patterns that appear from both sides of the brain, in regular rhythms of about three per second, are the electroencephalographic sign of petit mal, the form of epilepsy occurring mainly in children.

V146.27, B171.4, P149.5   during the Lübeck raid   In 1942, Britain's Royal Air Force bombed the city of Lübeck in northern Germany. The raid occurred at night, on Palm Sunday, against a target with no strategic value. Hitler was enraged. The firebombing sparked his first threats of using the *Vergeltungswaffen* or "revenge weapons." Yet those weapons (the buzz bombs and V-2s) were still more than two years away from production and Hitler settled instead for "Baedeker raids" on historic English towns of no strategic importance. Here, the temporal symmetries are notable: Lübeck was bombed on Palm Sunday, March 28, 1942, exactly three years before the last V-2 was launched on London, during Easter week of 1945.

V147.1, B171.23, P149.20–21   the winds of karma   Here Pynchon uses the term "karma" almost as a substitution for the word "fate." But the Hindu-Buddhist sense of karma is different from fate: it has to do with the cumulative effects of one's actions during successive stages of being, in all one's incarnations, the way those cumulative effects determine one's destiny. In American sixties slang the term "karma" was cheapened to mean simply "luck."

V147.7, B171.30–31, P149.27   tuned in to the same aethereal Xth Programme   As though the BBC had, beyond its General Forces and Home Service programs, some Tenth Programme for the dead to enjoy.

V147.13, B171.37–38, P149.33–34   What are we to make of Gavin Trefoil   He appeared earlier at the séance, in secret conversation with Carroll Eventyr (V33.30). Here, the narrator explains the boy's so-called autochromaticism, his (fictional) ability to willfully change skin pigmentation. This is what makes him a star in the film produced under the aegis of Operation Black Wing—the plan to frighten Germans with the prospect of Black Rocket Troops, a fictional outfit (in the propaganda film) that amazingly becomes (in the narrative) a reality. Later, Gavin's sexual promiscuity will be another basis for Slothrop's recollection of the boy (at V215.30–32). Thus we have been well prepared when the narrator gets around to noting (at V276.30–31) that Gavin has a "face as blue as Krishna." A trefoil is any of the lotoslike, three-petaled flowers common in Eurasia. In Hinduism the divinity is symbolized as a three-fold flower, the Trimurti composed of Brahma the Creator, Vishnu the Preserver, and Shiva the Destroyer. But Brahma has nothing to do with material being, leaving earth to the dialectical battle between love and hate, white and black, salvation and destruction, Vishnu and Shiva. Note that these are very much the contraries driving the novel. Still more, in myths Vishnu is represented as appearing to man in ten different avatars, of which the bluish-black, sexually promiscuous boy, Krishna, is the eighth. Following Krishna are the two last avatars: Buddha, who is in Hinduism a red herring, a false deity masquerading as Vishnu; then Kalki, the white avatar who signals a final transformation of material being back into its divine potentiality.

V147.39–40, B172.28–29, P150.19–20   tales of Jenny Greenteeth waiting

out in the fens to drown him   One source may be Katharine Briggs's *Faeries in English Tradition and Folklore* (46–47): "Lesser spirits with whom the young were threatened a short time ago, were perhaps nursery creations, invented by careful mothers to frighten their children away from danger. One of these was Jenny Greenteeth, who lurked in stagnant pools, grown over with weeds." And yet there is more. For instance, Pynchon correctly identifies the locality of the Jenny Greenteeth tales as Lancashire; the idea of Jenny's shapelessness is also quite accurate. For like the deeply buried fears or bogeys haunting Rollo Groast's psychological research, Jenny rarely shows herself, generally remaining below the surface. Roy Vickery of the Folklore Society (London) has sent me more (unpublished) details: pools of standing water in Lancashire are covered in summer with floating mats of duckweed (*Lemna minor*); if an unsuspecting child were to run out on them, he would be quickly swallowed up and possibly drowned. For many children, Vickery reports, Jenny Greenteeth was simply another name for the duckweed. Other children believed in Jenny as an actual bogey; one sixty-eight-year-old respondent told Vickery in 1980 that Jenny was sometimes thought to have "pale green skin, green teeth, very long green locks of hair, long green fingers with long nails, and . . . a pointed chin with very big eyes." Pynchon is remarkably concise about all this; *his* source for the details is unknown.

V148.4, B172.35–36, P150.26   Mr Tyrone Guthrie's accustomed murk Guthrie (1900–1971) was director of the Old Vic Theatre in London from 1936 to 1948 and renowned for his dark, chiaroscuro stage productions of *Richard III* and *Hamlet*.

V148.37–38, B173.36, P151.18   Fragments of vessels broken at the Creation   In Kabbalistic myth, the "vessels" or bodies of physical being were thought to have received the divine light at the moment of creation. They were meant eternally to contain it, as instruments of divine being. Instead they shattered under its impact. This moment, "the breaking of the vessels," is the decisive crisis of all divine and created existence, when temporality supplants eternity, and alienation becomes the lot of being in general. As Gershom Scholem (*On the Kabbalah* 112–13) explains: "Nothing remains in its proper place. Everything is somewhere else. But a being that is not in its proper place is in exile[,] . . . in need of being led back and redeemed. The breaking of the vessels continues into all the further stages of emanation and Creation; everything is in some way broken, everything has a flaw, everything is unfinished." On earth, the most abysmal of those shattered, lightless vessels are the Qlippoth, the "shells of the dead" that appear elsewhere in *GR* (see, e.g., V176.14–15n).

V149.7, B174.5, P151.28   the faille gown   Faille is a rubbed woven cotton or silk.

V150.6, B175.11–12, P152.27   Abdullas and Woodbines   Two medium-priced British cigarette brands, short and unfiltered, regularly advertised in the *Times* of London.

V150.13, B175.20–21, P152.34–35   a strange mac of most unstable plastic   A raincoat, or "mackintosh." Anticipates the suit of Imipolex G worn by Gottfried for the launch of Rocket 00000 and perhaps also the "Postwar Polyvinyl Chloride Raincoat" at V615.10.

V150.16–23, B175.24–33, P152.37–153.4   Nora-so-heartless . . . the progress through his hands   Ronald Cherrycoke's exploration of Nora's clothes and accoutrements calls to mind Graves's description of the White Goddess (72). Nora's clothes, the objects on her person, the palms and "Central Asian rugs," as well as the "rising snarls of incense" (V149.4–5), all tally with the description Graves provides from Apuleius. In part 2, Slothrop's erotic encounters with Katje Borgesius and her "Other Order of Being" (V222.17) are reminiscent of the moment here. In part 3, his encounters with Margherita Erdmann are another instance, and Frau Erdmann even thinks of herself as an avatar of the White Goddess—the Shekinah of Kabbalistic myth. Ronald is, incidentally, the descendant of the Reverend Wicks Cherrycoke in *Mason & Dixon*.

V151.23, B176.40–41, P154.5   the fussy Norden device   In the twenties, American engineer Carl L. Norden developed the bombsight that bore his name. Beginning in 1943, the United States put it to use in all B-17 and B-24 bombers. The sight was linked to an autopilot. All one had to do was aim the aircraft over its target and the Norden device made all required steering corrections. It even dropped the bombs, and Norden used to claim that with it he could put "a bomb in a pickle barrel" from twenty-five thousand feet. But the device was also very delicate. Rough weather and antiaircraft fire too easily caused malfunctions.

V151.29–30, B177.5–6, P154.12–13   his rainbowed Valkyrie over Peenemünde   In Norse mythology (for example in the *Verse Edda*) the Valkyries serve as Odin's handmaidens. Hovering over battlefields, they wait to conduct the souls of slain warriors up to Valhalla. Valkyries were sometimes depicted on horseback, and they always made their way back to Valhalla by way of the rainbow bridge called Bifröst. Behind that figural sense of airman Blowitt's vision, there is also the historical fact that in 1942 the German rocket engineers working at Peenemünde recorded the first successful launches of the V-2 rocket. The contrails from these test rockets were reported by pilots and provided British intelligence with the first piece of evidence that the Nazis had a rocket program.

V151.31, B177.7, P154.14   his Typhoon's wings   The Typhoon was a single-seat fighter aircraft produced in Britain from 1941 until the war's end.

V151.39, B177.17–18, P154.23   a skyful of MEs   The German Messerschmitt aircraft works produced over thirty-five thousand fighter planes during the war; its ME-109 was the most abundant model.

V152.1–2, B177.21–22, P154.26 problems with . . . Judgment, in the Tarot sense The picture in Ouspensky's *Symbolism of the Tarot* is telling. There, card twenty, entitled Judgment, appears as an angel whose red wings are unfolding from a white cloud, with "an ice plain" below her (*Symbolism* 31). The image is suggestive of Basher St. Blaise's angelic visitation over Lübeck. Waite's interpretation (*Pictorial Key* 80–81) of the card is also helpful. He sees it as an image of the Last Judgment and as a messenger of the Empress, card three of the Major Arcana. The Empress signifies "desire and the wings thereof, as the woman clothed with the sun. She is above all things universal fecundity and the outer sense of the word." The Empress also represents an "entrance into the beyond . . . which is communicated to the elect." The Empress is very much the White Goddess in her materialistic, fecund aspect; Judgment is her "messenger" in a millennial, apocalyptic sense. It could be a call for spiritual awakening, renewal. Such are the "problems" our narrator seems to have in mind.

V152.6, B177.27, P154.31 the Weimar decadence That is, Germany in the twenties. The Weimar Republic lasted from 1919 until 1933, when Hitler took power.

V152.8, B177.29–30, P154.33 in Neukölln In Berlin's Innere Stadt, or central city, the Neukölln am Wasser is a street running parallel to the south side of the Spree River.

V152.11–12, B177.34–35, P154.37 More than any mere "Kreis" . . . full mandalas During these séances Eventyr experiences more than a mere "circle," symbolizing physical dismemberment, that is said to appear in the air during them. Instead whole mandalas appear before his eyes, symbolizing a recuperated totality of being.

V152.16, B177.40, P154.41 "Taurus" In astrology, Taurus is the Bull, second house of the astrological year; the sun is in the house from April 20 to May 20. Hence also "Minotaur," the Bull of Taurus.

V152.17, B177.41, P155.1 "Hieropons" A fictional drug; in the spirit of Holopon and Nealpon (V345.8), Pynchon has created this one from the Greek root "*hieros*," that which is "holy," "of the gods," or "supernatural."

V152.19, B178.1, P155.4 Wimpe the IG-man In the next episode we learn more about this fictional agent, or *Verbindungsmann*, for the German chemical cartel IG Farben (V166.18n).

V152.21, B178.3–4, P155.6 Lieutenant Weissmann, recently back from South Africa Though prefigured in earlier references as "Blicero" (see V30.12n and V94.21–22n), Lieutenant (and, by 1944, Captain) Weissman ("white-man"; hence Blicero, death-as-bleacher) gets his first formal mention as such here. His 1922 service in the German colony of South-

West Africa is the subject of "Mondaugen's Story," chapter 9 of Pynchon's *V.*

V152.24, B178.7, P155.9   high-albedo stockings   The Latin *"albedo"* means "whiteness." In technical usage, albedo is the percentage of radiation thrown back by any surface, such as the moon or a woman's silkstockinged calves.

V152.34, B178.17–18, P155.18   good fill-light throw a yellow gel   In photographic use "fill light" is radiation that is directed on a subject in order to eliminate any shadows cast by one's main light source. A yellow gel is used to filter out shadowy blue from the opposite side of the color spectrum. On the yellow/blue symbolism see also V101.19–20n.

V152.39–40, B178.23–24, P155.22–23   mba rara m'eroto ondyoze . . . mbe mu munine m'oruroto ayo u n'omuinyo   The first phrase was taken directly out of Brincker's grammar of the Herero language (168), except that Pynchon has chosen to regularize Brincker's transliteration of the Herero to make it consistent with Kolbe, his English source on the language. Brincker gives the first phrase as "mba rara me roto ondjoze" and translates it "Ich habe ein Alptraum vertraumt" (I have dreamed a nightmare). Brincker uses the phrase as an instance of the word *"ondjoze,"* meaning "nightmare" (*"Alptraum"* or *"Alpdrücken"* in German). The second phrase is also an example of the use of the word, this time out of Kolbe: he translates it as "I saw him in my dream as if he were alive" (36). Fowler (*A Reader's Guide to "Gravity's Rainbow"*) doesn't identify these translations, but he does make an important secondary observation: the Herero lexicon involves an elaborate pattern of meanings organized around motions that are animate (like a spider's) and inanimate (like the wind) and around things in a state of rest (a stone). For instance, *ondjoze* ("nightmare" or "phantom") stems from the motion of a spider, and this spins us into the "giant web" and the "twisting of yarns or cordage" in Pynchon's following lines.

V153.6, B178.33, P155.30   the veld   An Afrikaans term for open grassland in South-West Africa.

V153.11, B178.39, P155.36   the S.P.R.   The London-based Society for Psychical Research (V89.36n).

V153.12, B178.40, P155.36   Altrincham   A suburb of Manchester, England, known for its villas built by industrial magnates.

V153.15, B179.1, P155.39   chi-square fittings that refuse to jibe   See V40.18n.

V153.40, B179.31, P156.23   the K.P.D.   The *Kommunistische Partei Deutschlands*, or German Communist Party that Hitler outlawed in 1934.

V154.7, B179.42, P156.31   the rocket facility at Reinickendorf   Located five miles northwest of Berlin's Innere Stadt, Reinickendorf was a major industrial center in the thirties and home to the *Raketenflugplatz* (rocket launching site) built for the first testing of rockets. In 1932 the increasing involvement of Germany's Army Weapons Department in rocket development brought about a move, first from Reinickendorf to a military proving ground at Kummersdorf, seventeen miles southeast of Berlin (Dornberger, *V-2* 20–23), and then, in 1937, to the site on the island of Peenemünde, on the North Sea.

EPISODE 19

A brilliant analepsis to pre-Hitler Berlin, circa 1929–30. The episode centers on Franz and Leni Pökler, especially her dissatisfaction with his idealistic devotion to Western science, depicted here as a dynastic succession. Pynchon's presentation of German geography (from Baedeker), economics (from Sasuly), cinema (from Kracauer), and rocketry (from Dornberger) is also closely interwoven with references to occult and astrological lore. These aspects of German life taken together reveal the historical background to the collective Germanic death wish, a Piscean striving for the Other Side.

V154.13–14, B180.8, P156.37–157.1   second Reich   Germany's second empire or Reich lasted from 1871 until 1919, from the accession of Bismarck until the fall of Kaiser Wilhelm.

V154.19, B180.14–15, P157.6   Die Faust Hoch   "The Raised Fist," though close to the commonly used imperative expression, "hoch die Faust!" (Raise the Fist!). The gesture was historically common among international Communists and leftist radicals; hence its adoption among American sixties-era radicals and dissident blacks. The phrase also riffs on "Die Fahne Hoch" (Raise the Flag), the tune known in Nazi Germany as the "Horst Wessel Song" (V443.2n).

V154.24–25, B180.22, P157.12   a woman born under the Crab, a mother   Leni was born under the astrological influence of Cancer (the Crab [June 21–July 22]). Like her husband, Franz, who is a Pisces (V154.35), Leni is also a "water person." And it is a desire for all-inclusiveness symbolized in the water sign that stands behind her uncertainty over the "nasty earth-sign belligerence" (V154.30) of her lover, Peter Sachsa, for earth-sign persons are supposed to be known as "the most critical or exacting" of the four types (Jones, *Astrology* 58). Among the water signs, Cancer differs from Pisces in being practically and not abstractly minded. Cancers are supposed to have a strong sense of possession, and this is why Leni's deserting Franz with just "one valise" seems out of character. Cancer is also a very maternal sign—on the body, it rules the breast—so it underscores Leni's concerns for her daughter.

V154.35–36, B180.35, P157.22   her Piscean husband . . . death-wish,

rocket mysticism   A winter sign (February 19–March 20), Pisces or the Fishes, twelfth and last house of the astrological year, signifies death and endings. Pisces individuals supposedly yearn for the dissolution of self and to move toward wholeness in the abstract. Jones notes a special predilection for mysticism among Pisces types.

V155.3–4, B181.2–3, P157.26–27   another Ufa masterpiece . . . token Jewess   In this foursome (including Leni) seemingly out of an Ufa studio film (see V98.24n), Rudi resembles one of the *Studenti* in act 2 of Giacomo Puccini's 1895 opera *La Bohème*, Vanya's the "token Slav," and Rebecca the "token Jewess."

V155.5–6, B181.4–5, P157.28–29   not even in the Kinos, no German *October*   The German cinema houses are called *Kinos*. Kracauer (172–75) reports that in the twenties German production companies, and Ufa in particular, kept steadfastly away from depictions of Bolsheviks or leftist revolutionaries of any kind. This is why German cinema would not produce anything like *October*, the 1927 film by Russian director Sergei Eisenstein, made especially to commemorate the tenth anniversary of the Russian Revolution and subtitled "Ten Days that Shook the World" in honor of John Reed's book.

V155.7–8, B181.7, P157.31   Rosa Luxemburg   Writer, activist, and Marxist revolutionary Rosa Luxemburg (1871–1919) was a cofounder of the German Communist Party or KPD and deeply opposed to Socialist nationalism. Disparagingly known as "Red Rosa," she was jailed for three years during World War I, released, and rearrested for her leadership during the Berlin uprisings of January 1919. Then on January 15 she and KPD founder Karl Liebknecht (V621.40n) were taken to Berlin's Eden Hotel, clubbed nearly to death, then shot in the head. Luxemburg's body was thrown into an icy canal from the Lichtenstein Bridge and not recovered until April 1919.

V155.12, B181.12, P157.35   AN ARMY OF LOVERS CAN BE BEATEN   This slogan painted on the wall reverses an old idea from Plato's *Symposium*, in which Phaedrus argues that an army of (homosexual) lovers *cannot* be beaten. As he puts it: "If only there were a way to start a city or an army made up of lovers and the boys they love! Theirs would be the best possible system of society, for they would hold back from all that is shameful, and seek honor in each other's eyes. Even a few of them, in battle side by side, would conquer the world, I'd say."

V155.22–23, B181.26–27, P158.6   "approaches . . . to that Absolute Comfort"   As with other approaches to Absolute Zeros, to various "Holy Centers" in *GR*, this one is also depicted as unobtainable. Still more, in this passage the "trope of the unavailable insight," a promised or prophecied revelation that does not happen (Hite, *Ideas of Order* 26), is referred to as a mass cultural tool, a means of socially conditioning the *Volk*.

V156.18, B182. 27, P159.1   the Judenschnautze   Pynchon means "die Schnauze," the German for the "mouth" or "jaw," hence a "Jewish-mouth." The narration is focalizing through Leni here; that's why in her anti-Semitic fantasy she next images Rebecca's "flashes of tongue against thick lips." In common usage also during the Nazi period, *Judenschnauze* signified "Jewish-nose."

V156.20, B182.29, P159.3   not just with another woman   The Bantam misprints this as "women." And the point of this line is that Leni is intimate (and identifying) with "a Jewess" in a nation tipping into virulent anti-Semitic fascism.

V156.40–41, B183.12, P159.24   the Mausigstrasse   A fictional Mousey Street.

V157.22, B183.39, P160.6   the gassen   German side streets or alleys.

V157.35, B184.12, P160.19   Old Gymnasium friends   Friends from grammar school.

V158.8–10, B184.29–31, P160.34   the President . . . asking the Bundestag . . . clogged and nasal voice   Paul von Hindenburg, Germany's president between 1925 and 1934, when Hitler became dictator, was known (and satirized) for such a voice. His addressing the Bundestag, or lower house of the parliament, in this way is Leni's fantasy of a bloodless revolution.

V159.9, B185.36, P161.35   Δt approaching zero   In calculus, Δt (delta-t) represents the time interval separating instantaneous values in the range of a function; thus it is a vanishingly slight change of time or interval along the slope of the graphed curve connecting those points. When "approaching zero" (i.e., no interval), it—and the graph itself—becomes more precise. Note that Franz and Leni disagree about what happens as delta-t approaches the zero. For Leni, the zero-moment would symbolize unity, continuity. For cause-and-effect man Franz, it signifies the end, annihilation.

V159.19, B186.4, P162.4   *Nibelungen*   Franz Pökler dozed off during the second part of Fritz Lang's 1924 silent epic. Entitled *Kriemhild's Revenge*, it depicts the marriage of Attila to Kriemhild (whose first husband, Siegfried, has been killed). She encourages the Hun massacre of the Burgundians, a scene Kracauer (*From Caligari to Hitler* 93–94) describes as "an orgy of destruction" in which Attila, having invited the Burgundians to a feast, then sets the dinner hall ablaze. Lang unfolds it all as a carefully orchestrated sequence of "causes and effects" where "nothing is left to chance. An inherent necessity predetermines the disastrous sequence of love, hatred, jealousy, and thirst for revenge." But note: Pökler had drifted off to sleep; this is why he mistakenly thinks Lang had Attila and his army "sweeping in from the East."

V159.33, B186.22, P162.18   They saw *Die Frau im Mond*   Another Fritz Lang film for Ufa, this one from 1929. Here is Kracauer (151): "Lang imagined a rocket projectile carrying passengers to the moon. The cosmic enterprise was staged with surprising veracity of vision; the plot was pitiable for its emotional shortcomings."

V159.38–39, B186.28–29, P162.24   the Jewish wolf Pflaumbaum   The name means "Plum tree." Throughout this chapter, in her sexual fantasies and references to other Berlin Jews, Leni, despite her leftist radicalism, has mindlessly fallen into the habit of Nazi-style anti-Semitism, here and in the rest of the paragraph blaming paint-factory owner Pflaumbaum for setting fire to the building, thus putting her husband Franz out of work: "All for the insurance" (V160.6–7). These details are later confirmed, with the further suggestion that Lyle Bland also profited from the arson (see V582.3–5n). Therefore when she herself is trundled off to the concentration camps, "her face darkened, Judaized" (V219.41), the novel metes out a kind of poetic justice.

V160.11, B187.2–3, P162.37   the T.H. Munich   That is, the Technische Hochschule, or Technical College, located in Munich.

V160.13, B187.5, P162.39   Max Schlepzig   From the German verb *schleppen* (to drag or tug in a slow, tedious manner).

V160.15, B187.8, P162.41   the tenement's Hinterhöfe   These are "back courts" within the *Höfe* that Baedeker (*Berlin* 53) describes as "huge, many storied buildings, often enclosing three or four interior courts."

V160.26, B187.21, P163.11   Reinickendorf   See V154.7n.

V160.35–36, B187.33–35, P163.20–21   before the World War, he'd gone to Schaffhausen . . . electric tram to the Rhine Falls   Of Franz's memory of a pre–Great War family holiday, Baedeker's *Southern Germany* (65–66) characterizes the Bavarian village of Schaffhausen on the Rhine River as very picturesque, with a "fine view" of the Alps. Its main attraction is the Rhine Falls, two miles to the south. Baedeker describes it as "one of the grandest cascades in Europe . . . reached either by railway or electric tramway." The other details included here—stairway, pavilion, tour boats—are all derived from Baedeker. Note also that the waterfall as a form "of energy, abstractions" (V161.8–9) would be especially significant to the Piscean Franz.

V161.18, B188.20, P164.3–4   the silver thing blew apart   The source is Dornberger's description (*V-2* 23–26) of a rocket engine that exploded on its test stand at Reinickendorf during the late twenties.

V161.22, B188.25–26, P164.7   Kurt Mondaugen   The last name translates to "Moon eyes," but possibly with the sense that he is a "pop eye." On his origin in Pynchon's *V.*, see also V152.21n.

V161.30, B188.35, P164.15   drafty mansarde in the Liebigstrasse in Munich   A mansard is so called for its distinctive roof, with a shallow slope near the peak and steeper near the eaves, designed by the seventeenth-century architect François Mansart. In Munich the Liebigstrasse is located about two-thirds of a mile from the Technische Hochschule; according to Baedeker, a statue of the German chemist Justus von Liebig

(d. 1873) used to stand in a plaza just off the end of Franz's street (*Southern Germany* 289).

V161.34–35, B188.40–41, P164.19–20   true succession, Liebig to . . . Jamf   Laszlo Jamf is fictional; on the origin of his name, see V48.25n. For a discussion of these patriarchs of modern chemistry, see below (V166.1–9n).

V161.36, B189.1, P164.21   Schnellbahnwagen   One of Munich's electric trolleys (Baedeker, *Southern Germany* 237).

V161.39, B189.5, P164.24–25   some kind of radio research project   Mondaugen's South African project involved "sferics," atmospheric radio waves. Pynchon has described his southern sojourn in chapter 9 of *V*, "Mondaugen's Story."

V162.12, B189.22, P164.39–40   kind of Wandervögel idiocy   Plural form of *Wandervogel* (see V99.2n).

V162.13–14, B189.23–24, P164.41   the Society for Space Navigation   The Verein für Raumschiffart, or VfR, organized in the twenties as an amateur group; many early members (like Wernher von Braun) went on to Peenemünde and worked on the V-2. Pynchon's source is Dornberger (20).

V162.15–16, B189.25–26, P165.1–2   in Lübeck . . . kleinburger houses beside the Trave   The city of Lübeck is nearly encircled by the river Trave that loops around it and leaves an opening to the north. Note that Leni's former residence there provides a thematic link to the prior episode, with its reference to the 1942 raid on the city.

V162.20–21, B189.32, P165.6–7   fussy Biedermeier strangulation   The Biedermeier style of furniture was a nineteenth-century German imitation of French Empire style (see V202.17–18n), but plainer and less ostentatious than its predecessor. The emphasis was on *Gemütlichkeit* (comfort, coziness). The name was a portmanteau word, from Biedermann and Bummelmeier, comical characters in a Berlin journal who were meant to satirize bourgeois values.

V162.28, B189.42, P165.15   detestable Bügerlichkeit   The "middle-class reflexes" of V163.14.

V162.38, B190.11, P165.25   "oh, Leni, your wings"   See V97.27n.

V163.17–18, B190.34–36, P166.3–4   Wines . . . the great '20s and '21s, Schloss Vollrads, Zeltinger, Piesporter   Respectively, a Rheingau and two Moselle wines. Lichine (Fifield, ed., *Alexis Lichine's Encyclopedia of Wines and Spirits* 488) hails the wines from the Schloss Vollrad vineyard as "the best of the Rhine wines." The term "Zeltinger" designates any of the Moselles from the Zeltingen district, just as "Piesporter" wines come from the district of Piesport. The years 1920 and 1921 yielded very good vintages.

V163.19–23, B190.37–42, P166.5–9   the late foreign minister . . . Die gottverdammte Judensau   A statesman, industrialist, and writer, Walter

Rathenau was assassinated in 1922. His father, Emil, had purchased European patent rights to Edison's inventions and then amassed a fortune in the electrical power industry. Emil Rathenau founded the AEG (Allgemeine Elektrizitäts-Gesellschaft), and his son Walter inherited it. For thirteen months Walter Rathenau was also the Albert Speer of World War I; he organized a special board to oversee wartime production. Later he criticized the armistice of 1918 because it seemed an unconditional surrender. His 1918 book *Die neue Wirtschaft* (The New Economy) argued for a fully rationalized system of industrial self-government, free of any treaty constraints. The book won him a post as a minister in Karl Joseph Wirth's reconstruction cabinet. However, fanatical nationalistic groups decried Rathenau's negotiations with the Allied governments over reparations. They saw him as selling out to international big capitalism, and Rathenau's Jewish faith only added to their suspicions; on June 24, 1922, a radical group called the Organization Consul assassinated him. Pynchon's likely source for the "anti-Semitic street refrain" is Kessler (*Walter Rathenau* 365), though Pynchon seems to have altered it slightly; it translates like this:

Blast the Jew Rathenau

The god-damned Jewish sow.

Duyfhuizen ("Critiquing the Cartel" 104–5) notes that another source was James Joll's *Three Intellectuals in Politics* (1960), in which he quotes the German rhyme. On Rathenau's contributions to the growth of the German cartel movement, see Sasuly (*IG Farben* 39–41).

V163.31–33, B191.9–12, P166.17–19   IG Farben . . . unlucky subsidiary Spottbilligfilm AG . . . OKW   The ties between IG Farben and the Armed Forces High Command (OKW) are well documented in Sasuly; Spottbilligfilm AG (Dirt-cheap Films, Inc.) is however a purely fictional subsidiary.

V163.37–38, B191.17–18, P166.24   The Götterdämmerung mentality   Oblique reference to the fourth libretto (*Twilight of the Gods*) of Wagner's *The Ring*.

V164.5, B191.24–25, P166.29   Chemical Instrumentality for the Abnormal   One of several fictional avatars of the CIA in *GR*.

V164.10, B191.30–31, P166.35   Generaldirektor Smaragd   In corporate circles the *Generaldirektor* is a managing director; "*Smaragd*" is German for "emerald."

V164.29, B192.10, P167.15   Death as validator   In the Celtic Method of tarot divination, the Validator is the tenth and last card drawn from the deck; it summarizes all previous cards and signifies "what is to come" (Waite, *Pictorial Key* 299–305). Should it be the thirteenth card of the Major Arcana, Death, it would confirm an overall sense of "mystical death . . . and the passage into a state to which ordinary death is neither the path nor gate" (ibid. 123).

V165.21, B193.8, P168.8   the Herrenklub   Literally, the "Men's Club." Sasuly (97) describes it as an elite inner circle of Berlin-based Junkers and financiers who used to meet regularly in the days before Hitler.

V165.26–29, B193.15–18, P168.13   blinking under the bulb . . . a net of information   The light bulb in this scene is, presumably, Byron the Bulb of *GR*, who spent time in Berlin (V647.25).

V165.41, B193.33, P168.28   your path, your Autobahn   A German divided highway. The first, connecting Hamburg, Frankfurt, and Basel, was built in 1929. During the thirties, Hitler poured resources into the idea, aiming both to unify Germany and to provide militarily useful transport routes. By the war's outbreak in 1939 Germany had an effectively networked, limited access high-speed highway system.

V166.1–9, B193.35–194.2, P168.29–37   "All right. Mauve . . . Herbert Ganister"   Here begins a dense, significant chain of references to the history of organic chemistry, specifically to the dye and pharmaceutical industries that burgeoned from it. Pynchon's main sources appear to be Sasuly (*IG Farben*) and a book Sasuly mentions, *This Chemical Age* by William Haynes. The English chemist Sir William Henry Perkin (1838–1907) was the discoverer of mauve dye, which he synthesized from coal tar in 1856. Prior to that, coal tar had been a waste by-product of the steel industry. But Perkin, working with results formerly obtained by his teacher, August Wilhelm von Hofmann (1818–92), produced the first synthetic dye and revolutionized the dyestuffs industry. Hofmann, in fact, had been "imported" to England from the University of Munich, where he had studied under Justus von Liebig (1803–73), the founding patriarch of organic chemistry. Perkin had been attempting the synthesis of quinine from naphthalene, a coal-tar derivative. The process was messy, smelly, and very sticky; worse still, he failed. Yet in the process he derived aniline purple as a precipitate, called the substance "mauve," registered it as British Patent No. 1984, and gave rise to the "Mauve Decade" of Victorian England, for Queen Victoria wore a mauve dress to an exhibition at the Crystal Palace in 1862, establishing the fashion trend of her reign. Other dye colors quickly followed: tyrian purple, alizarin, and indigo were the most important. Some of them, such as gentian, also became known for their pharmaceutical properties, thus opening up still wider business opportunities. In England the fortunes of Imperial Chemical Industries and, in Germany, the fortunes of IG Farben were raised on these discoveries. Herbert Ganister was one of the first researchers to experiment with such pharmaceutical compounds. His employer, the Bayer Company, soon merged with IG Farben.

V166.10, B194.3, P168.38   "Oneirine"   Another fictional pharmaceutical; its name stems from the Greek *oneiros*, "to dream." In chemical nomenclature, the "-ine" suffix signifies "from the family of."

V166.11, B194.4–5, P168.39   "cyclized benzylisoquinilines"   If the speaker (Rathenau's ghost) means one of the isoquinoline family, here with a benzyl radical attached, then he is talking rubbish, for the isoquinolines are not drugs but heterocyclic molecules left behind from the processing of coal tars and used industrially in coating the bricks of oxygen furnaces and, in some cases, in pharmaceuticals. The *quinolines* themselves have numerous pharmaceutical applications. Or maybe the reference is to quini*d*ines, an alkaloid used as a cardiac depressant? Or perhaps to quini*c*ine, another alkaloid?

V166.16–17, B194.11, P169.4   "von Maltzen . . . the Rapallo Treaty"   In 1922 Baron Ago von Maltzen was head of the Eastern Department of Germany's Foreign Office. Under Rathenau, in April, he negotiated the Rapallo Treaty, normalizing relations with Soviet Russia and establishing the terms of reparations payments agreed to in the Treaty of Versailles that ended World War I. With the treaty came a lifting of trade restrictions between Germany and the Soviet Union, and the Krupp works immediately began shipping steel and steel products—farm equipment, for example—to the Ukraine. Von Maltzen went on to become the German ambassador to the United States.

V166.18, B194.13, P169.5–6   "Wimpe, the V-Mann"   The acronym has nothing to do with the V-2 rockets, which weren't conceived as "revenge weapons" anyway until 1942. In the parlance of the IG Farben cartel, Wimpe is a *Verbindungsmann,* what we might call a "connection" or "go-between" or an "agent." Sasuly (*IG Farben* 105) explains: "These men were generally well-established sales representatives of the IG whose spy work could be carried on under the cloak of business" (see also Dubois, *Generals in Grey Suits* 58). V-men constituted a highly placed network of industrial spies whose connections provided a base of inestimable worth as World War II espionage became more complex. Wimpe reappears in part 3 (V344.11); the name, meaningless in the German, suggests the American slang "wimp"—a weakling.

V166.23–29, B194.19–27, P169.15–17   "coal tars . . . Earth's excrement . . . Passed over"   The mythology is certainly Pynchon's, yet listen to William Haynes (*This Chemical Age* 44) describe attitudes toward coaltar substances in Perkin's time: "Few chemists knew anything at all about coal tar. Certainly nobody suspected that it consisted of a mixture of more than two hundred different, definite substances, six of which would shortly become the material for the manufacture of many thousands of new chemical products. Inky black, evil smelling, oily, it is nasty to handle, and with the apparatus then available it was hard to work with." Thus for decades chemists had literally passed over coal tar; it was a preterite material and seemingly satanic, yet out of it emerged a virtual rainbow of colors.

V167.29–30, B195.35, P170.18   Heinz Rippenstoss   In German, *der Rippenstoss* is a nudge, dig, or kick in the ribs.

EPISODE 20

A Christmas Eve party at "The White Visitation." Slothrop is safe on the Riviera. Here in the cold, white North, Pointsman troubles himself over Slothrop as a "miracle and human child" (V168.3), another satiric inversion of the Christian Nativity story.

V167.36–168.1, B196.4–7, P170.26–28 And the crowds they swarm in Knightsbridge, and . . . Pointsman's all alone Note the ballad meter and rhyme. Crowds swarmed in the Knightsbridge area because shoppers were buying gifts from such exclusive London department stores as Harrod's and Harvey Nicholls.

V168.2, B196.8, P170.29 any Spam-tin dog See V133.3–4n.

V168.10, B196.17–18, P170.37 News from the Riviera In other words, news about Slothrop, who has recently been taken to the south of France.

V168.17–18, B196.27–28, P171.7–8 the Latin *cortex* translates into English as "bark" It does, and the etymological workings of this joke show how to solve the following riddle.

V168.21–22, B196.32–34, P171.11–13 jokes . . . such as the extraordinary "What did the Cockney exclaim to the cowboy from San Antonio?" The *Oxford English Dictionary* records a Cockney exclamation, *Cor!*, as a corrupt form of *God!*, citing an example from J. B. Priestly's *Angel Pavement* (1931): "Cor! You're in the wrong part of the theatre, boy." So the simplest answer to this riddle (and something of a groaner), is that the Cockney would exclaim: "Cor! Tex." Another solution: take as a model the etymological play of the *cortex*/bark/dogs/trees example above. The word "cockney" derives from the Middle English *"cokeney,"* or "cock's egg," archaic slang for a male homosexual. We recall Crutchfield, the "White Cocksman of the *terre mauvais*" (V69.1–2) in Slothrop's sodium amytal session. Just as the "White Cocksman" has his "little pards," so would the "cowboy from San Antonio" have his "Cockney," who might exclaim "I'll be your Rose of San Antone," echoing the famous song (see V559.36–37n for the lyrics). This is underscored when we recall the anal-erotic significance of the "rose" for Weissmann and *his* "Cockney," Gottfried, at V104.7.

V168.24–25, B196.35–36, P171.14–15 closet full of belladonna . . . thistle tubes Belladonna is the poisonous plant *Atropa*, also called "deadly nightshade." Its roots and leaves yield the drug atropine, used as an anesthetic (and to dilate the eyes). A "thistle tube" is a glass funnel with a flared, conical top, a large bulb below it, and then a spigot designed into the tube itself that is used to separate immiscible liquids. With the belladonna and the background music on the gramophone, McCarron ("A Pynchon 'Waste Land' Scene in *Gravity's Rainbow*") finds allusions to the Madame Sosostris *mise en scene* in T. S. Eliot's *The Waste Land*.

V168.29, B196.41, P171.19   "gam"   Thirties slang for a woman's leg, corrupted from the French *"jambe."*

V168.41–169.1, B197.14–16, P171.31–33   amphetamine sulphate, 5 mg q 6 h, last night amobarbital sodium 0.2 Gm. at bedtime   In plain English, Pointsman has been medicating himself with stimulants and depressants. He took five milligrams of amphetamine sulfate, a powerful stimulant, every six hours during the day; before bed at night he took a fifth of a gram of amobarbital, a depressant, to encourage sleep. Incidentally, "amobarbital sodium" is another name for sodium amytal, the drug that induces Slothrop's hallucinations in episode 10. Pointsman takes the drug in capsule form, which contains the least powerful dosage; according to the pharmacological handbooks his two-tenths of a gram would be appropriate to relieve anxiety and relax muscles.

V169.7–8, B197.23–24, P171.39   some piece by Ernesto Lecuona, "Siboney" perhaps   Lecuona was a composer and pianist, best known for his *Andalucia*, a suite that was pillaged for music to compose a number of popular forties songs. "Siboney" was a hit for him in 1929, when Grace Moore sang it in the film *When You're in Love*. It appears again in the music for a 1941 film, *Get Hep to Love*.

V169.22, B197.41–42, P172.13   this Pavlovian's Progress   We've had a Hogarth-like "Slothrop's Progress" (V25.6–7n); here we have its counterpart.

V169.31–33, B198.11–13, P172.23   all the way to Stoke Poges . . . from Luton Hoo, Bedfordshire   This is pure whimsy. The airfields were located to the west of London, and Stoke Poges seven miles further west of the fields. (It was from the churchyard of Stoke Poges that Thomas Grey wrote his famous elegy.) The village of Luton, in Bedfordshire (due north of London) would be about fifty miles distant from Gwenhidwy's singing.

V169.34, B198.14–15, P172.24   singing "Diadem"   The former Wesleyan turned independent British pastor Edward Perronet (1726–92) first published the verses (in 1780), and hymn composer James Ellor (1819–99) set them to music in 1838, as "Diadem"—often called "The National Anthem of Christendom":

> All hail! the power of Jesus' name,
> Let angels prostrate fall;
> Bring forth the royal diadem,
> And crown Him king of all.
>
> Crown him, ye martyrs of our God,
> Who from His altar call;
> Extol the stem of Jesse's rod,
> And crown Him lord of all.

It continues in this manner. The hymn has been translated into numerous languages and remains one of the ten most reprinted.

V169.36–37, B198.17–19, P172.26–27   beef tea, grenadine . . . lady's slipper   Gwenhidwy's mixture would gag an ox. Beef tea is brewed from the prolonged simmering of lean beef parts. Grenadine is thick sweet syrup prepared from red currants or pomegranates. "Blue scullcap" (in the Viking and the Bantam) is a misprint; it should be "skullcap," a plant with helmet-shaped flowers prescribed as a remedy for hydrophobia. Valerian root, the source for valerian (a liquid used in flavorings, perfumes, and pharmaceuticals), is known for its mildly sedative qualities. Motherwort gets its name from the fact that this purple-flowered weed was once used to ease uterine discomforts. Finally, the lady's slipper is an orchidaceous plant whose balsamic extracts were once widely used in cough syrups and ointments.

V169.39–40, B198.21–23, P172.31–32   the Welshman in *Henry V* who ran around forcing people to eat his Leek   This is Fluellen, who wears a leek on St. David's Day (March 1) in honor of the Welsh patron saint. A Welsh nationalist, Fluellen takes offense when the English soldier Pistol disparages the custom. So he forces Pistol (pronounced "pizzle") to "eat, look you, this leek; because, look you, you do not love it, nor your affections and your appetites and your digestions doo's not agree with it, I would desire you to eat it" (5.1.25–28). This sexual punning becomes more blatant when Fluellen commands Pistol to eat, "Or I have another leek in my pocket, which you shall eat" (65–66). In staging the only invasion of Europe that English forces would try, before the Normandy invasion of June 6, 1944, *Henry V* resonated powerfully with early-1940s audiences. This is why Laurence Olivier played the role of King Henry V on the London stage in 1942, and why his acclaim for that performance led to his both directing and starring in the late-1944 film that would win him a 1946 Oscar award. In a 1946 review of the film for *Time* magazine, James Agee concisely states its dominant themes: "an intensely masculine, sanguine drama of kinghood and war."

V170.4–5, B198.28–30, P172.37–38   Ashkenazic Jews . . . never heard in Harley Street   The Ashkenazic or Central European Jews occupied London's East End, so their accents would not be heard among the immensely successful doctors whose offices are on London's Harley Street (see V88.11n).

V170.10, B198.36, P173.2   some BMRs   Acronym for a patient's basal metabolism rate, a measure of the amount of energy required to maintain vital functions in a state of rest.

V170.13, B198.40, P173.5   Vincentesque invaders   That is, germs carrying the trench-mouth infection. A severe gingivitis presenting symptoms of foul odor, pain, and pallid coloring around the inflicted gums, it was named for French pathologist Jean Hyacinthe Vincent (1862–1950), who diagnosed it among trench-bound soldiers of the Great War.

V170.24–25, B199.11–12, P173.17   the Welsh once upon a time were Jew*ish* too   See Robert Graves's *The White Goddess* (19): "The Cymry, who we think of as the real Welsh, and from whom the proud court-bards were recruited, were a tribal aristocracy of Brythonic origin holding down a serf-class. . . . [T]hey had invaded Wales from the north of England in the fifth century A.D." The Cymry held fast to the belief that they were descended from Japhet and had wandered north from Israel to Britain.

V171.7, B199.40–41, P173.40   humming "Aberystwyth"   One of a host of hymns by Charles Wesley (1707–88), first published in 1740; Welsh composer Joseph Parry (1841–1903) wrote a score for it, "Aberystwyth," in 1881.

Jesus, Lover of my Soul,
Let me to Thy bosom fly;
While the nearer waters roll,
While the tempest still is high.

Hide me, O my Savior hide,
Till the storm of life be past;
Safe into the haven guide,
O receive my Soul at last.

Other refuge have I none,
Hangs my helpless Soul on Thee;
Leave ah!, leave me not alone,
Still support and comfort me!

All my trust in Thee is stayed;
All my help from Thee I bring;
Cover my defenseless head
With the shadow of Thy wing.

Aberystwyth is, in addition, a principal Welsh city and home of the University College of Wales, site of the activities mentioned below.

V171.37, B200.36, P174.30–31   Death's white Gymanfa Ganu   A Welsh festival organized around the singing of hymns, with hundreds of (here, white-robed) singers taking different parts, held annually at Aberystwyth, Wales, on St. David's Day, March 1.

V173.29, B202.38, P176.24   several enormous water bugs   The British would likely call them cockroaches. The name "water bug" is American and common mostly among Manhattanites. The cockroach population of New York City exploded in the nineteenth century when the Croton Aqueduct was completed, so Manhattanites often called the little vermin Croton bugs or water bugs, as Pynchon (a sometime Manhattanite) would have heard.

EPISODE 21

Part 1 of *GR* concludes on Boxing Day, December 26, 1944. The day when the British exchange gifts in celebration of Christmas, Boxing Day is in particular a day of rest for England's servant classes. The setting here is the London flat of Jessica's sister. The German *Märchen* of *Hansel and Gretel* reappears in this episode, once more in connection with the V-2 rocket. The astrological sign of Pisces, the Fishes, broods over the day.

V174.11, B203.24, P177.7 Penelope sits The Bantam misprints this as "Penelope sit."

V174.19, B203.34, P177.15 a golliwog Now regarded as an infamous racist caricature, the golliwog was a doll with jet black skin, large white eyes, clownishly large lips, and nappy hair—usually the doll was male and dressed up in a servant's suit. The "Golliwogg" (as initially spelled) was the brainchild of writer Florence Kate Upton (1873–1922), who re-membered playing with a "Negro minstrel doll" as a little girl in Flush-ing, New York. For *The Adventures of Two Dutch Dolls* (London, 1895), Florence Upton drew the illustrations and her mother Bertha (an English immigrant) wrote the verse narrative. Two white dolls, Peg and Sarah Jane, loose in a toyshop, encounter "a horrid sight, the blackest gnome." This Golliwogg rather became the star of the Uptons' twelve subse-quent books. Golliwog dolls were produced by English and German manufacturers beginning in 1908 and then in 1909 a trademarked "Golly" image appeared on jar labels and in advertisements by the James Robertson and Sons company, English manufacturer of jams and jellies (see MacGregor, "The Golliwog").

V174.21–22, B203.37–38, P177.18 The pantomime ... was *Hansel and Gretel.* Pantomimes are a part of British tradition on Boxing Day. For the Christmas of 1944, various groups were presenting shows for chil-dren, but the December 23 *Times* of London does not list *Hansel and Gretel* among them.

V176.14–15, B205.30, P179.9 the Qlippoth, Shells of the Dead See also V148.37–38n. The Kabbalists held that the godhead, initially whole and androgynous, was at Adam's fall sundered not only into masculine and feminine aspects but also into a spray of "sparks" that mingle with ma-terial being, penetrating it and redeeming materiality from an otherwise hollow duration. The "shells" or Qlippoth are these hollow containers; they may assume demonic attributes, and it was thought that only a messiah could banish the Qlippoth and restore being to its whole state.

Meanwhile, they are emissaries from the world of the dead who stalk the familiar world.

V176.38–39, B206.18, P179.35　Quisling molecules have shifted　A political personification of molecular events. Vidkun Quisling (1887–1945) was head of the Norwegian government from 1940 to 1945 and a Nazi puppet throughout that time. Thus: traitorous, collaborationist molecules.

V177.7, B206.30, P180.4　mindless hours of the day　Pynchon's original title for *GR* was "Mindless Pleasures," and these phrases (indeed these paragraphs closing the novel's first part) in which "second-class trivia" bloom with significance amidst "love, dreams, the spirit"—all qualities that "work and government" would submit to rationalization and control—point to its thematics.

V177.11, B206.34–35, P180.7–8　the rationalized power-ritual that will be the coming peace　A further reference to Weber's theory of the "rationalization [or routinization] of charisma" (see V81.8–9).

V177.28–29, B207.13–15, P180.25–26　Hark, the herald angels sing / Mrs. Simpson's pinched our King　The reference is to the abdication of the Prince of Wales, Edward VIII (king for eleven months, from January to December 1936), so that he could marry American divorcée Bessie Wallis Warfield Simpson. Edward Mendelson ("Gravity's Encyclopedia" 187) first pointed out the source of these lines: "This fractured carol is used by Iona and Peter Opie, near the opening of their classic book *The Lore and Language of Schoolchildren*, to illustrate the possibility of communication in a manner 'little short of miraculous.' The children's version of the carol, which could not have been broadcast or printed or repeated in music halls, managed to spread across all of England in the course of a few weeks, during school term, when there could have been little travelling to spread its transmission."

Part 2 Un Perm'
au Casino
Hermann
Goering

PART 2, whose French title means "A Furlough at the Hermann Goering Casino," opens around Christmas 1944 in Monaco. It ends five months later with Tyrone Slothrop departing from Nice for "the Zone" of occupied Europe and, back in England, with Pointsman and Company visiting Dover for Whitsunday, May 20, 1945. Thus part 2 of *GR* is bounded symbolically and ironically by the birth of a savior and the proof of his resurrected glory, two key moments on the Christian liturgical calendar. The dominant astrological sign of part 2 is Aries, the Ram, a fire sign and an omen of spring but more especially a sign of strong personal identity. The irony here is that Slothrop *loses* his identity in episode 2, when Katje Borgesius literally makes "one American lieutenant disappear" (V198.13) under a red damask tablecloth, a ruse she engages in so that Slothrop's papers and clothing can be stolen. This leaves him without official identity papers until episode 7, when he assumes the role of "ace reporter" Ian Scuffling (V256.35–36), the second of his eight avatars. In this part of the novel, Pynchon's principal sources treat the technology of the V-2 rocket, as well as the political background of its development in Germany and its detection in England. Pavlovian physiology continues to lend detail. Part 2 has eight episodes, a key number throughout the narrative. Its epigraph derives from a *New York Times* feature of September 21, 1969, entitled "How Fay Met Kong; or, The Scream That Shook the World" (sec. 2, 17). Fay Wray's story opens like this:

"You will have the tallest, darkest leading man in Hollywood." Those were the first words I heard about *King Kong*. Although I knew the producer, Merian C. Cooper, was something of a practical joker, my thoughts rushed hopefully to the image of Clark Gable. Cooper, pacing up and down in his office, outlined the story to me . . . about an expedition to some remote island where a discovery of gigantic proportions would be made. My heart raced along, waiting for the revelation. I enjoyed his mysterious tone, the gleeful look in his eyes that seemed to say "Just wait until you hear who will be playing opposite you."

Cooper paused, picked up some pocketsized sketches, then showed me my tall dark leading man. My heart stopped, then sank. An absolutely enormous gorilla was staring at me.

EPISODE I

This episode, set in the Riviera shortly after Slothrop's arrival there just before Christmas, is one of the most stagy in the narrative: Slothrop's British associates Bloat and Tantivy do a singing number, and Slothrop "saves" Katje Borgesius from Octopus Grigori, whose conditioning was planned with just this moment in view. Slothrop quickly suspects the whole venture but willingly plays along, lured as he is (or as is his magical penis?) by Katje's expert sexual wiles. Setting these contrived events at the (fictional) casino, named for Nazi air force chief Goering, establishes once more the conflict of causality and chance.

V181.1–2, B211.2, P183.2   wood-soled civilian feet   When they defeated Western European nations, occupying Nazi forces quickly grabbed up available supplies of leather and rubber. Civilians were forced to wear wood-soled shoes during the war.

V181.4, B211.5, P183.5   slow faro shuffle   See V69.12n. But the casino at Monte Carlo has never offered this Wild West card game to its patrons.

V181.5–6, B211.7, P183.6   along the esplanade   The beachside promenade in Monte Carlo, according to Baedeker's *South-eastern France*.

V181.10, B211.12–13, P183.11   along the *Cap*   Probably the Cap Martine, a spit of land located three miles eastward, across the bay from Monte Carlo.

V181.16, B211.20, P183.16   electric fire   British term for an electric-coil heater.

V181.25, B211.31, P184.2   Hispano-Suizas   The last word in prewar, luxury auto transportation for the wealthy. After 1914, Hispano-Suizas were assembled in Paris and shipped out of Spain. Until the factory closed in 1938, they were famous among Europe's rich and ruling elite, touted as the most commodious, quiet, high-powered car in the world.

V182.4, B212.10, P184.17   "I'm some kind of a Van Johnson"   With his good looks and gentlemanly ways, Johnson (b. 1916) was a favorite screen lover of the forties. Slothrop might well have in mind such films as *Two Girls and a Sailor* (1944) and *Thirty Seconds over Tokyo* (1944).

V182.6, B212.13, P184.19   green pack of Cravens   A medium-priced cigarette brand: "Craven Plain—This GOOD Cigarette, in GREEN packets," as the *Times* of London ads used to remind folks.

V182.10, B212.17–18, P184.23   "a gang of those section 8s"   See V114.5n.

V182.17, B212.26–27, P184.32   "you all turn into Valentinos"   Screen heartthrob Rudolpho Alfonzo Raffaele Pierre Filibert Guglielmi di Valentina d'Antonguolla changed his name to Rudolph Valentino in 1917. He was on screen from 1918 to 1926, when he died of appendicitis at the age of thirty-one.

V182.23, B212.34, P184.38   FOX-TROT   A dance song in 2/4 or 4/4 time, with alternating slow and fast sections.

V182.35, B213.4, P185.8   a sort of e-rot-ic Clausewitz   Prussian military theorist Carl von Clausewitz (1780–1831) was the author of *Vom Kriege* (*On War*), a three-volume masterpiece of military strategy.

V183.8, B213.16, P185.18   "Moi Tantivy, you know, Tantivy"   The girls might well be confused by an apparent pun: Tantivy's name sounds

like the idiomatic French *"tente ta vie"*—literally, "chance your life,"
but in common usage, "take a chance."

V183.10, B213.19, P185.20 "J'ai deux amis, aussi" I have two friends,
too.

V183.17, B213.27, P185.27 "où, you know, déjeuner" Where, you
know, [is] breakfast?

V183.24, B213.35, P185.34 "sur la plage" On the beach.

V183.29, B213.41, P185.38 "an Impressionist." A Fauve. Full of light
The fauves (literally, wild beasts) were a loose association of Parisian
turn-of-the-century painters, Henry Matisse chief among them. Fauves
extolled the beauty of pure colors, of tints displayed as if in unmediated
light. They were greatly influenced by the late-impressionist works of,
for example, Paul Cézanne. Like the impressionists, the fauves also
strove for the immediate, uninterrupted rendering of experience.

V183.31, B214.2–3, P186.1 Berkshire Saturdays When Slothrop used to
get his hair cut, in the fictional town of Mingeborough, in the Berkshire
Mountains of western Massachusetts.

V184.4, B214.16, P186.13 sporty Bing Crosby pompadour Like the famous American crooner and film star (see V38.19n), Slothrop combs his
hair in a well-oiled upsweep from his forehead.

**V184.14–15, B214.28–29, P186.23–24 Norfolk jacket . . . Savile Row es-
tablishment** Tantivy offers Slothrop a belted woolen jacket, pleated in
the back, that was purchased from one of the fashionable clothiers on
Savile Row in London's Piccadilly area.

V184.33, B215.8, P187.1 César Flebótomo He takes his moniker from
the Etruscan/Latin title for a dictator and the Greek word "phleboto-
meia" (bloodletting).

V184.39, B215.15–16, P187.7 Messerschmitt squadron See V151.39n.

V185.8, B215.28–29, P187.17–18 drab singlet, Wehrmacht issue Under-
shirts from the *Wehrmacht*, or German regular army, were green, as distinct from black ones worn by SS.

V185.12, B215.32–33, P187.22 lingua franca Common language, from
the Italian referring to a mixture of Italian, French, Spanish, Greek, and
Arabic and more generally referring to a language that speakers of different languages use as a common one.

V185.19, B215.42, P187.29 Antibes A cape seventeen miles west of
Monte Carlo.

V185.21, B216.2, P187.30 the chines Ridged intersections formed by
the sides and bottom of a flat- or V-bottom boat.

V185.22, B216.3, P187.31 prewar Comets and Hamptons Sailboats recalled from Slothrop's vacation days back at Cape Cod: the Hampton,
also known as the Hampton One Design, or HOD, was designed in 1934
by Hampton, Virginia, boat builder Vincent "Pappy" Serio. A Pappy
HOD was therefore an original, Serio-built sloop-rigged eighteen-foot

craft, made famous in the thirties by competitors out of the Hampton Yacht Club and now a rarity. Undoubtedly this is the origin of the character name for Pappy Hod, who first appears in Pynchon's *V.*, then in *GR* (see V715.2). The Comet, designed by boat builder C. Lowndes Johnson in 1932 and popularized in that decade as a low-cost craft by Thompson Brothers boat builders of Cortland, New York, now designates a *class* of sixteen-foot sailboats; like the Hampton, it is a sloop-rigged day-sailor with a large mainsail.

V185.25, B216.7, P187.34   a *pédalo*   Pedal-driven paddleboat available for hire by the tourists at Monaco.

V186.3, B216.32, P188.12   black bombazine frock   This is the cocoa-brown silken dress that Katje wore when Osbie Feel filmed her for the conditioning of Octopus Grigori (see V94.3–5n), a dress so dark brown it seems black, or "charcoal-saturated" (V94.11), against the light. Pynchon takes care over Katje's clothing, and the transitions run as follows: from brown-black, here, to a "long Medici gown of sea-green velvet" (V190.21), to a "white pelisse" (V194.27), to a "rainbow striped dirndl skirt of satin" (V208.8), then back into black (V224.23), and finally to "a red gown of heavy silk" (V225.38).

V186.5, B216.34, P188.14   guiches   Little side curls that frame the face, also known as "kiss curls."

V186.40, B217.34, P189.9   its cruel tetanus   Here, sharp muscular contractions brought on by a repeated stimulus (of Katje's "poor hand" in this passage).

V188.14–15, B219.21–22, P190.25–26   Puritan reflex of seeking other orders behind the visible   Referring to the practice of hermeneutical interpretation among Puritan divines, which in their hands resulted in a rigidly orthodox, deterministic mode of textual analysis. In a seventeenth-century treatise on the subject, William Whitaker (qtd. in Bercovitch, *Puritan Origins of the American Self* 111) defined their understanding of their task: "When we proceed from the thing to the thing signified, we bring no new sense, but only bring to light what was before concealed in the sign."

V188.18, B219.26, P190.29   no "found" crab   That is, not a randomly determined sign. In the "ready-mades" or "found objects" of modernist art, one enjoys the intellection of coincidental design in everyday things.

V188.37, B220.7, P191.8   "nessay-pah?"   For *n'est-ce pas?* (is it not?).

EPISODE 2

The episode opens on the evening of Slothrop's encounter with the "devilfish" (V192.19), Grigori, now safely back aboard ship with his keeper. Katje continues to play her role, setting up an assignation with Slothrop at midnight, "her hour" (V205.26), because it is the witching hour. Early next morning she contrives to make him "disappear" (V198.13). They frolic beneath a red tablecloth, and then the next morning, as they still lie beneath it, a cat burglar makes off with his clothes and papers of identity. Slothrop gives chase but his body is betrayed by gravity.

V189.20, B220.37, P191.34 Grischa Diminutive form of the Russian proper name Grigori.

V189.25, B221.4–5, P192.1 the Bukharin conspiracy Nikolai Bukharin (1888–1938) was a Trotskyite, revolutionary theorist, and author of the influential critique *Imperialism and Capitalist Economy* (1920). When the Stalinist regime brought him to trial in 1938, Bukharin "confessed" to a myriad of trumped-up "crimes," most of which involved ideological differences between the Trotskyite and Stalinite factions. He was executed on March 15, 1938, and the confessions tortured out of him sent more to their deaths.

V190.8, B221.28, P192.20 a warm pirozhok A small Russian pie or tart.

V190.23, B222.4, P192.35 "RHIP," sings Tantivy, shuffling off sarcastic buffaloes Servicemen's shortened form of the saying, "Rank Hath Its Privileges." In the film *42nd Street* (1933), actor Dick Powell does a song-and-dance routine called "Shuffle Off to Buffalo."

V190.32, B222.14, P193.3 "It's the Wormwood Scrubs School Tie." See V33.31–32n.

V190.40, B222.24, P193.11 some bird Colonel In the U.S. Army, a full colonel (see V80.20–22).

V191.2, B222.27, P193.14 their sets Their burrows (*OED*).

V191.20, B223.6, P193.32 White lightning Illicit grain alcohol that's not been aged, but here it's been given a touch of the mythic: "mulled with the hammers of Hell" (V191.23) recalls the manner in which Thor cured liquor with his great hammer, named Mullicrusher.

V191.25, B223.11, P193.37 the Uttermost Isle Continuing the allusions to Teutonic mythology, Utgarth, or "Outgard," is the "uttermost" island in the north and home to Loki, mischief-maker among the gods (see also V709.39n).

V192.1, B223.25, P194.11 Durban to Dover A port city in eastern Africa and another in southern England.

V192.2, B223.26, P194.12 four shaky sheets to the gale Extrapolating from the slang metaphor describing one who is drunk as sailing "three sheets to the wind."

V192.4, B223.28, P194.14 steeps of Zermatt Alpine resort of Switzerland.

V192.5, B223.29, P194.15 Plimsoll mark A line or set of markings on the hulls of ships that indicate the amount of water "drawn" when loaded; named for Samuel Plimsoll (1824–98), a member of the British Parliament who legislated the use of such marks.

V192.6, B223.30, P194.16   He's been game to go off on a bat!   American thirties and forties slang for one who's been anxious to begin a drinking binge.

V192.8, B223.32, P194.18   the high-sign   A discreet, usually secret, gesture used to indicate it's time to depart.

V192.15–16, B224.4–6, P194.26–27   humming "You Can Do a Lot of Things at the Sea-side That You Can't Do in Town"   Mark Sheridan (1888–1918) was a popular British music-hall performer of the World War I era, known for songs such as "At the Football Match Last Saturday" and, during the war, "Belgium Put the Kybosh on the Kaiser" as well as the tune Tantivy whistles here. This allusion is however shadowed by the fact that Sheridan walked out of a 1918 show in Glasgow, Scotland, and into Kelvin Grove Park, where he shot himself to death.

V192.38, B224.31, P195.10   "He is with Supreme Headquarters"   SHAEF (see V17.7n).

V193.31–32, B225.26–27, P196.1–2   "beyond Turl Street, past Cornmarket"   In Oxford, England, Turl and Cornmarket streets bracket Jesus College, originally established for Welsh students. Cornmarket is also home to the Union Society, a renowned debating and undergraduates' club that was founded in 1823 and known for training some of the best orators in Parliament.

V194.6–7, B226.1–2, P196.18–19   On to the Himmler-Spielsaal and chemin-de-fer till midnight.   A (fictional) Monte Carlo gaming room named for dreaded Nazi SS chief Heinrich Himmler. According to Baedeker, Monaco's gaming rooms closed promptly at midnight; chemin de fer (railroad) is a variant of baccarat.

V194.9, B226.5, P196.21   rotogravure   Nineteenth-century process for mass producing photographic images by transferring them to plates mounted on a rotary press.

V194.18, B226.17–18, P196.31   red-dogging Choate boys   Choate was the boys' preparatory school of Wallingford, Connecticut (now Choate-Rosemary Hall); indeed, John F. Kennedy attended Choate when Slothrop would have been attending *his school*. In football, "red-dogging" is the (now archaic) term for an all-out defensive rush on the quarterback or backs, known in post–World War II jargon as a "blitz."

V194.24, B226.25, P196.37   malachite nymphs   Slothrop ascending the stairs passes figures carved from a green and black mineral stone, a carbonate of copper, used for decorative and bas-relief statuary. Note, too, at the top, a "single bulb," which could be the ubiquitous Byron the Bulb (whose story begins on V647.16; but see other single-bulb-illuminated scenes at V299.25, V304.4, V427.3, V506.2, V642.1, and V745.21).

V194.26–27, B226.29, P196.40   a white pelisse   From the Latin *"pellis"* (skin), a pelisse is a jacket, usually with a chain across the throat; it is an item of the Napoleonic-era military uniform won by the light cavalry. It is also a lady's housecoat, which is clearly the reference here, one that in the forties was typically made of silk and had close-fitting long sleeves, a high standing collar, and an opening at the center front with no fastenings and that was usually worn over a gown. Note also the color shift, brown-black to white.

V195.13–14, B227.21–22, P197.28–29 maze of taffetas, lawn, and pongee ... passementerie Katje's handlers have carefully selected sheer, expensive fabrics for her wardrobe (depicted here as a "maze," thus figuring Slothrop as Theseus). Taffeta is a thin, woven, glossy fabric; lawn, thinly woven linen; and pongee, a loosely woven, knotted silk. Passementerie is decorative trimming. In any case Slothrop realizes these gowns are props when he picks up the scent from them of "carbon tet," the carbon tetracholoride dry-cleaning fluid.

V195.23, B227.32, P197.38 "got out by way of that Arnhem, then, right?" In fact Pirate Prentice snatched Katje out of Holland by way of Scheveningen, as we know from V97.11–12, but Katje lets Slothrop think she escaped from Arnhem, during the Allied "Operation Market Garden" offensive (September 17–26, 1944), which would have meant a dangerous crossing of the Neder Rijn (Lower Rhine) River at German-occupied Arnhem (see also V104.30–31).

V196.21, B228.30, P198.33 Katje's skin is whiter Her skin, the moonlight over this scene, the way parts of her darken with a "red animal reflection" (V196.29), and the various objects she wears like talismans— these details all suggest that Katje plays the White Goddess, like Nora Dodson-Truck of part 1 (see V150.16–23n).

V197.1, B229.12, P199.14 a plastic shell Recalls an earlier reference to the "shells of the dead," or Qlippoth (V176.14–15n). And it anticipates the black plastic shell of Imipolex G, designed for Gottfried's last ride in Rocket 00000. Note that Katje refuses to be "mounted by a plastic shell" of a man; but in part 3 Greta Erdmann will recall being dressed in the new plastic, Imipolex, and "mounted" by such a shell (see V488.2n).

V198.8–9, B230.28, P200.22 a big red damask tablecloth Yet another prop, and carefully selected. Recall the prevalence of the color red in Slothrop's sodium amytal session of episode 10, part 1. Clearly "They" have provided the tablecloth with such associations in mind. A reference to the red tablecloth, as a magician's prop, also appears later (V377.7).

V198.19, B230.40–41, P200.32 "My little chickadee" This is W. C. Fields's line (as Cuthbert J. Twillie) to Mae West (Flower Belle Lee) in the film *My Little Chickadee* (1940). Miss Lee requires a consort for legal reasons and takes on Twillie, but through a series of hoaxes she frustrates his hope of a consummated marriage. In one scene she leaves a goat behind in her bed and, in the dark, Twillie makes florid declarations of passion to the blanketed animal, as Slothrop describes it here.

V198.33, B231.14–15, P201.5–6   S'd against the S of himself   Excepting the image of S-shaped spokes in a wheel (V4.19), this is the first of *GR's* many "sigmoid" images: another sign of disease and disjunction.

V200.21, B233.16, P202.38   "That blighter"   In British slang the epithet signifies anyone whose presence blights; an egregious person.

V200.28–30, B233.24–26, P203.4–6   *"sauerkraut in the Strand! . . . your name would be Brun*hil*de"*   Running along the north bank of the river Thames, the Strand is a major thoroughfare connecting the West and East Ends of London; here, the phrase alludes to the specter of Nazis having taken over London and then populating it with wives named after the warrior woman of the Valkyrie in the *Nibelungen* saga.

V200.39, B233.39, P203.16   Kilgour or Curtis   London tailors, located in Whitechapel.

V201.15, B234.18, P203.34   "it's Lawrence of Arabia!"   Thomas Edward Lawrence (1888–1935) began his career as an archaeologist after graduating from Oxford, but the onset of war in 1914 found him in the Sinai carrying out reconnaissance for the British War Office under cover of a scientific expedition. He enlisted, became an intelligence officer stationed in Cairo, and, by late 1916, the liaison officer for Turkish insurgents rebelling against their country's German-allied regime. His operations in Turkey won Lawrence the respect of local sheiks. They admired Lawrence's innovative tactical leadership and guerilla strategies that brought the rebels significant victories at Aquba in 1917 and Damascus in 1918. An ardent supporter of Arab independence, Lawrence was disillusioned at war's end with the sheiks' factionalism that arose as victorious allies carved up the Middle East. During the interwar years Lawrence continued to serve sporadically in the armed forces, but the fame that came to him after *Seven Pillars of Wisdom* was first published in 1926 made it difficult for him to remain the ordinary soldier (and airman) he had been before its debut, and he regretted this. Before his untimely death in a May 1936 motorcycle accident, Lawrence worked for the RAF as an aircraft designer.

V201.23–24, B234.29, P204.2–3   Bristly Norfolk jacket   See V184.14–15n.

V201.33, B234.39–40, P204.12   Savile Row uniforms   See V184.14–15n.

V201.35–36, B234.42–43, P204.14–15   flimsies . . . a piece of Whitehall   "Flimsies," as noted at V105.20n, are thin, multicolored papers used for making carbon copies (British slang). So neatly stacked, here, they are a synecdoche for the secretarial routinization of Britain, and specifically Whitehall, home of the War Office, Admiralty, and such.

V202.2, B235.9, P204.22   "Didn't they teach you at Sandhurst to salute?"   Home of the Officer's Candidate Training Unit (or OCTU), Sandhurst is a military college south of London.

V202.17–18, B235.27–28, P204.40   Empire chairs   A style of furniture imposed practically by an edict of Napoleon. The designs were based on the rectilinear forms of classical Greek and Roman architecture: furniture made in this style was massive and sumptuous, with laurel wreaths and torches adorning the design (in metal attached to wood).

V202.30, B235.41, P205.11   What hangs from those hooks?   Given these hooks' appearance in the Himmler-Spielsaal with its "Nazi foolishness," recall that Hitler's regime sometimes executed prisoners by hanging them from meat hooks. In 1943 the execution chamber at Plötzensee Prison just outside Berlin was rigged for this purpose (with eight hooks) and used to execute high-profile political prisoners and alleged spies. Similar arrangements for executing "undesirables" were also reported at Büchenwald.

V202.34–35, B236.4–5, P205.15–16   golden, vaguely rootlike or manlike figure   A mandrake root, a sign of secular crucifixion that will reappear in part 4 when Slothrop "becomes a cross himself, a crossroads" (V625.3–4).

V203.11, B236.22–23, P205.32   the rainbow edges of what is almost on him   This is Slothrop, feeling the anxieties of *Erwartung* (V101.9n). Later, when he tries to explain his worries to Katje, she will remind him of his experience in this room, and she will connect it to one of her dresses, a "rainbow-striped dirndl skirt," sign of a related anxiety (V208.8).

V203.34, B237.8, P206.15   Bwa-deboolong   The Bois de Boulougne, the Paris promenade well known as the turf of prostitutes. Larsson ("A *Companion*'s Companion") points out the allusion to the lyrics of a turn-of-the-century music-hall song by songwriter Fred Gilbert, "The Man Who Broke the Bank at Monte Carlo," which was still popular by 1945 (it was used in Orson Welles's 1942 film *The Magnificent Ambersons*). The lyric's speaker has just returned to Paris, to declare:

As I walk along the Bois de Boulogne
With an independent air,
You can hear the girls declare,
"There goes a millionaire!"
You can hear them sigh, and wish to die,
You can see them wink the other eye,
At the man who broke the bank at Monte Carlo.

Larsson also hears an echo of this song's meter in the "Vulgar Song" at V213.20–30 and in the untitled song at V244.13–16.

V204.1–4, B237.16–20, P206.22   back to 1630 when Governor Winthrop came . . . that *Arbella* and its whole fleet, sailing backward   Aside from the remarkable, extended use of hysteron proteron in this paragraph, with its image of the fleet "sailing backward" to England, the historical allusions are also significant. John Winthrop (1588–1649) was the first governor of the Massachusetts Bay Colony, elected to that post in 1629 before the Puritan fleet set sail from England and reelected seven times thereafter. Winthrop's flagship was the *Arbella*. Thomas Pynchon's ancestor, William, was aboard the *Ambrose*, serving as "rear admiral" of the four-ship fleet. Along with other Puritan leaders, William Pynchon came aboard the *Arbella* once during the journey, about halfway across, when Winthrop invited the other patentees to dine with him. According to Samuel Eliot Morison ("William Pynchon" 73), they were each rowed to the flagship during "a small gale." Pynchon imagines the scene: heaving swells and a spilled pewter kettle and William Slothrop in attendance as "mess cook."

V204.33–35, B238.13–15, P207.13   abbreviated version of *L'Inutil Precauzione . . .* in *The Barber of Seville*   In act 2 of Gioacchino Rossini's opera *The Barber of Seville*, there occurs an opera-within-the-opera entitled "The Vain Precaution." In the frame story, Rosina promises to sing the aria from this work to Doctor Bartolo, her guardian but also—with strong hint of incestuous desire—one of several men who are pressing Rosina for marriage. She sings the aria because the mini-opera concisely parallels her own situation: duty bound to Doctor Bartolo, but in love with the dashing young Count Almaviva (Count "Good-life").

V204.39, B238.19–20, P207.19   a lively Rossini tarantella   Dance music in 6/8 time, perhaps from *The Barber of Seville*.

V205.7–8, B238.31–32, P207.28   *And if you need help, well, I'll help you*   Tantivy's words, from V194.3–4.

V205.13–14, B238.38–39, P207.34–35   messieurs, mesdames, les jeux sont faits   "Ladies and gentlemen, the bets are down." The croupier at a roulette table calls this out and then he spins the wheel. In the film *Casablanca* (1943), for instance, one hears Emil the croupier (Marcel Dalio) calling out these words in dour, nasal tones to the patrons of Rick's Café Americaine.

EPISODE 3

His identity stripped, Slothrop begins his crash course in rocket dynamics. This instruction puts him in contact with the Allies' vast archive of intelligence and captured documents pertaining to the V-2 rocket, contact itself designed (by "White Visitation" experts, among others) to uncover the mechanism of his magical penis. The time of this episode is indistinct, though it clearly ranges over a period of some weeks ending in "midwinter" (V224.25), that is, mid-February. The narration turns the reader's attention to language, its etymology, and how the lexicon of technology is suffused with an older, mythic lexicon. Another analepsis to pre-Hitler Berlin discloses how Peter Sachsa died. At episode's end Katje leaves Slothrop for England but not without first giving him a veiled warning.

V206.5, B239.30, P208.23   "Oink, oink, oink," sez Slothrop   Generations of Slothrops were swineherds (V555.5), and Slothrop himself will become a ceremonial pig (V567.34).

V206.14, B240.3, P208.32   arrow-stable trajectories These involve the use of external fins to stabilize a projectile (Dornberger, *V-2* 122–24).

V206.15–16, B240.4–6, P208.33–34   German circuit schematic whose resistors look like coils, and the coils like resistors See, for instance, the electrical schematics in Kooy and Uytenbogaart (*Ballistics of the Future* 356, 358). They follow the German system of designating an induction coil by means of a sawtooth line, which American technicians would understand as a resistor.

V206.20, B240.10, P209.1   Foreign Office P.I.D. Sir Stephen Dodson-Truck (whose moniker suggests the postwar brand of light truck, the Datsun, the now-abandoned brand name of the Nissan Motor Company Ltd.), works for the Political Information Division of the British Foreign Office.

V206.24–25, B240.16–17, P209.5–6   "Old Norse rune for 'S,' *sôl* . . . German name for it is *sigil*" The source here is Grimm (*Teutonic Mythology* 620), whose etymological research discloses that "the sun was likened to a wheel of fire" represented symbolically by a circle with an axis point at its center: a mandala, in other words. Ancient Goths used this figure or rune to represent the sun; later, "the Norse rune for S was named *sôl* sun," which, according to Grimm, is the Anglo-Saxon and Old High German "*sigil*" or "*sugil*." *GR*'s representation of this breakdown from mandala to sigmoid line as a discontinuity in historical process is not an imposition on Grimm's etymological details. Overall, his work documents the linguistic breakdown pursuant to the shattering of European tribal structures between A.D. 350 and 600.

V206.37, B240.31, P209.18   a Plasticman comic Plasticman, or "Plas," was the creation of writer/artist Jack Cole, who took his own life in 1958. Plasticman, however, still in print decades later, has achieved a kind of immortality for comic-book heroes. Plas made his debut appearance in a January 1941 issue of *Police Comics*. His real name was Eel O'Brien, a petty crook who fell into a vat of acid while burglarizing the Crawford Chemical Works. Eel ran, awoke next day in a monastery, discovered that his entire body had become rubbery and pliable, and thereafter dedicated his life to stopping crime. By spring 1943 Cole had his own book for Plasticman, published by Quality Comics, that ran until 1956; it was taken up in 1966 for ten issues by DC Comics and has been reprinted sporadically since then. It was a truly comical strip. Cole's plots hinged on slapstick humor, fast-paced and intelligent dialogue, and Plas's limitless ability to shape-shift and stretch. In fact, even a brief glimpse at the diction and rhythms of Cole's dialogue will suggest how much, and how often, the narrative voice in *GR* will slide into the rhetorical mode of *Plasticman*. One additional note on color: except for his outrageous white-frame glasses, Plas *always* appears in red.

V207.8, B241.6, P209.31   "Telefunken radio control" According to Dornberger (*V-2* 133–36), the Telefunken Radio Company of Germany worked on a centimetric guidance beam that would have delivered V-2 rockets over a distance of 150 miles and with "a dispersion of less than one thousand yards." If the system had gone operational, which it did not, the rockets would have become devastatingly accurate.

V207.12, B241.11–12, P209.35 **"it suggests *Haverie*"** Sir Stephen's etymological ramblings are accurate. The slang "*abhauen*" translates from the German as something like "Scram!," which is what the V-2 did on takeoff. "*Hauen*," or "smashing someone with a hoe or a club" (V207.14–15), anticipates the analepsis to Peter Sachsa's murder (narrated in this episode, V220.31–39).

V208.8, B242.15, P210.33 **a rainbow-striped dirndl skirt** This is Katje's fourth principal change of clothes before once more donning her brown-black dress. On the rainbow significance of this one, see V225.2n.

V208.20, B242.30, P211.4 **before Arnhem** See V195.23n.

V208.21, B242.32, P210.5–6 **Palmolive and Camay** Slothrop nostalgically remembers western Massachusetts girls, into whose soap-smelling ears he once uttered seductive *carpe diem* phrases. Even those sweet moments are haunted by cartelization, however. Palmolive brand soap was the product of three soap-making giants that merged in 1928: New York–based Colgate, Milwaukee-based Palmolive, and Kansas City–based Peet Company. Colgate-Palmolive-Peet was simply trying to compete with the gigantic Cincinnati-based Procter and Gamble, whose Camay brand was one of the first so-called beauty soaps.

V208.23, B242.34, P211.7 **Moxie-billboard** See V63.5n.

V209.20–21, B243.39–40, P212.8 **"I was in 's Gravenhage"** That is, in The Hague.

V209.25–26, B244.3–4, P212.12 **"the data on our side of the flight profile, the visible or trackable"** This corresponds with an idea presented in the novel's opening episode. That is, any naturally occurring rainbow wants to be a full circle, and if Earth did not intrude it would be (V6.33–35n). So there are two halves of the rainbow arch, just as there are two "sides" of "the flight profile." One side is visible; the other is not, for it is given up to gravity (see also V726.19–20n).

V210.16–17, B245.1, P213.5 **sent away to that Johnson Smith** Then based in Racine, Wisconsin (now in Bradenton, Florida), the Johnson Smith Company distributes one of the most extensive lines of mail-order novelty goods in the United States.

V210.17–18, B245.2–3, P213.6 **from Fu Manchu to Groucho Marx** Fu-Manchu wore a long, wispy-thin mustache. Groucho Marx (1895–1977) wore a grease-paint mustache covering his entire upper lip, like an upside-down canoe.

V210.27, B245.14, P213.16 **"What about Wyatt Earp?"** That is, the legendary lawman of Tombstone, Arizona. Slothrop's idea of Earp (1849–1929) derives from Stuart N. Lake's book, *Wyatt Earp, Frontier Marshall*

(1931), the first biography to use extensive interviews with its subject, as well as interviews with those who recalled him from the Dodge City and Tombstone epoch. This was crucial, because Earp had previously been unwilling to discuss his past. Even more, Lake discovered a trove of documents hidden in Prescott, Arizona, that revealed Earp's questionable business dealings from the period. There had always been speculation that Earp was greedy and involved in graft, and the documents tended to support that view. Lake, however, chose to believe Earp's justifications; thus he presents (5) a "good" Wyatt, a man of "swift and decisive action," a leader "in the vanguard of those hardy, self-reliant pioneers who led the course of empire across the wilderness." This Wyatt met the rough-and-ready frontier on its own terms, willing to make shady deals for the good of all. Later historians, those "revisionists" (V210.30) the narrator refers to, have taken a much less generous view of the man.

V210.31, B245.20, P213.20   a General Wivern   In heraldry, the wivern or wyvern is a two-legged, winged dragon with a barbed tail; it is depicted in the Welsh coat of arms.

V210.34, B245.22, P213.23   "So did John Wilkes Booth's"   Moustaches are still the subject of conversation. Booth (1838–65), Lincoln's assassin, had one whose ends were curved downward by gravity, as the encyclopedia daguerreotypes show.

V211.10–12, B245.41–246.1, P213.40–41   salvaged by the Polish underground . . . genuine SS shit and piss   The source for this detail is Irving (*Mare's Nest* 285). Allied intelligence made an important breakthrough when members of the Polish underground, along with several British scientists, followed the Russians into a V-2 test-firing site near Blizna, Poland, in September of 1944. The Russians had ravaged the site for anything technically significant, but one of the British scientists thought to check the latrines for discarded documents: "Sure enough," Irving writes, "in a pit which had been fouled by Russian militia no less than by German troops, he found a portion of a rocket test sheet." From this scrap, Allied intelligence determined that liquid oxygen and alcohol were the principal fuels for the V-2. The "genuine SS" excrement is Pynchon's flourish.

V211.15, B246.5, P214.3   peroxide and permanganate lines   In the V-2, hydrogen peroxide and sodium permanganate were combined to yield intense heat, which then created superheated steam that drove a turbine that then pumped the rocket's supplies of liquid oxygen and alcohol, thus driving the main engine (see p. 136). It was a chemically simple but mechanically complex system; see Kooy and Uytenbogaart (*Ballistics of the Future* 337–42).

V211.40, B246.33, P214.28   a drinking game, it's called Prince   The drinking game once famous among collegians who variously named it

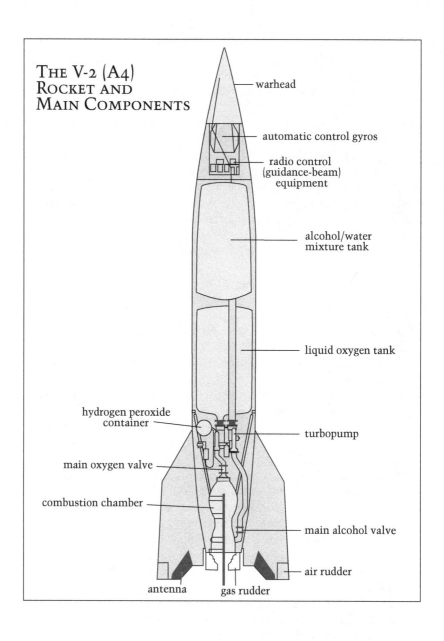

THE V-2 (A4)
ROCKET AND
MAIN COMPONENTS

warhead

automatic control gyros

radio control
(guidance-beam)
equipment

alcohol/water
mixture tank

liquid oxygen tank

hydrogen peroxide
container

turbopump

main oxygen valve

combustion chamber

main alcohol valve

air rudder

antenna   gas rudder

"Prince," "Wales Tails," or "Whales Tales." Of unknown origin, it apparently reached its heyday from the late thirties (after the Prince of Wales, King Edward VIII, renounced the throne to marry Wallis Simpson; see V177.28–29n) through the early to mid-sixties, when it appears to have faded in popularity. Pynchon outlines the very complicated rules for this drinking game, which requires players (usually five, plus the one who names himself Prince, making six) to seat themselves around a circular table and to remember concisely their ever-changing numbered places in relation to others. In calling the number of a seated player, as in this scene, the "Prince" literally accuses that one of stealing his tails (his dress coat); he must emphatically reply "Nay!" (denying the theft); the Prince then responds "Who?" (If not you, then which one of the others?), and the accused offers a number, requiring contestants to count that many spots counterclockwise (including the Prince), who must then respond as the previous accuser did. One objective is to move rapidly through these changes, increasing the chance that players will forget their constantly changing numbered places. As they err, and thus are forced to drink, each new round winnows away the field.

V212.3, B246.38, P214.32   clockwise around the table   Sources claim that play (unlike most card games) moves to the Prince's *right* (counterclockwise), so perhaps there are different versions, or Pynchon's players have made a mistake, or (better) Slothrop's playing it this way *for a reason*. Recall that clockwise is, according to Jung, the "correct" direction, the one involved with conscious process (V137.20n). This coincides with Slothrop's canny use of the "Prince of Wales has lost his tails" game toward a well-reasoned end: he wants to loosen Sir Stephen's tongue, to find out "Their" designs.

V212.18–19, B247.16, P215.8   "comprendez?"   Americanized French, from *Comprenez-vous?* meaning "Understand?"

V212.27, B247.27–28, P215.16   jeroboam of Veuve Clicquot Brut   A jeroboam of champagne holds four quarts; Veuve Clicquot is one of the prestige champagnes, produced in Reims; "Brut," a dry variety.

V212.33, B247.36, P215.22   a Highlander in parade trews   A member of one of the six Highlander regiments wearing his ceremonial tartan plaid trousers.

V212.41, B248.4, P215.30   dates of *degorgement*   The dates when bottles of champagne are opened to decant the deposits. Here, as those dates progress "into the war years," the champagnes become younger, less valuable.

V213.26, B248.36, P216.16   Chateaubriand   A richly seasoned double cut of tenderloin steak.

V213.27, B248.37, P216.17   ten-shilling panatelas   At 1945 exchange rates, cigars costing about a dollar—*very* expensive ones for the time.

V213.35–36, B249.4, P216.23   black Épernay grapes   In the Champagne district of France, Épernay is a town on the Marne River, whose fields produce some of the finest blancs de noirs (white champagnes from black grapes).

V213.36, B249.4–5, P216.24   noble cuvées   The term derives from the French for a vat ("*cuve*"); a *cuvée* is thus a "vatting" or, in plainer terms, a batch.

V214.2, B249.9, P216.28   sweet Taittinger   Because it's not produced in the Champagne district, a bottle from the Taittinger vineyard would be known among discriminating palates only as a "sparkling wine." Still worse, it is sweet. Another sign that vintage quality regresses as this game progresses.

V214.4–5, B249.12–13, P216.31   playing "Lady of Spain"   There are multiple copyrighted versions of this song, all based on a 1931 B-flat composition by Tolchard Evans (with lyrics by Erell Reaves). The accordian or "wheezebox" version was by Stanley J. Damerell and Robert Hargreaves. Reaves's lyrics however remain the same:

> Lady of Spain, I adore you—
> Right from the night I first knew you,
> My heart has been yearning for you;
> What else can my heart do?
>
> Lady of Spain, I'm appealing—
> Why should my lips be concealing,
> All that my eyes are revealing;
> Lady of Spain I adore you.

V214.11, B249.20–21, P216.39   a floating crown-and-anchor game   A favorite game of chance among sailors, who use three dice, the six faces of which will show either a crown, an anchor, or up to four "aces." The aim is to roll combinations of these. In underworld slang, a "floating" game is mobile, so as to elude the law.

V214.35, B250.7–8, P217.23   of course Empire took its way westward   Echoes Bishop Berkeley's famous paean to westward settlement in America, the "fourth act" of a historical drama before the revelation of Christ's millennial kingdom inaugurates the fifth and final act. The last stanza of his poem, "Verses on the Prospect of Planting Arts and Learning in America" (1752), declares:

> Westward the Course of Empire takes its way;
> The first four Acts already Past,
> A fifth shall close the Drama with the Day;
> Time's noblest Offspring is the last.

This was the ancient idea of the *translatio studii*, originally a classical concept about the westward progress of civilizations: Greece to Rome to Europe and then beyond. Berkeley's line supplied the title for American painter Thomas Cole's five-canvas series, "The Course of Empire" (1834–35), and Emanuel Leutze's "Westward the Course of Empire Takes Its Way" (1861), the most famous among other examples.

V214.40–41, B250.14–15, P217.29–30   the Angel that stood over Lübeck See V146.27n.

V215.5, B250.21, P217.35   the night-going rake Lord Death That is, Dominus Blicero.

V215.18, B250.37, P218.7   no milliards of francs A milliard is a thousand million (a billion); a franc is the French monetary unit.

V215.29, B251.7–8, P218.18   "the *News of the World*" London news periodical.

V215.31, B251.10, P218.20   "that kid who-who can *change his color*" Slothrop remembers how Nora Dodson-Truck was "caught" with Gavin Trefoil, whose "autochromatism" was the subject of earlier speculation (V147.13n).

V215.36–37, B251.17–18, P218.25–26   "good chaps at Fitzmaurice House" See V76.32–33n.

V216.3–4, B251.27, P218.33   "even a *touch* now and then" This is Sir Stephen, thinking about the needs of his wife, Nora. On the "miracle touch," see also V119.37n.

V217.14–16, B253.4–6, P220.3–5   Carroll Eventyr . . . and his control Peter Sachsa Recalls the séance of episode 5, part 1 (see V29.31n).

V217.18, B253.8, P220.7   Sammy Hilbert-Spaess The name suggests why he is the "most ubiquitous of double agents." In non-Euclidean geometry, Hilbert space (named for German mathematician David Hilbert, 1862–1943) is an abstract space. In ordinary space any point has three-dimensional coordinates. Any point in Hilbert space, on the other hand, has a theoretically infinite number of coordinates, and any point in Euclidean space can be identified with an infinite-dimensional point in Hilbert space, so that the one is a "subspace" of the other. Sammy reappears in part 3 (V540.28).

V217.20, B253.10, P220.9   scombroid face Referring to the Scombroidei, a suborder of marine fishes that includes the mackerel.

V217.24, B253.16, P220.13   Gallaho Mews The mews of London are its stable alleys. This (fictional) one is the location of the novel's imaginary Twelfth House. Pynchon may well have derived the name from Chief Inspector Gallaho of Scotland Yard, a figure who appears in *The Trail of Fu-Manchu* (see V277.34–38).

V217.26–27, B253.18–19, P220.15–16   They know . . . how to draw pentacles too See V145.20n.

V218.10, B254.5–6, P220.40   "a Zaxa or two"   The source once again is
Jacob Grimm (*Teutonic Mythology* 203–05): a "*zax*," from the Old High
German "*sax*," is a hatchet-like tool used to cut roofing slates. The
point of this wordplay, when we recall Sir Stephen's etymological discourse on "*sigil*" and "*hauen*," is to get at what happened, in 1930, to
Peter Sachsa (his head was smashed in, as if in fulfillment of his own
name). There is more: Grimm mentions that the Saxons were so called
either because they wielded such an ax-like weapon (the *saxum*) or because they worshipped a god by the name of Saxneat, a son of Wodin
who wielded the weapon in battle. This god is Eventyr's "old Zaxa" of
the next line.

**V218.31–32, B254.31–32, P221.20–21   She has swept with her wings an-
other life**   See Franz, to Leni, at V162.38.

V219.8, B255.12, P221.39–40   the Hamburg Flyer   Express train from
Berlin to Hamburg; the source may well be Baedeker's *Berlin.*

V219.9, B255.13, P221.40   industrial towers of the Mark   Short for the
Markisches Museum, a group of tall, plain buildings "dominated by a
massive tower," as Baedeker (*Berlin* 257) notes. In "Old Berlin" the
Mark was located several blocks from a railway station; thus Leni sees
it as a (backward) reflection in the train window.

V219.41, B256.10, P222.31   her face darkened, Judaized   See V159.38; her
empathic identification, her almost *passing* as a Jew, continues.

V220.31, B257.5–6, P223.21–22   Schutzmann Jöche   Peter's killer serves
as a *Schutzmann* or constable; "*Joche*" (no umlaut) is the German plural
for "yoke" (as used with draught oxen).

V221.13, B257.32, P224.3   A rain-witch   Another of the etymological
puns derived from Grimm (*Teutonic Mythology* 1088), who notes that
"in Germany witches were commonly called . . . *wetterhexe, wetterkatze*," that is, "weather witches" or "weather cats." It was believed
that they whimsically brought rain and storm; thus we have Katje, the
wetterkatze often seen looking out on the rain.

V222.2, B258.26–27, P224.33   I'm the Cagney of the French Riviera   In
The Public Enemy (1931), actor James Cagney plays the role of a Prohibition gangster. In one scene he punches a grapefruit into the face of gun
moll Mae Clark, the image Slothrop references here.

V222.32, B259.20, P225.23   "the boundary-layer temperatures"   Kooy
and Uytenbogaart (*Ballistics of the Future* 384–86) run through calculations for increases in the skin, or "boundary-layer," temperatures during
the phases of the V-2's ascent and descent.

V222.37, B259.27–28, P225.28   The bridge music   In cinema, a transitional device comparable to the "segue" in broadcasting (V70.36n). Of
the songs mentioned subsequently, "School Days" is a Will Cobb and
Gus Edwards tune from 1907 (and, given the S-M motif in *GR*, perhaps

its line "readin' and writin' and 'rithmatic/ Taught to the tune of a hick'ry stick" is significant), "Come Josephine" is a 1910 song by Alfred Bryan and Fred Fisher, and "There'll Be a Hot Time" an 1886 song written by Theodore Metz for the McIntyre and Heath Minstrels but a favorite during the 1898 Spanish-American War (both the titles of these last two contain obvious sexual puns).

V223.8–10, B259.41–260.1, P225.40–41   Nusselt heart-transfer coefficients . . . Reynolds numbers   All three editions contain the same error; it should be "heat-transfer." The Nusselt number is a constant used in the calculation of forced convection, when a measure of total heat transfer is required. The Reynolds number, named for physicist Osborne Reynolds (1842–1912), appears in formulas for calculating flow rates through a tube when factors such as velocity, tube diameter, fluid viscosity, and liquid density are known.

V223.13, B260.4, P226.3   jet expansion angles   From Kooy and Uytenbogaart again (*Ballistics of the Future* 310–12), and here referring to the angular expansion of the gas flow on exiting a jet nozzle owing to increased heat, and corresponding with Poisson's law for the increase in the pressure of flowing gases.

V223.19, B260.11, P226.9   called the rocket Der Pfau. 'Pfau Zwei'   There's no evidence that SS troops (or others) referred to the A4 rocket as "*Pfau,*" or "Peacock." So what is the logic here? Possibly because the peacock (or *Pavonia christatus*), with its rainbow tail, is a bird often linked symbolically with Christ—a key motif-nexus in *GR*. More importantly, though, we have another of Pynchon's interlingual puns: the "p" in "*Pfau*" is silent; and "*fau*" is the German pronunciation of the letter "v"; thus in English *Pfau Zwei* sounds like "Vee-two," for *Vergeltungswaffe-zwei.*

V223.32, B260.27, P226.22   draw-shots   In the jargon of pocket billiards, a draw shot is when a player strikes the cue ball on its lower hemisphere, thus spinning the cue backward when it hits the object ball and *drawing* it back toward the shooter (Byrne, *Byrne's New Standard Book of Pool and Billiards* 12).

V224.14–15, B261.8–10, P227.3–4   Professors Schiller . . . Wagner . . . Pauer and Beck   On Professor Beck, who designed "a circular slit injection nozzle" while at the Dresden College of Engineering, see Dornberger (*V-2* 132); on Professor Wagner of Darmstadt, coinventor of the "integrating accelerometer" used in the V-2, also see Dornberger (232). Professors Pauer and Schiller are unknown.

V224.25, B261.23, P227.15   the midwinter sea   If read literally, this fixes the date around February 3, 1945.

V225.2, B262.2, P227.33   "the skirt I was wearing"   This is Katje's "rainbow striped dirndl skirt" (V208.8n), and note that she offers this clue (or "clew") to Slothrop with her (determinist) "mask of no luck, no future" (V225.5), dropped for a moment. And Slothrop will remember this hint: in part 3 (V285.18n) he examines documents showing the lifelong conspiracy against him, and his thoughts return, as Katje intended, to the moment in Monaco's Himmler-Spielsaal when she wore that rainbow-colored skirt, which is the sign of a covenant he dreads.

V225.35–36, B262.41–42, P228.26   Benny Goodman   Jazz clarinetist Benjamin David Goodman (1909–86), leader after 1932 of his own band and, after 1937, of the first integrated jazz band to hit the big time. But the idea here is that *GR's* perverse Pavlovians did not behaviorially condition Slothrop to have "European reflexes" at the sound of clarinet music; he associates clarinets with jazz and hot dance tunes, while Europeans associate clarinets with *opera buffa,* with "clowns or circuses"— stuff that, for Slothrop, requires "a *lotta* kazoos!" (V225.37–38).

EPISODE 4

Back to England and "The White Visitation"; the time, late February, after Katje's return from Monte Carlo. Pointsman and colleagues discuss problems with government funding and with keeping Brigadier Pudding in line. In the guise of a Teutonic witch, Domina Nocturna, Katje disciplines Pudding by means of an elaborately contrived, satirical inversion of the Kabbalistic ascent to the Merkabah, or divine throne.

V226.17–22, B263.26–33, P229.7–12   "Ordinarily in our behavior . . . reactions in the given setting."   This quotation is from "The Book," Pavlov's *Lectures,* volume 2, lecture 52, "An Attempt to Understand the Symptoms of Hysteria Physiologically" (109). The paper was delivered before the Academy of Sciences of the USSR in 1932, when (as Pynchon notes) Pavlov was eighty-three.

V226.33, B264.7, P229.23   an old *gorodki* stick   Here is Pointsman's attempt at a dramatic monologue in the manner of T. S. Eliot, using the dramatic persona of Ivan P. Pavlov carrying this stick. As in Eliot's "Love Song of J. Alfred Prufrock," Pointsman's poem takes the subject of old age (referred to in the Pavlov quotation at 226.17–22) as its theme. In the line reference here, "*gorodki*" means "little towns" and designates a game. The source is Horsley Gantt's introduction to the second volume of Pavlov's *Lectures* (34):

> *Gorodki* is an ancient game popular among the peasants of Russia, played with the same informality and ubiquity as "horseshoes" in this country. Two squares about the size of a small room are marked out on the ground some 60 to 80 feet apart, and into these are placed a number of six inch blocks of wood. The members of the opposing

teams attempt to get all the blocks out of the square by throwing from a distance of 50 to 60 feet sticks about the size of baseball bats but much heavier. As soon as all the blocks are out, another formation is arranged to be knocked out, until a series have been set up, representing castles, fortresses, etc. The side which removes the blocks in the fewest number of strokes is the winner. Pavlov was a champion player until the age of 80, outlasting and out playing all his youthful companions.

The game also comes up in the 1957 novel *Pnin* by Pynchon's Cornell University English professor Vladimir Nabokov: "I still hear the *trakh*!, the crack when one hit the wooden pieces and they jumped in the air," Pnin recalls (105) after telling his guests the rules of the game. The hurled stick is called a *bita*, and its parallel with the V-2 rocket is of course the obvious analogy at work here: both projectiles fall on their targets according to the statistical laws of distribution, which is why Russian peasants may wager on *gorodki*.

V227.31–32, B265.1, P230.22   a Savile Row serenity   The serene confidence of high, conservative fashion (see V184.14–15n).

V228.1–2, B265.13, P230.33–34   inquiries down from Duncan Sandys   A member of Parliament since 1935, a disabled veteran after 1940, a parliamentary secretary to the Ministry of Supply after 1941, and husband of Winston Churchill's daughter, Diana, Duncan Sandys (1908–87) was named head of Britain's intelligence-gathering work on the German V-weapons program in 1943.

V228.5, B265.17, P230.37   "Funding," IF you can keep your head   An allusion to Rudyard Kipling's, "IF" (from his *Rewards and Faeries*, 1910), a poem whose opening stanza supposes:

If you can keep your head when all about you
Are losing theirs and blaming it on you,
If you can trust yourself when all men doubt you
But make allowance for their doubting too

And concludes, after a lengthy catalogue of such suppositions:

If you can fill the unforgiving minute
With sixty seconds' worth of distance run,
Yours is the Earth and everything that's in it,
And—which is more—you'll be a Man, my son!

V228.16–17, B265.29–30, P231.7–8   "took an organic chemistry course or two together back at Manchester . . . ICI"   That is, at Victoria University of Manchester; ICI is the acronym of Imperial Chemical Industries, whose dealings (especially its work on synthetic polymers, i.e., plastics) are treated in greater detail at V250.36–39.

V228.18, B265.32–33, P231.9–10   "working out of Malet Street"   Malet Street, London, WC1, runs parallel to Gower Street along the southwest side of London University.

V228.37, B266.13–14, P231.28   "this whole show can prang"   That is, crash or be destroyed. Pynchon probably picked up this bit of British slang from McGovern (*Crossbow and Overcast* 31), who quotes a use of it as a noun meaning "destruction." Following the Allies' successful 1943 night raid against the German rocket facility at Peenemünde (see V423.5–6n), "Flight Lieutenant Mickey MacMichaelmore sums it up— 'An excellent prang has been achieved.'"

V229.8, B266.28–30, P231.41   kidneys . . . vulnerable after a while to bromide therapy   Pavlov used injections of potassium bromide to aid the inhibitory process, calming even the most excitable of his dogs. Nowhere that I know of does he mention kidney problems resulting from bromide therapy; indeed, "The Book" (*Lectures* 2:95) claims that "large doses of bromides given daily for many weeks or months have proved in our hands to be free of any harm."

V229.14, B266.37, P232.7   da screw   Underworld cant for "the jailer."

V229.34, B267.20, P232.27   PAVLOVIA (BEGUINE)   A beguine is a slow dance number, from the French *béguin* (flirtation). In 1930 the Russian village of Koltushy, site of Pavlov's laboratories, was renamed Pavlovo in his honor (Lectures 2:80). See also V75.30–31.

V229.37, B267.23, P232.30   Lysol   Originally imported from Germany, Lehn and Fink Products began U.S. production of Lysol brand spray disinfectant in 1912.

V230.21, B268.7, P233.14   PWD   The Psychological Warfare Division (V76.36).

V230.21–22, B268.7–8, P233.14–15   urges the Volksgrenadier: SETZT V-2 EIN!   Hitler's home guard, composed primarily of old men and boys conscripted for the last-ditch defense of the fatherland, was called the Volksgrenadier. But if this (fictional?) Allied propaganda was designed to have surrendering Germans simply raise their hands, its language punningly stumbles: the German verb *"einsetzen"* ("to put in," "insert" and, when used with certain prepositions, "to stand up or erect") gives a possible sexual pun: "Erect V-2!" Or: "Put V-2 in!"

V231.14, B269.2, P234.5   asleep under the *Daily Herald*   London morning newspaper oriented to Labour Party interests.

V231.24–25, B269.15, P234.16   "I am blessed Metatron."   Here begins a satirical inversion of the Kabbalistic ascent to the Merkabah. In Kabbalistic myths Metatron is foremost among the angelic host and is sometimes depicted as standing beside or "keeping" Jahweh's throne, the Merkabah. Pynchon's source here and in the following paragraphs is Scholem's chapter on Merkabah mysticism in *Major Trends in Jewish Mysticism* (40–79). As he defines it, the visionary ascent to the throne takes the initiate through seven antechambers, each confronting the aspirant with a test. One of Scholem's sources puts it this way (78): "When I ascended to the first palace I was devout (*hasid*), in the second palace I was pure (*tahore*), in the third sincere (*yashar*), in the fourth I was wholly with God (*tanim*), in the fifth I displayed holiness before God; in the sixth I spoke the *kedushah* (the trishagion) before Him who spoke and created, in order that the guardian angels might not harm me; in the seventh palace I hid myself erect with all my might, trembling in all limbs." The main theme of such visions, Scholem argues, is the soul's ascent from earth and its return home through the hostile antechambers and into God's fullness and light, all of it signifying redemptive process.

Note how Pynchon satirically inverts this process. Brigadier Pudding descends into a private hell, into the darkness signified by the muds of Passchendaele and symbolized in the Domina Nocturna herself. And each of the seven anterooms through which Pudding passes inverts the comparable motif in Kabbalistic lore. In the first, a "hypodermic outfit" (V231.38) signifies not devotion but addiction. In the second, allusions to "Severin" (see the next note) point to depravity instead of purity. In the third Pudding finds not sincerity but scientific objectivity, and in the fourth an empty skull mocks the idea of being "wholly with God." His trials go on like this until, instead of standing erect before his God, Pudding kneels in abject servility (but sexually erect) before an avatar of the Shekinah, the mother of material being and of dissolute death.

V232.6, B269.39–40, P37   brand name is Savarin . . . it means to say "Severin"   The Savarin brand of coffee was frequently advertised in the *Times* of London. Severin is the protagonist of Leopold von Sacher-Masoch's novel *Venus in Furs* (1878). At Severin's insistence (and later with no urging at all), Wanda (Venus) takes him as her slave, ordering Severin to stand in attendance while she bathes. Later they call in a painter to "immortalize" on canvas their master/slave union—she dressed in furs, whip in hand, and posed with one foot on his back.

V232.15, B270.7–8, P235.5–6   copy of Krafft-Ebing   The massive study of deviant sexuality, *Psychopathia Sexualis* (1886), by Richard von Krafft-Ebing.

V232.16–17, B270.9, P235.7   fifth, a Malacca cane   These canes, made from the stems of rattan palms and often with a ball on the upper end, come from the Malaysian state of Malacca; symbols of constabulary discipline and autocratic power, characters in Rohmer's Fu-Manchu fictions often appear with them in hand.

V232.20, B270.13–14, P235.10–11   a tattered tommy up on White Sheet Ridge   A corpse of a British infantryman ("tommy") that Pudding recalls from a ridge in the Ypres Salient.

V232.21, B270.14, P235.11   Maxim holes   Bullet holes from an air-cooled machine gun named for its designer, Hiram S. Maxim of the United States. During the Great War, Britain, Germany, Russia, and the United States all used versions of it.

V232.21–22, B270.15, P235.12   eyes of Cléo de Mérode   She was a notorious dancer who became the mistress of King Leopold II of Belgium, on whose soil were fought some of the nightmare battles Pudding recalls here.

V232.33, B270.30–31, P235.24   a tall Adam chair   A neoclassical design well known for its proportionality and geometrical patternings; it was created by eighteenth-century British architects Robert and James Adam.

V232.35, B270.33, P235.26   "Domina Nocturna . . . shining mother and last love"   The source for Pudding's appellation is Grimm (*Teutonic Mythology* 1056), who discusses the diabolical "night-riding" of witches: "Night-women in the service of *Dame Holda* rove through the air on appointed nights, mounted on beasts; her they obey, to her they sacrifice. . . . These *night-women, shining mothers, dominae nocturnae* were originally demonic elvish beings, who appeared in women's shape and did men kindnesses." Like the Valkyries, the *dominae nocturnae* were thought to hover over battlefields to take off the souls of the dead. In this scene Katje appears to Pudding in the trappings of a White Goddess, the "shining mother" in her destructive aspect. On Dame Holda and her residence beneath Venusberg, see V364.22n and V374.39–375.2n.

V232.41, B270.40, P235.32   recco photographs   From air reconnaissance; this bit of military shorthand occurs in Irving (*Mare's Nest*, passim).

V233.21, B271.23, P236.13   Archies   In World War I service slang, "to archie" meant to fire on an aircraft; "Archies" were antiaircraft guns.

V233.23, B271.26, P236.15   a star shell   A canister containing phosphorus that—when shot aloft from a large mortar or canon—burns and illuminates a battlefield in white light.

V233.25–26, B271.28–29, P236.17–18   she stood in No-man's Land   The ground between the trenches of opposing troops.

V234.7–8, B272.11–12, P236.40–41   "At Badajoz . . . a bandera of Franco's Legion advanced"   The town of Badajoz, on the Portuguese frontier, was the site of one of the earliest and the most cold-blooded massacres of the Spanish civil war. After joining the struggle late, Franco won the assistance of both Hitler and Mussolini in flying his Army of Africa back to Spain over the Strait of Gibraltar. The Loyalist militiamen were quickly put into retreat and bottled up on August 16, 1936, in Badajoz, where the remaining two thousand of them were herded into the town's bullring and machine-gunned.

V234.28, B272.38, P237.21   that Gourd Surprise   See V80.2–3.

V234.33, B273.2, P237.26   gold tasseled fourragère or his own Sam Browne   On the Sam Browne belt see V9.40n. The *fourragère* is a braided cord worn around one's left shoulder.

V235.38, B274.16–17, P238.24–25   the smell of Passchendaele   See V79.41n.

V236.32, B275.17–18, P239.30   effects of *E. coli* Abbreviation for the bacteria *Escherichia coli*, a naturally occurring symbiont of the human lower intestine (or colon); toxic if orally ingested.

EPISODE 5

Back to Monte Carlo, where Slothrop's instruction continues, minus Katje; the time is March 20–21, 1945, the spring equinox. Slothrop uncovers perplexing evidence of collusion between businesses with interests in opposing sides of the war. He also inches closer to finding the links between his "conditioning" as an infant, the plastic called Imipolex G, and the rocket.

V236.36–37, B275.21–22, P239.33–34   The great cusp . . . watersleep to firewaking This phrasing describes the spring equinox, separating the astrological house of Pisces (February 19–March 20) from the house of Aries (March 21–April 19). Pisces, the Fishes, is the twelfth and last house of the astrological year, a water sign, and associated with dreaming, dissolution, and death. Aries, the Ram, is the first house of a new astrological year, a fire sign, and tied to identity, freedom, and rebirth. This transition is important in *GR*. Pisces dominated part 1, but Aries now takes over as the astrological sign under which events occur. As Marc E. Jones (*Astrology* 161) has put it, Aries symbolizes "the absolute freedom from social conditioning," and Slothrop will shortly slip free (or, at least think he's slipped free) of "Them." Jones also comments that the watchwords of the Aries type are "I AM," an idea the narrator will soon develop in playing on the name "Jamf" (I am?) as well as in quoting from Rilke's *Sonnets to Orpheus*: "To the rushing water speak: I am" (V622.21). Finally, it is a notable moment because—if the calculations at V624.18n are correct—then Slothrop may have been born on this date, in 1918.

V237.1, B275.23–24, P239.35   up in the Harz in Bleicheröde The Harz Mountains are in central Germany. The town of Bleicherode (no umlaut on the "o") takes its name from *"Bleich"* ("bleach," "white"), *Der Bleicher* ("Bleacher," a nickname for Death), and *"-rode"* (a clearing, as in a forest), thus a pale-white clearing. Bleicherode is near Nordhausen, where A4 rockets were manufactured underground, and the scene for early episodes in part 3. Note also the symmetry: von Braun in his "white waste" and Pointsman at his "chalk piece of seacoast" (V237.6) near Dover.

V237.1–2, B275.24–25, P239.35–36   Wernher von Braun . . . his 33rd birthday Von Braun broke his arm in an automobile accident on March 18, 1945. In his memoir, *Peenemünde to Canaveral* (148), Dieter Huzel recalls the celebration of von Braun's thirty-third birthday (Jesus's age when crucified), on March 23. Looking down from their perch in the Harz, the partying rocketeers glimpsed signs of advancing Russian divisions.

V237.4, B275.28, P240.2   storks   Misprinted in the Bantam edition as "stroks."

V237.9, B275.33, P240.7   Lloyd George is dying.   Former Prime Minister David Lloyd George became gravely ill in early March; the *Times* of London carried almost daily reports on his condition until his death on March 26.

V237.12–13, B275.37–276.1, P240.12–13   miles of secret piping . . . roast German invaders   In 1940 the plan, should Germany have attempted a landing on Britain's south coast, was to set the waters aflame with gasoline. Gas pipes were laid in the tidal zone with that possibility in mind.

V237.14, B276.2, P240.13   hypergolic ignition   Occurs when a proper mixture of fuel components spontaneously ignites, as with hydrogen peroxide and sodium permanganate in the turbine drive of the V-2 (V211.15n).

V237.16–20, B276.4–8, P240.16–20   Carl Orff's lively . . . Totus ardeo   Orff (1895–1978) was a German composer known especially for his interest in reviving primitive rhythms and melodies. The lyric here is from his musical arrangements for the *Carmina Burana* (1936), a thirteenth-century codex of song lyrics that was made public in the nineteenth century when the monastery from which it came was secularized. Orff was taken by the irreligious qualities of the songs, which Helen Waddell (*The Wandering Scholars* 208) also praised, in 1927, as "the last flowering of the Latin tongue." Bavarian monks had used the goddess Fortuna, with her wheel, as a frontispiece to their book, and the songs are all remarkable for their treatment of hedonistic motifs, which are linked to the seasons of the year. Insofar as this episode occurs on "the great cusp" (V236.36) of spring, the narrator appropriately selects from the *Carmina Burana* a spring dance lyric, called "Tempus est iocundum" (The Time Is Agreeable). To back the lyric, Orff arranged a fast-paced combination of wind and percussion instruments. The Latin translates to

Oh, oh, oh,
I bloom entirely!
Now virginal love
Burns me entirely . . .

V237.21, B276.9, P240.21   Portsmouth to Dungeness   That is, from the west to the east end of Britain's coastal South Downs, with a lighthouse marking each port city.

V238.7–8, B276.38–40, P241.5–6   has Roland been whispering from eight kilometers . . . one of the Last Parabolas   The last V-2 of the London Blitz was launched from Holland on March 28, 1945; it struck the village of Orpington, in Kent, at 7:45 P.M. on Ash Wednesday. Following that strike, a few final rockets were launched against advancing American positions in Europe, but apparently none were used after April 1, which was Easter Day. Here, Roland Feldspath occupies one of those final trajectories at an altitude of "eight kilometers." Why eight? Because he is (or rather his spirit is) operating as "one of the invisible interdictors of the stratosphere now," and the troposphere, beginning at Earth's surface, extends to an altitude varying between eight and fourteen kilometers, with the stratosphere extending above that to an altitude of about fifty kilometers, and the mesosphere above it, to an altitude of about eighty-five kilometers, approximately the altitude to which the V-2 rocketed, at the apex of its parabolic path. Space having been "bureaucratized" by military-industrial rocketry, Feldspath here patrols his assigned boundary.

V238.22, B277.17–18, P241.21   His cryptic utterances that night at Snoxall's   See V30.26–36, about the "control" being put "inside" the vehicle.

V238.25, B277.22, P241.24   Schwärmerei   Idolization, fanaticism.

V238.30, B277.27–28, P241.29   the Cybernetic Tradition   The reference is anachronistic. Cybernetics is the science of communication and control in and between animals and/or machines. But its father, Norbert Wiener, indicates "the term cybernetics does not date further back than the summer of 1947" (*Cybernetics* 12).

V239.18–19, B278.22, P242.18   demons—yes, including Maxwell's   British physicist James Clerk Maxwell (1831–79) introduced the idea of the "sorting demon" in his *Theory of Heat* (1871). His aim was to cast a comically doubtful light on the second law of thermodynamics, which holds that producing "any inequality of temperature or of pressure" within a closed system is impossible without the expenditure of work, which expends energy, thus bringing the system back into equilibrium. Maxwell's "sorting demon" would however place himself in the passageway between two linked vessels. He would "see" individual molecules and select the faster ones for vessel A and the slower ones for vessel B: the faster the molecules, the higher the temperatures and conversely so for the other vessel. Thus without an expenditure of work the demon would create an inequality of temperatures and pressures, contradicting the second law. There are many counterproofs. For instance, the demon needs light to "see" the molecules, but the introduction of light would add energy to the system, negating any effect the demon might have on it. Pynchon plays extensively with the idea of Maxwell's Demon in *The Crying of Lot 49*, and for an excellent summary of this background as well as applications to cybernetic theory, read Mangel ("Maxwell's Demon, Entropy, Information: *The Crying of Lot 49*" 87–89).

V239.24, B278.28–29, P242.24   motion under the aspect of yaw control
The formula Pynchon quotes is from Kooy and Uytenbogaart (*Ballistics of the Future* 247).

V239.26–27, B278.31–32, P242.26–27   Scylla and Charybdis . . . to Brennschluss   In the Strait of Messina, Scylla is a legendary rock standing opposite a whirlpool called Charybdis. Homer personified the two seafaring hazards in book 12 of *The Odyssey*. On *Brennschluss* see V6.37n.

V240.5, B279.12, P243.6   Plattdeutsch   A German dialect spoken in the low country of the northern provinces, Schleswig-Holstein and Niedersachsen, part of the British zone after May 8, 1945.

V240.5, B279.13, P243.6–7   Thuringian   The central German province of Thuringia includes the Harz Mountains and what was then the main rocket works at Nordhausen. U.S. Army units got there before the Russians, but in accordance with the Yalta agreements of February 1945, Nordhausen was transferred to Soviet hands in June.

V240.11–18, B279.20–29, P243.12–19   seems that early in 1941, the British Ministry of Supply . . . first successful test in August of '42   All details here derive from Irving (55). Compare the account in *GR* to that in *The Mare's Nest*:

> The remarkable story of Lubbock's petrol-oxygen rocket goes back to early 1941, when a £10,000 Ministry of Supply research contract was finally awarded to Shell International Petroleum Company to develop an assisted take-off rocket, using any fuel other than cordite, which was to be in short supply. In comparison with the millions of pounds spent by the Germans on rocket research, this sum was not impressive; and Shell had to pay all costs other than the cost of the actual materials and fuel.
>
> Isaac Lubbock decided to experiment with aviation fuel and oxygen, moderating the temperature with water. The Ministry of Supply placed at his disposal a part of the Petroleum Warfare Establishment at Langhurst, near Horsham. . . . a five-second trial was successfully carried out at Langhurst on 15th August 1942.

V240.19, B279.29–30, P243.20   Lubbock was a double first at Cambridge
The reference is to Lubbock's having scored two "firsts," or the highest marks, on the tripos exams at Cambridge (V31.17n). The source, again, is Irving (154): "The Shell engineer had taken a Double First at Cambridge."

V240.20–22, B279.32–33, P243.21–23   Liquid Oxygen Research . . . sour stuff . . . Geoffrey Gollin   Gollin was Isaac Lubbock's chief assistant at Shell, according to Irving (56). He helped find the excrement-stained documents mentioned earlier (V211.10–12n). The "sour stuff" is oxygen (from the German "*der Sauerstoff*").

V240.23, B279.35, P243.24   "an Esso man myself"   In other words,

Slothrop would gas up his Hudson Terraplane at a Shell Oil Company rival, Esso (for Standard Oil), the brand name of gasoline marketed by New Jersey–based Standard Oil. Esso remains an international brand (now owned by Exxon-Mobil). In the prewar years, "3-Star" was Esso's premium grade gasoline, and if his Terraplane behaved like "a gourmet" then this would have been his brand and grade of choice.

V240.25, B279.38, P243.26 "whole bottle of that Bromo" Bromo seltzer, an American brand of antacid, for mild, transient stomach disorders.

V240.35, B280.7–8, P243.36 "That's Bataafsche Petroleum Maatschappij, N.V.?" Slothrop inquires about the Royal Dutch Shell Company. For details about the Nazis' use of Shell company headquarters on "the Josef Israelplein" (a city street, spelled "Jozef Israëlsplein") for siting a "radio guidance transmitter" (V241.3–4), see Kooy and Uytenbogaart (*Ballistics of the Future* 287).

V240.37, B280.10, P243.38 a recco photograph See V232.41n.

V240.41, B280.15, P244.1 like Cary Grant The English-born but naturalized American actor (1904–86) with the cute British accent; Slothrop parodies him at V294.11.

V242.9–15, B281.31–38, P245.11–16 a DE rating . . . OKW . . . directs Slothrop to a Document S G-l . . . "a state secret" The source for these details was a photocopy of the "Contract for 12,000 A4 Rockets" given as an illustration in Irving (opposite 299). Documents pertaining to the rocket were given a "DE 12" security rating—the "highest priority," as Irving comments and Pynchon repeats. The OKW was the German Oberkommando der Wehrmacht, or Armed Forces High Command. On the photostat in Irving, the SS stamp and the warning *Geheime Kommandosache* ("Top Secret"; literally "Secret Command matter") are clearly visible, along with the (numerical) legal reference that Pynchon translates.

V242.38–39, B282.24, P246.1–2 "more of that specific impulse data" Slothrop uses the European expression for "specific thrust," a measure of thrust usually given in foot/pounds. The source here, and for the data quoted in the lines to follow, is Kooy and Uytenbogaart (*Ballistics of the Future* 395–98).

V243.17, B283.2–3, P246.21 Alkit uniforms As their ads in the *Times* of London used to indicate, Alkit, located in Cambridge Circus, WC2, was a provider of top-shelf "Gentlemen's Coats and Hats."

V243.28–29, B283.16–17, P246.32–33 a gold benzene ring with a formée cross in the center See V249.24–25. It was Kekulé von Stradonitz who discovered the hexagonal benzene ring; a "formée" (that is, "styled") design would resemble a Maltese cross, but it would have curved rather than flat edges along the outer side of the crosspieces. A heraldic insignia used by the Templars (indeed common to other secret societies).

V243.39, B283.30–31, P247.3 George ("Poudre") de la Perlimpinpin Derives his name from the French *"poudre"* (powder) and the French slang *"perlimpinpin"* ("a dash," "a soupçon"); but the meaning changes when they are used together, as in *C'est de la poudre de perlimpinpin!* (That's a bunch of baloney!).

V244.11, B284.2, P247.14–15   nattering through, in clear   London has been sending teletype messages but without encoding them for secrecy.

V244.18, B284.10–11, P247.22   the trente-et-quarante table   Also known as "red and black," *trente-et-quarante* is, with chemin de fer, one of the principal card games played at the Monte Carlo casino. Six decks of cards are shuffled together and dealt in two rows (one called "rouge," the other "noir"). Face cards and tens carry a value of ten; aces, one; and the rest, their numerical values. The dealer lays out the rows until they total thirty-one or more; the row most closely approaching thirty-one wins. There are side bets placed on what the color of the first card in each row will be.

V244.21–22, B284.15–16, P247.26–27   a wiry civilian, disguised as the Secret Service's notion of an Apache   When founded in 1865 the U.S. Secret Service was charged with protecting federal currencies and financial institutions against counterfeiting and fraud; Congress assigned it to protect domestic and foreign dignitaries after the 1901 assassination of President William McKinley. So it would be unusual for Slothrop to be tailed by an American SS officer here. But the idea is that whoever this "wiry civilian" is, he is doing a poor job of trailing him, evidently in a weak "notion" of an "Apache," the term coined (by either Arthur Dupin or Victor Morris, both French journalists) in 1902 to describe teenaged members of Paris street gangs specializing in petty theft, prostitution, and protection scams. In later decades, the term was applied to a whole range of garishly clad youth gang members throughout France (comparable to forties-era zoot-suiters, see V246.4–5n).

EPISODE 6

During the spring of 1945, Slothrop attends a party thronged with underworld types. One of them, Blodgett Waxwing, confirms Slothrop's suspicion that the octopus incident was a manufactured event. Slothrop is now ready to make his escape from Monaco, and Waxwing gives him the address of a hideout in Nice.

V244.26, B284.20, P247.30–31   a hundred grams of hashish in the Hollandaise   The Bantam misprints "Hollandaise" as "Hallandaise"; in any case, if the sauce has been spiked with that much—nearly a quarter pound—of hashish, then no wonder "What's happening is not clear."

V245.27, B285.24, P248.31   Saxophony and Park Lane kind of tune   Park
Lane forms the eastern boundary of London's Hyde Park and lies two
blocks from Slothrop's former office near Grosvenor Square. Once a residential street for the wealthiest of Londoners, by 1945 it was lined with
shops, offices, and hotels like the Dorchester and the Grosvenor House,
with their facilities for ballroom dancing. In this context, "Saxophony"
makes a kind of sense as another of the narrator's etymological puns. In
the nineteenth century Adolphe Sax invented the instrument that bears
his name, but readers will also recall *saxo*, the etymological root from
which the hatchet-wielding Saxons took their name (see V218.10n). In
addition, Clarence Major's work on African American slang records how,
among jazz musicians of this period, an "ax" designated "any musical
instrument but usually a saxophone." In these Park Lane ballrooms and
at Perlimpinpin's party, then, what we have is "Saxophony" imitations
of the genuine article, faked attempts at the real jazz.

V245.29, B285.26–27, P248.32   nodded out on a great pouf with Michele
Stoned on that hollandaise, Mr. Bounce naps on a hassock—in French,
called a "*pouf*" (though in British slang a pouf is a male homosexual).

V245.36, B285.35–36, P249.2   Tom Mix shirt . . . a Percheron horse
American cowboy-actor Thomas Hezekiah Mix (1880–1940) used to
favor the old cavalry-style bibbed shirtfronts, with lots of piping and
silver buttons. A Percheron horse is a comical incongruity; the breed is
a large French draught horse, usually dappled and large-hooved.

V246.1, B285.37, P249.3   Bokhara rug   A Turkish style, with black and
white octagons set on a background of red, sienna, and tan.

V246.4–5, B286.2–3, P249.7   a white zoot suit with reet pleats   The zoot
suit is obscure in its origins. Some attribute its elaborately pegged and
pleated trousers—the "reet pleats" billowing out over one's thighs—to
the style of trousers and long coats popular among American college
boys of the twenties and thirties. An article in *Newsweek* (June 21,
1943) claims that the style also owes something to Clark Gable's costumes for *Gone with the Wind*. The zoot-suit coat was double-breasted,
with billowing arms, padded shoulders, and a knee-length cut ("the
drape shape"). In March of 1942 the U.S. War Production Board virtually
banned the zoot suit by severely restricting the amounts of material that
could be used in men's clothes. As a result, bootleg tailors sprang up in
Harlem and East Los Angeles. In 1943 the War Frauds Division cracked
down on this underworld commerce, forbidding sales of zoots at shops
in New York, Chicago, and Los Angeles. The crackdown had racial overtones that were rather obvious: the main "zootsers" were Hispanics and
blacks. After the Zoot-Suit Riots of June 1943, the Los Angeles City
Council passed an ordinance making the wearing of the zoot a misde-
meanor offense (see V249.4–5n).

V246.9, B286.8, P249.11   a Shirley Temple   A glass of soda pop with a cherry on top named for the child screen star (V466.4n); here it indicates that Slothrop's intending to stay sober.

V246.14–15, B286.16, P249.18   Jean-Claude Gongue   Perhaps from the American underworld slang "gonga" or "gongue" (anus).

V246.21–22, B286.24, P249.24–25   American Army yellow-seal scrip   A United States paper currency issued for use in the occupied zones of Europe; widely counterfeited and used in black marketeering, it was withdrawn from circulation in May 1945 (see also V438.9).

V246.25, B286.28, P249.29   a Groucho Marx voice   Because this sort of inane pun, on Tamara/tomorrow, is characteristic of those that Julius ("Groucho") Marx used to interject—for example, in movies like *A Day at the Races* (see V619.1–4n).

V246.32, B286.36, P249.35   "42, medium"   Knowing Slothrop's suit size, we can estimate that he was about five-ten or six feet tall and around 175 pounds.

V246.35, B286.40, P249.39–40   Blodgett Waxwing, well-known escapee from the Caserne Martier   The Waxwing (genus *Bombycilla*) is a crested-head, brownish-black bird with waxy red-tipped wings. As Larsson ("A *Companion*'s Companion") notes, Pynchon's Cornell University English professor and writer Vladimir Nabokov develops his novel *Pale Fire* (published in 1962, by which time Pynchon was long gone from the campus) around a long poem that begins: "I was the shadow of the waxwing slain / By the false azure of the windowpane." However much, or little, such context may add to our sense of this character, the prison from which Waxwing escaped housed many of the European theater's most flagrant and dangerous black marketeers and criminals. Its name is misspelled in all three editions; it should be "the Caserne Mortier." Pynchon's source was a feature article in *Life* magazine for March 26, 1945 (25–29), entitled "GIs Involved in Black Market Held in Caserne Mortier." There are lots of photos: the stockade, a grim, closely guarded brick structure; the inmates, all of them rugged, hardened-looking characters; and the guards, who look equally case-hardened. There isn't much of a written story. Most inmates, the *Life* correspondent notes, were charged with murder, rape, theft of military or civilian property, or black marketeering. Escape, according to the jailers, was next to impossible.

V246.36, B286.41, P249.40   the ETO   Acronym for European theater of operations.

V246.37, B286.42, P249.41   PX ration cards   Issued to ration a soldier's purchases (of cigarettes, for example) at the post exchange.

V246.37, B287.1, P250.1   Soldbücher   The pay books issued German soldiers.

V246.38–39, B287.2–3, P250.2   AWOL . . . since the Battle of the Bulge

See V52.23–24n. Waxwing has been absent without leave since mid-December 1944.

V247.2, B287.7–8, P250.6 deuce 'n' a half ruts An army truck, load-rated at two and a half tons, with dual rear wheels that would leave wide, UU-shaped ruts in the dirt.

V247.5, B287.12, P250.10 known to hot-wire In underworld slang, to reroute the ignition wires in order to steal a car. The inspiration for this detail is probably the *Life* article on Caserne Mortier once more; car thefts were a major problem for the Allied governments, and the writer even mentions how a soldier in possession of electrical gear for a jeep could be charged.

V247.6–7, B287.13–14, P250.11 to see a good old Bob Steele or Johnny Mack Brown Before making his talking-pictures debut for the Tiffany Pictures studio in *Near the Rainbow's End* (1930), Bob Steele (Robert Adrian Bradbury, 1907–88) was the star cowboy in a number of silent films produced by the FBO (Film Booking Offices) studio owned by Joseph Kennedy Sr. (father of the future president). Through the thirties Steele averaged seven cowboy pictures per year, becoming, in spite of his small size, a matinee idol of the period, known for whirlwind fighting and a hot-dog horse-riding style. Johnny Mack Brown (1904–74) was a college football All-American (at Alabama) who led his team to a national championship and a 1926 Rose Bowl victory (over Washington). He made his film debut in 1927 and had his first starring role with Wallace Beery in King Vidor's version of *Billy the Kid* (1930). Like Bob Steele he became a matinee idol: handsome, dynamic, and above all a young cowboy, for it was Steele and Brown who, in contrast to the older generation of silent screen cowpokes, successfully made the transition into talkies.

V247.8–9, B287.15–16, P250.13 thousands of snowdrops' brains In U.S. service slang, "snowdrops" are the military police, whose helmets, puttees, gloves, and belts are all white.

V247.9, B287.16, P250.13–14 he has seen *The Return of Jack Slade* And, given the time of these fictional 1945 events it is a remarkable feat, because the film wasn't made until a decade later. Edward Mendelson first pointed out the anachronism in his essay "Gravity's Encyclopedia" (184). We might well ask why Pynchon makes the error, and one answer would be that he meant to work out a certain parallel. In *GR*, director Gerhardt von Göll plans a film version of José Hernandez's two-part Argentinian epic poem, *Martín Fierro*. The second part of the poem treats the "return" of that outlaw gaucho. Similarly, *Jack Slade* (1953) and *The Return of Jack Slade* (1955) were also based on a literary text, Mark Twain's *Roughing It*, chapters 9–11. As Twain tells the story, Slade was a decent but ruthless man, a vigilante who was hanged in Virginia City for the "crime" of stamping on a court order. On the gallows he broke down and wailed for his wife. Taking its cue from Twain, *Jack Slade* attempted to show the mitigating circumstances that turned a law-abiding cowboy into a ruthless killer. The first film was something of a matinee hit, so director Harold Schuster decided to go for the double play. *The Return of Jack Slade* brings on the vigilante's son, who tries to restore his father's tarnished reputation. The notable thing, here, is that the young man "sells out"; he becomes a Pinkerton agent, and that is exactly the sort of sell-out to "Them" that Pynchon also condemns in the *Return of Martín Fierro* (see V387.12–13).

V247.11, B287.18–19, P250.16   a typical WWII romantic intrigue   Perhaps because the plot might be taken as a parody of some popular wartime cinema thriller. Also, the Tamara-Italo-Waxwing-Theophile connection makes yet another "progressive *knotting into*" (V3.25), or circling into, that is complicated but not irrational, if one sorts out the vehicle (an American-made Sherman tank) and the funding ("the money Tamara fronted [the middleman]") and the politics (Palestine was seething with intrigue as Zionists attempted to carve an Israeli state out of the chaos Germany left behind) and the decadent motive (Turkish opium). We may also think of it as a type, "another of them Tamara/ Italo drills," as the narrator soon notes (V261.39–40). They keep readers practiced at following and interpreting plots; and this circular "drill" also keeps one in an open-ended state of anticipation (or *Erwartung*), because nothing ever develops from it.

V247.30, B287.41, P250.34   a face like Tenniel's Alice   British graphic illustrator John Tenniel (1820–1914) drew the original illustrations for Lewis Carroll's "Alice" books: *Alice in Wonderland* and *Through the Looking Glass.*

V247.35, B288.5–6, P250.39–40   like the eyes of King Kong   In Merian C. Cooper's 1933 film, Kong's eyes have a way of "burning" when he first appears, crashing through the jungle to snatch away Fay Wray. Later, in New York, his eyes become pathetically lightless.

V248.2, B288.15, P251.6–7   "One coup de foudre!"   From the French, "One bolt [of lightning] from the blue!" Also, an idiom for "love at first sight."

V248.7, B288.22, P251.12   black-market Jell-O   "Delicate Delightful Dainty" the newspaper ads used to say of the American brand of flavored gelatin products invented (in 1897) by Leroy, New York, carpenter Pearle Wait, who sold it to the company that would become after a series of mergers the General Foods Company.

V248.17–18, B288.35, P251.23   swell enough looking twist   In American slang a "twist" is a chorus girl.

V248.28, B289.5–6, P251.33   Tamara is escorted   The Bantam misprints it as "Tamar."

V248.32, B289.10, P251.37   Errol Flynn   Known for his hard-living, swashbuckling style both on and off the screen, mustachioed Errol Flynn (1909–59) makes an ironic analogue here to girl-grappling Slothrop.

V248.40–41, B289.21, P252.4–5 a business card, embossed with a chess knight and an address on Rue Rossini On the Rue Rossini, see V253.33n. The point, Larsson ("A *Companion's* Companion") shows, is that Waxwing's card with the chess knight (*Springer*, in German) mimics that of hired-gun hero Paladin (played by actor Richard Boone) in the CBS western TV show, *Have Gun, Will Travel*, which lasted for 263 episodes, from 1957 to 1963. A clue, leading us to one of Slothrop's future code names (see V376.26).

V249.4–5, B289.26–27, P252.9–10 the Zoot Suit Riots of 1943 The fighting broke out first of all in East Los Angeles. On June 1, 1943, two sailors stationed in Long Beach made unwelcome advances toward several *cholitas*, so-called slick chicks who traveled with gangs of Chicano zoot-suiters. The girls' boyfriends mauled the sailors and tensions rose. On the night of June 4, bands of sailors skirmished through East L.A., tearing the zoots off any *pachucos* (the gang members) who would not voluntarily disrobe. Next night, *pachuco* gangs retaliated in force and large-scale rioting broke out. Six nights of street fighting left about 120 injured; 18 sailors were treated for serious injuries. In all, 94 Chicanos and 20 servicemen were arrested. The usual bureaucratic gestures followed: Nelson Rockefeller, coordinator of the Office of Interamerican Affairs under the Roosevelt administration, began a federal inquiry into the riots. Governor Earl Warren of California impaneled a five-man board of inquiry. Meanwhile, in late June the Zoot-Suit Riots began to spread, with violence breaking out between whites and black "zooters" in San Diego, Philadelphia, Detroit, and Toronto.

V249.5–6, B289.28, P252.11 Anglo vigilantes from Whittier Richard Nixon's hometown and home also to Whittier College, his alma mater; San Gabriel (V249.11) is a nearby suburb of Los Angeles.

EPISODE 7

Next day, Slothrop learns the ostensible uses of Imipolex G in the rocket and learns also—while he scans an old *Times* of London—of Tantivy's death. This news pushes him over the edge; he departs for an address in Nice. Secret Service agents ("Apaches") still trail him. He becomes involved with a group of Argentine anarchists and runs errands for them between Zurich and Geneva, Switzerland—losing the U.S. agents as he goes. When he's finished he spends the night on an Alpine peak, at the grave of Laszlo Jamf. In payment for his anarchist legwork, a messenger brings Slothrop documents that confirm Jamf's role in his past, but readers do not learn of their contents until the opening of part 3. In this episode Slothrop assumes the identity of his next avatar: "He is now an English war correspondent named Ian Scuffling" (V256.35–36).

V249.21, B290.5, P252.26   an aromatic heterocyclic polymer   In organic chemistry the aromatics are a class of compounds structurally related to, or based on, the six-carbon benzene ring. Strung together in still larger chains they form a polymer, a compound of very high molecular weight but based on simple, yet infinitely repeatable, units. For example, the "polyethers" of V250.2 are formed from benzene rings with attached ether radicals, all strung into larger chains. As metaphor, note the idea of regression, of cycles within cycles, consistent with structural aspects of *GR* itself.

V249.28, B290.14, P252.33–34   early research done at du Pont   Refers to the E. I. DuPont de Nemours and Company. In the twenties and thirties, this company's main research laboratories at Wilmington, Delaware, produced a score of new polymers, including nylon, neoprene rubber, and polyester fabrics.

V249.29–30, B290.16–17, P252.26   Carothers, known as The Great Synthesist   He is Wallace Hume Carothers (1896–1937). DuPont hired him in 1928 for his research into linear polymers, and during the next decade he made a series of discoveries, most notably the discovery of nylon, at first called "Fiber #66." At DuPont, Ira Williams used Carothers's research to develop neoprene rubber, and the work of Carothers and his assistant Julian Hill also led to the production of polyester fabrics and plastics. Carothers was a melancholy genius who took his own life in 1937.

V250.2–3, B290.28–29, P253.8–9   aromatic polyamides . . . polysulfanes   The polyamides comprise the nylon family; polycarbonates are linear polyesters of carbonic acid, useful as injection-molded plastics; the polyethers are another family of plastics; the polysulfanes, a linear polyester of sulfuric compounds.

V250.17, B291.9, P253.24   monomer   Any of the molecular units—the amides, for example—that can be polymerized.

V250.23–24, B291.17–18, P253.30–31   Psychochemie AG . . . Grössli Chemical Corporation   The first company ("Psychochemistry Incorporated") is a Pynchon fiction; the second is a German name of an American company called Grasselli Chemical Corporation, which had connections to the IG Farben cartel throughout the twenties; part of it was openly acquired by the company in 1928 (see V284.15–16n).

V250.25–27, B291.18–21, P253.32–34   Sandoz . . . Ciba, and Geigy   Originally a Swiss dyestuffs manufacturer, the Sandoz company branched out into pharmaceuticals during the twentieth century. In 1943 Dr. Albert Hofmann of Sandoz was experimenting with a synthetic preparation of lysergic acid when he accidentally ingested a portion of it and experienced hallucinogenic effects. The acid, one of the two principal ingredients in the manufacture of LSD, is an indole compound. Ciba-Geigy and Sandoz merged in 1997, forming Novartis AG, which is based in Basel, Switzerland.

V250.36, B291.33, P254.3 between ICI and the IG This is the British firm Imperial Chemical Industries, of London, a cartel organized in 1926 to match the power of the German IG firm. By 1939 ICI was "second only to IG in Europe" and had reached agreements with the German firm concerning territories and trading rights (Sasuly, *IG Farben* 49).

V250.41, B291.38, P254.8 the Schokoladestrasse, in that Zurich A fictional Chocolate Street, for the fictional firm Psychochemie AG.

V251.10–12, B292.9–11, P254.18–19 Mr. Duncan Sandys . . . the Ministry of Supply located . . . at Shell Mex *House* All of this is historically accurate, though the suggestion that British Shell or Sandys colluded with the Germans is entirely that of Pynchon's speaker. On Sandys, see V228.1–2n. The details about his offices at the Shell Mex House come from Irving (*Mare's Nest* 70). The Shell Mex House is an office building on the Embankment, near Waterloo Bridge. The location of the German radar-guidance tower, atop the Royal Dutch Shell building in The Hague, was mentioned earlier (V240.35n).

V252.4, B293.10, P255.12 "S-Gerät, 11/00000" Pynchon's first extended discussion of the *Schwarzgerät* (black device) and the rocket number (the quintuple zero) it went into. All V-2 rockets were given five-digit serial numbers, as Huzel (*Peenemünde to Canaveral* 87) explains: "For a reason I have never discovered, the first production missile number was 17,001. At war's end the assembly lines were turning out missiles in the 22,000 numbering block." "*Schwarzgerät*" might also translate as "black box," in reference to the usage in both psychology and engineering to represent part of a model or design that, although its exact internals are (yet) unknown, is posited or projected as performing the desired function.

V252.14, B293.22, P255.22 last Tuesday's London *Times* Probably the *Times* of London for Tuesday, April 24, 1945. Slothrop's remark to himself two lines later—"Allies closing in east and west on Berlin"—corresponds with the headlines and map on p. 2, the *Times*'s main news page. On April 1–7, the fighting was still some distance from Berlin; on Tuesday, May 1, the Russians had already entered the city. Slothrop also remarks on an advertisement from the Ministry of Foods on p. 5 of the April 24 edition. Entitled "Bacon and Eggs," it gave the (regulated) price of powdered eggs as "one and three," just as Slothrop comments to himself. The names he reads in the "Fallen Officers" column are all fictional. At the Empire Cinema throughout this period, however, was not *Meet Me in St. Louis* (1944), but another Judy Garland picture, *Under* *the Clock* (1945). If this "last Tuesday's London *Times*" is indeed that for April 24, then the date of this scene must be late April, perhaps around the thirtieth.

V253.10, B294.25–26, P256.18   down the Corniche   Leaving Monte Carlo, Slothrop drives west on the Moyenne Corniche, a twisting, switchbacking road initially built for Napoleon that links the coastal cities of southern France.

V253.15, B294.32, P256.24   a black Citroën   During the prewar years, the Citroën Motor Works of France produced several models of powerful, comfortable, "saloon-type" automobiles.

V253.17, B294.33–34, P256.25   a flopping Sydney Greenstreet Panama hat   Best known for his role in *Casablanca* (1943), in which he appears as a fez-wearing café owner, the reference here is certainly—given Pynchon's interest in this novel in ghosts, revenants, and otherworldly life—to the 1944 film *Between Two Worlds*. Based on Sutton Vane's morality play *Outward Bound*, this film is set in London during the Blitz and features characters (played by Paul Henried, Eleanor Parker, and John Garfield) trying to escape England for America. One couple commits suicide when their escape is frustrated; others die when a bomb strikes the vehicle transporting them to the dockside. Excepting the two suicides (Henried and Parker) the characters do not know that they have died and so, reassembled as (essentially) ghosts aboard a ship bound for nowhere, their task is to work through their fate principally by understanding the kind of person they are: whether altruistic or timorous, cynical or naive. Greenstreet's role aboard ship in his floppy Panama hat as the Reverend Tim Thompson, "The Examiner," is to pass final judgment.

V253.19–20, B294.37, P256.28   off Place Garibaldi   Named for Italian anarchist Guiseppe Garibaldi (1807–82), whose so-called redshirts brought Europe its first inkling of its intensely militaristic nationalist/fascist future. Here as elsewhere, Pynchon's geographical references are concise. Coming into Nice, the Corniche would deliver Slothrop directly to the Place Garibaldi, near the center of town. He "ditches the car" there, walks south about a third of a mile toward the Mediterranean, then snacks in the Old Town district just east of the port (called the Port Fausse, or False Port, because it was excavated). Next, he walks the three-fourths of a mile into the Quartier de la Croix of Nice, to the address on Rue Rossini.

V253.26, B295.2, P256.34   April summertime   Because by April the weather in Nice had become so warm that (at least in the forties) the tourist season ended.

V253.27, B295.3, P256.35   vortex of redeployment from Europe to Asia   With the war wrapping up in the European theater Allied forces commenced the redeployment of troops to the Asian theater during April–

May, 1945, a movement imagined here as a "vortex" sucking "souls" (servicemen, who "cling" to tranquil places like Nice) down European rivers and into port cities such as Marseilles, France, and Antwerp, Belgium—thus reversing their deployment in another hysteron proteron.

V253.33, B295.11, P256.41   the Rue Rossini   A street of residential flats and pensions running through the Quartier de la Croix named for the Italian composer Gioacchino Rossini and significant in light of the Beethoven/Rossini debate that will develop in part 3 of *GR*. Recall also the Rossini music playing at the Casino Hermann Goering (V204.33–39).

V254.5, B295.26, P257.13–14   an old motherly femme de chambre   A chambermaid.

V254.33, B296.16, P258.1   Apache sideburns   Recall the Secret Service man decked out as "an Apache" (V244.23) as he tails Slothrop.

V254.33–34, B296.17, P258.1–2   a braided leather sap   In underworld slang, a braided leather tube or sock-like weapon packed with stones or metal shot.

V254.38, B296.22, P258.6   canary yellow Borsalini   Pynchon's plural for the Borsalino, usually a black felt hat with a narrow brim turned down in front and up in back—a favorite of Mafioso gangsters.

V255.20, B297.7–8, P258.29   "it's Dumpster, Dumpster Villard"   See V65.20.

V256.2–5, B297.36–39, P259.12   "Jenny, I heard your block was hit . . . the day after New Year's . . . took me to that Casino"   She was one of Slothrop's former "stars" from London and appears now from the Other Side because her block was rocketed (one must suppose). His dream thoughts also confirm the earlier chronology: that he arrived on the Riviera around Christmas.

V256.11–12, B298.4–5, P259.21–22   bend . . . like notes on a harmonica   The player's ability to "bend" notes is an important but difficult harmonica skill. Slothrop has mastered it by part 4 (V622.14n).

V257.8, B299.5, P260.18   like Katje on her wheel, off on a ratchet   The image is of a roulette wheel, knocking Katje like a ball "from one room to the next, a sequence of numbered rooms whose numbers do not matter, till inertia brings her to the last" (V209.6–7). Slothrop saw it that way during the revelatory moment in the Himmler-Spielsaal, when Katje wore her "rainbow striped dirndl skirt." Now, if Slothrop were on top of his game he would realize that, like Katje's, his moves are still under "Their" control and that (as Clive Mossmoon later puts it), he is being sent out into the Zone "'to destroy the blacks'" (V615.36). He doesn't, and this is another case of a missed message.

V257.35–36, B299.40–41, P261.6–7   Hotel Nimbus . . . in the Niederdorf or cabaret section   The Nimbus appears to be a fictional hotel, but networked to other images of shadows, nimbuses, shades, and eclipses scattered through the novel; the Niederdorf district lies in the central part of Zurich, on the west bank of the Limmat Canal, which divides the city in two.

V257.39, B300.2, P261.10   the Limmatquai   Main arterial running parallel to the canal, through Niederdorf.

V258.3, B300.6, P261.13–14   lieder   Songs.

V258.4, B300.6–7, P261.14   pours gentian brandy   French and Swiss liqueur distilled from the roots of gentian plants; also called Enzian, "one of the most aristocratic forms of schnapps" (Fifield, ed., *Alexis Lichine's Encyclopedia of Wines and Spirits* 250).

V258.9, B300.13, P261.20   Moxie   See V63.5n.

V258.26–27, B300.35, P261.38–39   Ultra, Lichtspiel, and Sträggeli   These are probably fictional nightclubs. Grimm (*Teutonic Mythology* 934) notes that at "some places in Switzerland the *Sträggeli* goes about on the Ember Night, Wednesday before Christmas, afflicting girls that have not finished their day's spinning." The word means "specter," a "play of light" (or "*Lichtspiel*"); in the same context, "ultra" refers to the very high frequency light waves in any spectrum of illumination.

V258.32, B301.1, P262.5   rösti   German-style fried potatoes.

V258.37, B301.6, P262.9   séracs   Glacial ice pinnacles in the Swiss Alps.

V259.39–40, B302.12, P263.14   singing "Three card monte on the *side*, walk"   An old scam in New York City, three-card monte is outlawed. In the "game," three cards are shown to a spectator and then the cards are shuffled and laid face down. The spectator is then asked to locate one particular card of the three. But skilled dealers have multiple ways of manipulating the cards; wise city denizens therefore know: if the dealer allows one to bet, one has *already* lost.

V260.30, B303.4, P264.11   "You interested in some L.S.D.?"   The source, here, of a monetary pun (pounds, from "libra," a Roman unit of weight, shillings, from "solidus," a Roman coin, and pence, from "denarius," another Roman coin) but also a premonitory reference to the Sandoz company's hallucinogenic indole compound.

V261.4, B303.20–21, P264.25   indole people   Those who focus their research on compounds of indole, a white, powdered coal-tar derivative with various pharmacological uses—for instance, it's part of what constitutes LSD. Note that in all respects the drug LSD is linked in *GR* with the North, the color white (symbolic of death), IG Farben, and an "elect" of researchers and business tycoons who are imagined "at the end of a long European dialectic" (V261.9) of progress that moves toward Death's "other kingdom."

V261.17, B303.36, P264.38   the Uetliberg   Southeast of Zurich, an hour away by tram, the Uetliberg is a peak rising to an altitude of 2,841 feet.

V261.29, B304.5, P265.9   the Gemüse-Brücke   Literally, the "Vegetable

Bridge." But of the thirteen Zurich bridges across the Limmat Canal, Baedeker and other maps record none by this name.

V262.5–6, B304.27–28, P265.28–29 William Tell Overture Music from Rossini's opera by that name, a melody also popularly known as the theme music to the *Lone Ranger* program on American radio (nearly 3000 episodes aired on Mutual Broadcasting System stations from 1930 to 1954) and television (1949–57).

V262.11, B304.34, P265.34 the Luisenstrasse Street In the northwest industrial quarter of Zurich.

V262.35, B305.19, P266.17 the Odeon James Joyce, Vladimir Ilyich Lenin, Leon Trotsky, Albert Einstein, and Tristan Tzara (the Dadaist) all lived in Zurich, circa 1916, and all used to frequent the Café Odeon, which opened for business in 1912 at Limmatquai 2, in the Niederdorf district. The fact is fairly well known: Richard Ellman mentions it in his biography of Joyce, and Tom Stoppard's 1975 play, *Travesties*, brings Joyce, Lenin, and Tzara together there.

V263.18, B306.5, P266.41 Argentine poet Leopoldo Lugones During the early decades of the twentieth century Lugones (1874–1938) became Argentina's leading literary figure. A liberal in politics, he always demonstrated sympathies with Argentina's disenfranchised people.

V263.20, B306.8, P267.2 the Uriburu revolution This coup occurred September 6, 1930, when army general Jose F. Uriburu, nephew of a former Argentine president, seized power after the Radical Party failed to resolve the havoc that worldwide depression was wreaking in the country. Uriburu stepped in because the military elite had decided that only its forceful guidance could save the nation from what was seen as a divisive party politics of bickering intellectuals (like Lugones).

V263.24–26, B306.13–15, P267.7 Graciela Imago Portales, hijacked . . . U-boat in Mar de Plata Her name means Graciela "Window Image," and she hijacked the German submarine at the Argentine port city of Mar del Plata, misspelled in the Viking and corrected in the Bantam, but not in the Penguin.

V263.33, B306.24, P267.15 Rivadavia At 46 degrees southern latitude, a port city that is the southernmost of Argentina's populous cities.

V263.34, B306.25–26, P267.16–17 "with Perón on his way" Juan Domingo Perón (1895–1974) was among a group of army officers who seized power in June of 1943. Appointed to head the Argentine Department of Labor and Social Welfare, then installed as Minister of War, Perón rallied the union workers, appealed for welfare reform, and thus swiftly established himself as champion of Argentina's lower classes, whose votes gave him the vice presidency in the 1944 elections. Pressing his case still harder with working people, Perón soon earned the distrust of President Ramirez, who well understood (by early- to mid-1945, the time of this scene) that the upstart threatened his hold on the presidency. Following an attempted coup in the early fall of 1945, Ramirez packed Perón off to the island of Martín Garcia where he was meant to be a prisoner for two years, but he ended up staying there only a matter of days. In Buenos Aires, Perón's wife Eva had rallied working people *en masse*; they demanded and won the future president's release. In April 1945, then, Squalidozzi's remark is therefore hopeful but on the mark.

V263.34–35, B306.26, P267.17 **"our last hope was Acción Argentina"** A militant Catholic organization, outlawed in 1945.

V263.39, B306.31, P267.21 **"He already has the *descamisados*"** Somewhat anachronistic, because while Perón had rallied the *descamisados* or "shirtless ones" for the 1944 elections, it was not until October 17, 1945, several days after his release from prison and return from exile, that Perón addressed a mass demonstration of workers in the Plaza de Mayo of Buenos Aires and cemented his hold on power. The crowd that day included many of the nation's most impoverished people, and it was then that the nation's elites coined the term *descamisados* in derogation of Perón's movement. He hurled the term back at the elites, using it as a rallying cry for social reform.

V264.4, B306.38, P267.27 **"*Pero ché, no sós argentino*"** In slangy, Argentine Spanish: "But man, you're not Argentine." Or, still better, "But fella, you ain't Argentine."

V264.6–7, B306.41–42, P267.29–30 **Bob Eberle's seen toasts to Tangerine raised in ev-ry bar** The allusion is to the third stanza of "Tangerine," the song written by Johnny Mercer that was a hit for Bob Eberle in 1941. On screen he sang it in the 1942 musical *The Fleet's In*. The lyrics:

> Tangerine! She is all they claim,
> With her eyes of night,
> And her lips bright as flame.
>
> Tangerine! When she dances by
> Señoritas stare
> And caballeros sigh.
>
> And I've seen toasts to Tangerine
> Raised in every bar
> Across the Argentine.

V264.8, B307.1–2, P267.31 **Europe's groaning, clouded alembic** In alchemical terminology, an alembic is the sealed vessel in which the adept seeks to achieve a conjunction of all opposites to produce gold. Here, the European counterpart of the American "melting pot."

V264.15, B307.7, P267.38 **In the Kronenhalle** Since the late nineteenth century one of Zurich's most famous restaurants, located in a five-story Beidermeier building at Rämistrasse 4 (just off the Limmatquai). Known for its Swiss (and French) cuisine and bar, it was a hangout (again) for the likes of Joyce, Trotsky, Thomas Mann, and Picasso.

V264.26–27, B307.24, P268.8 "Look at Borges" Squalidozzi refers to the dichotomy of openness and rationalized space, the latter being the "labyrinth" that is a common symbol in the work of Argentine poet and fiction writer Jorge Luis Borges.

V264.27, B307.25, P268.8–9 "The tyrant Rosas" Juan Manuel de Rosas, a cruel and repressive dictator, ruled Argentina from 1829 to 1851. His relentless persecution of the Indians, and his practice of dragooning the gauchos into military service to kill Indians, forms the historical backdrop to José Hernández's epic poem, *Martín Fierro*.

V264.36–37, B307.35–36, P268.17–18 quoting Saturday-afternoon western movies dedicated to Property if anything is Slothrop probably quotes from some of those Bob Steele and Johnny Mack Brown matinee westerns mentioned earlier (V247.6–7). Many of them, such as Steele's *No Man's Range* and Brown's *Rustlers of Red Dog* (both filmed in 1935) are plotted around range wars, cattle rustlers, and the need of ranchers eventually to fence in their properties and protect them by appealing to the law.

V265.37, B308.42, P269.20 a battered DC-3 Pynchon uses the aircraft's designation as a twin-engine commercial transport. But to the military, for whom the Douglas Aircraft Corporation produced over ten thousand after 1940, it was known as the C-47 "Skytrain" (if you were an American) or as the "Dakota" (if you were British).

V266.7, B309.14, P269.32 Spencer Tracy American actor Tracy (1900–67) played Welsh explorer Henry Norton Stanley for the 1939 film *Stanley and Livingstone*, about the exploration of central Africa—the basis, in pop culture, for Slothrop's understanding of "the Dark Continent" and its denizens. (On Livingstone see also V587.36.)

V266.11, B309.18, P269.39 Richard Halliburton An adventurer and popular writer. *The Royal Road to Romance* (1925), *The Glorious Adventurer* (1932), and *Seven League Boots* (1935) were his most famous works. He died in March 1939, when the ship on which he was traveling went down in heavy North Pacific seas.

V266.23–24, B309.33–34, P270.7–8 Lowell Thomas, Rover and Motor Boys . . . National Geographics Thomas (1892–1975) was a popular American adventurer, radio and television commentator, and writer: *With Lawrence in Arabia* (1924) made him famous. The Rover Boys were the creation of Arthur M. Winfield (1862–1930), author of more than sixty books "For Young Men and Boys," mostly on themes of adventure, heroism, and patriotic history. Under the pseudonym Edward Stratemeyer he published nine Rover Boys books from 1900 to 1922. The Motor Boys were the creation of Clarence Young, who published their motorized adventures (boat, plane, car) in twelve books between

1902 and 1916. The *National Geographic* is of course the well-known magazine published by the National Geographic Society, continuously in print since 1888.

V266.31, B310.2, P270.16–17   Cointrin   A *commune* (township) three miles northwest of Geneva and the site of its airport.

V266.34, B310.4–5, P270.20   Mont Blanc . . . lake sez howdy   At an altitude of 4,856 meters (15,782 feet), the peak of this "White Mountain" (south of Geneva) is the highest of the Alpine chain; the lake is Lake Geneva.

V266.38, B310.9, P270.24   Café l'Éclipse   Unknown, probably fictional.

V267.10, B310.25, P270.36   *Como no, señor*   Of course, sir!

V267.15–16, B310.32, P271.1   He gets off at Schlieren   A suburb of Zurich. Slothrop disembarks the Geneva-Zurich train here, instead of riding it into the main depot (or Bahnhof). Thus he gives his followers the slip. (*Schlieren* incidentally refers to the shadowy pressure waves photographed during wind-tunnel experiments: see V452.30–31n.)

V267.17–18, B310.34, P271.2–3   St. Peterhofstatt   Hitching a ride from Schlieren, Slothrop arrives here, at a street in central Zurich some three or four blocks from his room at the Hotel Nimbus in Niederdorf. And his precautions appear to have been effective; in the next episode we learn through Pointsman that "military intelligence lost him in Zurich" (V270.5).

V267.19–20, B310.36–37, P271.4–5   connects to Ivy League quadrangles   For example, at Harvard University, Slothrop's alma mater and site of his conditioning by Laszlo Jamf.

V267.26, B311.3, P271.12   Fatimas, Castile soap   Fatimas are the cigarettes that Dashiell Hammett's Continental Op smokes, a Turkish and domestic blend that was produced in the U.S. by the Liggett and Myers company and that was the first popular brand sold in twenty-cigarette packs. Castile is a kind (not a brand) of soap made (often at home) from lye and a base of olive, palm, and cocoanut oils, sometimes fragranced with (for example) lavender.

V267.36, B311.15, P271.22   Zwingli's town   Theologian Huldrych Zwingli (1484–1531), the leader of the Swiss Reformation, is fourth from the end in volume 24 of the Chicago edition of the *Encyclopaedia Britannica* (1944).

V268.1, B311.22, P271.28   *Vanitas*, Emptiness   From the Latin: *"vanus,"* "empty." *The Harvard Lampoon*'s well-known insignia features a jester on horseback bearing a shield with the motto VA-NI-TAS graven upon it, their parody of the Harvard crest, featuring the Latin for "truth," VE-RI-TAS.

V268.2, B311.24, P271.29–30   Allen Dulles   Brother to John Foster Dulles, who became Dwight Eisenhower's secretary of state, Allen

Dulles (1893–1969) was the wartime master spy of the OSS. From 1942 to 1945 he was posted in Switzerland and assigned to gather information about anti-Nazi Germans inside the Reich. His 1947 book, *Germany's Underground*, discusses some of these operations. When the OSS was renamed the CIA, in 1947, he returned to lead it into the fifties.

V268.6, B311.29, P271.32–33   *oss*, the late, corrupt, Dark-age Latin   The classical Latin for "bone" was "*os*," from the Greek "*osteon*"; but in medieval Latin the spelling was corrupted to "*oss*," from the stem "*oss*" (as in "*ossuarius*," "of bones"). The OSS was founded in 1942 with William ("Wild Bill") Donovan as its head.

V268.17, B311.42, P272.3   when Shays fought   A reference to Shays's Rebellion of 1786–87, the result of five years' dissatisfaction among the farmers of Massachusetts. High taxes and declining farm income contributed, but the decisive factor was the repeal of legal-tender status for paper currency. This meant that debts had to be repaid in scrip, which carried a 6 percent surcharge. Daniel Shays was a former officer in the revolutionary army; he led the insurrectionists as they descended on Springfield, Massachusetts, where they attempted to seize the federal arsenal. Tyrone Slothrop may have a "bland ignorance" (V268.24) of the topic but Thomas Pynchon does not, for his ancestor William Pynchon founded Springfield in the seventeenth century, and that ancestor's great-great-great-grandson, Major William Pynchon (1740–1808), served among the federal troops that ended Shays's revolt.

V268.18–19, B312.2–3, P272.5   sprigs of hemlock in their hats   To distinguish themselves from the federals who wore white-papered hats, the Shaysites put sprigs of this evergreen tree (genus *Tsuga*) in theirs. The tree is common throughout North America and especially in western Massachusetts where, in the Berkshires, it was logged off and pulped in the paper mills, a detail Pynchon would have cribbed from copy of *The Berkshire Hills* (see V28.2). Not to be confused with the European hemlock bush (genus *Conium*) known for its "white flowered, mousey-smelling" blossoms that supplied the poison used to execute Socrates and that is sacred to the White Goddess (Graves, *The White Goddess* 12).

V269.9–10, B312.39, P272.35–36   dream of Atlantis, of the Suggenthal   Atlantis is the mythical kingdom that Plato discusses in his *Timaeus* and in his unfinished work, *Critias*. British Masonic philosopher Francis Bacon used that background in developing the idea of his utopian society in *The New Atlantis* (1625). Pynchon's source on the "Suggenthal," or sunken city of Teutonic mythology, was Grimm (1982–84), who notes that in some versions of the *Nibelung* saga, this city houses the Nibelungen gold hoard.

V269.13, B313.2, P272.39   Lucky Strike   See V20.18–19n.

EPISODE 8

Part 2 of *GR*, which opened on Christmas, now closes on Whitsunday, May 20, 1945, with Pointsman, Roger, Jessica, and Katje at a seaside resort, probably Brighton. This feast day occasions some light parody. On Whitsunday, or Pentecost, Christians celebrate the descent of the Holy Ghost on Christ's disciples; in this scene Pointsman, a kind of disciple to the mock-hero Slothrop, hears voices. They intimate the same delusions of power that have dogged Pointsman all along. Pynchon also takes the opportunity to sum up their relationship now that peace has descended.

V269.26, B313.17, P273.11   Whitsun   The feast of Pentecost, which falls on the seventh Sunday, or fifty days, after Easter. That holiday having been celebrated on April 1 in 1945, the feast of Pentecost fell on May 20. In England Whitsun, or "White Sunday," derives its name from the medieval practice of clothing newly baptized Christians in white robes on this day.

V269.30, B313.22, P273.15   parkinsonism   Not the muscular tremor of Parkinson's disease (these people are "frozen"), but the stooping posture and facial distortions caused by it.

V269.32, B313.24, P273.15   Trafalgar Square on V-E Night   During the noon hour on May 8, over sixty thousand Londoners listened to the king's victory broadcast over loudspeakers; that night, the *Times* of London reported, more than a hundred thousand celebrated around Nelson's brightly lit column, skyrockets and firecrackers bursting around them.

V269.33–35, B313.26–28, P273.17–19   the Blavatskian wing . . . White Lotos Day pilgrimage to 19 Avenue Road, St. John's Wood   Elena Petrovna Blavatsky (1831–91) was the founder of the Theosophical Society. Its three aims were to promote the unity of mankind; to promote the comparative study of religion, philosophy, and science; and to explore human psychic faculties. Theosophists adopted the Hindu white lotos, a symbol of the Trimurti, or threefold godhead, as a sign of these unified aims. To them, the lotos also symbolized the unity of world religions: in Hinduism it is *padma*, birthplace of the gods, and in Buddhism it is the Buddha's throne, just as in Egyptian religions the lotos was Horus's seat. It came to Christianity as the multifoliate rose. Blavatsky died on the Buddha's birthday, May 8, 1891, at the address Pynchon gives on Avenue Road, just north of Regents Park in St. John's Wood. Thus, fifty-four years later, on V-E Day, the day both Harry Truman and Thomas Pynchon celebrated their birthdays (the one was sixty-one, the other eight), these fictional Blavatskians from "The White Visitation" make their "pilgrimage" in her honor.

V270.4–5, B313.33–34, P273.24   no word of Slothrop for nearly a month . . . lost him in Zürich   Readers previously saw (at V267.17–18n) that

Slothrop's evasive maneuvers in Zürich might have easily given his pursuers the slip (or at least those pursuers sent by Pointsman, for others—such as Clive Mossmoon—seem to think that Slothrop, out in the Zone, is still under their watchful eyes). These lines underscore that reading and also confirm the chronology: Slothrop slipped free in late April, "nearly a month" before this remark.

V270.6, B313.35, P273.26 browned-off British service slang from World War I meaning "bored," "disgusted with," or "embittered" (Partridge, *Forces' Slang* 28).

V270.14–15, B314.8–9, P273.34–35 the Tennysonian comfort of saying "someone" has blundered An allusion to stanza 2 of Tennyson's famous poem "The Charge of the Light Brigade" (1854):

"Forward, the Light Brigade!"
Was there a man dismay'd?
Not though the soldier knew
Someone had blunder'd.
Theirs not to make reply,
Theirs not to reason why,
Theirs but to do or die;
Into the valley of Death,
Rode the six hundred.

V270.16, B314.9, P274.1–2 Floyd Perdoo If they've lost Slothrop, then it's ironic that they've assigned Perdoo (from the French "*perdue*," "lost") to fix their blunder and find the man.

V270.19–20, B314.14–15, P274.4–5 Munchkins ... into the erotic Poisson. Don Giovanni's map Munchkins are the midget beings in the film *The Wizard of Oz* (1939); in Oz, they help start Dorothy along the Yellow Brick Road. Here, they are imagined skipping off into the Poisson distribution of Slothrop's erotic adventures, envisioned as mapped conquests of the legendary Don Juan. Act 1 of Mozart's *Don Giovanni* includes a long list of the Don's conquests, organized by nation (in Leporello's "Madamina" aria).

V270.23, B314.19, P274.8 mindless pleasures Once again, the working title of *GR*.

V272.19, B316.28–29, P276.7 young Sigmund Freud's This is the initial reference to Freud (1856–1939) and his research into deviant sexuality, circa 1905, which reappears in a similar context at V737.6. Here Pointsman makes specific reference to Freud's *seduction theory*, which explained away the testimonies of women claiming to recall being sexually abused by their fathers when they were children (hence Pointsmen's derogatory reference to "Papi-has-raped-me-stories"); to Freud these claims were instead unconscious, projective, wish-fulfillment fantasies: hence not actual truths but, as Pointsmen says here, "the truth *clinically*."

V272.32–34, B317.2–5, P276.20–23   Special Projectiles Operations Group . . . Operation Backfire . . . Cuxhaven   Dennis Joint is a fictional "representative" but these bureaucracies are not. SPOG was a subsidiary organization of CIOS (Combined Intelligence Objectives Subcommittee), created by "British-American Combined Chiefs of Staff in the Summer of 1944 to plan and administer an orderly exploitation of German scientific targets" (McGovern, *Crossbow and Overcast* 102). The British name for the recovery and testing of V-2 rockets was Operation Backfire; in October 1945 this program did succeed in launching three rockets northward from Cuxhaven (Huzel, *Peenemünde to Canaveral* 200–04). The comparable American effort, code-named Project Hermes, involved the transfer of one hundred partially completed V-2 rockets to White Sands, New Mexico, for test-firings.

V272.37, B317.8, P276.25   a l'etat c'est moi frame of mind   It was Louis XIV who announced, in 1651, before the assembled parliament of France, "I am the state."

V273.3, B317.16, P276.32   They took Peenemünde in the spring   The Russian army advanced on the Rugen Peninsula, and the island of Peenemünde, in mid-April 1945.

V273.3–5, B317.17–18, P276.32–34   they will be given . . . Nordhausen . . . dealings at Yalta   In accordance with boundary lines drawn at the Yalta Conference of February 4–11, 1945, Roosevelt, Churchill, and Stalin agreed that the Russian zone of occupation would extend through Thuringia and include Nordhausen, located in the Harz Mountains, where, unbeknownst to any of the Allies, Germany was producing V-2 rockets at an underground factory. The Americans overran Nordhausen in April and plundered as much of the hardware as possible; then under the Yalta accords it was ceded to Soviet control in June. Bower (*The Paperclip Conspiracy* 107–30) provides an excellent summary of Allied efforts, after taking the territory, to spirit out German rocket experts prior to the scheduled handover.

V273.5, B317.19, P276.34–35   VIAM, TsAGI, and NISO   The source here is McGovern (*Crossbow and Overcast* 126): "A special council under the Council of People's Commissars, headed by Malenkov, had . . . been formed in 1944. Representatives of VIAM, the All-Union Institute of Aviation Materials; TsAGI, the Central Aerodynamics and Hydrodynamics Institute; NISO, the Scientific Research Institute for Airplane Equipment; and engineers from various other commissariats had been given special powers and a mission." They were charged with gathering scientific intelligence on the V-weapons, especially the rocket.

V273.10–11, B317.25–26, P276.40–41   von Braun and 500 others . . . at Garmisch   Huzel's account is the best, and most likely it was Pynchon's source. Through his brother, Magnus, Wernher von Braun arranged for his own surrender and that of his entire technical staff on

Wednesday, May 2, 1945. They gave themselves up to the Americans, who decided to detain five hundred of them at the Bavarian town of Garmisch-Partenkirchen. They remained there for several months under interrogation until finally the Allied governments decided they would not be tried for war crimes.

V273.24, B318.12–23, P277.13   the Dodgem cars   Details here suggest that the seaside resort is Brighton, with its promenade of amusements that Baedeker describes (*Great Britain* 108). These electrically powered cars (hence the "ozone" smell), often known as "bumper cars," were trademarked in the U.S. by Dogdem Cars Ltd. in 1922. In 1928 William Butlin—having seen the cars in Canada—brought them to England where they became a favorite ride at seacoast amusement piers.

V273.30, B318.8, P277.18   Eton hats   Little flat-top hats with narrow, flat brims, so called for the students who wear them at England's exclusive private school for boys, Eton College, Windsor, founded in 1440 by "Scholar King" Henry VI. The likes of the Duke of Wellington, Thomas Gray, Percy Bysshe Shelley, and William Ewart Gladstone were educated there.

V273.37–41, B318.17–18, P277.26–29   Rossini's overture to *La Gazza Ladra* . . . without snaredrums or the sonority of brasses   The opening bars of Rossini's overture to *The Thieving Magpie* commence with a long snare-drum roll and conclude with the brasses laying down a sonorous melody line for the violins. Without them, then, the piece would be severely diminished.

V274.18, B319.2, P278.12   dubbed "Twelfth House"   Probably because Pisces is the twelfth house in astrology and a sign of dissolution and death.

V274.25, B319.11–12, P278.20   like Rita Hayworth   Her 1939 film *Only Angels Have Wings* was the first big film role for American actress Rita Hayworth, and *Cover Girl* (1944) capitalized on her popularity among U.S. servicemen, yielding the famous photo of her.

V275.1, B319.27–28, P278.33   a Wheel of Fortune   A carnival game, like an upright roulette wheel.

V275.11, B319.40, P279.3   her Fay Wray number   The second time Jessica has deployed it (see V57.8n).

V275.13–14, B320.1, P279.5–6   the Fist of the Ape . . . lights of electric New York white-waying into the room   Referring to the big scene in *King Kong*, when the ape grabs Ann Denham (Wray) from her room and takes her to the top of the Empire State Building, at Fifth Avenue and 34th Street, but with the lights of Broadway ("The Great White Way") glimmering below them.

V275.25–26, B320.16–17, P279.17   Murphy's Law . . . restatement of Gödel's Theorem   A humorous axiom of engineers everywhere, Murphy's Law holds that "when nothing can go wrong, something will" (or, in another version, "if anything can go wrong, it will"). Gödel's theorem is named for German mathematician Kurt Gödel (1906–78), whose famous paper of 1931 addresses the long-standing problem of "axiomatic consistency." Before Gödel, it appeared that Alfred North Whitehead and Bertrand Russell's monumental *Principia Mathematica* (1910) had established the consistency of all axioms within the system of arithmetic. Whitehead and Russell had employed a method of "mapping," or translating, arithmetical expressions onto sentences of formal logic. These sentences could then be verified and tested for consistency as purely logical statements. But the results would also be applicable, by reversing the mapping, to the system of arithmetical axioms: for example, the axioms governing multiplication. *Principia Mathematica* ran to three cumbersome volumes. Gödel's relatively succinct paper, "On Formally Undecidable Propositions in *Principia Mathematica* and Related Systems" (1931), overturned the work of Russell and Whitehead in just over thirty pages. Using the same methods of "mapping" as appear in *Principia*, Gödel was able to produce a sentence that demonstrated that Russell and Whitehead's work, "or any related system," was inherently incomplete. There would always exist, within the rules of the system, the possibility of a sentence or proposition the validity of which could not be decided by the rules themselves.

   Half a century later, Gödel's theorem now stands with Einstein's relativity theory and Heisenberg's undecidability principle as one of the cornerstones of modernist science. In *GR*, Gödel's incompleteness theorem is a hopeful sign. When it crops up again (V320.19), it is in the context of an infinite postponement of suicide, because some thing might be missing from one's catalog of worldly disgusts and denials. In formal logic and metamathematics, the incompleteness theorem establishes that formal closure, completeness, and the internal consistency of any complex, logical system may all be pipe dreams. As such, it makes a telling background to Pynchon's representations of closed versus open fields, of being "shut in by words" (V339.36–37) as opposed to breaking free by means of them. Some twenty pages back Slothrop thought to himself: "Free? What's free?" (V256.33). As metaphor, Gödel's theorem— in its vernacular version, Murphy's Law—begins to answer that question.

V275.34–35, B320.26–27, P279.26–27   legend of the black scapeape . . . tallest erection in the world   The reference is to *King Kong*, machinegunned from atop New York's Empire State Building in the closing scenes of Merian Cooper's 1933 film.

V276.21, B321.16, P280.13–14   the Tavistock Institute   Founded in 1920 by Dr. Hugh Crichton-Miller, a specialist in shell shock and similar war-related neuroses, the Tavistock Institute of England brought psychoanalytical techniques, both Freudian and Jungian, to England. In 1946 the group was reconstituted as the Tavistock Institute of Human Relations, administered through the newly established National Health Service.

V276.30–31, B321.28, P280.23   Gavin Trefoil, face as blue as Krishna On Gavin Trefoil, his role in the Operation Black Wing films, and his resemblance to Krishna, see V147.13n.

V277.14, B322.16, P281.7   gemütlich   German for "genial," or "cozy."

V277.24, B322.27–28, P281.17   like Lord Acton always sez   The reference is to Acton's famous comment in an 1887 letter to Bishop Creighton: "Power tends to corrupt; absolute power corrupts absolutely."

V277.34–38, B322.40–323.3, P281.28–31   the eloquent words of Sir Denis Nayland Smith to young Alan Sterling . . . "the best ointment for the burns"   The quotation is from *The Trail of Fu-Manchu*, the 1934 sequel by Sax Rohmer (Arthur Sarsfield Ward) to his *The Bride of Fu-Manchu* (1933). The earlier book had left its romantic hero, a young American named Alan Sterling, engaged to Fleurette Petrie, daughter of a friend of Nayland Smith, intrepid detective of Scotland Yard. In *The Trail of Fu-Manchu*, the "insidious yellow doctor" kidnaps Fleurette, and the words quoted here are Nayland Smith's advice to Sterling. There are few extant library copies of the book (New York: Doubleday, Doran, 1934), but readers can find a serialization of the narrative in *Collier's* magazine; the quotation here is from the edition of May 5, 1934 (15).

V277.38–39, B323.4, P281.32   what Nayland Smith represents   Mostly he represents a single-minded, puritanical devotion to work and a chivalric devotion to battling the dragons of evil.

V278.16, B323.27, P282.10   "Yang and Yin"   See V88.34n.

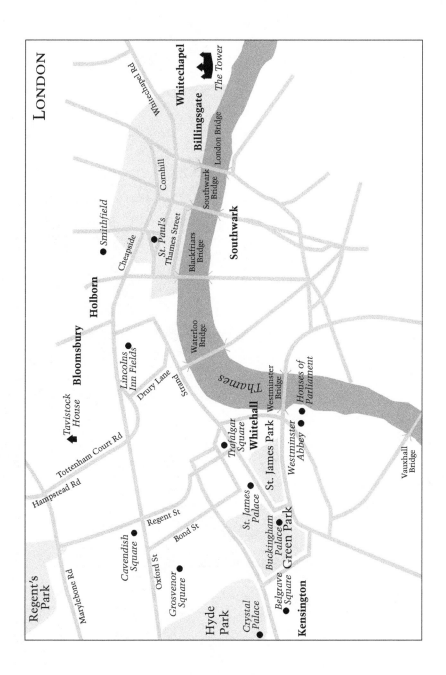

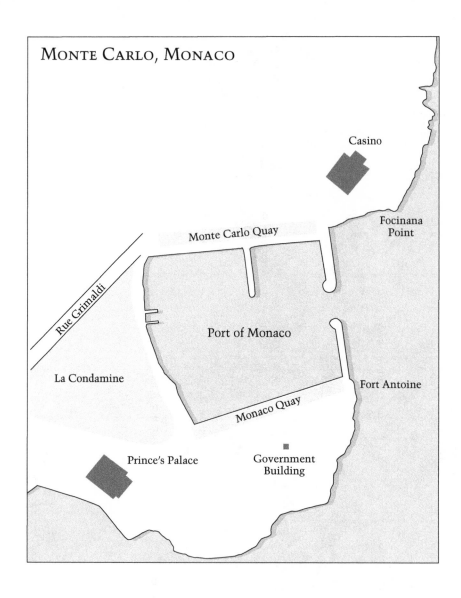

MONTE CARLO, MONACO

Casino

Focinana
Point

Monte Carlo Quay

Rue Grimaldi

Port of Monaco

La Condamine

Monaco Quay

Fort Antoine

Prince's Palace

Government
Building

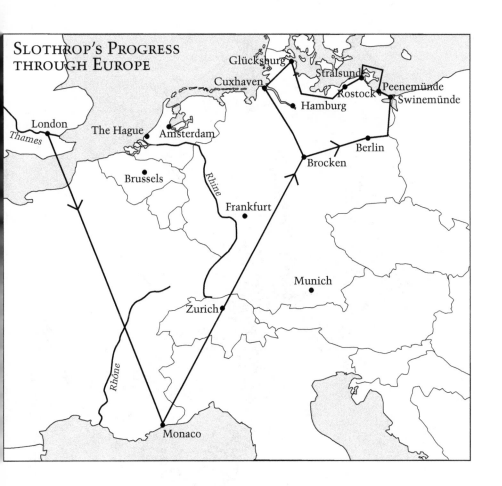

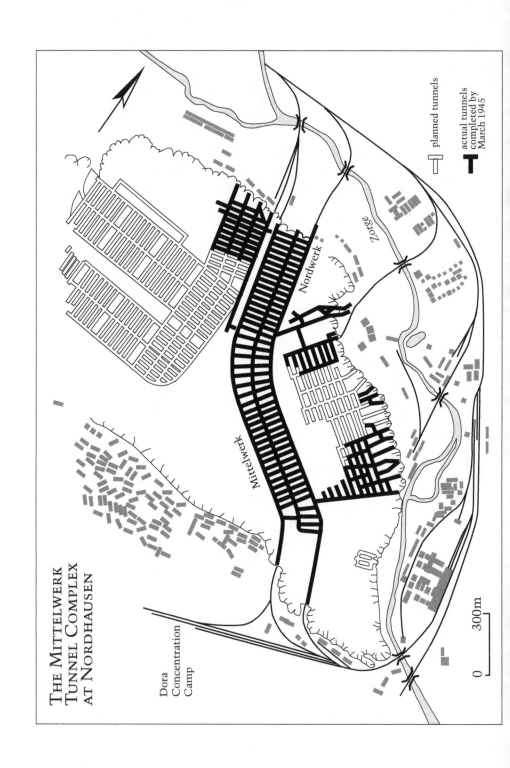

THE MITTELWERK
TUNNEL COMPLEX
AT NORDHAUSEN

Dora
Concentration
Camp

Mittelwerk

Nordwerk

Zorge

planned tunnels

actual tunnels
completed by
March 1945

0   300m

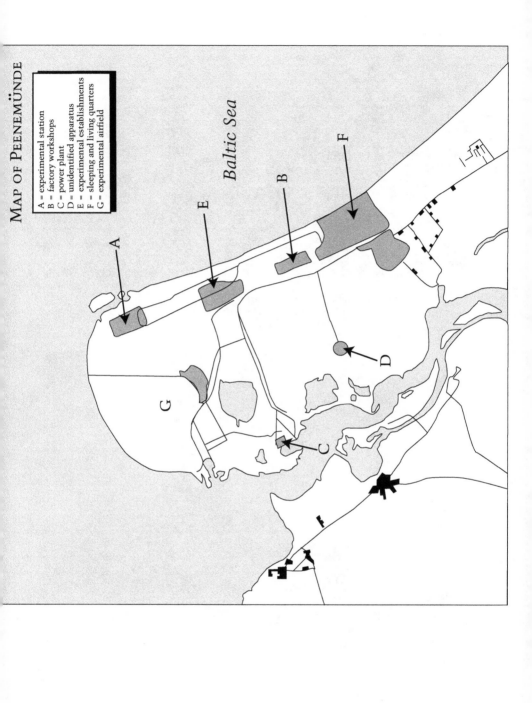

MAP OF PEENEMÜNDE

A = experimental station
B = factory workshops
C = power plant
D = unidentified apparatus
E = experimental establishments
F = sleeping and living quarters
G = experimental airfield

Baltic Sea

Production of V-2 rockets in caverns near Nordhausen. Courtesy of National Air and Space Museum, Smithsonian Institution (SI 79-13166).

Rocket on Meilerwagen. Courtesy of Foto Deutsches Museum.

Left: Three rockets raised atop their Bodenplatte. Courtesy of Foto Deutsches Museum.

Below: Rubble-strewn entrance to Mittelwerk in May 1945. Courtesy of National Air and Space Museum, Smithsonian Institution (SI 79-13171).

Wernher Von Braun (in cast) and Walter Dornberger (with cigar) at Garmisch, following their May 1945 surrender. © Corbis. All rights reserved.

Part 3   *In the Zone*

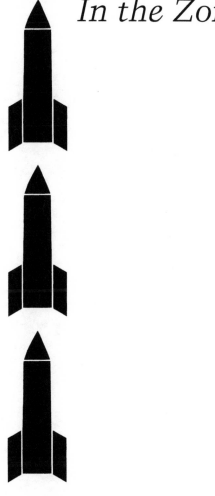

"FREE? What's free?" Slothrop wondered during his first day in Nice. Part 3 of *GR* explores that question. Set in the occupied zone of middle Europe during the summer of 1945, its dominant astrological sign is Leo, a fire sign and, as Marc E. Jones (*Astrology* 263) has phrased it, a time when "the bringing of facts into a simple conformity to the ideals held for them is a necessity." Here the possibilities for Slothrop's freedom are put to the test. Is there any way for him to wrest his being away from the logics and mechanics of submission and control, from the dominion of the war machine that seems to have determined his being? What in any case does Slothrop *want*? What role does the sovereign state play in this drama? Have agencies of the state in fact *planned* Slothrop's run for "freedom," and if they have, then what nefarious purposes guide them? Indeed, in the seemingly stateless "Zone" of occupied Europe, with streams of displaced persons flowing past Slothrop, a larger question is whether traditional sovereignties have been reconfigured according to the needs of an emergent corporatized, globalized network of control. This new state of late modernity assumes authority over the rubble and the land and its peoples—however displaced. Its power is galvanized in this part of the novel by the Rocket and nuclear weaponry—technologies literally and figuratively melded and then *translated* from Germany to the Allied West and the Soviet East. The action begins around May 18, several days before the end of part 2, on Whitsunday. Part 3 will end just before dawn on August 6, 1945, the Feast of the Transfiguration, the celebration of the radiance of Jesus's divinity revealed to his disciples on a mountaintop. In the novel Slothrop will experience a parody of that sacred revelation as part 4 begins, but part 3 will draw to a close on the morning of August 6, when the *Enola Gay* and the atomic bomb it cradles are approaching the city of Hiroshima.

The epigraph, "Toto, I have a feeling we're not in Kansas any more," derives from the film *The Wizard of Oz* (1939). In Dorothy's trauma-induced dream, her house has just fallen to the ground of Oz, killing the Wicked Witch of the East. This is her first comment on stepping through the door into a brilliantly colored world, the drab black-and-white of Kansas now behind her.

Part 3 of the novel includes thirty-two episodes, perhaps because the gravitational pull on matter is a constant thirty-two feet per second and perhaps because the number is significant in Kabbalistic mythology, where it is associated with the acquisition of wisdom. Specifically, Yahweh is thought to have inscribed his being in thirty-two paths of knowledge, comprising the ten numbers of the Sephiroth and the twenty-two letters of the Hebrew alphabet. C. G. Jung (*Collected Works* 12:205–06) quotes one Kabbalistic text in which the number thirty-two represents "the differentiation which appears in the organic world; not creative generation, but rather the plan and arrangement of the various forms of created things which the creator has modeled." In the open field of "the Zone," a geographical slate momentarily wiped clean, Tyrone Slothrop thus begins his quest for wisdom. Along the way he will change his outward self four more times: as part 3 begins he is still Ian Scuffling, war correspondent; but soon he becomes Rocketman, then Max Schlepzig (a Russian soldier), and finally Plechazunga (a pig hero). As Plechazunga he narrowly escapes castration at the hands of Edward Pointsman's agents from the now-declining "White Visitation."

EPISODE I

Internal references place the date of this episode as around May 16–18, 1945. Slothrop has traveled from Zurich to the Harz Mountains of central Germany. He arrives in Nordhausen to pursue simultaneously information about the rocket and details of his own childhood. Reading over documents handed to him in episode 7 of part 2, he is stunned to learn the welter of ties binding him to Laszlo Jamf, Imipolex G, and the V-2 rocket.

V281.1–2, B327.1–2, P285.1–2   the Eis-Heiligen—St. Pancratius, St. Servatius, St. Bonifacius, die Kalte Sophie   These "Ice Saints" are, in order: Pancratius and Servatius, whose feast days occur on May 12 and 13, respectively; Boniface of Ferentino, a Pope (608–15), whose feast day is May 14; and "Cold Sophie," for Saint Sophia, on May 15, a figure added to the pantheon of *die Eisheiligen* by German unification in the modern period, for her feast was originally honored by residents in southern Germany, Austria, and Switzerland. All four are known as the "Ice Saints" because their feast days coincide with a final cold spell that often arrives in mid-May (farmers and wine growers used to burn wet wood, green twigs, and soil, raising a thick smoky fog over the valleys to help protect new growth and blossoms from frost). The Ice Saints' days are a threshold, as gardeners wait until mid-May has passed before planting many seedlings.

V281.11–12, B327.14, P285.12–13   dragon's teeth, fallen Stukas   In the Hellenic myth of Cadmus, the hero kills a dragon guarding the pond where he means to establish the city of Thebes, unaware that the creature is sacred to Ares, the god of war. Athena appears and orders Cadmus to make reparation by sowing half the dragon's teeth; he no sooner does so than an army sprouts up and begins squabbling. Five *sparti* (sown men) remain after the fighting concludes, and they form the nucleus of Theban culture. Cadmus, meanwhile, is also forced to give eight years' service to Ares. In any case, the "dragon's teeth" of this scene are the steel-reinforced concrete pilings sown, as it were, in the ground to thwart the movement of armored vehicles such as tanks. *Stukas* are German dive-bombers (V102.29n).

V281.14–15, B327.17–18, P285.15–16   The vintage . . . will be fine   Vintage calendars note that 1945 was indeed a fine year for German white wines.

V281.20, B327.24–25, P285.21   some DP   The abbreviation for a "displaced person."

V281.23–24, B327.27–29, P285.24   red tulip . . . reminder of Katje   Because tulips are virtually the national symbol of Holland and perhaps also because Katje made Slothrop "disappear" under a red tablecloth (V198.8–9n). Tulip season in northern Europe runs from mid-April to mid-May.

V281.25, B327.30, P286.1   the Zone   Slothrop stands in what is at the moment the American zone of occupied Germany, ceded to the Soviets in June–July 1945.

V281.33, B328.2, P286.9   Herero beliefs about ancestors   The Herero believe that their dead ancestors dwell in the North (V327.11–17n), a myth that gathers resonance as Slothrop arrives in Nordhausen ("North dwelling" or "to dwell in the North"). Also, the Herero believe that cattle are gifts from dead ancestors (V316.28–29n), an idea present, here, in the image of "God clamoring" to black-coated Puritans (the white Anglo-Saxon protestants or "WASPs") in "every turn of a leaf or cow" (V281.35–36).

V282.6, B328.14–15, P286.19   Major-General Kammler's rocket units   An SS general, Hans Kammler was appointed deputy special commissioner for A4 matters by Hitler in 1943 at the request of the SS head, Heinrich Himmler. Thereafter, Kammler proceeded to wrest control of the rocket program from the regular army, a power play Dornberger (*V-2* 196–99) describes with some bitterness. Five battalions of rocket troops operated under Kammler from 1944 to 1945.

V283.5, B329.21–22, P287.20   the lovely little Queen of Transylvania   This is the last line of the "Vulgar Song" from the Casino Hermann Goering in part 2 (V213.21–32).

V284.15–16, B330.34–36, P288.29   on the board of directors of the Grössli Chemical Corporation as late as 1924   Here and in the following paragraphs Pynchon weaves the fabric of Laszlo Jamf's life from Sasuly's disclosures in *IG Farben* (especially 180–90). IG Farben acquired the dyestuff manufacturer Grasselli in stepwise fashion, beginning in 1925. This is why Jamf's tie-in, until "as late as 1924," assumes significance. IG Farben took over the company's dyestuffs production in 1928 and several days later DuPont purchased Grasselli's chemical operations. Then, in 1929, IG Farben formed the American IG Company, a hodgepodge of interests that included Agfa-Ansco (producers of photographic materials), as well as a firm with the fine Puritan name of Winthrop Chemical. All of these American companies under the IG Farben umbrella maintained close ties with DuPont, which had clearly been compensated for IG Farben's American push by the acquisition of Grasselli back in 1928. This, at least, was Sasuly's contention. If the calculations at V624.18n are fairly close, then Slothrop is six years old in

1924, and this is how his file, with all its data on his conditioning, passes into the institutional labyrinth of these corporate cartels.

V284.23, B331.7, P288.37   the Hugo Stinnes operation in Germany Once more the details are adapted from Sasuly (42–44). Compare, for example, Pynchon's "Based out of the Ruhr, where his family had been coal barons for generations" (V284.24–25) with Sasuly's "His family had been prominent in the coal industry of the Ruhr for generations" (42). The details of Pynchon's narration about how Stinnes put together a "super-cartel" (V284.31) of electric and coal/iron industries (the Siemens-Schuchert firm, the Rheinelbe Union, mentioned in the following passage) derive in similar fashion from Sasuly.

V284.37, B331.24–25, P289.14   he was blamed for the Inflation Stinnes engineered the inflation of 1921–25 as a means of negating the stiff reparations payments levied against Germany by the Treaty of Versailles. The details on Stinnes's arrangements with the German financiers Krupp and Thyssen derive from Sasuly (45–47).

V285.9, B331.39, P289.25   another of Hjalmar Schacht's many bookkeeping dodges The interestingly named Horace Greeley Hjalmar Schacht headed Germany's Reichsbank during the carefully orchestrated inflation of the twenties. Like Stinnes's, his strategy was to drive down the value of German marks so that the reparations payments could be made in devalued currency. At the same time he supplied German manufacturers with another, secret currency, the *Notgeld*, for transactions among themselves. In the thirties, with Krupp von Bohlen and steel magnate Albert Vogler, he arranged massive donations of cash that sealed Nazi Party victories in the crucial elections of 1933. Known worldwide as "Hitler's Banker," Schacht was acquitted of war crimes at the Nuremberg Tribunal and acquitted of being a Nazi functionary at the Lüneburg trials. He died in 1970 at age ninety-three.

V285.18, B332.9, P289.34   these eight ink marks That is, in the name "Slothrop." Yet the number eight has widespread significance throughout *GR*: there were eight episodes in part 2; Slothrop assumes eight different identities in the narrative; V-E Day, White Lotos Day, and Pynchon's birthday all fell on May 8; the text references Krishna, eighth avatar of Vishnu (V147.13n).

V285.37, B332.33, P290.13   Jim Fisk style Vermont-born James "Jubilee Jim" Fisk (1834–72) quit school early, worked for a circus barker, became a traveling salesman, and then, during the Civil War, dealt cotton smuggled through Union blockades—a risky business in which he made and lost a fortune. As a stockbroker after the war he rebuilt his fortune, again on the illicit side. With partners Daniel Drew and Jay Gould he tried to use his ownership in the Erie Railroad to destroy competition in western Massachussetts; when that fell through, he then attempted to hoard gold and ruin the stock market. In January 1872, Fisk was shot to death by a man who was his rival for the hand of a woman. His rambunctious career is well documented in Robert Fuller's *Jubilee Jim*, in Henry and Charles Adams's *Chapters of Erie* (1871), and in chapter 3 of Mathew Josephson's *The Robber-Barons* (1934). He reappears at V378.16, and V438.15–17.

V286.5, B333.1, P290.22   Schwarzknabe   That is, "black boy."

V286.6, B333.3, P289.23   Schwindel   "Giddiness" but also "swindle," an apt code name for a double-dealer like Stinnes.

V287.1–4, B334.4–7, P291.19   dictionary of technical German . . . JAMF . . . definition would read: I   A paranoid Slothropian fantasy.

V287.23, B334.30, P291.41   hitched a lift on a P-47   This would have been difficult, or at the least very cramped, since the American-built P-47 "Thunderbolt" fighter plane was designed as a single-seat attack aircraft. But Marvy could have "hitched a lift" on a C-47 transport plane (see V265.37n), an aircraft much more likely to be flying the skies during peacetime between two medium-sized cities like Kassel and Heiligenstadt in Thuringia.

V287.25–26, B334.33–34, P292.2–3   Project Hermes people from General Electric   Under the code name Hermes, GE and U.S. Army Ordnance worked to sneak one hundred dismantled A4 rockets out of Germany to White Sands, New Mexico, for extensive testing. Pynchon's source on these details is McGovern (*Crossbow and Overcast* 101–02).

V287.36, B335.4, P292.13–14   Old Blood 'n' Guts   Nickname of U.S. Army general George S. Patton (1885–1945), whose armored divisions defeated German general Erwin Rommel in the north African deserts. In 1943, he led the Seventh Army's invasion of Sicily; in 1944, he took command of the Third Army, leading it from France through Belgium, Germany, Austria, and Czechoslovakia.

V288.2, B335.13, P292.21   P/Ws   Another abbreviation for prisoners of war (in British usage).

V288.4, B335.15, P292.23   "Russkys, frogs, limeys"   Slang for Russians, Frenchmen, and Englishmen.

V288.25, B335.41–42, P293.3   A crescent moon has risen   A waxing crescent moon appeared in the night sky from May 16 until May 18, 1945.

V288.26, B336.1–2, P293.4   introduces himself, in English, as Oberst Enzian   Not to nitpick, but in English he would say "Colonel [or Group Captain] Enzian." On the character's name and its origins in Rilke, see V101.23–26n.

V289.12, B336.31, P293.31   Quit kvetchin', Gretchen!   From "*kvetch,*" Yiddish verb meaning "to complain."

V289.18–19, B336.39, P293.38   makeshift PXs   A military-sponsored marketplace or "post exchange."

V289.28, B337.10, P294.7   long-looted by the slave laborers . . . the Dora camp   The Nazi SS operated the top-secret Dora concentration camp next to the Nordhausen Mittelwerke. It was liberated on April 11, 1945, when troops of the U.S. 104th Infantry Division, which had been advancing rapidly across Thuringia, drove up to the wire enclosure and survivors threw open the gates, the guards having previously left on an eastward forced-march of the relatively healthier inmates. Inside the gates Americans found thousands of bodies laid out in rows, and several hundred starving, desperately ill survivors, who had indeed looted the surrounding buildings. At its peak, the Dora inmates—shipped mainly from Buchenwald—had numbered around forty thousand and were employed chiefly in extending the existing tunnel system for V-weapons production, although some with special skills assisted in production work (McGovern, *Crossbow and Overcast* 79, 121–22). Wegener recalls a March 1945 visit to the *Mittelwerke* and his shock on seeing those inmates. The "skilled people from many different countries" who had been brought from other camps to Dora were given "just enough food to survive and still perform the required work." He observed that they were restive, and well aware of events outside the wire boding the war's end; indeed they had secreted weapons throughout the tunnels for what would prove to be a futile resistance, as the bodies that soldiers of the 104th Infantry came across attested to. Wegener further records that during his visit he was told how some workers accused of sabotage had been hanged from a crane, and their bodies "left hanging for all to see" (94–95).

V289.29, B337.11, P294.8   those *fags* still around . . . 175 badges   The badges designated them as prisoners interned for violating paragraph 175 of the German Penal Code, "which exacted punishment for certain abnormal sex practices" (Kracauer, *From Caligari to Hitler* 45).

V290.7, B337.29, P294.25   Under the rose   From "sub rosa," the Latin phrase indicating that which is secret, spoken in confidence. Also the title of a short story Pynchon published in *Noble Savage* (1961), later rewritten as chapter 3 of *V.*, subtitled "In which Stencil, a quick-change artist, does eight impersonations" (so will Tyrone Slothrop, in *GR*).

V290.15–16, B337.37–39, P294.33–34   Her name turns out to be Geli Tripping . . . a Soviet intelligence officer named Tchitcherine   Notice the onomastic pun in her name: the German-sounding name Geli Tripping and the English verb yield "gaily tripping," no doubt also in the sixties slang sense of "tripping," as in a drug-induced fantasy. There is a historical echo as well. Geli Raubal was Adolf Hitler's niece, twenty years old when he met her for the first time in 1928 while living at Obersalzburg in Austria. They soon became deeply affectionate; indeed, Geli Raubal would travel and make public appearances with Hitler. Heini Hoffman in his 1955 book *Hitler Was My Friend* refers to Geli as "a child of nature"; other memoirists and historians (such as Alan Bullock, in his 1952 book *Hitler*) record that Geli became quite jealous when Hitler, then in his early forties, took up with a still younger girl, Eva Braun, just seventeen, beginning a relationship that would last until his suicide. In September 1931, after an argument that may have had to do with Eva Braun's increasing influence, Geli Raubal took her life by shooting herself in the chest with a pistol. As for the name of this Tchitcherine who gives Geli Tripping the balalaika for this scene, the source may have been Theodore von Kármán's book *The Wind and Beyond*: "Frank Tchitcherine was of Russian origin, and in fact had been related to the first Minister of Education in the Kerensky government. This Tchitcherine helped convince the Germans to disclose their hiding place for literally tons of research documents pertaining to the rocket and supersonic flight" (276). Yet David Seed ("Pynchon's Two Tchitcherines") adds that Pynchon may have also meant to reference the Georgi Tchitcherine who negotiated the Rapallo Treaty of 1922 between Germany and the USSR, enabling the German army secretly to produce weapons banned by the Treaty of Versailles, though Pynchon writes that his "Vaslav" is "no relation" to him (V238.3–4).

V290.21, B338.5–6, P295.1 Nordhäuser Schattensaft A fictional wine: a *Schattensaft* would be a "shadow juice" (one of many shadows, nimbuses, etc.). In any case Nordhausen is not a wine-producing region.

V290.39, B338.27, P295.20 even G-5 See V125.22n.

V291.32, B339.23, P296.12 a Baby Ruth Registered trademark of the American candy bar, first marketed by the Curtiss Candy Company in 1921.

V292.25, B340.20, P297.4 "like that Ernest Hemingway" The subject once more is moustaches. Future novelist Ernest Hemingway was still a cub reporter for the *Kansas City Star* in 1917; later, while recovering from his war wound, he worked as a correspondent for the *Toronto Daily Star*, and by that time had grown a moustache.

V292.41, B340.39–40, P297.20 best Cary Grant imitation See V294.11n.

V293.10–11, B341.8–9, P297.30 "if the *Guardian* will even be interested" Slothrop fakes an employer, probably the Manchester *Guardian*, an English weekly newspaper.

V293.14–15, B341.14–15, P297.35 "I posed once for a rocket insignia . . . I was voted the Sweetheart of 3/Art. Abt. (mot) 485" There was just such an insignia but no such squadron. Klee and Merk (*The Birth of the Missile* 38) include a photograph showing Dr. Thiel's propulsion specialists at Peenemünde posing before an experimental rocket, which exploded after only forty-five seconds of flight. On the lower end of the rocket fuselage is the figure of a witch in a white dress, broom over her shoulder. Another such picture (33) depicts a lingerie-clad woman in a sickle-shaped moon, seated with her legs crossed; the rocket bears the legend A4 on its fuselage. The emblem was itself inspired by Fritz Lang's

1929 film, *Die Frau im Mond* (see Schmundt-Thomas, "Grab-bagging in *Gravity's Rainbow*" 93). The German troop designation Geli mentions here appears to be fictional though the numbering system derives from Collier (*Battle of the V-Weapons* 108). It would be the Third Motorized Squadron of the 485th Artillery Division. Collier shows the organizational chart for General Kammler's rocket squadrons, which were divided into northern and southern groups. The 485th was Gruppe Nord, operating out of The Hague; it was divided into First and Second Squadrons. There was no third.

V293.17, B341.17–18, P297.37   "been up to the Brocken yet?"   Jutting peaks of the Harz Mountains, site of the *Walpurgisnacht*, or eve of May Day, celebrations. In part 1 of Goethe's *Faust*, on the night of April 30, Mephistopheles conducts Faust to the Brocken, an area known for its strangely beautiful light, the so-called *Brocken-Gespenst*, or Brocken specter. Goethe (*Goethe's Color Theory* 89) experienced it in December 1777:

> During the day, owing to the yellowish hue of the snow, shadows tending towards violet had already been observable; these might now be pronounced as decidedly blue, as the illuminated parts exhibited a yellow deepening to orange. But as the sun last was about to set, its rays greatly mitigated by the thicker vapors began to diffuse a most beautiful red color over the whole scene around me, the shadow-color changed to a green, in beauty to the green of an emerald. The appearance (Gespenst) became more and more vivid: one might have imagined oneself in a fairy world, for every object had clothed itself in the two vivid and so beautifully harmonizing colors.

Goethe had witnessed the phenomenon of complementarity across the rainbow spectrum of colors. The moment would spark him to use Germanic legend to situate his demonic festivities in *Faust* atop the Brocken; it also inspired his scientific researches into "the color wheel"—a way of representing the color complements in a circular, mandala form. For a description of the Brocken itself, and a note on Pynchon's source for its modern amenities, see V330.9–11n.

V293.26, B341.29–30, P298.5   a Nagant blazing   In 1895 the Russian army adopted as its service revolver this six-shot pistol designed by the Nagant brothers of France. Russian officers used it through the forties.

V293.28, B341.32, P298.7   a Stalin tank   The main Russian battle tank, a heavy vehicle that complemented their T-34; first commissioned for service in 1943 and in use until war's end.

V293.38, B341.43, P298.18   "In clear"   That is, an uncoded message.

V294.5, B342.9, P298.26   "Blodgett Waxwing"   Slothrop guesses wrong here. The man waiting for him will be *"Der Springer,"* Gerhardt von Göll. On Mr. Waxwing see V246.35n.

**V294.11–12, B342.16–17, P298.32 "Cary Grant. Ge-li, Ge-li, Ge-li. . . .
Listen, Swinemünde, that's in the Soviet zone"** Slothrop here mimics
the supposed exclamations of pilot Geoff Carter (Cary Grant) to "Ju-dy,
Ju-dy, Ju-dy" (Rita Hayworth) in the Howard Hawks film *Only Angels
Have Wings* (1939). But he never says exactly that; rather, he once greets
her like this: "Hello, Judy. Come on, Judy. Now, Judy." Nonetheless
Grant was famous for and hounded all his life about the supposed exclamation. Swinemünde, a town on the island of Usedom (actually, as Wegener remarks [*The Peenemünde Wind Tunnels* 13], it is a peninsula
bisected by a small river, so that it is like an island) in the Stettin Bay
of the Baltic Sea, was the site of a German naval base. Ceded to Poland
according to agreements made at the Yalta Conference, the town was
indeed, as Slothrop remarks, located in the sector controlled by Soviet
forces, and with its cession the town took the current Polish name,
Świnoujście.

EPISODE 2

Next day, Slothrop arrives at the Nordhausen Mittelwerke, and here several strands of myth are woven together. First, the episode is scattered
with items from the lexicon of Teutonic myth, signified in references to ancient runes, and the Tannhäuser legend. Second, there are references to ancient Herero myth and custom. Finally these two strands—northern and
southern, the white and the black—converge in a contemporary, technological mythology of rocketry. Slothrop's journey into the Nordhausen works,
whose tunnels have been fictionally altered for this thematic convergence,
provides a locale for the main action—a Hollywood-style chase scene, with
Major Duane Marvy hot on Slothrop's trail.

V295.13, B343.23, P299.35 This rail Here and throughout *GR*, slang for
a lieutenant in the U.S. Army, after the brass bar insignia, or "rail."
V295.15, B343.25, P300.1 English SPOG See V272.32–34n.
**V295.27–28, B344.2–3, P300.14 Nick De Profundis, the company lounge
lizard** From the Latin "*de profundis,*" "out of the depths." The reference
is to Psalm 130: "De profundis clamavi ad te Domine" (Out of the depths
have I cried to thee, O Lord). The Psalm was famously set to music by
Mozart (*De Profundis Clamavi,* for mixed choir and orchestra, K.93, composed in Salzburg in 1771). In American slang, a "lounge lizard" is one
who spends most of his waking hours basking in the alcoholic glow of
cocktail lounges; he is usually a sponger and perhaps also a gigolo.
**V295.34, B344.11, P300.20–21 acorn diodes . . . looted out of the Tele-
funken units** They've taken diodes—thermionic semiconductors func-

tioning indeed like "valves"—that use heat rectify the current, converting it from AC to DC, from the radio-guidance machinery built for the rockets by Telefunken AG, a German electronics firm.

V295.36, B344.14, P300.22   there's "Micro" Graham . . . lurks in the Stollen   *Stollen* are tunnels (here in the underground rocket works). "Micro" Graham's name plays on "microgram" (a unit of weight).

V296.14–16, B344.31–32, P300.37–38   "When the Americans liberated Dora . . . a rampage after the material"   U.S. forces that liberated the Dora camp on April 11, 1945, also were surprised by the cache of V-1 and V-2 material left behind at the Nordhausen works. During the ensuing weeks, with the area slated for takeover by Soviet forces, a race commenced to get out valuable parts and other intelligence. That was one kind of turmoil, and McGovern (*Crossbow and Overcast* 156) describes another: shortly after the Dora liberation, a full-scale "rampage" erupted as former internees began looting the barracks of their former guards (see also V299.29–30n). Wegener (*The Peenemünde Wind Tunnels*) further describes how this resistance had been planned for months before the liberation itself.

V296.21, B344.39, P301.3   the elegant Raumwaffe space suit wardrobe . . . Heini of Berlin   A wardrobe for the "space weapon," or V-2 itself. In American slang, one's "heinie" is one's "butt"; and in German "Heini" is the shortened form of the name Heinrich. "Heini of Berlin" is probably fictional, though the allusion may point to Heinrich "Heini" Hoffman (1885–1955), Hitler's photographer/press secretary and the Führer's constant companion. Heini Hoffman's 1932 book of photographs, *The Hitler No One Knows*, was masterful public relations work designed to set before nervous citizens of Germany (and Europe) a man who was, as Hoffman put it in the book's introduction, both "strong" and "good," a gentleman of learning and taste.

V297.12–13, B345.38, P301.37   The milk calabashes   Pynchon's source was Luttig (*The Religious System and Social Organization of the Herero* 33–36), who explains that milk from the sacred cattle was stored in the gourds of calabashes. Only women milked the cattle, and the liquid was stored in the center of the Herero's mandala-shaped village.

V297.20, B346.5–6, P302.3–4   "The Promise of Space Travel"   From the brief comments, Pynchon probably has in mind the 1924 treatise by German rocket pioneer Hermann Oberth, *Wege zur Raumschiffart* (The Way to Space Travel).

V297.29, B346.17, P302.13   this salt underground   The Nordhausen Mittelwerke was constructed in a former salt mine; hence the blazing white walls of this scene.

V297.38, B346.28–29, P302.22   the bristlecone pines outracing Death   The *Pinus aristata* or bristlecone pine is a small species (fourteen to forty feet) that grows only in the western United States. One stand of trees near Wheeler Peak, Nevada, includes a four-thousand-year-old specimen, earth's oldest living organism.

V297.40, B346.31, P302.24   especially *polymerized* indoles   See V249.21n.

V298.15, B347.6–7, P302.40   the young tanker   Army idiom for anyone associated with tanks, like this eighteen-year-old. However, to old navy hands the term also signifies those shipmates whose filthy work it is to maintain the fuel-oil tanks. In American underworld slang, it also signifies anyone who spends his nights in the city drunk tank. This is the sense Pynchon has in mind in "The Secret Integration" (*Slow Learner* 180) when he has McAfee, the drunken black bass player, recalling "tanks he had known."

V298.19–20, B347.12, P303.3–4   The Albert Speer Touch   Trained as an architect, Speer had ambitions that led him to become Hitler's designer for civil works projects in Berlin and eventually Minister of Armaments and War Production. Though he had nothing directly to do with designing the Nordhausen works, Speer did inspect the factory in December 1943, when the SS was readying it for full production. In his memoir (366–71), Speer recalls the visit and the scene: "In enormous long halls prisoners (from the Dora Camp) were busy setting up machinery and shifting plumbing. Expressionlessly, they looked right through me, mechanically removing their prisoners' caps of blue twill until our group had passed them." Appalled at their mistreatment ("sanitary conditions were inadequate, disease rampant"), Speer futilely urged SS general Kammler to make improvements. To give them credit, Speer and Wegener are the only memoirists to acknowledge forthrightly the brutal slavery used to construct the V-weapons. Huzel and Dornberger and von Braun, who became American citizens while Speer was imprisoned at Spandau for war crimes, entirely sidestep the moral issue to concentrate instead on the romance of rocketry. Here, the detail about parabolas is a Thomas Pynchon touch. Speer was no more enamored of the parabola than any other form. In any case, Pynchon may have in mind Speer's well-known design for a Berlin Arch of Triumph that Hitler wanted built. It never was.

V298.24, B347.17–18, P303.8   a Speer disciple named Etzel Ölsch   A fictional character, whose first name stems (we're told a few lines further on) from Attila (the Hun). The last name appears to derive from the German "*öl*," "oil": so an oily Attila.

V298.25, B347.19, P303.10   u.s.w.   The German abbreviation for *und so weiter* (and so forth), the equivalent of "etc."

V298.36–37, B347.31–32, P303.20–21   the colonel heading up the American "Special Mission V-2"   He was Colonel Holger Toftoy, who became the prime mover behind American efforts to ship secretly one hundred dismantled V-2 rockets out of Europe (McGovern, *Crossbow and Overcast* 112).

V298.37–38, B347.33–34, P303.22   B Company, 47th Armored Infantry, 5th Armored Division   According to McGovern (156), these troops were responsible for "cordoning off" the *Mittelwerke* during May and June 1945, when the Project Hermes people removed their hundred rockets.

V299.10, B348.5–6, P303.35   how long you sfacim-a dis country   From the Italian noun *"sfacimento"* ("wreck" or "ruin"). Thus, "How long you been wreckin' dis country?" Note also the pun on *Dis*, Dante's underground hell.

V299.13–14, B348.10, P303.39   Tannhäuserism   The tragic error of Tannhäuser—for example, in Richard Wagner's operatic version of the myth—was to postpone his quest in order to linger for one year of sensual, "mindless pleasure" with the goddess Venus under her mountain called Venusberg. Grimm (*Teutonic Mythology* 934–35), Pynchon's source, has shown that in German folk tradition Frau Holda, a White Goddess who leads (like Wuotan) a "furious host," is virtually equivalent to Venus, and it was to savor her delights that the hero descended in medieval versions of the myth.

V299.20, B348.18, P304.4   a Minnesinger   A troubadour, a singer of folk tunes like Henry Tannhäuser in the Teutonic myth. Denis de Rougement has shown that the German *Minnesänger* were nurtured on twelfth-century Catharist heresies and symbolism, a source of references as *GR* closes (see V732.22–24n).

V299.29–30, B348.30–31, P304.15   When the Dora prisoners went on their rampage   Again, see McGovern (156). He notes that when liberated, former prisoners joined citizens of Nordhausen to scavenge the factory works, "stealing such items as light bulbs."

V299.33–34, B348.34–36, P304.19   in Germany the word for electric socket is also the word for Mother   Well maybe: German standard and technical lexicons indicate that the word for an electrical socket is *"Anschlussdose"* and that for a sleeve socket (for example, in plastic piping) is *"Muffe"*—also slang for the vagina.

V299.38, B348.40–41, P304.23   Picture the letters SS each stretched lengthwise   Descriptions of the underground *Mittelwerke* can be found in every one of Pynchon's sources: in Dornberger (*V-2* 241–42), Huzel (*Peenemünde to Canaveral* 86), Irving (*Mare's Nest* 144–45), and McGovern (*Crossbow and Overcast* 78). There are photos available in Irving and McGovern. All agree: instead of Pynchon's forty-four cross-tunnels (*Stollen*) linked to two main tunnels in ladderlike fashion, there were forty-seven rather irregularly spaced cross-tunnels. The double-S configuration is also Pynchon's fiction, a sigmoid fraud that becomes suggestive in its links to related images. Some have seen the configuration Pynchon specifies as referring to the double-helical structure of a DNA molecule, what Dalsgaard (102) reads as a "genetic justification as well as the symbolic basis for the totalitarian regime's desire to exterminate 'subhumans'" such as the Dora inmates. On the DNA imagery see also Larsson ("A *Companion*'s Companion").

V300.4, B349.5–6, P304.29 Apprentice Hupla Or "hoopla"; from the French *houp-là* (confusing or botched speech). Also, in American slang "a commotion."

V300.38–39, B350.4–6, P305.23 a double integral . . . Summe, Summe, as Leibniz said In the seventeenth century Baron Gottfried Wilhelm von Leibniz demonstrated methods of double integration that could be used in describing the trajectories of moving objects. "*Summe*" is the German for "integration" or "an adding up." More extensive treatments of the calculus can be found in Slade (*Thomas Pynchon* 218–19) and Ozier ("Calculus" 193–99).

V301.13, B350.26, P305.40 pulling gs Engineers' (or pilots') slang for a body (or a mechanism) under the influence of gravitational pull because of acceleration.

V301.21, B350.37, P305.7 coil, transformers . . . one tetrode A coil or solenoid functions as a switch, an electrolytic cell (or battery) stores power, the transformer boosts the current, the diodes would rectify it (from AC to DC; see V295.24n). The tetrode is a vacuum tube with four internal electrodes: a cathode, an anode, and two wire grids. One of the wire grids would carry the signal; the second would "screen away capacitive coupling inside the tube," that is, shield its (initially) weak input from interference before amplification: this is what our narrator names "an elaborate dance of design precautions."

V301.26, B350.41–42, P306.12 "A life of its own," she said For Katje's remark see V209.23.

V301.31, B351.5–6, P306.17 a Wheatstone bridge Measures resistances in electronic circuits by comparing them to known values and balances automatically any difference in them, whence the current is transmitted to (or, charges up) "a capacitor," which stores only temporarily (unlike a battery) the energy created in a field (by being joined to equal but oppositely charged conductors on either side).

V301.33, B351.8, P306.19 this so-called "IG" guidance Because in German it was called an *Integrationsgerät* (integration device). Willy Ley (*Rockets* 224) refers to it as "one of the most important inventions that went into the A4." Once more, though, Pynchon has stretched the historical facts to suit his sigmoid fraud. All versions of the A4 were fitted with a double-integrating device that controlled the steering vanes (Dornberger, *V-2* 45). But the device controlling *Brennschluss* was more complex. Dornberger explains that all operational models of the A4 rocket were fitted with the ground-control device manufactured by Telefunken. When the rocket reached a set velocity, as recorded by ground-controlled telemetering equipment, a radio command was beamed to the rocket, ending the burn. This method had inherent disadvantages; for instance, it was "susceptible to interference by suitable counter-measures," wrote Dornberger (231). The solution was an "integrating accelerometer," built by Kreiselgeräte GmbH according to designs developed at the Technical College of Darmstadt. However, this "IG" was fault-ridden, and while rockets fitted with it were tested over the fields of Poland in 1944, the revised design never went into production (Dornberger 232). Pynchon may have been following Kooy and Uytenbogaart (*Ballistics of the Future* 351), who leave the mistaken impression that some IG accelerometers were used in combat.

V301.37–38, B351.13–16, P306.21   Brennschluss exactly here would make the Rocket go on to hit 1000 yards east of Waterloo Station Where, Larsson ("A *Companion*'s Companion") points out, it would impact London's America Street.

V302.2–3, B351.20–21, P306.29–30   the ancient rune that stands for the yew tree, or Death Either a red herring or an error. According to Graves (*White Goddess* 194–95, 245–46), the yew (or *Taxus*) was represented by the rune "I," and its day on the calendar was the last of the year, corresponding to the pagan Saturnalia and to the Judeo-Christian feasts of Hanukkah and Christmas. The rune "SS" signified the blackthorn (*Bellicum*), a tree symbolizing "strife" and appearing on the calendar at April 15.

V302.20–21, B352.1–2, P307.7   a 13th sign of the Zodiac Not as offbeat as it initially seems. Some astrologers hold that there always was a thirteenth sign or house of the zodiacal calendar and that this house is Christ's. In astrology, writes Fern Wheeler (*The Thirteenth House* 15–20), each of the twelve houses is characterized by an offsetting, countervailing force: Aries, for instance, is a house of love, the ruling planet of which is Mars, symbolic of war. But the thirteenth house has no opposites because it integrates all such polarities in the body of Christ. He was the thirteenth person at the Last Supper, claimed to unite within himself the twelve tribes of Israel, and was certainly—as the narrator would put it—an "interface" between "one order of things and another." In short, we may take this as a further sign of messianic hope in *GR*.

V302.39, B352.25, P307.25   The Penis He Thought Was His Own Sir Stephen Dodson-Truck's vulgar song of V216.38–217.11.

V303.19–20, B353.9, P308.7   the legendary ship *Marie-Celeste* Under the command of Captain Benjamin Spooner Briggs, the *Mary-Celeste* (note the actual spelling) sailed from New York on November 7, 1872. Aboard were Briggs, his wife, his daughter, and a crew of seven. Three weeks later the two-masted ship was discovered virtually abandoned, yet still under partial sail. Everyone aboard vanished without a trace or clue, and a board of inquiry failed to resolve the enigma.

V304.10–11, B354.5, P308.40–41 **"Ah, so reizend ist! . . . Hübsch, was?"** "Ah, it's so enticing! . . . Pretty, eh what?"

V304.31, B354.32–33, P309.21 **expansion nozzles** Details of size and shape probably stem from drawings appended to the back of Kooy and Uytenbogaart's *Ballistics of the Future.*

V304.36, B354.38–39, P309.26 **Lally columns** Engineering term for steel tubes sometimes filled with concrete and used to support girders or other floor beams in building construction.

V305.6–7, B355.11–12, P309.39 **a red von Hindenburg mustache** Paul von Hindenburg was president of Germany from 1925 until 1934, when Hitler assumed full powers. His very large moustache drooped broadly down and across his cheeks.

V306.2, B356.5, P310.27 **A fat cracker** According to the *Dictionary of American Regional English*, "cracker" is a slang term generically designating any white, southern backwoodsman; specifically the term often designates one from Georgia.

V306.4, B356.8. P310.29–30 **"how to run these in the WPA"** President Roosevelt's Depression-era job-relief and civil works corps, the Works Progress Administration (1934–40).

V306.34, B357.3, P311.22 **"i-it's *Tarzan* or something!"** On film, the talkie Tarzans began with Johnny Weissmuller in the starring role for *Tarzan the Ape Man* (1932). Buster Crabbe got the part in 1933, with *Tarzan the Fearless,* but it became Weissmuller's again in 1934, for what became a series of seven more Tarzan films before 1945, the time of this episode.

V307.32, B358.5, P312.19 **"here to see that GE"** See V287.25–26n.

V308.36, B359.16, P313.24 **"Gruss Gott!"** A common German greeting, on the order of "good morning!" but difficult to translate: "Greet (you with) God!" or simply "Hello!"

V309.2, B359.21, P313.30–31 **blue racks of cold-rolled sheets . . . bar stock** Varieties of aluminum and aluminum alloy sheet metal (for fairing), ingots (for machining), and bar stock (for framing) the A4 parts.

V309.7, B359.29–30, P313.36 **Monel bars** Bars of corrosion-resistant nickel alloy, named for manufacturer Ambrose Monell, president of the International Nickel Company in 1904, when the patent was awarded.

V309.11–12, B359.35–36, P313.41–314.1 **Glimpf, Professor . . . of the Technische Hochschule, Darmstadt** This fictional professor's name derives from the German adjective meaning "lenient" or "mild." Faculty at the Technical College of Darmstadt developed the integrating accelerometer (V301.33n).

V310.6, B360.33, P314.36 **sharp "Himmel"** Another exclamation, short for "Gott im Himmel!" (God in Heaven!).

V310.27, B361.15, P315.16 **Shouts go dopplering** Pynchon's verb derives from the Doppler effect, where the frequency of sound or light waves appears to vary because the source emitting the waves and the observer receiving them are in rapid motion relative to one another, usually going in opposite directions.

V311.6, B361.35, P315.33   the course-gyro battery   In the Rocket, an electrolytic cell stored power to run the gyroscope that functioned to keep the missile stable on its course.

V311.32, B362.24–25, P316.22   the Icy Noctiluca   An "Icy Night-light," caused here by the explosion of the white phosphorous flare in the white salt tunnel. Symbolically, it's the night-light of the frozen North.

V312.17, B363.7, P317.2   giant white Stetson . . . two .45 automatics   With his prestigious Stetson brand of cowboy hat and his modern automatic service pistols, Marvy is a mix of western cowboy and modern U.S. Marine.

V312.21, B363.12, P317.6–7   the Amatol   Each V-2 warhead carried a ton of this explosive.

V313.11, B364.9, P317.39   Thunderbolts   The American P-47 fighter plane.

V313.14, B364.13, P318.1   deuce-and-a-half   U.S. service slang for a two-and-one-half ton truck.

V313.27, B364.28, P318.13   "Zwitter"   In German the man's name signifies a hermaphrodite.

V313.32, B364.34, P318.18   from the T.H. in Munich   Franz Pökler's alma mater (V160.11n).

V313.40, B364.43–365.1, P318.26   GEHEIME KOMMANDOSACHE   See V242.9–15n.

V314.2, B365.5, P318.29–30   Frederick the Great hairdos   That is, hair mounted in tight waves encircling the head in layers from the ears up, like a beehive.

EPISODE 3

The time of this episode is indistinct. It provides, as background for Pynchon's fictional Schwarzkommando, an extended introduction to Herero folkways and mythology. Motifs introduced here—the mandala symbolism, a culture's intercourse with the dead—correspond with signifiers the narrator finds in other, European, cultures.

V314.30, B365.34, P319.16 Bleicheröde   See V237.1n.

V315.8, B366.8, P319.30   Steve Edelman   He will reappear in the closing moments of *GR* as a "Kabbalist spokesman" (V753.9) and as a blues-harpist (V755.21). The etymology of his name: "*Edelman*" is German for a nobleman and Stephen comes from the Greek "*stephein*," "to encircle."

V315.15, B366.17, P320.1–2   Jaeger underwear   A kind of wool union

suit with a drop seat, introduced for German men and women by Dr.
~~Gustave Jaeger in the 1880s (*Fairchild's Dictionary of Fashion* 297).~~

V315.17–18, B366.19–20, P320.4   the great Herero rising of 1904–06
See V317.2n.

V315.21–22, B366.25, P320.8   Germany's plan for the Maghreb   The
Maghreb region of north Africa includes what are now the nations of
Libya, Tunisia, and Algeria. During World War II, Germany's plan, had
Rommel been successful in holding north Africa, was to use garrisons
there as bases from which to reclaim former South-West African
colonies.

V315.27–31, B366.32–37, P320.15   Among the Ovatjimba . . . in the open
Compare this passage to its source paragraph in Luttig (*The Religious
System and Social Organization of the Herero* 53, my emphasis): "The
Ovatjimba may at present be *considered as a group of outcasts, as they
do not possess the requisite number of cattle* necessary for social significance. This explains the fact that *they do not live in villages* as do the
rest of the tribe. *They live a scattered existence in the veld.* Possessing
small herds of cattle, in sufficient [sic] for subsistence, they are forced *to
dig their food from the ground.*" Luttig follows this discussion with a
derivation of the name: "*Ova-*" is the Herero prefix signifying "people,"
while "*-tjimba*" signifies the "ant bear"—the aardvark, or *Erdschwein*.
Hence they are the "ant-bear people"; and they do not eat the animal because of their spiritual, totemic association with it.

**V315.38–316.13, B367.4–21, P320.26–40   who was the woman alone in
the earth . . . The holy aardvark has dug her bed.**   The source again is
Luttig (53), who notes that the aardvark's power as a totem among the
Ovatjimba is suggested by one tribal myth relating how a woman, all of
whose children had been stillborn, was cured after having been placed in
an ant-bear hole: "Als sie wiederschwanger war, sagte man, man solle
sie in eine Erdschweinhöhle stecken, um sie su entzaubern, dann wür-
den ihre Kinder am Leben bleiben. So geschah es, sie wurde in eine Erdschweinhöhle gesteckt und bekam lebensfähige Kinder" (that is, "When
she was pregnant again, it was said that she should be planted in an
aardvark hole, to disenchant her, then her children would be able to survive [birth]. So it happened, that she was planted in the aardvark hole
and she bore viable children"). Pynchon's fictional rendering of this legend is addressed to a second-person narratee, a hypothetical old South-
West African hand who (in a passage that well represents the embedding
of narrative perspectives in *GR*) is called upon to exhibit remarkable
powers of empathy in the face of such strange practices.

V316.6–7, B367.13–14, P320.34   the village calabashes   See V297.12–13n.

**V316.16–19, B367.25–29, P321.2–5   Inside the Schwarzkommando there
are forces, at present, who have opted for sterility and death . . . it is political struggle**   Luttig (107) clarifies why, for the Hereros, a plan involv-

ing "tribal suicide" might be construed as an act of "political struggle." The reason is that for them suicide could also be an act of "blood vengeance." He explains: "A person who commits suicide under these circumstances is also actuated by the thought that the dead are capable of bringing about evil and death more effectively than the living." So, imagine the whole tribe going into an avenging battle from the Other Side.

V316.22–23, B367.32–33, P321.8–9   Otyikondo, the Half-breed The name derives from Kolbe (*An English-Herero Dictionary*), who gives the Herero noun for "mulatto" as "*otyi-kondo*."

V316.28–29, B367.40–41, P321.14–15   Eanda and oruzo have lost their force Herero society was organized around a system of double descent, a combination of matrilineal and patrilineal clans. In the *eanda*, all trace their descent to a single matriarch; in the *oruzo*, to a single patriarch. These clan designations used to play a key role in the distribution of cattle, but in the twentieth century, these organizations, like much else in Herero society, disintegrated (Luttig 68–70).

V316.31, B368.1–2, P321.17   the Rhenish Missionary Society See V100.7–8n.

V316.31–35, B368.2–7, P321.18–21   as noon flared . . . the omuhona took from his sacred bag, soul after converted soul, the leather cord . . . and untied the birth-knot The source here, again, is Luttig (72): after a child's birth the "funicle, when it has fallen off, is handed over to the priest chief (or *omuhona*) to be preserved in a sacred skin bag. In this bag leather straps with knots are kept, and each knot relates to a particular member of the oruzo. These knots are untied if the child should die or go over into Christianity." The untying of such knots "as noon flared" is Pynchon's touch, consistent with similar moments of judgment in *GR*.

V316.38, B368.11, P321.25   Otukungurua Kolbe (*An English-Herero Dictionary* 177) gives "*kungurua*" as a plural noun for emptied containers—for example, the Herero milk calabashes. The substitution of the inanimate prefix "*otu-*" for the animate "*omu-*" shows that the "Empty Ones" already consider themselves to be among the dead, perhaps like the Kabbalistic "shells of the dead," or Qlippoth (see V148.37–38n).

V317.2, B368.17–18, P321.30   after the 1904 rebellion failed A brief sketch of German colonial and Herero history will help. After the first Rhenish Missionary Society members arrived in southwest Africa in 1842 (see V100.7–8n), they assisted German administrators in establishing settlements, assessing the colony's mineral wealth, and in keeping peace by pitting the Herero and their old tribal enemy, the Nama, against one another. As German colonial administrators became more knowledgeable about the tribes and more adept at managing their strife, they also learned to pit Herero and Nama tribesmen against a common enemy, the Dutch Boers. Increasingly, however, they found it necessary to manage this delicate balance by using armed force, usually with the help of these mission workers. Indeed by 1870 the Rhenish missionaries' true colonialist objectives were unmasked with the founding of the Missions-Handels-Aktiengesellschaft, a trading company capitalized in Germany and specializing in the not-so-secret importing of weapons and ammunition into the colony (Drechsler, *"Let Us Die Fighting"* 18–19). In 1884 Bismarck declared the *Südwest* a German territory, and five years later in order to safeguard its diamond mines he made the territory a formal protectorate. Meantime, colonist Adolf Lüderitz had begun encouraging middle-class colonists to seek their fortune in *Südwestafrika*, which increased the tension (and caused frequent armed clashes) between the colonists and Herero and Nama tribespeople. During the next two decades German military commanders sought to consolidate their power by backing the rise of a single Herero *omuhona* or chief, a centralizing move that was strange to the previously scattered tribes. Samuel Maherero, picked as that new ruler, realized all along that he was being played as a puppet. He turned against the German overlords in 1904, leading his newly united tribes in revolt. The war itself was brief. Under General Lothar von Trotha, the Germans embarked on a plan of extermination. Von Trotha's infamous *Vernichtungsbefehl* (extermination order) stipulated that German soldiers could with impunity take the life of any Herero found outside the settlements. Samuel Maherero escaped to neighboring Bechuanaland, whose chieftain, King Khama, had provided the fleeing Hereros with assistance in making the grueling trek across the Kalahari Desert (see below, V323.10–11). Pynchon could have pieced together the account in *GR* from chapters in many of his sources on German Southwest Africa, for example Bley (*South-West Africa under German Rule*), Drechsler (*"Let Us Die Fighting"*), Goldblatt (*History of South-West Africa*), Hardinge (*History of South-West Africa*), and Vedder (*"The Herero"* and *Southwest Africa in Early Times*).

V317.7, B368.24, P321.35–36   whites looked on as anxiously as they would have at an outbreak of rinderpest   The comparison is to a deadly cattle plague that also renders the animal's flesh poisonous to humans. The analogy between a declining Herero birthrate and cattle plague of course underscores a cornerstone of the German colonists' white supremacy: that natives are like cattle. But the reference also bears a heavy historical weight. The Herero economy like that of all southwest African peoples depended on animal husbandry and on customs that permitted cattle to graze freely on tribally held lands. Drechsler estimates that when German colonization commenced "the Herero's livestock population . . . ran into the hundreds of thousands"; then came a decade of withering "acquisitions" of both cattle and lands ordered by colonial governors coveting meat for occupying troops (117). At the same time devastating outbreaks of rinderpest irrupted, which Drechsler (98–99, 118) indicates the German colonials rather encouraged; indeed the rinderpest undoubtedly came from Europe. German colonials routinely vaccinated their own cattle but would only quarantine Herero cattle in vast tracts and then watch as both cattle and tribesmen died of disease and starvation. A particularly devastating epidemic of rinderpest broke out in 1897, and Bley (125–26) argues that it "resulted in the immediate impoverishment of the Herero" and was a direct cause of the bitterness leading to the Herero uprising of 1904. During the epidemic Herero cattle losses in some areas ran as high as 90 percent; by 1902 their herds had diminished to a mere fifty thousand head (118–19). The point on this (animal) side of the analogy is that these "whites looking on . . . anxiously" had themselves either passively or actively contributed to massive deaths of Herero cattle. The point holds on the other (human, Herero) side, as well, where German policies had equally horrific consequences for tribespeople.

V317.21, B368.41–42, P322.9   the poppy, and cannabis and coca   Respectively, the opium poppy, the marijuana plant, and the plant source of cocaine.

V317.22, B369.1, P322.10   ergot and agaric   Ergot is the fungal source material for LSD; agaric, the white mushroom formerly used as a cathartic and as a coagulant in medicine and as a fixing agent in the dye processing of fabrics.

V317.30–33, B369.10–13, P322.17–19   rational men of medicine attributed the Herero birth decline to a deficiency of Vitamin E . . . long and narrow uterus of the Herero female   The source is Steenkamp (*Is the South-West African Herero Committing Race-Suicide?* 22). He discusses the hypothesis of others who had connected infertility to diets deficient in vitamin E and notes as well that after the European incursions a typical Herero diet, formerly consisting of milk products and beans rich in E vitamins, began revolving around vitamin-deficient white rice. Steenkamp himself is one who advanced the "narrow organ" hypothesis, although Pynchon misstates several of its suppositions. Here is Steenkamp (my emphasis): "The Herero woman is tall and slender. Her legs are very long and so are her fingers and arms. . . . This brought me on the idea that all the other organs in the body must be proportionately longer. I thereupon began to examine *the length of the cervix* with Herero [women] . . . and found to my surprise that this was the case. . . . In one instance I even found a cervix so long that it was impossible with a digital examination to feel the body of the womb (*corpus uteri*). This much longer cervix must thus logically and virtually form a much longer incubation bed *for the development of the gonococcus.*" Note that in Steenkamp's view the long Herero cervix (not the uterus) was an anatomical contributing factor to female infertility, and gonorrhea (not

Pynchon's "poor chances of fertilization") was its supposed mechanism. Steenkamp's theories are the source of still more detail at V519.14.

V318.18, B370.5–6, P323.6–7   they are spieling earnestly   That is, "gaming," but in the sense of playing to or pitching a product to someone.

V319.7, B371.1, P323.37   Josef Ombindi   His name derives from the Herero *"ombinda,"* a noun meaning "wild pig" (Kolbe, *An English-Herero Dictionary* 369).

V320.8–9, B372.8–9, P324.37   Der Bingle . . . that darn "bu-bu-bu-boo"   Respectively, the nickname of Bing Crosby (V184.4n) and the phrasing often used by crooners mimicking or mocking him.

V320.12, B372.12, P325.2   Mothers who used to be baby vamps   In *This Side of Paradise* (1920), F. Scott Fitzgerald (65) defines the jazz age as a time when "the flirt had become the 'baby vamp.'" The sense here is the same: a sexual teaser who affects a childish manner.

V320.14, B372.14, P325.4   the Cards or Browns   Baseball's St. Louis Cardinals, of the National League, and the St. Louis Browns, formerly of the American league. The World Series of 1944 pitted these two neighboring teams against each other in what became known as the "Streetcar Series" (the Cards won, four games to two).

V320.19, B372.19–20, P325.9   by Gödel's Theorem   See V275.25–26n.

V321.3–4, B373.8–9, P325.31   the village built like a mandala   Luttig (*The Religious System and Social Organization of the Herero* 32–34) and Vedder ("The Herero" 168–69) both describe the traditional Herero village as circular, with the cattle pens (the *kraals* in Afrikaans) located in the center and the villagers disposed around the circumference according to certain rules: concubines to the north, unmarried boys to the south, the senior wife of the *omuhona* to the east, and everyone else (including the *omuhona*) to the west. As in a mandala, the arrangement's meaning is defined by opposite signifiers held in equipoise. However, by the time of Gibson's article in the mid-fifties ("Double Descent and Its Correlates among the Herero of Ngamililand"), this order had degenerated to an arch or bow shape, designed only with the aim of protecting the village from prevailing winds.

V321.6–7, B373.12, P325.33–34   sneaking Whoopee Cushions into the Siege Perilous   In chivalric romances and Arthurian legend not just the castle but the Round Table itself was the "seat" of sovereign power, which is why these "jokers around the table" bring in fart cushions to slide "under the very descending arse of the grailseeker" in this scene.

V321.19–20, B373.28–29, P326.7–8   before the continents drifted apart   Geologist Alfred Wegener (uncle of Peenemündan and memoirist Peter Wegener) first put forward the theory of "continental drift" in 1914 in his book *The Origins of Continents and Oceans.* For decades the majority of geologists laughed at his theory. Then in the sixties they dusted it off, transforming it into a new theory we now know as plate tectonics.

Interestingly, former Peenemünde rocketman Willy Ley also produced a book on the topic, called *The Drifting Continents* (1969), giving a lay (Ley?) explanation of plate tectonics and locating the origins of the new theory in Wegener's work.

V321.26–27, B373.39–40, P326.15–16   the name Enzian . . . for chanting See V101.23–26.

V321.40–322.1, B374.13–15, P326.27–29   the south pole of his Adam's apple . . . pole . . . axis . . . axle-tree . . . Tree . . . Omumborombanga . . . Mukuru . . . first ancestor   The ellipses are Pynchon's; the source is Luttig's *The Religious System and Social Organization of the Herero*. In Herero creation myth the *Omumborombanga* is "a great fig-tree which is thought of as a seat of all ancestors" and thus a "tree of life, from which all life emanates; its location is in the North" (25). Mukuru is regarded as the "first ancestor" (21), like the Judeo-Christian Adam; as a god, Mukuru was thought to have sprung from the great tree. His color is red, and he is "intimately associated" with the holy fire and the sacred cattle (30). Mukuru's name means, simply, "the old one" (18). The Herero think of Mukuru as one who will be "present in the grave" with them (21), just as he is present during everyday life by his extension (symbolized in the "birth-knots") through the patrilineal clans.

V322.6, B374.21, P326.34   each sunset is a battle   All details in the surrounding passage, including the killing of the sun, whence it passes into the North (land of the dead), thus to rise newly born each morning, are in Luttig (12–13).

V322.21–22, B374.40–42, P327.8–10   in mythical times, when the sly hare who nests in the Moon brought death . . . instead of the Moon's true message   Luttig (15) explains that the moon is referred to as a "hare's nest" (*ein Nest des Hasen*), and he relates the story: "The hare functioned as the messenger of the moon, and was responsible for the appearance of death among mankind by the wrong interpretation and delivery of a message from the moon to humanity. For this the hare was punished by the moon." Furthermore, the moon is associated in Herero mythology with the netherworld, abode of Ndjambi Karunga, a deity who is, as Pynchon notes a few lines further, "both the bringer of evil and its avenger." Finally, this is why "the Herero sang of the Germans: 'Sie kommen daher wo der Mond ist,' i.e. out of the Netherworld . . . [for when] European ships emerged from the horizon, West Coast tribes thought they were coming up out of the spirit land and were confirmed in their opinion by the pale skins of the mariners. . . . So was Hahn, the first [Rhenish] missionary among the Herero, addressed as Karunga, the god of the netherworld" (Luttig 15). The story of the hare and the moon will reappear at V730.4–6.

V322.29–30, B375.9–10, P327.18   "Blicker," the nickname the early Germans gave to Death   On this Teutonic myth see V30.12n.

V322.41, B375.23, P327.29   the Kakau Veld   Dry range lands bordering on the Kalahari Desert and home to the Herero bushmen or *Ovatjimba*.

V323.4, B375.27–28, P327.33   had the child out of wedlock   For more details on Enzian's birth and lineage, see V349.37–352.7. Note, however, that in being born "out of wedlock" and in being "passed over" by a Herod-like figure, his birth and infancy parallel Christ's.

V323.10–11, B375.35–36, P327.39–40   Samuel Maherero's great trek across the Kalahari   See V317.2n.

V323.25–27, B376.22–24, P328.14–15   to work on the railroad the Germans were building . . . others died eating cattle dead of the rinderpest   When hostilities erupted in early 1904 the German colonials had recently begun constructing the 355-mile Otavi Rail Line from the Atlantic port of Swakopmund eastward to Windhoek, at the colony's center. Initially the Otavi-Gesellschaft's principal labor force consisted of six hundred Herero but, when these men either deserted or were dismissed with the onset of warfare, the company replaced them with Italian contract workers, who soon went on strike in protest against low wages and poor food. Construction stalled through 1904, but by 1905 when General von Trotha's policies had resulted in the extermination of most resisting Herero tribes and the imprisonment of the rest in what German chancellor Heinrich von Bülow named *Konzentrationslager* (concentration camps) in his written orders, any surviving men capable of laboring were enslaved for work on the rail line (Drechsler, *"Let Us Die Fighting"* 153–55, 165–66). Such are the contexts for Pynchon's allusion. On the rinderpest, see V317.7n.

V323.41–324.1, B376.31–32, P328.31–32   the move from Peenemünde down here to the Mittelwerke   The move occurred in February–March of 1945, as Russian troops advanced across Poland toward Rügen Island, forcing all staff still involved in research to move south to Nordhausen, where A4 rockets were already in full production.

V324.10, B377.2, P328.41   Bürgerlichkeit played to Wagner   A bourgeois drama acted out to the strains of a Richard Wagner operatic score.

V325.3, B377.42, P329.34   the Autobahns   The national highway system (see V165.41n).

V325.4–6, B378.2–4, P329.36–37   the women . . . having their breasts milked into pails   An amusing error in the Bantam: "their beasts."

V325.29–30, B378.31, P330.20   "almost as a 'routinization of charisma'"   See V81.8–9n.

V325.31, B378.32, P320.22   Outase   Brincker (*Wörterbuch und Kurzgefässte Grammatik des Otji-Herero* 229) defines this Herero word as *"Frischer, weicher Kuhmist"* (fresh, soft cow dung), Kolbe (*An English-Herero Dictionary* 170) as "the dung of large cattle, if fresh."

V325.36, B378.38, P330.26–27   Schwarzkommando use the 50 cm band . . . the Rocket's Hawaii II guidance   They transmit and receive on a radio band tuned to a 50 centimenter wavelength; on the A4 guidance see V207.8n.

V326.4, B379.6, P330.35   the second dog watch   In U.S. naval idiom, the twenty-four-hour day is divided up into six "watches." Also, the watch between 4:00 and 8:00 P.M. is further "dogged," or halved, in order for sailors to eat their supper; the "second dog watch" thus runs from 6:00 to 8:00 P.M. On duty, Andreas is transcribing Morse code but sometimes also "keying" it—that is, tapping out and transmitting his answers in code, thus endangering them all.

V326.17, B379.22–23, P331.7–8   Celle, Enschede, Hachenburg   These are all towns along the way from Hanover to Lüneburg, which the Schwarzkommando here traverse in search of clues that Blicero's crew might have left behind, during the war's last weeks. Hachenburg is a mid-sized town about sixty-five miles northwest of Frankfurt; Eschede is a small town about midway between Hanover and Lüneburg (though there is a chance Pynchon [or the text] is confusing it with Enschede, a larger industrial town that would more likely be a "rocket town").

V327.5, B380.16, P331.6   flummeries   Of Welsh origin, and initially signifying a coagulation of oatmeal, the word now signifies someone's empty triflings and gestures.

V327.11–17, B380.24–32, P332.2–8   a symphony of the North, of an Arctic voyage . . . it is a return   The reason why a northward journey would be both "a return" and a trek into Death's kingdom is made clear in Luttig (*The Religious System and Social Organization of the Herero* 13): "When mention is made among the Herero of the 'land over the sea' or the 'region of the north' reference is made to the underworld. It is to this world that the dead depart, for they are buried facing that region." The North is not only a "place of annihilation, but is also a place where new life is created," for the North is where the first ancestor appeared from the Omumborombanga tree; and it is the place to which all Hereros hope to return after death.

V327.34, B381.11, P332.25–26   SCHWARZE BESATZUNG AM RHEIN!   Or, "Black Garrison on the Rhine!" A significant bit of historical detail that contributes to Pynchon's fictional critique in *GR* of race and fascism. The Treaty of Versailles ending European hostilities in 1918 provided that allied troops would be garrisoned along the Rhine River, and immediately after the armistice of November 11, 1918, France moved into the region, bringing troops recruited from its African colonies. By late 1919 and early 1920 they numbered as many as forty-five thousand, of whom about ten thousand were "fully black" soldiers officered by whites. From the beginning these garrisons were a source of tension for their placement was, Keith Nelson finds, a deliberate strategy of French commanders like General Charles Mangin ("father of the black forces") who wanted to humiliate the defeated Germans ("'The Black Horror on the Rhine'" 611). Realizing the psychological strategy of the French, Prussian and German statesmen had become increasingly vehement in their complaints against the "black occupation," and during the U.S. presidential election season of 1920 they mobilized German Americans to make "the black horror on the Rhine" an international cause célèbre by getting them to spread stories of black-on-white rapes. French consular officials countered in 1921 that black troops along the Rhine had been drawn down until only five thousand remained and that during the conflict Germans themselves had conscripted black troops from their own African colonies. Nonetheless the campaign achieved some success—for example, it mobilized women's petition drives in Norway, Italy, and even France; at the same time stories in U.S. magazines (the *Nation*) and newspapers brought the crisis to somewhat of a head in 1922 (that familiar *annus mirabilis* in *GR*), after which the French began fully to draw down the African garrisons. Notably, Nelson also mentions that German responses to black troops on the Rhine also included Munich-produced films featuring a "*Schwarze Besatzung*" that was depicted terrifying white Rhinelander women (619), a tantalizing historical counterpart to *GR*'s fictional *Schwarzkommando* films produced to stir up Germans. On black African troops serving in French regiments, see also McCloy (*The Negro in France* 191–99) and Shelby Davis (*The French War Machine* 117–19).

V328.7, B381.17, P332.31   Onguruve   His name is synonymous with the *ombinda*, or wild pig, of V319.7.

V328.25, B382.6, P333.19   Pervitins   First introduced on the market in 1938, Pervitin is the proprietary name of a methamphetamine stimulant produced at the Berlin-based Temmler pharmaceutical company. During World War II, German servicemen on land, in the air, and at sea were given liberal quantities of Pervitin to keep them awake over long, stressful periods of time and to give them seemingly superhuman intensity and drive. Pervitin is popularly known in America as "speed" because of its stimulant effects. Enzian keeps a plentiful supply (see V522.6).

V328.29–30, B382.12–13, P333.24   okanumaihi, the little drinker of sweet milk   Kolbe (*An English-Herero Dictionary* 187) identifies it as "the evening star" (the planet Venus), which appears at milking time.

EPISODE 4

Internal references place the time of this episode as May 28, 1945. The location: Slothrop and Geli stand atop the Brocken, site of the *Walpurgisnacht* celebrations on the night of April 30. Slothrop makes a madcap escape to Berlin in a hot-air balloon.

V329.13–14, B383.4–6, P334.8–9   May Day Eve's come and gone . . . nearly a month later   May Day Eve (*Walpurgisnacht*) was April 30. See also V330.9–11n.

V329.15, B383.7, P334.10   Kriegsbier   That is, "war beer." During both World Wars German breweries faced shortages of barley, which was being diverted for bread, and so the brewers were forced by law to weaken their formulas. Some brands had alcohol levels as low as 1.5 to 2.0 percent.

V329.19, B383.11, P334.14   "the devil's kiss"   According to Grimm (*Teutonic Mythology* 1065, 1070, 1077), newly admitted witches were "marked by the prick of a needle, while they cursed their maker, and signified their faith and homage to the Evil one, as to worldly rulers, by a kiss." This "blood mark," which was often stained with inks, was thought to be without feeling ever afterward.

V329.23, B383.16, P334.18   the sus. per coll. crowd   From the Latin "*suspendatur per collum*" (hanged by the neck), an entry common in legal registers next to the names of those convicted and executed for capital crimes. In his Introduction to *Colonial Justice in Western Massachusetts*, treating seventeenth-century Springfield, Massachusetts, Joseph H. Smith (24–25) notes that in June 1645 (exactly three centuries before these fictional events), William Pynchon sat on the General Court at which Margaret Jones, a Bay colonist, was indicted, found guilty, and executed—*suspendatur per collum*—in the first American case of capital punishment for witchcraft. In Springfield William Pynchon also tried and convicted the second such person, Mary Parsons, brought up on a witchcraft charge but found guilty of murdering her child (a charge she acknowledged to be true). Mary Parsons was also sentenced to hang but appears to have died in prison in 1657. These two cases preceded by forty years the more widely known witchcraft trials in Salem.

V329.25, B383.18–19, P334.20   Amy Sprue . . . turned Antinomian   She is fictional. "Sprue" is an archaic medical term for a type of throat infection; now it figures in the name of a gluten-sensitive enteropathy called celiac sprue (also known as celiac disease), a chronic disease of the digestive tract caused by an intolerance to the gluten in, for example, bread or pasta. The name "Antinomian" was given to those radical, charismatic Puritans who held that faith alone was sufficient for the attainment of salvation.

V329.26–27, B383.20, P329.21–22   Crazy Sue Dunham   In his 1964 short story "The Secret Integration" (*Slow Learner* 151), Pynchon identifies her as "that legendary and beautiful drifter who last century had roamed all this hilltop country [of western Massachusetts] exchanging babies and setting fires." Pynchon's source, Larsson notes ("From the Berkshires to the Brocken"), was *The Berkshire Hills* (256).

V329.28, B383.22, P329.23   Snodd's Mountain   Fictional locality named (one supposes) for an ancestor of Grover Snodd, a character in "The Secret Integration" (*Slow Learner* 142) and a resident (like Tyrone and Hogan Slothrop) of the fictional Berkshire hill town of Mingeborough, Massachusetts.

V329.30–31, B383.25, P329.25–26   young skipping Dorothy's antagonist
In the film *The Wizard of Oz* there are two "wicked" witches: the
Wicked Witch of the East, killed when Dorothy's house crash-lands
on her, and the Wicked Witch of the West, who tries to incinerate
Dorothy's friend the Scarecrow and who melts away when Dorothy
splashes water about in rescuing her straw-headed friend.

V329.32, B383.27, P329.27   headed for Rhode Island   Because that was
home to Separatist and Antinomian leaders Anne Hutchinson (1591–
1643), who was banished there in 1637, and Roger Williams (1603–83),
who established the colony in 1636.

**V330.9–11, B384.1–4, P335.2   six toes on each foot . . . Nazi transmitter
tower up on the Brocken**   The descriptive details of this scene derive
from a May 28, 1945, story in *Life* magazine (122–24). Pictures show the
Brocken with a hotel and radio tower perched atop it. Inside the transmitting tower are the murals, photos of which show the women riding
black rams; the *Life* caption reads: "GI who is inspecting mural found
one witch with six toes." The accompanying, brief story goes on, in the
alliterative style of the magazine:

> On the eve of May 1, according to German legend, weird witches whip
> wildly through space, riding broomsticks and goats, with long-tailed
> monkeys under their arms. On their mad way they bring blight, drain
> cattle dry, spread havoc. They gather at the *Teufelskanzel* (Devil's Pul-
> pit) on Brocken and hark to the exhortations of their master, the devil.
> Then, after devouring a great dinner of toads and mice, they dance and
> revel until dawn around the bonfire lit before the pulpit.
>
> In 1933 the celebration of this pagan ritual called Walpurgisnacht
> (Walpurgis was a medieval saint) was adopted as a ceremonial of the
> Hitler Youth. Until this year they gathered from all over Germany on
> Brocken, which is the highest peak of the Harz mountains southeast
> of Hanover, and listened to the demoniacal diatribes of their leaders.
> This year there was again a fire burning on Brocken before the Devil's
> Pulpit. It was lit by a cold and bored American sentry who saw no
> witches.

This story and its accompanying photographs were the source for details
of this scene.

V330.13, B384.7, P335.7   von Bayros   See V71.27n.

**V330.21–22, B384.16–18, P335.15–16   past Clausthal-Zelterfeld . . . to-
ward Weser**   Cities that lie in a west-northwesterly direction from the
Brocken, opposite the rising sun.

**V330.22–24, B384.18–20, P335.17–18   "By golly . . . it's the Specter." You
got it up around Greylock in the Berkshires too.**   Slothrop's recognition
of the American version of the German *"Brockengespenst"* in this scene
stems precisely, Larsson ("From the Berkshires to the Brocken") has
shown, from *The Berkshire Hills* (42): "Of the stories and legends about

[the mountain] Old Greylock, the one about the 'Specter' is most popular . . . [for its] gigantic shadow of an object reflected in a cloud is so well
known as to have a German name, Brockengespenst (Specter of the
Brocken) from Brocken, the highest peak in the Hartz [sic] Mountains."

V331.2, B384.42, P335.37   Atlantis   See V269.9–10n.

V331.3, B385.1, P335.38   Brockengespenstphänomen   The "Brocken
specter phenomenon." See V293.17n.

V331.12, B385.10, P336.6   *warum*   Why?

V331.32–33, B385.35, P336.27   down in Bad Harzburg, Halberstadt   Resort towns on the lower northern slopes of the Harz Mountains, an hour
or so by car from the Brocken.

**V332.4, B386.8–9, P336.39–40   those Rolls Roycers who were after him
in Zürich**   That is, the "Apache" Secret Service men to whom Slothrop
gave the slip in part 2 (see V267.17–18n).

V332.5–6, B386.10, P336.40   GE, that's Morgan money   Backed with
capital from financier John Pierpont Morgan, Charles Coffin (1844–
1926) founded the General Electric Company in 1892.

V332.15, B386.21, P337.9   K-rations   During World War II the U.S. Army
issued K rations to troops in the field, in packages containing breakfast,
supper, and dinner, and accessories such as matches, dextrose tablets, or
caramel candies. They were distinct from C rations, which came in the
form of a gold-toned laquered twelve-ounce can, providing one meal
(such as a meat and vegetable stew), or from D rations, which were an
emergency field snack (typically a four-ounce fortified candy bar).

V332.16, B386.23, P337.10   the Goldene Aue   Baedeker's *Northern Germany* describes it as a fertile valley located nineteen miles east of Nordhausen in the Harz Mountains. The town of Eisleben, home of Protes-
tantism's father, Martin Luther, lies on its edge.

V332.19, B386.26, P337.13   "Liebchen"   German for "sweetheart" or
"lover."

**V333.14–15, B387.29–30, P338.9–10   Nordhausen: Cathedral, Rathaus,
Church of St. Blasius**   This is Slothrop's view, as he peers down from
the balloon. But Pynchon was looking down at his Baedeker (*Northern
Germany* 370): "The cathedral is a fine late-Gothic edifice . . . the
Church of St. Blasius contains two pictures by Cranach, an Ecce
Homo, and the Raising of Lazarus . . . near the Rathaus rises a Roland's
Column."

V334.3, B388.21, P338.40   "Kot!"   Here and afterward throughout *GR*,
the German exclamation "Shit!"

V334.12, B388.32, P339.8   the pitch amplifier   In the Rocket's guidance,
a two-stage DC circuit designed to detect slight degrees of "pitch" as the
missile flies and to amplify that signal to the vane servomotors so that
they can move it and thereby keep it on course.

V335.11, B389.33, P340.6   the vane servomotor   Inside the A4's thrust chamber were four graphite vanes to guide it; these vanes were controlled by servomotors.

V335.24, B390.9, P340.19   a LOX generator   To pump liquid oxygen, one of the A4's principal fuels.

V335.29, B390.14, P340.23   volplaning along   That is, in aeronautical terms, gliding along with the engine throttled back.

V336.12, B390.39–40, P341.6   "the Ur-Markt"   German for the "primeval market."

V336.18–19, B391.6–7, P341.12–13   "At this latitude the earth's shadow races across Germany at 650 miles an hour"   Schnorp (or Pynchon) is roughly correct. Relative to an equinoctial sun, a point on the earth's equator spins at roughly 1,100 miles per hour. But here, at 51.5 degrees of northern latitude, and with the sun nearly at its northernmost solstitial latitude, the shadow would be moving at approximately 640 miles per hour. Similarly, over the French area of Carcassonne, at 43.2 degrees, the shadow would be speeding along at roughly 770 mph, 32 mph faster than the speed of sound. Still, a "shadow" never breaks the sound barrier (V336.26–32).

EPISODE 5

The time is now "full summer" (V336.33) or around June 21, 1945. This episode brings the first extensive treatment of Vaslav Tchitcherine, Slothrop's Soviet antagonist. As with Pynchon's Hereros, an elaborate amount of research went into constructing this analepsis to the Soviet province of Kyrgyzstan, which *GR* represents during a time of linguistic and cultural upheaval in the twenties and thirties.

V337.17, B392.13, P342.12–13   stvyehs and znyis   As Terrill Shepard Soules ("What To Think about *Gravity's Rainbow*" 106) explains: "These are suffixes. (*Sdravstuyeh* means hello, for example; *nebreznieh* means careless.) Just catch these typical word endings on the wind and you know you're hearing Russian."

V337.31, B392.31, P342.27   TsAGI   See V273.5n.

V338.3–5, B393.5–7, P342.41–343.1   no relation at all to the Tchitcherine who dealt the Rapallo Treaty with Walter Rathenau   On Walter Rathenau, see V163.19–23n; on the Rapallo Treaty, V166.16–17n. David Seed has noted that a Georgi Tchitcherine helped Rathenau negotiate the Rapallo Treaty in 1922, settling the questions of reparations payments to the Soviets. The same Tchitcherine also participated in the Lausanne treaty that brought formal peace with Turkey in 1923. At that time, Georgi Tchitcherine met young reporter Ernest Hemingway, who wrote him up in the Toronto *Daily Star*. Georgi was, as Pynchon notes, "a long-term operator, a Menshevik turned Bolshevik" who was forced to flee Russia and take exile in Germany, where he evidently found it easy to cooperate with a capitalist like Rathenau. Vaslav, on the other hand, remains true to his "anarchist" beliefs.

V338.21–22, B393.29–30, P343.17–18   a remote "bear's corner" (*med-vezhy ugolok*), out in Seven Rivers country   The source for this bit of detail is a 1916 travelogue by Stephen Graham, a British adventurer who passed through Kyrgyzstan in 1914–15. His book is entitled *Through Russian Central Asia*, and in treating one of the smaller towns in Semi-retchenskaya Oblast, or "Seven Rivers Land," he comments (192) that it "is what the Russians call a *medvezhy ugolok* (a bear's corner), a place where in winter the wolves roam the main streets as though they did not distinguish it from their peculiar haunts."

V338.25, B393.33, P343.21   played *preference*   According to Hoyle, this Russian card game is a variant of vint, a contract game that hybridizes hearts and bridge. Preference, or Russian preference, is played with a deck of thirty-two cards (7 through ace). The point-value suit is hearts (preference); three active players (plus an inactive dealer) bid, declare trumps, and attempt to make their contracts.

V338.26, B393.35, P343.23   the Moisin   This is misspelled in all three editions. It should be "Mosin," for the Russian bolt-action rifle that uses the 7.62-millimeter ammunition of V340.3. The gun was the standard Russian infantryman's rifle from 1891 until 1945.

V338.28–30, B393.37–40, P343.24–25   because of the earthquakes . . . false fronts   The source again is Stephen Graham. Here (156) he describes Verney, capital city of Semiretchie: "It is so subject to earthquakes that it is difficult to see in it a permanent capital. No houses of two stories can with safety be built, so it is more suited to remain a military center and fortress than to be a great city. In order to look imposing, shops and stores have fixed up sham upper stories; that is, they have window-fronts up above, but no rooms behind the fronts."

V338.33–34, B394.2–3, P343.31–32   the local Likbez center . . . the "red dzurts"   These details derive from Thomas G. Winner's *Oral Art and Literature of the Kazakhs of Russian Central Asia* (142). He describes the Soviet campaign against illiteracy: "Individuals were hurriedly trained in the essentials of reading and writing in order to instruct the population. 'Red caravans' and 'Red dzurts' on the model of the Russian 'red clubs' became the centers for the anti-illiteracy campaign, or, as it was officially called, 'liquidation of illiteracy' (*Likbez*)." A *yurt*, or *dzurt*, is the "tent-like conical felt structure in which the nomadic Turks of Central Asia live" (ibid. 14n).

V339.1, B394.11, P343.39   the NTA   In his 1952 essay on alphabetic reform in central Asia, Winner describes how, in the twenties and thirties, Soviet-trained teachers attempted to substitute a Latinate alphabet for the Arabic script used by the nomadic Turks. The new letters were dubbed the "New Turkic Alphabet."

V339.11, B394.23–24, P344.8–9   dessiatinas of grasses   A Russian land measure: one *dessiatina* equals 2.7 acres.

V339.17, B394.30–31, P344.14–15   in naked Leningrad encounters with the certainty of his death   Indicating that Tchitcherine was one of the two hundred thousand Red Army defenders at the three-year German siege of Leningrad that began in the fall of 1941 continued until the early winter of 1944. In one year alone, two-thirds of the city's million residents may have died just of starvation.

V339.35, B395.11, P344.33   the verst-long dive   Another Russian measure: three versts equal two miles (a verst is just slightly longer than a kilometer). Note the motif of winged flight and the dive, recalling the "wings" of Katje Borgesius (V97.27) and of Leni Pökler (V162.37), as well as the death-dealing angel swooping in on Walter Rathenau (V164.37).

V340.1, B395.19, P344.40   Dzaqyp Qulan   His first name means "Jacob"; *"qulan"* is the Kirghiz word for a wild horse (Winner, *Oral Art* 63n).

V340.1–3, B395.20–22, P344.41–345.1   black theodolites . . . 7.62 mm rounds . . . chunks of lepeshka   A theodolite is a commonly used surveying instrument, the 7.62-millimeter bullets would be for the Mosin rifle, and the *lepeshka* are flat, hard loaves of bread. A photograph in Stephen Graham's *Through Russian Central Asia* (opposite 84) shows a stack of such loaves, like stones, for sale in an open-air market.

V340.7–8, B395.27–28, P345.6–7   the 1916 rising . . . Kuropatkin's troops   When compulsory military service was imposed on all Russians in 1916, the Kazakhs rebelled against the crown, and a detachment of cavalry under Colonel Kuropatkin was sent to suppress the revolt. The czar had been moving settlers into Kyrgyzstan for some decades, and many of these Russians used the revolt as a pretext for seizing land and ousting dissident Kazakhs, sometimes murdering them at random (Winner, *Oral Art* 133–34).

V340.27, B396.10–11, P345.27–28   The Georgian has come to power   Joseph Stalin, or Iosif Vissarionovich Dzhugashvili, was a young Communist from the Georgian Soviet Socialist Republic (SSR); he came to power in 1922 and then became premier in 1941.

V340.33–34, B396.19, P345.34   among the auls   Soules ("What To Think about *Gravity's Rainbow*" 106) mistakenly identifies these "auls" as the "tents of the nomads" (the *dzurts* are the tents). *Auls* are subclans of several nomadic families, traveling together; thus a clan-based caravan (Winner, *Oral Art* 5–6).

V341.18–19, B397.8–9, P346.19–20   O, wie spurlos zerträte ein Engel den Trostmarkt   Line 20 of Rilke's tenth Duino elegy; Leishman and Spender translate: "How an Angel would tread beyond trace their market of comfort." Pynchon's rendering, "to trample spoorless the white marketplace" (V341.38), neatly preserves the excremental sense of *spur-los*, which is apt for a street trod by horses. "White" is a curious reading for *"Trost"* (comfort); perhaps it is meant to distinguish between a black market and a white (or legitimate) one. Note that Pynchon has omitted a preposition from the German; it should read *"ein Engel inhem den Trostmarkt."*

V342.11, B398.7–8, P347.12–13   an Appaloosa from the United States named Snake   We're later informed (see V482.34n) that this is the horse ridden by Greta (Margherita) Erdmann in her film *Weisse Sandwüste von Neumexiko;* evidently it is also the one ridden by Crutchfield the Westwardman of Slothrop's sodium amytal fantasy (episode 10, part 1).

V342.15–17, B398.3–5, P347.17   the famous bucking bronco Midnight   Foghorn Clancy, the most famous rodeo radio announcer of all time, relates the "true story" of Midnight in his autobiography (174–75, 212, 264). Pynchon's "remittance horse," Snake, has outdone even the legendary Midnight.

V343.15–16, B399.22, P348.18   the winged rider, red Sagittarius   Sagittarius is the Archer, ninth house of the astrological year (November 22–December 21). The winged red horse was also a symbol adopted by the Red Army during the 1917 Revolution.

V343.19–20, B399.26–27, P348.21–22   some whistling sweep of quills across her spine   Here, the direct reference is to the Red Army symbol of the winged horse (see above). Behind that, one hears an allusion to the myth of Leda, forcibly taken by Zeus, who adopted the shape of a swan. Pynchon may also, finally, have had in mind the Kazakh legend of Tulpar the Winged Horse, though Winner (*Oral Art* 239–40) mentions it only in passing (and none of the details he does supply match the context here).

V343.28, B399.37, P348.31   Horse-fucking Catherine   The reference is to Catherine II, empress of Russia from 1762 to 1796; her alleged sexual appetites quickly became the subject of folklore (for evidently it was mainly lore).

V343.30, B399.40, P348.33   neo-Potemkins   Prince Grigori Potemkin (1739–91), a Russian army officer and Catherine the Great's favorite paramour (see also V388.27–28n).

V344.4, B400.17–18, P349.7   Ostarzneikunde GmbH   Eastern Pharmaceuticals Incorporated, one of Pynchon's fictions.

V344.7, B400.21, P349.10   "NW7"   The code number for IG Farben's top-secret intelligence-gathering office, based out of the cartel's Berlin office building (Sasuly 97–101).

V345.1–2, B401.23, P350.5–6   cyclized benzylisoquinolines   On the problems with this chemical nomenclature, see V166.11n. The significant thing is that a (fictional) compound mentioned by the spirit of Walter Rathenau in a séance, circa 1930, has attained reality in Wimpe's office.

V345.6–16, B401.29–38, P350.10–20   "Eumecon ... Eucodal"   All the drugs listed in this catalogue are opium alkaloids (eucodal or oxycodone, for example, is a semisynthetic derivative of a codeine compound made from Asian poppies, more potent and addictive than codeine itself), but only Pantopon (proprietary name for the popular narcotic analgesic first produced in 1909 by Roche pharmaceutical company of Grenzach, Germany) appears to have been available in the United States as an injection for pain (Gilman, *The Pharmacological Basis of Therapeutics* 509). Trivalin SF is an ethoxydiglycol used in cosmetics.

V345.17, B402.1, P350.21   Valerian Dried roots of *Valeriana officinalis* were formerly used as a mild sedative.

V345.35–36, B402.23–24, P350.39–40   It's magnificent, but it's not war General Bosquet's exclamation once again (see V10.28n).

V346.2–3, B402.33–34, P351.7   deadly ogive of their Parabellum rounds In architecture, an ogive is a bullet-shaped, gothic-style arch; in statistical applications it is the graphic representation of a frequency distribution. "Parabellum" was originally the telegraphic address of the Deutsche Waffenund Munitionsfabrik (DWM, the German Weapons and Munitions Factory) of Berlin. DWM manufactured the famed Luger pistol, chambered for a uniquely bottle-nosed cartridge of 7.65-millimeter caliber, known from 1900 on as a "Parabellum round."

V346.4, B402.35–36, P351.11–12   Napoleon's *on s'engage, et puis, on voit* His widely attributed (but variously remembered) advice to generals: "One engages, and then one sees." Or sometimes: *on s'engage l'enemie, et puis, s'on voit:* "One engages the enemy, and then, one sees."

V347.6–7, B404.5–7, P352.11–12   everything from Mille-Feuilles . . . La Surprise de Vésuve That is, everything from Brain Fondue in Puff Pastry to Vesuvius Surprise.

V347.32, B404.37, P352.37   an old *Enbeksi Qazaq* A newspaper (whose name translates as the Kazakh Toiler) founded in 1920 as the official Communist journal (Winner, *Oral Art* 176).

V347.35, B404.41, P352.40   red and yellow repetitions over Britannia metal Tchitcherine's hashish pipe is made of an alloy of tin, copper, and antimony normally used for inexpensive tableware but here engraved in repetitive patterns.

V348.8, B405.16, P353.13   the ACS Journal *Journal of the American Chemical Society*, the official publication of that professional organization since 1878.

V348.12, B405.22, P353.17–18   Carothers of du Pont See V249.29–30n.

V348.21, B405.32–33, P353.26   the Heisenberg situation Leipzig University–educated physicist Werner Heisenberg (1901–76), the father of quantum mechanics (for which he received the 1932 Nobel Prize in Physics), formulated the indeterminacy principle in 1927. It states the impossibility of determining simultaneously both the position and the velocity of a particle: the more exactness achieved in the measurement of the one, the more indeterminacy results in the measurement of the other.

V348.31, B406.2, P353.37   Weltschmerz   German for a sense of world-weariness.

V349.28, B407.7, P354.35   Chemnyco of New York   See Sasuly (*IG Farben* 101) and Dubois (*Generals in Grey Suits* 25). Sasuly explains that "the United States was so important in German plans that IG [Farben] found it necessary to set up a special organization—called Chemnyco, Inc., of New York—to siphon out technical data of military importance." This dummy corporation was established in 1931, and most of its secret information was sent to Germany through the NW7 office (V344.7n).

V349.38, B407.18, P355.4   the Krasnyy Arkhiv   The Red Archive of Moscow, a trove of documentary materials. From 1922 until 1941 the archivists also edited a sociohistorical journal, eventually published six times annually. It published articles and archival materials on the Bolshevik Party, the October Revolution, the civil war of 1918–20, and outstanding figures of the Communist Party. Tchitcherine's research involves prerevolutionary materials, which may explain some of his fears about how "They" will use the information.

V349.39, B407.19–20, P355.5   the epical, doomed voyage of Admiral Rozhdestvenski   The Russo-Japanese War began in the spring of 1904 and, after months of being under siege, the main Russian garrison at Port Arthur fell just after Christmas of 1904. However, in October the Russian Baltic Fleet had been dispatched under the command of Admiral Rozhdestvenski with orders to relieve the beleaguered garrison. The fleet had rounded the Horn of Africa by late December, and the admiral was informed of the Russian defeat at Port Arthur when he arrived at Madagascar in January 1905. There was some discussion of turning back, but Rozhdestvenski took his fleet into the South China Sea, then into the Strait of Tshushima, off what is now Korea. Japanese squadrons under Admiral Togo managed to bottle up the Russians on May 27; that day the *Suvorov*, Rozhdestvenski's flagship, was sunk, and later that night Togo's torpedo boats cut up the remainder of his fleet, most of which sank.

V350.2–3, B407.25–26, P355.10   a touch of Dante . . . Simple talion   In Dante's *Inferno* the damned are carefully classified and situated in one of the circular "bulges" or levels, each according to his or her sin. The term "talion" derives from the Latin "*lex talionis*" (retributive justice).

V351.6, B408.37–38, P356.14   the Jablochkov candles   Named for Russian inventor/engineer Pavel Yablochkov (1847–94), who developed this electric carbon arc lamp in 1876. The lamp worked by discharging electricity between two carbon electrodes, yielding an intensely bright light. They were useful only for lighting streets and buildings because it was unbearable to gaze at them; they were also impossible to regulate. Though supplanted within years by Edison's light bulbs, the so-called Jablochkov Candle was used into the twentieth century in military engagements and in film projectors.

V351.17–18, B409.9–11, P356.25–26   kari . . . means "the drink of death"
This stems from Steenkamp (*Is the South-West African Herero Commit-ting Race-Suicide?* 23): "They [the Hereros] brew a potent beer called Kari, which translated into English means 'The Drink of Death.' It is brewed from potatoes, peas, sugar, and yeast. It makes them, in Captain Bowker's words, 'fighting mad.'"

V351.35, B409.32, P357.3   a few bars of *Madame Butterfly* This music would be especially appropriate here, because Giacomo Puccini's opera was introduced in 1904, when Tchitcherine's father was en route to Port Arthur, and because its plot concerns a woman left pregnant by a sailor.

V352.10–11, B410.10, P357.19–20   the era of Feodora Alexandrevna, she of the kidskin underwear That is, Alexandra Feodorovna (1872–1918), the granddaughter of Queen Victoria of England and the empress of Rus-sia following her 1894 marriage to Czar Nicholas II. She was a woman of endless scandal because of her relations with the mystic Grigori Rasputin, a favorite of the royal family. Her highly refined tastes in clothes (the "kidskin underwear" here, whose specific source is un-known) only added to that reputation. In any case, she died when Tchit-cherine was about twelve or thirteen, so the liaison described is highly unlikely. The historical figure, though, probably gives the name to Tchitcherine's fictional lover.

V352.15–16, B410.15–17, P357.24–25   how his own namesake and the murdered Jew . . . at Rapallo On Georgi Tchitcherine's role in working out the 1922 Rapallo Treaty for Walter Rathenau, see V338.3–5n.

V352.23, B410.25, P357.32   apparatchik A Soviet Party functionary, a bureaucrat.

V352.26–27, B410.29–30, P357.35–36   first plenary session of the VTsK NTA From Winner's "Problems" (139). The abbreviation stands for the All-Union Central Committee on the New Turkic Alphabet. The group first met in plenary session in Baku, during 1927, to establish a head-quarters for the literacy movement in central Asia.

V352.30, B410.33, P357.39   a kind of G, a voiced uvular plosive The New Turkish letter was *tenth* in the alphabet (Winner, "Problems" 140).

V353.24, B411.35, P358.33   zapekanka In Russia, a baked pudding.

V354.15, B412.31–32, P359.25–26   on the model of one ratified at Bukhara in 1923 In a footnote, Winner reports in "Problems" (135n) that an Arabic script was "ratified in Bukhara in 1923 . . . but did not take hold."

V354.21, B412.39, P359.31–32   the Night of Power In Islamic myth, the night when Allah gave to Mohammed the alphabet in which he was to write the Koran.

V355.37–39, B414.24–26, P361.10–12   Tiflis . . . Samarkand . . . Tashkent Tiflis (now Tbilisi) was the capital of the Georgian SSR; Bishkek (for-merly Frunze) is the capital of Kyrgyzstan; Samarkand is the former cap-ital of Uzbekistan, while Tashkent is its present capital city.

V356.10, B415.1, P361.26   an ajtys—a singing-duel   In *Oral Art* (29–30),
Winner describes this social convention as "a singing competition between two individuals, professional bards or amateurs, or two groups.
In such duels the words were generally improvised and the most successful improviser was declared the winner. The content of the songs
was usually drawn from everyday life. Each party might recite as many
simple tales as could be recalled or the competition might be carried on
in the form of a witty debate, or a mock love duel in words and song."

V356.13, B415.5, P361.29   qobyz and dombra   The source again is Winner, *Oral Art* (46): "Generally, legends and tales were recited and were
accompanied by the music of the *dombra* (a plucked instrument similar
to the *balalaika*) or the *quobyz* (a 2-stringed instrument with a round
body, open at the top)."

V356.25, B415.20, P362.3   qumys   An intoxicating drink made from
mare's milk.

V356.33, B415.29, P362.11   aqyn   Kazakh name for a professional bard
(Winner, *Oral Art* 26n).

V357.1, B415.35, P362.17   lepeshka   See V340.1–3n.

V357.29, B416.27, P363.9   Džambul   Winner (*Oral Art* 158) reports that
by the twenties Džambul Džabajev (1846–1945) had become "the most
significant Soviet *aqyn*, celebrated not only in Kazakhstan but throughout the entire Soviet Union."

V357.33, B416.31, P363.13   older than Qorqyt   In Kazakh legend, Qorqyt
is the patriarch of song. Legend has it that, "unable to accept the idea of
death, Qorqyt flees from the people to eternal nature. But nature in the
shape of trees, mountains, steppes, and forests tells him that even she
does not have the power of immortality. Qorqyt then fashions from the
wood of the tree *Sryghaj*, the first qobyz, and plays on it the first Kazakh
song" (Winner, *Oral Art* 47).

V357.37, B416.35, P363.17   the Kirghiz Light   Pynchon's fiction.

EPISODE 6

We left Slothrop high over the Harz Mountains in Schnorp's hot-air balloon. He has now been in occupied Berlin for several weeks, and by
the time this episode concludes he will be on his way to Neubabelsberg
where he will find himself in the midst of the Potsdam Conference of July
17 through August 2, 1945. The writing in this episode brims with local
color gleaned from journalistic accounts of Berlin after V-E Day. Slothrop assumes his next disguise: Raketemensch, or Rocketman.

V359.24, B418.27, P365.7   the Tiergarten   Six hundred acres of paths,
ponds, statuary, and forest situated to the immediate west of central
Berlin.

V359.27–28, B418.30–31, P365.10–11 the center of the bulb is deadly poison The genus *Tulipa*, like many members of the lily family, stores in its bulbs a yellowish alkaloid gum, colchicine, which can cause gastroenteritis, coma, and death.

V360.10, B419.16, P365.28–29 the reflection from her Gold Star brightening See V134.38n.

V360.13, B419.22, B356.27 Hallucinating Rolls Royces and bootheels Slothrop, fearing he's being hunted down by those "Apache" agents (see V267.17–18n, V332.4n).

V360.25, B419.34, P366.9 in Basic American service slang for the basic training given new recruits and inductees into the armed forces.

V361.5, B420.19, P366.31 one insigne in common Latin for an identifying sign or mark ("insignia" is the plural).

V361.7–13, B420.23–28, P366.35–367.1 Adapted from insignia the German troopers wore . . . Klar, Entlüftung, Zündung, Vorstufe, Hauptstufe The source was most likely the photo illustrations in Bley (*South-West Africa under German Rule*) showing German troopers circa 1900 wearing the "wideawake" hat, the brim pinned up with a circular pin (a light circle against a dark background) that was perhaps an inch and a half in diameter (see also Schneider, *Die Kaiserliche Schutz- und Polizeitruppe für Afrika*, and Selmici and Henrichsen, *Das Schwarzkommando*). But Herero tribesmen serving German colonial troops also wore these hats and German military garb. Bley includes a fascinating picture (illus. 16) of Herero chieftain and insurgency leader Samuel Maharero dressed this way, his wideawake pinned up with just this pin (see also V75.12n). The five-position switch plate used to fire V-2s from the mobile launch vehicle is illustrated in the *A-4 Fibel*. After being filled with propellants and preheated at key places, the A4 rocket was attached by wires to an armored "firing control car" or *Feurlitwagen*. In it sat a "firing officer" and his two assistants. They controlled the launch according to the following five-stage declarations: "*Klar*," or "clear," indicated that all hoses and cables had been disconnected from the rocket and that the area was clear of people; "*Entlüftung*," or "ventilation," meant that the first flow of alcohol and liquid oxygen had been released into the combustion chamber; "*Zündung*," or "ignition," was their call when the mixture was ignited by a spark plug; "*Vorstufe*," or "first stage," meant that the flow of auxiliary fuels (hydrogen peroxide and calcium permanganate) had begun driving the turbopumps to increase the flows of alcohol and oxygen; and "*Hauptstufe*," or "main stage," meant that those primary fuels had begun to lift the A4. Kooy and Uytenbogaart (*Ballistics of the Future* 375–76) give an overview of the launch sequence, also available in Dornberger (*V-2* 6–8). Pynchon's best source was certainly the *A-4 Fibel*; however, if he used the English version (virtually the only publicly available one), he also chose to use the German terms.

V361.18–19, B420.35–36, P367.7–8 *Der Meistersinger* The Bantam edition corrects a pronoun error in the Viking; the "Der" should be "Die," as in *Die Meistersänger von Nürnberg* (*The Master Singers of Nuremberg*), Richard Wagner's 1863 opera. Its plot centers on a lover's pursuit that is fulfilled (with the aid of a cobbler, Hans Sachs) on Midsummer's Day, by means of a singing contest.

V361.22, B420.39–421.1, P367.11   Wernher von Braun's birthday   See V237.1–2n; it comes up again in connection with African adventurer Dr. Livingstone (V588.1–2n).

V361.23–25, B421.2–4, P367.12–13   rolled flower-boats through the towns . . . young Spring and deathwhite old Winter   Such equinoctial celebrations on March 21 were many and varied throughout Europe. Grimm (*Teutonic Mythology* 763–65) discusses some Teutonic variants, including the flower-laden carts accompanying the person of Spring, who drives out the personified figure of aging Winter.

V362.12–13, B421.36, P367.41   Search-and-destroy missions   A phrase widely used by U.S. military strategists and personnel during the Vietnam War. It meant, simply, to send out patrols to search out and destroy enemy forces and then withdraw immediately (in contrast to the traditional "clear and hold" mission, where the idea was to conquer the enemy forces in a territory and hold the position indefinitely).

V362.14, B421.38, P368.1–2   butcher named von Trotha   See V317.2n.

V362.17, B421.41, P368.4   "mba-kayere"   "I am passed over." "*Mba-*" is the Herero first-person prefix and "*-kayere*" is a verb signifying any overhead motion, as of birds (Kolbe, *An English-Herero Dictionary* 361).

V362.38, B422.25, P368.27   "Was ist los, meinen Sumpfmenschen?"   Or, "What's up, my swamp-men?" But Enzian's German is a bit off; the plural possessive would be "*meine.*"

V363.3, B422.31–32, P368.32   a couple of muddy trimtabs poke up   Trimtabs were the control surfaces on the back end of each of the A4's four tailfins.

V363.13, B422.43–423.1, 369.1   "der Fünffachnullpunkt"   The "quintuple zero." On the five-digit numbering of the rockets, see V252.4n.

V364.22, B424.15, P370.11   Tannhäuser, the Singing Nincompoop   Here and in what follows Pynchon alludes to the Teutonic legend of Tannhäuser, the troubadour who succumbs to the temptations of sensual pleasure and spends one year underground with Venus (Dame Hulda or Frau Holda in some versions). Boredom and jaded appetites eventually get the better of him, and he returns home. There he boasts of his dalliance during a competition of minnesingers (troubadours), shocking his beloved Lisaura, the girl who had awaited his return. That is his first stupid error: kissing and telling, as it were. Judged guilty of violating the conventions of courtly love, Henry Tannhäuser makes a pilgrimage to Rome. The pope denies him absolution, declaring (in Richard Wagner's operatic version):

Thou art forever accurs'd!
And as this staff I hold
Ne'er will put forth a flower or leaf,
Thus shall thou never more behold
Salvation or thy sin's relief!

Hearing this, Lisaura wastes away and dies of grief, and Henry is doubly overcome by what Calvinists would name his preterition, Catholics his damnation. But then the compounding irony: word comes that the pope's staff has miraculously bloomed. Medieval versions (related in Grimm) used to end here; Wagner, however, adds a romantic coda: Lisaura's sacrifice wins Tannhäuser an eternal love in heaven.

V364.25–26, B424.19–20, P370.15–16   William Slothrop . . . that Arbella   See V204.1–4n.

V364.36, B424.32, P370.25–26   Along the Havel in Neubabelsberg   The community of Neubabelsberg (situated on an arm of the river Havel about fifteen miles southwest of central Berlin) became the center of the German film industry after World War I.

V364.39, B424.36, P370.29   a magenta gel   Magenta is a purple-red coal-tar dye (discovered in 1859 and named for the bloody Battle of Magenta of that year). Impregnated in a photographic gelatin, it serves as a filter. But thrown over a "key light," it would make Greta Erdmann appear red, the color opposite to green—the dominant color pair in these episodes (see Hayles and Eiser, "Coloring Gravity's Rainbow" 18–19).

V365.3, B424.42, P370.34   Chanel suits   Probably the signature cardigan jacket and little black dress introduced during the Roaring Twenties by Paris designer Coco Chanel (1883–1971). During World War II, Chanel (a longtime anti-Semite) began an affair with Nazi officer Hans Gunther van Dincklage, who allowed her to reside in the Ritz Hotel, a collaboration that brought disgrace on her name for years afterward.

V365.10, B425.8–9, P370.41   mangel-wurzel   German name for a species of Goosefoot (the genus *Chenopodium*), a yellowish beet that thrives in high-alkali soils (including the Argentine pampas).

V365.13, B425.13–14, P371.3   near the Grosser Stern   Translated, "Great Star"; a traffic circle in Berlin's Tiergarten where five streets intersect, forming a star-pattern.

V365.17, B425.18–19, P371.7   a REEFER!   Underground slang for a marijuana cigarette. Some say it derives from the verb "reef," to roll up a sail; more likely it originated from a phonetic spelling of Er Rif, the Moroccan hills known for their production of marijuana. Thus Pynchon's comment on "the Rif's slant fields" in the next lines.

V365.23, B425.26, P371.14   "Säure"   German for "acid" (as in vinegar). Thus Emil's name ("Emil" as in the homophone, "Amyl," name for the organic radical C_5H_{11} common to many isomers) means "acid bummer," American sixties slang for an unpleasant experience while under the influence of LSD.

V365.37, B425.42, P371.27　Slothrop's faithful Zippo　Trademarked brand of cigarette lighters, from the Zippo Manufacturing Company. The flints for Slothrop's were strewn amidst the "godawful mess" on his desk back in London (see V18.8–38n).

V366.3, B426.7–8, P371.34　"the Tauschzentrale"　German for a "barter center." It's not necessarily a black market; rather it's a bazaar or trading post with used goods. In this instance, however, it's where Slothrop thinks Trudi and Magda will get needed money for these filched opera costumes.

V366.12, B426.21, P372.4　Tonto　On the *Lone Ranger* programs for American radio and television (see V262.5–6n), Tonto was the masked man's "faithful Indian companion." He saved the life of Texas Ranger Dan Reid, and after Reid became the Lone Ranger, Tonto rode along with him, doing good deeds and helping to search for the outlaws who dry-gulched Reid and his fellow rangers. For subsequent references see V435.21n and V752.7n.

V366.14, B426.22, P372.5　"Raketemensch!"　The correct German should be "Raketenmensch." But the real question here is why Säure would use "*-mensch*" (a "human being" or "person" or "individual") instead of "Raketemann" (Rocketman)? In any case, the comic-book character Rocketman (Cal Martin) made his debut with fiancée Doris Dalton as Rocketgirl in Harry A. (for "Anything") Chesler's *Scoop Comics* (no. 1), published in 1941. They used Cal's rocket pack to zoom around fighting crime; the pair also migrated to different comics, for example *Hello, Pal Comics* (in 1943). In 1952 Ajax/Farrell Comics published a single *Rocketman* issue (all devoted to his adventures), featuring a former stunt pilot named Cliff Secord. Recently, Pacific Comics revived the character under a slightly different moniker, *Rocketeer*, doubtless a ploy to avoid copyright trouble. The Ajax Rocketman comes into the accidental possession of a rocket pack coveted by both Allied and Nazi forces and operated by hand controls. He uses it for heroic and patriotic deeds. His getup—a finned helmet that covers his face, except for eye and mouth vents, a brown cavalry waistcoat, tight riding breeches, and knee-high boots—is much like Slothrop's attire here.

V366.24–25, B426.32–33, P372.14–15　people bring him food, wine and maidens in a four-color dispensation　Slothrop, in short, sees himself enacting the fantasy-life of a "four-color" comic-book hero.

V366.28, B426.39, P372.19　"any armies?"　Servicemen's slang for generic army-issue cigarettes.

V367.19, B427.35, P373.12　"Listen, Kerl"　The term is conversational German for a guy or fella.

V367.27–28, B428.4–5, P373.21–22　Like the ballroom in St. Patrick's . . .

none in these trousers here   An old locker-room pun. In New York City, St. Patrick's Cathedral (which has no ballroom) is located in midtown, at Fifth Avenue and 51st Street.

V368.9, B428.32, P374.5   pisscutter   Partridge (*Forces' Slang*) claims that the word, used here in reference to a men's cap, means "top-notch" and he traces it to Canadian naval slang from World War II. In popular usage, it meant anything cordially, fraternally approved.

V368.13, B428.37, P374.9   Reichstag building   The Reichstag, located on the eastern boundary of Berlin's Tiergarten, was the parliamentary seat of German government prior to Hitler's takeover. The July 16, 1945, issue of *Time* magazine includes a photo, one of the first taken after the Allies were allowed into the Russian-occupied sector of the city. Here is how the correspondent described the scene (28–29): "In the rubble-heaped city, now opened to Anglo-U.S. forces for the first time since its capture ten weeks ago, two things at once impressed the Americans: the mark of Death, and the mark of the Russians. Death stared from the cadavers of mighty buildings; the smashed, charred bones of the Reichstag . . . the stench of death rose too from corpses still rotting under debris, from the corpse-clogged . . . canal, from the hasty shallow graves dug in every park and platz." As to the "mark of the Russians," see below.

V368.17, B428.41–429.1, P374.13   a big chromo of Stalin   This is the "mark of the Russians" on devastated Berlin. The *Time* story (see above) includes just such a picture of Stalin's face staring down on passing Berliners from a huge chromolithograph. *Time*'s correspondent noted (29) that after taking Berlin the Russians "placarded the ruins with portraits of Stalin" (see also V493.39).

V368.28, B429.14, P374.24   GI fartsack   Normally, in U.S. service slang, a sleeping bag, but here used metaphorically to refer to a body bag.

V368.37, B429.24, P374.33   M.O.s   Services acronym for medical officers.

V368.41, B429.30, P374.37–38   John Dillinger   Photos of the legendary 1930s outlaw, and the FBI's "Public Enemy Number One," would be appropriate decor for this (evidently fictional) bar because John Dillinger (b. 1903) was gunned down outside Chicago's Biograph Theater on July 22, 1934 (see also V741.6–26).

V369.18, B430.7, P375.15   mountain of hash!   Hashish.

V369.20, B430.9, P375.17   the Romilar River   Romilar is the registered trademark of a dextromethorphan hydrobromide cough pill that first won FDA approval in 1958. In 1967, Australian physicians Angus Dodds and E. Revai reported in the *Medical Journal of Australia* (2:231) a case of Romilar abuse in which a twenty-three-year-old male addict, having ingested twenty tablets, experienced "marked visual and auditory hallucinations, and associations of sounds with colours (synaesthesia)." These findings were widely reported in mainline and underground media, and a spike in reported recreational use led in the early seventies to Romilar's removal from pharmacy shelves so that the company could work out another delivery mode. Remarketed in syrup form, Romilar lost popularity in the drug subculture because achieving hallucinogenic effects required mass quantities (a "river") of Romilar, and the syrupy sweetness tended to induce vomiting.

V369.28, B430.17, P375.25   Panama Red   More sixties-era underworld slang; here, for the red-tinted variety of Panamanian marijuana.

V369.34, B430.23, P375.31   a narco man   A narcotics agent.

V370.5–6, B430.34–35, P376.2–3   "Potsdam . . . the Wilhelmplatz"   Potsdam is located across the Havel from Neubabelsberg and was the site for the Potsdam Conference of late July and early August 1945. The Wilhelmplatz is a large square located in the center of town.

V370.25, B431.13, P376.22   "the CBI"   The China-Burma-India theater of operations.

V370.36, B431.24–25, P376.33   "not a devotee of the Green Hershey Bar, mm?"   The "decadent young woman" taunting Rocketman/Slothrop here refers not to a Hershey chocolate bar but—in underworld slang—to a pressed and packaged chunk of Nepalese hashish.

EPISODE 7

In full Rocketman regalia, Slothrop makes a raid on the "Berlin White House" in the neighborhood of Neubabelsberg occupied by President Harry Truman. The approximate date is July 18, 1945. Slothrop recovers a kilogram of the Nepalese hashish buried below Truman's window, makes his way back to central Berlin, is intercepted by Tchitcherine and, as the episode ends, slides once more into a sodium amytal–induced hallucination.

V371.32–33, B432.26, P377.30   villa at 2 Kaiserstrasse, in Neubabelsberg   President Truman's address for the Potsdam Conference. Journalistic accounts of the house, located on the south shore of the Griebnitz See, agree that it was an unattractive squat building and not white but yellow.

V371.34–35, B432.28, P377.32   the Avus Autobahn   This highway runs southwest out of Berlin through the middle-class suburb of Zehlendorf, through Neubabelsberg, then over the river Havel to Potsdam.

V372.10, B433.2, P378.7   "Plunging fire"   U.S. Army handbooks define it as gunfire from high emplacements that strikes earth at an oblique angle.

V372.12, B433.5, P378.9   an AGO card   Issued through the Adjutant General's Office of the U.S. Army to military personnel who are awaiting, or in the midst of, either a reassignment or some special assignment.

V372.23, B433.18, P378.21 "back to Cuxhaven" The North Sea town where, by this time, English rocket experts were beginning to study and test the A4 rocket for Operation Backfire.

V372.29–30, B433.25–26, P378.27–28 Mare's-tails . . . the Berliner Luft Mare's-tails are white cirrus clouds. Ancient Europeans regarded them as hairs from the White Goddess (*Albina*), sometimes known as Rhiannon or Demeter, a premonitory sign of an *Alpdrücken* or "nightmare." The "Berliner Luft" is the Berlin "air," with the sense of its singularity. In reference to the traditional popular song, "Berliner Luft," the idea also involves the city's comical uniqueness, the result—suggests the lyric's opening line ("Das macht der Berliner Luft, Luft, Luft") of Berlin's air or ambiance. Teague ("A *'Gravity's Rainbow' Companion* Companion") provides a sample verse and its translation:

> Ich frug ein Kind mit jelbe Schuh
> Wie alt bist do denn, Kleene?
> Die sagt sie schnippisch: "Du? Nanu
> Ick werd' schon nächstens zehne?"
> Doch fährt nach Britz sie mit Mama'n
> Da sagt die kleine Hexe
> Zum Schaffner von der Straßenbahn:
> Ick werd' erscht nächstens sechse!

> [I asked a kid wearing yellow shoes,
> "How old are you, little one?"
> She came back, "Hey? Well,
> I'll be ten my next birthday!"
> As she and her mama were going to Britz,
> I heard the little witch
> Tell the streetcar conductor,
> "I won't be thikth till my nekth birthday?"]

V372.33–38, B433.30–36, P378.32–33 Where's the city Slothrop used to see back in . . . National Geographic? . . . the City Sacramental The reference and source, as McCarron points out ("Slothrop, Berlin, and Pynchon's Use of Periodicals"), is to the February 1937 *National Geographic* lead article, forty-six pages of pictures and text on "Changing Berlin," spotlighting the Nazi regime's immense architectural remake of the city it imagined as sacred center of the Third Reich, which is represented in *GR* as an exercise in "necropolism."

V373.19, B434.21, P379.18 the Winterhilfe one-course The *Winterhilfswerk* (Winter Relief Project) was a 1933 brainchild of Nazi propaganda chief Josef Goebbels. It began as a campaign to raise funds for social relief, originally to purchase items of food but later clothing and other articles. Donors to the program were given WHW lapel buttons and stickers for their front doors announcing: "We gave." The WHW also established one Sunday each month as a "one-course Sunday," when a simple meal of pickled meat was to be substituted for the usual multicourse spread. The dispensation of goods to the needy took the form of mass feedings, free clothes, and the like (Heiber 185–86).

V373.26–27, B434.30–31, P379.26–27   giant photographs are posted out in the Friedrichstrasse   And indeed they were. Truman, Stalin, and Churchill were all in a row at the intersection of Unter den Linden and the Friedrichstrasse (see the photograph in *Time*, July 23, 1945, 21).

V373.32, B434.38–39, P379.32   "Roosevelt died back in the spring"   Specifically during the afternoon of April 12, 1945, while Slothrop was "jiving on the Riviera" (V374.10).

V373.39–40, B435.4–6, P379.40–41   Slothrop was going into high school when FDR was starting out in the White House   Roosevelt took office on March 4, 1933. If Slothrop were born in March 1918 (see V624.18n), he would have been about fifteen and a high school freshman.

V374.22–23, B435.34, P380.24   posing in the black cape at Yalta   In February 1945, Roosevelt, Churchill, and Stalin met in the Crimean city of Yalta to discuss plans for the occupation of Germany and Europe. The picture of Roosevelt in the black cape, flanked by the other two allies, was widely published (for example, in *Time*). He died two months later.

V374.39–375.2, B436.11–16, P380.40–381.3   the Evil Hour, when the white woman . . . comes out of her mountain . . . offering the Wonderflower . . . with long teeth   A reference to Dame Holda (V364.22n), from Grimm's *Teutonic Mythology*. The goddess appeared under two aspects: as a kind and helpful maid, white as and often associated with the glittering snow, and as an ugly old woman (in Grimm's description [269] "an old witch with long teeth" who has a dark and dreadful disposition). The "Wonderflower" or *Wunderblume* is a folk talisman, a key to open Dame Holda's mountain wherein lies its miraculous treasure. Usually the Wonderflower is a white forget-me-not and associated with Dame Holda in her helpful aspect. In many of these stories the hero has been banished to the mountains; in order to redeem his freedom, he must recover the enchanted treasure, "and the white woman, the snake woman, or simply snake and dragon, are they that guard it (ibid. 970). In this context, Grimm also notes that Christ was frequently interpreted as a "treasure" who went down to harrow hell. The "Evil Hour" thus explains itself: Christ was crucified at noon, and the noon hour gathers significance as *GR* unfolds: see also V439.37, V500.40, V625.5, V667.3–4, and V674.19–20.

V375.4, B436.18, P381.4   Black P-38s   Lockheed Aircraft produced nearly ten thousand of these twin-engine fighter planes, nicknamed "Lightning." The models built for the U.S. Army Air Corps were green and black; those for the Navy, silver and blue.

V375.7, B436.21–22, P381.8   a "stick" of "tea"   More underworld slang for a cigarette of marijuana, although very self-consciously done, as the scare quotes indicate.

V375.16, B436.33–34, P381.17–18   It was our "Captain Midnight"   *Captain Midnight* was a radio program that got its start in 1940 over the Mutual Broadcasting Network out of Chicago. By 1943 it was carried nationwide every weekday evening. Captain Midnight was an agent whose wartime job was so secret that his identity, beyond the code number SS-1, was unknown even to his superiors. Ovaltine sponsored the show, and for a dime plus the label from one jar, a kid could buy membership in the Captain's "Secret Squadron," which earned him or her a "decoder badge" to decipher messages broadcast at program's end.

V375.21, B436.39–40, P381.23   "Something in that rocket needed potassium permanganate"   In the A4 rocket, permanganate of *calcium* was used in the autocatalytic ignition of hydrogen peroxide to power the turbines. In underworld use, as Pynchon describes it here, permanganate of potassium can indeed be used to process cocaine. In aqueous solution, as permanganic acid, it is a purple liquid (the "Purpurstoff"); hence the "purple target" (V376.6) on the blotting paper. Notice also the reversal or hysteron proteron: in this case, the target materializes from the outside in, the outermost rings being the most valuable.

V375.31–32, B437.8–9, P381.34–35   "So . . . there crept over Berlin a gigantic Laurel and Hardy film, silent, silent"   Stan Laurel (1890–1965) and Oliver Hardy (1892–1957) made their first film together in a silent short, *Lucky Dog* (1917). Ten years later they formalized their partnership with director Hal Roach and proceeded to make a series of shorts and features, nearly all with sound. But Säure is referring here to the ways that the A4 rocket's demands for raw materials, like calcium permanganate, seem (to him) to have affected *markets*, white and black, including the cocaine market, in which shortages created an unspeakable wackiness.

V376.26, B438.7–8, P382.29   "der Springer"   The German name given to the knight in games of chess (remember, back at V248.40–41, the card Blodgett Waxwing gave to Slothrop featured a knight). Ludwig "Der Springer" was moreover an eleventh-century Thuringian king remembered in Baedeker's *Northern Germany* (369) for erecting churches in the vicinity of Nordhausen.

V376.27–28, B438.9–10, P382.31   "to spend my last several decades as the Sublime Rossini did"   Italian composer Gioacchino Rossini (1792–1868) retired from the public eye in his thirties. For three decades thereafter he continued to write songs and instrumental pieces but lived mainly for pleasure's sake.

V376.36, B438.20, P382.39   "Zorro? The Green Hornet?"   Two more American heroes. In 1920 actor Douglas Fairbanks played the sword-dazzling lead in the silent film *The Mark of Zorro*, a story set in Spanish California about a wealthy ranchero's son who secretly fights against a corrupt colonial government on behalf of ordinary farmers. The young man, Don Diego de la Vega, is soon known as Señor Zorro (Mr. Fox). From 1936 until 1952 *The Green Hornet* was a regular feature of the Mutual Radio network. He hunted down "the biggest of all game, public enemies that even the G-men cannot reach!" as the announcer used to exclaim in the show's opening moments. The Hornet was Britt Reid, son of Dan Reid (the Lone Ranger). With "his faithful valet, Kato," he matched wits with the underworld, always won, and like his famous dad forswore the use of deadly force.

V376.41, B438.26, P383.4   "Glück"   That is, "luck," as in "Good luck."

V377.2–4, B438.28–31, P383.6–8   the mountain has closed . . . that White Woman   Dame Holda once again (see V374.39–375.2n).

V377.7, B438.35, P383.11–12   Katje, her damask tablecloth   Slothrop recalls how Katje made him "disappear" beneath it at V198.8–13.

V377.11, B438.39–40, P383.16   Suomis or Degtyarovs   The Degtyarev (as it's usually transliterated, not -ov) is a Russian submachine gun with a forty-seven-shot magazine, an infantry standard during World War II. The Suomi (Finnish) submachine gun used a drum magazine located below the barrel (see also V513.15n).

V377.25–26, B439.16, P383.32   "Stiefeln, bitte"   "Boots, please." But the sentry's German is off: the plural form should be "Die Stiefel, bitte."

V377.30, B439.21, P383.36   the Funkturm   The radio tower.

V377.35, B439.28, P384.1   A SNAFU FOR ROCKETMAN   From the popular servicemen's acronym for "Situation Normal, All Fucked Up."

V378.7, B439.42, P384.13   "Stimmt, Herr Schlepzig"   Or, "[It's] in order, Mr. Schlepzig."

V378.12, B440.6–7, P384.18   what the Book of Changes calls Youthful Folly   See V13.1n. The image from *The I Ching; or, Book of Changes* is of a mountain with a lake or spring pond below it. The setting here resembles that image: the waters of the Griebnitz See are at Slothrop's feet, and above him is the "White House," looming like a mountain, from beneath which he must snatch a treasure.

V378.16, B440.11, P384.22   Jubilee Jim   The second reference to James "Jubilee Jim" Fisk (1834–72), the notorious robber baron and womanizer, known also as "The Barnum of Wall Street" for the spectacle he made. Fuller's book, a likely source, narrates how with Jay Gould he masterminded a takeover of the Erie Railroad, which was at the time (in 1868) laying track through western Massachusetts. (See also V285.37n and V438.15–17n; see also Larsson ["From the Berkshires to the Brocken" or "A *Companion*'s Companion"], who notes Fisk's appearances in *The Berkshire Hills*.)

V379.25–26, B441.26–27, P385.29–30   back on Midsummer Eve . . . fern

seed fell in his shoes Midsummer's Eve is the solstice (June 22). On the fern seed Pynchon's source was Grimm (*Teutonic Mythology* 1210): "Fern seed makes one invisible, but it is difficult to get at: it ripens only between 12 and 1 on Midsummer Night, and then falls off directly, and is gone. A man, who on that night happened to be looking for a lost foal, passed through a field where fern seed was ripening, and some fell in his shoes. Next morning he was invisible."

V380.6, B442.10, P386.9   Amateur Fritz von Opels Opel was a member of the German family that began producing automobiles in 1898, but he distinguished himself for daring feats of speed. In 1927, for example, he called on Society for Space Travel expert Max Valier, who designed for him a rocket-propelled automobile. On Berlin's Avus Autobahn, Opel pushed the car to speeds of over 125 miles per hour, setting a new land-speed record.

V380.11, B442.16, P386.14   Garbo fedoras Perhaps a hat like the fedora that actress Garbo wore in *Anna Christie* (1930).

V380.14, B442.20–21, P386.17   a lean gray Porsche The Porsche trademark did not exist on automobiles until 1948. Before the war, however, Ferdinand Porsche did design automobiles for Steyr, Mercedes, and Volkswagen. In VW's Stuttgart plant, he also built three streamlined sports cars for the Rome-to-Berlin road race of 1939. But when the war intervened these designs were never raced, and Dr. Porsche ended up dedicating his facilities to the German *Wehrmacht* by designing and producing parts (especially engines) for numerous vehicles, including Panzer tanks. His automobiles sat in storage through the war and were hauled out as prototypes for the first Porsche production cars built in 1948. If this "lean gray Porsche" was one of those three, then Slothrop has had what auto enthusiasts would call a religious experience.

V380.25–26, B442.34–35, P386.29   Hey! Leaps broad highways in a single bound! The narrator riffs on the radio announcer's introduction of Superman, who "leaps tall buildings in a single bound!" An interesting sidenote: an April 20, 1995, story in the *Los Angeles Times* relates how Pynchon lived, during the late sixties, at 217 Thirty-Third Street in Manhattan Beach, in a small downstairs apartment next door to a little café called the Fractured Cow. Coincidentally, across the street lived Phyllis Coates, famous as the original Lois Lane (from 1952 to 1953) in the television show *The Adventures of Superman*. According to the story, Pynchon dated Coates's daughter.

V380.37, B443.7, P386.40   BMW limousines Like the Porsche reference, above, a puzzling one. The Bayerische Motoren Werke of Eisenach and Munich was known, from the time it commenced production in 1928 until well after the war, as a manufacturer of sports cars and "drophead" (convertible) coupes. A production-line "BMW limousine" is undocumented and probably a Pynchon fiction.

V381.6, B443.18–19, P387.9–10   Some think he is Don Ameche, others Oliver Hardy   Perhaps these servicemen are blind, or else Slothrop really is next to invisible. The Kenosha, Wisconsin–born Ameche (1908–93) was the thin, boyish star who made his screen debut in 1936 and for years was best known for his roles in *The Story of Alexander Graham Bell* (1939), in which he played the great inventor, and in *Heaven Can Wait* (1943), a comedy by former Ufa director Ernst Lubitsch. Oliver ("Ollie") Hardy (see also V375.31–32n) was in contrast the fat, mustachioed member of the Laurel and Hardy duo.

V381.10–14, B443.24–29, P387.14–17   Miss Rheingold 1946 . . . Dorothy Hart . . . Helen Riickert   Every summer the Liebmann Breweries Incorporated (in Brooklyn, New York) sponsored a contest to find the new poster girl for their Rheingold Beer, with patrons casting their votes "at Rheingold Stores and Taverns Everywhere," as the ads used to note. Hart, Rickert (note the actual spelling), and Darnley were—with Jean Welch and Maggie Long—the losers in balloting that closed on August 31, 1945. The winner, blonde Rita Daigle, received three thousand dollars and a modeling contract that would lead to her picture being displayed in ads and on billboards throughout the greater New York City area. Dorothy Hart went on to roles in a few B-grade movies of the late forties.

V382.3–4, B444.25–26, P388.8   "Don't Sit Under the Apple Tree" . . . Andrews Sisters   The song (by Brown, Tobias, and Stept) was a 1942 hit for the Glenn Miller Orchestra and a hit once again in 1944 for the Andrews Sisters. The lyrics are in parts. First the male voices sing:

Don't sit under the apple tree
With anyone else but me [repeat twice, then the whole stanza]
Till I come marching home.

Don't go walking down lover's lane
With anyone else but me [repeat as before]
Till I come marchin' home.

Well I just got word, from a guy who heard
From the guy next door to me;
The girl he met just loves to pet,
And she fits you to a tee—

But don't sit under the apple tree
With anyone else but me [repeat as before]

Then the female voices come in:

Don't give out with those lips of yours
To anyone else but me [repeat as before]
Till you come marchin' home.

So watch the girls on those foreign shores,
They'll have to report to me [repeat as before]
When you come marchin' home.

You're on your own, where there is no phone,
And I can't keep tab on you;
Be fair to me, and I'll guarantee,
There's one thing I won't do—

I won't sit under the apple tree
With anyone else but you [repeat, all together now].

V382.15–16, B444.40–41, P388.20   Mickey Rooney . . . Judge Hardy's freckled madcap son   From 1936 to 1958 actor Mickey Rooney (b. 1920) made fourteen Andy Hardy films. During his early years, the films also featured Andy's father (played in the first film by Lionel Barrymore), a judge who always fought for the rights of little people. In *Judge Hardy's Children* (1938), he battles an electric cartel and its Washington lobbyists. It turns out that Rooney was touring Germany in the summer of 1945 with the U.S. Army but never made it to Potsdam or met President Truman. Larson ("Rooney and the Rocketman") has made an interesting find, however. The first issue of *Hello, Pall Comics*, which introduced Rocketman's second comic-book avatar, featured a cover photograph of Rooney.

V382.22, B445.7, P388.27   Minsky's   Beginning in the early twentieth century, the Minsky family operated several "variety theater" houses in New York. By far the most famous was Minsky's Burlesque, which opened in 1934 in the former Apollo Theatre building at 223 W. 42nd Street. Shows featured comedy, chorus lines, and striptease (including the renowned Gypsy Rose Lee), until Mayor Fiorello LaGuardia closed down the "burley houses" after a series of 1939 raids.

V383.1–2, B445.34, P389.7–8   hair combed lionlike . . . glimmering steel teeth   This is Tchitcherine, whose "steel teeth wink as he talks" (V337.22–23).

V383.2, B445.35, P389.8   eyes black and soft as that Carmen Miranda's   The Portugal-born singer, dancer, and actress (1909–55) famous for her fruit-filled hats and smokey eyes. Those eyes were a key focus in 1944 when she starred as "Chiquita Hart" in a piece of film candy for servicemen, *Something for the Boys*.

EPISODE 8

Aboard a hijacked German submarine, most likely off the coast of north Africa near the Azores, the Argentine anarchists lazily plan a film version of José Hernández's epic poem of the Argentine pampas, *Martín Fierro*. They propose to shoot this film on the Lüneburg Heath, the place (as it happens) where the quintuple-zero rocket was fired. The time of this episode is unspecified, but probably mid-July.

V383.10, B446.2, P389.16   Leopoldo Lugones   See V263.18n.

V383.11, B446.4, P389.17–18   the chug of the "billy-goat"   The sound of the submarine's bilge pump. Its below-decks compartment, in naval slang, is called "the goat hole" (used again at V594.38).

V383.12–13, B446.5–6, P389.19   El Ñato   He derives his moniker from a character in canto 22 of Hernández's *Return of Martín Fierro*. It means "pug nose."

V383.13–14, B446.7, P389.20   tristes and milongas   Respectively, Spanish for "laments" (or any sad songs) and "dances."

V383.18, B446.12, P389.24   Cipriano Reyes   Next to Juan Perón, Reyes was once one of Argentina's most charismatic political figures. During the summer and fall of 1945 he parlayed his leadership of the Packinghouse Workers Union into leadership of the entire Partido Laborista, the Labor Party. Reyes was an anarchist and also a Perónist in 1944–45. However, by the spring of 1946 he had broken with Perón over the role of the military, and by 1948 he was accused of plotting with U.S. diplomat John Griffiths to assassinate Perón. Reyes never recovered from that charge, which appears to have been trumped up anyway (Alexander, *The Perón Era* 54–60). Note also his first name: "Cipriano" means "of Kyprian Venus"; compare, for example, "Kyprinos" at V55.36 and "Cypridinae" at V690.40.

V383.19, B446.13, P389.25   Acción Argentina   See V263.34–35n.

V383.20–22, B446.15–17, P389.26–28   Borges ... ("El laberinto ... la disquietante luna")   Here is a curious puzzle. The quotation does not appear in the *Obras poéticas* (Poetical Works) of Jorge Luis Borges nor does it crop up in the course of his fictional works. It *is* neatly consistent with the rhythms and motifs in Borges's poems, and if the lines are not his then Pynchon has worked up a decent imitation—a neat trick, given the way Borges's fictions reinvent literary history. The lines translate: "The labyrinth of your uncertainty / detains me with the anxious moon."

V383.25–26, B446.20–22, P389.31–32   "pitos ... puchos ... mamao" El Ñato (like Pynchon) is showing off his facility with tough-guy, gaucho slang. The glossary appended to Walter Owen's translation of *Martín Fierro* provides most of the terms: a *pito* is a kind of knife blade; *puchos* derives from the gaucho exclamation "*la pucha!*" (the whore!); *caña* is a drink high in alcohol content and distilled from the juices of various fruits; *tacuara* is the gaucho term for a stout bamboo lance that the pampas Indians once used as a weapon. The term *mamao*, for "drunk," is of unknown origin.

V383.29–30, B446.26, P389.36 Beláustegui . . . from Entre Ríos His name is Basque; the place is an inland province of Argentina, located northwest of Buenos Aires.

V383.36–37, B446.35, P390.6 Lugones's "Pavos Reales" On Leopoldo Lugones see V263.18n. The "Pavos Reales," or "Peacocks," are six short lyrical poems (for those tracing the references to the number eight in GR, the poems are *octets*). Published in his 1922 book, *Las horas doradas* (Golden Hours), the six poems are arranged in a cyclical order, treating the theme of redemption. The Peacock (or *Pavos christatus*) provides a symbolic center for that theme, for it is the traditional symbol of messianic hope. In order the six poems are "La Pompa" (The Display), "La Rueda" (The Spread), "El Orgullo" (Arrogance), "La Aurora" (Dawn), "La Tarde" (Evening), and "La Noche" (Night). Finally, note that like many works and events referred to earlier—the *Duino Elegies, Erwartung,* Stalin's coming to power, and the second Herero uprising—the Lugones book appeared in 1922, one of the *anni mirabili* in GR.

V383.37, B446.36, P390.7 off Matosinhos A Portuguese coastal city.

V384.28, B447.30–31, P390.35–36 pero ché, no sós argentino See V264.4n.

V384.30–31, B447.34–35, P384.38–39 Rolls Royce with a sinister dome . . . green Perspex The Rolls Royce–driving "Apache" agents seem to be on Squalidozzi's trail, too (see V332.4n). Perspex is the British registered trademark for a transparent, very lightweight polymerized methyl methacrylate plastic (also known in the U.S. as Plexiglas) that is also capable of "piping" light around bends (see V487.24n).

V384.34, B447.38–39, P391.1 a harmonica factory Given their worldwide monopoly on the market, this can only be the Matteus Hohner Company in Trossingen, Germany, just over the Swiss border from Zurich.

V385.1, B448.6, P391.9 the Caligari gloves These are the "bone white" gloves with the black lines extending from the wrist to each knuckle from *Das Kabinet des Doktor Caligari.* The film itself is black-and-white, so the reference is anachronistic. Pynchon may have gotten the violet idea from the still photo of the gloves that was tinted that color (by the Princeton University Press) for the cover of Siegfried Kracauer's scholarly book *From Caligari to Hitler.*

V385.8, B448.14–15, P391.16 the smell of freshly brewed maté In *Martín Fierro,* the gauchos suck herb tea (called yerba maté), made from the maté plant, through metal straws projecting from gourds full of steaming tea (Hernández 309).

V385.20, B448.29, P391.28 a Bob Steele See V247.6–7n.

V385.32, B448.42, P391.40   his *nom de pègre* His gangster name.

V385.39–40, B449.9, P392.6–7   Edouard Sanktwolke Edward Saint-Cloud.

V386.6, B449.17, P392.14   "verdad?" "True?"

V386.16, B449.29, P392.24   *I Promessi Sposi* *The Betrothed*, Alessandro Manzoni's nineteenth-century novel, a melodramatic story of two peasants who fall in love and struggle against all socially determined odds—tyranny, poverty, disease, prejudice—to do the right Christian thing and marry.

V386.21–22, B449.36–37, P392.30–31   "the Gaucho Bakunin. . . . a Gaucho Marx" Respectively, Squalidozzi is an Argentine version of the nineteenth-century Russian anarchist Mikhail Bakunin (d. 1876); and, in a pun—perhaps derived, thinks Larsson ("A *Companion*'s Companion") from a scene in *The Manchurian Candidate*—he is a gaucho version of either film comedian Groucho Marx (1895–1977) or political philosopher Karl Marx (1818–83).

V386.37–387.2, B450.12–17, P393.5–10   Aquí me pongo a cantar . . . con el cantar se consuela This is the opening stanza of *Martín Fierro*. Giving himself wide latitude with the translation, in order to preserve the prosody, Owen translates:

> I sit me here to sing my song,
> To the beat of my old guitar;
> For the man whose life is a bitter cup,
> With a song may yet his heart lift up,
> As the lonely bird in the leafless tree,
> That sings 'neath the gloaming star.

V387.4, B450.19, P393.11   the estancia The ranch.

V387.5–6, B450.21, P393.14   General Roca's campaign It lasted six years, from 1880 to 1886, during which time Roca pursued a ruthless strategy against the Indians of South America. In this he shared the genocidal passion of the German general Lothar von Trotha in South-West Africa. Roca pursued his ends by dragooning other natives, the gauchos, into his army. The gaucho could ride and fight, he was also a dispossessed person, and (as we see in *Martín Fierro*) he could do little to resist, except desert and become an outlaw with a bounty on his head.

V387.14, B450.33, P393.24   Gesellschaft The term can signify a socioeconomic partnership or company; but here simply "society."

V387.29, B451.8, P393.39   Punta del Este Point of land on the northern Argentine coast.

V387.29–30, B451.9–10, P393.39–40   Anilinas Alemanas . . . Spottbilligfilm The first was German Anilines, a subsidiary of IG Farben based out of Buenos Aires (Sasuly, *IG Farben* 167–68). On the fictional Spottbilligfilm see V163.31–33n.

V387.36, B451.17, P394.5   *Alpdrücken* The dog in Edward Pointsman's dream, Reichssieger von Thanatz Alpdrucken (without the umlaut over the "u"), has fragmented and the parts of his name now begin to metamorphose. Here, *Alpdrücken* (Nightmare) is an imaginary film tying together any number of characters and events in *GR*. Margherita Erdmann acted in it; her daughter was conceived during the shooting of a scene from it; Franz Pökler watched that scene and was emboldened to go home and conceive his daughter, Ilse; and Slothrop will be sexually linked to both Margherita and Bianca. Tchitcherine will be linked to Margherita through a horse named Snake, his mount in central Asia; Snake was the first horse Greta ever rode (while in the U.S. filming *Weisse Sandwüste von Neumexiko*), and it's the horse of Crutchfield the Westwardman in Slothrop's sodium amytal nightmare. The term *Alpdrücken* derives from an old folk belief that the devil rode men as if they were horses, so that by morning their "mane" (hair) would be tangled and their bodies dripping with perspiration (Grimm, *Teutonic Mythology* 1246–47). Graves (*The White Goddess* 67) also discusses the etymology: "*Alpdrücken*, the nightmare or incubus, is connected with the Greek words *alphos*, meaning 'dull-white leprosy' (Latin albus) . . . and *Alphito*, the 'White Goddess.'"

V387.38, B451.20–21, P394.7–8   singing-duel between the white gaucho and the dark El Moreno   In cantos 29 and 30 of *The Return of Martín Fierro*, the gaucho competes with "a Negro" named El Moreno in a singing duel. A fight nearly breaks out at the end, but Martín and his sons ride peaceably into the west, to freedom.

V388.1, B451.24, P394.11   wipe   A transitional device in filmmaking, where the new scene "wipes" vertically, horizontally, or diagonally across the frame.

V388.13–15, B451.39–40, P394.23–25   "I can take down your fences . . . lead you back to the Garden"   Another of the novel's potential "returns." Also another instance of hysteron proteron.

V388.21–22, B452.7–8, P392.31–33   "Back to Gondwanaland . . . took the ferry not to Montevideo, but to Lüderitzbucht"   Still more hysteron proteron. In theory, Gondwanaland was a Mesozoic continent that once included South America, Africa, India, and Australia. They split and drifted apart (see also V321.19–20n), and this is why Felipe's "refugees" from the Mesozoic age (dinosaurs?) took the ferry, not to the port city of Montevideo, but to Lüderitzbucht, the southwest African port.

V388.27–28, B452.15–16, P394.38   Prince Potemkin's fake villages   During the winter and spring of 1787, Empress Catherine of Russia journeyed to the southern provinces ruled by her lover and adviser, Prince Grigori Potemkin (1739–91). He had wrought enormous changes in the south: ports had been constructed, a system of roads built, and imperial administration had been extended to even the smaller towns. Catherine made a float trip down the Dnieper River in May and saw for herself its scores of thriving villages and well-dressed people. In St. Petersburg, however, Potemkin's detractors insisted that it was all a show, that those people were slaves dressed up for the occasion who leap-frogged along the riverbank for Catherine's benefit. Even the villages were faked, they alleged. No proof was ever, or has ever, been introduced to prove this claim. Still, in German the phrase *"Potemkinsche Dörfer"* became synonymous with such fakery.

V388.35, B452.23, P395.4   "Der Aal! Der Aal!" The eel, wonders Graciela
The "aal" is a torpedo, not an eel, but in this linguistic stew or Tower of Babel, confusion reigns. The passage gives us an obscene (punning) image in the description of the torpedo being aimed and fired to "intersect the [USS *John E.*] *Badass*'s desperate sea-squirm about midships" (V389.15–16).

V389.3–4, B452.36–37, P395.13–14   Spyros ("Spider") Telangiecstasis
In medical terminology, telangiecstasia is a chronic vascular disorder in which groups of capillaries dilate, causing transient red blotches, like birthmarks, on the skin. The Greek word *"spyros"* designates a coil.

V389.23–24, B453.18, P395.33–34   writes Shetzline American novelist David Shetzline (b. 1937) was at Cornell University with Thomas Pynchon and Richard Farina (to whose memory *GR* is dedicated). Shetzline is the author of two novels: *DeFord* (1968) and *Heckletooth 3* (1969). He is also married to novelist and short story writer Mary F. Beal, one of whose fictions ("Gold") is the subject of an allusion at V612.33. The quotation here does not appear in Shetzline's published writings, so its reference is perhaps private.

V390.1, B453.40–41, P396.11   the Dreyfus Affair After French captain Alfred Dreyfus (1859–1935) was convicted of treason in 1895, following a long trial rife with anti-Semitic bias, French Zionists united in his defense. Dreyfus was retried, acquitted, and released in 1906.

V390.4, B454.1–2, P396.14   Will you go to the Heath? An important question, to whomever it is addressed. The Lüneburg Heath is the setting for Weissmann's last stand, during Easter/April Fool's of 1945, in the concluding episode of *GR*.

EPISODE 9

An exceptionally short episode set sometime in mid-July, outside Berlin. Tchitcherine, having taken half of the Potsdam hashish, puzzles over the results of Slothrop's latest sodium amytal session.

V390.7, B454.5, P396.17   Džabajev The fictional namesake of Džambul Džabajev, celebrated Kirghiz *aqyn* (see V357.29n).

V390.8–9, B454.7–8, P396.18–19   combs his hair like . . . Frank Sinatra

That is, in a slick pompadour, in the style of the American singer and actor (1915–1998).

V391.19, B455.24–25, P397.27 SPOG, CIOS, BAFO, TI On SPOG and CIOS, see V272.32–34n; TI is British Technical Intelligence, which intercepts and interprets data about enemy manufacturing and supply; BAFO was the acronym of British Air Force of Occupation.

V391.22, B455.28–29, P397.30 from the Hook of Holland all across Lower Saxony Retreating from their positions in Holland, German V-2 units were forced to exit The Hague northward along the Zuider Zee, skirt around Montgomery's divisions located just to the south, then turn east toward Hanover and the Lüneburg Heath. The units left on Thursday, March 28, 1945, and were in the Hanover area by Easter Sunday, April 1. Various sources (the *Times* of London, Irving [*Mare's Nest*], Huzel [*Peenemünde to Canaveral*]) agree that from there, around Easter, the last rockets of the war were fired on advancing Allied troops.

V391.33–34, B456.1, P398.2 Malenkov's special committee During the war Georgi M. Malenkov directed Russian heavy industry. In particular, he oversaw the production of planes and tanks. So when the Soviet army overran German rocket facilities at Peenemünde, in March–April of 1945, the gathering of information and the removal of equipment fell under his administrative purview.

V391.35, B456.2, P398.3 TsAGI See V273.5n.

EPISODE 10

Another short episode, which occurs later the same day as episode 9, now identified as occurring in a whitewashed room above a disused Neubabelsberg movie studio. Slothrop awakens from his sodium amytal session to encounter "his Lisaura," Margherita Erdmann. Her yellow and purple iris assumes, in this satirically inverted context, the power of a *Wunderblume* (V374.39–375.2n), a talisman associated with Venus and capable of unlocking secret treasures.

V393.11–12, B457.31–32, P399.21–22 phony-gemütlich love nests . . . Wagnerian battlements That is, phony comfortable love nests and battlements of the sort that Fritz Lang constructed for *Nibelungen*, his two-part screen epic that Kracauer's *From Caligari to Hitler* describes and reproduces stills from (93–94, ills. 10, 11).

V393.32, B458.15, P400.2 his helpless Lisaura Alluding to the Tannhäuser myth (see V364.22n).

V393.37, B458.21, P400.7 worked as a movie actress, at Templehof and Staaken Kracauer (17) reports that after World War I the German film companies were first established at Neubabelsberg and Tempelhof (the correct spelling; the text gets it wrong), both Berlin suburbs. Later, in the early thirties, the great director Fritz Lang moved his studio to Staaken, another Berlin suburb (ibid. 219).

V393.41–394.1, B458.26–27, P400.11–12   no Dietrich, nor vamp à la Brigitte Helm   Marlene Dietrich (1901?–1992) was the German actress best known for her role as Lola Lola in the film *Der Blaue Engel* (1930); Brigitte Helm played a series of "vamp" roles, most notably in a double role as lovely Maria and as robot Maria in Fritz Lang's *Metropolis* (1926), a key text in *GR* for its treatment of immachination; Helm also played a prostitute (in *Unholy Love*, 1928), a bourgeoise who loses herself in debaucheries (*Crisis*, also in 1928), and the lead in both *Anna Karenina* (1929) and *The Countess of Monte Cristo* (1932). Kracauer (passim) was probably the source here.

V394.2–3, B458.29, P400.14   nicknamed her the anti-Dietrich   If Greta achieved (fictional) stardom acting in German films "[t]hrough the twenties and thirties," then her role as "anti-Dietrich" would have been to play characters who were the opposite of the ultramodern man-eaters that Dietrich's director during the thirties, Josef von Sternberg, having taken her to Hollywood, cast her in in such films as *Blonde Venus* (1932) and *The Devil is a Woman* (1935). Greta would have played rather more *Volkisch* roles, characters with submissive personalities.

V394.23, B459.13, P400.35   Ludwig II   Hitler's favorite kaiser was Frederick the Great. Ludwig II was a nineteenth-century king of Bavaria; before he went insane, in 1886, he was known as a supporter of Wagner and as a patron of the arts. When his mind snapped, he murdered one of his attendants and then drowned himself. This is why von Göll's selection of Ludwig would probably have gotten the fictional director "blacklisted" by the Nazi regime.

V394.32–33, B459.25, P401.3   *Das Wütend Reich*   Literally, "the Mad Empire" but misspelled in *GR*; it should be *Wütende*.

V394.36, B459.29, P401.7   "Königreich"   "Kingdom."

V396.28, B461.35, P403.3   *singularities*   In mathematics, a point at which the rate of change approaches infinity. Lance Ozier's 1975 essay, "The Calculus of Transformation: More Mathematical Imagery in *Gravity's Rainbow*," identified the background here as mathematician Alexander Friedmann's calculation (in 1922, one of the *anni mirabili* in *GR*) for the phenomenon of redshifting. The theory described how light waves moving rapidly away from stars (from the point of observation) "shift" toward the longer wavelength portion of the spectrum, so that infrared shifts toward microwave, red shifts to infrared, and so on. Friedmann's theorem made way for the currently accepted big bang theory in cosmology, as well as the concept of "black holes"—singularities in which the density of matter approaches infinity, a state known as "gravitational collapse."

As Katherine Hayles (*The Cosmic Web* 190–91) has stated, the behavior of the function of calculus in which singularities are the points "ceases to be mathematically expressible, except in a purely formal way." The function has only an abstract reality; it escapes into a zone of the unknown. Hayles quite aptly sees the concept of a black hole as "a powerful metaphor of the absolute annihilation of no Return" figured throughout *GR* but errs in seeking to establish a textual link between astronomer Karl Schwarzschild, whose name has been given to the "event horizon" of a black hole (a zone beyond which there's no return), and Tyrone Slothrop. In *GR*, the code name for the infant Slothrop is Schwarzknabe (see V286.5), which could be read as "black boy," since *"schwarz"* means "black" in German and *"Knabe"* means "boy" (see V286.5n); "Schwarzschild," however, is not the same as "Schwarzchild" (and, of course, "child" is not in any event a German word; to make the name Schwarzschild a German word, one would have to read it as a combination of *"schwarz"* and *"schild"*—"black shield"). The connection Hayles suggests is thus tenuous: wholly reliant upon the reader's misreading "Schwarzschild" as "Schwarzchild."

V396.31, B461.39, P403.4   scenic Berchtesgaden   The Bavarian site of Hitler's mountain redoubt he called "Wolf's Lair." The place-name invokes a familiar mythic code: named for the Teutonic goddess Berchte, who is closely related to Dame Holda, it is derived (according to Grimm, *Teutonic Mythology* 272–74) from the etymological roots meaning "bright, luminous, glorious" and from an evil version of the White Goddess identified among children as a terror who slits open the bellies of disobedient boys and girls.

V396.33, B461.41–42, P403.7   the Russian mathematician Friedmann   See V396.28n.

V396.41, B462.10, P403.15   under the rose   Once more pointing to what is uttered in secret (sub rosa) and to the title of Pynchon's short story (see V290.7n).

EPISODE II

Note how this episode is linked to the one preceding it: that one ends with Slothrop whipping Margherita Erdmann into a passion at the Neubabelsberg movie studio where *Alpdrücken* was filmed and Bianca Erdmann conceived; this one begins with Franz Pökler remembering that film and how he went home from it to engender his daughter, Ilse. For a similar linking device, see the transition between episodes 15 and 16 in part 1, where the word "touch" provides a bridge. Here it consists of the words "Bianca" and "bitch." Several triads of characters overlap at this moment: there are Franz, Leni, and Ilse Pökler; Max Schlepzig, Margherita, and Bianca Erdmann; Slothrop (on paper, an avatar of Schlepzig), Margherita, and Bianca; also Weissmann, Katje, and Gottfried, for it was "the word bitch" that similarly brought Gottfried to arousal (see V103.25–26 and V429.21–22n). A theme of repetition and incest runs throughout. This episode is also the longest in the novel and is placed very much at its center. The time is July 1945, though the narration ranges back over sixteen years, its analepsis beginning in the late twenties, in Berlin, where the German rocket program began as an apparently innocent club, the Society for Space Travel. Franz Pökler's recollections of these and subsequent events, up to the present moment, stem largely from Walter Dornberger's memoir of the German rocket program, entitled *V-2*. As the episode ends, readers also learn some crucial bits of information about the time when Rocket 00000 was fired.

V397.28–29, B463.7, P404.7–8   the Ufa theatre on the Friedrichstrasse
See V98.24n.

V398.3–4, B463.21–22, P404.20   The onion-topped Nikolaikirche
Countless German towns and cities have their Nikolaikirche, or St. Nicholas church, as a glance through Baedeker's *Northern Germany* will show. So we cannot pinpoint the locale of Pynchon's fictional place Zwölfkinder (Twelve Children). The name, as well as the idea (a kind of German Disneyland?), is also unclear. We can only note that it sits somewhere north ("up," at V398.32) from Lübeck; from it one sees Denmark across the Baltic Sea (V398.36).

V398.4–5, B463.23, P404.21   the great Wheel   A Ferris wheel.

V398.8–9, B463.28, P404.25   a moon newly calved   The new crescent moon appeared in the nighttime sky on July 9, 1945.

V398.18–19, B463.39–40, P404.34–35   the dog with saucer eyes . . . the beard of the goat on the bridge, the mouth on the troll below
Here the salt encrusts figures at Zwölfkinder depicting, respectively, the dog "with a pair of eyes as large as teacups" who guards the treasure that the soldier must get, to satisfy the witch, in Hans Christian Andersen's fairy tale, "The Tinder Box"; and the third goat in Peter Christen Asbjörnsen's "The Three Billy Goats Gruff," who kills the troll lying in wait under the bridge and threatening to eat one of them.

V398.19, B463.41, P404.35–36   Frieda the pig   Named for Freya, sister of Frey, the etymology of whose name gives us *fried* ("peace" [see V94.26n]). Frieda is an apt name for Pökler's pig because the Teutonic goddess Freya often appears riding a sow or boar, sometimes one with gold bristles (Grimm, *Teutonic Mythology* 214–16, 299–303).

V398.20–22, B463.42–464.2, P404.38–39   The plaster witch . . . leans near the oven . . . corroded Hansel   More salt-encrusted, corroded figures at Zwölfkinder's entrance, this time representing figures from the Brothers Grimm version of "Hansel and Gretel" (see V174.21–22).

V399.19, B465.8, P405.36   strands of steel cable   In the Bantam edition, "steel" is misprinted as "steels."

**V399.38–39, B465.32–33, P406.15 tracing patiently the xs and ys, P (atü)
. . . moving always** All of these are measurable quantities—P (atü) is
atmospheric pressure, W is velocity in meters/second, and T is temperature in degrees Kelvin—that would need to be known when aiming the
rocket.

**V400.6–7, B465.42–466.1, P406.23 the coordinates switched from the
Cartesian x and y of the laboratory to the polar azimuth and range of
the weapon as deployed** That is, in aiming the missile, the rocket's
flight graphed on a two-dimensional X–Y axis must be translated for
global targeting. The rocket's line of flight, or azimuth, would be lined
up relative to polar north (that is, its "polar azimuth"), and its range, or
distance-to-target, would, when plotted, yield through another calculation the point—somewhere along the V-2's upward slope—for
"*Brennschluss*," or the engine's cut-off moment.

V400.25, B466.25, P407.1 "Kadavergehorsamkeit" German for "corpse
obedience"; a kind of zombie state, proverbially attributed to Prussian
troops under Otto von Bismarck during a series of short wars against
Denmark (1864), Austria (1866), and France (1870–71).

V400.30, B466.32, P407.6 Verein für Raumschiffahrt The Society for
Space Travel (V162.13–14n).

V401.6, B467.9, P407.22 Major Weissmann Note his rank. Sometime
between the early thirties and 1944, when we meet him in Holland,
Weissmann has evidently been "busted" from major back to captain (his
rank at V94.22).

V401.25, B467.32–33, P408.1–2 a weapon to . . . leap like a chess knight
The V-2 rocket as *der Springer*.

V402.5–6, B468.18, P408.23 the Spree The river running through
Berlin.

V402.11, B468.25, P408.29 to Kummersdorf Seventeen miles south of
Berlin, where the German army established Experimental Station West
to begin its initial experiments in rocketry (Dornberger, *V-2* 23).

**V402.29–32, B469.3–4, P409.6 a model no more than 4 or 5 centimeters
. . . manometers outside** The *Halbmodelle* (half-model) "solution" derives from Dornberger (118), who describes wind-tunnel testing: "The
models [of the V-2 rocket], 1.5 to 2.0 inches wide and 12 to 16 inches
long, were . . . halved along their longitudinal axis and mounted on
plates. The pressure changes were then simultaneously measured at as
many as one hundred and ten separate points over the body." In the
same context, he reports that they used manometers, that is, pressure
gauges, to monitor the models in the wind tunnel. Evidently Pynchon
translated the linear measurements back into metric equivalents.

**V402.38, B469.9–10, P409.14–15 the likes of Pökler, who would eat an
apple in the street** That is, a man with no manners, no genteel training
or breeding; from an old folk saying of German and Yiddish derivation.

V403.5, B469.25–26, P409.24 then, in '34 . . . Dr. Wahmke A description of his death, along with that of two others, when a rocket engine exploded on its test bed in March 1934, appears in Dornberger (29).

V403.11, B469.32–33, P409.30   reading Hesse, Stefan George, and Richard Wilhelm   Hermann Hesse (1877–1962) was a German poet and novelist, winner of the 1946 Nobel Prize for literature. His fictions often involve the theme of paired opposites, the possible reference here. Stefan George (1868–1933) was a German poet whose freedom with diction was counterbalanced by his adherence to the strictest of structural and prosodic rules. Richard Wilhelm was known chiefly as a translator of Eastern texts, for example, *The I Ching; or, Book of Changes* in 1923.

V403.19–21, B470.1–2, P409.38–39   There was also Fahringer . . . out in the woods . . . with his Zen bow . . . to practice breathing   A student of Zen Buddhism, Fahringer uses archery to achieve and/or sustain with respect to the Rocket the condition of satori: a stepping outside the self, a condition of spiritual freedom, and an outlook in which all phenomena are "of equal importance in its sight, the most trivial as well as the most significant by human standards. They all seem to have acquired absolute value." This is how Eugen Herrigel phrases it in his popular 1953 book *Zen in the Art of Archery* (67), which is probably the source here and in the lines that follow. There, Fahringer's advice to colleagues that they should learn not to "will" the rocket to its target but "to surrender, step out of the role of firer," could very well come from Herrigel, who between the world wars spent years studying in Japan under a bodhisattva (see below).

V403.23, B470.5, P410.1   "Folgsamkeitfaktor"   Literally, an "obedience factor" or "willingness to follow" (compare at V400.25). In ballistics, German researchers applied the term to problems of arrow-stable trajectories.

V403.30, B470.13–14, P410.8   Mondaugen was the bodhisattva here   That is, back in Germany, for having returned from the 1922 strife in Südwestafrika, Mondaugen among these rocketeers in Germany has already achieved, as bodhisattva, a level of enlightenment (in Buddhism) of near-nirvana; he has only postponed nirvana in order to train others in the path.

V403.35, B470.19–20, P410.13   uprising by the Bondelswaartz in 1922   Here Pynchon summarizes events he treated in chapter 9 of *V.*, "Mondaugen's Story." Another Bantu-speaking people of the German protectorate, the Bondels had risen up against the colonial administration beginning in 1903 and were brutally repressed for their boldness. Their tribal leader, Abraham Morris, fled the country until January of 1922, when he crossed the river and returned to his homeland. Colonial administrator Reitz Hofmyer issued a warrant for his arrest and after several failed attempts to capture him, about 160 Bondel tribesmen rebelled in May 1922, raiding homes and villages. On May 29, the Germans attacked with planes, canon, and machine guns. Next day the surviving Bondel tribesmen surrendered.

V404.4–5, B470.31–32, P410.23–24   the triode was as basic as the cross in Christianity   The triode is a three-terminal vacuum tube whose function was supplanted by the transistor; it was, in other words, foundational to the digital world on whose threshold these characters stand (with their "Signals. . . . now positive, now negative" a few lines further).

V404.12, B471.1, P410.32   "In the name of the cathode, the anode, and the holy grid?"   Pökler riffs, here, on the commandment of Jesus to the disciples (in Matt. 28:19) that they should baptize "In the name of the Father, the Son, and the Holy Ghost." In an electrolytic cell (or battery) the cathode and anode are the negatively and positively charged electrodes; when the battery is hooked up to a "grid," it is capable of transmitting or receiving electrons (its power).

V404.16, B471.5–6, P410.36   the Versuchsanstalt   The Research Institute at Kummersdorf.

V404.38–405.3, B471.33–41, P411.19–25   They used an ancient ferryboat . . . the late sun   These details are from Dornberger (*V-2* 42–43), who describes the move to Peenemünde in a more matter-of-fact way:

That Spring the tranquillity of the inlet had been interrupted. One day a number of small motor launches filled with building personnel and surveyors had arrived in the little harbor. Next came a large vessel of unusual appearance, such as had never been seen before on the Baltic. She carried building materials and equipment. Halliger had recollected that he had come across that antediluvian craft once before, in Stralsund. She had been a car and passenger ferry then. A typical example of mid-nineteenth century shipbuilding, she possessed large cabins with decrepit furniture upholstered in red plush, a quantity of gleaming brass fittings and mountings, towering upper works, and high funnel.

V405.10, B472.7, P411.32   Lot's wife   The allusion is to Gen. 19:26.

V405.26, B472.26, P412.8   good company at Herr Halliger's inn   Dornberger again (42): "Herr Halliger, owner of the island . . . attended with inexhaustible good humour to our bodily needs and to the warmth of the inner and outer man, a matter of dire necessity at this cold season of the year."

V405.34, B472.36–37, P412.16–17   ephedrine pre-dawns . . . ja, ja, stimmt   Ephedrine is a mild stimulant, taken here to ward off sleep while solving engineers' problems and nodding "yes, yes, correct."

V406.11–12, B473.17, P412.35–36   Stodda's treatise on steam turbines   Apparently fictional.

V406.13–16, B473.19–23, P412.37–40   the propulsion group were testing . . . exhaust velocities of 1800 meters per second   The data are from Dornberger (46).

V406.37–38, B474.7–8, P413.20   the A3, christened ... with flasks of liquid oxygen   More detail from Dornberger (44): "We baptized our rockets with liquid oxygen." The A3 measured 21 feet high and 2½ feet in diameter, less than half the size of an A4.

V407.1, B474.13–14, P413.25   the camera photographed the needles swinging on the gauges   See Dornberger (45), who recalls fitting test rockets with crude instruments: "A barograph, a thermograph, and a small motion picture camera for photographing these two instruments in flight."

V407.3–4, B474.16–17, P413.27–28   Heinkels were also dropping iron models of the Rocket from 20,000 feet   The Heinkel was a German bomber plane. Dornberger (57) explains its use in researching the flight of supersonic projectiles: "We built several iron models about 8 inches in diameter and 5 feet in length. . . . In September 1938 we began to drop these missiles from a Heinkel HE-111 at 20,000 feet. The trajectory was recorded by photo-theodolites and cinetheodolites."

V407.19, B474.36, P414.4   in Peenemünde-West   The home of a testing station for the German Luftwaffe (Air Force). The Messerschmitt-262, the world's first jet plane, was tested from this airfield.

V408.15, B475.39, P414.41   from a place in the mountains   Ilse has arrived from the Dora camp, next to Nordhausen in the Harz Mountains.

V410.11, B478.6–7, P416.37   crater in the Sea of Tranquillity, called Maskelyne B   In July 1969 the Apollo 11 astronauts landed, just as Ilse dreams it, "right on the rim" of this crater, and astronaut Neil Armstrong became the first man to walk on the moon. The rocket that took Apollo 11 there was built under the direction of Wernher von Braun, second in command at Peenemünde under Dornberger.

V410.34, B478.34–35, P417.19–20   Friedrich August Kekulé von Stradonitz, his dream of 1865   This is the second reference to the famous chemist (see V84.9–10n). Kekulé dreamed of the "cosmic serpent," Ouroboros, which devours its own tail. From this he intuited the cyclical, six-sided structure of the benzene molecule, opening the study of "aromatic" compounds in organic chemistry.

V410.38, B478.39, P417.23   nice of Jung to give us the idea of an ancestral pool   The reference is to Swiss psychoanalyst Carl Gustav Jung (1875–1961) and his theory of "the collective unconscious," a sort of ancestral-semiotic background from which emerge the elemental structures (here, a "mandala archetype") of dreams.

V411.16, B479.21, P418.1   Atlantes   The plural form of Atlas, Greek god who supports all heaven on his shoulders.

V411.19, B479.24–25, P418.4   Once again it was the influence of Liebig   See V166.1–9n.

V411.25–26, B479.32–33, P418.10–11   sorting-demon such as ... Clerk Maxwell once proposed   See V239.18–19n.

V411.34–35, B480.1–3, P418.19–20   Mrs. Clerk Maxwell's notorious "It is time to go home . . . you are beginning to enjoy yourself"   Her remark is probably apocryphal. Mrs. Maxwell was Katherine Mary Dewar, who married Maxwell in 1858. They were a deeply pious couple who used to write each other meditations on Scripture whenever they were forced to be apart. But Maxwell himself was known as a conversationalist and sometime practical joker. So his wife's remonstration seems plausible, even though undocumented (nothing even close, in Campbell and Garnett's biography).

V411.38, B480.6–7, P418.23–24   the double-integrating circuit in the guidance   See V301.33n.

V412.35, B481.10–11, P419.21   "the old refrain, 'I lost my heart in Heidelberg'"   So many echoes here: for most readers, it will call to mind crooner Tony Bennet's 1955 hit song "I Left My Heart in San Francisco," but before that there was "I Left My Heart at the Stage Door Canteen" (see V134.27). Finally, though, one of Larsson's correspondents ("A *Companion's* Companion") notes a German popular song of the twenties, "Ich hab / mein Herz in Heidelberg verloren" (I Lost My Heart in Heidelberg), by composer Friedrich Veseley (alias Fred Raymond) that he wrote for a musical by that title. Its speaker is a middle-aged man looking regretfully back to his youth when, at age twenty, overlooking the Neckar River, he gave a kiss and his heart to a young woman:

As by the gates she said: "Good-bye my lover,"
That last sweet kiss, it did confirm once more,
I'd lost my heart in Heidelberg forever.
My heart still beats on Neckar's shore.

V413.15–16, B481.37–38, P420.4   a quote from Rilke: "Once, only once . . ."   From Rilke's ninth Duino elegy. The poem speaks to the contradictoriness of human destiny, which is beyond yet also reliant on those transitional forms that lie around us. That which is absolute and eternal, Rilke argues, is merely a transformation of that which is ever changing around us. After asking the question, why long for this destiny? Rilke answers:

Not because happiness really
exists, that premature profit of imminent loss.
Not out of curiosity, not just to practice the heart
that could still be there in laurel . . .
But because being here amounts to so much, because all
this Here and Now, so fleeting, seems to require us and strangely
concerns us. Us the most fleeting of all. Just once,
everything, only for once. Once and no more, And we, too,
once. And never again. But this
having been once, though only once,
having been once on Earth—can it ever be cancelled?

This is the Leishman and Spender translation of the *Duino Elegies*; note that Pynchon works his own rendering of "Einmal / jedes einmal."

V413.22–23, B482.4–5, P420.11–12   a gold hexagon with the German formée cross   The same kind that bounces above Hilary Bounce's navel (V243.28–29n).

V414.35–415.3, B483.27–34, P421.24–30   Nur . . . ein . . . Op-fer! . . . Wer zum Teufel die Freiheit, braucht?   The narrator here riffs on the 1931 hit song for Louis Prima that Bing Crosby snatched from him, whence it appeared in several films. The song is "Just a Gigolo," a translation of a 1929 German hit, "Schöner Gigolo," music by Leonello Casucci and lyrics by Irvin Caesar, who also did the English translation:

> Just a gigolo, everywhere I go,
> People know what part I'm playing;
> Paid for every dance, selling romance,
> Ev'rynight some heart betraying.
>
> There will come a day,
> Youth will pass away,
> Then, what will they say about me?
> When the end comes, I know they will say
> Just a gigolo—
> As life goes on without me,
> Life goes on without me.

Reworking this lyric, Pynchon makes a mordantly masochistic macaronic, which translates:

> Just a victim
> In a vacuum
>
> Won't someone even take advantage of me?
> Just a slave without a master . . .
> Who the devil needs freedom?

V415.29–30, B484.23, P422.20   "The new planet Pluto"   In 1930 astronomer William Tombaugh confirmed the previous calculations of Percival Lowell, who had predicted, on the basis of gravity-related oscillations in the orbits of neighboring planets, the presence of a planet-size mass. This "new" (or, newly discovered) body was given the name Pluto in 1930; here, the significance of that name involves the way Nazi Party leaders were blaming Germany's economic woes on Jewish "plutocrats" like Walter Rathenau.

V415.31, B484.24–25, P422.21   long Asta Nielsen upper lip   Swedish-born film star Asta Nielson (1883–1972) gained her reputation as the "Duse of the Screen" because of her facial features: large passionate eyes, expressive upper lip, strong cheekbones. After moving her career to

Germany in 1910, she became Europe's pinup girl of World War I. Kracauer (*From Caligari to Hitler* ill. 29) includes a still photo from Georg Pabst's *The Joyless Street* (1925), in which the expanse of upper lip is well displayed.

V415.36, B484.31, P422.26–27 Brunhübner and that crowd That is, the astrologers working in Nazi Germany. Fritz Brunhübner (1894–1965) was the author of the astrological book *Pluto* (1934), the first to reckon the astral influences of this newly discovered planet.

V416.8, B485.3, P422.39 *Schicksal* That is, destiny.

V416.10, B485.5–6, P422.40 an uncontrolled series of A5s These launchings occurred in 1938. The A5 rocket used the same motor as the A3 but was somewhat larger in diameter. Most details in this passage are from Dornberger (*V-2* 56–58).

V416.13–14, B485.9–10, P423.3 vanes made of graphite . . . down to five degrees Once more, Dornberger (57) is the source: "The oscillations we had seen in no case exceeded 5 degrees."

V416.23, B485.21–22, P423.13 Poehlmann's work Ernst Pöhlmann (Pynchon uses the unaccented spelling) devised a method for irrigating "the inner wall of the chamber with alcohol" (Dornberger 53; also, Klee and Merk, *The Birth of the Missile* 24).

V419.2, B488.20–21, P425.38 nearly the end of peacetime Germany invaded Poland at dawn on September 1, 1939.

V419.32, B489.15, P426.28 Hugo Wolf An Austrian composer and disciple of Richard Wagner, Wolf (1860–1903) wrote some two hundred songs and a number of instrumental works.

V420.4, B489.32, P427.1 sastrugi Wind-plowed grooves in the snow; plural of sastruga (groove), a German word (derived from the Russian "*zastruga*") that has entered in English.

V421.32, B491.34–35, P428.28 Juch-heierasas-sa! o tempo-tempo-ra! An idiomatic German exclamation meaning "Hip-hip-hooray for Time!" And the refrain, we know through one of Larsson's correspondents ("A *Companion*'s Companion"), comes from a macaronic lyric by Emmanuel Geibel (1815–84): "Ein lustger Musikante Marschierte am Nil" (A Humorous Minstrel Marched on Zero).

V422.2, B492.6–7, P428.39–40 General von Trotha's brave men See V99.38n; they are "brave" only from the perspective of German imperialism.

V422.26–28, B492.34–37, P429.24 the great sphere, 40 feet high . . . 20 seconds of supersonic flow The description of this wind-tunnel vacuum chamber stems from Dornberger (114–15).

V423.5–6, B493.17–18, P430.3–4 In '43 . . . Pökler missed the British air raid on Peenemünde At midnight on August 17, 1943, the German V-weapon facility was attacked by over six hundred British bombers, collectively carrying over fifteen hundred tons of high explosives and several hundred tons of incendiary bombs. Among the research staff at Peenemünde, the most serious loss was Doctor Thiel. But by far the most tragic loss occurred (as the narrator notes here) at the nearby slave labor camp at Trassenheide, where 650 died. Dornberger cites a total of 735 dead. Research at Peenemünde was not seriously impeded, but shortly afterward the Germans relocated the aerodynamics research program to the Bavarian town of Kochel and transferred production of the A4 rocket to the *Mittelwerke,* at Nordhausen. On the raid see Collier (*Battle of the V-2 Weapons* 33), Dornberger (*V-2* 154–68), Huzel (*Peenemünde to Canaveral* 54–58), Irving (*Mare's Nest* 100–115), Klee and Merk (*Birth of the Missile* 43–44), McGovern (*Crossbow and Overcast* 16–31) and Wegener (*The Peenemünde Wind Tunnels* 57–63).

V423.21, B493.36–37, P430.19   the gradient was to run east to west   It happened just so, and this dispersal of bombs over the island explains why the Trassenheide camp was so severely damaged. Irving (106–12) explains how such a tragic error happened. Note, also, that this bomb pattern recalls how the devastation of V-2 rockets was greatest over London's East End, home of that city's poor (V15.12–13n) and how the devastation of Berlin was greatest in that city's poorer, eastern sector (V433.17n).

V423.23, B493.39, P430.21   "foreign workers," a euphemism   Dornberger (168) waves off the whole issue of concentration camp labor at Trassenheide by calling the camp a site for "foreign construction workers." Huzel tries the same moral sleight-of-hand, and in his writings von Braun never even mentions the workers. Wegener (in his 1996 memoir) is the only Peenemünde scientist to treat the forced labor issue. Out of sight, out of mind, as it were. Simpson (*Blowback: America's Recruitment of Nazis and Its Effects on the Cold War*) neatly sums up history's indictment of Dornberger et al. on this issue: "Dornberger . . . knew— or should have known—that the prisoners who worked on his rockets were being systematically starved to death. And he knew, for he said this much himself, that Germany's defeat was inevitable. Dornberger could have shut down the assembly line on some technical pretext. He could have demanded adequate rations for the prisoners. He could have cut back his missile orders to the number that Germany was capable of launching. He chose instead to accelerate production" (29–30).

V424.14, B494.32, P431.13   the test series at Blizna   In November 1943 field tests of the A4 began at Blizna in western Poland. They continued until the spring of 1944 (Dornberger 213–24).

V424.17–18, B494.36–37, P431.16–17   Maj.-Gen. Kammler's empirebuilding   Dornberger describes the appointment of SS General Kammler as special commissioner for A4 matters in chapter 22 of *V-2* (208–11).

V424.18–23, B494.38–495.2, P431.17–18   an airburst problem . . . perhaps

the insulation on the alcohol tank was at fault From Dornberger (218): "Von Braun declared that the alcohol tank and its ventilation were the culprit. I was more inclined to blame the oxygen tank."

V424.32–33, B495.12–14, P431.32–33 Green rye and low hills all around: Pökler was by a small trench . . . pointing his binoculars south Compare the narrator's account to this one, from Dornberger (220): "We were in a small observation trench at the foot of a long, low hill. . . . We were at exactly the spot marked on the map as the current target area. That morning the first rocket had come down successfully 150 yards away[;] . . . lumps of clay, almost as big as a man, lay scattered far and wide in the fields of green rye round the crater. We had never yet been able to catch with our binoculars the white cloud heralding an explosion."

V424.34, B495.15, P431.34 Erwartung See V101.9n.

V424.38, B495.19–20, P431.38 dark eels of rivers catching the sun From Dornberger's recollection (220) that "winding curves of a clear little stream sparkled in the sunshine."

V425.25–29, B496.13–17, P432.26–30 Chances are astronomically against a perfect hit . . . the Ellipse of Uncertainty. The historical details again derive from Dornberger (220–21). But note how this event constitutes a ballistic instance of what Hite (*Ideas of Order* 26) calls "the trope of the unavailable insight." Here, the rocket approaches "the very center . . . the holy X" (V424.39). Statistical probabilities are massively against a direct hit on the target, which is why it seems like the most reasonable place to sit. Another case, therefore, of what the narrator of *GR* will soon call "Holy-Center Approaching" (V508.35).

V426.5, B496.38, P433.6 the penetralia From the Latin *"penetralium,"* the deepest, innermost chamber of a temple.

V427.3, B498.1–2, P434.3 The bulb was explaining the plot to him This anticipates the story of Byron the Bulb (V647–55).

V427.29–30, B498.34, P434.30–31 "a 'flying laboratory,' as Dr. Thiel said" See Dornberger (215): "Could Dr. Thiel and the senior staff at Peenemünde have been right after all? Was our flying laboratory too much for soldiers to handle?"

V428.28–29, B499.36–37, P435.31 the gift of Daedalus Daedalus's gift was building, engineering. He built for Pasiphae a mock cow into which she could climb to mate with one of Poseidon's bulls (which resulted in the birth of the Minotaur). Daedalus also built the Cretan labyrinth to contain the Minotaur that nonetheless required—every ninth year—the sacrifice of seven maidens and seven young men. Once, one of these young men was Theseus. Daedalus gave Ariadne, who loved Theseus, a ball of thread and instructed her to have him unwind it as he made his way into the labyrinth (to slay the Minotaur) and then to wind it up again as he made his way back out.

V429.15, B500.28, P436.18   the Volkssturm   A creation of Martin Bormann, Josef Goebbels, and Heinrich Himmler for the last-ditch defense of Germany, these "People's Brigades" were christened on October 13, 1944, and their ranks filled with the Reich's young boys and aging men.

V429.21–22, B500.37–38, P436.25–26   who was the slender boy . . . so blond, so white   This would be Gottfried. The blond hair and white skin partly identify him. His link to the von Göll film, *Alpdrücken*, underscores the link. Here Ilse is Gottfried's female doppelgänger just as Katje was in part 1. And the Blicero-Katje-Gottfried triad now slides into place with the others, for Gottfried experiences a curiously Pavlovian reflex erection whenever "the word bitch" is spoken (V103.25) (and recall that the word "bitch" forms a bridge into this episode [V397.18]). A side point here: Gottfried was at Zwölfkinder in August 1944.

V429.27, B501.1–2, P436.31   Gnostic symbolism in the lighting   Because it involves a precise distinction between polar opposites: evil and good, Cain and Abel. That bipolarity was a major trait of Gnostic Christianity and (evidently) significant to the fictional director von Göll: see V394.18–20 on his use of light "from above and below."

V431.21, B503.7, P438.26   in the spring, he did see Weissmann again   When Pökler assists with the Imipolex *Schwarzgerät*. The timing is crucial: spring arrived on March 21, the equinox; the last V-2 rockets were fired during Easter week, from March 25 to April 1, 1945.

V431.29, B503.18, P438.35   SD   Acronym for Sicherheitsdienst (Security Service), the most feared of all the Nazi SS units. SD men wore black, with a silver or white death's-head insignia.

V431.36, B503.25, P438.41   one rocket, only one   Echoing the line from Rilke, at V413.15–16, and recalling Crutchfield the Westwardman, at V68.01.

V432.6, B503.38–39, P439.11   "Vorrichtung für die Isolierung"   The "insulation device" of V242.6.

V432.9, B503.42, P439.14   The first week in April   Once more the timing is crucial. Weissmann disappears with his Imipolex shroud in the "Spring" (that is, after March 21), leaving Franz to his own devices during "[t]he first week in April," that is, after April 1.

V432.13, B504.5, P439.18   "Gaudeamus igitur"   May very well be the oldest extant student song. Some sources claim that its lyric, expressing loose and lively student life, dates from the thirteenth century and the University of Paris. It was the most popular student song in the German universities of the eighteenth century, where it became known by the first line: *Gaudeamus igitur, juvenes dum sumus* (Therefore rejoice, so long as we have youth!).

V432.27, B504.23, P439.32   The Obersturmbannführer   Military rank of the *Waffen* SS (the military SS) and equivalent to a colonel.

EPISODE 12

Returning to Berlin, Slothrop travels to the city's Russian (eastern) sector to deliver the Potsdam hashish, less Tchitcherine's expropriation, to Säure Bummer. A musical debate ensues. Slothrop and Margherita resume their sadomasochistic pas de deux. The time: still the later half of July.

V433.17, B505.18–29, P440.22   the Russian sector . . . Königstiger tank
This area included all the industrial and working-class neighborhoods of east Berlin, neighborhoods that were the most devastated—as the narrator notes—because fighting there had progressed house-to-house before the advancing Russian divisions in April. The King Tiger was the largest German battle tank, with its "monster" 88-millimeter gun (see V91.37).

V433.32, B505.37, P441.1–2   DER FEIND HÖRT ZU   "The Enemy is Listening."

V434.26–27, B506.38, P441.35   Biedermeier chair   See V162.20–21n.

V434.29–30, B506.42, P441.38   *Tägliche Rundschau*   A Berlin newspaper nearly as old as the *Times* of London, whose title translates as The Daily Review.

V434.30–31, B506.42–507.1, P441.38–39   chalcedony doorknob . . . ferrocyanide   A doorknob made from this milky-gray quartz with its ferrocyanide compounds could, under the right circumstances, react with sodium or potassium salts and produce a deadly white powder, sodium or potassium cyanide (NaCN or KCN).

V434.31–33, B507.2–4, P441.41   B . . . or H . . . the rejected Locrian mode
A vexed business, but the general idea is that in German musical notation the "hard" or "square" "B" is written as an H, and only the "soft" or "rounded" "B" (the flat) is designated by the "B" itself. This detail plays a key role in Thomas Mann's *Doktor Faustus*, which may be on Pynchon's mind here. In *Faustus* the "H" allows composer Adrian Leverkuhn to devise a "note-cipher," his "haetera esmeralda," in honor of his beloved, the woman who is also the source of his disease. Yet this bit of musical nomenclature has no essential relation to the "Locrian" or "Hyperphrygian" mode of music handed down from Hellenic culture. In that mode, which has only a theoretical existence, the interval between the first and the fifth is a diminished rather than a true fifth.

V435.8, B507.24, P442.17   kids in George Raft suits   American actor George Raft (1895–1980) was on screen from 1929 until 1961, almost always in underworld roles that put him into a succession of high-grade gangster suits: neatly cut, with padded shoulders, in black or gray sharkskin, handkerchief neatly folded in the breast pocket. See, for example, *Scarface* (1932), *The Glass Key* (1935), or Fritz Lang's *You and Me* (1938).

V435.10, B507.27, P442.19   Gunsels   Partridge (*Macmillan Dictionary*) lists it as a variant spelling of "gonsel" or "gonzel," designating "a boy, a youth, with implications of sexual perversion; a passive male homosexual." Thus one of them "licks his lips and stares at Slothrop." A second meaning common to American detective novel cant—for example, in Dashiell Hammet's *The Maltese Falcon* (1930) and in Raymond Chandler's *The Big Sleep* (1939)—is "hired gun." Both meanings apply here.

V435.16, B507.35, P442.25   a quick veronica with his cape   Slothrop spins like a Spanish matador, flourishing his cape to fool this coughing kid.

V435.20, B507.39–40, P442.29   "Fickt nicht mit der Raketemensch!"   "Don't fuck with Rocketman!" Even so, there's a case error in Pynchon's German: it should be "dem Raketenmensch." (On other problems with the German see V366.14.)

V435.21, B507.40–41, P442.30   a hiyo Silver here   Slothrop imitates the call of ABC Radio's Lone Ranger (Bruce Beemer) to his horse, Silver.

V435.29, B508.9, P442.38   *Saturday Evening Post* faces   Edited by the Curtis Publishing Company of Philadelphia, the weekly *Post* was famous by the forties for covers that presented images of a folksy, homey America and its cute, or at least sweetly grotesque, faces in the crowd, all drawn by the likes of Stevan Dohanos, Mead Schaeffer, Albert Straehle, and Norman Rockwell. So taken was Rockwell by the desire to depict such scenes realistically that he would use dozens of photographs for a single picture. But these images, while they come to Slothrop on this fictional Saturday evening, are delivered by messengers from a sort of margin, "in from out of the long pikes"; the junkyard messages are available entirely on their "surface," perhaps like the empty Qlippoth.

V436.16–17, B508.42–43, P443.25–26   "As B/4" . . . Dillinger's old signoff   Details about outlaw Dillinger (1903–34), who also used to sign his letters to the FBI with "Bye-Bye" and "Johnnie," probably stem from Toland's *Dillinger Days*. See also V516.3n and V741.6–7n.

V436.24, B509.9–10, P443.33   the Chariot gleaming like coal   A reference to the copper sculpture atop the Brandenburg Gate in Berlin, which is located one block south of the Reichsstag and that constitutes the termination point of Unter den Linden, the linden tree–lined boulevard that led to the royal residence. Commissioned as a symbol of peace by Emperor Wilhelm II and built by Karl Gotthard Langhans from 1788 to 1791, the gate consists of twelve Doric columns patterned on the gateway to the Acropolis. Atop it: the Quadriga, a four-hourse chariot for the Goddess of Peace. From 1962 until the Berlin Wall's demolition in 1989 this was the principal gateway connecting East and West Berlin. Baedeker (*Berlin* 55) describes its former glory, and is a likely source.

V436.32, B509.19, P443.41   Hinterhöfe   As noted at V160.15n, these are the back courts of tenement buildings; here they are "nested" inside the building, and Slothrop passes through each one below a numbered parabolic arch: first ("Erster"), second ("Zweiter"), and so on.

V437.18, B510.9, P444.28 kif Hemp (marijuana) from the Maghreb region.

V437.21, B510.12–13, P444.31–32 Bosendorfer Imperial concert grand piano The text omits the umlaut over the first "o." This Austrian firm of piano makers was founded by Ignaz Bösendorfer in 1828 and made famous by Franz Lizst, who discovered theirs to be the only grand piano capable of withstanding his playing. Their "Imperial" concert grand has an extended compass in the bass register.

V437.28, B510.21, P444.38–39 the racetrack at Karlshorst In southeast Berlin, a steeplechase track that, according to Baedeker, operated in spring, summer, and fall.

V438.9–10, B511.6–7, P445.20–21 American yellow-seal scrip ... discontinued See V246.21–22n.

V438.15–17, B511.15–17, P445.28–29 what Jubilee Jim Fisk told the Congressional Committee ... in 1869 Specifically, in October 1869, while answering charges that he had conspired to corner the gold market in September of that year. When a congressman asked what happened to the fortune in railroad money Fisk had sunk into his scheme, he answered: "It has gone where the woodbine twineth." Asked what that meant, Fisk replied: "Up the spout" (Adams, *Chapters of Erie* 128).

V439.38, B413.2–3, P447.8 When Slothrop wakes up it's at the height of the Evil Hour See V374.39n.

V440.4, B513.11–12, P447.15 who is better, Beethoven or Rossini Here begins the Beethoven-Rossini debate, anticipated in *GR* for some time. Recall, for example, the "Rossini tarantella" heard at Monte Carlo (V204.39) or Slothrop's first night of freedom on "the Rue Rossini" of Nice (V253.33). The narrator dresses out this debate in plenty of satiric passementerie, elaborating on what is really an old contrast—as old, indeed, as the uncomfortable 1822 meeting between the two composers. Säure's arguments have been anticipated by Stendhal's 1824 biography of Gioacchino Rossini, the mainspring of which is the perceived difference between German (northern) music and the (southern) Italian style preferred by Stendhal. In fact, when his distinctions between the two are listed in a column, they look strikingly like the binary differences Pynchon weaves into his narrative:

Italian	*German*
warm, southern	cold, northern
simple, unsophisticated	complex, erudite
irrational	rational
organic	mechanical
emphasis on melody	emphasis on harmony
comedy (opera buffa)	tragedy (opera seria)
Scarlatti and Rossini	Bach and Beethoven

Stendhal (132) derogates the German emphasis on complex harmonics as "a scientific discipline of doubt and analysis applied to something one loves." Later (306), he describes harmony as "mechanical technique," an impersonal force "moving rapidly towards a state of perfection" that will make all the notes "equal," just as "ciphers" are equal. Beethoven's mania for harmony he therefore paints (128) as "a black night" that diminishes compassion in favor of "scientific knowledge." By comparison, he argues, Rossini's music expresses a simpler folk wisdom, a pure passion for song.

As for Gustav in this scene, his position is probably indebted to Schauffler's biography, *Beethoven: The Man Who Freed Music* (1933). This Beethoven "unshackled music" from "concreteness," from its referential and representational bonds, and brought it instead toward "imaginative liberty," to a dependence on instrumentation alone (69). To Schauffler, this music expresses a pure idealism, an "overarching transcendence" characterized, for instance, in a familiar signature that recurs in Beethoven's work, the so-called Mannheim rocket, an arpeggio rising sequentially through the scales (69). But Schauffler's Beethoven was also "eccentric, lonely, unattractive, in urgent need of a woman's loving companionship" (273). Worse still, he was paranoically locked inside himself. Like Pynchon's character Stencil, in *V.,* Beethoven used to address himself in the third person; he once scribbled a note to himself, lamenting that "there is no happiness from without, thou must create it all from within thyself, only in the ideal world findest thou friends" (273). Carved on the obelisk over Beethoven's grave is a striking symbol of this Germanic idealism: the worm Ouroboros devouring its own tail and, inside that, a butterfly.

Slothrop overhears but does not recognize in this debate the strains of a much larger ethical struggle between, on the one hand, empathy and the responsibilities of friendship and, on the other, an idealistic alienation made culturally fashionable. Slothrop has been prepared for this moment by various pieces of music and even street names, but the debate goes on, with musical compositions hurled back and forth like missiles—Rossini's *La Gazza Ladra* and *Tancredi* thrown against Beethoven's "Ode to Joy" from his Ninth Symphony—and through it all he is mute. As the debate ends, he will "paranoiacally" escape (V442.40).

V440.26–27, B513.38–39, P447.37   "Italian girl is in Algiers, the Barber's in the crockery, the magpie's stealing everything in sight!"   In order, these refer to the title characters of three Rossini operas: *L'italiana in Algeri* (1813), *Il barbiere di Siviglia* (1816), *La gazza ladra* (1817).

V440.31, B514.2, P448.1–2   Anton Webern is dead   An anachronistic allusion. The time of this fictional episode is late July, but Webern was shot on the evening of September 15, 1945, in the Austrian village of Mittersill. He was sixty-two. Pynchon has all the other details correct. Webern's brother was under investigation for dealing in illegal substances. That night, a contingent of Allied soldiers approached his brother's house in Mittersill; at the same moment Webern stepped out on his brother's patio to light a cigar. A jumpy American boy from North Carolina was startled by the light and shot Webern once with a .45 caliber pistol (Wildgans, *Anton Webern* 112–17).

V440.39, B514.11, P448.9   going on since Bach . . . music's polymorphous perversity   Implies an extension of the patriarchal line Stendhal discusses: Bach to Beethoven to Wagner to Schönberg to Webern. Moreover, the passage ascribes a logic to that lineage: "polymorphous perversity," derived from Norman O. Brown's *Life Against Death*. Brown (291) hypothesizes a man "freed from all sexual organizations—a body freed from unconscious oral, anal, and genital fantasies or return to the maternal womb. Such a man would be rid of the nightmares that Freud showed to be haunting civilization; but freedom from those fantasies would also mean freedom from that disorder of the human body, which Freud pitilessly exposed. In such a man would be fulfilled the mystic hope of Christianity, the resurrection of the body, in a form, as Luther said, free from death and filth." To be "polymorphously perverse" in this way is to delight in the full life of the body rather than in its separate, rationalized "sexual organizations" or "erogenous zones."

This is the one direct allusion in *GR* to Brown's psychoanalytical theory of history, although, as Wolfley ("Repression's Rainbow") has shown, its presence is strong throughout the text. To Brown, the metaphysics of human history is defined by repression—the repression of physical desire, which is compensated by man's sublimating, "civilizing," activity. "The dynamic of history," Brown argues (230), "is the slow return of the repressed" in ever more complex forms of violent technology. This much of the theory was orthodox Freudianism. Yet Brown foresaw two possible outcomes. First, the disappearance of man: the products of his sublimating activity (weapons, for instance) would lead to self-extinction. Second, the disappearance of history: this would mean, simply, the disappearance of repression, the rebirth of a "polymorphously perverse" erotic being that stands beyond guilt and even consciousness and that would embody the childish, "mindless pleasures" Pynchon represents in *GR*. Yet the psychosocial barriers to the second possibility are so great, and man is so inured to the first, that he has both feared and desired his death. Through this paradoxical law, Wolfley argues, repression gives form and "plot" to history just as gravity plots, or imparts form to, the Earth. In *GR*, then, gravity is "the ultimate metaphor" of the "human repression that is its theme" (Wolfley 104). And it is their own "gravity," their dream of annihilation, which characters both seek and seek to escape.

V441.2, B514.15, P448.12   "Another Götterdammerung"   *The Twilight of the Gods*, fourth and last opera in the *Ring* cycle of Richard Wagner.

V441.11, B514.25–26, P448.21   "do we have to start da capo with Carl Orff?"   Taking it "from the top" with German composer Carl Orff might mean two things. First, Orff is well known for his programs of musical instruction designed for children. Second, his principal works (the *Carmina burana* among them) avoid harmony in favor of an archaic diatonic scale. Orff once said of his music that its purpose was "to achieve a unification of spiritual attitudes, which will lead to a binding and universally valid sense of community" (Leiss, *Carl Orff* 82). For Western music to progress toward this apparently millennial end, it would have to regress to ancient patterns of rhythm and tonality.

V442.8, B515.30, P449.19   "Fabelhaft, was?"   "Marvelous, isn't it?"

V442.9, B515.31, P449.20   They are a Mutt and Jeff routine   The girls Trudi and Magda, resembling (respectively) the tall and short characters in the newspaper comic strip (allegedly the first ever) pioneered in 1907 by Harry Conway "Bud" Fisher; initially, it featured just the gangly and mustachioed "A. Mutt," but after March 1908 the diminutive, mustachioed (and often top-hatted) Jeff joined him.

V442.14–27, B515.37–516.11, P449.25–38   "Hübsch . . . A trifle *stahlig* . . . more *zart* than that"   Säure and Gustav disagree over the taste of their marijuana, and in virtually the same pattern of binary differences as shapes their taste in music. Gustav opens the debate when he "allows" that the reefer is nice (*hübsch*), though rather metallic or steely (*stahlig*), perhaps even having an aftertaste of dirt ("*Bodengeschmack* [dirt flavor] behind its *Körper* [body]"), which he finds tasty (*süffig*). But instead of the metallic or dirty taste Säure finds the smoke to have a certain dampness or sprightliness (*spritzig*), even an aromatic (*bukettreich*) quality. Gustav counters that even though this "herbage" was grown in the High Atlas regions of Morocco, the dope has its manners (*Art*). He finds its flavor nutty (*kernig*) and, like the clean (*sauber*) marijuana from the Oued Nfis region of Morocco's northern slopes, piquant (*pikant*). Again Säure disagrees. He tastes, instead of these northern characteristics, a southern liveliness, as from Jebel Sarho (just above the Sahara) and as proof he cites the play (*Spiel*) of this smoke, which is smooth (*glatt*) and fragrant (*blumig*), having a suggestion of fullness (*Fülle*) in its seasoned (*würzig*) audacity.

V442.36, B516.23, P450.6   Zig-Zags   A package of the cigarette rolling papers produced by Braunstein Frères (they were Maurice and Jacques), the cover of which figures a picture of "Le Zouave" (see V91.41n). A gold medal winner at the 1900 Paris Universal Exposition, Zig-Zags have long been popular with U.S. cigarette- and marijuana-joint rollers.

V442.39–40, B516.28, P450.9–10   an Irving Berlin *medley*   In his long career, tunesmith Irving Berlin (1888–1989) wrote some nine hundred songs ("Alexander's Ragtime Band," "Cheek to Cheek," "God Bless America," and so on). There's a myriad to choose from in making this medley.

V443.2, B516.31–32, P450.12   Horst Wessel Song   The original title of this song was "Die Fahne Hoch" ("Raise the Flag"). A student of Josef Goebbels, Horst Wessel was a young copywriter and *Sturmführer* of Berlin's most notoriously violent faction of the SA (*Sturmabteilung*). In 1929 he was living with an ex-prostitute in a house belonging to a Frau Salm. She wanted Wessel and the woman out, they refused, and Salm invited comrades from the Red Veterans' Organization, a rival Communist storm troop, to eject the pair. When the Reds showed up, one of them shot Wessel. This was on January 14, 1930. But Wessel did Goebbels and the Nazis a great favor: he didn't die for six weeks, until February 23, by which time he had been transformed into a Nazi Galahad. "Die Fahne Hoch" had made its debut in 1929, and nobody cared much about the tune then (indeed, it was widely acknowledged that Wessel stole the melody from a Communist songbook). But Goebbels transformed Wessel's little opus, with its petty chauvinism ("The banners flutter / The drums roll, / The fifes rejoice, and from millions resounds the hymn / Of the German Revolution!"), into a national anthem. See also V653.14n.

V443.5–7, B516.34–37, P450.15–17   A parabola . . . tonic to dominant . . . to tonic   Aside from the pun ("to tonic"/Teutonic), here again is the symbol of the parabolic arch, this time as a symphonic structure. Beethoven, for example, is widely noted for his three- and four-part structures in the major symphonies. His so-called *per aspera ad astra* (from struggle to victory) motif works like this: (1) outer struggle, (2) comfort and reassurance, (3) internal struggle, and (4) victory. Beethoven's Fifth Symphony perfectly exemplifies this parabolic movement.

V443.10, B516.40, P450.20   the Mark   That is the "Mark Brandenburg," the old principality of which Berlin became the royal seat. The Brandenburg Gate and its surrounding park space were designed to be Berlin's centerpiece. Here, with "Russian cavalry" crossing the "soggy fields" of it.

V443.11, B516.41–42, P450.21   the Kurfürstendamm   In the former West Berlin's Charlottenburg district, a main arterial running southwest from the Brandenburg Gate and past the *Tierpark*, or Zoo.

V444.19, B518.15, P451.30   the Mungahannock   A fictional river, in fictional Mingeborough.

V444.22, B518.19, P451.33–34   "the president died"   On April 12 (V373.32n).

V445.14, B519.18, P452.26   yellow loach   A bewhiskered European freshwater fish.

V446.14, B520.25, P452.26   the Alexanderplatz   Just east of the Spree, this plaza in the former East Berlin used to be the home of the Berlin Police Headquarters.

V446.16, B520.27, P453.28   snowdrop   Here again: an American MP, or military policeman.

V446.16–17, B520.28, P452.29   the Titaniapalast   From its opening in

1927 at Schloßstraße 5, one of Berlin's most elegant and best known "Kinos."

V446.17–18, B520.29–30, P435.30   One Sunday out at Wannsee   Located on an arm of the river Havel running southwest from Berlin, Wannsee is a neighborhood of villas above a popular beachfront. Most notoriously, though, Wannsee was the site of a January 20, 1942, conference (on a Tuesday) where, at a villa located just off Am Grossen Wannsee Strasse, S.S. Obergrupenführer Reinhard Heydrich laid out the strategy of Hitler's "final solution" to eliminate German, and European, Jewry. In attendance and taking fifteen pages of notes that would help convict him (as well as others): Adolf Eichmann. In sum it's a haunted place; and surely this explains why Slothrop, there to enjoy the beach, must use charmed words to escape from "little kids in soldier hats" plotting to "sacrifice him"—a prefiguration of his end, perhaps? As a counterpart to Gottfried's obvious sacrifice?

V446.21, B520.34, P453.33   *Hauptstufe*   See V361.7–13n.

EPISODE 13

The time is still late July. Enzian and the Hereros interrogate Horst Acht-faden (the last name means "Eight-strand" or "Eight-thread"), an aero-dynamics engineer formerly of Peenemünde. As with Slothrop's journey down the toilet during his sodium amytal interrogation of part 1, so this "Toiletship" is evidently a hallucination of Achtfaden's. His fantasy recod-ifies, in terms of excremental process, the science of aerodynamics.

V448.3–4, B522.24–25, P455.16–17   the *Rücksichtslos* here lists . . . angle of 23° 27′   The angle at which the axis of the earth inclines, relative to the plane of the celestial equator. Put differently, on June 21–22, the summer solstice, the sun has climbed to its northernmost latitude and lies at the same angle, relative to the equator. The ship's name: the *Reckless.*

V448.23–24, B523.10–11, P455.36–37   like the American cowboy actor Henry Fonda   Early in his career, and before he played Tom Joad in *Grapes of Wrath* (1940), Henry Fonda (1905–82) appeared in a number of cowboy films like *The Trail of the Lonesome Pine* (1936) and *Jesse James* (1939), in which he played Jesse's brother Frank.

V448.25, B523.13, P456.1   RHIP   See V190.23n.

V448.28, B523.17, P456.4–5   a whole *Geschwader*   German for a squadron.

V448.30–31, B523.20, P456.7   Degenkolb was heading up the Rocket Committee by then   In 1943 the German general Gerhard Degenkolb was brought into the A4 project. In chapters 7–9 of his memoir, Walter

Dornberger describes the struggles he and von Braun had with Degen-kolb and his powerful Special A4 Committee.

V449.7, B523.36, P456.20   a gofer   Workplace slang for a lackey, one who "goes for" things; also, in British public school slang, a "fag" (see next line).

V449.11–12, B524.1–2, P456.26   hair . . . Rita Hayworth style   See V274.25n.

V449.15, B524.4, P456.28–29   Took her out to Buf-falo Bayou   Located in Houston, Texas, the Buffalo Bayou is the waterway running through the city and the site of its first French and Spanish settlements. Between 1911 and 1914, it was dredged to make the Houston Ship Channel. From early days, it was an area notorious for brawling, illegal gaming, and prostitution.

V450.24–25, B525.18, P458.6   BDM volunteers   Acronym for the Bund Deutscher Mädchen (League of German Girls), a support group compara-ble to Britain's Auxiliary Territorial Services.

V450.31, B525.26, P458.12–13   Wagner and Hugo Wolf   See V419.32n.

V450.34, B525.29–37, P458.15   from Swinemünde to Helgoland . . . sharp-shadowed   That is, the *Rücksichtslos* makes its way from the Baltic Sea bay that forms the mouth of the Swine River, just east of Peenemünde, westward to the small North Sea island on the coast of Schleswig-o. That it is "sharp-shadowed" means the ship was camou-flaged with irregular diagonal stripes to disguise its size and direction.

V451.1, B525.41, P458.22–23   listen to your VE-301 People's Receiver   "People's receiver" translated into German is *"Volksampfänger,"* which was an AM radio receiver mass produced in Germany during the thir-ties: it came in a Bakelite case, with Nazi insignia on either side of a dial marked with the Reich's approved stations (but it also featured a two-tube design that allowed the German *Volk* to pull in distant [Allied] stations).

V451.35, B526.40, P459.17   the Kiel Canal   North of Hamburg, the Kiel Canal (now called the Nord-Ostsee) links the city of Kiel on the Baltic Sea with the North Sea estuary of the Elbe River.

V452.1–6, B527.6–12, P459.23–24   1904 was when Admiral Rozhdest-venski sailed his fleet . . . the year the American Food and Drug people took the cocaine out of Coca-Cola   On Admiral Rozhdestvenski's doomed voyage of 1904, see V349.39n. But the statement about Coca-Cola and the FDA appears to be factually inaccurate on two counts. Coke historian E. J. Kahn writes (99, my emphasis): "Two words that ir-ritate the Coca-Cola company are 'cocaine' and 'caffeine.' In its forma-tive days, the drink did contain a minute quantity of cocaine, since this drug was not removed from the coca leaves that constituted a tiny frac-tion of its makeup, but *even before the passage of the Pure Food and Drug Act in 1906, the last trace of cocaine had gone.*" The FDA did not exist before the 1906 congressional action, and the Coke people evidently took out the cocaine entirely of their own volition.

V452.8, B527.15, P459.30　Ludwig Prandtl proposed the boundary layer
As Theodore von Kármán (*The Wind and Beyond* 61) explains it, Prandtl "ingeniously assumed that the total effect of friction on any part of the airplane can be estimated by the trick of restricting the investigation of the forces to a thin sheet of air close to the surface, which he called 'the boundary layer.'" As the narrator claims, this was in 1904 (another of the novel's *anni mirabili*), and it put the science of aerodynamics into business. Prandtl's *Essentials of Fluid Dynamics* provided the model for aerodynamics research, and Wegener recalls in his memoir that when he first reported to Rudolf Hermann (the head of the Aerodynamics Institute at Peenemünde), he was advised to immediately "start reading" the book.

V452.21, B527.31–32, P460.2　Hermann and Weiselsberger's tiny window
As head of the Aerodynamics Instititute at Peenemünde, Dr. Rudolf Hermann directed its research uses not only in rocketry but in aircraft design and ballistics work as well. Hermann got his start as assistant to Carl Weiselsberger, head of the Institute of Fluid Dynamics at the University of Aachen. Together, they arrived at Peenemünde and performed the first wind-tunnel experiments on designs for the A3 rocket, predecessor to the operational model, the A4 (Dornberger 49, 114; Wegener 23). The wind tunnel at Peenemünde operated on a simple principle: connected to the horizontal wind tunnel itself was a forty-foot-diameter steel sphere, which technicians evacuated using large pumps; then they opened a valve at the opposite end of the wind tunnel, pulling air back into the sphere, yielding velocities of flow up to Mach 5 and beyond for periods of ten to forty seconds. Technicians observed their mounted models through small plate glass windows in which they could also install cameras. This work could be dangerous. Wegener records his "miraculous" survival when one of the windows disintegrated as he was peering through it (25).

V452.26–27, B527.37–39, P460.7–8　Professor Wagner . . . air would liquefy　Carl Wagner, a physical chemist from the Technische Hochschule at Darmstadt, consulted at Peenemünde to assist with a previously unexplored problem. As wind-tunnel experiments reached Mach 5 and beyond, researchers were concerned that any atmospheric moisture would condense and liquify, perhaps even supersaturate and form a fog, in either case posing a flow problem at the nozzles in the wind tunnel itself. Dornberger evidently believed (perhaps with others) that this problem would also manifest itself at the "boundary layer" of the rocket traveling at supersonic speeds, but Wegener apparently did not (see Dornberger 232, Wegener 70–71).

V452.30–31, B527.42–528.2, P460.11–12　"Bingen pencils" we would call the helical contrails . . . The Schlieren shadows danced　Wegener gives an excellent summary of what researchers and their optical equipment observed and recorded. Using high-intensity light from mercury lamps that they directed by parabolic mirrors, they were able to see "substantial temperature changes attending the flow about a model" at supersonic speed; "in turn, this variation was made visible by the deflection of the light, which was recorded as light or dark areas on a ground-glass screen or a photographic plate" (26). The photographic or "Schlieren equipment," Dornberger relates (120), "had been built by Zeiss of Jena after protracted experiments undertaken in the wind tunnel." Directing the so-called Bingen pencils from the rear of the models was crucial, because the A4 guidance depended on graphite vanes at the bottom of the four fins; when the vanes overheated from a too-wide contrail or "pencil" emerging from the engine blast, the vanes burned up and the rocket veered off course and crashed.

V452.38–39, B528.11, P460.19–20 Cranz's *Lehrbuch der Ballistik* According to which "it was impossible for bodies with arrow stability to accomplish perfect flight at supersonic speeds" (Dornberger 34).

V452.39–40, B528.12–13, P460.20–21 memorized Ackeret, Busemann, von Kármán and Moore, some Volta Congress papers The Fifth Volta Congress of High Speed Flight convened in Rome in 1935. Major attendees included all the researchers mentioned here, and as von Kármán recalls in his autobiography (216), the talk was "seriously hinting of rockets to the moon and of speeds of thousands of miles per hour." Jakob Ackeret of Zurich was a friend of von Kármán, a pioneer in aerodynamics research, and director of an advanced wind tunnel at the Swiss Technische Hochschule; he subsequently immigrated to the U.S. and ended up working for NASA. Adolf Busemann did pioneering work on measurements of drag in wind-tunnel experiments, work that led to swept-wing designs for jet aircraft. Norton Moore studied for his Ph.D. under von Kármán in the early thirties at the California Institute of Technology. On all these men see von Kármán (216–20). Equally useful is Peter Wegener's memoir (22–24). Bower (*The Paperclip Conspiracy* 104–05) describes how von Kármán was instrumental in getting Adolf Busemann out of Germany before the Soviets could take him into custody.

V453.3, B528.18, P460.25 the Gomerians That is, inhabitants of La Gomera, one of the Canary Islands off the north African coast, where Columbus stopped on his way to the New World.

V453.6, B528.21, P460.28 the KdF ship "Kraft durch Freude" (Strength through Joy), one of many euphemistic slogans by Nazi propagandists. This one promoted a plan to increase industrial output. For example, the Volkswagen was originally called a "KdF-wagen," and at Peenemünde there was a so-called KdF Plant that produced rocket components. Here, one from a line of KdF cargo ships.

V453.9, B528.25, P460.31   mountains around Chipuda   Pynchon's source may well be Brown's 1898 travel guide, which describes Chipude (note the alternate spelling) as one of the oldest, pre-Spanish villages on the island of La Gomera, in the Canary Islands. Chipude is situated on a mountainous plateau in the island's central highlands. Brown also describes the native inhabitants' unique practice of communicating from village to village by loud whistles, comparable to the yodeling of inhabitants of the Swiss alps.

V453.20–21, B528.39–40, P461.3   Reynolds, Prandtl, Péclet, Nusselt, Mach   The Reynolds and Nusselt numbers have appeared earlier (V223.8–10n). Prandtl numbers are named for pioneer aerodynamicist Ludwig Prandtl and are used to calculate "drag" (von Kármán, *The Wind and Beyond* 60–61). Mach numbers, named for Ernst Mach, are the familiar numbers corresponding to multiples of the speed of sound. The Péclet number, named for Jean Claude Eugene Péclet (1793–1857), is used in the physics of heat transfer; it is a dimensionless number that relates the forced convection of a system to its heat conduction.

V453.35, B529.15, P461.16–17   Weichensteller, ask Flaum, and Fibel   All are fictional Peenemündans. A *Weichensteller*, in German railroading nomenclature, is a pointsman or switchman. *Flaum* is fluff or fuzz. A *Fibel* is an introductory handbook or primer; one of Pynchon's sources was the *A-4 Fibel* handed out to German rocket troops and translated into English at the Redstone Arsenal of Alabama.

V453.41–454.1, B529.22–23, P461.23–24   typewriters in Whitehall, in the Pentagon, killed more civilians than our little A4   Just off Trafalgar Square, Whitehall was (and still is) the administrative center of the British government. The Pentagon is its Washington, D.C., counterpart, begun in September 1941 and completed in January 1943, not only the U.S. military's administrative center but the largest office complex of its kind.

V454.6, B529.29, P461.29   mad Fahringer   While Fahringer is a fictional Peenemündan (see V403.19–21n), the pheasants are not. Dornberger (*V-2* 45) recalls hunting them with the troops; hence the sudden popularity of pheasant feathers in everyone's hats.

V454.13–14, B529.38–39, P461.36–37   *Chinesische Blätter für Wissenschaft und Kunst*   The Chinese Journal for Science and Art, published during the prewar years and based at the China Institute at Frankfurt; Richard Wilhelm published in the journal on Chinese alchemy and astrology, which might explain the mad Fahringer's interest in the journal referenced here.

V454.34–35, B530.19–20, P462.16   What is it that flies?—Los!   In a figurative sense, the German "*Los*" means "fate"; in a contrary and literal sense it means "free." As represented in *GR*, the V-2 flight profile embodies both. Hite (*Ideas of Order* 164, n4) also points out as a possible

context the Andrei Voznesensky (b. 1933) poem "Ballad of the Parabola"
(1960). It begins:
Fate flies
like a rocket, on a parabolic curve—
Mostly in darkness, but sometimes—
it's a rainbow.

**V454.36, B530.21–22, P462.18   the Wasserkuppe, rivers Ullster and
Haune**   The Wasserkuppe (water knob) is a volcanic mountain in cen-
tral Germany, just east of the Thuringian town of Fulda. The Ullster and
Haune rivers flow around it.

V455.7, B530.35, P462.29   the madness of Donar   Donar is "Thunderer,"
Old Saxon for Thor, the god who rules over clouds and rain. His signs
are the flash of lightning and the roll of thunder.

**V455.24–25, B531.12–13, P463.5   Gessner's section . . . Prof.-Dr.
Kurzweg's shop**   From Dornberger (*V-2* 116): "I was met by Dr.
Kurzweg, in charge of [wind-tunnel] research, and Chief Engineer Gessner, constructor of the wind tunnel." Wegener recalls Hermann Kurzweg
as the "exceptionally pleasant person" who directed aerodynamic research at the facility.

**V455.35, B531.24–25, P463.16   "'Spörri' and 'Hawasch' . . . I was called
'Wenk'"**   The first two are the names of the mad Dr. Mabuse's assistants in Fritz Lang's 1922 film *Doktor Mabuse der Spieler*, while Achtfaden's nickname, "Wenk," recalls State Prosecutor von Wenk, who pur-
sues Dr. Mabuse (Kracauer, *From Caligari to Hitler* 81–82).

V455.37–38, B531.28, P463.18–19   "CG for a device of a given weight"
The abbreviation for center of gravity.

V455.39, B531.29, P463.20   "something kilos. 45? 46?"   Or, 99 to 102
pounds, the approximate mass of a small human body; for example, the
boy Gottfried.

V456.37, B532.31, P464.17   "M'okamanga"   From Kolbe (*An English-
Herero Dictionary* 361), who translates the Herero "*mokamanga*" as
"instantly."

EPISODE 14

Slothrop and Margherita depart Berlin on a barge, journey to a fictional resort town called Bad Karma, link up with the *Anubis*, and head northward to Peenemünde. Margherita is reunited with her daughter, Bianca (a
name meaning "white"). Slothrop meets Miklos Thanatz, who was with
Blicero before the launch of Rocket 00000.

V457.1, B532.36, P464.21   the Spree-Oder Canal   This canal will carry
Slothrop and Margherita eastward out of Berlin to the Oder River, on

which they journey northward to Stettin and Swinemünde, on the Baltic Sea.

V457.2, B532.37–38, P464.22   Geli Tripping's clew   Again recalls Theseus's "clew" or ball of thread, the gift of Daedalus to help him wind his way back out of the Cretan labyrinth (see V88.17n, V428.28–29n).

V457.4, B533.2, P464.24   the Lublin regime   See V34.28–30n.

V457.26, B533.27, P465.10   "the Polish invasion"   Germany invaded Poland at dawn on September 1, 1939.

V457.30, B533.32, P465.14   Bad Karma   The pun's a groaner; the place is fictional, though patterned after such German resort towns as Bad Sachsa, in the Harz Mountains, or Bad Freienwalde, just off the Oder River north of Berlin. "Karma" is the Hindu term for the whole of a person's deeds, seen as determining his fate in future reincarnations. "Bad karma" was popular sixties countercultural slang for "bad luck."

V458.14, B534.13–14, P465.36   The Sprudelhof   A courtyard built around the curative mineral springs.

V458.36, B534.41, P466.26   the Kurhaus   A pavilion housing the curative mineral baths.

V459.10, B535.16, P466.34   the *Anubis*   This boatload of degenerates is named for the jackal-headed god of Egyptian mythology who conducted the dead to judgment. In Gerhardt von Göll's film *Alpdrücken*, the "jackal men" ravish Margherita Erdmann (see V461.15).

V459.14, B535.21, P466.37   spaetzle   German-style noodles.

V460.12, B536.25, P467.38   *Świnoujście*   Polish name for the city called Swinemünde by Germans.

V461.18, B537.39, P469.2   Goebbels   Josef Paul Goebbels (1897–1945), the Nazi Minister of Propaganda and, after July 1944, "General Plenipotentiary for Total War."

V461.20, B537.41, P469.4   at Bydgoszcz   The German name for this Polish industrial city 150 miles northwest of Warsaw was Bromberg.

V461.32, B538.15, P469.17   "Miklos Thanatz"   Thanatz's name derives from the Greek god Thanatos (Death). Grimm (*Teutonic Mythology* 840–41) describes him as "a genius, with hand on cheek in deep thought, or setting his foot on the psyche (soul) as if taking possession of her. . . . At times he appears black . . . or black winged." Grimm also connects Thanatos with the German Valkyries, who gather Wuotan's elect from the battlefields when they fall. "Thanatz" also closes the circle of references generated around the name of E. W. A. Pointsman's imaginary dog, Reichssieger von Thanatz Alpdrucken (see V142.32–33n).

V462.28, B539.19, P470.14   Marie-Celestial   Alluding again to the ship *Mary Celeste*; see V303.19–20n.

V462.38, B539.29, P470.24   the *Titanic*   The passenger liner that went down on April 14, 1912, in the midst of its maiden voyage from Southampton to New York.

V463.8, B539.38, P470.33   murmuring together in Wendish   The Wendish homeland is in Lusatia, in eastern Germany; though they had been long dominated by German nobility, the preterite Wends continued to speak their native west Slavik language, Sorbian.

V463.11–12, B540.1–2, P470.37–38   Baron de Mallakastra . . . Mme. Sztup   The baron is from a region in central Albania, the nation whose name links (on one theory—from the Indo-European *"albh"*) to the "white" powder he "sifts" into the drink. As to Mme. Sztup, her name is from the Yiddish verb *"sztup"* or *"shtup,"* which means "to push" or, by vulgar extension, "to fornicate with."

V463.19, B540.10, P471.3–4   that Bianca's a knockout, all right: 11 or 12   Wrong. She has to be 16 or 17 years old (see Duyfhuizen, "'A Suspension Forever at the Hinge of Doubt'" 3–6).

V463.26, B540.20, P471.11   a bitt   A vertical, phallus-like post for securing cables on board a ship.

V464.30, B541.29–30, P472.14   "a Max Weber charisma"   See V81.8–9n.

V465.11, B542.14–15, P472.35–36   "His name was Gottfried. God's peace"   On the etymology see V94.26n.

V465.14, B542.18, P472.39   "that terrible week"   Easter week of 1945, March 25 to April 1, when Weissmann's battalion fled eastward across Niedersachsen, the state in northern Germany.

V465.18, B542.23, P473.1   "the captain in *Wozzeck*"   Austrian composer Alban Berg's 1922 opera was based on the unfinished play *Woyzeck* (1837) by the German writer Georg Büchner, itself based on a historical case. In 1821 Johann Christian Wozzeck, a soldier and barber, murdered his adulterous wife and was publicly executed in Leipzig's public square. Büchner's play casts Wozzeck as the sacrificial victim of an autocracy represented by a doctor and captain determined to validate their superiority by making a humiliating spectacle and a blood rite of Wozzeck's execution. Büchner's manuscript was completed and published in 1909, and Berg was drawn to the potential for depicting Wozzeck's madness as the mentality of a helpless soldier caught in a vastly unjust machine, the merciless and selfish power of a ruling class that itself manifests insanity. As with the innovations of Schönberg's opera *Erwartung,* so the atonal shrieking Berg composed for his characters brought sharp criticism; but it was, like the expressionist cinema of the period, a powerful statement of the German spirit after the Great War. Here, Thanatz recollecting that Blicero (Weissman) had at war's end "screamed at the sky" and "reverted" to the hysteria represented in Berg's Hauptman (the captain) underscores in this scene how Gottfried, like Wozzeck caught in a seeming destiny against which he has no control, has been sacrificed. Or so, Thanatz suggests, have *all* of them, all of them having been "weighed in the balance and found wanting."

V465.22–23, B542.28, P473.6   "that ungodly coloratura"   The trills and high-register runs in Wozzeck's vocal score.

V465.30, B542.37–38, P473.13   "the Urstoff wakes, and sings"   An *Urstoff* is any primal substance. The allusion here is to Isaiah 26:19 (translation from the *Oxford Annotated Bible*):

> The dead shall live, their bodies shall rise;
> O dwellers in the dust, awake and sing for joy!
> For thy dew is the dew of light,
> And on the land of the shades thou wilt let it fall.

V466.4, B543.12, P473.27   "On the Good Ship Lollipop" . . . without a trace of shame   A Sidney Clare and Richard Whiting song written for Shirley Temple to sing in her starring role in the 1934 film *Bright Eyes*. The lyrics:

> On the goo-o-ood ship, Lolli-pop,
> It's a swee-e-eet trip, to a candy shop,
> Where bon-bons play,
> On the sunny beach of Peppermint Bay.
>
> Lemona-a-ade stands, every-where,
> Crackerja-a-ack stands, fill the air,
> And there you are—
> Happy landing on a chocolate bar.
>
> See the sugar bowl do the Tootsie Roll,
> With the big bad devil's food cake;
> If ya' eat too much—oooh, oooooh!
> You'll awake with a tummy ache!
>
> On the goo-o-ood ship, Lolli-pop,
> It's a ni-i-ight trip, into bed you hop,
> And dream away—
> On the good ship Lolli-pop!

The representation here of young Bianca Erdmann performing the song and obviously vamping her leering audience has a notable historical context, to which Larsson ("A *Companion*'s Companion") calls our attention. Shirley Temple (b. 1928) was a childishly cute seven-year-old child when *Bright Eyes* was shot but seemed older even two years later when she appeared in *Wee Willie Winkie*, the John Ford adaptation of Rudyard Kipling's 1888 tale, "Wee Willie Winkie: An Officer and a Gentleman." In the Kipling story Wee Willie is a lisping six-and-a-half-year-old Percival William Williams, child of a British officer garrisoned in colonial India (indeed, as the story says, "child of the Dominant Race"). For the film, Ford gives the role of Wee Willie, now a girl named Priscilla Williams, to Shirley Temple, who struts through a good bit of the film in kilts and pants, indeed positively vamps the crusty Scots regimental sergeant played by Victor McClaglan. Reviewing the film for the British magazine *Night & Day*, novelist Graham Greene zeroed in on Temple's cloying gestures: "the way she measures a man with agile studio eyes, with dimpled depravity"; "emotions of love and grief glissade across the mask of childhood, a childhood skin-deep. . . . [H]er admirers—middle aged men and clergymen—respond to her dubious coquetry, to the sight of her well shaped and desirable little body." Twentieth-Century Fox sued *Night & Day*, in what became a rather famous case.

V466.16, B543.26–27, P473.39   "'Animal Crackers in My Soup'" Another song written for Shirley Temple, this one by Ray Henderson for her 1935 film *Curly Top*:

> Animal crackers in my soup,
> Monkeys and rabbits loop-the-loop;
> Gosh oh gee!, but I have fun,
> Swallowin' animals one by one!
>
> I make 'em jump right through a hoop,
> Those animal crackers in my soup.
> When I get ahold of the Big Bad Wolf,
> I just push him under to drown,
> Then I bite him in a million bits,
> And I gobble him right down.
>
> [Repeat the chorus]
>
> Stuff my tummy like a "goop,"
> With animal crackers in my soup.

V467.1–2, B544.16, P474.26   building up a skew matrix of pain on Bianca's flesh A skew matrix graphs the divergence or displacement of a measured value (such as the intensity of pain) from some optimal or desired value. Usually consisting of two or more nonperpendicular scales, the tangent of their intersection defines the skew value. Here Slothrop inflicts pain on Bianca with an embossed steel ruler, the intensity of it correlating to the force of his blows, which may be variable (but not randomized), so that a particular skew value would be obtainable. Nonetheless the point involves how Slothrop uses objective science as barrier between himself and what he's doing to/with Bianca.

V467.8–29, B544.24–545.8, P474.32–475.13   Everyone is kind of aroused. . . . back down the Oder River a ways Notice the circularity of this orgiastic groping, which begins and ends with the "juicy blonde."

V468.5, B545.30, P475.31–32   "Chattanooga Choo Choo" A Mack Gordon and Harry Warren song for the 1941 film *Sun Valley Serenade* and a monumental wartime hit for the Glenn Miller Orchestra:

Pardon me boys, is that the Chattanooga Choo Choo?
Yes, yes!
Track twenty-nine!
Boy you can give me a shine.

Can you afford to board the Chattanooga Choo Choo?
I got my fare,
And just a little to spare.
You leave the Pennsylvania Station 'bout a quarter to four,
Read a magazine and then you're in Baltimore . . . [and so on].

V468.10, B545.36, P475.37　her chignon　The woman's hair, tied in a bun.

EPISODE 15

Still aboard the *Anubis*, and the time is still late July. Bianca and Slothrop couple violently, and doing so plugs Slothrop into the erotic fantasies of a host of others: Franz Pökler, Max Schlepzig, Miklos Thanatz, Gerhardt von Göll, even Tchitcherine.

V468.19, B546.6, P476.8　a statue of the White Rabbit in Llandudno　A resort town in northern Wales, on the Irish Sea, where the white statue mentioned here stands by the shore. Scholars have presented no evidence that Lewis Carroll ever visited the resort, but Alice Liddell's parents often took her there and this remains Llandudno's claim to Alice fame. Carroll, the Oxford mathematician (Charles Ludwig Dodgson, 1832–98), met Alice in July 1862, took her as his inspiration, and published *Alice's Adventures Underground* on July 4, 1865. Slothrop's tie to Lewis Carroll is, via the writer's passion for little girls, the whiff of pedophilia; for our hero here reads Bianca ("white")—most likely around 16 or 17 (see V463.19n)—as a sexually precocious child of "11 or 12."

V469.17, B547.12, P477.6　Alençon lace　Fine-quality lace and brocaded fabric from the French mill town of Alençon.

V470.10–11, B548.13–14, P478.2　this exploding *emprise*　The French term "*emprise*" signifies "mastery." Here it echoes the *sentiments d'emprise* or paranoid delusions over which Pavlov had debated Pierre Janet (V49.1–2n).

V470.11–12, B548.14–15, P478.3　sense of *waiting to rise*　That is, the sense of *Erwartung* (V101.9n).

V470.18, B548.22–23, P478.9　out the eye at tower's summit　A curious image, whose intratextual reference must be not only to Slothrop's penis but to Rocket 00000, with Gottfried's little window cut (somewhere) into it. Intertextually, it also recalls the mystical symbol of God's eye atop a pyramid or tower, as, for example, on the backside of an American dollar bill. In Masonic or Kabbalistic interpretations, such an eye represents the transcendent vision of an adept after his seven- or ten-stage climb toward the divine throne (see also V484.33).

V470.37–38, B549.3–4, P478.29–30 **The Pope's staff is always going to remain barren** Alluding once more to the Tannhäuser myth (V364.22n).

V471.8–11, B549.20–22, P478.41–479.3 **She dreams often about the same journey. . . . In a Pullman, dictating her story** Bianca's dream of traveling in a German *Schlafwagen* or sleeping car (in the U.S., a "Pullman," after the manufacturer), will recur later in part 3 as Leni Pökler (working as the prostitute "Solange") dreams of her daughter Ilse riding "lost through the Zone" in a train. The link between both scenes is Slothrop, lying next to Bianca here and next to "Solange" in the later scene (see V610.3–5n).

V471.24, B549.38, P479.17 **tin Moxie signs** Slothrop's nostalgic, homeward-tilting memory of advertisements for this American brand of soft drink (see V63.5n).

V471.28, B550.1–2, P479.22 **Murphy's Law** See V275.25–26n.

V471.30, B550.3, P479.23 **drowned Becket** As Larsson points out, the reference is to the town of Becket, in Berkshire County, Massachusetts, devastated by floods on November 4, 1927, after the collapse of nearby Bayou Dam (see *The Berkshire Hills* 220).

V472.20–21, B550.43, P480.16 **this Eurydice-obsession** In Greek myth, Orpheus was to be allowed to bring his wife Eurydice out of Hades, provided he did not look back. He did. So will Slothrop.

V472.35–36, B551.17–18, P480.30–31 **never threatened along any rookwise row or diagonal** In this chessboard analogy, applied to a grid of theater seats, all the moves are accounted for except those of the knight (*Springer*).

EPISODE 16

We are still aboard the *Anubis*. The subepisode entitled "Ensign Morituri's Story" reveals Margherita Erdmann as a destructive avatar of the Shekinah, a Kabbalistic version of the White Goddess. Greta's homicidal mania for children bodes ill for Bianca, her daughter.

V473.3–4, B551.27, P481.2 **Ensign Morituri** An ex-kamikaze trainee who derives his name from the greeting of Roman gladiators to their caesar: *morituri te salutant* ("those who are about to die salute you"). In Conrad's *Heart of Darkness* (1899), Marlow quotes it after visiting "the Company's offices" to get his commission for the African voyage (147). Also, as a spy or agent our Morituri may owe something to W. J. Lueddecke's spy thriller entitled *Morituri* (1964), made into a 1965 movie starring Marlon Brando and Yul Brynner. The plot: a German merchant ship carrying secret cargo sets sail for Japan, amid plentiful intrigue, during the middle of the Battle of the Pacific. In any case, given the lack of distinguishable "r" and "l" sounds in spoken Japanese, it's an impossible moniker for our ensign.

V475.11, B554.5, P483.4 *curanderos* In his notes for Hernández's *Martín Fierro* (332), translator Walter Owen defines the *curandero* of South America as a quack doctor, "expert in remedies which were a strange medley of nature lore, superstition, mother-wit, and pretension." Here, one among many healers—ranging from acupuncturists, to Freudian analysts to hypnotists—called in to cure Greta Erdmann. Hence her faith in the "greasy mud with traces of radium"; for nineteenth-century theories put great stock in the curative power of small-dose radium exposures.

V476.7, B555.8, P484.1 an aquatic *corso* From the Italian signifying a "contest" or "race."

V476.11, B555.13, P484.6 Garbo hats Such as the "Garbo fedora" referenced at V380.11.

V476.21, B555.25, P484.15 the Sprudelstrasse Street leading to the Sprudelhof, the courtyard with its mineral springs.

V476.39–40, B556.5, P484.35 the Trinkhalle Literally referencing the "drink hall," a pump room at a spa in which one could imbibe the curative waters.

V477.1–2, B556.9, P484.38 the Kursaal A main pavilion or hall at the spa, where *the Kur-Orchestra* would play the songs noted below.

V477.5, B556.13–14, P484.41–485.1 *The Merry Widow and Secrets of Suzanne* Franz Lehár's opera, *The Merry Widow*, with its famous waltz, premiered in 1906. *Susanna's Secret*, by Ermanno Wolf-Ferrari, premiered in 1909. (Her secret was smoking.)

V477.24, B556.37, P485.20 the Brodelbrunnen A bubbling, gurgling mud spring.

V478.14–17, B557.35–38, P486.13–14 "I wander all the Diaspora . . . you fragment of smashed vessel" The Kabbalists regarded Israel not only as a historical community but as an esoteric symbol, a container or "vessel" of the Shekinah. Members of the community are parts of it; thus, the Jews scattered throughout the European Diaspora all are considered "fragments of a smashed vessel," as Pynchon notes. The Shekinah is the earthly presence of Yahweh, usually the last of his ten emanations, or Sephiroth, and it is a feminine presence, "seen at once as mother, as wife, and as daughter" (Scholem, *On the Kabbalah* 105). After man's fall the Shekinah always wears black garments, like Greta's in this scene, for black is the token of mourning. The "righteous man" or Messiah would strip off these somber robes to reveal her rainbow radiance (ibid.

67). The proper home of the Shekinah is with the sun, symbol of Yahweh's masculine light. But she also has a dark side, appearing as the moon, a lightless receiver of light. As such, she is especially susceptible to domination from demonic powers from the Other Side, when she appears as the tree of death, symbol of punishment and retribution. Thus, in her black garments and through her connection with the preterite mud (Erdmann, again, signifying an "earth man"), Greta appears to the boy as exactly this demonic emissary from the other side. She is the Shekinah as destroyer, not as the rainbow symbol of Yahweh's covenant. Note, in addition, the presence of another hysteron proteron trope: the boy is a "fragment" (another of *GR's* many remnants) of a "smashed vessel" seeking to reconstitute itself.

V478.27, B558.8, P486.26   d'Annunzio's adventure at Fiume   After the Treaty of Versailles was signed in 1919, the Italian poet Gabriele D'Annunzio attempted to forestall the cession of Fiume, a valuable port city, to Austria. For two years he held it as self-appointed duce. Pynchon relates the story in his epilogue to *V.*

V479.1, B558.27, P487.1-2   next day was 1 September   Of 1939, the day (at dawn) the German *Wehrmacht* crossed the Polish frontier, beginning the war.

V479.10, B558.38, P487.11   "Oh, pip, pip, old Jap"   Another deliberate groaner of a pun, here on the British idiomatic farewell: "Pip, pip, old chap!"

V480.4–5, B559.37–38, P488.6–7   "Hiroshima . . . a city on Honshu"   This is the first reference to the city, anticipating the atomic holocaust of August 6, 1945, the historical backdrop that marks the end of part 3 and the beginning of part 4 (see V588.8 and V693.36). Morituri's thoughts on "radioactivity" (V479.17) thus take on an edge of dramatic irony.

V480.20, B560.13, P488.22   a black Italian maduro   From the Latin maturas (ripe); thus a dark, very strong cigar.

V480.23, B560.17, P488.25–26   "the face of a Jonah"   Like the Old Testament figure, Slothrop is also an underwater, in-the-belly-of-the-beast traveler; like Jonah he also flees his calling—and with "the face" of one recognizable as hexed; like Jonah, he will be pitched overboard during a storm.

V481.1, B560.38, P489.5   "There's only one free ride"   An old bit of colloquial wisdom whose completion is: "into hell" (which is where the Egyptian god Anubis conducts dead souls).

V481.5, B561.1, P489.9   One of the General Orders   In basic training, all newly recruited U.S. servicemen memorize the twelve "General Orders" pertaining to military conduct and discipline.

V481.21, B561.19, P489.25   crystal birds   Late sixties American slang. A "crystal ship" is a hypodermic syringe filled with any crystalline drug liquified for injection (such as methadrine or heroin); thus a "crystal bird" is the powdered form of a drug, when it flies up one's snoot.

EPISODE 17

A board the *Anubis:* this episode provides background on Greta Erdmann, her film roles, and the physical similarities between her child, Bianca, and Blicero's "young pet" (V484.17), Gottfried. Greta's recollections of Blicero and the last days at Lüneburg Heath add considerably to Slothrop's accumulating file on Rocket 00000 and the *Schwarzgerät*.

V482.15, B562.15, P490.19   Gretel   Diminutive form of Greta, from Margherita; it also links her to Katje Borgesius, who played the Gretel role (to Gottfried's Hansel) in part 1 of *GR*.

V482.18–19, B562.19, P490.23   comatic   From the Latin *"comatus"* (hairy) and the Greek *"coma"* (sleep).

V482.29, B562.31, P490.33   *Weisse Sandwüste von Neumexiko*   Literally, "white sand waste [desert] of New Mexico" but associatively it's White Sands, New Mexico, the southwestern military base where the first atomic bomb was test-detonated in 1945 and where the one hundred captured V-2 rockets and various German technicians were secretly brought in 1946.

V482.34, B562.37, P491.2   an American horse named Snake   Tchitcherine's central Asian mount from 1935 (see V342.11) and evidently the horse that Crutchfield rides in Slothrop's fantasy of episode 10, part 1.

V483.1, B563.2–3, P491.4   the Sagittarian fire   Sagittarius (the Archer, from November 22 to December 21) is a fire sign and ninth in the astrological year.

V483.25, B563.33, P491.28   Lotte Lüstig   Another onomastic pun, from the German *lustig*: fun-loving, comical, lusty.

V483.28, B563.36, P491.31   *Jugend Herauf!*   "Youth Arise!," a National Socialist propaganda slogan from the period, with a grim pun on the command *Juden heraus!* (Jews out!).

V484.10–11, B564.21–23, P492.13–15   Double and Triple Protars . . . Grundlach Turner-Reichs   A list of late-nineteenth- and early-twentieth-century German-manufactured large-format camera lenses— a Zeiss Protar in a "double" and another in a "triple" length, and so on.

V484.25, B564.40, P492.29   Croix mystique   See V16.15–16n.

V484.33, B565.10–11, P492.37   The Eye at the top of the pyramid   See V470.18n.

V485.13, B565.32, P493.16   a Hannomag Storm   The name is short for Hannoversche Maschinenbau AG, a manufacturer of road vehicles from

1905 on (the company still builds trucks). The Sturm, or "Storm," a very powerful, neatly appointed automobile popular with Germany's upper middle class, was introduced in 1928.

V485.32–34, B566.14–16, P493.36   at the Schußstelle . . . bleeding with beads of gum   Kooy and Uytenbogaart (*Ballistics of the Future* 289) describe similar damage to trees at the rocket-firing sites in Holland.

V485.35, B566.18, P493.39   "Blicero was a local deity."   See V30.12n.

V486.1, B566.25, P494.5   "into the Heath"   That is, the Lüneburg Heath.

V486.2, B566.26, P494.6   "*Jabos* flew over"   The term was German slang for the American P-47 fighter plane. The source of this detail is Huzel (*Peenemünde to Canaveral* 149–50), who recalls how the American *Jabos* harassed the Peenemündans as they made their escape.

V486.3, B566.27–28, P494.7   "a werewolf"   We could see this change coming over Weissmann, who earlier "screamed at the sky" (V465.21) and whose totem has been the wolf. The motif will come up once more (V640.23n).

V486.7, B566.32–33, P494.11   "my Ur-Heimat"   His primeval homeland.

V486.26, B567.16, P494.30–31   "I said, 'The Castle'"   Refers to card sixteen of the tarot deck, known as the Tower or Castle. In the Rider deck, the illustration on this card shows a white castle tower struck by lightning, its crown exploded off, fire belching from the windows, and its two occupants falling headlong to the ground. Waite (*Pictorial Key* 132) interprets the image as a portent of destruction in material creation: "the ruin of the house of life, when evil has prevailed therein."

V486.33–34, B567.36, P494.38   the silver stork flew wings-down   That is, the chrome hood ornament on the Hispano-Suiza motorcar in which they are riding.

V486.39–40, B567.32–33, P494.3   "I only recognized one: Generaldirektor Smaragd"   The IG Farben representative from the séance of part 1 (see V164.10n).

V487.24, B568.21–22, P495.29–30   "methyl methacrylate, a replica of the Sangraal"   See also Perspex, the light-bending plastic (V384.31n). Methyl methacrylate was synthesized during the thirties from acetone, methyl alcohol, cyanide, and sulfuric acid. Like polystyrene, it is a rigid plastic, and its ability to "pipe" light makes it useful in fiber optics. In Arthurian legend, the Sangraal is the Holy Grail, a chalice containing Christ's blood.

V487.40–41, B569.43, P496.5   "'butadiene,' and I heard *beauty dying*"   Butadiene is a liquid derivative from butane that is widely used in manufacturing synthetic rubber.

V488.2, B569.2, P496.7–8   "costume of some black polymer"   Donning the black plastic suit of Imipolex G designed as second skin for the white boy, Gottfried, Greta recalls the Qlippoth (see V176.14–15n and V197.1n).

EPISODE I 8

A s an evening storm tosses the ship, Slothrop slips from the decks of the *Anubis* and tumbles into the Oder Haff.

V488.36, B570.4, P497.4   the clinometer bob   The pendulum swings of this instrument indicate the angle of inclination of the ship as it rolls in the storm.

V489.3–4, B570.10, P497.9   the pelorus   Aboard ship, a device for taking one's bearings.

V489.6, B570.13, P497.11   Corposants   From the Latin signifying "holy bodies"; that is, the electrical phenomenon known as St. Elmo's fire (see V491.6).

V489.9, B570.16, P497.14   the Oder Haff   A bay formed where the river Oder dumps into the Baltic Sea, divided into the lesser or Kleines Haff to the west and the greater or Grosses Haff to the east. The pun on "other half" is coincidental.

V489.11–16, B570.18–25, P497.16–21   the passage being kept in grease-pencil . . . phosphor grass ripples across the A-scopes . . . is the pip you see there even a ship?   The A-scope was an early form of radar. Here, aboard the *Anubis*, the concern is that Russian radar men (like this Vaslav) are plotting with grease pencils the ship's passage across their screen, its changing position indicated by a "pip" or spike in their A-scopes' horizontal lines across the bottom.

V489.20, B570.29, P497.25   Fort-Lamy   Named for renowned French soldier-explorer F. J. A. Lamy (1858–1900), Fort-Lamy (now N'Djamena) is the capital city of Chad, a protectorate in French Equatorial Africa after 1910. During World War II it was a stronghold for Free French activities against Rommel's desert troops. It's also a way station along the route that brought Pirate Prentice his bananas (see V5.35–36).

V489.21, B570.31, P497.26   high albedo   See V152.24n.

V490.5, B571.18–19, P498.11   The second dog watch   That is, from 6:00 to 8:00 P.M. See also V326.4n.

V490.11, B571.25, P498.17   Dramamine   Trademarked name of the antiemetic drug dimenhydrinate marketed for the relief of motion sickness. It was developed by the G. D. Searle Company in the late 1940s and first released in 1949 (so these "stewards" would not be dispensing it in 1945 to the "Barfing aristocracy" aboard the *Anubis*).

V490.30, B572.5–6, P498.37   the September afternoon   Here, the afternoon of Friday, September 8, 1944, when the first V-2 rocket fell on London.

V491.21, B573.2–3, P499.29   the Iron Guard . . . screaming Long Live Death   See V11.35n.

V491.22–23, B573.3–4, P499.30   bodies of Jews and Leftists hung on the hooks   See V202.30.

EPISODE 19

A black marketeer named Frau Gnahb (the name, a backward spelling of "bhang," is the Hindu term for marijuana) plucks Slothrop from the storm-tossed waters of the Baltic Sea, then puts him in touch with Der Springer, Gerhardt von Göll. For a price, Springer offers to recover the *S-Gerät* for Slothrop. They make their way westward along the Usedom coast to Peenemünde, where the Russians detain von Göll.

V492.18, B574.14, P500.28 "the Silent Otto" He might be nicknamed after Nikolaus Otto (1832–91), the German inventor (along with Gottlieb Daimler and Wilhelm Maybach) of the four-stroke compression gasoline engine. For its smoothness, the engine was dubbed "The Silent Otto" (circa 1890). Or, more likely, he's named after German submarine captain "Silent Otto" Kretschmer (1912–98), credited with sinking forty-four Allied ships between early 1940 and March 1941, when he was captured by Allies who had given him the moniker because he attacked quietly under cover of darkness. His motto (consistent with Rilke, and Crutchfield the Westwardman): "One torpedo . . . one ship."

V493.7, B575.3, P501.19 Bohnenkaffee Bean coffee, the "honest-to-God" article instead of wartime *ersatzkaffee.*

V493.12–13, B575.9–11, P501.24–25 See the sugar bowl . . . big, bad, Devil's food cake Echoing Bianca's Shirley Temple song on board the *Anubis* (see V466.4n).

V494.21–22, B576.30, P502.36 about Anton Webern On the anachronism, see V440.31n.

V495.7–9, B577.19–21, P501.24 the same Klaus Närrisch that aerodynamics man Horst Achtfaden fingered for the Schwarzkommando See V456.33. The name Närrisch recalls the German for "foolish."

V496.23–24, B578.41–579.1, P504.38 Ulcerous impresario G. M. B. Haftung The German acronym GmbH stands for Gesellschaft mit beschrankter Haftung (limited liability corporation).

V496.33, B579.11, P505.9 "Deine Mutter" "Your mother."

V497.8, B579.27, P505.24 across the brow Fowler (*A Reader's Guide to "Gravity's Rainbow"*) mistakenly assumes this is a misprint for "prow." But in nautical terminology a "brow" is any inclined planking or gangway used in loading a ship, which is why Pynchon's boys and girls go "stevedoring" across one.

V497.15, B579.36, P505.31 film, *Lucky Pierre Runs Amok* One fictional night ten years later in *V.* (219), "Pig" Bodine will file these reels of film in his private collection of "depraved" movies stowed aboard his ship, the USS *Scaffold.*

V497.26, B580.8, P506.1 Crosscurrents tug at the boat Misprinted as "tug a the boat" in the Bantam.

V498.6, B580.30, P506.19   the Flying Dutchman   According to seagoing legend, a Dutch captain named Vanderecken swore by the gods Donner and Blitzen that he would safely beat a dangerous storm into harbor. At the very moment of his oath, the ship foundered and was condemned to sail on eternally. Sailors believe that seeing his ship portends doom. In Richard Wagner's opera *Der Fliegende Holländer*, every seven years Captain Vanderecken is allowed a sabbatical to swim ashore and seek the woman whose love can redeem him from his eternal sailing.

V499.17, B582.9, P507.31   "He's an OSS man"   That is, from the Office of Strategic Services, the precursor to the CIA run by "Wild Bill" Donovan (V268.6n).

V499.36, B582.32–33, P508.10   Helen Trent, Stella Dallas, Mary Noble Backstage Wife   Slothrop's mother, Nalline, would float away in "nameful recapitulating" (V499.34) at the mention of these programs because they were her favorite radio soap operas. *Stella Dallas* ran from 1937 to 1955 and billed itself as "the true-to-life story of mother love and sacrifice, in which Stella Dallas saw her beloved daughter Laurel marry into wealth and society, and, realizing the differences in their tastes and world, went out of Laurel's life" (but not entirely; she was an eternal outsider looking in). John Dunning (*Tune in on Yesterday* 568) has written that only *The Romance of Helen Trent* could ever match *Stella Dallas* in the "misery-per-episode quota." From 1933 to 1960 radio's Miss Trent was a model of purity, temperance, and equanimity in sinful Hollywood. The third program, *Backstage Wife*, featured the character "Mary Noble . . . a lovely girl from the Iowa sticks" (ibid. 54) who marries a matinee idol other women are forever trying to seduce. This show had a long run too, from 1935 to 1959.

V500.26, B583.28, P509.1   Dr. Mabuse   In Fritz Lang's 1922 film, the people who show a "glacial smile" are those prospective victims whom the evil doctor has hypnotized.

V500.40, B584.3, P509.15   Rocket Noon   Recalls the "Evil Hour" (V374.39–375.2n), and it anticipates another detail: Rocket 00000 was fired from the Lüneburg Heath at noon (V667.3–4n).

V501.5–6, B584.10–11, P509.21–22   scorched as Rossokovsky and the White Russian Army left it in the spring   "Rossokovsky" here is a misspelling. The Soviet general Konstantin Rokossovsky (1896–1968) fought with Bolshevik forces during the Revolution and was one of many army officers whom Stalin purged in 1937. Rehabilitated in 1940, Rokossovsky distinguished himself during the siege of Stalingrad (1942–43), in reward for which Stalin appointed him commander of the central front. He infamously kept his troops outside Warsaw during the tragic uprising of 1944. In January 1945 he was given command of the Second Belorussian (or White Russian) Front, a "Front" being a combination of armies, and he led the Soviet invasion of Prussia through Königsberg,

Danzig, and Rostock. On May 5, 1945, his troops entered Peenemünde and plundered it (but evidently, without leaving it "scorched") in the course of gathering intelligence on the German rocket program.

V501.6–7, B584.11, P509.22   On the maps, it's a skull   Just so, as the map in Irving's book (*Mare's Nest* 6) will show. Remember, too, that the "black scapeape" (V275.34) King Kong originates from Skull Island.

V501.10, 584.15–16, P509.26   a Wilhelm Busch cartoon face   German artist Wilhelm Busch (1832–1908) was the country's best-known and most beloved humorist. *Max and Moritz,* his illustrated children's book, appeared in 1865. These were also the names playfully assigned to two experimental A2 rockets fired from Borkum in 1934 (Klee and Merk, *The Birth of the Missile* 12). In addition, two members of Blicero's firing crew are named Max and Moritz (V757.26, 29).

V501.22, B584.30–31, P509.39   Bicycle Rider in the Sky   A vague and ambiguous allusion with at least three possible referents. First is the so-called Rider pack of tarot cards manufactured by William Rider and Sons of London: A. E. Waite and P. D. Ouspensky both used the Rider images in their interpretations of the tarot. Second is Rilke: in the eleventh of the *Sonnets to Orpheus* there appears a constellation called *Reiter* (Rider, Horseman), symbolizing human nature (the horse) guided by an unseen force astride it; it also appears in the sky over the new-found "Pain-Land" in the tenth Duino elegy. Third is the Norse god Odin: one of his frequent nicknames was "Atrithr," meaning "Rider" and signifying his role as a wind god galloping across the heavens. His horse, Sleipnir, was a gray with eight legs. In part 4 Blicero appears as the Knight of Swords, "the rider on a black horse" (V747.5–6).

V501.25–26, B584.35, P510.1–2   In the Tarot he is known as The Fool   In most interpretations the card is the twenty-second and last card of the Major Arcana, though its number is zero. Ouspensky (17) reads the image as "ordinary man . . . separate man. The uninitiate lower consciousness. The end of a ray not knowing its relation to the center." As "Fool," Slothrop will approach his "Holy Center" in the next episode but will not know the place. So "groweth his Preterition sure" (V509.37).

V501.40, B585.11, P510.16–17   half the Jonahs of falling Europe   On Slothrop as Jonah, see V480.23n.

V502.9–10, B585.21–22, P510.25–26   stations of the cross   In Roman Catholicism there are fourteen stations symbolizing events in the Passion of Jesus. Here, out of historical and numerological necessity, there are ten, one for each of the test stands at Peenemünde. From Dornberger, we know that only stands VII (for A4 rockets) and X (for experimental rockets) were used in actual liftoffs; the rest were used in various types of static tests.

V502.20–21, B585.35–36, P510.37   the red brick . . . cathedral in Wolgast   From Dornberger (*V-2* 3): "In the west the low hills on the far bank of the river Peene were dominated by the red brick tower of Wolgast Cathedral."

V503.35, B587.14, P512.10   unslinging his Tokarev   An automatic pistol similar to the German Luger (V505.22n), and the weapon of preference among Russian officers during the war.

V504.28, B588.9, P513.3   "Zu Befehl, Mutti!"   "At your command, Mommy!" "*Zu Befehl*" is the response of an inferior to the command of a superior—for example, in the military.

V505.22, B589.12–13, P513.41   a Luger   A German officer's semiautomatic pistol, designed by Georg Luger for the German Parabellum Company and in service from 1900 until 1947; if "fully loaded" (here), there would be eight rounds in its magazine.

V505.36, B589.29–30, P514.13   the orchestra plays *Tristan und Isolde*   Wagner's 1865 opera. Perhaps they would play the "Deliverance by Death" theme from the last act, or perhaps Isolde's song as she falls dead on the prostrate body of Tristan—the *Liebestod* (love-in-death) theme.

EPISODE 20

The time is now July 30, 1945. Klaus Närrisch leads Slothrop on a commando raid, springing Der Springer from his Russian captors. This raid supplies a pretext for touring the facilities at Peenemünde, a parody of the "Holy Center" in traditional mythology. In a scene that recalls the ending of *For Whom the Bell Tolls*, Klaus is left heroically behind as Slothrop and Springer escape. Details stem largely from Dornberger (*V-2*) and Irving (*Mare's Nest*).

V506.37, B590.38, P515.15   A sharp sickle of moon has risen   The moon entered its last quarter in late July, and on July 30 a sickle-shaped moon would have risen near midnight, the "twilight" of V505.37 having occurred between nine and ten that evening.

V508.9, B592.14, P516.27   Zitz und Arsch, downslope   The narrator's German is slightly off. "*Zitz*" is the noun for any chintz or calico fabric, and "*Zitze*" the noun for an udder, teat, or dug. *Arsch* is the bum, backside, or ass.

V508.22, B592.32, P516.40   toward Test Stand VII   Was—as Dornberger, McGovern, and Wegener all describe in varying detail—the site from which A4 rockets were test-fired at Peenemünde and so the "holy center" of rocketeers (see below; also, V725.16–20n).

V508.29–30, B592.39, P517.7   a holy Center   Mircea Eliade (*The Myth of the Eternal Return* 17) describes such a place as "preeminently the zone of the sacred, the zone of absolute reality." Symbolically, the center is that navel or omphalos from which all reality is thought to have unfolded. It is the locale of objects having "absolute" significance, like the trees of life, knowledge, and death. It also exists as a meeting place for all three cosmic regions: hell, earth, and heaven. Test Stand VII is a fitting center because of its ellipsoid shape, as though it truly were a cosmic "Egg" (V510.31). For further discussion see Eliade (12–18).

V508.39–40, B593.8, P517.17–19 Gauss curve will herniate toward the excellent . . . tankers the likes of Närrisch and Slothrop . . . weeded out See V40.13–14. The Gauss curve or "bell curve" in common parlance will peak at the vertical or y-axis, with desirable or "excellent" results on the right or positive side (along the x-axis) equally balanced by the nonexcellent or negative ones on the left. When it *herniates*, the number of excellent results exceeds the others and thus the bell curve shifts rightward, along the horizontal or x-axis (see also V709.33–35n). With that movement "tankers," which is to say intentional losers (from boxing slang, for when a fighter "goes in the tank" or deliberately loses a fight), will have been weeded out. Preterite souls like Slothrop, perhaps.

V509.33–34, B594.7, P518.11 the terrible Rider See V501.22n.

V510.1–2, B594.19–20, P518.21 forgive him his numbness, his glozing neutrality A condition that stems from his habit of always glossing, or annotating, events occurring around him (like we're doing here!). Later the narrator says: "Those whom the old Puritan sermons denounced as 'the glozing neuters of the world' have no easy road to haul down" (see V677.1–2n). Too studious of minor annotations on experience to recognize the "Egg the flying Rocket hatched from" (V509.41), Slothrop has the experience but not its meaning.

V511.22, B596.9–10, P520.4 unslinging his Degtyarov See V377.11n.

V512.39, B597.36, P521.21 the *budka* Russian for a sentry box.

V513.3, B597.41, P521.26 "It's your Schwarzphänomen" That is: Slothrop's "black phenomenon," the recurring presence of blackness in the "plot" of his being.

V513.9, B598.4, P521.32 gold starred *pogoni* In Russian the *pogon* is a shoulder strap, deriving from a Polish word for a "tail" or "whip."

V513.10, B598.6, P521.33 a Kurt Weill medley Probably from the composer's best German operas: *Der Neue Orpheus* (1925) and *Die Dreigroschenoper* (1927). Weill (1900–50) fled Germany for the United States in 1935.

V513.15–16, B598.12–13, P521.38–39 Suomi subs . . . drums as big as that Gene Krupa's That is, Finnish submachine guns with large drum-magazines. Gene Krupa (1909–73), who perfected the art of "kit" drumming, was the first to record with a pedal-operated bass drum—hence the allusion here.

V514.39, B600.1, P523.24 "Lebe wohl" "Farewell."

V516.3, B601.15, P524.34 John Dillinger, at the end Toland has related the story in *The Dillinger Days* (319–31). On July 22, 1934, Dillinger and

Anna Sage went to Chicago's Biograph Theater to see *Manhattan Melodrama*. In the film Jim Wade (played by William Powell) wins the governorship after prosecuting a childhood friend, Blackie Gallagher (Clark Gable), who has shot and killed the man running against Wade in the gubernatorial election. There are some mitigating circumstances and Governor Wade therefore extends a commutation of sentence to Blackie, who refuses it and goes to the electric chair just as the narrator relates it here. Cigar-smoking Melvin Purvis and his FBI G-men were waiting outside the Biograph. When Dillinger stepped out, they opened fire. Anna Sage, the Judas goat and so-called lady in red, had relayed Dillinger's plans for the evening.

V516.22, B601.39, P525.13   Der Müde Tod   Released with English subtitles as *Destiny* (though the German means "tired Death"), this is another film that Fritz Lang directed for Ufa (1921). Kracauer (*From Caligari to Hitler* 88–91) gives a synopsis: a young woman tries to save her lover from his mortal destiny by promising Death she will bring a substitute victim. She fails at the last moment and dies in a fire. As the film ends, "Death finally guides the dying girl to her dead lover, and, forever united, their souls wander heavenward over a blossoming hill."

V516.30, B602.8, P525.21–22   east with the Institute Rabe   RABE is an acronym for *Raketenbau und Entwicklung*, meaning "rocket manufacture and development"; it was a facility established by the Russians in Bleicherode near Nordhausen during the summer of 1945. They lured former V-2 engineers and technicians with promises of fantastic salaries, the prospect of remaining together with their wives, and employment in Germany. In 1946 the Russians reneged and moved them all to the steppes of Kyrgyzstan. Von Braun, Dornberger, Huzel, and other top rocket men all went "west," first to Cuxhaven (to assist with Operation Backfire) and then to America, for the "$6 a day" salaries mentioned in *GR*. Their wives weren't allowed to join them until much later. The Russians' biggest catch was Helmuth Gröttrup, whose wife, Irmgard, recorded her memories of these days in *Rocket Wife*, Pynchon's source here.

V517.12, B602.34–35, P526.4   "Cocaine—or cards?"   Dr. Mabuse's nightclub line to prospective victims in Fritz Lang's film *Doktor Mabuse der Spieler*.

V517.17, B602.41, P526.9   a Wien bridge   In electronic circuitry, a four-arm alternating-current bridge that measures capacitance or inductance. This device was used in the automatic steering of the rocket (Kooy and Uytenbogaart, *Ballistics of the Future* 353–59). In describing its use, the narrator adopts Pavlovian terminology (for instance, the "reflex arc") to characterize these events inside the rocket's "body" (V517.23, 24).

V518.6, B603.36–37, P526.41   Driwelling, and Schmeil   Unknown if not fictional Peenemünde technicians.

V518.8, B603.39, P527.2 elctro-decor A Viking error, corrected in the Bantam and the Penguin to read "electro-decor." And it's just that: the narrator lists a series of measuring devices manufactured by such German firms as Zeiss, Siemens, and Gülcher.

EPISODE 21

In Hamburg, in late July, Enzian and the Zone Hereros move to block an abortion. They also glimpse, in the seemingly ruined landscape, signs of transnational economic interests (cartels) just waiting to leap back into operation. Pavel, one of Enzian's assistants, experiences this immanent design during a gasoline-fume-induced hallucination. Enzian reasons that a quest for the rocket will endlessly divert his people from tribal suicide.

V518.31–32, B604.23–24, P527.24 coming on like Smith, Klein, 'n' French "Smith, Klein, 'n' French" is not a reference to some trio of "famous Prohibition agents" (Fowler, *A Reader's Guide to "Gravity's Rainbow"*) but rather to the famous Philadelphia drug firm (slightly misspelled) of Smith, Kline, and French. For decades the company's bestselling pharmaceutical product was the Thorazine brand of tranquilizer, which Pynchon's character Steve Edelman keeps in his "family-size jar" (V753.27–28). Thorazine is still prescribed for relief of psychotic symptoms, but in the late twentieth century SKF's best-selling product was the Contac brand of antihistamine cold and allergy remedy.

V519.1–2, B604.31, P527.30–31 their signature, their challenge Another Bantam error: "ther signature."

V519.14, B605.7–8, P528.7 Washing-blue is the abortifacient of choice One of the dyestuffs manufactured by IG Farben, "washing-blue" or Prussian blue is a source of a deadly toxin, hydrocyanic acid. Pynchon's source here, as earlier (see V317.30–33n), was the pamphlet *Is the South-West African Herero Committing Race-Suicide?* by W. P. Steenkamp, as T. S. Tillotson first pointed out. Among the abortifacient substances that Steenkamp (29) identifies as being in use among Herero women, "washing-blue" was one "used by them . . . since the contact with the white man"; it causes "a strong stomach irritation" that produces "uterine stimulation" and contractions powerful enough to expel the fetus.

V519.22, B605.17, P528.15 British G-5 See V125.22n.

V519.27, B605.22–23, P528.20 red-shifting, fleeing the Center Another reference to the Big Bang theory of cosmic creation and the phenomenon of red-shifting stars as they speed away from the center (see V396.33n).

V520.15, B606.15, P529.8 Jamf Ölfabriken Werke AG The fictional Jamf Oil Works Incorporated.

V520.20, B606.21, P529.13   the Kabbalists out here   Knowledge of
Kabbalistic wisdom derives from three texts: those rabbinical writings
collected in the Talmud, the Sephir Yetsirah drawn up in the second
century A.D. (though based on much older material), and the Sohar,
which was composed somewhat later in the second century. The central
doctrine of Kabbalistic theosophy is that divine wisdom can be received
directly from the close, hermeneutical study of these three holy texts.

**V520.24–25, B606.26–27, P529.17–18   orururumo orunene the high, ris-
ing, dead, the blazing**   From Kolbe's grammatical introduction (*An
English-Herero Dictionary* xxxi–xxxii). "*Orururumo*" signifies "a
flame," and "*orunene*" is an adjective signifying "immensity of size."
But note the shift in lines 25–26, where the narrator explains that the
Zone Hereros have already begun dropping the inanimate prefix ("*oru-*")
and, instead, attaching the animate one ("*omu-*") to the rocket, yielding
"*omunene*" (*brother*). In sum, even as they begin to represent themselves as emptied, inanimate shells of being (see V316.38n), the Zone
Hereros simultaneously represent the rocket as animate.

V520.26–27, B606.29, P529.20   our Torah   Strictly speaking, the capital
"T" signifies only those sacred writings collected in the Old Testament
Pentateuch. With a small "t" it would signify the whole body of Judaic
sacred literature.

V520.36–37, B606.42, P529.29–30   in the form of 8th AF bombers
While stationed in England the U.S. Eighth Air Force was instrumental
in the bombing of areas in Germany where rocket components were
manufactured. For example, Irving (*Mare's Nest* 123–24, 187–88, 242)
reports that squadrons of Eighth Air Force bomber planes hit various liquid oxygen plants, manufacturing areas, and petroleum works.

V520.38, B607.1, P529.31   Director Krupp   That is, Gustav Krupp von
Bohlen und Halbach (1870–1950), the German financier, steel magnate,
and director of the Krupp Steel Works.

V521.17, B607.25–26, P530.11   a Gaussian reduction   In mathematics,
a procedure used to find one solution, or a manifold of solutions, to a
given set of complex linear equations. Also called Gauss's algorithm, it
involves the systematic elimination of variables from the equations.
Gaussian reductions are now routinely handled using computer algo-
rithms that eliminate their time-consuming and mechanistic tedium.
Here, however, before computers, the Schwarzkommando has leveled
arguments against technology that are "as dogged and humorless as a
Gaussian reduction." That is, the argument goes into too much boring
detail to cover.

V521.38, B608.10, P530.33   Blohm & Voss   They produced nose cones
for the A4 rocket at their Hamburg manufacturing plant (Irving 136n).

V522.1, B608.14, P530.37   Pervitins   His "speed" (see V328.25n) or des-
oxyephedrine tablets (V731.33); and the keyword for the novel's lyric
that follows.

V522.6–8, B608.20–22, P531.2 Sort of a Hoagy Carmichael piano A reference to American composer and jazz pianist Howard Hoagland ("Hoagy") Carmichael (1899–1981). While a student at Indiana University he met Bix Beiderbecke, recorded with him, and then commenced a solo career. He is best remembered for his slow, graceful melodies set to romantic texts: "Georgia on My Mind" (1930), "In the Still of the Night" (1932), and "Skylark" (1942), for example.

V522.12, B608.27–28, P531.7 the Stars 'n' Stripes Official magazine for servicemen in the U.S. armed forces.

V522.29, B609.7–8, P531.24 chrome and Bakelite . . . Berliner Schnauze Weissman's Dictaphone is made of chrome metal and Bakelite, a brand-name of moldable, heat- and chemical-resistant plastic (some say, the *first* plastic) patented in 1910 by Belgian chemist Leo Baekeland and widely used thereafter in electrical appliances. Here, Enzian recalls speaking into the device with his nasal or "Berlin snout" voice—a consequence of all those drugs he has snorted.

V523.13–16, B609.33–37, P532.7–10 Leunagasolin . . . Moss Creature . . . Water Giant The fuel is a brand of gasoline manufactured at the Leuna works of Hamburg, a subsidiary of IG Farben (Sasuly, *IG Farben* 56). Recalls the sort of fantastic creatures often threatening Plasticman.

V523.34, B610.17, P532.28 'fore I drop my BVDs Men's underwear manufactured by the American Bradley, Vorhees and Day Company.

V523.39, B610.23, P532.33–34 3-sigma white faces That is, with lots of variation in the shades of white (see also V40.13–14n). Here Bing Crosby directs the white, green, and blue "faces" in this hallucination.

V524.11, B610.39, P533.6 the breath of Mukuru The Herero god (see V321.40–322.1n).

V525.24, B612.20, P534.20 Saint Pauli The St. Pauli district of west Hamburg is, like London's East End, a haven for the preterite. Here is Baedeker (*Northern Germany* 150), who graciously neglects specific mention of the prostitutes renowned for working the Reeperbahn in St. Pauli: "principally frequented by sailors, for whose amusement booths and shows of every kind abound. The scene witnessed here on a Sunday or Monday afternoon . . . is a highly characteristic phase of Hamburg low life. Hawkers and itinerant venders of every kind also thrive here." The street comes up again at V652.19–20.

EPISODE 22

Around noon on July 31, off the coast of Rügen, Slothrop boards the *Anubis* one last time. Bound northward, evidently toward Copenhagen, the ship contains in its engine room not only a package of contraband but, as Slothrop discovers, or hallucinates that he discovers, the dead body of Bianca Erdmann, the Eurydice this Orpheus will not bring up from hell (see also

V472.20–21n). Frau Gnahb puts him back ashore at Stralsund, where Slothrop begins a long trek across the Zone.

V526.13, B613.13, P535.9   very Savile Row   See V184.14–15n.

V526.16–17, B613.17, P535.12–13   Mitteleuropäisch   That is, middle European.

V526.39, B614.1, P535.8   Operation Backfire   Those connected with the British effort to test-fire several rockets from Cuxhaven (V272.32–34n).

V527.3, B614.6, P536.1   the Dorum road   Leads to the village of Dorum, about one or two miles south of Cuxhaven. From subsequent details (V602.6ff) we know that Slothrop and Springer arrange to meet on the night of August 5, about one week after this conversation (V602.34).

V527.19, B614.24, P536.17   crossfire from three Schmeissers   In World War II German infantrymen made widespread use of the Haenel MP38 and MP40 submachine guns, which the Allied troops dubbed "Schmeissers," after world-famous gunsmith Hugo Schmeisser (1884–1953), who designed the weapons.

V527.24, B614.29, P536.22   Schilling's best man   None of the historical accounts seem to mention this (fictional?) engineer from Peenemünde.

V527.25, B614.30–31, P536.23   outside of Garmisch   That is, Garmisch-Partenkirchen, the Bavarian village where the Allies detained the German rocket experts. By this time, however, most had been released or offered positions with the Operation Backfire/Operation Hermes group.

V527.36–37, B615.1–2, P536.34   *mythical Rügen off our starboard bow*   Is "mythical" because, as Baedeker explains in *Northern Germany* (204), this large island in the Baltic was initially inhabited by the ancient Germanic tribes of Rugii and then by Slavonic peoples who "resisted the influences of Christianity and civilization down to the middle of the 14th century." A residue of the Teutonic and Slavonic mythologies remains in the place-names scattered along the coast (see V528.9–10n, V528.13–15n). Heading west, Frau Gnahb steers them between the main coast and Rügen Island, encountering it off the starboard (right) bow.

V527.40, B615.5–6, P536.8   the *Greifswalder Bodden*   A bay to the southeast of Rügen Island.

V528.9–10, B615.17–19, P537.6–8   the Stubbenkammer . . . Cape Arkona   After searching several of the firths on the southeastern coast of Rügen, Frau Gnahb has turned northward, according to our mock tour guide, and these landmarks from the island's eastern coast (V528.5) slide by on the left, or port, side of the ship. The geographical details stem from Baedeker (*Northern Germany* 206–07), which notes that the island is dotted with mounds and altars used in ancient Slavic sacrificial rites. The Stubbenkammer is a set of rock steps in the chalk cliffs; further west is the Königstuhl, or "King's Seat," a chalk precipice looming four

hundred feet above the Baltic. Last, according to Baedeker, there is Cape
Arkona, the island's northernmost point, site of an old Slavonic temple
"consisting of a circular entrenchment 20–40 ft. high, and containing
the temple of their four-headed idol Swantewit" (ibid.).

**V528.13–15, B615.21–24, P537.10–12   Svetovid . . . Triglav . . . Porevit
. . . Rugevit**   The sources here are Baedeker and Grimm. The latter (*Teutonic Mythology* 201) treats the Slavonic god Svetovid or Swantewit in
several connections, equating him with the Teutonic god Tiw, a war god
analogous to Mars. Interestingly, the Saxon rune for Tiw was an arrow
pointing heavenward, rocket-like. The other names are variants of, or
nicknames for, this god.

V528.19, B615.28–29, P537.16   the Wissow Klinken   The source once
again is Baedeker's *Northern Germany* (206), which describes the place
as "a series of chalk cliffs resembling those of the Stubbenkammer."
Klinken are latches or latchkeys, so this white promontory might be
said to metaphorically probe "the wards of Slothrop's heart" here.

**V529.38, B617.13–14, P538.36   Guy Lombardo . . . "Running Between the
Rain-drops"**   A song written by Carroll Gibbons and James Dyrenforth,
and a hit for Guy Lombardo (1902–77) and his orchestra (the Royal
Canadians) in 1931.

V530.29, B618.9, P539.27   three bells strike   The ship's bells strike every
half hour, the number of rings increasing by one every half hour, so that
at the end of a four-hour watch, eight bells will strike. Since it is afternoon, and the cook aboard the Anubis is "peeling potatoes" for supper
(V529.21), the time must be 1:30.

**V531.27–40, B619.12–27, P540.26–40   His hand closes on stiff taffeta. . . .
the smell of . . .   *of***   The keyword here is "taffeta," for Bianca was wearing a "red taffeta" dress (at V469.10) when they coupled back in episode
14. But it is unclear whether our "buccaneering Slothrop," grappling
his way aboard the *Anubis*, has, or hallucinates, these experiences.
Duyfhuizen ("'A Suspension Forever at the Hinge of Doubt'") argues
that Bianca's appearances trouble "our readerly desire for causality" (9),
and most of all in this scene, which he reads as replaying Brigadier Pudding's ritualized approach to Domina Nocturna (in V232.35). Note also
that in a few lines, "[w]hen the lights come back on," whoever or whatever Slothrop confronts is not named. Neither is the smell, which may
just as equally be the smell of death, shit, or the *Schwarzgerät* he's chasing like a Grail. Or, chasing like Orpheus after his Eurydice.

V532.7, B619.35, P541.6   what's dancing dead-white   Note the wordplay:
Bianca/white. As if she were the sacrifice presaged by the references in
this episode to Teutonic and Slavonic custom, she dances the dance of
death.

V532.28, B620.19, P541.27   the wet Hafenplatz   The "harbor plaza" of
Stralsund.

EPISODE 23

Returns the narrative to England. Except for the remark that "Brigadier Pudding died back in the middle of June" (V533.10), the time of this episode is indistinct, though perhaps contemporaneous with episode 22 (July 31). Here Katje watches a reel of film that Osbie has left behind especially for her. The film images constitute a code, an allegorical call for her to leave "The White Visitation" for an as yet undefined "counterforce" (V536.23).

V532.32, B620.25, P541.32   Where is the Pope whose staff will bloom for me?   The reference, again, is to the Tannhäuser myth (V364.22n), and this question becomes the first line in the Petrarchan sonnet written, it appears, by Brigadier Pudding. Its details (the "whips," the "call" of its Lisaura at night, its speaker having "knelt" before her in confession) all recollect Pudding's coprophagic ritual of episode 4, part 2.

V532.33, B620.26, P541.33   vamps me   See V320.12n.

V533.9, B620.38, P542.10   No pentacles, no cups, no holy Fool . . .   Those ellipses are Pynchon's and suggest the modernity of this sonnet, for the traditional kind of Petrarchan sonnet requires closure at the end of its sestet. In tarot symbolism, Pentacles and Cups are two of the four suits in the Lesser Arcana. Pentacles (five-pointed stars) are generally associated with monetary motifs, Cups with matters of the heart and pleasure. On the tarot Fool see V501.25–26n.

V533.10–11, B620.39–40, P542.11–12   Pudding . . . a massive *E. coli* infection   See V236.32n.

V533.11, B620.40–621.1, P542.12   "Me little Mary hurts"   Soules ("What To Think about *Gravity's Rainbow*") identifies this as the idiom of British children complaining of stomachache, from J. M. Barrie's play *Little Mary* (1906).

V533.13, B621.3, P542.14   demobbed   That is, "demobilized" (British service slang).

V533.29, B621.21, P542.28–29   some northern coomb   Also spelled "coombe," a short, deep valley, sometimes nestled in a hillside.

V533.31–32, B621.24–25, P542.32   the day Osbie Feel was processing the Amanita mushrooms   That is, December 22, 1944 (in episode 14 of part 1).

V534.2, B621.38, P543.5   "with Nelson Eddy in the background"   With singer/actress Jeanette MacDonald, Eddy (1901–67) crooned his way through a fistful of movie musicals in the thirties, such as *Naughty Marietta* (1935), and *Rose-Marie* (1936).

V534.9–10, B622.5–6, P543.12–13   "Basil Rathbone and S. Z. ('Cuddles') Sakall"   Actor Basil Rathbone (1892–1967) played Karenin to Greta Garbo's Anna Karenina, the son of Baron von Frankenstein in *The Son of Frankenstein* (1939), and the villainous Mr. Murdstone in *David Copper-*

field (1934). But Rathbone was best known for his portrayal of Sherlock Holmes during the thirties and forties. A more unlikely cowboy cannot be imagined, unless it is Sakall, who fled Europe and Hitler's madness in 1939. Hungarian by birth, Sakall (1888–1955) appeared in his first English-speaking role in the 1940 Deanna Durbin film *It's a Date*. He learned his lines by means of phonetic transcriptions, but his thick Eastern European accent always remained. Sakall is best known as the plump waiter named Carl, at Rick's café in *Casablanca* (1942).

V534.11, B622.7–8, P543.14   the Midget who played the lead in *Freaks*
This was Harry Earles (1902–85), who starred with his wife, Daisy, in several other Tod Browning films before *Freaks*, Browning's 1932 masterpiece of horror. In that film Earles plays "little Hans," a midget who marries a beautiful but devious trapeze artist called Cleopatra. She only wants his money. For that, the other "Freaks" give her a fearful beating as they chant "One of us!" and after Cleopatra's death Hans marries "little Frieda" (Daisy). *Freaks* may be read in this context as a grotesque allegory on the theme of the beautiful and the damned, in which life's preterite get in their licks. See earlier references at V106.36, V125.3, and V151.9–10.

V535.17, B623.20–21, P544.21   the element of *Greed* must be worked somehow in . . . but the film runs out   The reference is to director Eric von Stroheim's film classic *Greed* (1924), apparently in its first, ten-hour version, a quite faithful screening of Frank Norris's novel *McTeague* (1899). But we'll never fully know that first cut; MGM producer Irving Thalberg forced von Stroheim to chop it down to four hours, then Thalberg himself chopped it in half again and, worse, destroyed the discarded footage (to extract twenty-three cents of silver from the emulsion, von Stroheim bitterly suggested)—all of it the context for why the "film runs out" in this scene.

V536.12, B624.8–9, P545.5   the windmill called "The Angel"   See V106.12n.

V536.18, B624.29, P545.22–23   *An Introduction to Modern Herero*   Fictional book. Yet what would, or does, "modern" Herero *mean* after modernity itself nearly wiped out the Herero people? How deeply inflected by the oppressor/exterminator would be or is the modern form of the language?

EPISODE 24

The time is as unspecified as the place. Katje and Pirate make an allegorical tour of a rather pleasant hell, an inversion of Dante's Inferno with its deeper levels of ever greater punishments. The version here is horizontally arranged, plastically changeable, and certainly not frightening. It does involve elements of tedium, as with the long list of illicit sexual encounters, but Pirate and Katje break into joyous dance at episode's end.

V537.1–4, B625.10–13, P546.1–4   Dear Mom, I put a couple of people in Hell today . . . (Oxyrhynchus papyrus number classified)   The Oxyrhynchus papyri were named for the Nile River village where they were discovered, near the turn of the century. They consist of forty-plus volumes of fragments, three of which (numbers 1, 654, and 655) include sayings ascribed to Jesus, eventually found to resemble other sayings contained in the Gospel of Thomas, a coptic Gnostic manuscript uncovered at Nag Hamadi. However, there is also an apocryphal Gospel of Thomas, commonly referred to as the "Infancy Story" of Jesus. It exists in four recensions, one each in Greek and Latin, two in Syriac. In it are narratives of Jesus's boyhood from his fifth to his twelfth years, narratives abounding with miracles: Jesus restores the dead to life, inflicts death on some who thwart his will, and makes birds out of clay and (like Satan in Mark Twain's *Mysterious Stranger*) causes them to fly. Pynchon may well have had this background in mind here. This epigraph, however, appears in neither of the gospels of Thomas, though it is consistent with the motif of youthful magic. Indeed, this episode of *GR* does "put a couple of people [Katje and Pirate] in Hell" for the day. On the Gnostic and apocryphal backgrounds to this bit of satirical play, see M. R. James (*The Apocryphal New Testament* 14–15, 49–69).

V537.16–17, P625.28–29, P546.17   fantastic pastry carts . . . big as pantechnicons   Big as those English furniture moving vans (see V19.30).

V537.33–34, B626.12–13, P546.34   like Route One . . . through the heart of Providence   As the narrator says, the road does provide a scenic tour. Entering Providence, Rhode Island, from the south, Route 1 arcs to the right over the Woonasquatucket River, turns left under George M. Cohan Boulevard, and then heads past the campus of Brown University.

V538.14, B626.33, P547.16   Beaverboard Row   Again, the pressed-board paneling dividing cubicles of offices (see V19.37n).

V539.12, B627.33, P548.14   Teilhard de Chardin   A Jesuit father, paleontologist, and philosopher, Pierre Teilhard de Chardin (1881–1955) wrote his best-known work, *The Phenomenon of Man*, while serving as a missionary in China during the early years of World War II. His philosophy attempts a synthesis of evolutionary science and mystical Christianity. The question of a "return" thus arises here because, in Teilhard's view, the evolution of material forms up to man is an evolution of spirit, and man is the "omega point" of a linear progress that Teilhard sees as an escape from entropy, a transcendence founded on love and unity. For mankind he projects no "return" to repressed, primitive forms but rather a continued evolution of that divine spirit.

V539.21, B628.4, P548.23   "Critical Mass"   This is the smallest amount of fissionable material necessary to sustain a nuclear chain reaction. But in this scene in *GR* it's probably late July of 1945 and the first A-bomb (or "Cosmic Bomb," as the news media dubbed it) will not become common knowledge until after August 6, the day of the Hiroshima blast. So the idea, here, is still "trembling in its earliness," as our narrator remarks.

V540.23, B629.13–14, P549.25–26   Charley-Charley, Hits 'n' Cuts, and Rock-Scissors-and-Paper   Children's games, mostly English. The Opies (*Children's Games* 133–35) describe Charley-Charley as a "Catching Game" in which one child, the odd man out, stands to one side of a street. To him, the other children call out "Charley-Charley, may we cross your golden river?" The child who is "Charley" replies: "You mayn't cross my river unless you have *blue*." Anyone wearing something blue may safely cross. Those who don't must rush across while Charley, assisted by the ones with blue, tries to catch them. It goes on this way until the colors are exhausted or none are left. The last one caught becomes the new "Charley." In the same book (25) the Opies describe hits-and-cuts as a game that involves the drawing of lots or straws, the loser becoming the chaser in a game of catch. Rock-scissors-and-paper is universally known, and the Opies (ibid. 26–27) suggest that it may well have come from the Orient. After chanting in unison with three thrusts of their fists, the players (three in all) expose an image made with their fingers. The winner is determined according to a circular formula: the "rock" (fist) blunts the "scissors" (a V-shape), which cut "paper" (flattened palm, held down), which enfolds the "rock."

V540.28, B629.19, P549.31   Sammy Hilbert-Spaess   The double agent of part 2 (see V217.18n).

V540.32–34, B629.24–26, P549.37   a black man . . . His name is St.-Just Grossout   In sixties-era slang "grossout" meant "disgusting" or "revolting"; here, with the man's first name, it also means "revolutionary." In episode 8 of part 4, the burgeoning "counterforce" stages an impromptu disruption at a dinner sponsored by one of "Them," Stefan Utgarthaloki. Specifically they stage what in the sixties became a sort of stoners' parlor game, a "grossout session" in which the goal was to duel verbally in quest of the most disgusting image (see V715.17). In this context it becomes notable that the black radical's first name invokes—as Larsson ("A *Companion*'s Companion") has noted—the French revolutionary Louis-Antoine-Léon de Saint-Just. See V715.17n.

V540.38, B629.32, P550.1   sitrep   A "situation report" or, as Noel's *Naval Terms Dictionary* puts it, "a report required when prescribed conditions exist without reference to the time lapse between occurrences." Exactly.

V541.23, B630.23, P550.28   Say a prayer for the common informer   This song by character "Merciful" Evans riffs on the Rolling Stones's 1970 anthem to the preterite, "Salt of the Earth," from their *Beggar's Banquet* album:

> Let's drink to the hard-working people,
> Let's drink to the lowly of birth;
> Raise your glass to the good and the evil,
> Let's drink to the salt of the earth.
>
> Say a prayer for the common footsoldier,
> Spare a part for his backbreaking work;
> Say a prayer for his wife and his children,
> Who burn the fires and who still till the earth.
>
> When I search a faceless crowd,
> A swirling mass of gray and black-white;
> They don't look real to me,
> In fact they look so tame.
>
> Raise your glass to the hard working people,
> Let's drink to the uncounted heads;
> Let's think of the wavering millions,
> Who need leaders but get gamblers instead . . . [etc.]

V541.24, B630.24, P550.29   a quim   Old-timey British vulgarism for the female genitalia.

V541.27, B630.27, P550.32   Kilkenny to Kew   Kilkenny is a poor county of southwestern Ireland; Kew, an aristocratic district west of London, home of the Royal Botanic Gardens.

V542.13, B631.17, P551.18   Gallaho Mews   Fictional London mews (alley) that is home to the fictional Twelfth House (V217.24n).

V542.39, B632.5–6, P552.3   Smithfield Market   This London square was famous as an execution site and as the home of the Bartholomew Fair from 1150 until 1855; today, it is surrounded by fish, meat, poultry, and produce markets.

V544.8, B633.26, P553.14   living in St. John's Wood   Pirate imagines his lost love, Scorpia Mossmoon, living in this upper-crust district of northwest London. Through it runs Abbey Road, on which the Beatles recorded their first album (at the Abbey Road Studios) and that is home to the famous crosswalk where the band was photographed for the *Abbey Road* album (1969).

V544.33, B634.15, P553.40   sufficient unto the day   "Sufficient unto the day is the evil thereof" (Matt. 6:34).

V545.4–5, B634.30–31, P554.12–13   young Porky Pig holding out the anarchist's ticking bomb   Porky Pig became a popular character from his introduction by Warner Brothers in a 1935 Technicolor cartoon, "I Haven't Got a Hat." In "The Blow Out" (1936) a penny-poor Porky, who wants an ice-cream soda, figures out that he can earn the coin needed for it by returning to people things they drop. Seeing a dark-suited man (who turns out to be the anarchist "Mad Bomber" terrorizing the city) leave behind a clock, Porky tries to return it—tries repeatedly as the Bomber runs to the top of a building, down a manhole, and other places until he ends up hiding in a police paddy wagon and Porky shoves in the bomb—which explodes. Irwin ("A Note on 'Porky Pig and the Anarchist' in *The Crying of Lot 49* and *Gravity's Rainbow*") and Larsson ("A *Companion*'s Companion") both point out that an allusion to this cartoon first appeared in *The Crying of Lot 49*, when Mr. Thoth asks Oedipa Maas about it ("Did you ever see the one about Porky Pig and the anarchist? . . . dressed all in black" [73]). It will be alluded to again in *GR* (see V586.38–39).

V546.24–25, B636.25–26, P555.37–38   Rexist meetings . . . Degrelle   In Belgium, in the late thirties, French separatists under the fanatical leadership of Léon Degrelle organized a fascist brotherhood known as the Rexists. The "realm of total souls" (V546.29) is actual rhetoric from Rexist propaganda, which emphasized a mystical nationalism. Luc Herman adds another interesting gloss. On December 14, 1944, the Rex movie theatre in Antwerp was struck and practically obliterated by a V-2 rocket strike; 567 moviegoers were killed as they watched William Wellman and Maureen O'Hara in a matinee showing of *Buffalo Bill*. While the "Rex" of this allusion refers to a fascist organization, its mention in connection with Antwerp is haunted by the Nazis' destruction of the Rex theatre, thus by the technology of cinema that also haunts *GR* (Herman, "Introduction: Approach and Avoid" 9).

EPISODE 25

This episode opens the day after episode 22, and so most likely the date is August 1. Slothrop continues his trek across northern Germany, near Rostock, about fifty miles from Stralsund. A short analepsis treats his Puritan ancestors, who are satirical representations of Pynchon's own. Slothrop joins up with a young boy looking for his lost lemming, and at episode's end Major Marvy once more crosses his path.

V549.1, B639.16, P558.14   the narrow gassen   "Lanes" in German.

V549.18–20, B639.42–43, P558.28   Vikings . . . sailing this great water-meadow   Because the north German lowlands sloping toward the Baltic Sea offer easy water travel to the south. The region is pockmarked with lakes carved out by receding glaciers of the last ice age, and the rivers offered the Vikings, predecessors of modern travelers, opportunities to sail the Vistula and Bug upriver into territories that the Soviets annexed in

1945. From there—after a portage—they took the Volga, Don, and other rivers right down to the Black Sea.

V549.21–32, B640.1–14, P558.34–559.10   The nationalities are on the move . . . streaming over the surface of the Imperial cauldron   Imagined as a reverse of prior migrations (*Völkerwanderung*) that spread Teutonic peoples throughout Europe and the British Isles, for example in the fourth and fifth centuries, and as the Zone's 1945 version of a "melting pot," we have in this passage an amazing catalogue of displaced persons streaming around occupied Germany; but they are decidedly *not* traditional Germans. Here instead are ethnic Germans. There are Poles who had been brought to Germany (perhaps for forced labor) and who took one side or another in the dispute over the Lublin regime (see V34.28–30n). Alongside them are Sudeten Germans who had been expelled by the millions in 1945 from various Balkan states, just as Germans in East Prussia were expelled as that area was carved up and annexed to Lithuania (the northernmost portion), the Soviet Union (the central region around Königsberg, renamed Kaliningrad), and Poland (the southernmost region). There are also the Lettish speakers from Latvia, "trekking north" with Estonians and Lithuanians (who perhaps collide with those Germans displaced from East Prussia). The Tosks and Ghegs are Albanians, but Christian and Muslim respectively. Vlachs in the Zone have come or been transported from Romania and their streaming melds with that of Bulgars, Czechs, Croats, Serbs, and Slovaks—all of whom have differing ethnic and religious affiliations that have led to long-standing enmities among them. The Circassians have perhaps the longest journey, back to the Caucasus region. The Spaniols would trace their descent from Jews expelled from Spain—Ashkenazik Jews who have migrated around Europe for centuries.

V550.3–7, B640.26–30, P559.20   Kazakh ex-P/Ws marching east . . . pale green farmworker triangles   Still more displaced persons: now, former Soviet fighters (originally from Kazakhstan) taken captive by the Germans and just released, along with Germans for whom these northern European landscapes (of Prussia) are also alien. Some in this mix are agricultural workers. As Allied occupying forces began to organize war-torn Europe after May 8 they devised a system of designating the occupational status of displaced persons with colored triangular cloth patches—a system haunted, certainly, by the Nazis' former practice of differentiating kinds of concentration camp prisoners—i.e., Jews, leftists, homosexuals—with vari-shaped and -colored patches.

V550.14–15, B640.38–40, P559.29–31   stripped by the SS . . . every fucking potato field . . . alcohol for the rockets   A bit of detail whose source was Dornberger (*V-2* 111). He describes the general concern, in 1943, that the SS would be unable to meet the army's need for alcohol to fuel nine hundred rockets per month: "How much alcohol we should have depended on the potato harvest." See also: V640.25–26.

V550.34, B641.21, P560.8 Allgeyer soldiers Johann Baptiste Allgeier (1763–1823) was an Austrian chess master whose writings on the game, and whose designs for the chess pieces, and whose meticulously designed, accurately painted toy soldiers (described in this line and the next) became nineteenth-century standards. Pynchon gives the correct spelling at V675.34–35.

V550.38–39, B641.27, P560.13 Vorsetzer rolls Rolls for the Welte-Vorsetzer brand of mechanical piano player, designed and first produced by inventor Edwin Welte of Freiburg, Germany, in 1904. Popular during the early twentieth century but superseded by internal players, the Vorsetzer was literally (as the German indicates) "set before" one's piano, whence its wooden, felted "fingers" commenced to play tunes coded onto the rolled red paper with holes for a specific composition. Welte's Vorsetzer players and red rolls were distinguished for being able to reproduce a fuller range of piano sounds by controlling the sustaining and softening of the pedals, even the volume.

V550.40, B641.29, P560.15 Jugendstil cups Literally, "youth style," the name for the German and Austrian version of art nouveau (1890–1920), a reaction against impressionism. *Jugendstil* (1896–1914) took its name from the Munich magazine *Jugend* and shared with the art nouveau movement an interest in decorative, often abundant, natural figuration. German, Austrian, and Swiss *Jugendstil* artists were known also for their interest in Germanic mythological motifs and in exotic forms and languid, melancholic expressions of decadence—of sex, death, and resurrection. Examples include the work of artist Gustav Klimt (1862–1918), designer Josef Hoffman (1870–1956), and writer Hugo von Hofmannsthal (1874–1929). *Jugendstil* also involved a strong focus on crafts, on household objects—Hoffman, for example, produced tableware and vases (hence these "cups"). After 1918 it was largely superseded by German expressionism.

V552.4, B642.40, P561.18 "where've you *been*, gate?" Here and throughout *GR*, "gate" is American forties slang indicating a person especially sensitive to swing music. It derives from the expression "to swing like a gate" (to have a sense of jazz). On Bob Hope's wartime radio show, comedian Jerry Colonna used the expression in a variety of rhyming slang greetings, as in "Greetings, gate! Let's deliberate."

V553.4, B644.7, P562.20 bleaching that to paper Recall the etymology of Blicero, the "Bleacher" (see V30.12n).

V553.27, B644.32, P563.4 Ludwig The kid's name recalls mad, suicidal King Ludwig II of Bavaria (V394.23n).

V553.31, B644.37, P563.8 Pritzwalk A town eighty miles south of Rostock.

V553.34, B644.41, P563.11 "One lemming, kid?" A fitting question for Slothrop to ask, given the motif in his sodium amytal nightmare of

episode 10, part 1, and Crutchfield's obsession: "One each of everything" (V67.36). Remember also the quotation from Rilke's ninth elegy:
"Once, only once" (V413.15–16n). Slothrop remarks here the improba-
bility of finding, among the lemming host rushing toward mass suicide,
the *one lemming* that might be saved from among the doomed. And
though the idea of lemmings running to their death is, alas, mythical,
Ursula would in any case be the One saved; thus she points up how Pynchon here begins to reroute the theme of the one, sole survivor figured
in Slothrop's Crutchfield fantasy and the Rilke allusion. Ursula represents the concept of "the saving remnant," in Hebrew the *sheris ha'p-
leyte* from Genesis 45:7. There, Joseph tells his fellow captives in Egypt
that despite their tribulations under Pharaoh, a "remnant" of them will
be saved for a great (and nation-founding) event. This idea has had enormous staying power and is significant in two main ways for readers of
GR. First, historians have long pointed out that the Puritans and other
dissenting protestants emigrating to New England believed deeply that
they themselves were the *sheris ha'pleyte*; also, that their "city upon a
hill" would accomplish in the New World the deliverance Joseph had
envisioned (see for example Cowing's historical study). Second, for Holocaust survivors the concept of themselves as a "saving remnant" gave
hope for a future and made real the prospect, especially, of establishing
Israel. Pynchon probably knew of this context through Herbert Agar's
well-known book of 1962, *The Saving Remnant: An Account of Jewish
Survival*, which was also a likely general source for background material
on the conditions of the Zone's displaced persons (DPs) in the immediate aftermath of V-E Day.

**V554.31–32, B646.3–5, P564.10–11   "what Jesus meant . . . venturing
out on the Sea of Galilee"**   Jesus has just been informed that John
the Baptist's head has been delivered to Herod, as the king ordered.
Thronged by grief-stricken crowds, Jesus works several miracles, healing the sick and feeding the five thousand. That night, his walking on
the water terrifies the disciples, who think he's a ghost. Peter tries it
and, seeing "the wind" on the water, sinks to the bottom, whereupon
Jesus upbraids his faithlessness: "O man of little faith, why did you
doubt?" (Matt. 14:31).

**V554.40–555.5, B646.13–21, P564.19–26   William Slothrop was a pecu-
liar bird . . . and his son John got a pig operation going**   Here Pynchon
begins a fairly close satire of his own seventeenth-century ancestors,
William and John, originally of Writtle, Essex County, England. William
Pynchon (1590–1662) was a moderate sort of Puritan who preferred to
continue his worship in accord with the Episcopal Book of Common
Prayer. He was learned in Latin, Greek, and Hebrew, was prominent in
the business affairs of Essex, and, in 1629, became one of the original
patentees of the Massachusetts Bay Company. With Winthrop, Salton-

stall, and others, Pynchon signed the famous Cambridge Agreement of August 26, 1629, promising they would all migrate to the New World colony and found a Christian commonwealth. Interestingly, William Pynchon was assigned the task of supervising the purchase of weapons for the colonists, and he appears to have become enough of an expert on ordnance that he was able to offer a "narration" on the topic before Governor Winthrop.

William Pynchon did not come to America aboard the *Arbella*, as did his fictional counterpart William Slothrop. Nor did he amass a fortune selling pigs. He did, however, establish the village of Roxbury and then, in 1634–35, the village of Agawam, now Springfield, Massachusetts. At the time, he became the westernmost frontiersman of the colony. With his son John, he commenced to build a sizable wealth through fur trading. Most sources agree that he was able to accomplish this by establishing policies of fair, humane dealings with the neighboring Indians. For further information, see McIntyre (*William Pynchon: Merchant and Colonizer*), Byington ("William Pynchon, Gent."), Winston ("The Quest for Thomas Pynchon"), and Morison ("William Pynchon, the Founder of Springfield").

V555.21–22, B646.41, P565.2   a little early for Isaac Newton   Indeed it was, for the famous physicist wasn't born until 1642, and his second law of motion (the subject here) wouldn't be formulated for another thirty years.

V555.24, B647.2–3, P565.5   his Gadarene swine   The story of how Jesus exorcised the demons from a man of Gadara, sending them into a herd of pigs that promptly plunged over a hillside, appears in Mark 5:1–17 and Luke 8:26–33. No saving remnant here; they're demoniac pigs.

V555.29–31, B647.9–12, P565.10   He wrote a long tract . . . called *On Preterition* . . . burned in Boston   Pynchon continues the satirical history of his own ancestors. While at Agawam, William Pynchon arranged for the private printing, in England, of a 156-page-long quarto volume entitled *The Meritorious Price of Our Redemption,* published by James Moxon of London in 1650. Copies reached Boston in August of that year, and the General Court promptly declared that they "detest and abhorre many of the opinions and assertions therein, as false, erronyous, and hereticale." As punishment, they ordered "the said book to be burned in the market place, at Boston, by the common executioner" (Byington 200–01). The sentence was carried out in October, and one result was that William Pynchon's tract became exceedingly rare; only four copies are extant in U.S. libraries.

The crux of the matter was a rather technical point in Puritan theology, generally related to the Arminian heresy. The orthodox view was that Christ suffered the full extent of hell torments because only thus could he fully discharge the debt of the elect and so secure their heavenly place. The Puritans therefore held that *all* sins of the elect, including their original sin inherited from Adam, were "imputed" to Christ. Only in this way would Christ's punishment fully release the elect from their sinfulness. William Pynchon disagreed. In an elaborate argument set out in dialogue form and laden with scriptural citation, he argued that Christ did not *need* to bear these sins by imputation and so did not suffer the hell torments of God's awful wrath. In closely argued chapters at the end, he held that Christ's obedience was, by definition, always and already perfect; therefore the question of punishing him was unnecessary. Christ's death on the cross was the final test of his total obedience to the Father's will, and so it fully redeemed God's covenants established with Adam after the Fall. Simply put, no need for Christ to harrow Hell, because he, having done God's will on the cross, had *already* redeemed the Damned.

In satirizing this technical point Pynchon has to simplify. Still, he remains faithful to the perceived threat of his ancestor's writings. *The Meritorious Price of Our Redemption* was banned because it undercut the doctrine of Puritan sainthood, with its absolute separation of elect from preterite. William Pynchon's argument implied that anyone might have access to divine grace, and that Christ died for elect and preterite alike. In thereby opening the doors, it might even be necessary, as Thomas Pynchon writes three hundred years later, "to love Judas too" (V555.40), even to extend that loving grace to animals such as the dodo (see V111.7–9).

V556.1, B647.26, P565.24   did finally 86 him out   See V21.36n.

V556.3–4, B647.29, P565.26   he sailed back to Old England   Frustrated with the legal proceedings against him, William Pynchon transferred the Springfield lands and businesses to his son John and, in 1652, sailed back to England where he retired to an estate in Wraysbury, Buckinghamshire. There he continued his theological writings. A 450-page defense of the 1650 tract appeared in 1655. He also wrote tracts on the Sabbath, another one entitled *The Jewes Synagogue* (1652), and another describing in elaborate detail God's covenant of grace with Adam (1662), a reprise of many of the arguments put forth in the "hereticale" tract of 1650.

V556.19, B648.5–6, P566.2   that anarchist he meet in Zürich   This was Francisco Squalidozzi (V263.16).

V557.19, B649.12, P567.2   Michaeliskirche   The Church of St. Michael, but many northern European towns have one by that name, and this particular one is unspecified.

V557.20, B649.14, P567.3   a Sterno fire   Sterno was the American brand of "canned heat." "Sterno fires" were tiny tins of paraffin fuel doled out to servicemen.

EPISODE 26

The time picks up from that of the previous episode: so, early August. Slothrop, in his next disguise—that of a Russian officer—bluffs his way through an encounter with Major Duane Marvy and a character from Pynchon's first novel, Clayton ("Bloody") Chiclitz (who takes his name from the Chiclets brand of American chewing gum, from which "Chiclets" also became commonplace street slang for "teeth"). Learning of Marvy's plans to raid the nearby encampment of the Schwarzkommando, Slothrop warns the Hereros away. He also gives Andreas Orukumbe a summary of what is known, thus far in the narrative text, about the firing of Rocket 00000.

V557.30–31, B649.26–27, P567.15   a Russian accent . . . like Bela Lugosi Or, more precisely, a voice with a molasses-slow, heavy middle European accent; American actor Bela Lugosi (1888–1956) was born in Hungary and spoke with an especially pronounced accent in his early roles such as when he played the count in Tod Browning's *Dracula* (1931) and Legendre in his *White Zombie* (1933).

V558.3, B649.38, P567.25   old Bloody Chiclitz A refugee from Pynchon's first two novels. In chapter 8 of *V.*, set in 1955, Chiclitz has become "president of Yoyodyne Incorporated, a company with factories scattered careless about the country and more government contracts that it really knew what to do with." By *The Crying of Lot 49*, set in 1966, Yoyodyne has burgeoned from this (1945) toy factory into an international cartel. His family name calls up Chiclets, invented by chewing-gum maker Henry Fleer and first marketed in 1906. Looking for a name to give his peppermint candy-coated gum squares, Fleer, head of a subsidiary of American Chicle Company, showed it around to others who dubbed it a "Chiclet." The name stuck, the product sold well, and by the 1930s the word had entered American slang: teeth became known as "chiclets," and a tough-guy threatening to give another a punch in the face might say: "How would you like a mouthful of bloody chiclets?" Hence this character's name.

V558.9–10, B650.7, P567.30–31   arms around each other's shoulders, two smiling fat men A visual allusion to Tweedledum and Tweedledee in their famous pose.

V558.15–20, B650.14–20, P568.1–5   equator-crossing festivities. . . . the Royal Baby. . . . the polliwogs' hair Aboard ship, those who have not previously made an equatorial crossing, the "polliwogs," are subjected to playful rites of humiliation, presided over by the gluttonous "Royal Baby," to whom they make their obeisance. Pynchon would have known this ritual from his own naval service aboard the USS *Hank*.

V558.21, B650.21–22, P568.6   the T-Force Military abbreviation for the

Technical Force; in this case the bureaucracy that includes SPOG, CIOS, and so on.

V559.11–14, B651.17–20, P568.37–40   Cecil B. De Mille . . . rowin' old Henry Wilcoxon   American film director Cecil B. DeMille (1881–1959) spotted tall, rugged Henry Wilcoxon (1905–84) on the English stage and brought him to Hollywood in 1934, where he played Mark Antony to Claudette Colbert's Cleopatra in the epical film *Cleopatra*. That is the referent of Marvy's allusion: "rowin' old Henry Wilcoxon away into th' sunset to fight them Greeks or Persians" is an image from DeMille's epic (see also V18.8–38).

V559.16–17, B651.22–23, P569.1–2   "For De Mille, young fur-henchmen can't be rowing!"   The most elaborately staged pun in all of *GR*. Camouflaged within it is the declaration "forty million Frenchmen can't be wrong," itself a variation on a phrase attributed to actress, speakeasy owner, and dance girl Texas Guinan (see V657.10–11n), who grabbed it from a popular phrase during the Great War, "fifty million Frenchmen can't be wrong," a phrase that became the title of a 1927 hit song by jazz singer Sophie Tucker. In 1931 Guinan attempted to take a troupe of forty-two girls to Paris, where she hoped to open a nightclub free from Prohibitionism and the harassments of J. Edgar Hoover's G-men. However, French officials refused to let the troupe disembark. Legal proceedings commenced, during which it became clear from the popular outcry that French males were delighted to have the Americans. Nevertheless, after ten days Texas and her girls were deported. Arriving back in New York on March 21, 1931, they were met by throngs of well-wishers and reporters. Texas proclaimed (getting the number wrong): "Forty million Frenchmen can't be wrong" about a sexy display of skin. Her saying stuck and has since been taken to comment in general on the (supposed) sexual preferences of Frenchmen. Note that Pynchon has fashioned an entire narrative digression about illicit trading in furs, oarsmen in boats, fur henchmen, and DeMille—all of it in order to launch this pun.

V559.30, B651.38, P569.15   muttering *da, da*   "Yes, yes" (Russian).

V559.36–37, B652.4–5, P569.21–22   Marvy bellowing "San Antonya Rose," his fav'rite song   Written in 1941 by Bob Wills, of Bob Wills and the Texas Playboys, the song "San Antonio Rose" remains a perennial favorite:

Deep within my heart lies a melody,
A song of old San Antone,
Where in dreams I live with a memory,
Beneath the stars all alone.

It was there I found beside the Alamo,
Enchantment strange as the blue up above;

A moonlit path that only she would know,
Still hears my broken song of love.

Moon in all your splendor, know only my heart,
Call back my Rose, Rose of San Antone!
Lips so sweet and tender, like the petals falling apart,
Speak once again of my love, my own.

Broken songs, empty words I know,
Still live in my heart all alone,
For that moonlit path, by the Alamo,
And Rose, my Rose of San Antone.

V560.5–6, B652.16–18, P569.31–32   Everything's been stripped . . . back to the hollow design envelopes of their earliest specs   Yet another hysteron proteron figure in *GR*. A "design envelope" is a rough-draft specification for basic design qualities and features of a product.

V560.21, B652.36, P570.6   "the Soviet CIC"   The Soviet's counterintelligence corps.

V560.25, B652.41–42, P570.11   holding up the mandala, cross to vampire   According to folk tradition, vampires will shrink away from a cross. In the Zone it is the KEZVH mandala, from the rocket, that works a spell against evil; it is thus another sign of redemptive sacrifice.

V561.26, B654.8, P571.12   LOOK-IN FAWR A NEEDLE IN A HAAAAY-STACK!   A song written by Con Conrad and Herb Magidson for a Fred Astaire–Ginger Rogers musical film, *The Gay Divorcee* (1934), in which Astaire, playing American dancer Guy Holden on vacation in England, through a mishap meets Mimi Glossop (Rogers) at a train station, regrets not getting her name and despairs of ever finding her again. It turns out she wants a divorce from her boring geologist husband, and after a series of mistaken identities gets it—and Guy Holden too. Early on, Holden (Astaire) sings the following song in despair of seeing her again:

It's just like looking for a needle in a haystack
Searching for a moonbeam in the blue
Still I've got to find you

It's just like looking for a raindrop in the ocean
Searching for a dewdrop in the dew
Still I've got to find you

I'll roam the town, in hope that we'll meet
Look at each face, I pass on the street
Sometimes I feel the beat of your feet
But it's just my imagination

'Though it's like looking for a needle in a haystack
Still I'll follow everything you do
'Cause I've got to find you.

This is why, in lines that follow, our narrator imagines Astair "reflecting on his chances of ever finding Ginger Rogers again."

V562.1, B645.23, P571.26   searchin' for a (hmm) cellar full of saffron
Slothrop, here, trying to recall the lyrics from *The Gay Divorcee* (above), fumbles—it seems—into the keyword in the opening line of a sixties pop hit, "Mellow Yellow" (1966), by Donovan (Leitch), with Beatle Paul McCartney singing backup: "I'm just mad about saffron / She's just mad about me / [repeat] / They call me mellow yellow / Quite rightly." After its release a widespread countercultural rumor had it that the song was about releasing hallucinogenic compounds from bananas by scraping fiber from the skins into a hot frying pan, then inhaling the fumes. None of it was true.

V562.7, B654.31, P571.31–33   a thumb-harp   Also known as a "finger-piano," comparable to the "thumb-piano" widely played in Africa, from where it migrated, but here, with a "German pine" soundbox and metal "reeds" fashioned from the springs of a "wrecked Volkswagen"—so, a very *large* version of the African original.

V562.25, B655.13, P572.11   "Where Mukuru wants us to go"   See V321.40–322.1n.

V563.6–11, B655.38–656.2, P572.33–38   "In our villages the women lived . . . on the northern half . . . men on the south . . . in the center . . . the sacred cattle"   On the traditional mandala-like arrangement of the Herero village, see V321.3–4n.

V563.24–25, B656.19, P573.11   A mezuzah   In Judaism, a small roll of parchment inscribed with the words from Deut. 6:4–9 and 11:13–21, invoking faith in Yahweh as the one God. Inside its small container, a mezuzah was assumed to work as an amulet against evil.

EPISODE 27

Later that evening, around midnight, Marvy, Chiclitz, and Tchitcherine huddle, apparently after attacking the Schwarzkommando encampment and finding their quarry has fled. They discuss how and why (see also V611.10–11). We get some technical information about Rocket 00000, and Marvy drops the names of some prominent American businessmen-politicians.

V563.29, B656.24–25, P573.15   Audie Murphy style   America's most decorated World War II soldier (he was awarded twenty-four medals), handsome young Murphy (b. 1924) became a Hollywood actor in 1948 and played in a handful of cowboy and war films before dying in a 1971 plane crash at the age of forty-seven.

V564.3, B656.38–657.1, P573.26 More precious than Ravenna The coastal city of northern Italy, here recalled for its beautifully intricate mosaics.

V564.31–32, B657.36, P574.18 visas to far Lemuria, to the sun-resorts of Sargasso Named for the lemures of Roman myth (they were terrifying specters of the dead), Lemuria was, like Atlantis (V269.9–10n), thought to be a sunken land between East Africa and India. On the opposite coast, between the Azores and the West Indies, the calm expanse of the Atlantic Ocean known as the Sargasso Sea grows vast, island-like masses of seaweed, sites of these fanciful "resorts" for dead sailors.

V564.37–38, B658.1–2, P574.24–25 si me quieres escribir you already know where I'll be staying Larsson ("A *Companion*'s Companion") identifies the source as a song from the Spanish Civil War that would have been sung by a loyalist fighter:

If you want to write to me
You know where you can always find me. [Repeat]
On the broad front of Gandesa
The front line of every battle.

See also V605.37–38n.

V565.11, B658.18, P574.40 "Dillon, Reed . . . Standard Awl" Pynchon's source for these references is Sasuly (*IG Farben*, ch. 9, esp. 197, 205). He details the economic forces that in the twenties brought IG Farben into a collision course with Standard Oil of New Jersey. Standard had a heavy stake in Europe, with subsidiary refineries in England, Denmark, Germany, and Italy. At the same time, the IG Farben cartel had developed a process for retrieving gasoline from hydrogenated coal, a process that might well have wrecked Standard's refining interests in coal-rich, oil-poor Europe. So the two monoliths struck an agreement: Standard Oil agreed to stay out of research into hydrogenation, while IG Farben agreed to shelve its plans for hydrogenation refineries. A crucial side effect, Sasuly argues, was a shortage of rubber goods in Allied countries during the first years of the war, a shortage that had no impact on Germany because IG Farben had continued with plans to manufacture butyl rubber from hydrogenated coal. And butyl rubber was vital for tires and other machine products necessary to conduct the Panzer Army's Blitzkrieg attacks. After V-E Day, the Truman Committee investigating these and similar corporate agreements reported that the policies of Standard Oil made Germany's initial military successes possible. And even as the Truman Committee was opening its inquiry—indeed, as early as June 1945—Standard Oil was actively assisting IG Farben in its recovery from the war, evidence that the cartel arrangements were in effect before, during, and after hostilities. One way the Standard/Farben agreements were maintained was through the work of General William Draper, who had worked at the Wall Street firm of Dillon, Reed and Company. As head of the Army Economics Division in occupied Europe, Draper was meant to have directed efforts to "de-Nazify" German industry. Instead, claims Sasuly, he probably headed the effort to reaffirm the old cartel arrangements.

Moore (*The Style of Connectedness* 143–46) has also located an important source in J. S. Martin's *All Honorable Men* (1950), a book that examines—from the viewpoint of an investigator on the ground in postwar Germany—the same business ties but that supplies other notable details, for example, Martin's recollections of a late-May 1945 journey to retrieve hidden documents at Bad Sachsa, "a few miles from the Devil's Pulpit on the Brocken, a traditional site of the Witches' Sabbath" (Moore 144).

V565.19–20, B658.27–28, P575.7–8   "Herbert Hoover . . . He came over and *fed* you people"   When the United States entered the Great War, President Wilson appointed Herbert Hoover to head the Food Administration, where he oversaw the distribution of almost nineteen million tons of foodstuffs to famine-stricken areas of western Europe. After the armistice was signed, he coordinated relief projects in Austria, Hungary, Armenia, and Russia, raising over $250 million for food and aid.

V565.24–26, B658.32–34, P575.12–14   "Mister Swope was ace buddies with old FDR . . . Electric Charlie's in there now . . . one-thim Brain Trusters. Jews, most of 'm."   Gerard Swope (1877–1957) worked first of all for Western Electric, then for General Electric. In 1922 he became president of the company. But in fact there were two Swopes: Herbert Bayard Swope (1882–1958) was Gerard's younger brother; he was the one-time head of the *New York World* newspaper and was more an "ace buddy" to Roosevelt than Gerard. Franklin D. Roosevelt's "Brain Trust" was formed during the 1932 campaign around a nucleus of Columbia University professors: Rexford Guy Tugwell, Adolf Berle, and Raymond Moley. Hugh Johnson, financial adviser to Bernard M. Baruch, was added later, and Gerard Swope was loosely associated with the group. In *GR*, Major Marvy's anti-Semitism stands out here; for Swope, Moley, and Berle were Jewish (though nonobservant). "Electric Charley" is a reference to the founder of General Electric, Charles Coffin (V332.5–6n).

V565.36, B659.5, P575.24   Carl Schmitz of the IG   Unknown or else fictional. Sasuly (*IG Farben* 101, 165) does mention Hermann and Dietrich Schmitz, both associated with IG Farben for decades, but neither had any connection to the German-based Siemens manufacturing company, mentioned here.

V566.1–2, B659.13–14, P575.32–33   his Eleanor Roosevelt routine . . . "my son Idiot—uh, Elliot"   Elliot Roosevelt (1910–90) was Franklin and Eleanor Roosevelt's fourth child. He came out of the war a brigadier general for his work with a photo-reconnaissance squadron of the U.S. Army Air Force. He had a reputation for being the family maverick; his son Elliot Jr. (b. 1936) is known for his string of mystery novels starring grandmother Eleanor as the detective (*The Hyde Park Murder* [1985] and *Murder in the West Wing* [1992], for example) in some of which characters like Joe Kennedy appear.

V566.14, B659.28, P576.4 **a very large white Finger** Appears to be a reprise of Adam Smith's "invisible hand" that guides the marketplace of laissez-faire capitalism (see V30.30n). This hand, however, also makes an obscene gesture.

EPISODE 28

At a town "near Wismar" (V567.32) in northern Germany, Slothrop adopts the last of his disguises or alter egos before part 4, when he fragments. From internal allusions the time of this episode would seem to be Thursday and Friday, August 2–3, 1945, although it is about here that the novel's chronology becomes more impressionistic. As Plechazunga, a (seemingly) fictional pig hero, Slothrop finds himself in the midst of a raid. He escapes, leaves yet another young girl beneath a rainbow archway, takes up with Franz Pökler's pig, Frieda, and as the episode ends meets Pökler himself.

V567.20, B661.7–8, P577.15 **the Askania films of Rocket flights** See V407.3–4n.

V567.22, B661.10–11, P577.18 **Treppengiebel shapes** The "step gables" of the houses.

V567.24–25, B661.13–14, P577.20 **playing Himmel and Hölle** Heaven and Hell, a popular German version of the children's game of hopscotch. Peesch, in his *Berliner Kinderspiel* (22–28) describes it as follows: the playing area is chalked out to form a cross, around which are drawn ten squares in all; children start play from a zero area called *Erde* (Earth), hop through the numbered squares with increasingly more difficult moves, the ninth (*Hölle*) being the hardest. The tenth square (*Himmel*) is home. It's a striking image, given the prevalence throughout *GR* of crosses, the number ten, and the desire to return "home."

V567.31, B661.21–22, P577.27 **singing Laterne, Laterne, Sonne, Mond und Sterne** The call in another German children's game, described again in Peesch as a form of hide-and-seek. The sun (*Sonne*) must catch the other children, who are the stars (*Sterne*), and bring them back to a holding area, usually a lantern post (*Laterne*). The moon (*Mond*) is a player who has the power to release those captives by invading the home base and pulling them out. The Opies mention the contest rules in *Children's Games* (173–74); Peesch (42–43) refers to the game as *Englische Versteckspiele,* or "English hide-and-seek."

V567.33, B661.23–24, P577.29   near Wismar   Slothrop has traveled to a point about fifteen miles southeast of Rostock. This unnamed coastal town with its Peterskirche and Roland Statue—common features in many northern German towns—is not specifically identifiable.

V567.34, B661.25–26, P577.30   Plechazunga, the Pig-Hero   This name apparently derives from a page of etymological ramblings in Grimm (178): "The lightning's flash, which we name *blitz,* was expressed in our older speech both by the simple *plih* . . . and by *plechazunga* . . . derived from *plechazan,* a frequentive of *plechan.* A Prussian folk-tale has an expressive phrase for the lightning: '*He with the blue whip chases* the devil,' i.e. the giants; for a blue flame was held especially sacred." In a footnote on the page Grimm adds: "While writing *plechazan,* I remember *pleckan* (pateria, nudari, bleak), MHG [Middle High German] blecken, blacte . . . which, when used of the sky, means: the clouds open, heaven opens, as we will say of forked and sheet lightning." Simply put, *plechazunga* belongs to a complex of Germanic words associated with Thor (Donnar, Thunar), whose weapon is lightning. The "Pig-Hero" business is Pynchon's fiction, but note that this *Schweinheldfest* occurs on a Thursday (Thor's Day), which is consistent with the details in Grimm. Also, note that this hero was not "tamed," that is, was not translated from the pagan into a Christian context, "into St. Peter or Roland," even though the ceremony does occur near the Roland Statue and Peterskirche mentioned above.

V568.6, B661.38–39, P577.40   Schraub the shoemaker   His moniker derives from the German noun "*Schraube,*" a screw.

V568.7–8, B661.40, P577.41–578.1   drafted last winter into the Volksgrenadier   Hitler's Home Guard or "People's Infantry," made up of old men and boys.

V568.36, B662.29, P578.29   a Wilhelm Busch original   Reminiscent of Busch's comic-strip characters (see V501.10n).

V569.2, B662.38, P578.36   "Well, Haferschleim is better than none, ho, ho"   This is Slothrop punning in the manner of Groucho Marx. *Haferschleim* is a gruel or porridge made from oats. And thus we have Pynchon still riffing on the earlier half-a-loaf and half-an-Ark allusions (see V14.7n, V68.1n).

V569.16, B663.13–14, P579.9–10   Quark . . . Gold-brown Kartoffelpuffer   Respectively, curds packed sausage-style in tubes and fried potato cakes.

V569.26, B663.26–27, P579.20   an hour's game of hammer-and-forge   In a sexual pun, our narrator uses the name of a German pub game, often known as *Glocke und Hammer,* to figure Slothrop's ideal escapade with not one but "TWO healthy young ladies."

V569.41, B664.4, P579.37   Plattdeutsch   The north German dialect spoken in these low-country areas, Rostock or Lüneburg, for example.

V570.3, B664.8, P579.40   Gemütlichkeit   Coziness, comfort.

V570.6, B664.10–11, P580.1–2   charabancs full of bluegreen uniforms   Figures a parody of the Keystone Cop routines of silent film fame. The uniformed "coppers," with their "starburst" badges, show up in two open buses (the French *char à bancs* is an open carriage with bench seats). Brutal pandemonium ensues.

V570.28, B664.37, P580.23   that erste Abreibung   The noun "*Abreibung*" (rubdown) used figuratively—"the first beating."

V571.26, B666.2, P581.22   dossed down   In underworld cant, to "doss down" is to sleep somewhere; during the thirties, drifters through depressed America would search out a cheap "doss-house" for the night (Partridge, *Macmillan Dictionary*).

V571.28–29, B666.5–6, P581.24–25   *Die Welt am Montag* . . . the Buchdrucherverband   The first is a weekly news magazine published in Berlin. The second involves a slight misspelling of the German: it should be *Buchdruckerverband*, literally, the Printer's Union.

V571.31–32, B666.8–9, P581.28   the German Wobbly traditions   In the early decades of this century "Wobbly" was the slang term given to the Industrial Workers of the World, a Socialist labor organization.

V572.30, B667.15, P582.26   "There's no moon"   The moon entered its last quarter on July 31 (see V506.37n); by August 2 the thin sliver of a moon did not rise over Europe until after 1:00 A.M. Earlier in the evening, as here, no moon would be visible.

V572.39, B667.25, P582.35   the Tauschzentrale   A bazaar; see V366.3n.

V573.11, B667.40–41, P583.7   through the ogival opening   That is, under a vaulted arch, whose "stairsteps" recall the narrator's earlier discussion of projectile calculus (V567.13–24). Notice that the young woman "makes no move to step through the arch" (V573.13–14) with Slothrop. One inference must be that his is no quest "over the rainbow," no joint venture—as in *The Wizard of Oz*—founded, like skipping Dorothy's, on mutual risk and compassion. Instead, Slothrop's journey takes him *under* the rainbow, alone.

V573.19–20, B668.7, P583.16   a Winkelhaken   Brand name of an Austrian printing press; perhaps here referring to the composing stick used by typesetters working on one.

V573.21, B668.8, P583.17   "You're a May bug"   An engaging metaphor for Tyrone Slothrop. The May bug, or cockchafer (*Melolontha melolontha*), emerges from its chrysalis in April or May, whence it commences to devastate the vegetation of Europe.

V575.14–16, B670.13–14, P585.10–12   pines thick with shreds of tinfoil, a cloud of British window . . . to fox the German radars   This detail stems from Irving (*Mare's Nest* 88–89): "At noon [on July 24, 1943]

Hitler raged at his Air Force experts for their incompetence; owing to the first use of *Window* by the R.A.F., their losses had been unusually low . . . the British had introduced a technique feared for a long time— dropping showers of metal foil; as a result, all radar except *Freya* had been jammed." Incidentally, the pig at Slothrop's side is named Frieda, for the Teutonic goddess Freya (see V398.19n).

V575.24–26, B670.24–27, P585.20–22   They fall asleep . . . waiting for morning and a child to claim him   According to an old Germanic folk belief, to dream in a pigsty will cause the dream to come true (Grimm, *Teutonic Mythology* 1146).

V576.35, B671.40, P586.31   "an aromatic polyimide"   From a class of film-forming plastics. This, however, is little help in specifying what Imipolex G actually *is*, for the handbooks advise that there are approximately 6.4×10^{15} theoretically possible molecular products of the reaction used to produce these plastics.

EPISODE 29

Insofar as the chronology is specified and trustworthy, this would be Friday, August 3, 1945. In response to Slothrop's questions about Laszlo Jamf and Imipolex G, Franz Pökler launches a lengthy digression that includes his thoughts about German expressionist cinema and his recollections of chemistry lectures by Jamf while Pökler was getting his technical schooling at Munich. The episode concludes with Jamf's fascist theories of chemical physics.

V577.10, B672.18, P587.7   "On D-Day"   June 6, 1944.

V577.28, B673.1, P587.25   back at the T.H.   The Technische Hochschule, in Munich.

V577.29, B673.2, P587.26   "the lion"   At this time in *GR*, action occurs under the astrological sign of Leo (July 22–August 21).

V578.7–9, B673.19–22, P588.4–6   Klein-Rogge was carrying . . . Brigitte Helm in *Metropolis*   A reference to Fritz Lang's film of 1927. Kracauer (*From Caligari to Hitler* 162–64) gives a helpful summary: downtrodden workers tend mammoth machines underneath a city of skyscrapers and lively streets. Brigitte Helm plays Maria, a young woman who—for the workers—stands as a symbol of saintly comfort, of heart. Rudolf Klein-Rogge plays an inventor, Rothwang, who constructs a robot Maria and then uses it to incite the workers, giving the bureaucratic leaders a pretext to crush the nascent dissent. The film thus develops into an allegory of the higher mind triumphing over heart, of a fascist and masculine reason coldly ruling over a feminine and irrational mass culture. In the key scene, Maria goes to the industrialists' office complex high above the city and there attempts to mediate between management and the work-

ers. But the compromise she achieves works mainly to the benefit of
Freder, the industrialist. As Kracauer (164) puts it, "The whole composition denotes that the industrialist acknowledges the heart for the purpose of manipulating it." Pynchon's image of the "magnificent-looking
suits" (V578.14–15) can be checked against a still photo that is illustration 27 in Kracauer's book.

Moreover, as C. A. Rothwang "der Erfinder" (inventor), Klein-Rogge
plays a significantly *doubled* figure. His inventions virtually *make* the
glories of Metropolis. Yet he also plays the deeply disturbed modern
man, nostalgic for premodern agrarianism and mysticism; indeed, he
figures an irrationality tipping toward madness, which is the flip side
of the city's thoroughgoing rationalization. Responsible for running
Metropolis, he lives outside of it, in a cottage adorned with symbols
out of European mystical traditions, and from there he plots the city's
destruction. In this sense, Rothwang's character capsulizes the split psyche of Nazi fascism: overhyped modernity and folkish nostalgia packed
together in such a way as to produce destructive impulses.

V578.22–23, B673.39, P588.20–21   whatever Käthe Kollwitz saw   At the
time of this fictional episode she may have been seeing it (death) again,
for the German artist Käthe Schmidt Kollwitz (b. 1867) died on August
22, 1945, at the age of seventy-eight. She was known principally as a
printmaker and a masterful draftsman, secondarily as a sculptor. Here
Pynchon has in mind a series of sketches she did from 1903 to 1935 on
the theme of death. One of these she transformed into a poster commemorating the murder of socialist Karl Liebknecht (see V621.40n). Carl
Zigrosser (*Prints and Drawings of Käthe Kollwitz* xviii) describes the
rest of the fifteen-drawing sequence as "a process or dance of death in
the grand tradition—visions of death violent and death serene." The
picture that Pynchon specifically means, imaging a "lean Death" swooping down "to hump Its women from behind," belongs to the violent category. In the Zigrosser edition of her work it is plate 71, "Death Seizes a
Woman." The subject's one visible eye is riveted ahead, her mouth open
in the beginning of a scream. The featureless, bony figure of Death is virtually sexless, an "It" that has wrapped lean but muscular arms around
her breast in a sure embrace.

**V578.25–26, B673.42–674.1, P588.23–24   deeper excursions into the
Mare Nocturnum**   That is, into the "Night Sea" (Latin).

**V578.31–33, B674.7–10, P588.29–31   Attila the Hun . . . come west out
of the steppes to smash . . . the Burgundians**   The reference is to Fritz
Lang's 1924 film *Die Nibelungen*, produced in two parts, *Siegfried* and
Kriemhild's Revenge. In the first Siegfried fights Fafnir the dragon and
proposes marriage to Kriemhild (sister to the Burgundian king, Günther),
Hagen uses a "magic hood" to trick Brunhild into marrying Günther,
and Siegfried dies as a result of another of Hagen's greedy schemes. In
the second film Kriemhild marries the barbarian chieftain, Attila, and

encourages him to sweep out of the east and lay waste to the Burgundian stronghold. See Kracauer (91–93).

V579.9, B674.31–33, P589.7–8   Klein-Rogge . . . as Dr. Mabuse   In Lang's 1924 film *Doktor Mabuse der Spieler*.

V579.10, B674.32, P589.8   Hugo Stinnes   See V284.23n.

V579.21–22, B675.3–5, P589.19   Bernhardt Goetzke as State Prosecutor von Wenk . . . Death in *Der Müde Tod*   As von Wenk in Doktor Mabuse, actor Bernhardt Goetzke (1884–1964) plays the public prosecutor charged with tracking down the sinister hypnotist and criminal. Wenk enlists the help of "the degenerate Countess Told, while Mabuse relies on his mistress, Cara Carozza" (Kracauer 81–82). But Mabuse falls in love with the countess and ravishes her, much as the narrator describes it here. For a plot summary of *Der Müde Tod* see V516.22n.

V579.30, B675.15, P589.29   Agfa plate   A photographic plate manufactured by Agfa of Berlin, a subsidiary of IG Farben. Note that Mabuse, as a "savage throwback" unpicturable on that plate, stands as another instance of hysteron proteron: here, a regression to primal savagery.

V579.36, B675.22–23, P589.34–35   white light, ruins of Atlantis   The reference is to Georg Wilhelm Pabst's 1932 film *Die Herren von Atlantis* (*Mistress of Atlantis*) shot with the blazing white sands of northern Africa as the backdrop (Kracauer 242).

V580.5–6, B675.34, P590.4   they sang *Semper sit in flores*   The narrator translates the Latin a few lines further: "be he always in flower." It's a line from the student song "Gaudeamus igitur" (see V432.13n).

V580.12–13, B676.1, P590.11   IG's Stickstoff Syndikat   Nitrogen syndicate. Levy (*Industrial Germany* 71–72) provides the context. IG Farben's interests in synthetic nitrogen production for use in fertilizers (and later, explosives) intensified during the 1920s and took shape as a horizontal and vertical monopoly entailing both processing and distribution as well as price fixing in European markets.

V580.15–16, B676.4–5, P590.14–15   scrawled C—H on his chalkboard . . . Si—N   The chemical notations for covalent bonds of carbon and hydrogen and of silicon and nitrogen. As the narrator notes, silicon is just below carbon on the periodic table of the elements, so it has the same valence.

EPISODE 30

A flashback concerning Lyle Bland, Slothrop's uncle, who conspired in selling the child to Laszlo Jamf. Bland's connections with the Masons and his attraction to Rosicrucian mysticism form, with pinball, the main focus of this episode.

V580.29–32, B676.20–23, P590.28–31   Just as there are, in the World machineries committed to injustice as an enterprise . . . at least in the

dance of things This passage paraphrases a quote from Ralph Waldo Emerson that Pynchon would use in *Vineland* (369). There, the character Jess Traverse quotes the Emerson from William James's *The Varieties of Religious Experience*, who got it from Emerson's 1878 essay, "The Sovereignty of Ethics." It warns that despite anything powerful men might do to avoid it, retribution nevertheless comes, even in "secret," and restores a "natural" balance. The Emerson:

> The idea of right exists in the human mind, and lays itself out in the equilibrium of Nature, in the equalities and periods of our system, in the level of seas, in the action and reaction of forces. Nothing is allowed to exceed or absorb the rest; if it do, it is disease, and is quickly destroyed. It was an early discovery of the mind,—this beneficent rule. Strength enters just as much as the moral element prevails. The strength of the animal to eat and to be luxurious and to usurp is rudeness and imbecility. The law is: To each shall be rendered his own. As thou sowest, thou shalt reap. Smite, and thou shalt smart. Serve, and thou shalt be served. If you love and serve men, you cannot, by any hiding or stratagem, escape the remuneration. Secret retributions are always restoring the level, when disturbed, of the Divine justice. It is impossible to tilt the beam. All the tyrants and proprietors and monopolists of the world in vain set their shoulders to heave the bar. Settles for evermore the ponderous equator to its line, and man and mote and star and sun must range with it, or be pulverized by the recoil.

In the case of Lyle Bland, who (among other things) apparently sold Slothrop into bondage, the balancing (here) comes through his affiliation with the Masons.

V581.24–25, B677.22, P591.24–25   commodity and retail, Harriman and Weinberg A contrast between old wealth and the nouveau riche, with hints of anti-Semitism. Sidney James Weinberg (1891–1969) was an investment broker and a member of the Business Advisory Council from 1933 to 1969. On Harriman, see below.

V581.29–30, B677.27–28, P591.29–30   Business Advisory Council . . . Swope of General Electric During the Great Depression, the Business Advisory Council was organized under the U.S. Chamber of Commerce, headed by Henry I. Harriman (1872–1950) of the venerable New England Harrimans. Gerard Swope, then the president of General Electric (see V565.24–26n), was also a member. In 1933 the council put forward a group of proposals, known as "The Swope Plan," calling for industry-wide controls on production and prices.

V581.34–35, B677.34, P591.35   the Alien Property Custodian This functionary was empowered to seize and redistribute assets of aliens for reasons of war, nonpayment of taxes, violations of immigration laws, and the like. During World War I, the APC seized many German firms, the IG Farben subsidiaries among them, shortly after the United States joined the hostilities in 1917. However, as Sasuly argues (*IG Farben*

178–83), seizure was one thing; not removing managers at those firms with ties to IG Farben was another. By failing to replace upper-management figures at seized firms, the APC made it easy for IG Farben to rebuild the old cartel arrangements during the twenties and thirties.

V581.41, B677.42, P591.41   Glitherius Paint & Dye, a Berlin firm   An apparently fictional company, its name of unknown origin.

V582.3–5, B678.5–7, P592.2–6   Bland got cash, securities . . . the same Pflaumbaum Franz Pökler worked for   See V159.38–39. The Bantam contains a misprint: "Frank Pökler."

V582.28–29, B678.36, P592.29–30   the annual Veiled Prophet Ball   During the November to January "season," a debutante living in St. Louis would hope to be presented at the Veiled Prophet Ball, the Midwest's most glamorous and exclusive cotillion. But there is more. In Masonry, the "Veiled Prophet" is Christ. According to Masonic scholar Albert Pike (839–40), Moses purified and "re-veiled" the "Occult Science of the Ancient Magi" when he brought down the tablets of stone: "He covered them with a new veil, when he made of the Holy Kabbalah the exclusive heritage of the people of Israel, and the inviolable secret of its Priests." But Jerusalem lost that occult wisdom through centuries of worshipping false gods imported by Syrians and Babylonians. But then Jesus, "a Prophet announced to the Magi by the consecrated Star of Initiation, came to rend asunder the worn veil of the old Temple, in order to give the Church a new tissue of legends and symbols, that still and ever conceals from the Profane, and ever preserves to the Elect the same truths." In addition, these secrets are only fully revealed to Masonic adepts in their last or "Thirty-Second Degree" of initiation (recall that part 3 of *GR* has thirty-two episodes).

V582.39, B679.7–8, P592.41   the Nieman-Marcus bowl, the Bauhaus-style furniture   The bowl is from Neiman-Marcus (misspelled in all three editions), the Dallas-based chain of specialty department stores with branches throughout the United States. The furniture is a mass-produced version of the high modernist designs generated from the German Bauhaus Institut, founded in 1919 and dedicated to functional and experimental designs in architecture and household furniture and products.

V582.40–41, B679.9–10, P593.1–2   little HO trains . . . cans 'n' reefers   The HO is one of two standardized sizes or gauges of toy railroad trains that emerged from British and U.S. manufacturers in the late twenties: HO was manufactured to 1/87 scale; OO to 1/76; and, in the lingo, "cans" are tank cars while "reefers" are refrigerator cars.

V583.3–4, B679.14–15, P593.6   "Even Laurel & Hardy doesn't work"   To make him smile, that is. On this comic duo of American cinema, see V375.31–32n.

V583.13, B679.27, P593.15   Mouthorgan, Missouri   Fictional town named after the harmonica.

V583.21–24, B679.36–40, P593.23–25   Oh Boys, Grand Slams . . . a Folies-Bergères   The subject is pinball machines, and a bit of pop history will help. Michael Colmer (*Pinball: An Illustrated History*) claims the pinball game was invented in 1931, when Raymond T. Moloney, a printshop owner, began manufacturing a purely mechanical game called Ballyhoo. It was a huge success, and before long the newly formed Bally Company was joined by a host of others: Chicago Coin, Keystone Novelty, and Gottlieb among them. Indeed, Tolbert and Tolbert identify David Gottlieb's game, Baffle Ball (also 1931), as the first pinball machine as we know it, with button-operated flippers. A Chicago Coin game, Beamlight, was the first electrically hopped-up machine, in 1938. But it ran on batteries; the first of the complex electrical boards was not designed until just before the United States entered World War II, and they were mass-produced only after V-E Day. Meanwhile, throughout the late thirties and early forties civic leaders everywhere vilified pinball games. Mayor Fiorello La Guardia had them banned from New York City in 1942 and led the charge by personally sledgehammering a bunch of them into junk. Here is the main point: the scene is Depression-era St. Louis, where Lyle Bland's friend, Alfonso Tracy, supposedly has a warehouse full of malfunctioning *electrical* pinball machines, which in the historical scheme of things haven't been invented yet. Still more anachronistic is the reference (at V584.31–32) to the drunken sailor playing an electrical machine (it has a "solenoid" at V584.36) in Virginia Beach on July 4, 1927. Of the machines listed here, the Oh Boy was a product of the Williams Company in 1964, with its table featuring a pair of leggy bathing beauties showing plenty of cleavage. The others are unattested in the literature.

V583.37, B680.19–20, P594.3   the solenoid thrashing, clonic, horrible   A solenoid is an electronic switch consisting of a coil around a metal plunger; when the current reaches a specific level, the plunger shoots out, usually operating a switch. But here it is "clonic," that is to say convulsing or "thrashing" wildly; hence the pinball horror.

V584.1, B680.21, P594.7   Katspiel   The background for this fantasy is Scholem (*Major Trends* 53), who explains that in the pre-Kabbalistic writings of many Merkabah mystics, the archons Domiel and Katspiel are "gatekeepers" of the sixth antechamber, the next-to-last stop for the adept during his ascent to the divine throne or Merkabah.

V584.9–10, B680.31, P594.12–13   Keokuk and Puyallup, Oyster Bay, Inglewood   Thomas Pynchon graduated from Oyster Bay High School, on Long Island, in 1953; he lived in Seattle, just north of Puyallup, from 1960 to 1962; and he was living in the Los Angeles suburb of Manhattan Beach, near Inglewood, by 1965. Then we lose his public trail. The reference here and in the lines that follow is to great marble shooters, "thumbs," whose performance has been damaged permanently ("good-by to another unbeatable and legendary thumb") by their having had to learn how to clean their M-1 service rifle in basic training and, while learning, having had the mechanism squash their thumb (the end result being what's known in service slang as an "M-1 thumb").

V584.12–13, B680.34–36, P594.15–16　dead on Iwo . . . gangrenous in the snow in the forest of Arden　The Pacific island of Iwo Jima, where U.S. Marines fought a fierce battle against Japanese defenders in the spring of 1945, and the forested area of the Ardennes, site of the Rundstedt offensive of December 1944. The allusion to Shakespeare's "forest of Arden" in *As You Like It* suggests what has been destroyed, scattered with Death's spawn, in the Bard's idyllic landscape.

V584.14, B680.38, P594.18　M-l　The standard service rifle of the U.S. armed forces during World War II.

V584.21, B681.4, P594.25　some Offenbach galop　A galop is a quick, lively dance tune in 2/4 time; with the waltz, polka, and quadrille it was one of the nineteenth century's most popular dance forms. There is a parody of the form in Jacques Offenbach's *Orphée aux enfers* (1858). A French composer of German origin, Offenbach (1819–1880), like Johann Strauss, was one of the outstanding figures in nineteenth-century popular music and is best known for gay, exhilarating, and tuneful comic operettas, such as *La belle Hélène* and *La vie parisienne*.

V584.32, B681.17–18, P594.36　ship went down at Leyte Gulf　Leyte is an island of the central Philippines. The battle to retake it from the Japanese began in early October 1944, when Allied troops landed there. The Japanese counterattacked, sending a large fleet of ships and nearly half their available fighter aircraft. During the naval battle, American submarines and surface ships cut up the fleet, which severely crippled the Japanese navy for the remainder of the war. In desperation, the Japanese employed suicidal kamikaze attacks, and losses in the U.S. Seventh Fleet were also fairly steep.

V584.40–41, B681.27–28, P595.3–4　check out the portrait of Michael Faraday in the Tate Gallery　Good luck! Museum director Norman Reid's 1967 catalog, *The Collections of the Tate Gallery*, lists no such portrait of British physicist Faraday (1791–1867). Larsson ("A *Companion*'s Companion") offers a *photograph* of a standing Faraday, right arm raised, as if saluting the viewer, and holding one of his inventions, a glass bar used in experiments. But this photo is evidently not from the Tate, and we can't tell much about Faraday's eyes, which so trouble Tantivy in this passage. The National Gallery in London presently owns ten different portraits of Faraday ranging from chalk sketches to daguerreotypes, lithographs, and oil paintings. The likeliest candidate: an 1841–42 oil-on-canvas portrait of Faraday by Thomas Phillips depicting the inventor standing, leaning against a table, hands clasped before his stomach, and wearing a black coat, white shirt, and black cravat. Looking rather "lambent" but not really "sinister" (V585.2).

V585.17–18, B682.8–9, P595.21–22   reprise of . . . "Bright Days for the Black Market"   See V495.26–36.

V586.17–18, B683.8, P596.20   play morra   Also known as "mora." Of Italian origin, it's a game in which one player guesses the number of hidden fingers another is holding up. Also, when applied to mules and horses, the Italian expression *giocare alla mora* (to play mora) means "to kick [somebody]."

V586.23, B683.14, P596.25   or if it has happened   In the Bantam, "or" is misprinted as "of."

V586.38–40, B683.34–35, P597.2–3   Silver-Streaking . . . Last we saw of Fibel   See V454.39; here, imagined as speeding like the "Silver Streak," or Pioneer Zephyr, a streamlined locomotive engine that in 1934 set a speed record from Chicago to Denver.

V587.7–8, B684.3–5, P597.11–12   Fibel happens to be working now . . . General Electric plant in Pittsfield   According to *The Berkshire Hills*, already in the thirties General Electric was a plant on the cutting edge of manufactured plastic parts for radios and appliances (80).

V587.17, B684.16, P597.22   a Schnipsel here and there   A shred or scrap.

V587.29, B684.32, P597.36   the Illuminati   Closely tied to Masonic and Rosicrucian writings since the beginning of these movements in the late sixteenth and seventeenth centuries is the idea of an elect, secret group, the Illuminati, scholar-statesmen learned in the ancient mysteries and banded together in brotherly love. The term was given a certain millennial character in the writings of Masonic philosopher Francis Bacon, especially in his *Advancement of Learning* (1605) and *The New Atlantis* (1627), published shortly after Bacon's death. Frances Yates (*The Rosicrucian Enlightenment* 125–29) has argued that the latter work, an allegory of the settlement of New England, is also a utopian representation of the Rosicrucian ideal, a state run by the Illuminati. As for the secret order itself, on May 1, 1776, Adam Weisshaupt (1748–1811) procured a royal Bavarian charter for a society called he called the "Order of the Perfectibilits," later the "Illuminati," and as "Brother Spartacus" he led the group, whose mission was to achieve moral perfection (just what Benjamin Franklin describes as his personal goal, in *The Autobiography*). The Jesuit-educated Weisshaupt was initiated into a Munich Freemasonry Lodge the following year. In popular culture, the Illuminati have long been described as a conspiratorial group dedicated to world dominion.

V587.32–33, B684.36, P597.39   Bakunin, Proudhon, Salverio Friscia   In his 1840 tract "What Is Property?" Pierre Joseph Proudhon (1809–65) adopted the term "anarchy" to define his system of "mutualist" exchange, which would be devoid of interest rates and profits that stem from the concept of possession. Mikhail Bakunin (1814–76) was one of Karl Marx's bitterest opponents and, incidentally, a Mason during the 1840s. In the last decade of his life he promoted schemes for an "International Brotherhood" of anarchists divided into "National Families"

and secretly controlled by an "International Family" opposed to all property ownership. Bakunin migrated to Italy in 1863, settling first in Florence and then (in 1865) in Naples, where three Italian anarchists became
his devoted followers. Saverio Friscia (1813–86) (Pynchon has misspelled
the first name) was one of them and, together with Alberto Tucci and
Giuseppi Fanelli, he founded the International Brotherhood in 1868.

V587.36, B684.41, P598.2   Doctor Livingstone   Dr. David Livingstone
(1813–73) was the Scottish missionary who took his medical practice
into central Africa. He was instrumental to British exploration of the region, and he *was* a Mason. Note also the narrator's recognition of a clue
in this passage—("living stone? Oh, yes")—which points up yet again
one of the novel's liminal states, between life and death, hinting of an
other side.

V587.40, B685.4, P598.6   a Masonic high sign   The upraised left hand,
palm open and expanded: "a symbol of equity and fair-dealing, of which
the left hand, as slower than the right, and more void of skill and craft,
is therefore the appropriate emblem" (A. Pike, *Morals and Dogma: The
Ancient and Accepted Rite of Freemasonry* 388). But we know better:
the left side is also the *sinister* side (see V137.20n).

**V588.1–2, B685.7–8, P598.8   like Wernher von Braun, was born close to
the Spring Equinox**   See V237.1–2n.

V588.5, B685.11, P598.12   Check out Ishmael Reed   Our narrator pays
homage to Reed's 1972 novel, *Mumbo Jumbo.* In his satire, Masonism
participates in a centuries-long effort to veil the real mysteries in racist,
destructive visions. The original mysteries out of Egypt, Reed's fiction
argues, had several revered black deities: Isis, Osiris, and others who are,
like Krishna, dark-skinned. Also, the real mysteries practice the magic
of the right hand, while, in Reed's satire, the evil "Atonists" (Knights
Templars and Masons, for example) practice the deceptive magic of the
left hand. Opposite page 210 in the Avon paperback edition of *Mumbo
Jumbo* is a photograph worth noting: captionless, it nonetheless clearly
shows rocket men Walter Dornberger and Wernher von Braun, his *right*
arm in a cast, shortly after the internment at Gammisch, in March 1945.

**V588.7–9, B685.13–16, P598.14–16   Missouri Mason Harry Truman . . .
this very August 1945 . . . his control-finger poised right on Miss Enola
Gay's atomic clit**   On August 3, having just departed Europe from the
Potsdam Conference, Truman issued orders to send Colonel Paul Tibbets aloft on the night of August 5 on a plane bound for Hiroshima.
Tibbets's plane, the *Enola Gay,* was named for his mother. If Truman's
finger is "poised," this must be during the period of August 3–5, and
probably the fifth, because Truman was capable of rescinding the mission down to the last hours. The grotesque, anticipatory image of a
"vapor-deposit of fat-cracklings" (V588.11) from immolated Japanese
will reappear in part 4 as a cloud circling the earth and "changing" the
color spectra at sunset (V642.31–41).

V588.27, B685.38, P598.35   home to Beacon Hill   The old residential district of central Boston.

V588.40, B686.13, P599.8   Belleau Wood   The forest near Chateau-Thierry, France, where in 1918 the U.S. Marines stopped the German advance on Paris. Bland is evidently a veteran of that battle.

V589.10, B686.26–27, P599.19   State Street   Runs through the heart of Boston's business and financial district.

V589.24–27, B687.2–5, P599.33–36   the Pearys and Nansens . . . Sir John Franklin and Salomon Andrée   A short catalog of Arctic explorers. Franklin (1786–1847) was one of the last mariners to believe in a Northwest Passage, and he died while trying to locate it. In 1897 Swedish balloonist Salomon Andrée (b. 1854) tried to navigate an airship over the Pole; a crash left the remains—discovered in 1930—of Andrée and two assistants spread out over several miles of polar ice. Robert Edwin Peary (1856–1920) was the American naval officer who made it to the North Pole in 1909; Fridtjof Nansen (1861–1930) was a Norwegian arctic explorer.

V590.12–13, B687.38–39, P600.23   having hugged to its holy center the wastes of dead species   The center of the earth as a (gravitational) "Holy Center." In the following paragraph of *GR* the idea becomes clearer: living beings "left on the outside of Earth," on its surface, blunder along; they are another instance of "Holy-Center-Approaching."

V590.28, B688.15–16, P600.40   a power series   In mathematics, a function expressed as a sum of powers of a variable multiplied by a coefficient. The formula for a Poisson distribution is a common example.

V591.3, B688.36, P601.13   holding a red rose   With the cross, the red rose is a principal symbol of Rosicrucianism, and Lyle Bland's experiment with astral projection confirms that sense. The surrounding details ("before sunrise," and so on) all correspond with Albert Pike's interpretation (291) of the rose as a symbol "of *Dawn*, of the Resurrection of light and the renewal of life, and therefore the dawn of the first day, and more particularly the Resurrection; the cross and the rose together are therefore hieroglyphically to be read, the *Dawn of Eternal Life* which all nations have hoped for by the advent of a Redeemer." To achieve this eternal life is Bland's aspiration.

V591.10–11, B689.3–4, P601.21   law firm of Salitieri, Poore, Nash, De Brutus, and Short   Outrageous pun on Thomas Hobbes's characterization (*Leviathan*, pt. 1, ch. 13) of cultural desolation in times of civil disorder and war: "No arts; no letters; no society; and which is worst of all, continual feare and danger of violent death; and the life of Man, solitary, poore, nasty, brutish, and short." See also V645.11–12n.

V591.18, B689.13, P601.30   Buddy left to see *The Bride of Frankenstein*   Universal Pictures' big 1935 sequel to their hit of four years earlier, in which Boris Karloff plays the monster and Elsa Lanchester both "bride" and Mary Shelley. Buddy Bland sees this film, perhaps significantly, on the day of his father Lyle's transcending; he'll be absent again for his father's funeral, when (perhaps with equal significance on that day) he takes in *Dracula* (see V652.12n).

EPISODE 31

If, using internal allusions as clues, we fix the time of this episode as just before the August 6 bombing of Hiroshima, then it would unfold around 10:15 P.M. on Sunday, August 5, 1945. All of this is however somewhat impressionistic and problematic, for while it is useful abstractly in the novel's chronological and circular design it also requires, practically, that Slothrop—previously afoot—has been whisked somehow the rest of the way across northern Germany. The setting in any case is Cuxhaven, the small city at the mouth of the Elbe River that Nazi rocketeers used for V-2 launches. There, medical officers Muffage and Spontoon prepare to castrate surgically our grail-seeking Tyrone Slothrop. At precisely this moment, in a different time zone near Japan, the *Enola Gay* is winging its way to Hiroshima, delivering the "Cosmic Bomb" anticipated in *GR* for some time. In this episode the circular dancing of the gathered preterite forms a symbolic counterpoint to the mushroom cloud that will form eight thousand miles to the east. The rosette pattern of the dancers also gives rise to a set of related allusions: to the Red Cross (or "rosy cross" of the Rosicrucians); to Major Duane Marvy's song, "San Antonio Rose"; and to Shirley, "the rose of no-man's land" (V601.15) in this episode. As for Slothrop, he beds down with Leni Pökler in a whorehouse located in Dorum, a village outside Cuxhaven. In a mix-up, Marvy dons the Plechazunga suit and suffers the sacrificial castration in Slothrop's stead.

V591.22, B689.19, P601.34   Queen Anne salutes   Characteristic of the British Royal Guards, a snappy salute used by sentries.

V591.24, B689.20–21, P602.1   deuce 'n' a halfs and civilian bobtail rigs   Slang terms for types of trucks: a two-and-a-half-ton model and a short-bed civilian model.

V591.32, B689.32, P602.10   junkie M.O.s   In other words: drug-addicted medical officers.

V592.5, B690.6–7, P602.21   stroking his full Imperial   A pointed beard grown only from the lower lip and chin.

V592.12, B690.16, P602.28   Weltschmerz   World-weariness.

V592.21, B690.26, P602.38   like James Mason   The voice of actor Mason (1909–84) was a blend of Yorkshire dialect and transatlantic drawl.

V592.22–23, B690.29, P602.40   Marston shelters   Half-cylindrical buildings also called "quonset huts." The picture of Britain's Operation Backfire headquarters at Cuxhaven, in Kooy and Uytenbogaart (*Ballistics of the Future* 268), clearly shows a row of these in the background.

V592.25–26, B690.32–33, P603.1–2   the General Forces Programme features Sandy MacPherson at the Organ   Here, the "distant radio" playing in the background establishes the time of these events. BBC programming schedules in the *Times* of London list Mr. MacPherson on Sunday night, August 5, at 10:15 P.M., and at no other time during this month. See also V13.39–40n, and note how this loops us back toward our narrative's beginning.

V592.29, B690.36–37, P603.5–6   sausage-limbed Petty Girl pin-ups   George Petty (1894–1975) was an American graphic artist and illustrator who began doing cartoons for *Esquire* magazine shortly after its 1933 debut. His drawings of fetching young women became increasingly popular, and for its December 1939 issue Petty drew the first foldout pinup girl. Through the war years Old Gold cigarette ads in magazines featured Petty Girls. Petty left *Esquire* in 1942, his place taken by the artist Alberto Varga, who continued the practice of lusty foldout displays. The sometimes rather scantily clad Petty girl was never exactly "sausage-limbed," except perhaps in the thighs.

V592.32, B690.39–40, P603.8   an American Bugs Bunny comic book   See V545.4–5n. Perhaps an issue of *Looney Tunes and Merrie Melodies Comics*, first released in 1941; or, as Larsson suggests ("A *Companion's* Companion"), a copy of Dell Comics' *Four Color Comics* that, starting with issue #3 (1943), featured Bugs, among others.

V592.35, B691.1, P603.11   M.I.6 or something   British military intelligence, in charge of overseas spying.

V592.36–37, B691.4, P603.12–13   a Nayland Smith   See V277.34–38n.

V593.7–8, B691.17–18, P603.24   "If they ever get one in working order"   "They" (the British) did. Three A4 rockets were launched from Cuxhaven in late September and October 1945 as part of Operation Backfire.

V593.15, B691.27, P603.32–33   the same General Wivern   After Katje departed Monte Carlo, Wivern took over Slothrop's rocket education (V237.27–29).

V594.7–8, B692.20–22, P604.23   boys circle clockwise, girls anticlockwise . . . a rose-pattern   The choreography seems straight out of a Busby Berkeley musical. Moreover, it is richly symbolic. The "rose-pattern" is reinforced by the color of the dancers' faces: "ruddy," tending, even, toward an "apoplectic mauve" (V593.14–15). To a Jungian, their direction of movement is also noteworthy: the "boys" move in the direction of consciousness, rationality, and analysis; the "girls" move in the direction of the unconscious mind and associative logic. Together, the movements give yet another image of opposites held in equipoise by a circular mandala. Also, General Wivern's erection and launch, stamen- and penis- and rocket-like, occurs at the center of this circle, as narratively glimpsed from above. This image suggests a target, or an atomic blast as seen from an airplane. August 5 came on the very eve of the atomic age;

the morning blast over Hiroshima occurred on the Roman Catholic Feast of the Transfiguration, and to a Rosicrucian, the rose is a symbol of such transfiguration, from material to spiritual existence. Indeed, Lyle Bland just accomplished that transformation, rose in hand, at the end of the last episode.

V594.17, B692.32–33, P604.33   the CBI theatre with . . . bhang   He's come back from the China-Burma-India theater of war with a ton (2,240 pounds!) of Indian marijuana.

V594.20, B692.36, P604.36   Runcible Spoon   Soules ("What To Think about *Gravity's Rainbow*") identifies their weapons: "Edward Lear coined *runcible spoon* in 1871. Sometime after that, the curved-like-a-spoon, single-cutting-edge pickle fork was either invented or rechristened."

V594.30, B693.5, P605.6   "Greetings, gate, need an opiate?"   Here and following, an imitation of comedian Jerry Colonna (V552.4n).

V594.31, B693.7, P605.7   Albert Krypton, corpsman striker   He derives his family name from the Greek for "hidden" and from the element on the periodic table whose atomic number is 36. In its normal form, it is a colorless, odorless, tasteless, and inert gas (present approximately one part per million in ordinary air); in its much more rare solid form, it comprises a white powder with a face-centered cubic structure. In naval nomenclature, any enlisted man in training for one of the specific technical ratings is called a "striker"; this fellow's in training to be a (medical) corpsman. Kryptonite is also, of course, the legendary (fictional) material that immobilizes and potentially even kills comic-book hero Superman.

V594.38, B693.15, P605.14   the goat hole   Location of the ship's bilge pumps.

V595.14, B693.35, P605.32   *La Forza del Destino*   *The Force of Destiny*, an 1862 opera seria by Giuseppi Verdi. The plot: a story of illicit love (between a young boy named Alvaro and a young girl Leonora); the woman goes into seclusion, the man into a monastery, while her brother (Carlo) vows eternal revenge. In the last act Carlo has his chance for revenge when he finds Alvaro in the monastery, surrounded by hungry beggars. Lots of knifeplay, with speeches about *destino* mixed in, leaves everyone united in death.

V595.19, B693.42, P605.38   "I've OD'd"   Underworld acronym for an overdose of any potentially lethal drug.

V595.35–36, B694.18–19, P606.14   an old *News of the World*   See V215.29n.

V596.13–14, B694.39, P606.31–32   the drape and hand of the pig's shag coat   That is, the drape and *texture*—the feel of its shag—to one's hand (fashion terms).

V596.41, B695.27–28, P607.18–19   "Follow the yellow-brick road"

Krypton sings the words that the Munchkins teach Dorothy, as they send her Oz-ward in the film *The Wizard of Oz.*

V599.9–10, B698.8–9, P609.28   a Deanna Durbin hairdo   In the film *Mad about Music* (1938), she appears with her hair pulled tightly back from her forehead, parted on the left, its curls framing her face in guiches. Actress Durbin never gave up that prim, cute, schoolgirlish look.

V600.19, B698.25–26, P610.37   Krypton now looting the cash register . . . "love in bloom."   Larsson ("A *Companion*'s Companion") suggests Krypton is riffing on a 1934 Bing Crosby tune for the film *She Loves Me Not.* But there is nothing here that jibes in any way with the lyrics, and "love in bloom" is such a universal idea and phrase, there may be no such connection.

V601.1, B700.11, P611.20   "Were those snowdrops back there?"   See V247.8–9n.

V602.6, B701.20, P612.26   off the Dorum road   Their prearranged meeting place (see V527.3n).

V602.12–13, B701.28, P612.33   toward Helgoland   The tiny North Sea island off the Schleswig-Holstein coast, which the ancient Teutons regarded as the home of dead souls.

V603.8, B702.31, P613.29   Solange   Plugging now into the triangle of Franz-Leni-Ilse Pökler, Slothrop beds down with Leni, who's under this assumed name.

V603.38, B703.26, P614.20   "San Antonio Rose"   Marvy's favorite song (V559.36–37n).

V603.39, B703.28, P614.21   reeling out   In the Bantam, "realing out," an interesting error.

V604.34, B704.30, P615.18   "Got your 'snow,' Major Marvy"   His cocaine, in underworld slang.

V604.39, B704.36, P615.23   "Call it a little lagniappe"   Louisiana creole (pronounced "lan-yáp"), from the Spanish *"la ñapa,"* meaning "a little extra," a bit more added on as a gratuity.

V605.1, B704.40, P615.26   "Boats"   Naval service slang designating a boatswains mate, or bosun mate or bosun.

V605.9, B705.6, P615.34   "It isn't the House of All Nations"   A legendary eighteenth- and nineteenth-century Paris brothel, catering exclusively to Europe's elite, operating in the Hôtel Chabanais Saint-Ponges.

V605.21, B705.20, P616.5   "Va-len-cia-a-a," sings Major Marvy   A 1925 French song by Lucienne Boyer and Jacques Charles, rendered in an English version by Clifford Grey; it was a number one hit for the Paul Whiteman Orchestra in that year for the Brunswick label. Its refrain: "Valencia! In my dreams it always seems / I hear you softly call to me."

V605.26, B705.27, P616.10   from the Asturias   On October 1, 1936, two years before civil war erupted in Spain, the socialist coal miners of the Asturias (mountains of Spain's northern coast) staged a revolt, quickly capturing each Civil Guard post in their separate valleys and cutting off all roadways. Their number has been put at sixty thousand. The government called in General Franco to suppress the miners, and he brought over his Moorish army troops stationed in Africa. It took the Moors two weeks—during which time they pillaged, raped, and committed random acts of murder—to end the revolt. Estimates are that three thousand of the revolutionaries were dead by October 18, when an uneasy peace was declared. Two years later Franco was leading the Moors back into Spain as the civil war erupted in earnest (V234.7–8n).

V605.33, B705.35–36, P616.17–18   the International Brigades   A collection of leftist militia from various countries who joined the antifascist Loyalist Party during the Spanish civil war in an effort to defeat Franco. American volunteers fought in the Lincoln Brigade.

V605.37–38, B705.40–42, P616.21–22   *Ya salimos . . . otros frentes, ay Manuela*   Larsson ("A *Companion*'s Companion") provides the gloss. The song is "Viva la Quince Brigade" (Long Live the Fifteenth Brigade), sung by the American Lincoln Battalion of the Spanish Civil War. The two last verses of the Spanish, the relevant part in this context, followed by the English version, are given below:

> En los frentes de Jarama
> Rumbala, rumbala, rum-ba-la [repeat]
> No tenemos ni aviones
> Ni tanques, ni canones, ay Manuela! [repeat]

> Ya salimos de España
> Rumbala, rumbala, rum-ba-la [repeat]
> Par luchar en otros frentes
> Ay Manuela, ay Manuela!

> [On the front at Jarama
> Rumbala, rumbala, rum-ba-la
> We have no planes above us
> Not a tank, nor any canons, ay Manuela!

> We have left the Spanish trenches
> Rumbala, rumbala, rum-ba-la
> To fight on other fronts,
> Ay Manuela, ay Manuela.]

V607.1, B707.14–15, P617.28   *puto and sinvergüenza*   Spanish slang for, respectively, a gigolo or prick (from "*puta*," "whore") and a rascal or scoundrel, literally a person "without shame"; these are Manuela's way—she's "enough of a professional"—to flatter the "limpening, nervous," and hence sexually ineffectual Marvy.

V607.18, B707.35–36, P618.4   the red-hatted 'suckers coming his way

That is, British military police in their red-banded hats, here referred to "'suckers," a shortened form of the obscene epithet "cocksuckers."

V608.40, B709.25, P619.32–33   the small moon . . . at its zenith   The thin sliver of a moon appeared in the night sky of August 5–6, 1945. On July 30 (see V506.37n) the waning moon was a "sharp sickle" in the night sky. A week later it's a waxing moon, still small and sickle-like. If the moon is this high up, the time would be early morning of August 6, perhaps at 5:00 A.M.

V609.6–7, B709.32–33, P619.39–40   "We're catching the C-47 at one"   The American-made transport plane, a Douglas DC-3; the departure time for Muffage and Spontoon is presumably 1:00 P.M., August 6.

V610.3–5, B710.36–38, P620.36–38   "Solange," oddly enough, is dreaming of Bianca too. . . . it's her own child Ilse . . . train that never seems to come to rest   The reason why Leni/Solange would dream of Bianca Erdmann is the sexual tie between Slothrop and Leni/Solange and between Slothrop and Greta—Greta and Bianca Erdmann and Ilse and Leni Pökler are bound together as homologous pairs (see V471.8–11n).

EPISODE 3 2

A prolepsis to some unspecified time *after* the botched castration of Lieutenant Slothrop, part 3 closes here with Tchitcherine arriving at the Lüneburg Heath to find Gerhardt von Göll filming scenes for his movie version of *Martín Fierro*. Then, in London, the time still indistinct, two lordly characters discuss Pointsman's ignominy following the accidental castration of Marvy, which has left Slothrop still on the loose.

V610.31, B711.26, P621.23–24   a copse of junipers   In the Bantam, "junipers" is misprinted as "jumpers."

V610.32–33, B711.27, P621.24–25   two men, one white, one black   Based on the singing duel in *The Return of Martín Fierro* in cantos 29 and 30. This scene also duplicates the *ajtys* that Tchitcherine witnessed ten years previously in Kyrgyzstan.

V611.10–11, B712.5, P622.1–2   Who tipped the Schwarzkommando off to the raid?   Recall that part 3, episode 27, commenced with a discussion about how the Schwarzkommando had been able to flee.

V611.13, B712.8, P622.4   Since his illumination that night   When the "large white finger" showed Tchitcherine, accompanied by Major Marvy and Clayton ("Bloody") Chiclitz, the existence of "A Rocket-cartel" (V566.14, 20).

V611.18, B712.14–15, P622.9   Mravenko, one of the VIAM people   On VIAM see V273.5n; Mravenko appears to be fictional.

V611.33, B712.32–33, P622.25   "Molotov isn't telling Vishinsky"

Vyacheslav Molotov (1890–1986) was the Soviet foreign affairs commissar from 1939 to 1945. Andrei Vishinsky (1883–1954) was state prosecutor under Stalin and best known as a ruthless leader of the great Soviet purges of 1934 to 1936.

V612.22, B713.26, P623.14   estancieros   Ranchers.

V612.27–28, B713.32–33, P623.19–20   Argentine legend . . . Maria Antonia Correa   Indeed as the legend has it, in the 1830s María Antonia Deolinda Correa resided in San Juan province. When her husband Bustos was dragooned into the militia of Juan Facundo Quiroga, a local gaucho warlord, so aggrieved was Deolinda that she journeyed after Busto, walking and carrying her newborn son, until finally, in the desert, she collapsed and died of thirst. When passing muleteers found her body days later they were amazed to find her infant son alive and nursing at her breast. Having found the name Correa on a pendant she was wearing, they buried her at a tomb under the name "Difunta Correa." As her story spread, Argentinians came to regard her as a saint, and people in need began to pray to her.

V612.33, B713.39–40, P623.25   M. F. Beal   Mary F. Beal (b. 1937) is a novelist (her first, *Amazon One*, appeared in 1973; a second, *Angel Dance*, in 1977) and a short story writer. She is married to novelist David Shetzline (mentioned earlier; see V389.23–24n). Here, the link to ideas of "mineral consciousness" calls to mind Beal's short story "Gold," included in Martha Foley's *Best American Short Stories of 1972*. The piece is a visionary allegory about mountain-dwelling ascetics who learn to create inwardly, and then excrete, small nuggets of "calculi," or gold. Yet achieving this mystical power also brings with it premonitions of "the end"; that is, achieving the story's "mineral consciousness" is an allegory of death's final victory.

V613.30, B715.1–2, P624.23–24   The boliche . . . the pulpería   Respectively, the tavern and the country store of the Argentine pampas, in Hernández's epic poem.

V614.10, B715.26–27, P625.4   Rin-Tin-Tin style   In 1918 Captain Lee Duncan of the U.S. Army found future canine star Rin Tin Tin (1916–32) cowering in an abandoned infantry trench. He brought the German shepherd to Hollywood, where the dog became a hero of silent films like *Rinty of the Desert* (1927) and serials like *Lone Defender*.

V614.12, B715.29, P625.6   Hund-Stadt   Or, "Dog City."

V614.18, B715.37, P625.13   G-5   See V125.22n.

V615.9–10, B716.37–38, P626.5   to finalize plans for the Postwar Polyvinyl Chloride Raincoat   A carryover from part 1, episode 18. By this point, though, it's reached the corporate planning stage, perhaps under the leadership of Sir Scammony, drinking his "Quimporto" (an undocumented and seemingly awful blend of quinine—the alkaloid for treating and preventing malaria—port wine, beef tea, Coke, and onion) and thinking about the coat as "source of great corporate fun" because of how—"unstable plastic" that it is (V150.13)—the coat falls apart on the wearer.

V615.15, B716.42, P626.11   "in Portobello Road"   See V107.26n.

V615.27–28, B717.16, P626.26–27   "if this show prangs"   Recalling Aaron Throwster's slang (V228.37n).

V615.28–31, B717.17–20, P626.27–30   "Ginger Groupers jamming my switchboard . . . *and* 1922 Committee coming in the windows"   In sum, foes from opposite sides of the political spectrum. A ginger group is a subset of a larger organization that serves as a motivating force within it. The name derives from United Mine Workers organizer Ginger Goodwin, a Canadian, who was gunned down during a 1918 strike; in 1924 a faction of progressive and radical Labour Party members in Canada who advocated socialism formed the first ginger group. In British politics the 1922 Committee consists of all backbench conservative members of Parliament, though when the party is in opposition frontbench members other than the party leader may also attend committee meetings, held every week. The idea took shape after the 1922 election, with the goal of giving backbench members a way to set their views before the Tory leadership.

V615.31–32, B717.21, P626.30–31   "Bracken and Beaverbrook go *on*"   Sir Brendan Bracken (1901–58) was an influential member of Britain's Conservative Party. He advised Churchill throughout the war, but Churchill and the Conservatives lost control of the government in the July 1945 parliamentary elections. William Aitken, Baron Beaverbrook (1879–1964), was another Conservative and a publishing magnate. After the election loss Beaverbrook continued to argue in print for stiff dealings with the Soviets, whose ambitions, he felt, must be thwarted even at risk of another war.

V616.4–5, B717.38, P627.3–4   "ex Africa semper aliquid novi"   The Latin means "always something new out of Africa."

V616.31–32, B718.28–29, P627.32   run . . . by no visible hands   Recalling Adam Smith's "invisible hand" running the laissez-faire marketplace (V30.30n).

Part 4 *The Counterforce*

ART 4, "The Counterforce," begins shortly after August 6, 1945, the Feast of the Transfiguration (in the Roman Catholic Church), though we also return to August 6 during an analepsis in episode 1, when Slothrop is shown miraculously recovering his long-lost mouth harp. This signals a transfiguration that inverts the Christian myth: here, Tyrone Slothrop becomes "The Fool" (V724.28–29), the eighth and last of his avatars in the novel. Stretched crosswise on the earth, he is Christ-like. With his ragged and ruddy appearance beneath the phallic sign of a "stout rainbow cock" (V626.17), he recalls Krishna, Vishnu's priapic avatar of fertility and dance. With his harp he is Orpheus, the dismembered Greek god. He embodies the acceptance of pain in Rilke's *Sonnets to Orpheus*, with their climactic expression of being and flux—"To the rushing water speak: I am." As "Fool," Slothrop is also the null or zero card of the tarot deck, a card that shows a youth skipping near the edge of a precipice, oblivious to danger. And by part 4 of *GR*, Slothrop has completed the long descent of part 3 and fallen, the "fragments" (V742.25) of him scattering everywhere. For those in the burgeoning "Counterforce," who begin to organize around his memory, Slothrop and the rocket become central figures in a nascent polyglot mythology. And perhaps this is why part 4 consists of twelve episodes, for twelve is the number associated with discipleship. Appropriately, too, the dominant astrological sign of this part is Virgo, a common earth sign and symbolic of assimilation, the maneuvering of people into new and practical configurations. Twelve is also the number of the astrological signs, organized mandala-like around the astrological year.

In a minimal nod toward conventionally realistic narrative, part 4 brings most of the novel's other main characters to well-defined ends. Pointsman's career has become a mediocre disgrace, wrecked after his botched attempt at castrating Slothrop. Roger Mexico, Pirate Prentice, Katje Borgesius, Osbie Feel, and others form the loosely delineated Counterforce. With the war now safely past, Jessica Swanlake slides back into middle-class comfort with Jeremy. In episode 11, Geli Tripping wins Tchitcherine through a successful exercise in white magic. Enzian guides his Herero Schwarzkommando to Lüneburg Heath and the firing of Rocket 00001—a repetition, and a counterpart (as one to zero, autumn to spring, and black to white), of the quintuple zero fired months ago.

But the Herero rocket raising occurs in conjunction with another Christian feast day, September 14, the Exaltation (or Raising) of the Holy Cross. In episode 12, the last of seventy-three, this moment triggers an almost simultaneous prolepsis and analepsis. The allusions that the many and skewed narrative voices—Kabbalistic myth, comic-book lingo, mock etymologies, and history—give rise to in these episodes are such that part 4 can be said finally to be all about Blicero's noontime sacrifice of Gottfried during the Easter/April Fool's weekend of 1945. But "Westward the Course of Empire takes its way," as Bishop Berkeley and the narrator have at times reminded us (see V214.35n), and after the Easter-time firing Weissmann/Blicero heads west. The narrator advises us to look for him among the present-day heads of corporate America (V749.9–12). This validates the novel's leap forward to Los Angeles and the Orpheus Theater, circa 1970. Its owner, a thinly disguised Richard M. Nixon, supplies the epigraph to part 4: a question, directed to no one in particular and perhaps most generally (and lamely) to the envisioned threat of nuclear winter—"What?"

This is how the published text of part 4 opens. Yet Clifford Mead, in a brief note, has commented that the epigraph for part 4 in the galley sheets was not the Nixon question but instead the fourth verse of Joni Mitchell's 1968 song "Cactus Tree":

> She has brought them to her senses,
> They have laughed inside her laughter;
> Now she rallies her defenses,
> For she fears that one will ask her
> For eternity
> And she's so busy being free.

EPISODE I

Part 4 opens with Pirate Prentice flying southward toward the Harz Mountains of central Germany. Given the chronology of part 3, which by the end is hard to pinpoint exactly, this episode would appear to unfold sometime after August 6, 1945. Slothrop plucks his recovered Hohner harmonica out of a mountain stream where he has been soaking its reeds. He begins to play. The narrative then moves back, by analepsis, to his recovery of that lost harp and his turning away from the quest for what Jamf and "the primal dream" (V623.31–32) of his infancy may mean. That recovery evidently occurred on August 6, "the day he became a crossroad" (V626.15–16) and a rainbow vision seemed to transform him forever. His transfiguration alludes, however, to the bombing of Hiroshima on August 6, and Slothrop will soon find a scrap of newsprint with a figure of that holocaust.

V619.1–4, B721.1–5, P631.1–4   Bette Davis and Margaret Dumont . . .
"Who Dat Man?" from *A Day at the Races*   The idea of dramatic heavy Bette Davis (1908–89) appearing alongside comedy star Margaret Dumont (1889–1965) is the stuff of oneiric whimsy. So too with the backdrop of Slothrop's dream: François de Cuvilliés was the architect who, in 1734, designed the rococo pavilion (with lots of curlicues) for Nymphenburg, a castle outside Munich. In the film *A Day at the Races* (1937), Chico and Harpo Marx wander into the back lot of a horse track. They begin to sing and play. Soon all the black stable boys, grooms, and other menials (in fact, it is Hollywood's all-black Crinoline Choir) have joined

in behind Harpo, on the pennywhistle, for a swing-time rendition of "Who Dat Man?" The lyrics have mock-millennial overtones. To the question that recurs in the refrain—"Who dat man?"—comes the answer in a refrain: "Ga-bri-el!" But Gabriel, ironically, is not God's trumpeter but Harpo, the foolish mute. In the film Margaret Dumont plays the wealthy Mrs. Upjohn, a hypochondriacal dowager. Groucho Marx plays Hugo Z. Hackenbush, the former horse doctor who—by a zany error—becomes her private physician. As the film ends, they all wind up at the racetrack again and everyone joins the Crinolines for one more chorus of "Who Dat Man?" As the narrator comments here, it is thus *"a day at the races"* in more ways than one.

V619.12, B721.15, P631.12 P-47 A single-seat fighter aircraft, also called the Thunderbolt but affectionately known as the "Jug" because of its rotund shape. For its first year of service during the war, 1943 to 1944, the P-47 had the "greenhouse canopy" (V619.16) Pynchon describes. After that, it was manufactured with a bubble canopy, giving pilots 360 degrees of visibility.

V619.23–25, B721.28–30, P631.24–25 over Celle . . . Brunswick . . . an Immelmann over Magdeburg Pirate flies an east-southeasterly course over towns situated just north of the Harz Mountains. In aeronautics, an Immelmann is a strategic maneuver, consisting of a roll combined with a loop, named for the German flying ace of World War I, Max Immelmann (1890–1916).

V619.33, B722.1, P632.8 Tooting Upper and Lower Tooting are, in Baedeker's description (*London* 196), two "uninspiring suburbs" of southwest London.

V619.36, B722.4, P632.11 Kaiser Bill That is, Kaiser Wilhelm II, German emperor from 1888 to 1918, when he abdicated and went into exile in the Dutch city of Utrecht. Hitler gave Wilhelm a full military funeral when he died in June 1941.

V620.25, B722.34–35, P632.36 painted Kelly green The U.S. Army's Eighth Air Force used gray on their Thunderbolts. Pirate's plane has been repainted green, color of the Counterforce in part 4.

V621.11–13, B723.22–25, P633.23–25 the Great Dying . . . northward march of black plague The Black Death or plague of 1347–51 swept out of Turkestan (like Attila) and then spread aboard ships with destinations to Mediterranean ports. Arriving in Sicily in 1347, it turned north: Spain and France were afflicted in 1348; northern Europe was devastated in 1349. The plague moved on to England and Scandinavia in 1350–51. In its wake some one thousand villages and towns were virtually emptied.

V621.26, B723.39–40, P633.37 Bakelite top . . . seal of Merck of Darmstadt On Bakelite plastic, see V522.29n. Merck AG, now an international corporation, was a Swiss manufacturer of pharmaceuticals. Its current seal: the letter "M" inside a shield.

V621.39, B724.14, P634.10   smooth as a Jo block   Named for Swedish machinist-engineer C. E. Johansson, who (according to the entry for "Precision Gauges" in the 1955 *Encyclopedia Britannica*) developed them in 1896. Any Johansson or "Jo" block would be part of a set of steel blocks with parallel ends, each one carefully milled and hand-lapped to specified lengths, so that their measurements were very accurate and their finishes very smooth. Coincidentally, the noun "joe" or "jo" is forties and fifties slang for a porcelain toilet, and Bummer's nasal passages might be as smooth as that, too.

V621.40, B724.15, P634.11   the Liebknecht funeral   Karl Liebknecht was a Socialist deputy in the Reichstag and an opponent of the Great War from 1914 on. His resistance won him a prison sentence, together with Rosa Luxemburg. From their cells they formed the Spartacus Party, in opposition to the majority Socialists. They were released in 1918 but imprisoned again on the fifteenth of January 1919 and then supposedly "shot while escaping" as the police euphemism would have it. In fact, Liebknecht had been brutally beaten before he was shot in the head at close range. His body was dumped off a bridge into the Spree-Oder Canal in Berlin and not recovered until the spring thaws. In 1922 a memorial was erected in his honor in Luxembourg.

V622.3, B724.20–21, P634.15   "why I listen to Spohr, Rossini, Spontini"   On Gioacchino Rossini, see V440.4n. Louis Spohr (1784–1859) was a German composer and violinist whose compositions were confined mainly to violin pieces he wrote for himself. Known until Paganini's heyday as Europe's best violinist, he passed most of his days as director of the orchestra at the court theater of Kassel. Gasparo Luigi Pacifico Spontini (1774–1851) was the son of a peasant and an Italian composer whose early fame was built on comic operas he wrote that were performed in Rome and then Paris. In 1814 Kaiser Friedrich Wilhelm III of Prussia brought him to Berlin, at an enormous salary. Thereafter he did little composing and, rather like Rossini, lived his remaining decades in regal splendor.

V622.14, B724.34, P634.27   the old Hohner   Focalized through Slothrop, the narrative here recalls his miraculous recovery of the long-lost blues harp, which fell down the toilet (in a vision) at Boston's Roseland Ballroom in 1939. But why a Hohner? First, Slothrop's harmonica must be a Hohner because the company holds a virtual lock on the market; no one would think of challenging the company's happy worldwide cartel. Hohner has offices and brand names scattered over the globe, but Slothrop's Blues Harp would have been manufactured at the company's Black Forest factory in Trossingen, north of Zurich. (Indeed, this must be the "harmonica factory" where Squalidozzi and Gerhardt von Göll plan the filming of *Martín Fierro*; see V384.34n.) In addition, Slothrop's Hohner is a sign of his identity with Orpheus, the mythic harp player and dismembered holy Fool. The Hohner is thus also a sign of Slothrop's preterition. In the coming pages the narration explains how a harpist "bends" notes on the Hohner's reeds, describing it as a transformation of pain: "you suck a clear note, on pitch, and then bend it lower with the muscles of your face. Muscles of your face have been laughing, tight with pain, often trying not to betray any emotion, all your life" (V643.28–31). This kind of transformation might well be taken as a synecdoche for the satire in *GR*—for the downward betrayal to pain and gravitas of one's smile and the human comedy reflexively triggering it. And so Slothrop's harmonica must be a Hohner for it will yield yet another of the novel's etymological puns: the German verb "*höhnen*" means "to deride or ridicule" (like the character Minne Khlaetsch, of V683.23–684.24, we have to not hear the umlaut); thus we have a *Höhner*, one who sneers or derides, a figure in satire. The Hohner Blues Harp thus emerges as an instrument of Slothrop's satirically transformed preterition. For such a "far-fallen" character as he is (V569.33–34), the Blues Harp becomes an expression of his being. Finally, the Hohner sound holes that are numbered ten (high) through one (low) recall the significance of ten in Kabbalistic myths and of the rocket with its countdown from ten. With its rainbow of notes, the Hohner Blues Harp may thus be read as a narrative counterpart to the rocket.

V622.17–21, B724.38–41, P634.30–34   Like that Rilke prophesied, "And though Earthliness forget . . . To the rushing water speak: I am"   The narrator quotes from the last of Rilke's *Sonnets to Orpheus* (pt. 1, no. 29). Since details from it filter through the context of this episode, it will help to reproduce the whole poem here. Note also that while the copyright pages to *GR* specify the Norton edition for translations of Rilke, here Pynchon provides his own translation. Compare his three lines to the last three as translated by M. D. Herder Norton:

> Silent friend of many distances,
> feel how your breath is still increasing space.
> Among the beams of the dark belfries let
> yourself ring out. What feeds on you
>
> will grow strong upon this nourishment.
> Be conversant with transformation.
> From what experience have you suffered most?
> Is drinking bitter to you, turn to wine.
>
> Be, in this immeasurable night,
> magic power at your senses' crossroad,
> be the meaning of their strange encounter.
>
> And if the earthly has forgotten you,
> say to the still earth: I flow.
> To the rapid water speak: I am.

In several respects Pynchon's is the better and more interesting translation. His last line, with "rushing" in place of Herder Norton's "rapid," preserves the onomatopoeic sibilance of Rilke's *Zu dem raschen Wasser sprich*. Pynchon's "And though Earthliness forget you" bends the grammar of Rilke's *Und wenn dich dass Irdische vergass* but preserves the tightness of that line. And his translation of *der stillen Erde* as "the still*ed* Earth" is striking: the participial adjective implies some victimized subject, some paranoid striving to surmount others' efforts to "perfect methods of immobility" (V572.20–21).

V622.30–31, B725.12–13, P635.3–5   In a week he mastered that dreamy tune Dick Powell sang . . . over and over, on the bagpipes   The song Slothrop learns, so absurdly, "on the bagpipes" and then (still worse) practices "over and over," is "The Shadow Waltz," one of many by songwriting duo Al Dubin, who wrote the lyrics, and composer Harry Warren. Originally composed for actor Dick Powell's role in the 1933 Busby Berkeley musical film *The Gold Diggers of 1933*, Bing Crosby afterward made it a number-one hit. For all Pynchon's play in *GR* with apparitions, phantasms, moirés (V625.38–39), nimbuses, scrims, shadows, and the like, and given Slothrop's awareness in this scene that something otherworldly may be "going on," and specifically that someone's *watching him* from just beyond the circle of his encampment, Dubin's lyrics make an apt accompaniment:

> In the shadows let me come and sing—to you.
> Let me dream a song that I can bring—to you.
> Take me in your arms and let me cling—to you.
> Let me linger long, let me live my song.
> In the winter let me bring the spring—to you.
> Let me feel that I mean everything—to you.
> Love's old song will be new.
> In the shadows when I come and sing—to you.
>
> Shadows on the wall, I can see them fall
> Here and there, everywhere.
> Silhouettes in blue, dancing in the dew
> Here am I. Where are you?

V622.35, B725.18, P635.8   Mangel-wurzels   Those yellowish, rutabaga-shaped beets again.

V624.1, B726.34, P636.15   Werewolf stencils   The Werewolves were an underground group of Nazi resistance fighters who pledged to keep fighting after V-E Day. See also V640.23n.

V624.2–5, B726.35–39, P636.16–17   WILLST DU V-2, DANN ARBEITE . . . WILLST DU V-4, DANN ARBEITE   The narrator translates these supposed Werewolf slogans but note also the (mindless, pointless?) puns:

"Will you be, too? Then work!" and "Will you before? Then work." But before what?

V624.18, B727.12–13, P636.32   Past Slothrops, say averaging one a day, ten thousand of them   Why not say so? If Slothrop is ten thousand days old on this August 6, 1945, and if we count backward, including the leap years, then Slothrop's birthday would fall on March 21, 1918. A coincidence? Perhaps, but if so he will have been born on "the great cusp," the "green equinox" when "dreaming fishes to young ram, watersleep to firewaking . . . bears down on us" (V236.36–37). There is remarkable symmetry in this. The young ram of Aries is, according to Marc E. Jones (*Astrology*), characterized by the assertion of individual being, the "I am." This would correspond with the great care Pynchon has taken over the Pisces/Aries cusp and explain why he also highlighted the birthdays of Wernher von Braun and Dr. Stanley Livingstone (see V588.1–2). Slothrop's being born on March 21, 1918, tallies with everything we know about him: his association with Jamf and Lyle Bland while an infant, his entering high school when Roosevelt was "starting out" as president (V373.39–40n), and his being at Harvard University in 1937. Slothrop would have been born as the Germans began their offensive in the Somme on March 21, 1918, and this narrative about his life opens with a parallel offensive, when the German *Wehrmacht* swept into the Ardennes during Advent 1944. Then there is, yet again, the numerological significance of ten: it's fitting that Slothrop should have counted down ten thousand days at this moment when he is transformed, when he says, "I am."

If March 21, 1918, is indeed Slothrop's birthday (a wild surmise), then we may also cast his natal horoscope. We can use noon and the coordinates for Lenox, Massachusetts, as a basis for computing his sidereal time of birth. The results are also quite remarkable. The sun entered Aries at exactly 12:03 P.M., or noon, on March 21, 1918. This means that the *Medium coelum* or midheaven of Slothrop's chart would be a perfect zero degrees of Aries; the celestial equator would be directly overhead at birth, the sun's declination at zero. A striking pattern of balanced oppositions also occurs in the chart itself. Slothrop's sun is in Aries, his tenth house while the moon counterbalances it in Libra, his fourth house. Similarly, Mercury in Pisces (his ninth) is neatly counterbalanced by Mars in Virgo (his third); Venus and Uranus in Aquarius (his eighth) are balanced by Neptune and Saturn in Leo (his second); and finally, Jupiter in Gemini (his twelfth) is balanced by Pluto in Sagittarius (his sixth). In sum, Slothrop's horoscope would demonstrate the motif of opposites held in equipoise that readers have noted in other mandala images in *GR*. Like the Fool, the null card in the tarot deck, Slothrop is astrologically zeroed out.

Or perhaps not. The one hitch in these naturalizing projections is that Slothrop's father, Broderick, laments having "a double Virgo" for a son (for further discussion, see V699.17n). The remark could easily refer to the presence of Mars in Virgo on Slothrop's natal chart. Or it could be that Slothrop is a Virgo (born between August 23 and September 22) and that chasing down these patterns sends one off on a fool's errand, another *poisson d'avril*. That uncertainty dogs the novel as a whole.

V624.20, B727.15, P636.34   fifth-columnists   Originally the term applied to those residents of Madrid who sympathized with Generalissimo Francisco Franco during the Spanish civil war. General Emilio Mora was leading four columns of troops against that city and hoping sympathizers inside would rise up as a "fifth column" and come to his aid. Ernest Hemingway defines the circumstances and the term in his introduction to *The Fifth Column* (v–vi). In general use now, the phrase indicates any sympathizers, saboteurs, and secret supporters who assist enemies of a nation from within that nation's borders.

V624.31, B727.26–27, P637.6   Frisch Fromm Frölich Frei   The Viking edition contains a misprint: "Frölich" should be "Fröhlich," as corrected in the Bantam (but not the Penguin). This Nazi motto might be translated "Fresh Faithful Frisky Free."

V625.3–4, B728.4–5, P637.16–17   he becomes a cross himself, a crossroads   See V622.17–21n and lines 9–11 of Rilke's sonnet.

V625.5, B728.6–7, P637.18–19   a common criminal . . . hanged at noon   This certainly recalls the noon execution of Jesus, flanked as he was by "common criminals." See also the discussion of "Rocket Noon" and "Evil Hour" at V500.40n and V374.39–375.2n.

V625.10, B728.13, P637.23–24   gnädige Frau Death   The gracious lady Madame Death.

V625.17, B728.22, P637.31   a mandrake root   This narrative digression stems from Jacob Grimm's discussion (*Teutonic Mythology* 1202–03) of the *Alraun*, or mandrake root:

> If a hereditary thief that has preserved his chastity gets hung, and drops water or seed from him, there grows up under the gallows the broad-leaved yellow-flowered mandrake. If dug up, she groans and shrieks so dismally, that the digger would die thereof. He must therefore stop his ears with cotton or wax, and go before sunrise on a Friday, and take with him a black dog that has not a white hair on him, make three crosses over the mandrake, and dig round her till the roots hold by thin fibres only; these he must tie with a string to the dog's tail, hold up a piece of bread before him, and run away. The dog rushes after the bread, wrenches up the root, and falls dead, pierced by her agonizing wail. The root is then taken up . . . washed with red wine, wrapt in silk red and white, laid in a casket, bathed every Friday, and clothed in a new little white smock every new-moon. When questioned, she reveals future and secret things touching welfare and increase, makes rich, removes all enemies, brings blessings upon wed-

lock, and every piece of coin put to her overnight is found doubled in the morning, but she must not be over-loaded. When her owner dies, she goes to the youngest son, provided he puts a piece of bread and a coin in her father's coffin.

V625.18, B728.23, P637.32 Heiligenschein Saint's halo; also, a luminescence around the shadow of a person's head caused by light diffracting through vapor or dew.

V625.29, B728.36–37, P638.2 Committee on Idiopathic Archetypes Note this "CIA."

V625.38–39, B729.5, P638.11 kif moirés The kif (or kef) is marijuana from the Maghreb region; a moiré is a pattern created by the superimposition of one repetitive design on the same or a different one, which typically results in a doubling effect where one image transforms, in the blink of an eye, into another (as, for example, in the work of M. C. Escher).

V626.2, B729.10, P638.15 "Chapter 81 work" Larsson ("From the Berkshires to the Brocken") provides a gloss from *The Berkshire Hills*. Depression-era Massachusetts maintained country roads in the Berkshires with publicly funded and administratively categorized improvement projects: "Chapter 81 work is for road improvement, during which a scraper removes sod and dirt from ditches and shoulders, followed by workers who clean out ditches and replace culverts and drains" (216).

EPISODE 2

The Counterforce begins to take shape. Roger Mexico learns that Jessica Swanlake has permanently deserted him for Jeremy, the "Beaver." Roger strikes back with a vulgar "commando raid" on one of "Their" board meetings. He urinates on their conference table. Also, more economic details treat the controls exercised on Slothrop when he was a child. Back at Pirate's Chelsea maisonette, Roger finds a host of other disaffected cast members joining him. The Counterforce now consists of Pirate and Katje, Roger, Stephen Dodson-Truck, Milton Gloaming, Osbie Feel, and Thomas Gwenhidwy.

V626.22, B729.35–36, P638.36 a pre-Hitler Horch 870B The Horch was Germany's version of the SS Jaguar: powerful, relatively quiet, well-appointed touring cars. There is no mention in the literature of an 870 model. In fact, the Horch 800 line first appeared in 1933, and that is no longer "pre-Hitler."

V626.24, B729.38, P639.2 Heidschnucken sheep Take their name from *Heide* (heath) and *Schnucken* (a little breed of sheep). These "little heath sheep" are common only to the Lüneburg region of northern Germany.

V628.4, B731.28–29, P640.21   optimum time is 8 May, just before the traditional Whitsun exodus   Recall that part 2 ends with Pointsman and crew spending "Whitsun by the sea" (V269.26n). This traditional British holiday weekend fell on May 20 in 1945. On the significance of V-E Day, see V269.32n.

V628.23–24, B732.10–11, P641.1   wide as a Fortress's wings   Another reference to the B-17 Flying Fortress bomber (with a wingspan of 104 feet).

V628.28, B732.16–17, P641.5   her ATS brogans   Jessica's work shoes were issued for her assignment in the (women's) Auxiliary Territorial Services (V17.26n).

V628.32, B732.22, P641.9–10   The day the rockets stopped falling it began to end for Roger and Jessica   Their wartime love ended, that is; the last V-2 fell at 7:45 p.m. on Ash Wednesday, March 28, 1945, on Orpington, Kent (see V238.7–8n).

V628.36, B732.26, P641.13   Woolworth's   The department store chain (see V114.19n).

V629.6–7, B732.41, P641.26   *News of the World*   The London weekly periodical dishing up news, alongside great helpings of gossip, scandal, the sensational.

V629.17, B733.13, P641.37   ganged to   In electrical terminology, the mating of two or more circuits to a common line, facilitating simultaneous control of them all.

V630.6–12, B734.9–16, P642.27–33   Josef Schleim . . . to work for Imperial Chemicals   Mr. Schleim (slime, mucus) is fictional, but the remainder of the detail here derives from Sasuly (*IG Farben* 95–108). Max Ilgner headed the industrial spy ring at IG Farben. His operating base was the Berlin office known as NW7, the largest section of which was innocently abbreviated VOWI, the statistical department of IG Farben, a section that was headed by a Dr. Reithinger, mentioned here in *GR*. His principal job was to gather financial and economic data on foreign countries, under cover of "scientific exchange," and to coordinate with the Army High Command (OKW) in disseminating that information. From the United States, data were funneled through the various IG subsidiaries: Chemnyco, General Aniline and Film (GAF), Ansco, and Winthrop Chemical. From England, information came through Imperial Chemical (not Chemicals, as in *GR*), IG Farben's main British contact.

V630.16, B734.20–21, P642.37   Geheime Kommandosache   See V242.9–15n.

V630.23, B734.29, P643.3   the Wehrwirtschaftstab   Very likely this is a misspelling in *GR* for *Wehrwirtschaftsstab* (literally, military economics staff), a unit of the OKW responsible for calculating the raw material requirements of the military.

V630.25, B734.31–32, P643.5   OKW . . . Vermittlungsstelle W   Or, the

Army High Command and the Liaison Office. Sasuly (108) quotes from a 1935 memorandum outlining its strategic objectives: "To the field of work of the Vermittlungsstelle W belongs . . . the continuous collaboration with regard to armament and technical questions between the authorities of the Reich and the plants of the IG." For the remainder of the details concerning this office, the source is Sasuly 106–10. Pynchon's representation of the *Sparte,* or "branch" system, stems from the organizational outline included in the Kilgore Committee report on IG Farben submitted to the U.S. Senate and appended to Sasuly's book (esp. 274–75). An *Abteilung* is a department.

V631.2, B735.10, P643.22   some name like Mipolam   According to the *A-4 Fibel,* Pynchon's source, Mipolam was the name of a plastic sheeting used to protect rocket components.

V631.5–6, B735.13–14, P643.26–27   Ter Meer was a Draufgänger—he and Hörlein   The narrator here singles out two of the most notorious *Draufgänger,* or go-getters, of IG Farben. Prior to World War I, Dr. Heinrich Hörlein headed the research laboratory of IG's Bayer (aspirin) subsidiary. He had the lab systematically testing *every* new coal-tar derivative and dye to determine if it had possible uses in medicine or industry. In 1909 the company obtained a patent on a brick-red dye that also turned out to have startling antibacterial properties: it was sulfanilamide. IG Farben hid the information. It was not until 1933 that an American IG subsidiary, Winthrop Chemical, first marketed this sulfadrug compound under the trade name of Prontosil. By this time, IG had a virtual lock on the sulfa-drug patents and stood to make a fortune on its worldwide monopoly over production and distribution. During World War II Fritz Ter Meer was, according to Sasuly (30–31), "one of the half-dozen most important men in the IG." He had knowledge of IG's development and use of tabun gas in the death houses at Auschwitz. Questioned at the Nuremberg trials about the ethics of such "research," he answered that it stood to benefit IG Farben in the long run and, besides, "no harm had been done to these KZ [concentration camp] inmates, as they would have died anyway" (ibid. 125–26).

V631.10–11, B735.20, P643.31–32   "rather thin chap with thick eyeglasses"   It was Weissmann/Blicero.

V631.25, B735.37–38, P644.5   the Jaguar   Pointsman has withdrawn the use of his "vintage Jaguar" (V38.38n) from the PISCES motor pool, leaving his colleagues with the Morris, one of Britain's least expensive workingman's cars.

V631.29–31, B735.42–736.2, P644.9   Nayland Smith campaign . . . Sax Rohmer's great Manichaean saga   See V277.34–38n. Pointsman's "visitation" on Whitsunday (episode 8, part 2) has blossomed into this "campaign."

V632.39, B737.20–21, P645.19   Vereinigte Stahlwerke   United Steel-

works, of Düsseldorf, a gigantic trust founded in 1926 and a vertical monopoly "of giant dimension" (Levy, *Industrial Germany* 55) linked to
the IG Farben cartel through its collieries and to the Siemens cartel
through its electrical works.

V633.1, B737.24–25, P645.22   "Miss Müller-Hochleben"   Punning on
"Miller High Life." Founded in 1855 in Milwaukee by brewer Frederick
J. Miller, the Miller Brewing Company introduced its popular "High
Life" brand in 1903.

V633.40, B738.30, P646.21   "the S.P.R."   The Society for Psychical Research.

V634.22, B739.14, P647.3   a Beardsley gown   Such as British artist
Aubrey Beardsley might have drawn for one of his imposing dames (see
V71.27n).

V635.35, B740.37, P648.18   3-sigma colors   That is, colors that are non-
standard, (way) outside the norm (see V40.13–14n).

V635.37, B740.39, P648.20   Atlantis   See V269.9–10n.

**V636.28–29, B741.34–36, P649.10–12   Phi Beta Kappa keys . . . Dewey-
for-President lapel pins**   An international catalog of badges of election.
Phi Beta Kappa is an American honorary society, and the key its principal symbol. The Legion of Honor, Order of Lenin, Iron Cross, and Victoria Cross ("V.C.") are medals of valor awarded to soldiers (and, at times,
civilians) by, respectively, the governments of France, Russia, Germany,
and Britain, and only for consummate heroism and extraordinary service
to the nation. The Republican Thomas E. Dewey (1902–71) twice ran for
the presidency of the United States: against Roosevelt in 1944 and
against Truman (to whom he narrowly lost) in 1948. In 1944 his plat-
form was raised on the promise that he would "get big government off
the back of business."

**V637.11, B742.21–22, P649.34–35   Douglas Fairbanks scampering across
that moon minaret**   The reference is to *Thief of Baghdad* (1924), a silent
film in which Fairbanks (1883–1939) stars as a scimitar-wielding swash-
buckler.

V637.13, B742.24, P649.37   Roger dives under . . . to button his fly   A
misprint in the Bantam has Roger diving under the table "to unbutton
his fly" (it is already unbuttoned).

**V637.37–38, B743.11–12, P650.21   "*Dick Whittington!*" . . . zooming
down Kings Road**   A mercer, adventurer, and three-time lord mayor of
London, Whittington (d. 1423), a member of the preterite raised to elite
status, has a monument to his honor in Hampstead Heath, one of London's upper-crust neighborhoods. Kings Road runs southwest out of central London, nearly parallel to the Chelsea Embankment. It got its name
in the seventeenth century when Charles II used it as his private route
to Hampton Court and his mistress, Nell Gwynne.

V638.12, B743.29, P650.38   "the Haig and Haig"   Brand of Scotch
whiskey.

V638.13, B743.31, P650.39 **"Chebychev's Theorem"** In everyday life as in statistical investigations of a theoretical nature, it is important to know if the probability of an event—say, a bridge collapsing or a nuclear material successfully fissioning—will be nearer to zero or to one, respectively. Using large numbers as a model, the Russian mathematician P. L. Chebyshev was able to create a formula for these types of calculations.

V638.33, B744.11, P651.17 **Jan Otyiyumbu** The last name means "fire-brand" (Kolbe, *An English-Herero Dictionary* 57), appropriate for a spy or "liaison man" placed in London.

V638.37, B744.16, P651.21 **a Porky Pig tattoo** Because the pig has been a totemic sign of the preterite throughout *GR*. Also, because Porky last appeared in a simile: Pirate looked like "Porky Pig holding out the anarchist's ticking bomb" to Katje, during their "tour" of hell (V545.4–5n).

V639.18–19, B744.42–43, P652.4–5 **Sabbatai Zvi's apostasy before the Sublime Porte** Amid the widespread messianism of seventeenth-century Europe, Sabbatai Zvi (or Zevi) emerged as one of the most charismatic and interesting figures. Despite his lowly origins (he was the son of a Smyrna poulterer), Zvi became well schooled in Kabbalistic doctrine. During the mid-seventeenth century he began to gather around himself a band of fanatical Jewish disciples who believed him to be the messiah. Zvi preached that the Torah had been inscribed without vowels and punctuation because of Adam's sin. As punishment, God arranged the letters into words treating only of earth and death. The same letters, proclaimed Zvi, will be rearranged with the coming of the true messiah, who will eliminate death altogether and thus interpret the Torah in a new way, in a way that rids it of its original sense of mortal chaos. The new reading, he believed, would say nothing of death and uncleanness and would contain no proscriptions against animals such as swine. Like Jesus of Nazareth, Zvi was in frequent danger. Jews and Muhammadans alike denounced Zvi as a false messiah and a heretic. Sources differ on the date, but it appears that on September 14, 1666, Holy Cross Day, he was arrested and brought before the Ottoman emperor, called the Sublime Porte or "High Gate" (from the Turkish *Bab-i Ali*). The emperor, Mahomed IV, demanded and got a complete renunciation out of Zvi, who became a Muhammadan on the spot and descended into obscurity.

V639.39, B745.24–25, P652.25 **a rosewood crwth** A traditional Welsh instrument, stringed and fretless like a violin, and played with a bow.

EPISODE 3

A colonel from Kenosha gets a horrifying haircut. Above him is a light bulb that has traveled widely throughout Europe, and also through previous episodes of *GR*. Outside his tent a harmonica player—evidently it's Slothrop—plays a mortal blues. "The Story of Byron the Bulb" extends Pynchon's paranoid conspiracies into the power and light industry. This weird salmagundi concludes with Private First Class Pensiero (from the Latin for deep, dark "thinking" and the Italian *"pensiero," "thought"*) poised over the colonel's jugular with a pair of haircutting shears.

V640.23, B746.10, P653.11   A certain lycanthropophobia or fear of Were-wolves   In the Bantam the "or" is mistakenly omitted. Recall that, as Greta Erdmann said, Blicero in his last days "had grown on, into another animal . . . a werewolf" (V486.3). There is also a historical precedent for the reference. In the last days of war and on into the summer of occupation, Allied troops clashed with so-called Werewolf Packs, German resistance fighters who refused to concede defeat. They had a song:

I am so savage, I am filled with rage—
Hoo, hoo, hoo!
Lily the werewolf is my name;
I bite, I eat, I am not tame—
Hoo, hoo, hoo!
My werewolf teeth bite the enemy,
And then he's gone, and then he's done—
Hoo, hoo, hoo!

An article in *Time* magazine for April 16, 1945 (40), describes the Werewolf threat and quotes this song. McGovern (*Crossbow and Overcast* 159) also mentions the Werewolves' postwar activities.

V640.25–26, B746.12–14, P653.13–14   Potato crops . . . all went to make alcohol for the rockets   See V550.14–15n.

V640.30–31, B746.20, P653.19–20   bright as dittany in July   The *Dictamus albus*, also called "burning bush" or "fraxinella," is a summer-blooming plant with white flowers and leaves so aromatic that even their vapors may be ignited.

V640.31, B746.21, P653.20   Eddie Pensiero   A marvelous pun deriving from the "La donna e mobile" aria of Giuseppe Verdi's 1851 opera, *Rigoletto*. The significant verse reads, in Italian:

La donna e mobile
Quai pluma al vento
Muta d'accento
E di pensiero

[Woman is fickle
As a feather in the wind,
She changes her tune
And her thoughts.]

V640.33–35, B746.23–26, P653.18–19   the divisional patch . . . all in black and olive-drab   Pynchon's source was probably the *Life* magazine spread entitled "Shoulder Insignia," in the issue of August 6, 1945 (41–47). The patch for the Eighty-ninth Division, which fought in central Germany, could (to Pensiero's drug-addled vision) resemble a cluster of three rocket noses, "seen out of a dilating asshole."

V641.10–11, B746.38–747.1, P653.34–35 has been growing in his brain a kind of discriminator circuit In radiation detection devices, a discriminator circuit distinguishes between and selects from different waveforms on the basis of pulse height—which is how Pensiero "reads . . . people's shivers."

V641.17, B747.8–9, P654.6–7 Fourier-analyzed into their harmonics In the analysis of periodic waveforms, physicists use the Fourier series, developed in 1811 by the French mathematician Jean Baptiste Joseph Fourier (1768–1830). The series represents all the frequencies that are present in the waveform, including overtones or harmonics in a musical tone.

V641.20, B747.13–14, P654.10 Howard ("Slow") Lerner Anticipates the title of Pynchon's 1984 collection of short stories, *Slow Learner*.

V641.30, B747.24, P654.20 the "benny" habitué Eddie Pensiero gets his single-minded focus from his addiction to Benzedrine, a brand of amphetamine tablets known in the drug underworld as "bennies." Benzedrine is marketed by the Smith, Kline and French company, which was mentioned in part 3 (V518.31–32n).

V641.40, B747.37, P654.30–31 A Tree Grows in Brooklyn This 1945 film was Elia Kazan's directorial debut. It won two Oscar awards, one for Peggy Ann Garner's portrayal of a sensitive girl growing up in the slums and another for James Dunn in a supporting role as her drunken father.

V642.32, B748.32–33, P655.23–24 "something has exploded . . . in the East" The atomic bombs used on Hiroshima (August 6) and Nagasaki (August 9). The island of Krakatoa was obliterated by volcanic eruption in 1883, and a cloud of ash and gases circled the earth for four years afterward. The A-blasts were thousands of times less powerful.

V643.1, B749.3, P655.34 "I'm from Kenosha, Wisconsin" So perhaps this colonel is "the Kenosha Kid" of episode 10, part 1?

V643.4, B749.7, P655.37 "Graves Registration" A division of the U.S. Army whose job it is to gather, autopsy, identify, and ship home the bodies of the dead.

V643.11, B749.14, P656.4 Atropos In Greek myth, one of the three Fates. Clotho spins out the thread of destiny, Lachesis winds it onto spools, and Atropos cuts it. A figure, then, of death.

V643.24, B749.30, P656.17–18 number 2 and 3 hole Bass and mid-range notes on the harmonica.

V644.15, B750.28, P657.11 dacoits The robber bands of Burma, figures of terror in Sax Rohmer's novels (see V13.28n).

V644.21, B750.38, P657.18 Oh, *will they*, Skippy? Beginning in 1923,

"Skippy" was a syndicated cartoon strip drawn by Percy Crosby (1891–1964) for the King Features Syndicate, and by the mid-twenties its title character—a street-smart nine-year-old American boy—was a household name. In the strips, which focused on Skippy's urban adventures, his dialogue looked on the pages more or less like Pynchon writes it here. For an example of how it sounded, see nine-year-old Jackie Cooper in the role in *Skippy* (Fox, 1931), for which he picked up an Oscar nomination in the Best Actor category.

V644.25–26, B750.42, P657.23   that A-sticker   Gasoline rationing, controlled through the Office of Price Administration, was imposed on U.S. consumers beginning in the spring of 1942. The administrators devised a system of cards, which were later replaced by stickers. An "A" sticker designated nonessential passenger use, "B" was for drivers who required an automobile for business, "T" for commercial transports, and so on. Throughout the war, A-sticker allotments of gasoline averaged five gallons per week.

V646.8, B752.31, P659.5   "I'm evading-room vino from Visconsin"   A pun: "I'm a waiting room wino from Wisconsin." This is why "the nurses run."

V646.12, B752.36, P659.9–10   an ingenious Osmo-elektrische Schalterwerke   A *Schalterwerke* is a switch works or switching device; and Osmo-elektrische is a trade-name designation of the German Siemens manufacturing cartel.

V646.14, B752.38, P659.11   Beeman's licorice flavor   In the 1880s, Dr. Edward Beeman began marketing his brand of chewing gum, combining pepsin with the basic gum (chicle) and promoting it as a cure for indigestion and even the insomnia caused by an upset stomach. In 1899, Beeman joined his company with three other manufacturers to form a sort of chewing gum cartel, the American Chicle Company (now a subsidiary of Cadbury Adams), producers also of Chiclets (see V558.3). A side note: Beeman's early advertisements claimed that "with pepsin, you can eat like a pig" and his wrappers featured the image of a pig (the pig was later replaced with Beeman's bearded visage).

V646.33, B753.18, P659.32   the Schokoladestrasse   The fictional Zurich street mentioned at V250.41 (see also the V250.41n).

V646.38, B753.25, P659.38   lieder   German for "songs."

V647.5, B753.34, P660.5   Osram light bulb   A European trade name, Osram light bulbs were available in England as well as on the Continent. Pynchon mentions other light bulbs in the course of this digression: Tungsram (Hungary, Czechoslovakia, and Romania), the Nitralampen brand produced by the Emil Rathenau–founded AEG company of Germany (see V163.19–23), Azos (an Austrian brand), and Philips (Dutch).

V648.4, B754.40, P661.5   this roach's abreaction   For a definition of this therapeutic term from psychoanalysis, see V48.14n.

V649.12–13, B756.17, P662.13–14   Herbert Hoover, Stanley Baldwin
Respectively, the U.S. president from 1929 to 1933, and the British
prime minister from 1923 to 1929 and 1935 to 1937, which would mean
these fantastical events are taking place in 1929.

**V649.15, B756.20–21, P662.17   "Phoebus," the international light-bulb
cartel**   Pynchon's source, Levy (*Industrial Germany*), explains that battles over patent rights and market pricing of tungsten filament light-
bulbs intensified greatly in the early decades of the twentieth century
and led to syndication and cartelization. Indeed, Levy (writing in 1935)
found that *"the most* prominent example of international interconnec-
tion in the electric industry is certainly represented by the history and
development of the electric lamp manufacture" (96), a strategy adopted
by the industry in its efforts to solve problems of competition. Thus
from several earlier syndicates there arose "a much more important international cartel, the *Internationale Glühlampen Preis-Vereinigung*
(I.G.P.) in 1921." When it was dissolved in 1924 because of increasing
overlap with competitors outside the cartel, representatives of companies like the German Siemans, Dutch Osram, Dutch Philips, and American General Electric (among others) worked up a new set of agreements,
signed in Geneva in December 1924, establishing the "Phoebus S.A.
Compagnie Industrielle pour le Developpement de l'Eclairage"—a new
"world-combine" or cartel estimated to have controlled 90 percent of
the world's lightbulb production and marketing (Levy 98).

V649.27, B756.35–36, P662.29   the statue of Wernher Siemens   According to Baedeker (*Northern Germany* 184), this statue commemorating
the founder is located on Franklin Strasse in the Charlottenburg district
of Berlin, in a park across the street from the old Siemens factory. Ernst
Werner von Siemens (1816–92; sources other than Baedeker give his
name as "Werner," and the "von" was added when he was raised to the
Prussian nobility in 1888) founded Siemens and Halske in 1847, which
initially specialized in the production of electric cable, then moved into
electric power engineering, and eventually invented and manufactured
(among other things) the electric tramway (1879) and the elevator (1880).

V649.34, B757.2, P662.36   prayers to Astarte and Lilith   The Syrian goddess Astarte has been widely identified with Aphrodite and Venus, the
Greek and Roman goddesses of love. In Hebrew mythology, Lilith was
Adam's first wife. After she left Adam she became a demonic female
spirit known for haunting children in forests and glades.

V650.12, B757.26, P663.15–16   The Phoebus Surveillance Room   A fantasy, here.

V650.14, B757.28, P663.17   ebonite   Also known as vulcanite, ebonite is
a hard, vulcanized rubber used in buttons, combs, and (here) electrical
insulators.

V650.30–32, B758.6–8, P663.33–36   every bulb, Azos . . . Monowatts and

Siriuses   Still more tungsten filament incandescent electric lamps from the early twentieth century, most of them European: on Azos and Nitralampen see above (V649.12–13n); the Just-Wolfram was the brand of the Austrian manufacturer Just-Hanamann of Augsburg; the Monowatt brand bulb was produced by A. Wolff and Company of New York, and the Sirius, produced by Kuzel-Sirius, was another Austrian brand.

V650.38–39, B758.16, P663.41–664.1   Committee on Incandescent Anomalies   Another CIA.

V651.24, B759.6–7, P664.28–29   young Hansel Geschwindig   The German adjective *"geschwindig"* means "speedy."

V652.11–12, B759.42–760.1, P665.15   Salitieri, Poore . . . Buddy at the last minute decided to go see *Dracula*   On Buddy Bland's moviegoing habits and his absences see V591.18n. Note also the return of Pynchon's wonderfully named law firm partners (see V591.10–11n) serving here as Lyle Bland's pallbearers.

V652.19–20, B760.10, P665.24   a Reeperbahn *prostitute*   The Reeperbahn, one of the principal thoroughfares in Hamburg's St. Pauli district, is famous for its thriving houses of prostitution.

V652.29, B760.22, P665.33   he reaches Helgoland   Again, the tiny island off the Schleswig-Holstein coast. Its name, "Holy Land," stems from the ancient Teutonic belief that it was a sacred home for dead souls. The *Hengst* (stallion) and the *Mönch* (monk) are two of the "rocks that have received fanciful names" on the island (Baedeker, *Northern Germany* 158).

V652.33–34, B760.27–28, P665.38   a certain 1911 Hochheimer   A fruity, mellow white wine from the Rheingau region of Germany, near Frankfurt; a high-quality wine, according to Lichine (Fifield, ed., *Alexis Lichine's Encyclopedia of Wines and Spirits*).

V652.35, B760.28, P665.38–39   the great Berlin Eispalast   The city's Ice Palace opened in 1908 on the Potsdamer Strasse.

V653.6, B761.2, P666.11   Mausmacher   His moniker means "mouse maker."

V653.14, B761.12, P666.19   "Die Fahne Hoch"   See V443.2n.

V654.27, B762.35–36, P667.33   the arrangement between General Electric and Krupp   Pynchon's source is Sasuly (*IG Farben* 175): "In 1938 the Krupps made an agreement with the American General Electric Company concerning tungsten carbide. . . . In Germany tungsten carbide was produced in quantity and sold for prices ranging from $37.00 to $90.00 per pound. In the United States [it] was made in small quantities and sold at prices ranging from about two hundred dollars to four hundred dollars per pound." An antitrust action burst this bubble in 1940. See also Levy, *Industrial Germany* (76–78).

V654.38–39, B763.7–8, P668.2   *Seele*, as the core of the earlier carbon filament was known in Germany   In technical German *die Seele* (the soul) indicates the core of any object, for example, an electrical cable, the bore of a gun, or the filament of a light bulb.

EPISODE 4

Katje Borgesius meets with Enzian and discloses to him what she knows of Blicero's last days in Holland. Coming upon the Herero troops, she is startled to see them performing a dance in which she herself figures as the "Golden Bitch" (V658.21) of Blicero's sadoerotic fantasies. In short, she's already the stuff of legend and ritual. Blicero's survival after the Easter launch of Rocket 00000 is disclosed to readers.

V656.34–35, B765.20, P670.1   the Sprudelhof   See V458.14n.

V656.36, B765.27, P670.2   Pan   The Greek god of woods and fields, half goat and half man. More significantly, however, Pan is the name applied to the "chief devil" during black magic rites.

V657.10–11, B765.34–35, P670.13–14   Diamond Lil or Texas Guinan Guinan was a medium for the key phrase in Pynchon's pun at V559.16–17. Born in 1884, she worked as a chorus girl, vaudeville trouper, and gun-girl heroine of numerous horse operas produced during the silent era of American cinema. With Prohibition, she opened a string of nightclubs (speakeasies), which brought rapid profits and fame. Prohibition agents were continually frustrated in their attempts to close down her businesses. One club, the Texas Guinan Club on West Forty-eighth Street in Manhattan, lasted for five tumultuous years, until a widely publicized 1929 raid forced its closure. By then, the term "Texas Guinan Clubs" applied to speakeasies in general. In 1930 she began touring with a troupe of forty dance girls; tried, and failed, to establish them in Paris; returned to the United States; and, during a tour of North America, died unexpectedly of ulcerated colitis in 1933. Honora ("Diamond Lil") Ornstein (1883–?) was a club dancer who achieved some notoriety in the early decades of the twentieth century. Her nickname derived from the diamond she had a dentist implant in one of her incisors and from the copious stones she wore about her person.

V657.17, B765.42, P670.20   Even Goya, couldn't draw ya   Francisco Goya (1746–1828) was, aside from a genius painter, a master draftsman, and his drawings of the monstrous (as in his series "The Caprichios") are famous examples of the grotesque style. In short, very grotesque.

V657.22, B766.5, P670.25   ENSA   Acronym for the Entertainers' National Service Association, the British sponsor of shows and entertainments for the Crown's servicemen stationed abroad.

V657.33–34, B766.18, P670.37   an Isadora Duncan routine   After the

American dancer who died in 1927, at the age of forty-eight, when her long scarf caught on the axle of a sports car in which she was riding.

V658.26–27, B767.15, P671.28   the great Kalahari rock painting of the White Woman   All the Bantu-speaking peoples of the Kalahari region, the Hereros included, used to draw such petroglyphs. The "White Woman," however, probably derives from Parrinder (*African Mythology* 27), who includes an illustration and comments that "Bushmen were great engravers and painters on rock surfaces in red, black, yellow, white, and brown. The subjects are usually hunting, fighting or dancing. The practice of the art has almost completely died out, as there are only a few thousand Bushmen left and the survivors rarely know the meaning of the designs. This is clearly a hunting scene and the central figure is called the White Lady, though no more is known about it than the color."

V658.33, B767.23, P671.35   leukemia of soul   Physiologically, the disease involves an uncontrolled proliferation of the leukocytes, or white blood cells.

V659.17, B768.9, P672.18   he got as far as the Lüneberg Heath   A misspelling in all three texts: it should be "Lüneburg."

V660.26, B769.28, P673.29   "All this I will give you, if you will but—"   The completion of this biblical quotation is "fall down before me" (Luke 4:6–7) and they are Satan's words to Jesus, when offering him the kingdoms of the world.

V661.21, B770.31, P674.25   "sadder that that?"   The phrase should be "than that"; it is a misprint in early printings of the Viking and in the Bantam edition but was ultimately corrected.

V661.27–28, B770.38, P674.30–31   Pan's grove   The meeting place of a witches' coven (see V656.36n).

V661.30, B770.41, P674.33–34   the Qlippoth   "Shells of the dead" in Kabbalistic lore (see V176.14–15n).

V661.39, B771.9–10, P675.1   smooth as that Cary Grant   See V13.34–35n and V240.41n.

V662.7, B771.19–20, P675.10   this Suave Older Exotic   Remember that Pirate Prentice was a commando with the SOE (Special Operations Executive). See V5.15.

V663.2–3, B772.16–17, P676.7–8   "someone who was with Blicero in May. Just before the end"   The timing is noteworthy. Blicero clearly goes his own way after launching Rocket 00000, before "the end" of hostilities on May 8, 1945. The mentioning of Blicero here is a key to Weissmann's fortunes after his Easter sacrifice of Gottfried, for Pynchon will soon disclose how we might look for him in positions of political and industrial power (see "Weissmann's Tarot," esp. V749.9–12). Weissmann's betrayal to the world, to mammon, may also be interpreted from an anagram given later (see V746.9n).

V663.6–7, B772.22–23, P676.11–12   like mischievous Ophelia just hav-

ing glimpsed the country of the mad   A reference to Ophelia's madness and suicide in *Hamlet* (4.7), hence her glimpsing *the other side.*

EPISODE 5

The time of this episode is indistinct, as is its exact location in the occupied zone of Germany. The narrator opens with a haughty "You will want cause and effect. All right." Then he proceeds to supply a full description of the rescue of Miklos Thanatz from the Baltic Sea, after he was swept overboard in the storm that tossed Slothrop from the *Anubis* in part 3. After Thanatz spent weeks wandering among Europe's preterite, the Schwarzkommando plucked him from a camp of displaced persons. To them Thanatz relates the story of Rocket 00000, fired from the Lüneburg Heath at noon.

V663.27, B773.8, P676.32   He's a digital companion   A points-man?

V663.37–664.1, B773.20–22, P677.5–6   Benjamin Franklin was also a Mason . . . practical jokesterism   According to Van Doren (*Benjamin Franklin* 132), Franklin's biographer, the earliest known Masonic Lodge in America was St. Johns's in Philadelphia, and its records date back to 1730. Franklin (1706–90) joined in February 1731, drafted its bylaws, and eventually became grand master of the province of Philadelphia. He helped build the first Masonic temple in the United States (1755). Franklin was an accomplished literary satirist and indeed given to practical joking. Van Doren tells (419) how he once hoaxed some French lords by promising to still some breeze-rippled waters. He walked around the pond and waved his cane three times over the water while mumbling some jibberish; within minutes all were amazed at its glassy surface. Franklin had released oil from a hollowed core in the cane.

V664.4–5, B773.25–26, P677.9–10   a sinuous curve with first derivatives at every point   That is, a sine wave or simple parabolic curve, every "point" or moment of which can be derived as the infinitesimal change (d) in the function (f) with respect to one variable (x), describable by the equation df/dx—a "first derivative" (see V641.17n). The "cusp" of such a curve (mentioned a few lines further down) is that point where two branches or sides of a curve meet, so that each branch is absolutely equal; the virtual peak of the parabola, therefore. At that point, in our narrator's fantasy here, the rate of change measured in infinitely small time units between points is positive on the upward curve and negative on the downslope. As Seed notices (*The Fictional Labyrinths of Thomas Pynchon* 202), the comic tone pulls the rug out from under all this theorizing.

V664.13, B773.37, P677.18   lammergeiers cruising there   Large predatory birds of Europe, the *Gypaetus barbatus*, called lammergeiers because they are said to swoop down on lost lambs, as on these lightning-struck souls.

V664.19, B774.2–3, P677.23–24   *Carmen Miranda* hats   Actress and singer Carmen Miranda's (1909–55) signature, especially when she starred opposite Don Ameche in, for example, *Down Argentine Way* (1940) and *That Night in Rio* (1941), was her extravagant high headgear, adorned with feathers and fruit.

V664.22, B774.5, P677.26   Wilhelmets   Pynchon's portmanteau word for the spike-top parade helmets or *Pickelhauber* that Kaiser Wilhelm II (1849–1941) and his German soldiers wore in World War I.

V664.26, B774.10, P677.30   like that sacrificial ape off the Empire State Building   In *King Kong* (see V275.13–14n).

V664.38, B774.25, P678.3   monthly magazine A Nickel Saved   The allusion is to Benjamin Franklin's maxim: "A penny saved is two pence clear; a pin a day's a groat a year" (from *Necessary Hints to Those That Would Be Rich*, 1736). But Franklin's saying was itself an inflated version of a still older, less greedy version: "A penny saved's a penny got" (anonymous).

V664.41–665.1, B774.28–30, P678.6–7   Mark Hanna's: "You have been in politics long enough . . . owes the public anything"   Mark Hanna (1837–1904)—Cleveland capitalist, nickel magnate, campaign manager for William McKinley in the 1896 presidential race, and then McKinley's appointee to a vacant Ohio Senate seat—wrote this advice to a young Ohio prosecuting attorney. The date was May 8 (Pynchon's birthday, V-E Day) in 1890; the occasion, the attorney's trust-busting suit against Standard Oil of Ohio (Josephson *The Robber-Barons* 353).

V665.8, B774.38–39, P678.14   got married Easter Sunday   In 1945, April Fool's.

V665.15, B775.5, P678.21   Hank Faffner   Named for Fafnir, the monster guarding the hoard of Nibelung gold in Teutonic myth and in Richard Wagner's *Ring* operas. Siegfried slays him, and Fafnir prophesies while dying (Grimm *Teutonic Mythology* 370–71).

V665.34, B775.29, P678.41   They are 175s   On this numerical designation in the German Penal Code and its application to homosexual inmates, see V289.29n.

V666.2–4, B775.40–776.1, P679.9   Schutzhäftlingsführer to . . . Läufer   In order of their appearance, these German nouns designate the Nazi warden and block leader at a concentration camp and then (among the inmates themselves) the camp head, block elder, trusty, foreman, house servant, and runner.

V667.3–4, B777.9–10, P680.12   noon on the Heath when 00000 was fired   This fixes the time of launch: "Rocket Noon," the "Evil Hour" (see V374.39–375.2n and V500.40n), the hour Christ was crucified.

V667.38, B778.7, P681.5   Too bad, les jeux sont faits   Once again the roulette croupier's call: "The bets are down."

V668.6, B778.18, P681.14   the gassen   Lanes.

V669.5, B779.20, P682.11   anti-Lublin   Persons opposed to the Russian-backed Polish Committee of National Liberation based in Lublin (V34.28–30n).

V669.23, B780.3, P682.30   Soldbuch   A German soldier's paybook.

V669.36, B780.18, P683.1   His daily bread is taken away by another DP   Thanatz, in other words, experiences the reverse of what is asked for when one recites the Lord's Prayer ("give us this day our daily bread"); that his bread is taken away rather than given to him is a sign of his preterition.

V670.15–16, B781.2, P683.21   black eyeball reflecting a windmill   Various references—to London's Windmill Theatre (V22.3n, V39.1–2n) and the Dutch windmill called "The Angel" where Pirate makes his rendezvous with Katje (V106.12n)—now culminate in this visionary moment when Thanatz, who has been referred to as "Angel Thanatz," recalls the reflection of a nonexistent windmill in Blicero's eyes as Rocket 00000 was readied for launch.

V670.20–21, B781.8, P683.26–27   snarling purple around a yellow   Significant colors in *GR*. Yellow and purple are color opposites that appear in the first stage of the Brocken specter (see V293.17n). Earlier, the narrator also identifies the colors with Weissmann's half brother, Enzian, the same name Weissmann gives to Gottfried during the Holland-based rocket launchings, and the name of Rilke's purple-and-yellow flower in the *Duino Elegies* (see V101.23–26). Then there is Margherita Erdmann, whose sign is the "purple-and-yellow iris at her breast" (V393.26).

V670.34, B781.25–26, P683.40   Wandervogel-limp   For the pre-Hitler youth movement in Germany, see V99.2n.

V670.38, B781.30–31, P684.3   about to don a wig, a Dragon Lady pageboy   The reference is to the hairstyle of comic-strip artist Milton Caniff's archvillainess, the Dragon Lady, in his *Terry and the Pirates* comic strip, syndicated for nearly five decades after its 1934 release by the Chicago Tribune syndicate. The strip focused initially on the story of Terry Lee and sidekick Pat Ryan searching for a mine discovered by Terry's grandfather. The Dragon Lady alternately seduces, humiliates, and attempts to murder our heroes. The addition of bangs to her pageboy hairstyle was evidently the addition of George Wunder, who took over *Terry* in 1946 when Caniff left to produce the *Steve Canyon* strip.

V672.8–9, B783.7, P685.13–14   Hamburg to Bydgoszcz in a purloined P-51 Mustang   Bydgoszcz is a city in central Poland, east of Hamburg; the Mustang was an American-made single-seat fighter aircraft.

V672.26, B783.28–29, P685.31   Zeros bearing comrades away   The Japanese Mitsubishi A6M8 fighter airplane (see V690.37–38n).

V673.37–38, B785.10–11, P687.2   iya, 'kurandye   The source was Kolbe (*An English-Herero Dictionary* 203). He gives *"indyo 'kurandye"* as "Come, my fellow." Pynchon appears to have taken *"iya"* as a variant of *"indyo"* ("to go," or "to come").

V673.38–39, B785.11–12, P687.2–3   the two palms do slide and brush, do touch   Here is that "miracle touch" that has appeared earlier (see V119.37n) and that will recur at novel's end.

EPISODE 6

In this episode the narration begins to fragment. A variety of discourses, modes, and forms are parodied in the twelve subsections, eleven of them titled. Two ("On the Phrase 'Ass Backwards'" and "Shit 'n' Shinola") may be read as parodies of the etymological/philological writing in Grimm's *Teutonic Mythology*, one of Pynchon's principal sources. Other subsections parody comic books (the opening section treating the "Floundering Four" and that treating "The Komical Kamikazes"), scientific writing ("Some Characteristics of Imipolex G"), travel handbooks ("Streets"), poetic forms (such as haiku and Miltonic verse), and letters ("Mom Slothrop's Letter to Ambassador Kennedy"). In the midst of it all, Slothrop finds a scrap of newspaper announcing the atomic blast at Hiroshima. The time range here is partly mid- to late August, though some fragments of the narration reference events of September. The action mainly occurs in northern Germany and Berlin, at Säure Bummer's flat on the (fictional) Jakobistrasse, with leaps to the United States.

V674.10, B785.25, P687.13   it's a giant factory-state here, a City of the Future   Perhaps on the model of Fritz Lang's sets for *Metropolis* (see V578.7–9n).

V674.19–20, B785.38, P687.24   the Radiant Hour   Phoebus (shining one) was a Greek kenning for the god Apollo. From prior references to the "Evil Hour" and "Rocket Noon," "the Radiant Hour" is probably high noon (see V374.39–375.2n).

V675.10–11, B786.33–35, P688.15   Club Oogabooga where Beacon Street ... with Roxbury winos   The club, whose name has obvious racist overtones, is a fictional Boston watering hole. Running southwest out of central Boston, Beacon Street skirts the Charles River and passes through the upper-crust community of Brookline (former home of the Kennedys), just southeast of which is Roxbury, the city's black ghetto at the time referred to here, which was founded by William Pynchon.

V675.15, B786.40, P688.21   Stephen Foster music   Perhaps "Old Black

Joe" or "My Old Kentucky Home," two songs by composer Stephen Collins Foster (1826–64) that might fit the context.

V675.18, B787.1–2, P688.24   the great conjurer Robert-Houdin   He was the renowned French magician of the nineteenth century; Erich Weiss (1874–1926) changed *his* name to Harry Houdini in order to pay homage to Robert-Houdin.

V675.23, B787.7–8, P688.29   hi-de-hoing in . . . one finger jivin' in the air   The image refers to zoot-suited Cab Calloway in the film *Stormy Weather* (1943). He dances and sings "Minnie the Moocher," with its refrain, "hi-de-hi-de-hi-de-hay! hi-de-hi-de-hi-de-ho!"

V675.32, B787.18–19, P688.38   the Floundering Four   The Foundering Four here are patterned on Marvel Comics' highly successful book series *The Fantastic Four*, which was first issued in 1961. The Fantastic Four are space-age types who ride a rocket into a belt of "cosmic radiation" and return to Earth transformed into superbeings. Sue Storm becomes "the Invisible Girl"; her brother, Johnny, becomes "the Human Torch," capable of blazing up unannounced (with no harm to himself); Ben Grimm becomes a super-strong "Thing," who looks like a cross between the Elephant Man and a stone fence; and Reed Richards becomes "Mr. Fantastic," capable of stretching and contorting himself much like Plasticman. Pynchon's Floundering Four also owe a debt to *The Wizard of Oz*. Like Dorothy's three traveling companions, Slothrop's also lack some essential quality: Maximilian (like the Cowardly Lion) lacks bravery; Marcel (like the Straw Man) lacks a "touch of humanity" (V675.37) in his brain; and Myrtle (like the Tin Woodsman) lacks heart, the "miracle" (V675.41) of love.

V675.34–35, B787.22, P688.40–41   little Johann Allgeier   The chess master, designer of board pieces and soldiers (V550.34n).

V676.4, B787.34–35, P689.10   Mary Marvel and Wonder Woman   In the early forties the Fawcett Comics group added a wrinkle to their highly successful *Captain Marvel* series. The captain was known in everyday life as Billy Batson, and in 1943 the Fawcett writers introduced Billy's long-lost twin sister, Mary, who reasons that if brother Billy has magic powers then so must she. Mary says the magic word—"Shazam!"—and becomes Mary Marvel, suited up in a red dress with a golden thunderbolt emblazoned across her ample chest. *Wonder Woman* was a comic book created by "Charles Moulton," the pseudonym of psychology professor William Moulton Marston. His superwoman was raised under the aegis of Aphrodite (Venus) on Paradise Island. She made her debut in the December 1941 issue of *Sensation Comics*, released through the Superman-D.C. Publications group. Her costume: a red strapless longline bra, golden headband, red culottes emblazoned with stars, and red boots. Her major weapon is a magic lasso worn girdle-like. When captured in it, feckless (male) criminals become immediately helpless.

V676.36, B788.33, P690.1   only a mutter   A misprint in the Viking and Bantam editions that was corrected in the Penguin to read: "only a matter."

V677.1–2, B788.41–42, P690.8–9   Those whom the old Puritan sermons denounced as "the glozing neuters of the world"   As David Seed has pointed out ("Thomas Hooker"), this is another quotation from Hooker's collection of sermons, *The Soules Implantation into the Natural Olive* (1637). To "gloze," according to the *OED*, is to veil a true meaning with specious comments or annotations, and in Hooker (238) there lies a middle ground between the "open enemies to Christ" and those who are merely "fawning hypocrites," namely, "all glozing Neuters of the world" who defer making any commitment. They are, he goes on (246), like "lukewarm water" that "goes against the stomacke, and the Lord abhors such lukewarme tame fooles." Hooker censures them, but in this passage (Seed notes) Pynchon pleads for the humanity. "When's the last time you felt intensely lukewarm? eh?" the narrator asks, concluding that "Glozing neuters are just as human as heroes and villains" (V677.5–7).

V677.26–27, B789.27, P690.34   "time for that *Pause that Refreshes!*"   As in, "A happy occasion is an occasion for a Coke, and the happy American custom, the *pause that refreshes!*" (a 1945 Coca-Cola advertisement).

V677.34, B789.36, P690.41   Kelvinator   Registered trademark of the Kelvinator Appliance Company of Grand Rapids, Michigan.

V677.36–37, B789.39, P691.2–3   "like Mawxies, 'n' big Baby Rooths"   Once again, Slothrop's favorite soft drink, Moxie, and favorite candy, Baby Ruth brand candy bars.

V678.14–15, B790.18, P691.19–20   in *love* with Chiquita Banana   The registered trademark of Chiquita Brands Incorporated, a subsidiary of what at the time was the United Fruit Company (see V678.26n). In the company's ads, she appeared as a leggy, south-of-the-border banana girl.

V678.21–22, B790.26–27, P691.26   the Spike Jones record of "Right in the Führer's Face"   Actually, the song was titled "Der Führer's Face." Oliver Wallace wrote it for a Walt Disney cartoon, "In Nutzy Land," featuring Donald Duck. However, when Spike Jones (1911–65) and his City Slickers made the song an overnight hit in 1942, Disney changed the name of Wallace's cartoon to that of the song. Spike Jones did the vocal, and Willie Spicer played a honking-farting instrument called the Birdophone. Here are the lyrics, with the honks:

> Ven der Fuehrer says ve ist da Master Race,
> Ve Heil! (honk), Heil! (honk) right in der Fuehrer's face.

> Not to love der Fuehrer iss a great dis-grace!
> So ve Heil! (honk), Heil! (honk) right in der Fuehrer's face.

Ven Herr Goebbels says ve own der World of space,
Ve Heil! (honk), Heil! (honk) right in Herr Goebbels' face.

Are ve not der Super-men, Aryan pure Super-men?
Jah ve iss der Super-men, Super-duper super-men!
Iss dis not zee land zo good?
Jah dis Nazi land iss good! Ve vould leave it if ve could!

Ve bring der world to order, heil Hitler's world to order (honk)!
Every one of foreign race will love der Fuehrer's face,
Ven ve bring der world dis-order (honk)!

In 1994, Pynchon wrote the liner notes for a Spike Jones CD, *Spiked!*
(Catalyst), in which he expresses a lifelong appreciation of Spike Jones's
musicianship and sense of humor. He also quotes Spike (from a 1945 interview) about the reasons why soldiers liked such music: "Soldiers just
don't go for stuff like 'Over There.' They want sentimental stuff or strictly
comic. We give 'em the comedy, and it's what the public goes for too."

V678.26, B790.32–33, P691.31   United Fruit's radio commercials   That
is, for Chiquita Bananas. United Fruit, the IG Farben of Central America
and the Caribbean basin, was formed in 1899 when Boston capitalist
Minor C. Keith unified two rival banana-importing firms, Boston Fruit
(owned by Andrew Preston) and his own Tropical Trading and Transport
Company. Keith's company was unrivaled for its extensive market and
Preston's company was famous for its so-called Great White Fleet (so-
called well before Theodore Roosevelt sent on a world tour, in 1907–9,
a battleship group also called the Great White Fleet). By 1940, United
Fruit handled almost 70 percent of the fruit and sugar business from the
Caribbean region; it also controlled lucrative mail contracts with the
United States and other governments; several thousand miles of railway;
telephone, telegraph, and electrification contracts for most of the region;
and its fleet. The UFC had political influence that made it possible
for it to remove and install governments almost at will. It lived by
exploiting cheap labor in Cuba, Jamaica, Nicaragua, Panama, Santo
Domingo, Guatemala, and Mexico. Throughout the thirties and forties
this cartel's repressive wage practices fueled labor unrest in Central
America.

V680.12–13, B792.33, P693.20   a pack of Armies   Service slang for packs
of generic, army-issue cigarettes.

V680.18, B792.40, P693.26   station Metatron . . . stall Malkuth   On the
angel Metatron in Kabbalistic lore, see V231.24–25n. Malkuth is probably Malkoth, or Malakoth, the female genitalia as represented on the
Kabbalist Tree of Life (see V747.41–748.5n).

**V681.20–21, B794.10, P694.29   message . . . back at the green edge of
Aries**   The "green" cusp of Aries would be at its end, around April 20–

23, as springtime fully emerges and Taurus takes over. In part 2 Slothrop takes the message from Squalidozzi, exchanges it, and returns to Zurich, where he fails to relocate the Argentine anarchist. The timing suggested here, April 20–23, jibes very well with chronological details from episode 7, which discloses that Slothrop's escape from Monaco occurred during the week of April 20–27, 1945.

V681.23–24, B794.14, P694.33   Rohr . . . just out of the Ravensbrück camp   Located sixty miles north of Berlin, the Ravensbrück concentration camp was built, in 1939, for the internment of women. By 1945 more than 92,000 of its 132,000 prisoners had been cruelly executed. Victims included mainly Jewish, Gypsy, and Communist women and their children, but later in the war a number of male religious prisoners, including Catholic priests and Jehovah's Witnesses, were also shipped to Ravensbrück.

V681.26, B794.17, P694.35   the local G-5   Political-administrative wing of the occupying U.S. Army (see V125.22n).

V681.30, B794.21–22, P694.39   a War Crimes Tribunal . . . in Nürnberg   On August 8, 1945, British and Soviet delegates agreed on Nuremberg as a site for the War Crimes Tribunal. Trials didn't begin until November 20.

V681.32, B794.24–25, P695.2–3   antisocial and mindless pleasures   Echoing a rejected prepublication title for *Gravity's Rainbow*.

V681.34–36, B794.27–30, P695.5   on 28,000 meters (the distance . . . in Griefswald, where Slothrop . . . newspaper photo)   The distance is equal to 17.2 miles, and it roughly tallies with the scaled distances on David Irving's maps of the Peenemünde area (*Mare's Nest* 6, 96). Slothrop's discovery of the news photograph showing Hiroshima will occur at V693.39–41.

V682.8–9, B795.2–3, P695.20   Nalline into . . . *What* was that word?   The word was doubtless Shekinah, unspeakable here because it's the black symbol of maternal punishment and death in Hebrew and Kabbalistic mythology. Wearing the black Imipolex G suit, Greta Erdmann "progresses into" (V682.7) the same archetype in part 3 (see V478.14–17n). On the moniker "Nalline" see V18.8–38n.

V682.10, B795.5, P695.23   AMBASSADOR KENNEDY   Joseph P. Kennedy (1888–1969) was the U.S. ambassador to the Court of St. James from December 1937 until November 1940, when he stepped down to "keep America out of war." A great friend of British Prime Minister Neville Chamberlain, Kennedy was "Jolly Joe" to Londoners, who remembered him for calling (then) Princess Elizabeth "a cute trick" (Whalen, *The Founding Father* 263). The ambassadorship came after his great successes as a financier, most notably his 1930 consolidation of Radio Keith Orpheum, the parent company of RKO Pictures. (Three years later the studio produced *King Kong*.)

V682.11, B795.6, P695.24   Listen: Jew-zeppy   That is, Joseph (see also "Ho-say" a few lines further down). Yet Pynchon has put a sharp edge of irony on Mom Nalline's salutation, for Joe Kennedy was dogged by charges of anti-Semitism, as Whalen (387–90) points out. In a 1944 interview with two journalists, Lawrence Spivak and Joe Dinneen, Kennedy tried to respond to these long-standing charges and succeeded only in revealing the ambivalence and prejudice of his time. He said (ibid. 388): "It is true that I have a low opinion of some Jews in public office and in private life. That does not mean that I hate all Jews; that I believe they should be wiped off the face of the earth; or that I favor pogroms or persecutions. I don't. It was inevitable that I should find myself in conflict at times with Jews. I do, and have done, business with them."

V682.14–15, B795.10–11, P695.27–28   what you said when . . . the PT boat   The story of John F. Kennedy's heroism in the South Pacific, from August 1 to 13, 1943, is widely known and available. Its most popular retelling was in Robert J. Donovan's *PT-109* (1962). Joseph Kennedy's remarks were widely quoted in news accounts of the time. The navy did not clear the story of Jack Kennedy's deeds until August 19, 1943, and a *New York Times* story from that day records what Joseph Kennedy said: "Former Ambassador and Mrs. Kennedy shouted in joy when informed of the exploit of their son. Mrs. Kennedy, first to hear the news by telephone at their summer home, expressed 'deep sorrow' for the two crewmen who lost their lives. 'That's wonderful,' Mrs. Kennedy said when told her son was safe. The former Ambassador then exclaimed: 'Phew. I think Mrs. Kennedy has said enough for both of us!'" In the fictional context, here, the most notable things about these remarks are their singular blandness and Joseph Kennedy's deference to his wife.

V682.20–21, B795.16–18, P695.33–34   your wonderful speech at the GE plant over in Pittsfield the other week   The reference to Kennedy's speech here is an instance of the fracturing of Pynchon's narrative in this episode, for the reference would date Nalline's letter to late September or early October, since it was during the second and third weeks of September 1945 that Joseph Kennedy Sr. barnstormed the manufacturing towns of Massachusetts on a speaking tour. The GE Plant in Pittsfield, in Berkshire County, was one of his stops. The trip was his attempt to reenter public life after his 1940 break with Franklin D. Roosevelt over whether America should join the war against Nazism and after two family tragedies (the deaths in action of Joe Junior and a son-in-law) and the much-publicized injuries to son Jack. In addition, the tour marked his return to Boston after living for some time in New York. *Time*, in a September 24, 1945, story (17), reported on the trip:

> In a midnight blue Chrysler, he rode like a Paul Revere through the textile, shoe, and machinery-producing towns in Middlesex, Essex,

and Berkshire counties. All the way from Greenfield to Salem, in some 30 speeches within ten days, he spread the alarm: "I'm willing to come back [to Massachusetts] to live because this is where my heart is. But I don't expect to come back to stay until I think there has been change for the better. For the past 25 years Massachusetts has consistently been losing business—in that time 2,300 industries have left the state. . . . We haven't done a blessed thing to find out why they are leaving or to keep them here. During the next five years Massachusetts will have its last chance to keep itself out of the grave."

Kennedy thus argued for governmental intervention in the form of tax incentives, stricter labor laws, and the like. Whalen also reports on the trip in his biographical study (390–91).

V682.24, B795.21, P695.37   the WLB   Acronym for the War Labor Board, established in January 1942 to mediate labor-management disputes when they threatened production goals during the war.

V683.22, B796.30–31, P696.36   a second-story man   A burglar adept at breaking into the upper stories of buildings.

V683.23, B796.32, P696.37   Minne Khlaetsch   From the Middle High German *"Minne"* (love) and the modern German *"Klatsch"* ("slap" or "gossip, scandal").

V683.26, B796.36, P697.1–2   overdose of Hieropon   Imaginary drug of the gods (see V152.17n).

V683.28, B796.39, P697.4   chess Läufer   That is, a bishop. But note that Minne cannot hear the German umlaut. So would it be nonsense to her (*Laufer*, un-umlauted, not appearing in any dictionary)?

V683.38, B797.10, P697.14   "Hubschrauber!"   As the German for "helicopter," the noun *Hubschrauber* does not enter the German lexicon until the later forties. As a compound, its etymology (here) is from the masculine noun, *"Hub,"* for the "lift" of a piston or valve, and from *"schrauben,"* the verb "to screw."

V684.4, B797.18, P697.20   "Deutschland, Deutschland Über Alles"   The harmonica player in this scene struggles to play the first bars of the German national anthem: "Germany, Germany above all, above all in the world!"

V684.15, B797.31–32, P697.30–31   "Spörri" of Horst Achtfaden's confession   See V455.35n.

V684.31–35, B798.9–13, P698.7–11   William Bendix . . . Cagney . . . Sam Jaffe   Before playing the lead in his television sitcom, *Life of Riley*, William Bendix starred in *Lifeboat* (1944) as a Lindy-hopping sailor whose injured leg must be amputated, *The Hairy Ape* (1944), and *A Bell for Adano* (1945), films that established him as a character actor. In the film *City for Conquest* (1940), Arthur Kennedy made his screen debut as Danny, the younger brother of a prizefighter (James Cagney) blinded in a bout that was to have earned him enough money to support Danny in his music lessons. In *Gunga Din* (1939), the film based on Kipling's poem, actor Sam Jaffe played Din to Cary Grant's Cutter. Bodine thus specializes in the roles of "second sheep," those actors who wear "a white-hat in the navy of life" (that is, they are not officers).

V684.39, B798.18–19, P698.16 some hypothetical Joachim Joseph Joachim (1831–1907) was Germany's most celebrated violin virtuoso of the nineteenth century. A prodigy who first performed at the age of seven, Joachim was a student of Schumann and was known principally as a quartet and solo player.

V684.40, B798.19–20, P698.17–18 the long-suppressed Rossini violin concerto (op. posth.) This is a Pynchon red herring. After his early retirement, Rossini did continue to score various types of musical works, many of them performed only for his friends. For almost a century these private pieces were generally unknown. In 1950 the Rossini Foundation began the task of editing them. Some scores were evidently unavailable, because lost, and the foundation knows of them only at second hand. Nevertheless, among all these later scores (the so-called *Péchés de viellesse*, or "Sins of My Old Age"), whether extant or known to be missing, there exists no record of a violin concerto.

V685.21–22, B799.5–6, P698.39–40 "My Prelude to a Kiss," "Tenement Symphony" Duke Ellington scored a 1945 hit song with "Prelude to a Kiss," whose opening stanza gives one the idea:

If you hear a song in blue
Like a flower crying for the dew
That was my heart serenading you—
My prelude to a kiss

The second song mentioned here, "Tenement Symphony," by Hal Borne, Sid Kullen, and Roy Golden, was initially recorded by singer Tony Martin in the 1941 Marx Brothers movie, *The Big Store*.

V685.29, B799.14, P699.6 a "box" Here, self-conscious slang for a guitar.

V685.36, B799.21, P699.13 La Gazza Ladra Rossini's opera, "The Thieving Magpie" (see V440.4n).

V685.38, B799.23, P699.15 *opening of the Beethoven 5th* That is, Beethoven's well-known "Victory" motif that begins his Fifth Symphony.

V685.39, B799.26, P699.16 Harry James An orchestra leader and singer (1916–83). His first big break came with a singing part in the film *Springtime in the Rockies* (1942). The following year James married GI heartthrob Betty Grable (see V9.3).

V686.19–21, B800.14–17, P700.1–3 morphine tartrate . . . amyl nitrite . . . tins of Benzedrine Respectively, these drugs are an opiate with depressant effects, a stimulant commonly prescribed for patients with heart trouble, and the brand name of a mild stimulant, in tablet form.

V687.25, B801.25, P701.8 "Schitt" The German for "shit" is "Scheisse"; this exclamation might roughly translate to "Bother!"

V687.31, B801.35, P701.23   Schein-Aula   Derives from the noun
"*Schein*" (a blaze, a seeming, and in some contexts a halo); and from the
noun "*Aula*" (an assembly hall, an auditorium); so, no relation between
"*Schein-Aula*" and "Shinola." More pointless and frustrating (to Bodine)
interlingual wordplay.

V688.28, B802.39–40, P702.8–9   Jack and Malcolm both got murdered
Malcolm X was assassinated on February 21, 1965, as he spoke in New
York City's Audubon Ballroom; John F. Kennedy was killed fifteen
months before that, in Dallas, on November 22, 1963.

**V688.36–37, B803.8–9, P702.17–18   Fay Wray . . . in her screen-test scene
with Robert Armstrong**   In the film *King Kong*, actor Robert Armstrong
plays Carl Denham, a director of jungle adventure movies. He takes star-
let Ann Darrow (Fay Wray) on a South Pacific cruise to Skull Island,
home of Kong. Her screen test, a long take of overtly erotic mugging for
the camera, occurs on board ship.

**V689.4–20, B803.17–33, P702.25–703.2   At that first moment . . .
whisper me a line**   Thus far in *GR*, Pynchon has parodied T. S. Eliot
(V226.33n), the Italian sonnet (V532.32n), and the Rolling Stones
(V541.23n). Shortly he will parody the Japanese haiku. Here, he takes up
the Miltonic blank verse line and, indeed, has a fine time with it. Note
the occasional spondee in this poem and how skillfully the caesural
pauses are moved around. Its colloquialisms, like the alliterative
spondee in "best bum actor's way" and the feminine ending in the
twelfth line of the page ("mooning sappy"), all work to lower the tone,
underscoring the Miltonic "Fall" of the eighth line. It is all charged, in
addition, with allusions to RKO Pictures' *King Kong*. The speaker of the
poem is Ann Darrow (Wray), who recalls how the natives on Skull Island
dragged her and tied her Christ-like to the posts outside their massive
gate. Their "flight" occurs when Kong appears to return with her to his
lair. The "Ravine," "tyrannosaurus," and "pterodactyl" are obstacles
and opponents Kong meets on his way. He jumps over the first and de-
feats the second in a wrestling match, using the "flying-mare," or kick.
In these lines Ann also remembers that while waiting for Kong she
prayed, not for Jack (Bruce Cabot), the sailor pacing the decks of the an-
chored ship, but for her director, Denham, who has used her, brought
her to this nightmare, and offered her up to this sexual symbol just as
Gerhardt von Göll offered up Greta Erdmann to the jackal-headed men
of *Alpdrücken*. Finally, in the line "making the unreal reel" one hears an
echo of French director Jean Cocteau's famous paean to film: "Long live
the young muse, cinema, for she possesses the mysteries of a dream and
allows the unreal to become real."

V689.26, B803.40–41, P703.8   a round black iron anarchist *bomb*   Recalls the comic book and cartoon cliché, for example, Porky Pig left
holding the round black bomb (see V545.4–5n).

V690.2, B804.16, P703.23   little Margaret O'Brien   The same age as Pynchon, she was five years old in 1942 when her film career began. At seven she won a special Oscar for her role in *Meet Me in St. Louis* and was widely hailed as a Shirley Temple for the forties.

V690.16, B804.34–35, P703.38–39   "Your closet *could* make Norma Shearer's look like the wastebasket in Gimbel's basement"   Gimbel's was a New York City department store on Thirty-third and Broadway; its basement is famous for its bargain goods. Actress Norma Shearer (1902–83) mainly played characters who were clotheshorses during the early years of her film career. In *Slave of Fashion* (1925), for example, she plays a young woman who accidentally comes into possession of a fabulous wardrobe and uses it to pass herself off as a New York socialite.

V690.27–28, B805.4–5, P704.9–10   Takeshi flies a Zero . . . Ichizo . . . an Ohka   The Mitsubishi A6M8 was the main fighter aircraft of the Japanese arsenal. Official Allied codebooks identified it as "Zeke," but U.S. servicemen dubbed it the "Zero." Beginning in 1944 the planes were fitted up for long-range kamikaze suicide attacks (from "*Kami kaze,*" or "divine wind," after a famous storm that sunk an invading Mongol fleet in A.D. 1274). The Ohka (Cherry Blossom) 11 was a much smaller aircraft, designed specifically as a suicide bomber and produced during the fall and winter of 1944–45. Built of flimsy wood and fabric, this stubby, rocket-propelled craft was fitted with a half-ton explosive charge that was dropped from the belly of a bomber. It had no landing gear, and the charge was rigged to go off on any impact. In sum, no going home in this piloted version of the German V-1 (see Inoguchi and Najakima, *The Divine Wind: Japan's Kamikaze Force in World War II* 32–34).

V690.36–37, B805.15–16, P704.18–19   The fighting is . . . at Leyte . . . Iwo Jima, moving toward Okinawa   The U.S. Marines invaded Leyte Island, in the central Philippines, in mid-October 1944. Iwo Jima was next, in February 1945. And extending this northward march of death, Okinawa was invaded on April 1, Easter of 1945. The main chronological parallel: just as Gottfried waits out the last terrible weeks of winter for the Easter weekend sacrifice, Takeshi and Ichizo simultaneously await their calling. Inoguchi and Nakajima (135–38), Pynchon's source, report the first, unsuccessful use of Ohka piloted bombs on March 21, 1945.

V690.40, B805.19, P704.22   Cypridinae   Family name of a tiny oceanic crustacean that phosphoresces when its surrounding waters are disturbed. The name stems from the Greek "*Kypridios,*" signifying that these little beings "belong to Aphrodite," the Cyprian Venus.

V691.16, B805.39–40, P704.36   PPI scopes   The acronym stands for "Plan-Position-Indicator," a standard air-radar device. The operator's position is at center screen and magnetic North is at the top; concentric circles radiate from the operator's position indicating distance.

V691.18–20, B806.1–2, P705.1–2   fatal mandala . . . screened eight-fold in a circle   On the radar screen (above): note the numerical and mandala symbolism.

V691.25–26, B806.9, P703.9–11   an improvised haiku   According to Japanese tradition, a haiku is supposed to express, in lines of five, seven, and five syllables, some distinct image that occasions spiritual insight. Old Kenosho's haiku adheres to the syllable rules, but his image puts across only a mundane irony.

V691.34–35, B806.20, P705.17–18   *Paranoid . . . For The Day!*   What follows is a mordant little parody of the broadcast game show *Queen for a Day*, first hosted in 1945 on NBC radio by master of ceremonies Jack Bailey and then on NBC (and later, ABC) network television from 1955 to 1964. The contest pitted four preterite women against each other, to see whose tale of woe and loss evoked the most audience approval, as registered on the "Applause-O-Meter."

V692.4, B806.29–30, P705.25   exotic Puke-a-hook-a-look-i *Island!*   See V635.14.

V692.19, B807.7, P706.1   STREETS   In this subsection of the episode we are given a list of streets and towns that Slothrop evidently has wandered through: Hafenstrasse (Harbor Street), Slüterstrasse (named for Protestant reformer Joachim Slüter [1492–1532]), and Wandfärberstrasse (Painter's Street) among them, streets suggesting common laboring jobs. Ben Teague identifies their origin: Semlower Strasse in Stralsund, Hafenstrasse in Greifswald, and the Petritor (tower of St. Peter's church) on Slüterstrasse in Rostock's east end.

V693.22–23, B808.20, P707.6   the Ortsschutz   The local constable.

V693.39–41, B808.40–42, P707.23–24   The letters / MB DRO / ROSHI   A newspaper headline, from circa August 7, 1945, announcing "ATOM BOMB DROPPED ON HIROSHIMA." In a proleptic comment, we were told that Slothrop would find this scrap during his rambles (see V681.35–36).

V694.3, B809.3–4, P707.27   3rd Armored treads 'n' triangle   Soldiers of the Third Armored Division of the U.S. Army wore a triangular shoulder patch with tank treads stitched in its center. Pynchon's source, again, is probably the article on "Shoulder Insignia" in the August 6, 1945, issue of *Life* (46).

V694.12–16, B809.16–21, P707.37–708.1   the pale Virgin was rising . . . The sun was in Leo   These astrological details are accurate. The atomic bomb was dropped on Hiroshima at 9:15 A.M., Hiroshima time, on August 6. The constellation Virgo, usually represented as a maiden dressed in a white gown, was rising in the east, at the angle the narrator gives here. The sun was midway through the house of Leo (July 23–August 22). Readers with a star wheel can roughly verify the figures, though an ephemeris table gives the exact fixes.

V694.19, B809.25, P708.5 cryptozoa A biological term (from circa 1895) signifying any class of organisms that live hidden lives—for example, the planaria worm, which comes out from under its seaside rocks only at night.

V694.25, B809.33, P708.11 Their Movieola Brand name of a film editor's device, capable of rolling the film one frame at a time, backward or forward, for cutting and splicing.

V695.25–28, B810.38–42, P709.10–13 Dungannon, Virginia . . . or Ellis, Kansas The "Sound-Shadow" (V695.23) involving these ten place-names is indeed, as Larsson ("A *Companion*'s Companion") finds by looking at historical maps, a matter of the time zones along which each happened to be arrayed in 1945 (the time zones have since been shifted westward). One may also plot these locations on a map and connect the points. The first five seem to sketch a sideways parabola, the second five a diagonal line. Put together, they seem to make something like a chalice (or Grail cup?) spilled toward Europe. Or maybe (again) it's all baloney.

V695.33–34, B811.7–8, P709.19 thine-alabaster-cities Echoing the last verse of "America the Beautiful":
O beautiful, for patriot's dream,
That sees beyond the years;
Thine alabaster cities gleam,
Undimmed by human tears.
America, America! God shed his grace on thee;
And crown thy good, with brotherhood,
From sea to shining sea.

V696.10–11, B811.28–29, P709.35–36 white tile greasy-spoon . . . (Kenosha, Wisconsin?) Fits the description of Frank's Diner, a fixture (with diner car) since the thirties at 508 58th Street in downtown Kenosha.

V696.28–29, B812.8–9, P710.13–14 voices far away out at sea *our position is two seven degrees two six minutes north* Inoguchi and Nakajima, the source for these details, append tables detailing all known kamikaze sorties, including map coordinates of their point of contact with Allied warships. Only one sortie matches these coordinates: on April 30, 1945, two kamikazes attacked the U.S. destroyer *Bennion*, seriously damaging it (ibid., app. C, p. 209). These "voices" would apparently be from those doomed pilots, broadcasting on *Walpurgisnacht* (V293.17n).

V696.30–40, B812.11–21, P710.15–21 a voice reciting in Japanese . . . the slogan of a Kamikaze unit . . . Power cannot conquer Heaven The source, again, was Inoguchi and Nakajima (138, n1), who report that the commander of the first Ohka squadron to attack American vessels, a lieutenant commander Nonaka, had flown a white pennant over the bivouac of his unit. This meditation was inscribed on it. The footnote explains: "This is the *on* or Chinese reading of the five ideographs in the pennant. Their literal meanings are, respectively: Injustice, Principle, Law, Power, Heaven." Pynchon quotes the remainder of the note, verbatim. A photo of Nonaka's squadron, and their HI, RI, HO, KEN, TEN pennant, appears in *The Divine Wind* (opposite 49).

V697.29, B813.15–16, P711.17   a Japanese Hotchkiss machine gun   The American-born gunsmith Benjamin Berkeley Hotchkiss developed his first machine gun, capable of firing six hundred rounds per minute, in 1876. This was in Paris. Governments the world over quickly bought rights to the design of his gun: the U.S. Army used a Hotchkiss (as the narrator notes) against Sioux Indians at Wounded Knee, South Dakota, during the Christmas 1890 massacre there. Ichizo's Model 92 is a latter-day Hotchkiss, from circa 1930.

V698.33, B814.29, P712.24   "Keying waves"   That is, keying messages in Morse code (see V326.4n).

V699.17, B815.18–19, P713.9   double Virgo fer a son   The term "double" identifies this astrological sign as one of the four "bicorporal" or "double-bodied" signs, including Pisces, Gemini, and Cancer. The designation "double Virgo" could be Slothrop's sun sign, indicating that he was born between August 23 and September 22. This would of course contradict the inferences drawn, in an earlier note, from V624.18. On the other hand, such bicorporal descriptions are also applied to other aspects of a subject's natal chart. And Slothrop's possible chart—cast for noon of March 21, 1918—*does* contain one noteworthy aspect: the planet Mars in Virgo, a sign of foolish, selfish pursuit of satisfaction, for which one might pay any price. That seems to fit the context here.

V700.19–20, B816.29–30, P714.13–14   Otyiyumbu Indeterminacy Relation   Jan Otyiyumbu is the Schwarzkommando "liaison man" for London (V638.33n).

EPISODE 7

Under the influence of drugs, Tchitcherine discloses the reasons for his obsessive pursuit of his half brother, Enzian. And it develops that Soviet agents let him track Enzian, just as Slothrop was allowed to escape into the Zone as a way of leading Allied agents to the Schwarzkommando. The time and setting of this episode are both indistinct.

V700.26–27, B816.38–817.1, P714.22   Nikolai Ripov of the Commissariat for Intelligence Activities   Yet another fictional CIA. "Ripov" here derives from American sixties slang "rip off," a verb form signifying "to steal" or "to defraud."

V700.33, B817.9, P714.28–29   subdeb cuties each a $65 fine   The reference is to a story Percy Knauth wrote for *Life* magazine (July 2, 1945, 26) indicating that in order to thwart "fraternizing" between American G.I.s and German women, the U.S. Army began imposing a $65 fine per infraction (see Schmundt-Thomas, "Grab-bagging in *Gravity's Rainbow*" 94–95).

V700.36–37, B817.12, P714.32   Fuder and Fass   Respectively, a cask (of wine) and keg (of beer).

V701.1, B817.14, P714.33   the Drunkards Three . . . what Frank Sinatra's doing   Perhaps the reference is to the DTs, as in delirium tremens? Or to the "Rat Pack," whose three best-known members—Frank Sinatra, Dean Martin, and Sammy Davis Jr.—performed together and clowned about their inebriety.

V701.18, B817.33, P715.13   Opiates of the people   Echoes Karl Marx's often-misquoted sentence from his 1844 "Introduction" to *A Contribution to the Critique of Hegel's Philosophy of Right* (John and O'Malley translation): "Religion is, at one and the same time, the expression of real suffering and a protest against real suffering. Religion is the sigh of the oppressed creature, the heart of a heartless world, and the soul of soulless conditions. It is the opium of the people."

V701.30, B818.6, P715.26   "natürlich"   Naturally, certainly.

V702.9, B818.31, P716.5   a number 26 point   Hypodermic needle of .26 millimeters in diameter, one of the smallest in use (so Tchitcherine won't feel it).

V702.15–16, B818.39–40, P716.12–13   recalling Tchaikovsky, salmonella . . . tunes from the *Pathétique*   Wimpe eyes the water tap "nervously" because *Salmonella* is the genus of pathogenic bacteria that causes stomach disease, especially when ingested via tainted water. Pëtr Ilich Tchaikovsky's last work was his Symphony No. 6, op. 74, also known as the *Pathétique*, a brooding, anguished, sorrowful work. One story has it that nine days after its first performance in 1893, Tchaikovsky committed suicide. Another is that the composer died after carelessly drinking a glass of unboiled water during a cholera epidemic. Still another is that he was poisoned—or, compelled to take his own life by drinking poison—in punishment for a homosexual liaison with a member of the Russian royal family.

V702.24, B819.8, P716.21   Polschuhen   That is, poles to construct a magnetic field.

V703.13–14, B820.4, P717.11   sedation (0.6 mg atropine subcut.)   Here, the prescription for a subcutaneous injection of six-tenths of a milligram of atropine, a central nervous system depressant derived from belladonna. The scholarly reference, to the *Journal of Oneiric Psycho-Pharmacology* (V702.40), is another of Pynchon's fictions.

V704.3, B820.37, P718.1   "We lost twenty million souls"   The Soviet

Union claimed an estimated twenty million dead as a result of German aggression, mostly peasants (referred to as *"dushi,"* meaning "souls").

V704.41, B821.42, P718.40   his Nagant   The Russian pistol (V293.26n).

V705.7–8, B822.8, P719.7   One is to examine the recently dead   Misprinted in the Bantam as "One is the examine."

V706.3, B823.7, P720.4   "TsAGI"   The Central Aerodynamics and Hydrodynamics Institute (see V273.5n).

V706.4–5, B823.9–10, P720.5–6   "We'll be taking German rocket personnel out to the desert"   Just as the Americans took their captured rocketry experts out to the desert of White Sands, New Mexico, so the Soviets took theirs to Semirechie, a region in modern-day Kyrgyzstan and Kazakhstan. Irmgard Gröttrup narrates the story of their 1946 move in *Rocket Wife.*

EPISODE 8

Appears to unfold later than other episodes, on the "brink of autumn" (V706.30), in Cuxhaven. Jessica tells Roger Mexico that she and Jeremy are planning marriage and a family. The Counterforce proposes that Rocket 00000 had to have been fired in a due-northerly direction, completing, in combination with the directions other V-2s were test-fired in, a mandala of compass bearings. Roger and "Pig" Bodine attend a dinner party, disrupting things with a boorish but zany verbal assault they have evidently learned from that connoisseur of indigestible delights, Brigadier Pudding, who has joined the Counterforce from the Other Side.

V706.27, B823.35, P720.28   an inn by the edge of a little blue Holstein Lake   Situated as it is on the south side of the Elbe River, Cuxhaven is in Lower Saxony, with the southern boundary of Schleswig-Holstein marked by the Elbe's opposite bank. Perhaps this inn is across the river. In any case, the area is dotted with lakes (nearly three hundred of them) that were carved out when the last ice age receded.

V707.4–5, B824.12–14, P721.4–5   a ghost-firing which, in the logic of mandalas, either has occurred, most-secretly, or will occur   The subject is mandalas, traditionally divided into four quadrants. The compass bearings of the V-2 test-firings were variously available to Pynchon in Kooy and Uytenbogaart (*Ballistics of the Future* 285), in Dornberger (*V-2*), and in Irving (*Mare's Nest*). The striking thing here, however, is the narrator's verb tenses: in the story time (or narrative *histoire*) the firing "has occurred" back on Easter weekend; but in the narration itself (the *discours*), it "will occur" in episode 12 of part 4.

V707.31, B825.2–3, P721.32–33   Der Grob Säugling, 23rd card of the Zone's trumps major   The narrator translates *"Grob"* from the German as "gross," but a better translation would be "coarse" or "rude." A *Säugling* is an infant, a "suckling" child. There are twenty-two cards in the Trumps Major (or Major Arcana) of the standard tarot deck. This additional symbol seems analogous to that of a thirteenth house in the traditional zodiac (see V302.20–21n).

V708.31, B826.11, P722.33   the ENSA shows   The British servicemen's entertainment organization (V657.22n).

V709.15, B827.1, P723.17   *Crime Does Not Pay Comics*   The *Overstreet Comic Book Price Guide* tells us that this comic, by Lev Gleason, made its debut as *Silver Streak Comics* but—with issue 22, in 1942—changed its title to *Crime Does Not Pay*. It contained adult themes and violence and was evidently the first comic targeted to adult readers.

V709.18, B827.4–5, P723.20–21   Is this Noel Coward or some shit?   Coward (1899–1973) was an English dramatist, actor, and songwriter; here, Pynchon's perennial dislike of Coward surfaces again (see V134.40–135.1n).

V709.23, B827.10, P723.25   Operation Backfire   V272.32–34n.

V709.33–35, B827.21–23, P723.35–37   "Little sigma, times . . . little-sigma squared."   In statistics, this is the equation for a "normal" or "Gaussian" distribution, a graph of which will yield a "normal" or bell curve (see V508.39n). The German mathematician Karl Friedrich Gauss (1777–1855) developed this equation, which later proved vital to work in statistics when observations showed that many populations, or distributions of events, adhere to it.

V709.39, B827.27–28, P723.41–724.1   the home of Stefan Utgarthaloki   He is named for the Teutonic god Utgarthaloki (Loki of Outgard), a giant and a personification of evil. Like Satan, Utgarthaloki lives far in the East, and to harrow (satirically) this satanic place is the simple reason for Roger's trip to "the Krupp wingding" (V711.16–17) at Stefan's house, but there is more. In Snorri Sturluson's tenth-century epic, *Gylfaginning* (ch. 44), we have a base text for the parody at work in this episode. That account of Utgarthaloki centers on a theme of deception. The god Thor journeys to Loki's castle in order to strive with the rival giant. First he challenges Loki to a drinking match and loses. Loki then challenges Thor to pick up a cat, and again Thor loses. And he loses yet again at wrestling an old hag. Before sending Thor on his way Loki sets the god a great feast. They eat most of the night, dining on strange delicacies from the world over. Next morning, with Thor too bloated to fight, Loki accompanies the great god to the gates of his stronghold, where he explains why Thor was so powerless the night before: Loki tricked him with three illusions. The drinking horn was connected to the oceans; Loki's cat was in reality the World Serpent, Ouroboros; and the old hag was really a great wrestler. Enraged, Thor seizes up his hammer, Mullicrusher, and swings at thin air, for Loki has vanished, a deceptive illusion like everything else in Outgard. Note that unlike Thor, however, Roger journeys to Utgarthaloki's stronghold with a friend.

V710.1, B827.31, P724.3   "there're a lot of snazzy NAAFIs about"   See V17.26n.

V710.40–41, B828.37–38, P725.2–4   "just a freckleface kid from Albert Lea ... on Route 69 where the speed limit's lickety-split"   A crude pun on the old venereal slang term "sixty-nine." Route 69 was once a major arterial running north-south, connecting Des Moines and Minneapolis. The town of Albert Lea, Minnesota, is ten miles north of the Iowa border.

V711.2, B828.38–39, P725.5–6   "used a safety pin through a cork for a catwhisker"   That is, used the safety pin in place of a fine wire inside his crystal radio set. To pick up a radio signal the operator moved the catwhisker tip over a galena crystal until he found the point where it would conduct electricity, thus tuning the radio.

V711.24, B829.23–24, P725.28   at your door, Fred and Phyllis   Another reference to Fred Allen's radio program, *Allen's Alley* (V44.17–18n). Here, the format has been inverted: someone comes to knock on Fred and Phyllis's door.

V711.29–31, B829.30–32, P725.34–35   suppressed quartet from the Haydn Op. 76 ... *Largo, cantabile e mesto*   Composer Josef Haydn's opus 76 is a set of six quartets that were written in 1799 and dedicated to Count Erdödy, for whom they are usually named. The fifth quartet, in D, is a set of free variations in the middle of which is a slow, sad song (largo, cantabile e mesto), meant to express a type of unearthly radiance. This middle movement of the quartet is scored in F-sharp major; Pynchon's fictional, "suppressed" movement for kazoos is "in G-flat minor."

V711.34, B829.36–37, P725.39   "a spiccato to a détaché"   Bow strokes. A spiccato is a "thrown" stroke, when the bow bounces off the strings of the instrument, such as a violin. A détaché is a downstroke of some length—one continuous, downward stroke, perhaps *really* drawn out, in which case it is *le grand détaché*.

V712.4, B830.7–8, P726.9   song from the movie *Dr. Jekyll and Mr. Hyde*   Not the 1932 version starring Fredric March, with Miriam Hopkins in the role of Ivy Pearson singing, but the 1941 remake with Ingrid Bergman singing a different song. The reason it's important is that each time before Dr. Jekyll (Spencer Tracy) transforms into Hyde, he hums a few bars of this tune. Larsson ("A *Companion*'s Companion") traces "You Should See Me Dance the Polka" to 1887 and composer George Grossmith, who also starred at the Savoy Theater for Gilbert and Sullivan. The lyrics:

You should see me dance the Polka
You should see me cover the ground;
You should see my coat-tails flying,
As I jump my partner 'round;

When the band commences playing,
My feet begin to go,
For a rollicking romping Polka,
Is the jolliest fun I know.

V712.9, B830.14, P726.13–14   this feeb's pizzicato   Another violin stroke, this time a "plucked" instead of a bow stroke. "Feeb" is slang for any feeble-minded person.

V712.11, B830.16, P726.15–16   Reps from ICI and GE   Representatives from the British firm Imperial Chemical Industries, the dyestuff and chemical manufacturer, and from the American General Electric Company, both of which were keenly involved in Project Hermes, the operation to recover and export to the United States one hundred of the V-2 rockets.

V712.21, B830.29, P726.26   early Virgo   The sixth house of the astrological year, Virgo holds sway from August 23 to September 22.

V712.25–26, B830.34–35, P726.31   "the 'Hydra-Phänomen'"   A Hydra phenomenon, named for the monster of Greek myths. Heracles (or Hercules, to the Romans) won his immortality by performing twelve extraordinary labors, the second of which was to slay the Hydra, a beast that grew two heads for each one that was lopped off.

V712.26–29, B830.36–39, P726.31–33   Natasha Raum . . . Proceedings of the International *Society of Confessors to an Enthusiasm for Albatross Nosology*   Note Pynchon's continuation of the PISCEAN motif. Nosology is the study and classification of diseases. Fictional author Raum derives her moniker from the German for "space"; in addition, according to Waite (*Black Magic* 178), the angel Raum is one of the "throne Angels" who "appears in the form of a crow, but assumes human shape when bidden" and is capable of both destroying cities and engendering love between foes.

V712.33–35, B831.2–4, P726.39–41   Pseudo-Goldstrassian . . . Mopp's Hedomeriasis   Fictional diseases. The second stems from the Latin "*hebdoma*" (seven); thus *hebdomeriasis* is any pathology that manifests itself during the first week of life.

V713.10, B831.24, P727.16–17   must have been dreaming for a minute here of the sweaty evenings of Thermidor: the failed Counterforce   If Roger Mexico is dreaming of these evenings, then his dreams contain a warning. Thermidor was the eleventh month of the French revolutionary calendar, corresponding to the period from July 19 to August 17.

Moreover, it was on the eighth of Thermidor, in the French Revolution's second year (in other words, July 27, 1794), that Robespierre, Saint-Just, and other leaders of massive redistribution of wealth and upheaval of the aristocratic order, known as the Reign of Terror, were arrested and, the next day, executed.

V713.33, B832.12, P728.1   a recco map   Produced from photographs taken by aerial reconnaissance.

V713.41, B832.22–23, P728.10–11   according to the menu, full of relevés, poissons, entremets   Respectively, spiced dishes, fishes, and side dishes.

V715.2, B833.33, P729.15   Pappy Hod   A refugee from Pynchon's first novel, *V.*, he's a shipmate of "Pig" Bodine's in 1955 aboard the USS *Scaffold*. His name recalls (see V185.22) the prewar Comet (Hampton One Design or "HOD") sailboats built by Vincent "Pappy" Serio. Also, a hod is a device slung over the shoulders for lugging bricks, and in Kabbalistic symbolism Hod (Majesty, or Glory) are the thighs on the anthropomorphized tree of life (see Scholem, *Major Trends* 213 and V747.41–748.5n).

V715.8, B833.39–40, P729.20   They are not "sensitive flames"   In reference to the technique used to detect frauds in "table rapping" (V29.31n).

V715.14, B834.5, P729.26   But is is through   An error in both the Viking and Bantam that was corrected in the Penguin edition.

V715.17, B835.9, P729.30   any *snot soup* on the menu   Just a bit earlier in this dinner table scene (see 714.36–37), Roger understands the word "ketchup" as a "code word," inviting him—and all the mock-revolutionaries in this scene—to commence what sixties-era dopers would recognize as a "grossout session" (see V540.32–34). As they ratchet up the disgusting images (*"menstrual marmalade!"* . . . *"discharge dumplings?"*) one of Utgarthaloki's guests even chimes in. From others of Them comes "a sound of well-bred gagging," while a sales representative from ICI flees. Thus, a successful counterattack.

V716.38, B835.39, P731.11   Lady Mnemosyne Gloobe   She takes her first name from the Greek goddess Mnemosyne (memory, mindful), the mother of all the Muses. Note that Mrs. Gloobe flees these "mindless pleasures."

V717.2–3, B836.4, P731.17   "the Scrubs"   Again, London's Wormwood Scrubs Prison (V33.31–32).

V717.8–9, B836.10–11, P731.23   Sixth Antechamber to the Throne   In *Merkabah* mysticism, the sixth antechamber is the next-to-last stop in one's ascent to the divine throne and is guarded by the archangels Katspiel and Domiel. It constitutes a supreme test of the mystic's faith; see also V231.24–25n, V584.1n, and V749.34–36n.

V717.18, B836.21–22, P731.32   "a Storm Trooper . . . like Horst Wessel"   On Wessel's life and his murder at the hands of a rival Communist storm troop, see V443.2n.

V717.19–22, B836.23–26, P731.33–35   "a Melvin Purvis Junior G-Man

... For Post Toasties"   During the thirties Purvis (1903–60) was special agent in charge of the Chicago office of the FBI. At the time all agents were nicknamed "G-men" (short for "government men"). In 1935 the General Foods Company developed the "Junior G-Men" as a promotional gimmick and began inserting badges and other paraphernalia as free gifts in boxes of their Post Toasties cereal.

V717.24, B836.29, P731.37   Tom Mix   The American cowboy-actor who made some sixty films and serials during his Hollywood career (see also V245.36n).

EPISODE 9

The time is late August or early September 1945. Geli Tripping continues her search for Tchitcherine in spite of reports that he has died. Her memories of kneeling before the chief devil, Pan, segue neatly into a key analepsis: Gottfried kneels before Blicero at the time of the spring equinox and just days before the launch of Rocket 00000, and he listens to Blicero's sermonette on the theme of sin: not "Original Sin" but "Subsequent Sin," on Europe and its obsessions with "Analysis and Death," and on America (722.29–32). Thematically this scene, a meditation on imperial America and the logics of colonial dominion, stands as one of the novel's touchstones.

V717.31, B837.1, P732.6   Adam and Eve root   Also known as "putty root," the *Aplectrum hyemale* is an orchidaceous plant with purple and yellow flowers and corms shaped like human bodies.

V717.35, B837.5, P732.10   her gallant Attila   Because Tchitcherine, like Attila, also swept down out of the steppes of central Asia.

V718.7, B837.14, P732.17–18   Bauernfrühstuck   A farm breakfast.

V718.33, B838.3, P733.5   The Hexes-Stadt   "Witch City."

V719.10, B838.26, P733.21–22   Beria's top man   Lavrenti Beria (1899–1953) was a member of Joseph Stalin's war cabinet (with Molotov and Malenkov). He headed the feared police agency in charge of Russian internal security, the NKVD (People's Commissariat of Internal Affairs).

V719.26, B839.1–2, P733.39   scurvy lot of tommies   British slang for "a lousy bunch of soldiers." "Tommies" are from "Tommy Atkins," a fictitious common soldier like the American GI Joe.

V719.39–40, B839.17–18, P734.12   she *feels the cross* the man has made on his own circle of visible earth   Another mandala symbol. The cross in a circle is, in addition, the astrological symbol of earth. To Geli, moreover, this member of the surveying party, standing arms out like a cross and rotating his body, crudely sighting a line, has (ephemerally) traced the sign.

V720.2, B839.23, P734.16   Pan   The reference pertains less to the Greek mythological figure than to the chief devil of European witchcraft. Grimm (*Teutonic Mythology* 1071), for example, describes Pan as a goat-man who "sits silent and solemn on a high chair or stone table in the midst of the ring" of gathered witches. They approach and "do him reverence by kneeling and kissing."

V720.13, B839.36, P734.27   it was the equinox   March 21, the "great cusp."

V721.12, B840.42–841.1, P735.26   his last ties   The masculine pronoun refers to Gottfried, whose last memories, circa March 21, have been neatly segued into Geli's recollections. Gottfried "kneels at [Blicero's] feet" (V721.26) here, just as Geli and the other witches had knelt before Pan.

V721.21, B841.11–12, P735.35   It's only a matter of weeks   To be concise, seven weeks from the spring equinox to V-E Day.

V723.28–29, B843.36–37, P738.32   "stories of us one day living on the moon"   Note that Gottfried's "stories" correspond to the bedtime stories that Ilse Pökler concocted with her father, Franz (V410.11n).

V724.21, B844.34–35, P738.26   latest spring torn across rainy miles   This comment, along with the mention of the "raw spring wind" (V724.11), confirms the time of Blicero's last firing: a matter of days after March 21.

V724.25–26, B844.40, P738.40–41   a card: what is to come   The tenth and last card drawn from the tarot deck in a divinatory reading. It is the culmination of all influences brought to light through the previous nine cards. See, for example, "Weissmann's Tarot" (V746.30n).

V724.28–29, B845.1–2, 739.2–3   like The Fool, no agreed assignment in the deck   As the zero card in the Major Arcana, the Fool's sequential place is disputed. Some tarot handbooks put the card first, others last or next to last. Ouspensky (*The Symbolism of the Tarot*) makes the Fool card number one in the sequence, a counterpart to the Magician, which turns him into a figure much like Blicero. Waite (*Pictorial Key*) places the Fool next to last, between the Last Judgment (number twenty) and the World (card twenty-one).

EPISODE 10

Early September, approaching the Lüneburg Heath. Enzian has managed to keep his Zone Hereros together and has done it in spite of continued attacks by unidentified white forces. His troops press on toward Lüneburg to fire Rocket 00001, the "second in its series" (V724.34). Their undertaking is still suffused by a polyglot mythology.

V725.13, B845.28, P739.24–25   you twelve struggled, in love, on this Baltic shore   Numerologically, recall that part 4 has twelve episodes and that Tchitcherine was rumored to have "a dozen" followers, even a "Judas Iscariot" among them (V719.19–20); additionally, Enzian's group will soon be attacked by a dozen hostile whites (V730.33). Here, there is a loose analogy to Christ's disciples struggling, "in love," on the shores of Galilee.

V725.16–20, B845.32–35, P739.31   at Test Stand VII . . . the holy place See V508.22n.

V725.23–24, B846.2–3, P739.34–35   at Siemens . . . centaurs struggling high on the wall   Another reference to the statuary outside the Siemens-Schuckertwerke of Berlin, its name as of 1903 when Siemens and Halske acquired a company founded by Joachim Schuckert (see V649.27n on Siemens and Halske).

V726.6–8, B846.32–33, P740.22   Constance Babington-Smith . . . at R.A.F. Medmenham discovered the Rocket back in 1943   The Royal Air Force office at Medmenham housed the Special Interpretations Unit. It was there, in the spring of 1943, that Mrs. Babington-Smith examined reconnaissance photos taken over Peenemünde. She identified the pencil-shaped, finned, A4 rocket cradled in its *Meilerwagen*. Her find supplied British intelligence with its first sure evidence that the rocket existed. Pynchon's source here was Collier (*The Battle of the V-Weapons* 31–32).

V726.15, B846.43, P740.31   toruses of Rocket range   In architectural usage, a torus is a geometrical figure or model that in three-dimensional space resembles a donut—or a donut-shaped target. In anatomy it is a protuberance or a tumorous bulge. Both meanings are at work here. The etymology of the word is similarly striking: in Hindu art, Shiva, the red god of destruction and waste, is frequently represented beneath a blazing *Torana*, a fiery arch (one-half of a geometrical torus) symbolic of death and dissolution.

V726.19–20, B847.4–5, P740.35–36   It Begins Infinitely Below The Earth And Goes On Infinitely Back Into The Earth   A reminder once more that the rainbow is not arch-shaped but is in its truest form a circle (like the geometrical torus; see also V6.33–35n and V209.25–26n).

V726.41, B847.30–31, P741.16   between quaternions and vector analysis in the 1880s   The reference is to an 1880s dispute between, on the one hand, physicists who were proponents of vector analysis and who proposed describing the motion of particles in space when the particle has a known direction and force, and, on the other, physicists who were proponents of quaternions, particles understood theoretically as scalar quantities, hypercomplex numbers in which four components (such as the spin of a particle) are "scaled" together, so as to provide a much more accurate description of their dynamic behavior.

V727.6–10, B847.38–43, P741.22–26   Gnostics . . . Kabbalists . . . Manichaeans   Gnosticism arose in the eastern Mediterranean during the early Christian centuries as a fierce opponent to Judaic mythology. Gnostics regarded the creation as a *pleroma*, a fullness that is hierarchically organized, in which each antechamber to the divine throne is occupied by angelic beings (the potencies, aeons, archons, and dominions that were soon adopted by Kabbalistic Judaism and Christianity alike). The central belief of the Gnostics was in a hidden God, whose throne one approached at death, the moment of redemption. Gershom Scholem (*Major Trends* 73ff.) has shown that early Kabbalism rose from these Gnostic beliefs. The throne or Merkabah mysticism of the second through the fourth centuries and the Neoplatonism of the medieval philosophers combined to yield in thirteenth-century Europe the first two exemplary Kabbalistic texts: the writings of Abraham Abulafia of Italy and the anonymous *Sefer Ha-Zohar*, or "Book of Splendor," that was written in Spain. In the third century, the Manichaeans gathered around their Persian prophet, Manes. Their fundamental belief was in the divinity of the soul, imprisoned in terrestrial matter symbolized by darkness and night. The soul's desire to seek the light is, however, checked by the jealousy of Venus, who wants to keep the soul locked up in dark matter. To be alive in the body is thus an absolute woe to the Manichaean, whereas death into a redeeming light is an absolute good. As Denis de Rougement has shown, it was from this Manichaean separation of divine and earthly love, the latter always connected with Venus, that the Tristan and Tannhäuser myths took shape among the Cathars of thirteenth-century Provence.

V727.11–12, B848.1–2   the sacred idiolalia of the Primal Twins   Enzian and Blicero are the twins, and the "sacred idiolalia" will soon appear as an anagram concerning their fates (V746.9n).

V727.17–18, B848.9, P741.34   the heretic's EEG   On the electroencephalograph see V146.1–7n.

V727.33–34, B848.29–30, P742.9–10   fennel . . . mallow leaves   Here Pynchon lists a variety of medicinal herbs common to Europe, all harvested in late summer. Medieval Europeans believed that fennel would ward off witches and evil spirits, and the herb is still used as a purgative. Its most potent form is its resinous sap, which one gets hold of by cutting the stems and drawing it off. Betony is a woodland plant of England, also called bishopswort, gathered late in the morning during summer after the dew has begun to evaporate. It is used to treat headaches and neuralgia. Whitsun roses, also known as guelder roses, grow in copses throughout England, producing snow-white flowers around Whitsun (mid-May) and berries in late summer. The berries and the bark are used as a nerve sedative and an antispasmodic. Sunflowers are nonnative European plants, introduced from South America during the sixteenth century. The seeds quickly became known for their diuretic properties.

Mallow grows all over Europe; its soft, velvety leaves are widely used to treat inflammation and soreness in the throat and chest.

V728.39, B850.2, P743.15 laager In Afrikaans, the language of southeast Africa, a caravan, in the sense of a migrating encampment, rather like the *auls* of central Asia (see V340.33–34), but also, during the 1904–06 Herero War in South-West Africa, a concentration camp.

V728.41, B850.4, P743.17 a sonic death-mirror As early as 1941 British intelligence experts had picked up rumors of such a German "death ray," supposedly in development. The thing was nothing more than a rumor (Irving, *Mare's Nest* 14).

V730.4–6, B851.18–19, P744.23–24 called "the Hare" . . . as in the old Herero story As a trickster, the hare (or Brer Rabbit, in Americanized versions) could never get any messages across in the way they were meant (V322.21n).

V730.30, B852.7, P745.9–10 Orutyene dead. Okandio, Ekori, Omuzire wounded The names of these dead and injured Hereros all stem from Kolbe's lexicon: *"orutyene,"* "steep" (471); *"okandio,"* "little bell" (151); *"ekori,"* "cap" (75); and *"omuzire,"* "shadow" (439).

V731.41, B853.28–29, P746.22 how's the head Mieczislav Misprinted in the Bantam as "how the head."

V732.22–24, B854.13–14, P747.5–6 full of Cathar horror at the practice of imprisoning souls in the bodies of newborns The Cathars derived the name of their Christian sect from the Greek *"katharos"* (spotless), which they chose in honor of Christ, the "spotless" lamb. They flourished throughout southern Europe, but especially in Provence during the thirteenth century. The Roman church declared Catharist beliefs heretical, which touched off the Albigensian crusades during which the sect was brutally exterminated. Denis de Rougement, who is surely Pynchon's source here, defines Catharist doctrine as originating from the Manichaean sects of Asia Minor, and before that from Gnosticism. The Cathars, or "Church of Love," held that good and evil exist in absolute separation, in two different worlds, one heavenly and the other earthly. Initiates to the sect, called the "perfect" or the "elect," were required to renounce the world fully and to devote their lives wholly to God, never to lie, never to kill or eat of an animal, and to abstain completely from sexual love. A second group, the "believers" or "imperfecti," were the only ones allowed to marry. De Rougement argues that despite the fierce persecution of the Cathars, their otherworldly beliefs survived in codified forms—for example, in courtly love poems. The doctrines lived on in the works of Europe's troubadours and minnesingers. They can also be found in the opera librettos for *Tannhäuser* as well as *Tristan und Isolde.* A. E. Waite (*Pictorial Key*) has argued that Catharism was also preserved in the symbolic images of tarot. He notes that the Hierophant, card seven in the Major Arcana, may correspond to the secret Catharist pope and that the Tower struck by lightning on card sixteen may represent the desired destruction of the Roman church.

V732.36, B854.30, P747.19   Djuro   Larsson ("A *Companion*'s Companion") identifies it as a Serbian male name and points out that while some Herero (like Enzian) have German names, others have Eastern European ones such as Vlasta (Czech) or Mieczislav (Polish).

V733.1, B854.36, P747.24–25   command frequency is by CW dots and dashes   CW is the abbreviation for a "continuous wave" transmission. When using a "key," the telegrapher in effect switches this frequency on and off and in this way creates the string of dots and dashes.

EPISODE I I

The novel's penultimate episode ends, not in fulfillment of the anticipated revenge of Tchitcherine on Enzian, but in coincidence and peace. In early September, near Lüneburg, Geli Tripping is at last reunited with Vaslav Tchitcherine. Her magical spell blinds him at the moment of his long-awaited confrontation with his half brother: they pass each other amicably, and even anonymously, at a roadside.

V733.24, B855.24, P748.7   terrenity   "Earthliness," from the Latin "*terrenus*" (of the earth) and by analogy with "*serenus*" (serenity).

V733.26, B855.27, P748.9   Stretchfoot   From the German *Streckefuss*, a nickname commonly applied to Lord Death, Dominus Blicero. Grimm (*Teutonic Mythology* 852) explains: "Death is called the pale *Streckefuss* or *Streckebein* (leg-stretcher) . . . because he stretches out the limbs of the dying."

V734.2, B856.5, P748.22   the mystery word   In this game of hangman the mystery word could be right in front of us: "*Gerät*," as in *Schwarzgerät*. But if we fill in the allotted spaces it is probably "generator" (same meaning and spelling in English as in German). Perhaps it is meant to designate the "LOX generator," or liquid oxygen generator. This turbo pump was a key piece of German rocket engineering, designed for the A4 (Irving, *Mare's Nest* 268–69).

V734.7–8, B856.12, P748.28   someone is swinging an ax-blade into a living tree   The "someone" is a member of Enzian's crew (V730.41), and the ax is yet another *saxum* or Zaxa (V218.10n).

V734.19–20, B856.27–28, P749.2–3   the Angels Melchidael . . . great Metatron   The spell Geli casts over Tchitcherine is Pynchon's variation on two spells described in Waite's *Book of Black Magic and of Pacts* (265–70), both of them designed to compel the presence and devotion of a beloved. In "The Experiment in Love" the practitioner makes a wax or clay figure of the beloved, inscribing it with a goose quill (Geli uses her fingernail). It is clothed (she uses "the silk crotch torn from her best underpants" [V734.13]) and conjured with; during those rites the angels (such as Melchidael, Yahoel, and Anafiel) are invoked along with the Names of Power.

V734.26, B856.35, P749.9   the last Names of Power   In "Solomonic" or black magic rites there are, according to Waite (*Black Magic* 240), seventy-two "Names of Power" for God. The practitioner will recite them at the close of a conjuring spell to bring about his or her desired end. Waite lists the last five names as "CREATOR, REDEMPTOR, UNITAS, SUMMUM BONUM, INFINITAS."

V734.34, B857.8, P749.17   mba-kayere   See V362.17n.

EPISODE 12

The last episode in *GR*, and like the sixth in part 4, this one is also subdivided. Here sixteen subepisodes detail Slothrop's dispersal (like the mythic Orpheus) and disclose at last the sacrifice of Gottfried. The episode begins on "a September morning" and insofar as it can be said to end, it ends on September 14, when Christians celebrate the Feast of the Exaltation of the Holy Cross, and the Zone Hereros are poised, ready to raise (exalt) their recovered Rocket 00001. The day is especially appropriate because it occasions the analepsis to the Easter weekend when Gottfried was sacrificed. There are, however, other, ambiguous temporal references, most notably, the analepsis or flashback to April that triggers a prolepsis or forward leap to Los Angeles and the Orpheus Theater, circa 1970, in the middle of the Nixon presidency.

V735.19, B857.35, P750.6   Queen of Cups   Here is Waite's reading of this tarot card in his *Pictorial Key* (200): "Beautiful, fair, dreamy—as one who sees visions in a cup. This is, however, only one of her aspects; she sees, but she also acts, and her activity feeds her dream."

V735.30, B858.11–12, P750.18   bleached colors of a September morning   Perhaps "bleached" because the spirit of Blicero rules.

V736.1, B858.22, P750.26   "our own boundary layer"   On this aerodynamic concept see V222.32n.

V737.17, B860.7, P752.3   It is the Lüneburg Heath, at last   The description in Baedeker (*Northern Germany* 144) gives the place just one word: "dreary." The area is remembered in pre-1945 history for two things, however. In 1417, after centuries of wandering, the gypsies made their first European home here; some say they brought with them the methods of tarot divination and that this is how Europeans learned of its occult powers (Waite, *Pictorial Key* 54). Also, on July 17, 1586, a secret meeting is supposed to have occurred here involving the kings of Navarre and Denmark, Elizabeth I of England, and a number of princes and electors. The object, supposedly, was to "form an 'evangelical' league of defense against the Catholic League" (Yates, *The Rosicrucian Enlightenment* 34). Supposedly Rosicrucianism was secretly founded at this meeting.

V737.22–23, B860.14, P752.9   the Messiah gathering in the fallen sparks A reference to the Kabbalistic belief that the divine illumination was scattered in the form of "sparks" at the moment of creation. The Messiah, it was believed, would once more gather in these dispersed sparks of light. The image was frequently given a world-historical interpretation: the "sparks" were taken as symbols of Diaspora Jews who would be gathered together at the Apocalypse. Here, the narrator satirically inverts that moment: the sparks are drawn into the "singularity," the gravitational collapse, of a black hole. Note, in addition, the hysteron proteron.

V737.41–738.1, B860.37–38, P752.27–28   the Kabbalists, the Templars, the Rosicrucians On the Kabbalists, see V727.6–10 and passim. The Knights Templar is a Catholic secret society that was founded in Jerusalem during the crusade of 1188. The best source on the Rosicrucian fervor of seventeenth-century Europe is Frances Yates's *Rosicrucian Enlightenment*. She argues that the manifestos of the movement reveal it as a conflux of Kabbalistic, Hermetic, and alchemical theory and symbolism. Yates sees the Rosicrucians—John Dee, Francis Bacon, and Frederick V, the elector of Palatine—as intermediaries between the Renaissance and the new science. She also sees the movement as decidedly antipapist and, after 1650, increasingly millennial in its beliefs— key aspects of its contextual use in *GR*.

V738.7–8, B861.4–5, P752.5   His cards . . . in the order suggested by Mr. A. E. Waite This is Slothrop's tarot, done in what Waite (*Pictorial Key* 299–305) describes as the "Celtic Method" of divination. First a "significator" is chosen from the pack; it must correspond to the query at hand. For example, if a legal matter is to be decided then the cartomancer would probably select Justice, card eleven of the Major Arcana. The significator is laid down and then the ten divinatory cards are randomly chosen from the deck and laid down in the shape of a patriarchal cross. The first of these ten cards is said to "cover" the significator and to set the conditions affecting the inquiry at hand. Getting the three of Pentacles in this position, especially after two tries, would definitely mean "mediocrity in work and otherwise, puerility, pettiness, and weakness." This is why Slothrop's tarot (though we know only three of its cards) is that of a "tanker and feeb," a loser and an idiot. Worse still, as his ninth card, which should indicate his "hopes and fears" (V738.17), he draws the Hanged Man, card twelve, but in a reversed position. This would signify "selfishness, the crowd, body politic." It is a card "of Martyrdom"; but its inverted position only underscores the satiric treatment Pynchon has given Slothrop's role as mock-Orpheus.

V738.19, B861.19, P753.5   analyst Mickey Wuxtry-Wuxtry   Named after the street-slang of American newsboys hawking their papers: "Wuxtry, wuxtry, read all about it!" "Wuxtry" meaning, for unknown reasons, "extra."

V738.26–27, B861.29, P753.14   an interview with the *Wall Street Journal*   The New York–based newspaper known for its conservative business outlook, founded in 1889 by Charles Dow and Edward Jones, with one of the largest U.S. circulations.

V739.3, B862.6–27, P753.29   A Raketen-Stadt Charlie Noble   After the war, atomic engineer Charles Carmine Noble (b. 1916) was the chief military officer for the Manhattan Project at Los Alamos, or "Atomic City." Hence the analogy to this radium-illumined stream of urine in the "Raketen-Stadt" (Rocket City).

V739.6–7, B862.11, P753.33–35   Typhoid Marys . . . caught some in the Underground   Mary Mallon (d. 1938) was an Irish cook living in the United States. She was infamous as a carrier of the deadly typhoid virus. The underground is London's metropolitan rail system, also known as the tube.

V739.22–24, B862.30–32, P754.8–10   why you see Gnostics so hunted . . . the Sangraal, is the bloody vehicle   The essence of Gnostic and Manichaean doctrine was to regard everything of flesh and blood as an absolute woe, the enemy of spiritual good. As de Rougement (*Passion and Society* 65) has written, "The fundamental dogma . . . is that the soul is divine or angelic, and is *imprisoned* in created forms—in terrestrial matter, which is Night." The reference in *GR* here to the black guard riding over half a continent through "stone night and winter day" perhaps alludes to the Celtic Gwyon's quest for the Grail, which was made of stone and could be said to contain the blackness of night through the symbolic power of Christ's blood.

V740.14, B863.24, P755.1   Humboldt County   On the northern California coast.

V741.6–7, B864.22–24, P755.32–33   "I was there . . . down the street from the Biograph"   "Pig" Bodine was a recent enlistee in the navy ("just a boot") in 1934 when he saw John Dillinger ambushed outside the Biograph Theater in Chicago. John Toland (*The Dillinger Days* 237) has described how the bystanders used handkerchiefs and articles of clothing to soak up Dillinger's blood from the sidewalk where Melvin Purvis's G-men gunned him down.

V741.13, B864.32, P755.39   "there's half my graduating class from Great Lakes"   As Schmundt-Thomas points out ("Grab-bagging in *Gravity's Rainbow*" 95), Bodine refers to the cohort ("in dress blues") who completed basic and specialized training courses with him at the Waukegan, Illinois, Great Lakes Training Center, forty miles north of Chicago.

V741.34, B865.15, P756.19   "I'm out of the Dumbo stage now"   In the Disney cartoon feature, Dumbo needed his feather to fly (see V106.33–37n). Bodine no longer needs his totem, the bloodstained T-shirt, in order to secure physical grace.

V742.2, B865.26, P756.28   Leverkusen   The western German city, near Cologne, that is home to the Bayer Works (below).

V742.5, B865.30, P756.31–32   the Bayer factory   Another IG Farben subsidiary and the original patentee of aspirin well before IG Farben was formed (Sasuly, *IG Farben* 27).

V742.22–23, B866.7–8, P757.7–8   Sprigs of woodruff . . . carried by the early Teutonic warriors   The woodruff, or *Asperula odorata,* has white flowers and fragrant leaves. Grimm (*Teutonic Mythology* 1199) mentions its use among Teutonic warriors.

V742.25, B866.10–11, P757.10   downtown Niederschaumdorf   A fictional locality. The name roughly translates to "Under the Foam Village" or "Under-foam Village."

V742.29, B866.15–16, P757.14   only record album ever put out by The Fool   Steven Moore ("Pynchon on Record" 57) notes that "there was indeed a rock group called The Fool. It put out one record in the late sixties, but beyond that it doesn't fit the description of the group with which Slothrop eventually plays . . . in part because the real Fool (whose album jacket is covered with Tarot imagery) consisted of only four members—two men and two women—and are not posed 'in the arrogant style of the early Stones, near an old rocket-bomb site.' There is, however, an unidentified harmonica player on the album." Larsson ("A *Companion*'s Companion") also points up a mention of the Fool in a March 21, 1969, cover story in *Time* magazine treating astrology and the occult (and rock 'n' roll).

V743.11–12, B867.3, P757.39   Maitrinke   Literally, "May drink"; the May wine of V742.20–21.

V743.35, B867.32, P758.22   too many Fortresses diving   Once again the American B-17 Flying Fortress bomber.

V744.1, B867.38, P758.27   THE OCCUPATION OF MINGEBOROUGH   Appears to take place during the spring, when the "apple tree . . . is in blossom" (V744.7). Perhaps it is shortly after Slothrop's escape from Monaco and Nice, in April of 1945. Many of the details in this incident can be checked against the description of fictional Mingeborough in Pynchon's 1964 short story "The Secret Integration."

V744.7–10, B868.5–8, P758.33–35   An apple tree . . . . Sitting under it, with anyone else but Slothrop   Riffing on the Andrews Sisters song (see V382.3–4n).

V744.21, B868.22, P759.7   old Cord automobiles   Front-wheel-drive autos manufactured by the Auburn Automobile Company, of Indiana, from 1929 to 1937.

V745.5, B869.11, P759.32   carburete   This is misspelled in all three editions: there shouldn't be an "e" on the end.

V745.19, B869.28, P760.8   Schadenfreude   Deriving joy or pleasure from others' injuries or troubles.

V745.35–39, B870.8–14, P760.24–29   Part of a reverse world . . . the corpse comes to life to the accompaniment of a backwards gunshot   Another elaborate hysteron proteron. For a similarly elaborate example of this rhetorical figure see Vonnegut's 1969 novel *Slaughterhouse-Five* (63–64), where the guns "sucked bullets and shell fragments" from airplanes and corpses; there, the scene is naturalized as a reversed film.

V746.9, B870.26–27, P760.39–761.1   medoshnicka bleelar medoometnozz in bergamot   This is the "sacred idiolalia of the Primal Twins" mentioned at V727.11–12. Puzzled out, the phrase might yield such words as "blicero," "enzian," "zero," "kabbala," "mammon," and "doomed," among many other possibilities. One possible reading: "Mammon doomed Blicero; the black Enzian gets zero." But any such efforts to discover benediction or malediction in the letters may of course be viewed as the imposition of system where none is invited. The bergamot, incidentally, is a small, spiny citrus tree of southern Europe, the *Citrus aurantium bergamia*, whose sour fruit yields oil that is used in perfumes.

V746.17–18, B870.37–38, P761.9   devotees of the I Ching   Or *Book of Changes* (see V13.1n); the trigger here too for an awful pun: "I Ching feet" (V746.20).

V746.21–22, B871.3, P761.13   Qlippoth, Ouija-board jokesters   The "shells of the dead" are from Kabbalistic lore (V148.37–38n); "Ouija-board jokesters" are those half-baked souls who believe in the Ouija board as a divinatory method.

V746.30, B871.13, P761.22   WEISSMANN'S TAROT   Unlike Slothrop's tarot, which is incomplete, Weissmann's is fully laid out. And while the narrator offers a reading, it will help to stand it alongside the comments of A. E. Waite, Pynchon's principal source. First, one would of course need to know the specific inquiry that Weissmann made, and there is one excellent clue: his significator, a Knight of Swords, which Waite identifies with chivalry and specifically with the Grail quester, Galahad (*Pictorial Key* 230). Weissmann could well have chosen this card had he inquired about the future of his romantic quest. Next come the ten cards drawn at random from the tarot deck. Weissmann's quest is "covered"— that is, limited or conditioned—by the Tower, a sign of "misery, distress, indigence, adversity, calamity, disgrace, deception, ruin" (286). This card symbolizes the chastisement of pride, the ruin of the "House of Life, when evil has prevailed therein" (132). Both Waite and Ouspensky speak of the card as a symbol of ruin coming to an entire body of doctrine, perhaps here the body of Weissmann's decadent romanticism.

Weissmann's query is also "crossed," or opposed, by the Queen of Swords, a sign of "female sadness and embarrassment, absence, sterility, mourning, privation, separation" (Waite, *Pictorial Key* 228). The narrator sees this as a sign perhaps of Weissmann "himself, in drag" (V748.21–22), but one might as easily take it as a reminder of his defeat when Katje deserted him. The King of Cups "crowns" Weissmann's quest. That is, it represents the best he can expect to achieve from it. Interestingly, this card foretells equanimity and success in business (Waite, *Pictorial Key* 198), which will correspond with other cards to come. "Beneath" that card, representing events already past, is the Ace of Swords, signifying "conquest, triumph of force" (252). Its image, a sword skewering a crown from its bottom, suggests Weissmann's sexual dominion over Katje and Gottfried, as well as the phallic insertion of Gottfried into Rocket 00000. In the fifth and sixth cards, Pynchon has reversed Waite's ordering ("behind" and "before"). The Four of Cups coming "before" in this case implies fatigue: "weariness, aversion, as if the wine of this world had caused satiety only," is how Waite (218) puts it. "Behind" Weissmann, waning in importance in his life, is the Four of Pentacles, signifying that his "surety of possession" is through (274).

Weissmann's remaining four cards are displayed in a line to the right of the circular mandala formed with the first six cards. The Page of Pentacles, representing his insensibility to messages around him (260), comes up as the sign of his self-attitude at the moment. His "house" card, showing the influence of his associates, comes up an Eight of Cups: Waite (210) notes that "the card shows the decline of a matter, or that a matter which has been thought to be important is really of slight consequence—either for good or evil." One can take this as yet another sign that the meaning of Gottfried's sacrifice during the Easter/April Fool's weekend is hopelessly equivocal: maybe a token of redemption or maybe just a fool's quest. Surely it did not culminate with the fulfillment Weissmann seems to have anticipated. This is confirmed in the penultimate card, that of his "hopes and fears": the Two of Swords shows a slide into conformity, equipoise, and business. The narrator's comment is particularly striking: "If you're wondering where he's gone, look among the successful academics, the Presidential advisers, the token intellectuals who sit on boards of directors" (V749.9–12). Something like that, incidentally, was the fate of Walter Dornberger, who settled in the United States and sat on the board of directors of the Bell Helicopter Corporation. Or of Wernher von Braun, who wound up as head of NASA, or Peter Wegener, who taught at Yale University.

In the Celtic method of cartomancy, all these divinatory possibilities

are supposed to conclude in the last card—"what will come." In Weissmann's spread, it's symbolized by the World, card twenty-one of the Major Arcana. It is a sign of emigration (to the United States?), of voyages,
new beginnings. Indeed, this is what all Weissmann's previous cards suggest *will* happen, now that his romantic quest has ended in ambiguity.
Here is Waite (157–59): "It represents the perfection and end of the cos-
mos, the secret which is within it, the rapture of the Universe when
it understands itself in God. It is furthermore the state of the soul in
the consciousness of Divine Vision, reflected from the self-knowing
spirit. . . . But it is perhaps more especially a story of the past, referring
to that day when all was declared to be good, when the morning stars
sang together and the Sons of God shouted for joy." The card is definitely also an apocalyptic sign. Ouspensky's reading (27) is also noteworthy: "A circle not unlike a wreath woven from rainbow and light-
nings, whirled from Heaven to Earth with a stupendous velocity."

How might readers interpret Weissmann's tarot in its whole gestalt?
One powerful suggestion is that the World is what Weissmann, like
many other characters, is still left with: no transcendence, no escape
into a sublime empyrean. As the borrowed phrase from Wittgenstein put
it in Pynchon's first novel, "The world is all that is the case." And (as
Tatham ["Tarot and *Gravity's Rainbow*"] aptly argues), the way to that
world is through the armed woman, the Two of Swords, a symbol of pas-
sivity in the face of the turbulent waters behind her. Surely, too, Weissmann's tarot points up the end of his romantic desire and its translation
into business, into conformity, into the cartelized military industrial
sovereignties of the postwar period, thus into the future threat of nuclear winter figured in *GR*'s allusions to Hiroshima. Recall that Weissman survived the April apocalypse and was seen as late as May. This
effectively underwrites the denouement of *GR*, where the prolepsis to
Los Angeles and the Nixon epoch hints at a new transmogrification of
Weissmann's apocalyptic desire. Blicero slips out of the Zone, but his
spirit presides over contemporary America.

**V747.14–15, B871.41–42, P762.5–6   The Oedipal situation in the Zone
these days is terrible**   In Sigmund Freud's classical formulation the
Oedipus complex configures every neurosis, developing at the peak of
infantile (phallic) sexuality and entailing the infant's desire for an opposite-
sex parent (here a postwar mother figured by our narrator in the following lines as "masculinized old worn moneybags of no sexual interest").
Thwarting the boy's desire in the classical formulation is a firm father
standing for the superego and laying down an incest prohibition understood as a moral absolute. That prohibition requires, Freud argues in his
later work, a crucial sublimation of libidinous desire that founds civilization itself. Acceding to that law by symbolically killing the father
through sublimation, the upside of the son's murderous urge against the

father for blocking him, also creates, according to Freud, the emotional space between Eros and Thanatos, Love and Death, in which humanity acts out its complicated being. Here, however, a generation of fathers (represented by the corporate/institutional madman Weissmann/Blicero in this passage) having not been either literally or symbolically killed circa 1945, are seen as establishing a reign of masochism leaving postwar fathers "no power today" and condemning us all "to impersonate men of power our own infant children must hate." Thus the passage takes on the guise of historical theory.

V747.33–34, B872.22–23, P762.25   a Gnostic or Cathar symbol for the Church of Rome   On the Gnostics and Cathars, see V739.22–24n and V732.22–24n. Waite discusses the tarot symbols as a secret code for antipapal Catharist messages in his introduction to the *Pictorial Key* (8). The Tower, in his view (8–9), typifies "the desired destruction of Papal Rome, the City on the Seven Hills, with the pontiff and his temporal power cast down from the spiritual edifice when it is riven by the wrath of God."

V747.38, B872.27, P762.29   the Order of the Golden Dawn   An organization of Christian Kabbalists centered around MacGregor Mathers, a reader at the British Museum. He attributed its origins to "secret sources" and to clairvoyant powers. In fact, he concocted it, in 1885, out of Rosicrucianism and Kabbalist symbolism. W. B. Yeats, the most famous member, joined in 1889 after a brief go-round with the theosophist movement of Madame Blavatsky. Yeats got to the fifth of seven levels, or "Elements," that initiates were supposed to master. The rest of Mathers's followers were more common sorts of Londoners and very much prone to squabbling. One of their rows caused Mathers to disband the order twenty years after establishing it.

V747.41–748.5, B872.31–37, P762.33–39   On the Kabbalist Tree of Life . . . Yesod, the sex and excretory organs   Kabbalist myths of creation variously represent it as a downward, unfolding process, as a tree, and as a human body. At the peak, corresponding to the crown of the tree or the cranium of the body, is Kether, an infinite source that contains all material being within it. Hakemah and Binah, Wisdom and Understanding, are often interpreted as the two lobes of the brain. Gedulah and Geburah, Benignity and Strength, are represented as the arms or two main branches. Tephareth, Beauty, is the trunk of the tree or the torso of the body. Netzach and Hod, Victory and Glory, are identified with the thighs or roots, and they are joined in Yesod and Malakoth, Foundation and Dominion, which are also the male and female genitalia, respectively. In their descending order, each of these ten Sephira, or Vessels, is thought to contain all that lies below. Furthermore, corresponding to these ten levels are the ten Qlippoth, the empty shells of creation. Pynchon rightly identifies the two Qlippoth that correspond to

Netzach and Hod; they are, respectively, Ghorab Tzerek, the Ravens of Death, and Samael, the Poison of God. His accuracy on these obscure points confirms that Scholem's *Major Trends* was his source in these matters.

V748.18, B873.11, P763.10   the Amanita muscaria   Or so-called flycap mushroom that supposedly gives visionary powers (see V93.2–3n).

V748.40, B873.38, P763.33   taken as "concord in a state of arms"   The phrase is quoted from Waite (*Pictorial Key* 250), on the Two of Swords.

V749.21–22, B874.20–21, P764.12–13   heathen Germans . . . in their old ceremonies   The source is Grimm (Teutonic Mythology 46–48), according to whom nothing so offended proselytizing Christians as the pagan Teutonic practice of propitiating their gods through the sacrifice of horses, the bodies of which were eaten, while the heads were hung on trees.

V749.34–36, B874.35–38, P764.25–27   an Aggadic tradition . . . that Isaac . . . saw the antechambers of the Throne   The source once more is Sholem's *Major Trends* (53, 61–63). He explains that of the major Judaic writings two classes stand out: Halakah, those writings occupied with sacred law, and Aggadah, which means "narrative" and indicates any writings consisting of folktales, dramatic monologues, parables, allegories, maxims, satires, wordplay, permutations of letters, acrostics, and so on. (In this sense, *GR* may be read as an Aggadic text.) The Aggadic writings are pre-Kabbalistic, dating from the first century B.C. until about the tenth century A.D. Among them is a fourth-century manuscript, "The Apocalypse of Abraham," which Scholem connects with the Merkabah mysticism of the time, for it is concerned with a sevenfold ascent through the antechambers to God's throne. However, Pynchon has worked a significant inversion of the tradition. In "The Apocalypse of Abraham" it is the patriarch and not his son who ascends throneward at the moment of sacrifice. On his way, Abraham hears a hymn "like the voice of the waters in the rushing streams" (*Major Trends* 61). It is the singing of angels who guard the Merkabah, and Abraham can hear them from the sixth antechamber. In Pynchon's version, it is "Isaac under the blade" (V750.9–10) who has this visionary experience.

V750.13, B875.17, P765.4   at Nymphenburg   See V619.1–4n. Larsson ("A Companion's Companion") also points up a possible reference to the Alain Resnais film *Last Year at Marienbad* (1961) that includes tracking shots down the corridors at mad king Ludwig's Nymphenburg palace in Bavaria.

V750.18–19, B875.24, P765.10   mad Ludwig and his Spanish dancer   An error. It was not "mad Ludwig" (the Second, who committed suicide) but his father, Ludwig I, who fell in love with the so-called Spanish Dancer, Lola Montez, an Irish beauty who was born Marie Gilbert.

V750.20–21, B875.26–27, P765.12   ascent to the Merkabah   That is, to God's throne.

V750.33, B876.2, P765.25   the Hand of Glory   Derives from A. E. Waite's *Book of Black Magic and of Pacts* (276–77). Why burglars, or "second-story men," would want to employ such a monstrous device to "light their way into your home" will be apparent from Waite's discussion:

> The Hand of Glory is indifferently the right or left hand of a criminal who has been gibbeted. The sorcerer obtains it as he can, and in the days of Tyburn Tree [London's infamous Hanging Tree] such requisites might have cost nothing beyond the personal risk of the adventure; it is indispensable, however, that it should be wrapped in a piece of winding sheet, and this suggests that the criminal must have been previously cut down with a view to interment. Thus enclosed, the hand must be well squeezed so as to force out any blood which may possibly remain in the member, after which it must be placed in an earthen vessel, together with some zimort, saltpetre, common salt, and peppercorns, all pounded. It should remain in this vessel for fifteen days, and when extracted should be exposed to the heat of the sun during the time of the dogstar until it is extremely dessicated. If solar warmth be insufficient, it may be placed in a furnace heated with bracken and vervain. The object is to extract all the grease from the member, and therefrom, in combination with virgin wax and sesame from Lapland, to compose a species of candle. Wheresoever this frightful object is lighted, the spectators will be deprived of all motion, and the sorcerer can do what he will. It is possible to destroy its influence by anointing the threshold of the door, or other places through which entrance may be gained to a house, with an unguent composed of the gall of a black cat, grease from a white fowl, and the blood of a screech owl. This should also be confected in the dog-days [i.e., in high summer].

Note also the color symbolism in this counterspell: black, white, and red. These colors are standard in occult literature and have dogged the narrative of *GR* since part 1.

P765.30   Not a Procrustean bed   A giant in Greek mythology, Procrustes would either hack off, or stretch, the legs of guests in order to fit them to his iron bed. Theseus killed him.

V751.11, B876.24, P766.4   the Zündkreuz   Literally, a "spark cross," a device affixed to a long pole and used to ignite the A4 rocket's fuels at the initiation of launch. Pynchon's source on the launch procedures is Kooy and Uytenbogaart (*Ballistics of the Future* 374–77).

V751.19, B876.33, P766.11   Ochsen-Augen   These are "oxen eyes" or round dormer windows, made of isinglass, that are found in upper stories of houses.

V751.33–34, B877.10–11, P766.25–26   Sir Denis Nayland Smith   See V277.34–38n.

V751.35, B877.12, P766.27   Superman will swoop boots-first   As a comic book, *The Adventures of Superman* was originally written by Jerry Siegel and drawn by Joe Shuster, its first issues published by Action Comics in 1936. Two years later the Mutual Radio Network debuted the program.

V752.1–3, B877.17–20, P766.29–32   Philip Marlow . . . the Bradbury Building   The address stems from one of the film versions of Raymond Chandler's detective stories and novels featuring hard-boiled Philip Marlow, who operated out of the Condor Building in many of Chandler's early stories of the thirties before moving into the fictional Cahuenga Building in the better known novels. In (the rather awful and misspelled) *Marlowe*, a 1969 adaptation of Chandler's *The Little Sister*, the detective (played by James Garner) works out of the legendary Bradbury Building, at 302 South Broadway (a building used with powerful effects in the 1982 sci-fi classic, *Blade Runner*). Designed by architect George H. Wyman and completed in 1893 for Los Angeles real-estate mogul Lewis Bradbury, the building exemplifies American Victorian architectural design and features a light-filled multilevel central court highlighted by filigreed iron railings and staircases.

V752.4, B877.21–22, P766.32   Submariner . . . will run into battery trouble   The Timely Comics company published *Submariner* from 1941 to 1949, and Atlas Comics picked it up for the period 1954–55, calling it Sub-Mariner. Both of these variant titles are used by Marvel Comics, which has been its publisher *since 1968*. The hero, pledged to the destruction of humanity, was Prince Namor of Atlantis, the underwater kingdom of myth and fable. In gathering together the remnants of his scattered realm, he traveled far and wide on "the surface world" (as the writers of *Submariner* called it). During the war years, this search brought him into frequent conflict with the forces of evil—Nazis and Fascists. Submariner's costume consisted of a red cape and blue swim trunks.

V752.5, B877.22, P766.32   Plasticman will lose his way   Jack Cole's comic book (see V206.37n).

V752.7, B877.25–26, P766.35   The Lone Ranger will storm in   Here the narrator parodies the CBS radio program that ran (initially only locally, from Detroit station WXYZ) after 1933; after winning national audiences in the late thirties and forties it migrated to ABC television in 1949. Tonto was the "faithful Indian companion" who saved Texas Ranger Dan Reid after he was ambushed and left for dead in a dry gulch.

V752.10, B877.29, P767.1–2   Tonto, god willing, will put on his ghost shirt   That is, he will reprise the fateful Ghost Dance movement of Plains Indian tribes during the late 1880s that was set in motion after Paiute mystic Wovoka—perhaps following the preachings of his father—prophesied a new age when whites would vanish and the tribes would be restored to a newly abundant land as well as to righteous behavior and peaceful community. In this millenarian vision, the Indians' *saving remnant* (see V553.34n) would be identified in their wearing the "ghost shirt"—a magical garment thought to protect them from all injury at the hands of foes. Still, Wovoka enjoined his followers "not [to] hurt anybody or do harm to anyone. You must not fight. Do right always . . . Do not refuse to work for the whites and do not make any trouble with them." Nonetheless, as the Ghost Dance movement spread among recently defeated Lakota tribes of the Great Plains it turned into an open insurgency culminating in the 1890 slaughter of Big Foot's band of Lakota Sioux at Wounded Knee. So, which version of the ghost shirt would this Tonto don: the pacifist's or the insurgent's?

V752.12, B877.31, P767.4 "Too late" was never in their programming Literally, it was not in the radio programs and comic books featuring these pop cultural heroes. But note, as well, that *GR* has come full circle: in the first episode Pirate Prentice saves Teddy Bloat from a fearsome fall; now the heroes arrive "[t]oo late."

V752.14, B877.34, P767.6 *Yes Jimmy* Superman, speaking to sidekick and *Daily Planet* reporter Jimmy Olson.

V752.29, B878.11–12, P767.21 Pavlov on his own deathbed, recording himself The subject here is Pointsman, ignominiously self-defeated, and the source once more is "The Book." In his introduction to volume 2 of the *Lectures*, Horsley Gantt (35) recalls of Pavlov that "in every illness he studied himself as he did his dogs in a laboratory experiment. The day of his death, February 27, 1936, while suffering a collapse, with a pulse rate of 150, he summoned a neuro-pathologist to know whether his symptoms might not be interesting to science and to discuss them."

V753.5–8, B878.33–37, P767.39–40 The countdown as we know it . . . Fritz Lang said The source is a footnote in Willy Ley's *Rockets* (284): After the "Viking Hall" at the Hayden Planetarium in New York had been opened with a count-down, Milton Rosen casually remarked that the count-down was a custom that had originated at the Raketenflugplatz. I assured him that we had not thought of it, but later I began to wonder who had. Thinking back, I realized to my surprise that it had first been used in the film *Frau im Mond*. This was a silent movie, and at one point the words "10 seconds to go" flashed on the screen, followed by numbers, "6–5–4–3–2–1–0 Fire!" Knowing that Fritz Lang had been in the Austrian Army in the First World War, I asked him whether he had adapted some military practice which used a countdown. He replied that he had thought it up for dramatic purposes when working on the film; on a proving ground nobody would possibly think of that side effect!

Note, once again, the hysteron proteron motif.

V753.9–21, B878.38–879.8, P768.3–16 "At the Creation . . . the Tree of

Life."   On the tenfold ordering of the creation, imagined as a tree of life, see V747.41–748.5n.

V753.23–24, B879.17, P768.19   the Bodenplatte . . . axis of a particular Earth   The *Bodenplatte* (ground plate) was the portable, folding steel launching pad, also called a "lemon squeezer" in reference to its shape— conical but with concave slopes, to deflect the rocket blast on liftoff (see Irving, *Mare's Nest* 274). Here, it assumes symbolic importance as what Mircea Eliade has called the *axis mundi*, or world axis. In most mythologies, the *axis mundi* becomes a meeting place for all the cosmic regions: heaven, earth, and hell. In the Christian mythology it is the site where Adam and Eve were created and buried, as well as the site where Christ was crucified. Thus, the "blood of the Savior falls on Adam's skull," Eliade (*The Myth of the Eternal Return* 14) notes, and that blood "redeems him." The symbolic play here, though part of the broader satire, is crucial. Finding the *Bodenplatte* (V754.3) stands as analogous to discovering the true Cross, celebrated on September 14, the day it was "exalted" or "raised" again, in the year 335.

V753.29, B879.22, P768.25   Thorazine   See V518.31–32n.

V753.40, B879.37, P768.37–38   for leads, mu's, numbering   Mu, the twelfth letter in the Greek alphabet, would show with its accompanying number the capacitance value of a "wafer capacitor," with its two wire leads projecting from it and identifying it as something other than a pill.

V754.34, B880.37, P769.33   (PNS)   Fowler thinks PNS indicates a "Pynchon News Service," but the reference instead is surely to the Pacific News Service, founded in 1969 as an alternative source for news and analysis on the U.S. role in Vietnam as well as on worldwide antiwar efforts. It was syndicated initially out of the Berkeley, California, radio station KPFA-FM, the founding station (started up in 1949 by legendary pacifist Lewis Hill) in the listener-supported Pacifica Radio Network. PNS began distributing written stories soon after its founding and until 1996, when it was reorganized (out of San Francisco) as a source for youth- and ethnic-oriented stories and commentaries.

V754.38, B881.4, P769.37–38   "the Adenoid"   As in the adenoid that terrorized London, in Pirate Prentice's fantasy (V14.30ff).

V755.3–4, B881.8–9, P770.3   "our Bengt Ekerot / Marie Casarès Film Festival"   Swedish actor Bengt Ekerot (1920–71) played the role of Death in Ingmar Bergman's cinema classic *The Seventh Seal* (1956). Spanish-born Mariá Casares Quiroga (1922–96) sought asylum in France after Franco's victory in 1938 and subsequently played Death in Jean Cocteau's 1950 film *Orpheé*.

V755.6–8, B881.12–14, P770.6–8   throwing his arms up into an inverted "peace sign" . . . exposing . . . white French cuff   The pacifists' peace sign of the Vietnam era was an upside-down "V" divided in two by a vertical line, inside a circle; in a hand salute, this became the two-fingered

"V" (a victory sign in World War II). The gesture described here, with the white cuffs exposed, unmistakably identifies Richard M. Zhlubb as Richard M. Nixon, photographed just so in 1971.

V755.19, B881.26, P770.19   in Atascadero   The California Penal Facility located just north, and inland, from San Luis Obispo. LSD guru Timothy Leary was incarcerated there after his arrest in 1969.

V755.28, B881.36, P770.29   the black Managerial Volkswagen   The VW is improbable as a managerial limousine, but it is perhaps implicated here because VW plants at Fallersleben and Magdeburg manufactured V-weapon parts (Irving, *Mare's Nest* 199, 291).

V755.29–36, B882.1–5, P770.34–40   Near the interchange of the San Diego and the Santa Monica . . . the Pasadena . . . the Harbor   A tally of some principal freeways in the Los Angeles basin. The San Diego Freeway (Interstate 405) begins its southward run in San Fernando, through what were, circa 1970, the valley's middle-class ("white and well-bred") suburbs and over the Santa Monica Mountains and down through Westwood and Long Beach; in west Los Angeles it interchanges with the east-west-running Santa Monica Freeway (Interstate 10), "the scene of every form of automotive folly known" perhaps because of its wide ethno-racial diversity. The narrower and winding (hence "treacherously engineered") Pasadena Freeway (State Highway 110) runs southwest from Pasadena then due south after intersecting with the Santa Monica, whence it becomes the Harbor Freeway (Interstate 110), which runs through the predominantly black enclaves of Watts and Compton (hence "ghetto-suicidal").

V756.22–23, B882.37–38, P771.25–26   dark Lincolns, some Fords, even GMCs, but not a Pontiac   If there is any logic to this list perhaps it is that the Pontiac was named for the eighteenth-century chief of the Ottawa Indians, the likes of whom had to be pitchforked further west by whites such as Abe Lincoln and Henry Ford.

V756.39, B883.15–16, P772.3–4   Heading up the Hollywood freeway . . . a mysteriously canvassed trailer rig and a liquid-hydrogen tanker   The south-north-running stretch of State Highway 101 is known as the Hollywood Freeway until it intersects with State Highway 134 where it becomes the Ventura Freeway. Circa 1970 these tractor-trailer rigs might well be hauling, respectively, a nuclear-tipped ICBM missile (directly descended from von Braun's A4 rocket design) and its liquid hydrogen fuel. These rigs were thus then-contemporary versions of the Nazis' portable rocket-firing rig that Pynchon images for us in this closing scene.

V757.17–758.24, B883.39–885.11, P772.22–773.33   "Räumen. . . . Steuerung klar? . . . Stecker 1 und 2 gefallen"   With these calls from Captain Blicero and Moritz to the launch crew, the ascent of Rocket 00000 begins. Seed (*The Fictional Labyrinths of Thomas Pynchon* 218) thinks one source may have been the opening launch sequence in *Oper-*

ation Crossbow, the 1965 film starring George Peppard and Sophia Loren, in which Peppard plays an Allied spy on a mission to parachute into Peenemünde and destroy the Nazis' V-1 and V-2 capability. A more likely source, however, was the *A-4 Fibel* (see also V361.12–13n), though once again Pynchon has put the terms back into the original German. Blicero and his launch assistants, Max and Moritz (see V501.10n), begin to call out a string of technical commands, warnings, and inquiries. *"Räumen"* is Blicero's command to unnecessary members of the launch crew, ordering them to clear the space. With the question *"Steuerung klar?"* one of the boys asks if the controls or steering vanes are clear of obstructions. The *Treibwerk* is the A4's fueling or propulsion system, which the operator verifies as functioning normally. The *Luftlage* is the launch site itself. So the actual liftoff commences. *"Durchschalten"*: "Switch on." Moritz presses a button marked *"VORSTUFE,"* meaning "first stage." *Entlüftung:* ventilation. *"Beluftung klar"*: "Takeoff cleared." *Zundung:* ignition. *Hauptstufe:* main stage. At this point the *Stecker* or plugs would be blasted from the main engine nozzles and the rocket would have begun its ascent.

V759.24, B886.20, P774.35 a Brocken-specter On the unusual plays of light visible from atop the devilish Brocken in Germany's Harz Mountains, see V293.17n.

V759.29, B886.26, P774.40 Streckefuss Again, Blicero's nickname, "Stretchfoot" (see V733.26n).

Bibliography

This is a bibliography of works cited or consulted. Textual evidence shows that Thomas Pynchon included many of them in his reading for *Gravity's Rainbow*. Among these source materials, the *Times* of London, circa 1944–45, played a very large role indeed. The *Times* supplied so much background—in politics, military history, material and popular culture (household brands and pop bands, for example), even the weather—that the individual references are too numerous to list here. Source materials from the *Times* of London are cited, instead, within annotations. Pynchon also made use of such American periodicals as *Time, Life,* and the *New York Times,* and those items are listed in this bibliography when the text of *Gravity's Rainbow* shows a clear debt to the original.

A-4 Fibel [A-4 Handbook]. Trans. John A. Bitzer and Ted Woerner. Redstone Arsenal, Ala.: Army Ballistic Missile Agency, 1957.

Adams, Henry. *The Education of Henry Adams*. Ed. Ernest Samuels. Boston: Houghton Mifflin, 1974.

Adams, Henry, and Charles Adams. *Chapters of Erie*. 1871. New York: Kelley, 1967.

Adorno, Theodor. *Philosophy of Modern Music*. Trans. Anne G. Mitchell and Wesley V. Blomster. New York: Seabury, 1973.

Agar, Herbert. *The Saving Remnant: An Account of Jewish Survival*. New York: Viking, 1962.

Alexander, Robert J. *The Péron Era*. New York: Russell, 1965.

Anastazi, Anne. *Psychological Testing*. 3rd ed. New York: Macmillan, 1968.

Angellucci, Enzo. *The Rand-McNally Encyclopedia of Military Aircraft*. New York: Rand-McNally, 1980.

Asquith, Margot. *More or Less about Myself*. New York: Dutton, 1934.

Baedeker's Handbooks Inc. *Belgium and Holland*. 14th ed. New York: Scribner, 1905.

_____. *Berlin and Its Environs*. 4th ed. Leipzig: Baedeker, 1910.

_____. *Great Britain*. 5th ed. London: Dulau, 1901.

_____. *London and Its Environs*. 21st ed. New York: Macmillan, 1955.

_____. *Northern Germany*. 14th ed. Leipzig: Baedeker, 1904.

_____. *South-eastern France*. 3rd ed. London: Dulau, 1898.

_____. *Southern Germany*. 12th ed. New York: Scribner, 1904.

Bakhtin, Mikhail. *The Dialogic Imagination: Four Essays*. Ed. Michael Holquist. Trans. Caryl Emerson and Michael Holquist. Austin: U of Texas P, 1982.

_____. *Rabelais and His World*. Trans. Helene Iswolski. Cambridge, Mass.: MIT P, 1968.

Baring-Gould, S. *The Lives of the Saints*. 16 vols. New York: Longmans, Green, 1898.

Baynes, Cary E., trans. [from Richard Wilhelm's 1923 German edition]. *The I Ching; or, Book of Changes*. Bollingen Series. Princeton, N.J.: Princeton UP, 1967.

Bercovitch, Sacvan. *The Puritan Origins of the American Self*. New Haven, Conn.: Yale UP, 1975.

Black, Joel Dana. "Pynchon's Eve of Destruction." *Pynchon Notes* 14 (1984): 23–28.

Blackett, P. M. S. *Fear, War, and the Bomb*. New York: McGraw, 1955.

Bley, Helmut. *South-West Africa under German Rule*. London: Heinemann, 1971.

Borges, Jorge Luis. *Ficciones*. Ed. Anthony Kerrigan. New York: Grove, 1962.

Borkin, Joseph. *The Crime and Punishment of I.G. Farben*. New York: Free P, 1978.

Bower, Tom. *The Paperclip Conspiracy: The Hunt for Nazi Scientists*. Boston: Little, 1987.

Branston, Brian. *Gods of the North*. New York: Thames and Hudson, 1955.

Braun, Wernher von. *Space Frontier*. Greenwich, Conn.: Fawcett, 1969.

———. "Why I Believe in Immortality." In *The Third Book of Words to Live By*, ed. William Nichols. New York: Simon, 1962. 119–20.

———, and Frederick Ordway. *History of Rocketry and Space Travel*. New York: Crowell, 1968.

Briggs, Katharine. *The Faeries in English Tradition and Folklore*. Chicago: U of Chicago P, 1967.

Brincker, P. H. *Wörterbuch und Kurzgefässte Grammatik des Otji-Herero*. Leipzig: Buttner, 1886.

Brown, A. Samler. *Madeira and the Canary Islands: A Practical and Complete Guide for the Use of Invalids and Tourists*. London: Sampson Low, 1898.

Brown, Norman O. *Life Against Death: The Psychoanalytical Meaning of History*. 1959. Middletown, Conn.: Wesleyan UP, 1970.

Brunhübner, Fritz. *Pluto*. Trans. Julie Baum. New York: McCoy and Masonic Supply, 1934.

Bullock, Alan. *Hitler: A Study in Tyranny*. 1952. New York: Harper, 1991.

Byington, Ezra Hoyt. "William Pynchon, Gent." In *The Puritan in England and New England*. Boston: Roberts, 1896.

Byrne, Robert. *Byrne's New Standard Book of Pool and Billiards*. New York: Harcourt, 1998.

Campbell, Lewis, and William Garnett. *The Life of James Clerk Maxwell*. 1882. New York: Johnson, 1969.

Carman, W. Y. *A History of Firearms*. London: Routledge, 1955.

Clancy, Foghorn. *My Fifty Years in Rodeo: Living with Cowboys, Horses and Danger*. San Antonio: Naylor, 1952.

Clerc, Charles. "Film in Gravity's Rainbow." In Clerc, *Approaches* 103–52.

———, ed. *Approaches to "Gravity's Rainbow."* Columbus: Ohio State UP, 1983.

Clouston, William Alexander. *Popular Tales and Fictions: Their Migrations and Transformations*. 2 vols. London: Blackwood, 1887.

Collier, Basil. *The Battle of the V-Weapons*. New York: Viking, 1965.

Colmer, Michael. *Pinball: An Illustrated History*. New York: NAL, 1976.

Conrad, Joseph. *Heart of Darkness and Other Tales*. Ed. Cedric Thomas Watts. New York: Oxford UP, 2003.

Cooksley, Peter G. *Flying Bomb: The Story of Hitler's V-Weapons in World War II*. New York: Scribner, 1978.

Cooper, Peter. *Signs and Symptoms: Thomas Pynchon and the Contemporary World.* Berkeley: U of California P, 1983.

Cowart, David. *Thomas Pynchon: The Art of Allusion.* Carbondale: Southern Illinois UP, 1980.

Cowing, Cedric. *The Saving Remnant: Religion and the Settling of New England.* Urbana: U of Illinois P, 1995.

Cowke, L. W., and John Selwin Gummer. *The Christian Calendar.* Springfield, Mass.: Merriam, 1974.

Crumb, Michael. "Uroboric Imagery in Thomas Pynchon's *Gravity's Rainbow.*" *Readerly/Writerly Texts* 1.1 (Fall 1993): 65–86.

D'Annunzio, Gabriele. *The Triumph of Death.* Trans. Arthur Hornblow. Boston: Page, 1917.

Davis, Shelby C. *The French War Machine.* London: Allen and Unwyn, 1937.

Dickinson, Emily. *The Poems of Emily Dickinson.* Ed. Thomas H. Johnson. 2 vols. Cambridge, Mass.: Harvard UP, 1955.

Dictionary of American Regional English. Ed. Frederic G. Cassidy. Vol. 1 (A–C). Cambridge, Mass.: Belknap, 1985.

Donovan, Robert J. *PT-109: John F. Kennedy in World War II.* Greenwich, Conn.: Fawcett, 1962.

Dornberger, Walter. *V-2.* Trans. James Clough and Geoffrey Halliday. New York: Viking, 1955.

Drake, Francis S. *The Town of Roxbury.* Roxbury, Mass.: By the Author, 1878.

Drechsler, Horst. *"Let Us Die Fighting": The Struggle of the Herero and Nama against German Imperialism (1884–1915).* Trans. Berndt Zölner. Berlin: Akademie-Verlag, 1966.

Dubois, Josiah Ellis. *Generals in Grey Suits: The Directors of the International "IG Farben" Cartel, Their Conspiracy and Trial at Nuremburg.* London: Bodley Head, 1953.

Dunning, John. *Tune in on Yesterday: The Ultimate Encyclopedia of Old-Time Radio.* Englewood Cliffs, N.J.: Prentice-Hall, 1976.

Duyfhuizen, Bernard. "Critiquing the Cartel: Anti-Capitalism, Walter Rathenau and *Gravity's Rainbow.*" *Pynchon Notes* 34–35 (1994): 88–106.

———. "A Long View of V-2." *Pynchon Notes* 5 (1981): 17–19.

———. "'A Suspension Forever at the Hinge of Doubt': The Reader-Trap of Bianca in *Gravity's Rainbow.*" *Postmodern Culture* 2.1 (Sept. 1991): 1–23.

Ehrenburg, Walter. "Maxwell's Demon." *Scientific American* 217 (November 1967): 103–10.

Eliade, Mircea. *The Myth of the Eternal Return.* Trans. Willard R. Trask. New York: Pantheon, 1963.

Ewen, David. *All the Years of American Popular Music.* Englewood Cliffs, N.J.: Prentice-Hall, 1977.

Fairchild's Dictionary of Fashion. Ed. Charlotte Mankey Calisibetta. New York: Fairchild, 1975.

Federal Writers' Project of the Works Progress Administration of Massachusetts. *The Berkshire Hills.* New York: Funk and Wagnalls, 1939.

Fifield, William, ed. *Alexis Lichine's Encyclopedia of Wines and Spirits.* New York: Knopf, 1968.

Fitzgerald, F. Scott. *This Side of Paradise.* New York: Scribner's, 1920.

Fowler, Douglas. *A Reader's Guide to "Gravity's Rainbow."* Ann Arbor, Mich.: Ardis, 1980.

Frazer, James George. *Adonis, Attis, Osiris.* Vol. 2, part 4 of *The Golden Bough.* 3rd ed. New York: Macmillan, 1935. 12 vols. 1906–15.

Frenssen, Gustave. *Peter Moor's Journey to Southwest Africa: A Narrative of the German Campaign.* Trans. Margaret Ward. Boston: Houghton, 1968.

Fuller, Robert H. *Jubilee Jim: The Life of Colonel James Fisk.* New York: Macmillan, 1928.

Georgano, G. N., ed. *The Complete Encyclopedia of Motor Cars, 1895–1965.* New York: Dutton, 1968.

Gibbon, Edward. *The History of the Decline and Fall of the Roman Empire.* 1776. London: Chatto, 1960.

Gibson, G. D. "Double Descent and Its Correlates among the Herero of Ngamililand." *American Anthropologist* 58 (1956): 109–39.

———. "Herero Marriage." *Rhodes-Livingstone Journal* 24 (1959): 1–37.

Gilman, Alfred. *The Pharmacological Basis of Therapeutics.* New York: Macmillan, 1980.

Giovanetti, Len, and Fred Freed. *The Decision to Drop the Bomb.* New York: Coward-McCann, 1965.

Glover, Tony. *Blues Harp.* New York: Oak, 1965.

Goethe, Johann Wolfgang von. *Faust: A Tragedy in Two Parts.* Trans. Bayard Taylor. London: Oxford UP, 1963.

———. *Goethe's Color Theory.* Ed. Rupprecht Matthei. Trans. Herbert Aach. New York: Reinhold, 1971.

Gold, Robert. *Jazz Talk.* Indianapolis: Bobbs-Merrill, 1975.

Goldblatt, Irving. *History of South-West Africa.* Cape Town: Juta, 1971.

Graham, F. Lanier. *The Rainbow Book.* Berkeley: Shambala, 1975.

Graham, Stephen. *Through Russian Central Asia.* New York: Cassell, 1916.

Graves, Robert. *The Greek Myths.* New York: Penguin, 1967.

———. *The White Goddess: A Historical Grammar of Poetic Myth.* New York: Farrar, 1966.

Greene, Richard Leighton. *The Early English Carols.* Oxford: Clarendon, 1935.

Grimm, Jacob. *Teutonic Mythology.* Trans. James Steven Stallybrass. 4 vols. [Paginated consecutively.] New York: Dover, 1966.

Gröttrup, Irmgard. *Rocket Wife.* Trans. Susi Hughes. London: André Deutsch, 1959.

Hanson, Stephen, and Frank Magill. *Magill's Survey of Cinema.* Englewood Cliffs, N.J.: Salem, 1981.

Hardinge, Rex. *South-African Cinderella: A Trek through Ex-German South-West Africa.* London: Herbert Jenkins, 1937.

Harmon, Jim. *The Great Radio Comedians.* New York: Doubleday, 1970.

Harrison, Max. *Charlie Parker.* New York: Barnes, 1961.

Hayles, N. Katherine. *The Cosmic Web: Scientific Field Models and Literary Strategies in the Twentieth Century.* Ithaca, N.Y.: Cornell UP, 1984.

Hayles, N. Katherine, and Mary B. Eiser. "Coloring Gravity's Rainbow." *Pynchon Notes* 16 (Spring 1985): 3–24.

Haynes, William. *This Chemical Age.* New York: Knopf, 1942.

Heiber, Helmut. *Goebbels.* Trans. John K. Dickinson. New York: Hawthorne, 1972.

Hemingway, Ernest. Introduction. *The Fifth Column*. London: Cape, 1939.

Herman, Luc. "Introduction: Approach and Avoid." *Pynchon Notes* 42–43 (Spring-Fall 1998): 9–11.

Hernández, José. *The Gaucho Martín Fierro*. Trans. Walter Owen. New York: Farrar and Rinehart, 1936.

Hite, Molly. "'Holy Center-Approaching' in the Novels of Thomas Pynchon." *Journal of Narrative Technique* 12.2 (1982): 121–29.

———. *Ideas of Order in the Novels of Thomas Pynchon*. Columbus: Ohio State UP, 1983.

Hoffman, Heinrich. *Hitler Was My Friend*. London: Burke, 1955.

Hogg, Ian V. *The Complete Illustrated Encyclopedia of the World's Firearms*. London: Quarto, 1978.

Hollingsworth, Derek. *They Came to Mauritius*. London: Oxford UP, 1965.

Hooker, Thomas. *The Soules Implantation into the Natural Olive*. 1637. London: AMS, 1981.

Hume, Kathryn. *Pynchon's Mythography: An Approach to Gravity's Rainbow*. Carbondale: Southern Illinois UP, 1987.

Huzel, Dieter. *Peenemünde to Canaveral*. Englewood Cliffs, N.J.: Prentice-Hall, 1962.

Inoguchi, Rikihei, and Tadashi Nakajima. *The Divine Wind: Japan's Kamikaze Force in World War II*. Ed. Roger Pineau. Westport, Conn.: Greenwood, 1978.

Irving, David. *The Mare's Nest*. London: Kimber, 1964.

Irwin, Mark. "A Note on 'Porky Pig and the Anarchist' in *The Crying of Lot 49* and *Gravity's Rainbow*." *Pynchon Notes* 28–29 (1991): 55–57.

Jackson, Stanley. *The Sassoons*. New York: Dutton, 1968.

James, Montagu Rhodes. *The Apocryphal New Testament*. London: Nash and Grayson, 1924.

Jones, Marc Edmund. *Astrology*. London: Penguin, 1969.

Josephson, Mathew. *The Robber-Barons*. 1934. New York: Harcourt, 1962.

Jung, Carl Gustav. *The Collected Works of C. G. Jung*. Ed. G. Adler et al. Trans. R. F. Hull. 2nd ed. Vol. 9, *Mandala Symbolism*. Vol. 12, *Psychology and Alchemy*. Vol. 16, *Practice of Psychotherapy*. Bollingen Series. Princeton, N.J.: Princeton UP, 1968–69, 1968, 1966.

Kármán, Theodore von. *The Wind and Beyond*. Boston: Little, 1967.

Kastrup, Edwin K. *Facts and Comparisons: A Pharmacological Handbook*. St. Louis: Facts and Comparisons, 1979.

Katz, Ephraim. *The Film Encyclopedia*. New York: Crowell, 1979.

"Kennedy Hits the Trail." *Time* 24 Sept.1945: 17.

Kessler, Harry Graf. *Walter Rathenau: His Life and Work*. New York: Harcourt, 1930.

Klee, Ernst, and Otto Merk. *The Birth of the Missile: The Secrets of Peenemünde*. Trans. T. Schoeters. Intro. Wernher von Braun. New York: Dutton, 1965.

Kolbe, F. W. *An English-Herero Dictionary with an Introduction to the Study of Bantu in General*. Cape Town: Juta, 1883.

Kooy, J. M. J., and J. W. H. Uytenbogaart. *Ballistics of the Future: With Special Reference to the Dynamics and Physical Theory of the Rocket Weapons*. London: McGraw, 1946.

Kahn, Ely Jacques. *The Big Drink: The Story of Coca-Cola*. New York: Random, 1960.

Kozminski, Isidore. *Numbers and Their Magic*. New York: Weiser, 1972.

Kracauer, Siegfried. *From Caligari to Hitler: A Psychological History of the German Film*. 1947. Princeton, N.J.: Princeton UP, 1969.

Lake, Stewart M. *Wyatt Earp, Frontier Marshall*. Boston: Houghton, 1931.

Larson, John A. *Lying and Its Detection*. Chicago: U of Chicago P, 1932.

Larsson, Don. "From the Berkshires to the Brocken: Transformations of a Source in 'The Secret Integration' and *Gravity's Rainbow*." *Pynchon Notes* 22–23 (Spring–Fall 1988): 87–98.

———. "Rooney and the Rocketman." *Pynchon Notes* 24–25 (1989): 113–15.

———. "A *Companion*'s Companion." Dec. 2002 ed. 8 May 2005 <http://www.english.mnsu.edu/larsson/grl.html>.

Lee, Stan. *Origins of Marvel Comics*. New York: Simon, 1974.

Leiss, Andreas. *Carl Orff*. London: Calder and Boyers, 1966.

Levine, George, and David Leverenz, eds. *Mindful Pleasures: Essays on Thomas Pynchon*. Boston: Little, 1976.

Levy, Hermann. *Industrial Germany: A Study of its Monopoly Organizations and Their Control by the State*. Cambridge, U.K.: Cambridge UP, 1935.

Ley, Willy. *The Drifting Continents*. New York: Weybright and Talley, 1969.

———. *Rockets, Missiles, and Space Travel*. New York: Viking, 1959.

Lichine, Alexis. *Encyclopedia of Wines and Spirits*. New York: Knopf, 1967.

Loranger, Carol Schaechterle. "'His Kipling Period': Bakhtinian Reflections on Annotation, Heteroglossia and Terrorism in the Pynchon Trade." *Pynchon Notes* 44–45 (1999): 155–68.

Lueddecke, W. J. *Morituri*. Greenwich, Conn.: Fawcett, 1964.

Lugones, Leopoldo. *Obras Poeticas*. Madrid: Aguilar, 1959.

Luttig, Hendrik Gerhardus. *The Religious System and Social Organization of the Herero: A Study in Bantu Culture*. Utrecht: Kemink en Zoon, 1933.

Lykken, David T. *A Tremor in the Blood: Uses and Abuses of the Lie Detector*. New York: McGraw, 1981.

MacGregor, Robert M. "The Golliwog: Innocent Doll to Symbol of Racism." *Advertising and Popular Culture: Studies in Variety and Versatility*. Ed. Sammy R. Danna. Bowling Green, Ohio: Bowling Green State UP, 1992. 118–36.

Marx, Karl. *Marx's Critique of Hegel's Philosophy of Right*. Ed. Joseph O'Malley. Trans. Annette John and Joseph O'Malley. Cambridge, UK: Cambridge UP, 1970.

McCarron, William. "Pynchon and Hogarth." *Notes on Contemporary Literature* 16.5 (1986): 2.

———. "The Openings of *Ulysses* and *Gravity's Rainbow*." *CCTE Studies* 53 (1988): 34–41.

———. "A Pynchon 'Waste Land' Scene in *Gravity's Rainbow*." *Notes on Contemporary Literature* 17.4 (1987): 5.

———. "Slothrop, Berlin, and Pynchon's Use of Periodicals." *Notes on Contemporary Literature* 18.5 (1988): 10–13.

McCloy, Shelby T. *The Negro in France*. Lexington: U of Kentucky P, 1961.

McGovern, James. *Crossbow and Overcast*. New York: Morrow, 1964.

McHale, Brian. "Modernist Reading, Postmodern Text: The Case of Gravity's Rainbow." *Poetics Today* 1.1 (1979): 85–110.

McIntyre, Ruth A. *William Pynchon: Merchant and Colonizer*. Springfield, Mass.: Connecticut Valley Historical Museum, 1961.

Major, Clarence. *Dictionary of Afro-American Slang*. New York: International, 1970.

Malcolm X (Malcolm Little). *The Autobiography of Malcolm X*. New York: Grove, 1966.

Mangel, Anne. "Maxwell's Demon, Entropy, Information: *The Crying of Lot 49*." In Levine and Leverenz 87–100.

Marriot, David. "*Gravity's Rainbow*: Apocryphal History or Historical Apocrypha?" *Journal of American Studies* 19 (1985): 69–80.

Marriot, John A. *The Eastern Question*. Oxford: Clarendon, 1958.

Mead, Clifford. Untitled note. *Pynchon Notes* 11 (Feb. 1983): 64.

Mendelson, Edward. "Gravity's Encyclopedia." In Levine and Leverenz 161–96.

_____, ed. *Pynchon: A Collection of Critical Essays*. Englewood Cliffs, N.J.: Prentice-Hall, 1978.

Mesher, David. "Corrigenda: A Note on *Gravity's Rainbow*." *Pynchon Notes* 5 (Feb. 1981): 13–16.

Moore, Steven. "Pynchon on Record." *Pynchon Notes* 10 (Oct. 1982): 56–57.

Moore, Thomas. *The Style of Connectedness: "Gravity's Rainbow" and Thomas Pynchon*. Columbia: U of Missouri P, 1987.

Morison, Samuel Eliot. "William Pynchon, the Founder of Springfield." *Massachusetts Historical Society Proceedings* 64 (1931): 67–107.

"Moxie Plus." *Saveur*. May/June 1996: 51–56.

Nabakov, Vladimir. *Pnin*. New York: Avon, 1969.

Nagel, Ernest, and James R. Newman. *Gödel's Proof*. New York: New York UP, 1958.

Nelson, Keith L. "'The Black Horror on the Rhine': Race as a Factor in Post–World War I Diplomacy." *Journal of Modern History* 42.4 (1970): 606–27.

Newman, Ernest. *The Wagner Operas*. New York: Knopf, 1963.

Newman, Robert D. *Understanding Thomas Pynchon*. Columbia: U of South Carolina P, 1986.

Noel, John V. *Naval Terms Dictionary*. 2nd ed. Annapolis, Md.: U.S. Naval Academy, 1966.

Novikoff-Priboy, V. *Tsushima*. New York: Holt, 1948.

Nussenzweig, H. H. "The Theory of the Rainbow." *Scientific American* 236 (Apr. 1977): 116–27.

Official Overstreet Comic Book Price Guide. 34th ed. New York: Random, 2004.

Opie, Iona, and Peter Opie. *Children's Games in Street and Playground*. Oxford: Clarendon, 1969.

_____. *The Lore and Language of Schoolchildren*. London: Oxford UP, 1959.

Orff, Carl. *Carmina Burana: Cantiones profanae, cantoribus et chorus cantandae*. New York: Schott, 1937.

Ouspensky, Petr D. *The Symbolism of the Tarot*. Trans. A. L. Pogossky. New York: Dover, 1976.

Oxford Annotated Bible. Ed. Herbert G. May and Bruce M. Metzger. New York: Oxford UP, 1962.

Oxford Dictionary of Quotations. 3rd ed. New York: Oxford UP, 1979.

Ozier, Lance. "Anti-Pointsman/Anti-Mexico: Some Mathematical Imagery in *Gravity's Rainbow*." *Critique* 16.2 (1974): 73–90.

_____. "The Calculus of Transformation: More Mathematical Imagery in *Gravity's Rainbow*." *Twentieth Century Literature* 21.2 (1975): 193–210.

"Paris Black Market Robs U.S. Army." *Life* 26 Mar. 1945: 25–29.

Parrinder, Geoffrey. *African Mythology*. London: Hamlyn, 1967.

Partridge, Eric, ed. *A Dictionary of Forces' Slang, 1939–45*. London: Secker, 1948.

———. *The Macmillan Dictionary of Historical Slang*. New York: Macmillan, 1974.

Pavlov, Ivan Petrovitch. *Conditioned Reflexes*. Trans. and ed. G. V. Anrep. Oxford: Clarendon, 1928.

———. *Lectures on Conditioned Reflexes*. Trans. W. Horsley Gantt. Vol. 1, *Twenty-five years of Objective Study of the Higher Nervous Activity of Animals*. Vol. 2, *Conditioned Reflexes and Psychiatry*. New York: International, 1928–41.

Pearce, Richard, ed. *Critical Essays on Thomas Pynchon*. Boston: Hall, 1981.

Pearsall, Ronald. *The Table-Rappers*. New York: St. Martin's, 1972.

Peesch, Reinhard. *Das Berliner Kinderspiel der Gegenwart*. Berlin: Akademie-Verlag, 1957.

Perle, George. *Serial Composition and Atonality: An Introduction to the Music of Schoenberg, Berg, and Webern*. 3rd ed. Berkeley: U of California P, 1970.

Pétillon, Pierre-Yves. "Thomas Pynchon and Aleatory Space." Trans. Margaret S. Langford and Clifford Mead. *Pynchon Notes* 15 (Fall 1984): 3–46.

Pike, Albert. *Morals and Dogma: The Ancient and Accepted Rite of Freemasonry*. Richmond, Va.: Jenkins, 1906.

Pike, Nicholas. *Sub-tropical Rambles in the Land of the Aphanapteryx: Adventures in and Wanderings in and around Mauritius*. London: Sampson Low, 1873.

Plater, William M. *The Grim Phoenix: Reconstructing Thomas Pynchon*. Bloomington: Indiana UP, 1978.

Poirier, Richard. "Rocket Power." *Pynchon: A Collection of Critical Essays*. Ed. Edward Mendelson. Englewood Cliffs, NJ: Prentice-Hall, 1978. 59–64.

Pynchon, Thomas Ruggles (1823–1904). *Introduction to Chemical Physics*. New York: Van Nostrand, 1881.

Pynchon, Thomas Ruggles, Jr. *The Crying of Lot 49*. New York: Lippincott, 1966.

———. *Gravity's Rainbow*. New York: Viking, 1973; New York: Bantam, 1974.

———. Introduction. *Been Down So Long It Looks Like Up to Me*. By Richard Fariña. New York: Penguin, 1983. vii–xviii.

———. "Is It O.K. to Be a Luddite?" *New York Times Book Review* 28 Oct. 1984, sec. 1: 40–41.

———. "Journey into the Mind of Watts." *New York Times Magazine* 12 June 1966: 34–35, 78, 80–82, 84.

———. *Slow Learner*. Boston: Little, 1984.

———. "Under the Rose." *Noble Savage* 3 (1961): 233–51.

———. *V*. New York: Lippincott, 1963.

Pynchon, William (1590–1662). *The Meritorious Price of Our Redemption; or, Christ's Satisfaction Explained and Discussed*. London: Thomas Newberry, 1655.

———. *The Time When the First Sabbath Was Ordained*. London: Printed by R.G., and to be sold by T. N. at the Three Lions in Cornhill, 1654.

Pynchon and Co. *The Aviation Industry*. New York, 1929.

Qazi, Javaid. "Source Materials for Thomas Pynchon's Fiction: An Annotated Bibliography." *Pynchon Notes* 2 (Feb. 1980): 7–19.

Reed, Ishmael. *Mumbo Jumbo*. New York: Avon, 1972.

Reid, Norman. *Collections of the Tate Gallery*. London: Tate Gallery, 1967.

Rilke, Rainer Maria. *Duino Elegies*. Trans. J. B. Leishman and Stephen Spender. New York: Norton, 1967.

———. *Sonnets to Orpheus*. 1922. Trans. J. B. Leishman. London: Hogarth, 1957.

———. *Sonnets to Orpheus*. 1922. Trans. M. D. Herder Norton. New York: Norton, 1942.

Rougement, Denis de. *Passion and Society*. Trans. Montgomery Belgion. London: Faber, 1957.

Sacher-Masoch, Leopold von. *Venus in Furs*. Trans. Friedrich Schaffhausen. London: Sphere, 1969.

Sadoul, Georges. *Dictionary of Films*. Trans. Peter Morris. Berkeley: U of California P, 1972.

Safer, Elaine B. "The Allusive Mode and Black Humor in Pynchon's *Gravity's Rainbow*." 1980. In Pearce 157–68.

Sargent, William Walters. *The Battle for the Mind*. 1957. New York: Major, 1997.

Sassoon, Siegfried. *Memoirs of an Infantry Officer*. London: Faber, 1931.

Sasuly, Richard. *IG Farben*. New York: Boni and Gaer, 1947.

Schaub, Thomas R. *Pynchon: The Voice of Ambiguity*. Urbana: U of Illinois P, 1981.

Schauffler, Robert R. *Beethoven: The Man Who Freed Music*. New York: Doubleday, Doran, 1933.

Schmundt-Thomas, Georg. "Grab-bagging in *Gravity's Rainbow*: Incidental (Further) Notes and Sources." *Pynchon Notes* 26–27 (1990): 90–95.

Schneider, Reinhard. *Die Kaiserliche Schutz- und Polizeitruppe für Afrika*. Stegen am Ammersee, Germany: Druffel and Vowinckel Verlag, 2005.

Scholem, Gershom. *Major Trends in Jewish Mysticism*. 1941. New York: Schocken, 1954.

———. *On the Kabbalah and Its Symbolism*. Trans. Ralph Mannheim. New York: Schocken, 1965.

Schwab, Gabriele. "Creative Paranoia and Frost Patterns of White Words: Making Sense in and of Thomas Pynchon's *Gravity's Rainbow*." Working Paper No. 4. Milwaukee: Center for Twentieth-Century Studies, 1985.

Seed, David. *The Fictional Labyrinths of Thomas Pynchon*. Iowa City: U of Iowa P, 1988.

———. "Pynchon's Hereros." *Pynchon Notes* 10 (Oct. 1982): 37–44.

———. "Pynchon's Two Tchitcherines." *Pynchon Notes* 5 (Feb. 1981): 11–12.

———. "Thomas Hooker in Pynchon's *Gravity's Rainbow*." *Notes on Modern American Literature* 8 (1984): item 15.

Selmeci, Andreas, and Dag Henrichsen. *Das Schwarzkommando: Thomas Pynchon und Die Geschichte der Herero*. Bielefeld, Germany: Aisthesis Verlag, 1995.

"Shoulder Insignia." *Life* 6 Aug. 1945: 41–47.

Siegal, Jules. "Who Is Thomas Pynchon . . . and Why Did He Take Off With My Wife?" *Playboy* 34 (Mar. 1977): 97, 122, 168–74.

Sillar, Frederick C. *The Symbolic Pig*. London: Oliver and Boyd, 1961.

Simpson, Christopher. *Blowback: America's Recruitment of Nazis and Its Effects on the Cold War*. New York: Weidenfeld, 1988.

Skinner, B. F. "Pigeon in a Pelican." In *Cumulative Record: A Selection of Papers*, ed. B. F. Skinner. New York: Appleton, 1972.

Slade, Joseph. *Thomas Pynchon*. New York: Warner, 1974.

Smith, Adam. *An Enquiry into the Nature and Causes of the Wealth of Nations.* Ed. Edwin Cannan. London: Methuen, 1981.

Smith, Joseph H., ed. *Colonial Justice in Western Massachusetts: The Pynchon Court Record.* Cambridge, Mass.: Harvard UP, 1961.

Smith, Marcus, and Khachig Tololyan. "The New Jeremiad: *Gravity's Rainbow.*" In Pearce 169–86.

Soules, Terrill Shepard. "What to Think about *Gravity's Rainbow.*" *Esquire* Oct. 1980: 104–07.

Speer, Albert. *Inside the Third Reich.* New York: Macmillan, 1970.

Steenkamp, Willem Petrus. *Is the South-West African Herero Committing Race-Suicide?* Cape Town: Unie-Volkspers, 1944.

Stendhal [Marie-Henri Beyle]. *Life of Rossini.* 1824. Trans. Richard N. Coe. New York: Orion, 1970.

Tabbi, Joseph. *Postmodern Sublime: Technology and American Writing from Mailer to Cyberpunk.* Ithaca, N.Y.: Cornell UP, 1995.

Tanner, Tony. *Thomas Pynchon.* London: Methuen, 1982.

Tatham, Campbell. "Tarot and *Gravity's Rainbow.*" *Modern Fiction Studies* 32 (Winter 1986): 581–90.

Taylor, A. J. P. *English History, 1914–45.* Oxford: Clarendon, 1965.

Taylor, A. Marjorie. *The Language of World War II.* New York: Wilson, 1948.

Teague, Ben. "A '*Gravity's Rainbow*' Companion Companion." June 2005 <http://www.benteague.com/books/titles/gravitys.html>.

Thompson, Don, and Dick Lupoff. *All in Color for a Dime.* New Rochelle, N.Y.: Arlington, 1970.

_____. *The Comic-Book Book.* New Rochelle, N.Y.: Arlington, 1972.

Thompson, Stith. *Motif-Index of Folk Literature.* 6 vols. Rev. ed. Bloomington: Indiana UP, 1955–58.

Tillotson, T. S. Untitled Note. *Pynchon Notes* 5 (Feb. 1981): 29.

Toland, John. *The Dillinger Days.* New York: Random, 1963.

Tölölyan, Khachig. "Fishy Poisson: Allusions to Statistics in *Gravity's Rainbow.*" *Notes on Modern American Literature* 4 (1979): item 5.

_____. "War as Background in *Gravity's Rainbow.*" In Clerc, *Approaches* 31–68.

Twain, Mark. *Roughing It.* Ed. Hamlin Hill. New York: Penguin, 1981.

Van Doren, Carl. *Benjamin Franklin.* New York: Viking, 1964.

Vedder, Heinrich. "The Herero." In *Native Tribes of South Africa.* Cape Town: Cape Times Limited, 1928.

_____. *Southwest Africa in Early Times.* Oxford: Clarendon, 1938.

Vonnegut, Kurt. *Slaughterhouse-Five; or, The Children's Crusade.* New York: Delacorte, 1969.

Waddell, Helen J. *The Wandering Scholars.* 1927. London: Constable, 1938.

Waite, Arthur Edward. *The Book of Black Magic and of Pacts.* Ed. I. W. Laurence. 1898. Chicago: de Laurence, 1940.

_____. *The Pictorial Key to the Tarot.* San Francisco: Harper, 1971.

"Walpurgisnacht Is Celebrated by G-Is." *Life* 28 May 1945: 122–24.

Ward, Arthur Sarsfield [pseud. Sax Rohmer]. *The Trail of Fu-Manchu.* New York: Doubleday, Doran, 1934.

Watson, John B., and Rosalie Rayner Watson. *The Psychological Care of Infant and Child.* New York: Norton, 1928.

Weber, Max. *The Protestant Ethic and the Spirit of Capitalism.* Trans. Talcott Parsons. New York: Scribner, 1958.

_____. *The Theory of Social and Economic Organization.* Trans. Talcott Parsons and A. M. Henderson. New York: Oxford UP, 1947.

Wegener, Peter. *The Peenemünde Wind Tunnels: A Memoir.* New Haven, Conn.: Yale UP, 1996.

Weiser, Francis. *Handbook of Christian Feasts and Customs.* 2 vols. New York: Harcourt, 1958.

Whalen, Richard J. *The Founding Father: The Story of Joseph P. Kennedy.* New York: NAL, 1964.

Wheeler, Fern. *The Thirteenth House: Lost Chapter in Spiritual Astrology.* Seattle: Lowman and Hanford, 1939.

Wiener, Norbert. *Cybernetics.* 1948. Cambridge, Mass.: MIT P, 1961.

Wildgans, Friedrich. *Anton Webern.* Trans. Edith Roberts and Humphrey Searle. New York: October, 1967.

Winner, Thomas G. *Oral Art and Literature of the Kazakhs of Russian Central Asia.* Durham, N.C.: Duke UP, 1958.

_____. "Problems of Alphabetic Reform among the Turkic Peoples of Soviet Central Asia." *Slavonic and East European Review* 31 (1952): 133–47.

Winston, Mathew. "The Quest for Thomas Pynchon." In Levine and Leverenz 251–64.

Wister, Owen. *Padre Ignacio; or, A Song of Temptation.* New York: Harper, 1900.

Wolfley, Lawrence. "Repression's Rainbow: The Presence of Norman O. Brown in Pynchon's Big Novel." 1978. In Pearce 99–123.

Wray, Fay. "How Fay Met Kong; or, The Scream That Shook the World." *New York Times* 21 Sept. 1969, sec. 2: 17–18.

Yates, Frances Amelia. *The Rosicrucian Enlightenment.* Boston: Routledge, 1972.

Yule, George U., and M. G. Kendall. *Introduction to the Theory of Statistics.* 14th ed. New York: Hafner, 1950.

Zigrosser, Carl, ed. *Prints and Drawings of Käthe Kollwitz.* New York: Dover, 1969.

Zipf, George Kingsley. *Human Behavior and the Principle of Least Effort.* Cambridge, Mass.: Addison-Wesley, 1949.

_____. *The Psycho-Biology of Language.* Boston: Houghton, 1935.

"Zoot Suits and Service Stripes: Race Tension Behind the Riots." *Newsweek* 21 June 1943: 35–40.

Index

This listing references the various allusions, brand names, characters, contexts, items, motifs, persons, place names, sources, subjects, substances, and texts in *Gravity's Rainbow*, as well as the principal texts consulted for notes in the *Companion*. Indexed items are to things discussed in the annotations and use page- and line-number references to the Viking-Penguin editions. (A few entries also contain cites to discussion of items in the frontmatter and the introductory sections of the *Companion*, and two entries are discussed only in an introductory section; these page-number references are to the text and are given below in brackets.) As such, this index may also double as a partial index to the novel; readers wanting a full index should consult *An Index to "Gravity's Rainbow,"* compiled by Khachig Tölölyan and Clay Leighton, published by *Pynchon Notes* 36–39 (1995–96): 83–138.

1922 Committee, 615.27–28

"Aberystwyth" (Wesley), 171.7
Abreaction, 48.14
Absolute zero, 3.34
Acción Argentina, 263.34–35, 383.19
Ackeret, Jakob, 452.39–40
Acton, Lord, 277.24
Agfa, 71.24, 579.30
Aggadah, 749.34–36
Ajtys, 356.10
Alasil, 132.16
Albedo, 152.24, 489.21
Alexanderplatz (Berlin), 446.14
Alexandrevna, Empress Feodora, 352.10–11
Alien Property Custodian, 581.34–35
"Allen's Alley," 44.17–18, 711.24
Allgeier, Johann Baptiste, 550.34, 675.34–35
Allport and Vernon's Study of Values, 81.23–24
Alpdrucken/*Alpdrücken,* 18.8–38, 142.32–33, 387.36
Amanita muscaria ("flycap"), 93.2–3, 748.18
Ameche, Don, 381.6
"America the Beautiful," 695.33–34

Amphetamine, 168.41
Andrée, Salomon, 589.24–27
Andrews Sisters, 382.34
"The Angel" (windmill), 106.12
Anilinas Alemanas, 387.29–30
"Animal Crackers in My Soup" (Henderson), 466.16
Arbella, 204.1–4, 364.25–26
Arch, 709.33–35; Gauss curve, 508.39; ogive, 573.11; parabola, 443.5–7; rainbow, 6.33–35, 151.29–30, 208.8, 209.25–26, 225.2, 726.19–20; "reflex arc" (Pavlovian theory), 56.14; torus, 726.15
Ariadne, 88.17, 143.16
Aries (astrology), 236.36–37, 681.20–21
Arkona, Cape, 528.9–10
Arrow (shirt), 63.14
Armstrong, Robert, 688.36–37
Aspinwall Hotel, 28.38
Asquith, Margot, 78.12
Astaire, Fred, 561.30–31
Astarte, 649.34
Astrology, as motif, 34.21–22, 152.16, 154.24–25, 154.35–36, 236.36–37, 302.20, 483.1, 624.18, 681.20–21, 694.12–16, 699.17, 712.21, 712.29
Atlantis, 269.9–10, 331.2, 635.37

Atropine, 703.13–14
ATS (Auxilliary Territorial Services),
17.26
Avus Autobahn, 371.34–35
Azos (light bulb), 650.30–32

Babington-Smith, Constance, 726.6–8
Baby Ruth, 677.36–37
Bach, Johann Sebastian, 440.39
"Backstage Wife," 499.36
Badajoz (Spain), 234.7–8
Baedeker guides, as source, 160.35–36,
161.30, 161.36, 181.5–6, 181.10,
332.16, 333.14–15, 525.24, 527.36–
37, 528.9–10, 528.13–14, 528.19,
649.27, 652.29
Bakunin, Mikhail, 386.21–22, 587.32–
33
Baldwin, Stanley, 649.12–13
The Barber of Seville (Rossini), 204.33–
35
Barrie, J. M. (Little Mary), 533.11
Bataafsche Petroleum Maatschappij
N.V. (Royal Dutch Shell Corporation),
240.35
Bayer Corporation, 742.5
Bayros, Franz von, 71.27, 330.13
BDM (Bund Deutscher Mädchens),
450.24–25
Beal, Mary F., 612.33
Beardsley, Aubrey, 71.27, 634.22
Beaton, Cecil, 78.12
Beaverbrook, Baron William Aitken,
615.31–32
Beck, Prof., 224.14–15
Beckett, Thomas à, 471.30
Beeman's gum, 646.14
Beethoven, Ludwig van, 440.4, 685.38
Belladonna (Atropa), 168.24–25
Bendix, William, 684.31–35
Bennet, Tony, 412.35
Benzene ring, 243.28–29, 249.21
Berg, Alban, 465.18
Beria, Lavrenti, 719.10
Berkeley, Bishop George, 214.35
The Berkshire Hills, 27.31–34, 28.33–
34, 268.18–19, 330.22–24
Berlin, Irving, 442.40

"Berliner Luft," 372.29–30
Bernreuter Inventory, 81.23–24
Between Two Worlds, 253.17
Beveridge proposal, 57.31
Biedermeier (style), 162.20–21, 434.26–27
Big Ben, 133.29–30
Bingen pencils, 452.30–31
Biograph Theater (Chicago), 741.6–7
Blackett, P. M. S., 12.14–15
Black plague, 621.11–13
Blavatsky, Elena Petrovna, 269.33–35
Bleicheröde (Germany), 237.1, 314.30
Blicero (Dominus Blicero), 30.12, 94.21–
22, 215.5, 322.29–30, 485.35, 727.11–
12, 735.30, 759.29; as Streckefuss,
733.26, 759.29
Blizna (Poland), 424.14
Bond Street (London), 25.28, 119.11
Bonifacius, St., 281.1–2
Booth, John Wilkes, 210.34
Borges, Jorge Luis, 137.20, 264.26–27
Bosquet, Gen. Pierre, 10.28
Bovril, 23.10
Boxing Day, [9], 132.26
Bracken, Sir Brendan, 615.31–32
Bradbury Building (Los Angeles), 752.13
Brandenburg Gate (Berlin), 436.24
Brain trust, 565.24–26
Braun, Wernher von, [8], 237.1–2,
Brennschluss, 6.37, 239.26–27
The Bride of Frankenstein
(Laemmle), 591.18
Briggs, Katharine (The Faeries in English
Tradition and Folklore), 147.39–40
Brincker, P. H. (Wörterbuch und Kurzge-
fässte Grammatik des Otji-Herero),
152.39–40, 325.31
Bristlecone pines (Pinus aristatus),
297.38
Britten, Benjamin, 59.1–2
Brocken (Germany), 293.17
Bromo seltzer, 240.25
Brown, Johnny Mack, 247.6–7
Brown, Norman O., 440.39
Buffalo Bayou (Texas), 449.15
Bugs Bunny, 592.32
Bukharin, Nikolai, 189.25
Burma Shave, 65.9

Busch, Wilhelm, 501.10, 568.36
Busemann, Adolf, 452.39–40
Business Advisory Council, 581.29–30
"Bye, Bye, Blackbird" (Dixon), 61.24–36

"Cactus Tree" (Mitchell), [322]
Cagney, James, 222.2, 684.31–35
Calloway, Cab, 675.23
Camay, 208.21
Cancer (astrology), 154.24–25
Cap d'Antibes (Monaco), 185.19
"Captain Midnight," 375.16
Carmichael, Howard ("Hoagy"), 522.6–8
"Carmina Burana" (Orff), 237.16–20
Carnegie, Dale, 77.35–36
Carothers, Wallace Hume, 249.29–30,
    348.12
Casablanca (Conway), 205.13–14,
    253.17
Casarès, Maria, 755.3–4
Caserne Mortier (Paris), 246.35
Castle (tarot), 486.26
Castle Walk (dance), 60.26–29
Catharism, 732.22–24, 747.33–34
Catherine the Great, 343.28
Cavendish Laboratory, 15.26
Chardin, Teilhard de, 539.12
"The Charge of the Light Brigade" (Ten-
    nyson), 270.14–15
Charleston (dance), 60.26–29
Charley-Charley (game), 540.23
"Chattanooga Choo-Choo" (Gordon and
    Warren), 468.5
Chebychev's theorem, 638.13
Chelsea Embankment (London), 5.21–22
Chemnyco Incorporated, 349.28
"Cherokee" (Noble), 63.23–24
*Chinesische Blätter für Wissenschaft
    und Kunst*, 454.13–14
Chiquita Brands Incorporated, 678.14–
    15
Chi-square test (statistics), 40.18, 153.15
Choate School, 194.18
Churchill, Sir Winston, 135.38, 373.26–
    27
CIOS (Combined Intelligence Objec-
    tives Subcommittee), 272.32–34,
    391.19

Civvie Street, 9.6
Clark bar, 63.6
Clausewitz, Karl von, 182.35
clew, 88.12–17, 428.28–29, 457.2
Clive, Baron, 82.36–37
Coca-Cola, 677.26–27
Collier, Basil (*The Battle of the V-
    Weapons*), 293.14–15, 726.6–8
Comet (sailboat), 185.22
Continental drift, 321.19–20
*A Contribution to the Critique of
    Hegel's Theory of Right* (Marx),
    701.18
Corydon (Gide), 5.21
Coué, Emile, 77.35–36
Coward, Noel, 134.40–135.1, 709.18
Crime Does Not Pay Comics, 709.15
Critical mass, 539.21
Croix mystique, 16.15–16, 484.25
Crosby, Bing, 38.19, 184.4, 320.8
Cross: as motif, 100.34–38, 101.1–2,
    560.25, 567.25, 719.39–40, 751.11,
    753.23–24; *croix mystique*, 16.15–16,
    484.25; *Kreis*, 152.11; Slothrop as,
    625.3–4; stations of, 502.9–10; *Zünd-
    kreuz*, 751.11
Crown-and-anchor (game), 214.11
Curtis (London tailor), 200.39
Crystal Palace (London), 3.7
Cuvilliés, François de, 619.1–4, 750.13
Cuxhaven (Germany), 272.32–34,
    372.23
Cybernetics, 238.30
Cypridinae, 690.40

Daedalus, 428.28–29
Daily Herald (London), 231.14
"Dancing in the Dark" (Dietz and
    Schwartz), 36.11–12
D'Annunzio, Gabriele, 478.27
Dante (Dante Alighieri), 350.2–3
Darnley, Jill, 381.10–14
Davis, Bette, 619.1–4
A Day at the Races (Weingarten),
    619.1–4
Death (tarot), 164.29
Degenkolb, Gen. Gerhard, 448.30–31
Degrelle, Léon, 546.24–25

DeMille, Cecil B., 71.30, 559.16–17
"De Profundis Clamavi" (Mozart),
  295.27–28
Descamisados, 263.39
Devil's kiss, 329.19
Dewey, Thomas, 636.28–29
"Diadem" (Perronet), 169.34
Dickinson, Emily, 27.26, 28.12–13
Dietrich, Marlene, 393.41–394.1
Dillinger, John, 368.41, 436.16–17,
  516.3, 741.6–7
Dillon, Reed, and Company, 565.11
Dodgem cars, 273.24
Doktor Mabuse der Spieler (Lang),
  500.26, 517.12, 579.21–22
Domina nocturna, 232.35
Don Giovanni (Mozart), 270.19–20
Donne, John, 12.22
"Don't Sit Under the Apple Tree"
  (Brown, Tobias, and Stept), 382.3–4
Doppler effect, 310.27
Dora prison camp, 289.28, 296.14–16,
  299.29–30, 408.15
Dornberger, Walter (V-2), [8], 6.37, 7.5,
  154.7, 161.18, 206.14, 207.8, 224.14–
  15, 282.6, 402.29–32, 403.5, 404.38–
  405.3, 405.26, 406.13–16, 406.37,
  407.1, 407.3–4, 416.10–14, 416.23,
  422.26, 423.23, 424.18–23, 424.38,
  425.25–29, 427.29–30, 452.21–31,
  454.6, 455.24–25, 502.20–21, 550.14–
  15, 640.25–26
Dorum Road (Cuxhaven, Germany),
  527.3
Dracula (Browning), 37.19–20, 652.12
Dracula (Stoker), 82.3
Dragon Lady, 670.38
Dragon's teeth, 281.11–12
Dramamine, 490.11
Dreyfuss, Gen. Alfred, 390.1
Dr. Jekyll and Mr. Hyde (Mamoulian),
  712.4
Dulles, Allen, 268.2
Dumbo (Disney), 106.33–37, 135.2–3,
  741.34
Dumont, Margaret, 619.1–4
Duncan, Isidora, 657.33

DuPont (E. I. DuPont de Nemours &
  Company), 249.28
Durbin, Deanna, 599.9–10
Dzabajev, Dzambul, 390.7

Earles, Harry, 534.11
Earp, Wyatt, 210.27
Eberle, Bob, 264.6–7
Eddy, Nelson, 534.2
Edward VIII, 59.16, 177.28–29
EEG (electroencephalogram), 34.6,
  145.36–37, 146.1–7, 727.17–18
Eight (numerical motif), 147.13, 238.7–
  8, 285.18, 290.7, 691.19–20
Eighty-sixed, 21.36
Eiser, Mary B. ("Coloring Gravity's
  Rainbow"), 101.19–20, 364.39
Eisheiligen, 281.1–2
Ekerot, Bengt, 755.3–4
ELAS, 34.28–30
Eliade, Mircea (*The Myth of the Eternal
  Return*), 508.29–30, 753.23–24
Eliot, T. S., 35.26, 121.29
The Embankment (London), 145.4
ENSA (Entertainers' National Service
  Organization), 657.22, 708.31
Entre Ríos (Argentina), 383.30
Equivalent phase (Pavlovian
  theory), 48.38–39, 78.39
Erwartung (Schönberg), 101.19, 424.34
Esso, 240.23
Eucodal (opiate), 345.6–16
Eumecon (opiate), 345.6–16
Eurydice, 472.20–21
Eventyr, 29.31
Evil Hour, 374.39–375.2, 440.4, 500.40

"Die Fahne Hoch" ("Horst Wessel
  Song"), 443.2, 653.14
Fairbanks, Douglas, 637.11
Falkman and His Apache Band (BBC),
  32.26
"Fantastic Four," 675.32
Faraday, Michael, 584.40–41
Faro (game), 69.12, 181.4
Fatima (cigarette), 267.26
Die Faust Hoch, 154.19

Fauvism, 183.29
Fields, W. C., 12.30, 198.19
Fifth-columnists, 624.20
Fisk, James ("Jubilee Jim"), 285.37, 378.16, 438.15–17
Fitzgerald, F. Scott, 320.12
Fitzmaurice House (London), 76.29–33
"Flotsam and Jetsam" (BBC), 73.34
Flying Down to Rio (Cooper), 106.33–37
Flying Dutchman, 498.6
Flynn, Errol, 248.32
Fonda, Henry, 448.23–24
Fool (tarot), 501.25–26, 533.9, 724.28–29, 742.29
Formby, George, 9.5, 18.8–38
Fort-Lamy (Chad), 489.20
La Forza del Destino (Verdi), 595.14
Foster, Stephen, 675.15
Fourier analysis, 641.17, 664.4–5
Franco, Generalissimo Francisco, 234.7–8
Franklin, Benjamin, 663.37, 664.1, 664.38
Franklin, Sir John, 589.24–27
Die Frau im Mond (Lang), 159.33
Freaks (Browning), 106.33–37, 534.11
Frederick the Great, 314.2
Fred Roper and his Wonder Midgets, 37.10–11
Free French, 34.28–30
Freud, Sigmund, 272.19
Frick & Frack, 22.4
Friedmann, Alexander, 396.34
Friscia, Saverio, 587.32–33
Fu-Manchu (Sax Rohmer [A. S. Ward], *The Trail of Fu-Manchu*), 65.19, 83.25, 210.18, 277.34–38, 592.36–37, 631.29–31

Gannister, Herbert, 166.1–9
Gantt, Dr. Horsley, 88.3, 226.33
Garbo, Greta, 127.19–20, 380.11, 476.11
Garmisch-Partenkirchen (Bavaria), 527.25
Garrard and Company Ltd., 17.7
"Gaudeamus Igitur," 432.13, 580.5–6
Gauss curve, 508.39
Gaussian distribution, 709.33–35

Gaussian reduction, 521.17
The Gay Divorcee, 561.26
La Gazza Ladra (Rossini), 273.37–41
General Electric Company, 332.5–6, 654.27
George, David Lloyd, 237.9
George, St., 24.14–15
George, Stefan, 403.11
Gibbon, Edward (*The Decline and Fall of the Roman Empire*), 67.8–9, 101.1–2
Gide, André 5.21
Gilbert and Sullivan, 5.3, 116.35
Ginger Group, 615.27–28
Girl Guides, 13.11, 39.7
Glastonburys, 86.32–33
Gnosticism, 429.27, 727.6–10, 739.22–24, 747.33–34
Gödel's theorem, 275.25–26, 320.19
Goebbels, Josef, 461.18
Goethe, Johann Wolfgang von, 293.17
Goetzke, Bernhardt, 579.21–22
Going My Way (McCarey), 38.19
Gold Star Mothers, 134.38
Gollin, Geoffrey, 240.21–22
Golliwog, 174.19
Goodman, Benny, 225.35–36
Gorodki (game), [7], 226.33
Gospel of Thomas, 537.1–4
Goya, Francisco, 657.17
Grable, Betty, 9.3
Graham, Stephen (*Through Russian Central Asia*), 338.21–22, 338.28–30
Grant, Cary, 13.34–35, 240.41, 292.41, 294.11, 661.39
Graves, Robert (*The White Goddess*), 170.24–25, 302.2–3
Greed, 535.17
Greene, Richard Leighton (*The Early English Carols*), 129.8–16
"The Green Hornet," 376.36
Greenstreet, Sidney, 253.17
Greenwich (England), 11.10–11, 20.4
Griebnitz, 370.5–6
Grimm, Jacob (*Teutonic Mythology*), 72.27–28, 73.23–27, 94.26, 108.12–13, 206.24–25, 218.10, 221.13, 232.35, 258.26–27, 269.9–10, 329.19, 361.23–

Grimm, Jacob (*Teutonic Mythology*)
(continued)
25, 374.39–375.2, 379.25–26, 398.19,
528.13–15, 567.34, 625.17, 733.26,
742.22–23
Grössli Chemical Corporation, 250.23–
24, 284.15–16
Grosvenor Square (London), 17.11
Gröttrup, Irmgard (*Rocket Wife*), 516.30
Guinan, Texas, 559.16–17, 657.10–11
Gunga Din, 13.34–35
Guthrie, Tyrone, 148.4
Gymanfa Ganu, 171.37
Gypsy Wildcat, 121.13–14

Haig, Sir Douglas, 79.31–32
Hall, Jon, 121.13–14
Halliburton, Richard, 266.11
Hamlet (Shakespeare), 663.6–7
Hammer-and-forge (game), 569.26
Hampstead Heath, 15.20–21, 19.12–14
Hampton (sailboat), 185.22
Hand of Glory, 750.33
Hanna, Mark, 664.41–665.1
Hansel and Gretel, 174.21–22
Hardy, Oliver, 375.31–32, 381.6
Hare (in Bantu mythology), 322.21–22,
730.4–6
Harley Street (London), 88.11, 141.2
Harriman, Henry I., 581.24–30
Harrison, Max (*Charlie Parker*), 63.32–
37
Hart, Dorothy, 381.10–14
Harvey Nicholls, 94.3–5
Have Gun, Will Travel, 248.40–41
Haydn, Josef, 711.29–31
Hayles, N. Katherine (*The Cosmic
Web*), 396.28
Hayles, N. Katherine ("Coloring Gravi-
ty's Rainbow"), 101.19–20, 364.39
Hayworth, Rita, 274.25
Heart of Darkness (Conrad), 93.25,
473.3–4
Heisenberg, Werner, 348.21
Helgoland, 652.29
Helm, Brigitte, 393.41, 394.1, 578.7–9
Hemingway, Ernest, 12.22, 292.25,
624.20

Henry V (Shakespeare), 169.39–40
Herero uprising of 1904–6, 315.17–18,
317.2
Hermann, Dr. Rudolf, 452.21
Hermeneutics, 188.14–15
Hernández, José, 383.12–13. See also
Martín Fierro and *The Return of
Martín Fierro*
Hesse, Hermann, 403.11
"Hickory, Dickory, Dock," 37.24
Hilbert space, 217.18, 540.28
Himmel und Hölle (game), [6], 567.24–
25
Hindenburg, Paul von, 158.8–10, 305.6–7
Hiroshima (Japan), 480.4–5, 588.7–9,
642.32, 693.39–41, 694.12–16
Hite, Molly (*Ideas of Order in the Nov-
els of Thomas Pynchon*), 101.19–20,
454.34–35
Hits-and-cuts (game), 540.23
Hobbes, Thomas (*Leviathan*), 591.10–11
Hofmann, August Wilhelm, 161.34–35,
166.1–9
Hohner harmonicas (Matteus Hohner
Company), 384.34, 562.37, 622.14
Holy Center, 508.29–30
Holy Grail (Sangraal), 739.22–24
Hooker, Thomas, 22.24–27,
677.1–2
Hoover, Herbert, 565.19–20, 649.12–13
"Hop Harrigan, " 117.15
Hörlein, Heinrich, 631.5–6
"Horst Wessel Song" ("Die Fahne
Hoch"), 443.2, 653.14
Huxley, Aldous, 132.37
Huzel, Dieter (*Peenemünde to Canaver-
al*), 237.1–2, 272.32–34, 273.10–11,
486.2

Iasi (Romania), 11.35
I Ching, 13.1, 378.12, 746.17–18
ICI (Imperial Chemical Industries Ltd.),
228.16–17, 250.36
"If" (Kipling), 228.5
IG Farben, 71.12, 163.31–33, 250.23–24
"I Left My Heart in San Francisco" (Ben-
net), 412.35
Illuminati, 587.29

"I Lost My Heart in Heidelberg" (Veseley), 412.35

Impressionism, 183.29

Industrial Germany (Levy), 580.12–13, 632.39, 649.15

Inoguchi, Rikihei, and Tadashi Nakajima (*The Divine Wind*), 690.27–28, 690.36–37, 696.29, 696.30–40

Institute Rabe, 516.30

"Invisible hand" (Adam Smith), 30.30, 566.14, 616.31–32

Iron Guard, 11.35,491.21

Irradiation (Pavlovian theory), 144.13–14

Irving, David (*The Mare's Nest*), 24.30, 211.10–12, 240.11–18, 240.19, 240.21–22, 242.9–15, 423.21, 501.6–7, 575.14–16, 681.34–36, 753.23–24

Isaiah (Bible), 465.30

Jablochkov candles, 351.6

Jaeger underwear, 315.15

Jaffe, Sam, 684.31–35

James, Harry, 685.39

Janet, Pierre, 49.1–2, 88.29–31, 144.1–2, 470.10–11

Jell-O, 248.7

Jenny Greenteeth, 147.39–40

Jesus, 554.31–32

Joachim, Joseph, 684.39

Jo block, 621.39

John the Baptist, 14.4

Johnson, Van, 182.4

Jonah (Bible), 480.23, 501.40

Jones, Spike, 678.21–22

Josephson, Mathew (*The Robber-Barons*), 664.41–665.1

Joyce, James (*Ulysses*), 6.9

Judge Hardy's Children (Seitz), 382.15–16

Judgment (tarot), 152.1 -2

Jugendstil, 550.40

Jung, Carl Gustav, 48.14, 137.20, 410.38

Jungfrau, 9.29

"Just a Gigolo" (Casucci and Caesar), 414.35–415.3

Just-Wulfram (light bulb), 650.30–32

Kabbalism, 148.37–38, [177], 717.8–9, 727.6–10, 737.22–23, 737.41, 747.41–748.5

Das Kabinet des Dr. Caligari (Pabst), 385.1

Kakau Veld (South-West Africa) 322.41

Die Kalte Sophie, 281.1–2

Kammler, Gen. Hans, 282.6, 424.17–18

Kari (alcoholic drink), 351.17

Karlshorst (Berlin), 437.28

Karma, 147.1

Kármán, Theodore von (*The Wind and Beyond*), 290.16, 452.8, 452.39–40

Katspiel (Kabbalah), 584.1

Kekulé von Stradonitz, Friedrich August, 84.9–10, 410.34

Kendall, M. G., (*Introduction to the Theory of Statistics*), 140.5–10

Kennedy, John F., 65.33, 682.14–15, 688.28

Kennedy, Joseph P., 682.10, 682.11, 682.14–15, 682.20–21

Kenosha (Wisconsin), 643.1

Kenosha Kid, 381.6

"The Kenosha Kid" (Parkhill), 60.8

Kilgour (London tailor), 200.39

Kilroy, 27.13

Der Kinderofen, 94.20

King Kong (Cooper), [7], 57.8, [123], 247.35, 275.13, 275.13–14, 275.34–35, 688.36–37, 689.4–20

King's evil, 119.33

Kings Road (London), 80.17–18

Kinos, 155.5–6

Kipling, Rudyard, 13.30–31, 228.5

Kirghiz Light, 357.37

Klein-Rogge, Rudolf, 578.7–9, 579.9

Knights Templars, 737.41–738.1

Kolbe, F. W. (*An English-Herero Dictionary*), 316.22–23, 316.38, 319.7, 325.31, 328.29–30, 456.37, 520.24–25, 673.37–38, 730.30

Kollwitz, Käthe, 578.22–23

Kooy, J. M. J. (*Ballistics of the Future*), 95.17, 96.18–22, 100.34–38, 101.1–2, 101.7–9, 104.19, 113.11, 206.15–16, 211.15, 222.32, 223.13, 239.24, 240.35, 242.38–39, 361.12–13, 517.17

KPD (Kommunistische Partei Deutschlands), 153.40
Kracauer, Siegfried (*From Caligari to Hitler*), 98.24, 155.5–6, 159.19, 159.33, 289.29, 385.1, 393.11–12, 516.22
Krafft-Ebing, Richard von (*Psychopathia Sexualis*), 232.15
Krasnyy Arkhiv, 349.38
Kreis (cross), 152.11–12
Kreml hair tonic, 18.8–38
Kriegsbier, 329.15
Krishna, 276.30–31
Krupa, Gene, 513.15–16
Krupp von Bohlen und Halbach, Gustav, 520.38, 654.27
Kurfürstendamm (Berlin), 443.11
Kuropatkin, Col. Aleksey, 340.7–8
Kurzweg, Prof.-Dr. Hermann, 455.24–25
Kyprinos Orient (cigarette), 55.36–39

La Bohème, 155.3.4
Labyrinth, 137.20
"Lady of Spain" (Reaves and Evans), 214.4–5
Lake, Stuart N. (*Wyatt Earp, Frontier Marshall*), 210.27
Lammergeiers, 664.13
Lang, Fritz, 112.33, 159.19, 159.33, 578.31–33, 753.5–8
Larson-Keeler test, 84.21
Lassie, 44.20
Laterne, Laterne (game), 567.31
Laurel, Stan, 375.31–32
Lawrence, T. E. (Lawrence of Arabia), 201.15
Lecuona, Emesto, 169.7–8
Lehár, Franz (*The Merry Widow*), 477.5
Leo (astrology), 694.12–16
Let Us Die Fighting (Drechsler), 317.7
Ley, Willy (*Rockets, Missiles, and Space Travel*), 301.33, 753.5–8
Liebig, Justus von, 161.34–35, 411.19
Liebigstrasse (Munich), 161.30
Liebknecht, Karl, 621.40
Life (magazine), as source, 246.35, 330.9–11, 640.33–35, 694.3
Lilith, 649.34

Little Mary (J. M. Barrie), 533.11
Livingstone, Dr. David, 587.36
Llandudno (Wales), 468.19
Lombardo, Guy, 529.38
"The Lone Ranger" 366.12, 435.21, 752.7
"Looking for a Needle in a Haystack," 561.26
LSD, 260.30
Lubbock, Isaac, 240.19
Lübeck raid (1942), 146.27
Lubitsch, Ernst, 112.33
Lublin regime, 34.28–30, 457.4, 549.23
Lucky Strike (cigarette), 20.18, 269.13
Ludwig I, 750.18–19
Ludwig II, 394.23
Luger, 505.22
Lugones, Leopoldo, 263.18, 383.10, 383.36–37
Lugosi, Bela, 106.33–37, 557.30–31
Luisenstrasse (Zurich), 262.11
Luke (Bible), 660.26
Lüneburg Heath (Germany), 390.4, 737.17
Luttig, Hendrik Gerhardus (*The Religious System and Social Organization of the Herero*), 100.2–3, 297.12–13, 315.27–31, 315.38–316.13, 316.16–19, 316.28–29, 316.33–35, 321.3–4, 321.40–322.1, 322.6, 322.21–22, 327.11–17
Luxemburg, Rosa, 155.7–8, 621.40

MacDonald, Ramsey, 77.23
Mach, Ernst, 453.20–21
Mackenzie, Sir Anthony Edward Montagu Compton, 115.32–33
MacPherson, Sandy (BBC), 13.39–40, 592.25–26
Madame Butterfly (Puccini), 351.35
The Magnificent Ambersons (Welles), 203.34
Malcolm X (*The Autobiography of Malcolm X*), 62.22, 63.3, 63.22, 63.23–25, 64.24, 67.31, 688.28
Malenkov, Georgi M., 391.33–34
Malkuth (Kabbalah), 680.18, 747.41–748.5

Mallon, Mary ("Typhoid Mary"), 739.6–7
Maltzen, Baron Ago von, 166.16–17
Mandala: as motif, [9–11], 137.20, 152.11–12, 212.3, 275.1, 285.38, 321.3–4, 398.4–5, 560.25, 563.6–11, 594.7–8, 691.19–20, 707.4–5, 719.39–40; Herero village as, 321.3–4, 563.6
Mandrake root, 202.34–35, 625.17
Manichaeanism, 727.6–10
"The Man Who Broke the Bank at Monte Carlo" (Gilbert), 203.34
Mares' tails, 372.29–30
Marie-Celeste (ship), 303.19–20, 462.28
Marlow, Philip, 752.1–3
Martín Fierro (Hernández), 383.25–26, 385.8, 386.37–387.2, 387.38, 475.11, 610.32–33, 613.30
Marvel, Marv, 676.4
Marx, Julius ("Groucho"), 210.17–18, 246.25, 386.21–22
Marx, Karl, 701.18
The Marx Brothers, 619.1–4
Maskelyne B (Lunar crater), 410.11
Mason, James, 592.21
Masonic Order, 27.11, 587.40, 663.37–664.1
Matthew (Bible), 544.33, 554.31–32
Mauritius, 108.17–18
Max and Moritz, 501.10, 757.26–29
Maxim gun, 232.21
Maxwell, James Clerk, 239.18–19, 411.34–35
Mayfair (London), 15.12–13
McGovern, James (*Crossbow and Overcast*), 228.37, 272.32–34, 273.5, 287.25–26, 289.28, 296.14–16, 298.36–37, 299.29–30
McTeague (Norris), 535.17
Meloids, 17.5
Mendelson, Edward ("Gravity's Encyclopedia"), 247.9
Mendoza (rifle), 107.23
Merck, A. G., 621.26
Merkabah (Kabbalah), [5], 231.24–25, 584.1, 717.8–9, 749.34–36, 750.20–21
Mérode, Cléo de, 232.21–22
The Merry Widow (Lehár), 477.5

Metatron (Kabbalah), 231.25, 680.18, 734.19–20
Metropolis (Lang), 578.7–9
Mezuzah, 563.24–25
Midnight (famous horse), 342.15–17
Midsummer Eve, 379.25–26
Milton, John, 689.4–20
"Mindless pleasures," 270.23, 681.32
Mingeborough, 26.30
Minotaur, 142.14
Minsky's Burlesque, 382.22
Miranda, Carmen, 383.2, 664.19
Mistress of Atlantis (Pabst), 579.36
Mitchell, Joni, [322]
Mix, Tom, 245.36, 717.24
MMPI (Minnesota Multiphasic Personality Inventory), 21.3–4, 81.22–24, 90.8
Modern Analysis (Whittaker and Watson), 55.11–12
Monel bars, 309.7
Montez, Maria, 121.13–14
Moore, Prof. Norton, 452.39–40
Morgan, Dennis, 32.36
Morgan, John Pierpont, 332.5–6
Morituri, 473.3–4
Morra (game), 586.17–18
Morrison shelter, 24.30
Motor Boys (Clarence Young), 266.23–24
Moxie, 63.5, 258.4, 471.24, 677.36–37
Der Müde Tod (Lang), 516.22, 579.21–22
Murphy, Audie, 563.29
Murphy's Law, 275.25–26, 471.28

Nabokov, Vladimir (*Pnin*), 226.33
Nansen, Fridtjof, 589.24–27
Napoleon, 346.4
Nathan of Gaza, 14.4
National Geographic (magazine), 266.23–24
Ñato, El, 383.12–13
Nayland-Smith, Sir Denis (Fu-Manchu novels), 83.35, 277.34–38, 277.38–39, 592.36–37, 631.29–31, 751.33–34
Ndjambi Karunga (Herero god), 100.2–3, 322.21–22
Neubabelsberg (Germany), 371.32–33

News of the World (London), 215.29
Newton, Isaac, 555.21–22
Die Nibelungen (Lang), 159.19, 578.31–33
Niederdorf (Zurich), 257.35–36
Nielson, Asta, 415.31
Nieman-Marcus, 582.39
Nimbus Hotel, 257.35–36
NISO (Scientific Research Institute for Airplane Equipment, Soviet Russia), 273.5
Nitralampen (light bulb), 647.5
Nixon, Richard M., 249.5–6, [322], 755.6–7
Noble, Charles, 739.3
Noon, as motif, 625.5, 667.3–4, 674.19–20. *See also* Evil Hour
Norden bombsight, 151.23
Nordhausen (Germany), 333.14–15
Novi Pazar, 14.34–37
Nuremberg War Crimes Tribunal, 681.30
Nussbaum, Mrs. Pansy ("Allen's Alley"), 44.17–18
Nusselt number, 223.8–10, 453.20–21
Nutria, 38.6
Nymphenburg (castle), 619.1–4, 750.13

O'Brien, Margaret, 690.2
October (Eisenstein), 155.5–6
Odeon Café, 262.35
Oder Haff (Germany), 489.9
Offenbach, Jacques, 584.21
Ogive curve (arch), 346.2–3
Ombindi, 319.7
Omuhona (lord), 316.31–35
Oneirine, 166.10
"On the Good Ship Lollipop" (Clare and Whiting), 466.4
Opel, Fritz von, 380.6
Operation Backfire, 272.32–34, 526.39
Ophelia (*Hamlet*), 663.6–7
Opie, Iona and Peter: *The Lore and Language of Schoolchildren*, 177.28–29; *Children's Games in Street and Playground*, 540.23
Order of the Golden Dawn, 747.38
Orff, Carl, 237.16–20, 441.11

Ornstein, Honora ("Diamond Lil"), 657.10–11
Orphée (Cocteau), 755.3–4
Osram (light bulb), 647.5
OSS (Office of Strategic Services), 76.34, 268.6, 499.17
Otukungurua, 316.38
Ouspensky, Petr Demianovich, 30.37, 77.35–36
The Ovatjimba, 315.27–31
OWI (Office of War Information), 76.34

Pabst, Georg, 112.33
Padre Ignacio (Wister), 94.38
Palmolive, 208.21
Pan, 656.36, 661.27–28, 720.2
Pancratius, St., 281.1–2
Pantopon (analgesic), 345.6–16
Parabellum (pistol), 346.2–3
Parabola (arch), 443.5–7
Paradoxical phase (Pavlovian theory), 48.38–39, 136.25
Parker, Charlie ("Yardbird"), 63.32–37
Park Lane (London), 245.27
Parrinder, Geoffrey (*African Mythology*), 658.26–27
Passchendaele, 79.41, 235.38
Patton, Gen. George S., 287.36
Pavlov, Ivan Petrovich (*Lectures on Conditioned Reflexes*), 37.32, 47.3, 48.38–39, 49.1–2, 55.29–30, 56.14, 75.30–31, 76.2–7, 78.32–33, 84.39–85.3, 87.32–34, 88.9–11, 144.13–14, 226.17–22, 226.33, 229.8, 229.34, 470.10–11, 752.29
"Pavos Reales" (Lugones), 383.36–37
Pearsall, Ronald (*The Table Rappers*), 29.31
Peary, Robert Edwin, 589.24–27
Peesch, Reinhard (*Das Berliner Kinderspiel der Gegenwart*), 567.24–25, 567.31
Pentecost (Whitsunday), 269.26
Perkins, Prof. William, 161.34–35, 166.1–9
Perón, Juan Domingo, 263.34
Perronet, Edward, 169.34

Pervitins (methamphetamine), 328.25, 522.1, 731.33
Petrova, M. K., 49.13–14
Petty Girl, 592.29
Phoebus cartel, 649.15
PID (Political Information Division), 206.20
Pigs: as motif, 59.30, 82.31, 114.12–13, 121.14–15, 206.5, 545.4–5, 554.40– 555.5, 555.24, 638.37; "pigs" (impure iron), 139.36; Plechazunga, 567.34; Porky Pig, 545.4–5, 638.37
Pinball, 583.21–24
The Pirates of Penzance, 5.3
Pirozhok, 190.8
Pisces, as motif, 34.21–22, 154.35–36, 236.36–37, 712.29
Place Garibaldi (Nice), 253.19–20
Plasticman (Cole), 206.37, 752.5
Plechazunga, 567.34
Pluto, 415.29–30
Pöhlmann, Ernst, 416.23
Poisson equation, 54.25, 85.37, 138.35– 36, 270.19
Police Comics, 206.37
Pollitt, Harry, 135.38
Portobello Road (London), 107.26
Potassium permanganate, 375.21
Potemkin, Prince Grigori, 343.30, 388.27–28
Potsdam (Germany), 370.5–6
Powell, Dick, 622.30–31
Power series, 94.35–37, 140.5–10, 590.28
Prandtl, Ludwig, 452.8, 453.20–21
Preference (game), 338.25
Primo Scala's Accordion Band (BBC), 115.19
Project Hermes, 287.25–26
I Promessi Sposi (Manzoni), 386.16
Proudhon, Pierre Joseph, 587.32–33
Purcell, Henry, 129.8–16
Purvis, Melvin, 717.19–22
PWD (Psychological Warfare Division), 76.36, 230.21
Pynchon, Thomas Ruggles, Jr., 27.5–6; *The Crying of Lot 49,* 558.3; *Slow Learner,* 329.26–27, 329.28, 641.20;

V., 290.7, 396.41, 403.35, 497.15, 558.3, 715.2
Pynchon, William, 27.5–6, 329.23, 554.40–555.5, 555.29–31, 556.3–4

Qazi, Javaid ("Source Materials for Thomas Pynchon's Fiction"), 12.14– 15, 290.16
Qlippoth (Kabbalah, "shells of the dead"), 148.37–38, 176.14–15, 197.1, 661.30, 746.21–22
Qorqyt, 357.33
Quaternions, 726.41
"Queen for a Day," 691.35–36
Queen of Cups (tarot), 735.19
Quisling, Vidkun, 176.38–39
Qumys, 356.25

"The Radio Doctor" (BBC), 133.14–15
Raft, George, 435.8
Rainbow, as motif, 6.33–35, 151.29–30, 203.11, 208.8, 209.25–26, 225.2, 726.19–20. *See also* arch
Raketemensch, 366.14
Rapallo Treaty (1922), 166.16–17, 338.4–5, 352.15–16
Rathbone, Basil, 534.9–10
Rathenau, Walter, 163.19–23, 338.3–5
Ravensbruck concentration camp, 681.23–24
Rayner, Rosalie, 84.3–5
Realpolitik, 50.22
Reciprocal induction (Pavlovian theory), 144.13–14
Red cap, 14.12
"Red River Valley," 68.12
Red Ryder, 68.23
Reed, Ishmael (*Mumbo Jumbo*), 588.5
Reflex arc (Pavlovian theory), 56.14
Regents Park Zoo (London), 121.14–15
Reichstag (Berlin), 368.13
Reinickendorf (Berlin), 154.7, 160.26
The Return of Jack Slade (Schuster), 247.9
The Return of Martín Fierro (Hernán- dez), 383.12–13, 387.38
Reyes, Cypriano, 383.18

Reynolds number, 223.8–10, 453.20–21
Rheingold (beer), 381.10–14
Rhenish Missionary Society, 100.7–8,
    316.31, 317.2
Rhine Falls (Germany), 160.35–36
Rider, 501.22, 509.33–34
"Right in the Führer's Face" (Wallace),
    678.21–22
Riickert, Helen, 381.10–14
Rilke, Rainer Maria: *Duino Elegies*,
    98.1–2, 98.7, 99.34–35, 101.23–26,
    341.18–19, 413.15–16, 431.36; *Son-
    nets to Orpheus*, 97.17–18, [321],
    622.19–21
Rin Tin Tin, 614.10
Roca, Gen. Julio A. 387.5–6
Rocketman, 366.14, 435.20
Rocket Noon, 500.40, 667.3–4. *See also*
    Evil Hour, noon
Rock-scissors-and-paper (game), 540.23
Rogers, Ginger, 561.30–31
Rohmer, Sax (Arthur Sarsfield Ward),
    631.29–31
Rohrschach test, 81.34–35
Rokossovsky, Gen. Konstantin, 501.5–6
Roland Peachey and His Orchestra,
    121.35–36
The Rolling Stones, 541.23
"The Romance of Helen Trent," 499.36
Romilar, 369.20
Rooney, Mickey, 382.15–16
Roosevelt, Eleanor, 566.1–2
Roosevelt, Eliot, 566.1–2
Roosevelt, Franklin D., 373.32, 374.22–
    23, 444.22
Rosas, Juan Manuel de, 264.27
Roseland Ballroom (Boston), 63.3
Rosicrucianism, 591.3, 737.41
Rossini, Gioacchino, 204.33–35, 204.39,
    262.5–6, 273.37–41, 376.27–28,
    440.4, 622.3, 684.40, 685.36
Rossini (Nice), 248.41, 253.33
Rover Boys (Arthur Winfield), 266.23–
    24
Roxbury (Boston), 675.10–11
Rozhdestvenski, Adm. Zinovi P.,
    349.39, 452.1–6
Rundstedt offensive, 52.23, 131.11

"Running Between the Raindrops" (Gib-
    bons and Drenforth), 529.38

Sacher-Masoch, Leopold von (*Venus in
    Furs*), 232.6
Sagittarius (astrology), 343.15–16, 483.1
Saint Pauli (Hamburg), 525.24
St. Felix, 37.24
St. James Park (London), 15.38
St. John's Wood (London), 269.33–35,
    544.8
St. Louis Browns, 320.14
St. Louis Cardinals, 320.14
St. Paul's Cathedral (London), 115.16–
    17
Sakall, S. Z. ("Cuddles"), 534.9–10
Salome, 82.37–38
"Salt of the Earth" (The Rolling Stones),
    541.23
"San Antonio Rose" (Wills), 559.36–37,
    603.38
Sandhurst (England), 202.2
Sandoz, 250.25–27
Sandys, Sir Duncan, 228.1–2, 251.10–12
Sangraal (Holy Grail), 487.24
Sassoon, Siegfried, 79.31–32
Sasuly, Richard (*IG Farben*), 163.19–23,
    163.31–33, 165.21, 166.18, 284.15–
    16, 284.23, 344.7, 349.28, 387.29–30,
    565.11, 581.34–35, 630.6–12, 630.25,
    631.5–6, 654.27
Savarin, 232.6
Savile Row (London), 184.14–15,
    201.33, 227.31–32, 526.13
The Saving Remnant (Agar), 553.34
Saxa (*saxo-*, Sachsa), 218.10, 245.27
Schacht, Horace Greeley Hjalmar, 285.9
Schaffhausen (Germany), 160.35–36
Schauffler, Robert H. (*Beethoven*), 440.4
Schlieren (pressure waves), 452.30
Schlieren (Zurich), 267.15–16
Scholem, Gershom: *Major Trends in
    Jewish Mysticism*, 231.24–25, 584.1,
    749.34–36; *On the Kabbalah*,
    148.37–38, 478.14–17
Scylla and Charybdis, 239.26–27
"The Secret Integration" (Thomas Pyn-
    chon), 329.26–27

The Secrets of Suzanne (Wolf-Ferrari), 477.5

Section eight, 114.5

Seed, David ("Thomas Hooker in Pynchon's *Gravity's Rainbow*"), 22.24–27, 677.1–2

Semiretchie (Soviet Central Asia), 338.28–30

Sentiments d'emprise: 144.1–2; and Pavlovian theory, 49.1–2

Servatius, St., 281.1–2

The Seventh Seal (Bergman), 755.3–4

Severin, 232.6

SHAEF (Supreme Headquarters, Allied Expeditionary Force), 17.7, 192.38

Shays's Rebellion, 268.17

Shearer, Norma, 690.16

Shekinah, 478.14–17

Shetzline, David, 389.23–24

"Siboney" (Lecuona), 169.7–8

Siegal, Jules ("Who Is Thomas Pynchon . . . And Why Did He Take Off with My Wife?"), 82.31

Siege Perilous, 321.6–7

Siemens, Wernher, 649.27

Siemens Electrical Works, 725.23–24

Sigma (letter), as motif, 40.13, 198.33, 206.24–25, 299.38, 300.38–39, 411.38, 523.39, 635.35, 709.33–35

"Si Mi Quieres Escribir," 564.37–38

Simpson, Wallis, 177.28–29

Sinatra, Frank, 390.8–9

Singularities, 396.28

Sirius (light bulb), 650.30–32

Skinner, B. F., 77.35–36

"Skippy," 644.21

Slippery elm throat lozenges (Thayer's), 18.8–38, 24.34, 116.24–25

Smith, Adam (the "invisible hand" and *The Wealth of Nations*), 30.30, 566.14, 616.31–32

Smithfield Market (London), 542.39

Smith, Klein, and French, 518.31–32

Snake (horse), 342.11, 482.34

The Social Register, 28.4–5

Sodium amytal, 61.17, 168.41–169.1, 512.1

SOE (Special Operations Executive), 5.15

Soho district (London), 22.4

Somerset Club (Boston), 28.4–5

Son of Frankenstein (Lee), 106.33–37

Soules, Terrill Shepard. ("What to Think about *Gravity's Rainbow*"), 11.34, 17.36–37, 337.17

Sous le Vent, 30.39–40

Southwest Africa Under German Rule (Bley), 317.7

"The Sovereignty of Ethics" (Emerson), 580.29–32

Spam tins, 134.3–4, 168.2

Speer, Albert, 298.19–20

SPOG (Special Projectiles Operations Group), 272.32–34, 295.15, 391.19

Spohr, Louis, 622.3

Spontini, Gaspare, 622.3

SPR (Society for Psychical Research), 89.36, 153.11, 633.40

Stage Door Canteen, 134.32–33

Stalin, Iosif, 340.27, 368.17, 373.26–27

Standard Oil, 565.11

Steele, Bob, 247.6–7, 385.20

Steenkamp, W. P. (*Is the South-West African Herero Committing Race-Suicide?*), 317.30–33, 351.17–18, 519.14

"Stella Dallas," 499.36

Stendhal (Marie-Henri Beyle), 440.4

Stinnes, Hugo, 284.23, 284.37

Stockholm (Sweden), 141.21–33

Stoke Poges (England), 169.31–33

Sträggeli, 258.26–27

The Strand (London), 200.28

Streckefuss ("Stretchfoot") 733.26, 759.29. *See also* Blicero

Submariner, 752.4

Sue, Eugène, 13.26–27

Suggenthal, 269.9–10

Superman, 751.35

Suso, Heinrich, 129.8–16, 136.6–7

Suspendatur per collum, 329.23

Svetovid, 528.13–15

Swinemünde (Germany), 460.12

Swope, Gerard, 565.24–26, 581.29–30

Symposium (Plato), 155.12

Tallis, Thomas, 129.8–16
"Tangerine" (Mercer), 264.6–7
Tannhäuser, 299.13–14, 364.22, 393.32, 470.37–38, 532.32
Tarot: as motif, 152.1–2, 164.29, 486.26, 501.25–26, 533.9, 707.31, 724.25–26, 724.28–29, 735.19, 742.29; Slothrop's, 738.7–8; Weissmann's, 746.30
Tarzan, 306.34
Tatham, Campbell ("Tarot and *Gravity's Rainbow*"), 746.30
Taurus (astrology), 152.16
Tavistock Institute, 276.21
Tchaikovsky, Petr, 702.15–16
Tchitcherine, Frank, 290.16
Tchitcherine, Georgi, 290.16, 338.3–5, 352.15–16
Telefunken radio control, 207.8
Temple, Shirley, 24.39, 246.9, 466.4, 466.16
Tenniel, Sir John, 247.30
Tennyson, Alfred, 270.14–45
Ter Meer, Fritz, 631.5–6
"Terry and the Pirates," 670.38
"There! I've Said It Again" (Evans and Mann), 121.35–36
Theseus, 88.17
This Is the Army, 134.32–33
Thomas, Lowell, 266.23–24
"The Three Billy Goats Gruff" (Asbjornsen), 398.18–19
Three-card monte, 259.39–40
Three Intellectuals in Politics (Joll), 169.19–23
Tiergarten (Berlin), 359.24
Time (magazine), as source, 368.13, 368.17, 640.23, 682.20–21
The *Times* (London), as source, 6.26–27, 17.9, 19.31–32, 20.1–3, 31.2, 32.26, 34.28–30, 35.21, 39.1–2, 53.25–26, 55.36–37, 72.34, 73.34, 86.39, 93.25, 115.19, 121.13–14, 121.35–36, 129.8–16, 130.24, 132.2–4, 133.3–4, 134.24–25, 134.40–135.1, 136.6–7, 168.2, 174.21–22, 182.6, 237.9, 252.14, 269.32
"The Tinder Box" (Andersen), 398.18–19
Titaniapalast (Berlin), 446.16–17

Titanic, 462.38
Toftoy, Col. Holger, 298.36–37
Toland, John (*The Dillinger Days*), 516.3, 741.6–7
Tölölyan, Khachig ("Fishy Poisson: Allusions to Statistics in *Gravity's Rainbow*"), 140.5–10
Tonto ("The Lone Ranger"), 366.12, 752.7
"Totus Ardeo" (*Carmina Burana*), 237.16–20
Tower Hill (London), 19.12–14
Tracy, Spencer, 266.7
Trafalgar Square (London), 269.32
The Trail of Fu-Manchu (Rohmer [Ward]), 217.24
Transfiguration, Feast of, [10], [177]
A Tree Grows in Brooklyn (Kazan) 641.40
Trefoil, 147.13, 276.30–31
Trente-et-quarante (game), 244.18
Triglav, 528.13–15
Tristan und Isolde (Wagner), 505.36
Trivalin, 345.6–16
Trotha, Gen. Lothar von, 317.2, 362.14, 422.2
Truman, Harry, 371.32–33, 373.26–27, 588.7–9
TsAGI (Central Aerodynamics and Hydrodynamics Institute), 273.5, 337.31, 391.35
Tunbridge Wells (England), 38.37
Tungsram (light bulb), 647.5
Turl Street (Oxford), 193.31–32
Twain, Mark (*Roughing It*), 247.9

Ufa-Theatre (Berlin), 98.24
"Under the Rose" (Pynchon), 290.7, 396.41
United Fruit Company, 678.14–15, 678.26
Uriburu, José, 263.20
Utgarthaloki (Loki of Outgard), 191.25, 709.39
Uytenbogaart, J. W. H. *See* Kooy, J. M. J.

"Valencia" (Bayer and Charles), 605.21
Valentino, Rudolf, 182.17

Valerian, 345.17
Validator (tarot), 164.29
Valkyries, 151.29–30
Varieties of Religious Experience (James), 580.29–32
"Variations on a Theme by Frank Bridge" (Britten), 59.1–2
Vauxhall Bridge (London), 11.24–25
Vector analysis, 726.41
V-E Day (May 8, 1945), 9.4, 269.32
Vedder, Heinrich, 321.3–4
Veiled Prophet Ball, 582.28–29
Venus, 88.17
Verbindungsmann, 152.19, 166.18, 344.12
Verdi, Giuseppi, 595.14
Vermittlungsstelle W, 630.25
Versteckspiele (hide-and-seek game), 567.31
VfR (*Verein fur Raumschiffart*), 162.13–14, 400.30
VIAM (All-Union Institute of Aviation Materials), 273.5, 611.18
Vincent's infection (trench mouth), 170.13
Virgo (astrology), 694.12–16, 699.17, 712.21
Vitamin E, 317.30–33
"Viva la Quince Brigade," 605.37–38
Volkswagen, 755.28
Vorsetzer (roll piano player), 550.38–39

Wagner, Prof. Herbert, 224.14–15, 452.26–27
Wagner, Richard, 324.10, 361.18–19, 393.11–12, 441.2, 450.31, 505.36
Wahmke, Dr. Kurt, 403.5
Waite, A. E.: *The Book of Black Magic and of Pacts*, 145.20, 734.11, 750.33; *The Pictorial Key to the Tarot*, 164.29, 735.19, 738.7–8, 746.30
Walpurgisnacht, 293.17, 329.13–14, 463.2
Wandervogel, 99.2, 162.12, 670.34
Wannsee Conference, 446.17–18
Ward, Arthur Sarsfield, 277.34–38. *See also* Sax Rohmer
Washington, George, 254.10

Watson, John B., 84.3–4
Weber, Max, 81.8–9, 464.30
Webern, Anton, 440.31, 494.21–22
"Wee Willie Winkie" (Kipling), 466.4
Wee Willie Winkie (1937), 466.4
Wegener, Alfred, 321.19–20
Weill, Kurt, 513.10
Weinberg, Sidney James, 581.24–25
Weisse Sandwüsste von a Neumexico, 482.29
Werewolf, 486.3, 624.1, 640.23
Wessel, Horst, 443.2, 717.18
Wheatstone bridge, 301.31
Whitehall (London), 144.26, 453.41
White Lotos Day (May 8), 269.33–35
White Rabbit (Llandudno), 468.19
White Zombie (Halperin), 106.33–37
Whitsunday (Pentecost), [9–10], [168], 269.26, 628.4
Whittington, Dick, 637.37–38
Wiener, Norbert (cybernetics), 238.30
Wilcoxon, Henry, 559.11–14
Wilhelm, Richard, 403.11
Wilhelm II, 619.36
William Tell Overture (Rossini), 262.5–6
Willkie, Wendell, 135.38
Windmill ("the Angel"), 106.12, 536.1–2, 670.15–16
Windmill Theatre (London nightclub), 39.1–2
Winkelhaken (printing press), 573.19–20
Winner, Thomas G.: *Oral Art and Literature of the Kazakhs of Russian Central Asia*, 338.33–34, 339.1, 340.1, 340.7–8, 340.33–34, 343.19–20, 347.32, 356.10, 356.13, 356.33, 357.29, 357.33; "Problems of Alphabetic Reform among the Turkic Peoples of Soviet Central Asia," 352.26–27, 354.15
Winterhilfswerk, 373.19
Winthrop, John, 204.1–4
Wister, Owen, 94.38
Witchcraft Act (1736), 33.26
The Wizard of Oz (Le Roy), [177], 270.19–20, 329.30–31, 596.41
WLB (War Labor Board), 682.24
Wolf, Hugo, 419.32, 450.31

Wolgast (Germany), 502.20–21
Wonder Woman, 676.4
Woolworth's (London), 114.19
Wormwood Scrubs prison (London),
    33.31–32, 190.32, 717.2–3
Wozzeck (Berg), 465.18
WPA (Works Progress Administration),
    306.4
Wray, Fay, 57.8, [123], 275.11, 688.36–37
Wuotan, 72.27, 110.6

Yang and yin, 278.16
Yew tree, 302.2–3
"You Can Do a Lot of Things at the Sea-
    side" (Sheridan), 192.15–16

Yule, George U. (*Introduction to
    the Theory of Statistics*), 140.5–
    10

Zener cards, 40.18, 78.6
Zig-Zags (cigarette rolling papers),
    442.36
Zipf, George Kingsley, 32.5–11
Zodiac, 302.20–21
Zoot suit, 246.4–5, 249.4–5
Zorro, 376.36
Zouave tribe (Algeria), 91.41
Zündkreuz, 751.11
Zvi, Sabbatai, 639.18–19
Zwingli, Huldrych, 267.36

CPSIA information can be obtained
at www.ICGtesting.com
Printed in the USA
LVHW08s0040170718
584032LV00001B/104/P

9 780820 328072